The New York Times
Guide to
New York City
2005

The New York Times
New York, New York

Please send all comments to:
The New York Times Guide to New York City
122 E. 42nd St., 14th Floor
New York, NY 10168

Published by:
The New York Times
229 W. 43rd St.
New York, NY 10036

Copyright © 2005 The New York Times Co.
All rights reserved

ISBN 1-930881-10-X
First Printing 2004
10 9 8 7 6 5 4 3 2 1

For the *New York Times*: Thomas K. Carley, President, News Services; Nancy Lee, Vice President, Business Development; Alex Ward, Editorial Director, Book Development; Mitchel Levitas, Executive Associate.

Correspondents for the *Times*: Randy Archibold, James Barron, Joseph Berger, Ben Brantley, Barbara Crossette, David W. Dunlap, Leslie Eaton, Grace Glueck, Paul Goldberger, Abby Goodnough, Laurel Graeber, Clyde Haberman, Anemona Hartocollis, Amanda Hesser, Stephen Holden, Bernard Holland, Leslie Kaufman, Randy Kennedy, Michael Kimmelman, Anna Kisselgoff, Douglas Martin, Jesse McKinley, Herbert Muschamp, Robin Pogrebin, Frank Prial, Ben Ratliff, Anne Raver, Rita Reif, Tracie Rozhon, Susan Sachs, Roberta Smith, Jennifer Steinhauer, Anthony Tommasini, Amy Waldman, Claire Wilson.

Maps: Charles Blow, Natasha Perkel

Prepared by Elizabeth Publishing: *General Editor:* John W. Wright.
Senior Editors and Writers: Alice Finer, Alan Joyce, Cheryl Farr Leas, Lisa Renaud.
Writers: Julia Chaplin, Kurt Hettler, Jerold Kappes, Gloria Levitas, Richard Mooney, Elda Rotor, Heidi Sarna.
Associate Editors: Christina P. Colon, James McCaffrey, Robert Murphy, Fred Riccardi, Patti Sonntag.

Design and Production: G&H SOHO, Inc., Hoboken, N.J.: Jim Harris, Gerry Burstein, Mary Jo Rhodes, Christina Viera, Gerald Wolfe.

Cover Design: Barbara Chilenskas, Bishop Books

Distributed by St. Martin's Press

Table of Contents

MAPS

PHOTOS

Manhattan Highlights

Visiting New York

GETTING THERE

By Plane

New York City is served by three major airports: John F. Kennedy (JFK) International Airport in Queens (about an hour's drive from Midtown), La Guardia Airport (LGA) in Queens (about a half-hour drive from Midtown), and Newark Liberty International Airport (EWR) in New Jersey (about a 45-minute drive from Midtown). Information about the airports, including ground transportation options, is available at *www.panynj.gov* or by calling (212) 435-7000.

Almost every major carrier serves at least one of these airports; many serve two or all three, so it's worth your while to compare fares. For the best fares, try an Internet search on one of the major travel sites, such as **travelocity.com** or **expedia.com.** *Hint:* Enter "NYC" as your destination and the search engines will check service to and from all three New York airports at once.

JetBlue has expanded its service in and out of JFK, but the nation's leading discount airline, Southwest, doesn't serve any of New York's major airports. The closest airport served by Southwest is in Islip, an 80-mile drive from Manhattan.

Getting into the City from the Airports

BY TAXI Once you arrive, the easiest option is to hop into a cab. Each airport has a taxi stand with uniformed dispatchers, and lines tend to move quickly. Fares do not include tolls and tips. From La Guardia to Midtown, expect to pay $20–$30. From JFK, there's a flat fare of $45 from the airport to anywhere in Manhattan (the flat-fare structure does not apply when going from Manhattan back to JFK). From Newark, you must take a New Jersey taxi; the dispatcher will give you a written slip with the fare based on your destination. It'll usually run $50 or more. Tolls and tip are not included in these prices. A New York taxi driver expects a 10–15 percent tip for good service.

BY CAR SERVICE Private car and limousine services offer door-to-door service from the airports to your destination. They are slightly more expensive than taxis, and service can be uneven, but because they have flat fares, you don't have to worry that your taxi meter is ticking ever upward in rush-hour traffic. (Taxis always make sense from JFK, with its flat $45 fee for yellow cabs.) Call 24 hours in advance, and choose between indoor pickup (more expensive, since you have to pay for parking) or curbside pickup (you call the service as soon as you land, and your car usually arrives by the time you pick up your bags). You can usually pay by credit card when you reserve. You can also reserve pickup at your door when you're ready to return to the airport.

Among the major car services are Allstate (212-333-3333), Carmel (212-666-6666), Legends (888-LEGENDS) and Tel-Aviv (212-777-7777).

BY AIRTRAIN FROM NEWARK   From Newark Liberty International Airport, you can take the efficient **Airtrain** (*www.airtrainnewark.com*) to get into Manhattan. From your airport terminal, follow the Airtrain signs. Board the free monorail at the terminal and get off at the Rail Link station, where you switch to a New Jersey Transit train to Penn Station. Service runs every five to seven minutes; the fare is $11.55. Travel time is 20 minutes.

BY VAN OR SHUTTLE BUS   **Super Shuttle** (212-BLUE-VAN or 800-622-2089; *www.supershuttle.com*) offers door-to-door service from all three airports. Vans run every 15 to 30 minutes around the clock and do not require reservations; just go to the ground-transportation desk or use the courtesy phone in the baggage claim area. When you're ready to return to the airport, you do need to make a reservation a day or two in advance. Fares run $13–$22 per person, depending on the airport and your destination.

New York Airport Service (718-875-8200; *www.nyairportservice.com*) provides van service every half hour from JFK and La Guardia to Grand Central, the Port Authority, Penn Station and select Midtown hotels. The fare is $10 from La Guardia to Manhattan ($12 for specific hotel drop-off), $13 from JFK to Manhattan ($15 for hotel drop-off).

Olympia Airport Express (877-894-9155 or 212-964-6233; *www.olympiabus.com*) provides frequent motorcoach service from Newark Airport to Manhattan (stopping at Penn Station, the Port Authority and Grand Central). The fare to Manhattan is $11–$14.50, depending on your destination (discounts are available for seniors and disabled passengers). For an extra $5, you can transfer at Grand Central to a shuttle that serves select hotels.

If you use a van or bus service for your return trip to the airport, be sure to allow lots of time before your departure in case traffic is bad.

BY PUBLIC TRANSPORTATION   All public transportation options from the New York airports are poor; they all involve lengthy travel time and multiple transfers. The only option worth recommending is available from JFK (and even this one is a 90-minute hassle, and only for those with an extremely tight budget). From the JFK terminal, take a free shuttle bus (which says "Long-Term Parking") to the Howard Beach station. From here, you can get the A subway train to Manhattan. For more information call the Metropolitan Transit Authority (M.T.A.) at (718) 330-1234.

By Car

It's not a great idea to bring a car into Manhattan: traffic is horrendous; street parking is tough to find; and garages charge astronomical fees. If you must drive to Manhattan, plan to put your car in a garage and keep it there until you're ready to leave. Call your hotel beforehand to inquire about parking fees; private garages may be cheaper.

Directions from the South: From the New Jersey Turnpike (I-95) to Midtown Manhattan, take exit 16E to the Lincoln Tunnel, which will bring you to 42nd St. and Ninth Ave. To get downtown, get off at exit 15W and take the Holland Tunnel, which will leave you on or near Canal St.

Directions from the West: I-80 leads directly to the George Washington Bridge. For the west side of Manhattan, exit almost immediately after you cross the bridge, onto the Henry Hudson Parkway (a.k.a. the West Side Highway). For the east side of Manhattan, look for the exit to the Harlem River Drive , which leads to the FDR Drive (a.k.a. the East River Drive).

Directions from the North: The New York State Thruway (I-87) becomes the Major Deegan Expressway as you enter the Bronx. To get to Manhattan's west side, exit at the Cross Bronx Expressway (west) and take the Henry Hudson Parkway south exit (a.k.a. the West Side Highway). If you cross the George Wahington Bridge, you've gone too far. Be aware, however, that the Cross Bronx Expressway can be jammed at any hour of the day or night. An alternative route to the west side of Manhattan from the Thruway is to take the Sawmill River Parkway (not far below the Tappan Zee Bridge) south to the Henry Hudson Parkway. For the east side of Manhattan, stay on 87 past Yankee Stadium to the Third Ave. Bridge (no toll), or a little farther to the Triborough Bridge ($4 toll). Both lead to the FDR Drive. (Warning: avoid this route before or after a Yankee game.)

Directions from New England: Take I-95 to the Bruckner Expressway (I-278) to the Triborough Bridge to the FDR Drive (for the east side); for the west side take I-95 to the Cross Bronx Expressway (west) to the Henry Hudson Parkway (a.k.a. the West Side Highway). Again, you might want to avoid the oft-congested Cross Bronx. Alternatives to the north are to take the Cross Westchester Expressway west to the Saw Mill River Parkway, and the Saw Mill south to the Henry Hudson Parkway; or the Cross Westchester to the Hutchinson River Parkway south to the Saw Mill.

By Train

The train is a terrific way to reach New York. **Amtrak** (800-USA-RAIL; 800-872-7245; *www.amtrak.com*) has frequent service to and from cities along the Northeast corridor between Boston and Washington, including service on high-speed Acela Express trains. There are also less frequent trains from Florida, Chicago, and the rest of the country. Amtrak trains arrive at New York's **Penn Station,** which is in the heart of Midtown Manhattan (at Seventh Ave. and 32nd St.). From here, it's easy to make subway connections or find a taxi.

Penn Station is also a hub for the **Long Island Rail Road (LIRR)** (718-217-5477, 718-558-3022 [TTY] or 516-822-5477; *www.lirr.org*), a commuter railroad for residents of Long Island. Other major LIRR stations are in Brooklyn (Flatbush Ave.) and Queens (Jamaica Center Station).

New Jersey Transit (800-626-7433 or 973-762-5100; *www.njtransit.com*) trains connect Penn Station with points throughout New Jersey, including Atlantic City.

Metro North (212-532-4900, 800-METRO-INFO, or 800-724-3322 [TTY information line]; *www.mta.nyc.ny.us/mnr*), the commuter railroad for New York's Westchester, Putnam and Dutchess Counties, and Connecticut's Fairfield and New Haven Counties, runs in and out of Grand Central Terminal (42nd St. at Park Ave.; *www.grandcentralterminal.com*), as well as the 125th Street Station. The New Haven and Harlem lines also stop at Fordham University (Fordham Rd. at Webster Ave. in the Bronx).

By Bus

Almost every intercity and interstate bus arrives in New York at the **Port Authority Bus Terminal** (between Eighth and Ninth Aves., 40th to 42nd Sts.). For schedules, call (212) 564-8484.

Greyhound (800-231-2222; *www.greyhound.com*) serves the entire country, as well as points in Canada and Mexico. In addition to stopping at the Port Authority, Greyhound serves Queens Village (219–17 Hillside Ave.).

Peter Pan (800-343-9999; *www.peterpan-bus.com*) serves the Northeast corridor from Boston to Washington, D.C., as well as all of New England.

New Jersey Transit (800-772-2222 or 973-762-5100; *www.njtransit.com*) commuter buses serve areas throughout New Jersey (including Atlantic City and the Jersey Shore), as well as Philadelphia; Wilmington, Delaware; and Washington, D.C. These buses also arrive at Port Authority; some make stops at the George Washington Bridge Bus Station (179th St., between Broadway and Ft. Washington Ave.).

Hampton Jitney (800-936-0440 or 631-283-4600; *www.hamptonjitney.com*), which provides service to and from the Hamptons area of Long Island, has four pickup locations on the East Side: 86th St. between Lexington and Third Aves.; 69th St. at Lexington Ave.; 59th St. at Lexington Ave; and 40th St. between Lexington and Third Aves. When requested, buses make dropoffs on the West Side of Manhattan. Fares are $21–$25 one-way; $40–$45 round trip.

VISITOR INFORMATION

New York has lots of resources to help you find your way and plan your time. There are two visitor information centers in Midtown West. Both have bus and subway maps, and much more.

Before you leave home, contact the **New York Convention & Visitors Bureau** at (800) NYC-VISIT or (212) 397-8222 (*www.nycvisit.com*) and order the bureau's Official NYC Visitor Kit. It includes a pocket-size guide to New York, a fold-out map, a newsletter about upcoming events and brochures from various New York attractions. It's $9.95 for rush delivery, $5.95 for non-rush or

Useful Web Sites

www.nyc.gov
Official New York City Web site

www.mta.info
Official site of the Metropolitan Transportation Authority, with info on
subways, buses, MetroCards and trips out of town

www.nycvisit.com
Web site of the New York City Convention and Visitors Bureau

www.nytimes.com   *www.newyork.citysearch.com*
www.timeoutny.com   *www.metronewyork.com*
www.villagevoice.com   *www.newyorker.com*

For arts and entertainment, restaurant reviews, shopping, sports, news,
weather, info on city activities and events, and more.

free for the city guide only. (A less comprehensive guide can be mailed to you
for free, but can take up to three weeks to arrive.) To address specific questions
to a travel specialist, call (212) 484-1222.

The New York Times offers a wealth of helpful information online, including
the latest on New York City events, arts and entertainment, restaurants, shopping, sports, news and weather. Go to the newspaper's home page at
www.nytimes.com, scroll down to the heading "Features" and click on "NYC
Guide."

The Times Square Visitors Center

1560 Broadway (between 46th and 47th Sts.) (212) 869-1890. The center has
an information desk where help is available in five languages. You'll also find
racks and racks of brochures and discount coupons; an MTA booth selling
MetroCards (fare cards; see p. 7) and offering maps and information; a row of
computer terminals where you can spend 10 free minutes on the Internet; an
out-of-town newspaper stand; a New York City souvenir shop; a full-price theater ticket desk; a sightseeing desk selling Circle Line cruises and Gray Line
bus tours; ATMs and currency exchange machines; and clean bathrooms. The
center is open daily from 8 A.M. to 8 P.M.

New York City & Co.

810 Seventh Ave. (between 52nd and 53rd Sts.) (212) 484-1222 or (800) 692-
8474. This center, operated by the New York Convention and Visitors Bureau,
has an information desk with a multilingual staff. Touch-screen terminals offer
information on events and attractions (you can also use them to buy tickets to
attractions, saving yourself a wait on line). You'll also find racks of brochures, an
ATM, a MetroCard machine, a one-hour photo developer and discount coupons.

GETTING AROUND

New York is a walking city, and your own two feet are usually the best way to go. But there are three additional modes of transportation for getting around the city: subways, buses and taxis.

Subways and buses are run by the **Metropolitan Transportation Authority (MTA),** which has a Travel Information Center available 6 A.M.–10 P.M., seven days a week, offering directions by telephone at (718) 330-1234. The Web site, *www.mta.info*, has extensive information, including maps and service updates. Subway stations and cars have subway maps, too; some buses have bus maps. *The inside back cover of this book has a full-color subway map.*

MetroCard®

Now that tokens have been offically retired, MetroCard is the way to pay your subway or bus fare (although buses still accept exact change in coins—no bills). You can buy MetroCard in subway stations and at 3,000 other locations—news-stands, restaurants, hotels, pharmacies and wherever you see an orange-and-blue MetroCard sign. All subway stations have automated vending machines that allow you to pay by cash, credit card or debit card.

- The **regular fare** for a single ride, from and to anywhere in the system, is $2.
- A **$7 Fun Pass MetroCard** permits unlimited rides on buses and subways for one day (from first use until 3 A.M. the next day). Fun Passes may be purchased from machines in subway stations that accept cash, credit and debit cards—not from token clerks—as well as at the tourist information centers mentioned earlier and at many MetroCard vendors.
- A **$21 weekly MetroCard** permits unlimited rides during the seven days after you first use it. A **$70 monthly card** permits unlimited rides for 30 days after the first use; if purchased with a credit or debit card, it is auto-matically insured against loss or theft.

Otherwise, you can pay per ride and put any value on the card that you choose (minimum of $4, or two rides). If you buy a MetroCard for $10 (5 rides), you automatically get a 6th ride free. The readers on the turnstiles will tell you how much value you have left on your card after each use.

To use a MetroCard, just swipe it through the slot at a subway turnstile or dip it into a bus fare box. Sometimes a turnstile will tell you to swipe the card again . . . and again . . . and again. The key is to place the card all the way down in the slot, hold it firmly and run it all the way through quickly and smoothly. If all else fails, go to the station booth clerk, who should then let you through the "special entry" turnstile.

Transfers: MetroCard permits transfers between subways and buses and vice versa, and between buses and buses, so long as you do not transfer to the same route you started on. After you use your card, you have two hours to transfer to another route, not necessarily connecting with the first leg of your trip, at no extra charge. (The card "knows" when your two hours have expired.) Note: When you pay a bus fare with cash, you can ask the bus operator to give you a transfer for another bus ride (but *not* a subway ride) within two hours.

The Subway System

Subways are the fastest way around town and the preferred mode of transit for New Yorkers themselves. The New York subway system may be one of the oldest in the world, but it is also one of the most efficient. It runs 24 hours a day, 365 days a year and covers every area of the city except Staten Island. There are over 722 miles of track and 468 stations.

While it's true that parts of the subway are run-down, and the screeching noise from older trains can cause jangled nerves, one look at the traffic jams in Midtown and at the bridges and tunnels will tell you why millions of New Yorkers ride the subway every day. There's a massive crush of people during morning and evening rush hours, but trains run frequently.

Subways are safe, but be alert, especially when you're packed tight on a crowded train. Beware of pickpockets, a crafty lot. Keep your hands on your purse and your wallet; don't leave valuables near the top of a backpack slung behind you. Don't wear flashy jewelry. At night, don't ride in the last cars, which tend to be the emptiest and riskiest. If you're nervous, ride in the middle car, where the train conductor works. Subways run less frequently late at night, so in the interest of both speed and safety, you may want to take a cab instead.

Service changes are increasingly common as the MTA attempts to upgrade this century-old system. Take note of posted signs that tell you if trains will not be running or be re-routed (often on the weekends) because of construction. Loudspeaker announcements are almost always unintelligible. Don't hesitate to ask someone for directions—you'll be amazed at how New Yorkers like to show off their knowledge of the subway system.

The Metropolitan Transportation Authority's Travel Information Center is available 6 A.M.–10 P.M., seven days a week, at (718) 330-1234, but it is not always completely informed about weekend service. It can, however, give directions. The MTA also posts service notices on its Web site, *www.mta.info*. A free copy of the subway map is available at any subway station booth.

Manhattan:

West Side: served by the A, B, C, D, 1, 2, 3 and 9 trains. The A, D, 2 and 3 are express lines. The C, 1 and 9 are local trains, which stop more frequently. E, F and V lines run local north–south service south of 50th St., then head east for crosstown stops on 53rd. The N and R run north–south below 57th St., then head east for crosstown stops on 60th St.

East Side: served by the 4, 5 and 6 trains. Trains run along Lexington Ave. north of 42nd St., and along Park Ave. to the south. The 4 and 5 are express trains; the 6 is local. They all have interchanges with the E, F, N, R, the 42nd St. Shuttle (S) and the 7 line.

Bronx: Served by the B, D, 1, 2, 4, 5, 6 and 9 trains.

Brooklyn: Served by the A, C, F, G, L, M, Q, R, W, 2, 3, 4 and 5 trains.

Queens: Served by the E, F, G, J, M, N, R, V, W, Z and 7 trains.

The Bus System

Buses are slower than subways, but they allow you to take in the scenery as you go, and offer many more alternatives for going crosstown (east and west) than the subway does.

Very important: You **must** have a MetroCard or $2 in coins (no pennies or half dollars) when you board. The driver does not handle money. You pay your fare with exact change or by dipping a MetroCard in the fare box. If you are pay-ing cash and do not have the right coins, you might be able to find someone on the bus who can make change for your paper money or pay for you with a Metro-Card and take your cash—if not, you'll have to get off.

City bus lines run the length and breadth of Manhattan and throughout other boroughs. They are especially useful for getting across town. All routes within Manhattan begin with the letter M. Many of the crosstown routes have the same number as the street on which they cross. Traffic on the principal crosstown streets runs in both directions; all the rest are one-way. As a general rule, even-numbered streets are one-way from west to east, and odd-numbered streets run east to west.

Here are the crosstown routes:

M-8 runs on 8th and 9th Sts. from Avenue D and 10th St. to Christopher St.

M-14 operates on 14th St.

M-16 and **M-34** operate on 34th St.

M-23 operates on 23rd St.

M-27 and **M-50** operate on 49th and 50th Sts.; the **27** goes to the Port Authority Bus Terminal.

M-31 crosses 57th St., then up Madison Ave. and across E. 72nd St.

M-42 operates on 42nd St.

M-66 operates on E. 67th St. westbound and crosses Central Park at 66th St.; eastbound it operates on W. 65th St. until it crosses Central Park, then contin-ues on E. 68th St.

M-72 operates on W. 72nd St. and E. 72nd St., crossing Central Park at 65th St. eastbound and 66th St. westbound.

M-79 operates on 79th St. and crosses Central Park on that street.

M-86 operates on 86th St. and crosses Central Park on that street.

M-96 operates on 96th St. and crosses Central Park on that street.

M-106 operates on 106th St. east of Central Park, and 96th St. west of the park.

M-116 runs across 116th St. to Manhattan Ave., then down to W. 106th St.

M-100, **M-101** and **Bx-15** operate on 125th St.

M-60 runs from W. 105th St. north on Broadway, east on 125th St., and then to La Guardia Airport.

Taxis

Taxis authorized to pick up passengers on the street have a distinctive orange-yellow color. A taxi's roof light will tell you if it is available. Look for cabs with the center section lit. They are empty, looking for customers. If the center section is off and the two ends are lit, they say "OFF DUTY" and the driver is not interested in you. If the entire light is off, don't bother with frantic waving—the cab has a passenger. Unlike in some other cities, cabs with passengers do not stop to pick up more. Hailing taxis in the rain is maximum frustration; consider some other way to go. And don't try to take a cab in Midtown during rush hour or right before theater curtains rise. Taxis cannot pick up more than four passengers.

Hailing a cab: Just stick your arm out and all the way up, and don't be shy. Yell "taxi" if necessary—no one in New York will look strangely at you for yelling. Get off the sidewalk if there is a lot of traffic or if parked cars will prevent taxis from seeing you. Be watchful of cars and trucks swerving into the lane where you may be standing. Don't jump ahead of other passengers who were trying to hail a cab before you arrived.

If you can't find a cab on the street, there are taxi stands at major hotels, Penn Station, Grand Central Terminal, and the Port Authority Bus Terminal.

Rules and Traditions: First of all, you should always remember that a New York taxi driver is *required* by law to take you anywhere within the city—even to the far ends of Brooklyn or Staten Island—as well as to Newark Airport and Westchester or Nassau Counties. Drivers may not want to take you to these locations, but they are obligated to do so. Cabs are required to accommodate you if you have a seeing-eye dog or are in a collapsible wheelchair. While some drivers have less-than-adequate English skills, most New Yorkers will tell you that they are far more courteous and respectful than drivers of earlier periods. Unfortunately, the long hours and low pay often lead to aggressive and reckless driving, so:

- Buckle your seat belt.
- Tell the driver to slow down if you become fearful. Don't be afraid to insist that the driver refrain from using a cell phone.
- Take a fare receipt from the cab driver when you get out. It gives the trip number and the taxi's official medallion number—information you need if you want to make a complaint or trace something you may have left in the cab. It also shows the 24-hour consumer hotline, (212) NYC-TAXI.

Fares: Yellow cab fares start with an initial charge of $2.50. The fare rises by 40 cents for every 1/5 mile traveled and 20 cents for every minute in stopped or slow traffic. There's a rush-hour surcharge of $1.00 per trip between 4 and 8 P.M. and a 50-cent surcharge per trip from 8 P.M. to 6 A.M. The metered fare does not include a tip; add 10 to 15 percent.

Yellow cabs are regulated by the city, which makes them a safer bet than unmarked car services, also known as **gypsy cabs**. Gypsy cabs are not allowed to pick up passengers on the street, but many do anyway, especially when cabs are scarce, such as during rush hour or when it's raining. Gypsy cab rates aren't metered, so their drivers often promise lower fares, but they may also fleece the unsuspecting.

Tips on Tipping

Restaurants: Tip the waiter 15 to 20 percent of the total bill before tax, according to quality of service. (Note: An easy way to calculate a reasonable tip in New York City is to double the 8.6 percent tax.) In more upscale restaurants that have a sommelier or wine steward, tip 8 to 10 percent of the cost of wine (and don't forget to subtract the cost of wine from the bill when calculating the waiter's tip).

Some restaurants automatically add a gratuity for large parties (usually 15 to 20 percent for parties of six or more). Customers should be informed in advance, but some restaurants are less forthcoming than others. Don't be shy about asking about this policy when dining with larger groups so you can avoid double-tipping.

Hotels: *Shuttle bus driver:* $1. *Bellhop:* $1 per bag. *Maid:* $2-$3 per night. *Room service:* 10 to 15 percent of the bill. *Parking attendant:* $2 per trip.

Taxis: We urge visitors to tip generously if the ride is satisfactory; drivers depend on tips to raise their pay to a decent level. Tip 10–15 percent of the fare, more if the driver helps with your luggage. Never tip less than $1.

Beauty Salons: A beautician, barber or manicurist should receive anywhere from 10 to 20 percent of the cost of the service, depending on how long it takes and how labor-intensive. Never tip less than $2.

Limousine and Car Services

There are dozens of limousine and car services, from long white Lincolns equipped with bars and TVs to regular sedans. They often cost more than taxis, but will come when you want them. You must call for them in advance. Among the major companies are **Tel Aviv** (212-777-7777), **Carmel** (212-666-6666), **Sabra** (212-777-7171) and **Allstate** (212-333-3333).

Exploring New York

New York reveals itself in fascinating ways to those who take the time to walk its streets. No other American city is more inviting to explore on foot, more geared to the pedestrian rather than the car.

Only by walking can you begin to sense New York's trademark energy and drive, its swirl of cultures and its layers of history. You'll learn much more about New York by strolling its streets than you will from the top of a tour bus.

You'll want to read this chapter carefully as you plan an itinerary. It's also a good idea to consult the chapter on **The Arts,** which has complete listings for all the top art museums, galleries and performing-arts institutions.

Street Smarts

Most first-time visitors have never experienced the hazardous traffic conditions found in New York. Cars, trucks, buses and aggressive bicycle messengers all compete for a favored place on the road; people on foot are seen as just another impediment.

The traditional pedestrian's right of way is, as Shakespeare wrote, "more honored in the breach than the observance." So walk defensively: Assume that a taxi will run a red light, or a truck or van will turn rapidly into the crosswalk without waiting for all the pedestrians to cross.

You'll notice almost immediately that New Yorkers on foot pay no attention whatsoever to traffic lights (it's that New York state of mind, the part that asks: Why trust a sign? I have eyes!). But if you're new here, obey the lights for a few days until you get the hang of crossing when it's safe.

Don't stand blocking the middle of the sidewalk while you're talking, studying a map or looking up at a tall building. Always step back toward the buildings. New Yorkers are an impatient lot, and they will shove right past you. And yet, you needn't hesitate to ask any reasonable-looking New Yorker a question. He or she will more than likely be glad to tell you anything you need to know.

Crime Safety

For city with such a tough reputation, New York has quite a low crime rate. The city is much safer now than it was in the 1980's and early 1990's—in terms of statistics, this is one of the safest big cities in America. Still, it's always smart to err on the side of caution. Here are some commonsense rules:

- Avoid desolate areas at night. Subways run infrequently late at night, and platforms may be a little creepy, so take a cab home after a late night out.
- Don't walk in Central Park at night unless there is a major event or you've attended a play at the Delacorte Theater.
- Keep your money in an inconspicuous place. Women should grasp their pocketbooks or wear them across the body; men should be sure a wad of

money is not bulging conspicuously in their pants pocket. Be conscious of keeping backpacks and purse zippers closed and within your view; bury your valuables at the very bottom of large bags, so pickpockets can't get at them without attracting your notice.

- Don't wear valuable necklaces that can be ripped off easily.

Public Bathrooms

New York City is notorious for its lack of public bathrooms. Here are a few places where you can find relief as you stroll around the city:

- Department stores
- Hotel lobbies
- Bryant Park (behind the Public Library on the 42nd St. side)
- Mid-Manhattan Library (across Fifth Ave. from the Public Library)
- Donnell Library (across 53rd St. from the Museum of Modern Art)
- Grand Central Terminal
- Times Square subway station (below the station entrance on 42nd Street at Seventh Avenue. An attendent will buzz you in.)
- Pennsylvania Station
- Port Authority Bus Terminal (though they won't pass a white-glove test.)
- Central Park Boathouse
- Coffee bars
- Barnes & Noble branches
- Visitor centers (Broadway between 46th and 47th Sts.; Seventh Ave. between 52nd and 53rd Sts.)

Finding Your Way

New York City is made up of five boroughs and stretches for 10 to 20 miles in several directions. If you can spend more than a few days in the city, take the time to venture beyond Manhattan to visit such wonderful places as the Bronx Zoo and the Brooklyn Museum. These world-famous institutions shouldn't be dismissed just by reason of location. You'll find descriptions of outer-borough highlights at the end of this chapter.

But the focal point for most leisure visitors is the island borough of Manhattan. As the accompanying maps make clear, Manhattan—or "the City," as many natives call it, much to the annoyance of Brooklynites—is one of the easiest places in the world to visit. The island is only 13 1/2 miles long and 2 1/3 miles wide at the center (not even a mile wide at its southern tip). Here's a brief guide to Manhattan's layout:

Avenues: run north to south. North is synonymous with "uptown"; south is "downtown." The higher the number in a building's street address, the farther uptown it will be.

Streets: run east to west on the grid above 14th Street.

East Side–West Side: The dividing line is Fifth Avenue. Addresses on the east side of Fifth begin at 1 East; on the west side of Fifth they begin at 1 West. The higher the number in the address, the farther east or west the location is from Fifth Avenue (for example, 200 W. 50th St. is farther west than 100 W. 50th St.).

    Streets are for the most part numbered consecutively and laid out in a grid. From 14th Street north to 181st Street (and beyond), you will always know where you are relative to, say, 42nd Street. South of 14th Street, in Manhattan's oldest neighborhoods, the streets have names and are not laid out according to any logical master plan. You'll need to a good map to navigate these areas.

    Many (but not all) *avenues* are also numbered. Starting at the East River, the East Side avenues, in order, are York, First, Second, Third, Lexington, Park, Madison and Fifth. After Fifth Avenue, which divides East Side from West Side, the West Side avenues are the Avenue of the Americas (more commonly referred to as Sixth Avenue), Seventh, Eighth, Ninth, 10th, 11th and 12th Avenues. Uptown (above Midtown on the Upper West Side), the West Side avenues assume new names (Eighth Ave. becomes Central Park West; Ninth becomes Columbus Ave.; 10th becomes Amsterdam Ave.; 11th becomes West End Ave.; and 12th becomes Riverside Dr.).Broadway cuts diagonally across the city from southeast to northwest, forming squares where it intersects with other avenues.

NEW YORK'S
TOP 25 ATTRACTIONS

American Museum of Natural History
Brooklyn Bridge
Bronx Zoo
Brooklyn Botanic Garden
Cathedral of St. John the Divine
Central Park
Chrysler Building
Ellis Island
Empire State Building
Grand Central Terminal
Guggenheim Museum
Lincoln Center
Metropolitan Museum of Art
Museum of Modern Art
New York Botanical Garden (Bronx)
New York Public Library
Radio City Music Hall
Rockefeller Center
St. Patrick's Cathedral
Staten Island Ferry
Statue of Liberty
Times Square
United Nations
Whitney Museum of American Art
Yankee Stadium

CityPass

CityPass is a great deal if you're planning on serious sightseeing. Adults pay just $48 ($34 for kids ages 6–17) for admission to six top attractions: the American Museum of Natural History, the Guggenheim, MoMA, the *Intrepid* Sea-Air-Space Museum, Circle Line Harbor Cruises and the Empire State Building. That's a whopping $48 savings on combined admission fees to these attractions for adults ($34 off for kids). You have nine days to visit each attraction (only once) beginning the day you first use your CityPass. You can purchase CityPass at any of the individual attractions, or buy online (*www.citypass.com* or *http://citypass.net*). The deal clincher? Once you've got CityPass, you can skip all the ticket lines—just present your booklet on the way into each attraction. (Tickets are void if removed from the CityPass booklet.)

SUGGESTED WALKING TOURS

Each of these walks can easily serve as a day's sightseeing itinerary. They link together many of Manhattan's top attractions, while offering you plenty of opportunity to go with the flow of New York's street life—shopping and noticing wonderful architectural details as you go.

Lower Manhattan

Lower Manhattan was the birthplace of New York City. It was first settled in the 17th century, when the Dutch founded the colony of Nieuw Amsterdam on the site of today's Financial District. It boasts a spectacular array of architecture, dense canyons of neo-classic temples and soaring skyscrapers.

Tragedy forever marked this neighborhood, of course, on September 11, 2001. Our walk will take in many historic streets where life carries on just as before, but we'll also stop at the site of the fallen towers, where so many visitors feel compelled to pay their respects in person.

Those of you with a surfeit of time and energy should start out by taking the A or C train to High Street in Brooklyn and hoofing it back into Manhattan. There's no more beautiful walk in New York than the stroll along the wooden pedestrian path of the **Brooklyn Bridge,** where the skyline views are still magnificent, if sadly changed now. The Brooklyn Bridge remains a marvel of engineering. Its soaring Gothic support towers stand tall as a monument to modern New York's ingenuity and ambition.

If the 30-minute bridge crossing has left you hungry, you can turn right (north) once you arrive in Manhattan. You're on the edge of **Chinatown,** which offers a huge array of dining options. You can also turn south toward **South Street Seaport,** which offers everything from an authentic British pub to sit-down seafood meals.

Those of you who couldn't muster the energy to walk the Brooklyn Bridge can join the tour at at the foot of **City Hall Park.** Branching to your right is Park Row, where Greeley, Pulitzer, Hearst, Ochs and other newspaper titans held forth for most of the 19th and some of the 20th century. No. 41 was the original *New York Times* building, now part of Pace University.

City Hall itself, housing the offices of the mayor and the city council, is an elegant Georgian and French Renaissance–style marble building built in 1803. It presides over the northern edge of elegantly manicured City Hall Park. On the northern edge of the park stands **Tweed Courthouse,** a magnificent structure built in the 1870's by "Boss" Tweed, who pilfered public construction funds on a massive scale (his plasterwork contractor was paid over $45,000 for a single day's work!). Stroll across the park, admiring its lovely gardens, until you emerge on Broadway.

On Broadway at Park Place, Cass Gilbert's opulent **Woolworth Building** is a study in Gothic splendor, complete with gargoyles, spires, lacy stonework and flying buttresses. The structure reigned briefly as the tallest building in the world when it opened in 1913. Be sure to peek inside the sumptuous lobby, with its vaulted ceiling of blue and gold mosaics; don't miss the architect's jest, a whimsical carving of Woolworth counting his nickels and dimes.

Continue south on Broadway. Just past Vesey Street, you'll see historic **St. Paul's Chapel,** New York's only intact pre-Revolutionary church. George Washington worshiped here on the day of his inauguration in 1789, and continued to attend during the months when New York was the capital. His pew is to the right as you enter. More recently, St. Paul's served as a place of rest and refuge for the rescue workers of Ground Zero.

Now you've arrived at **Ground Zero** itself, the site of the fallen Twin Towers (see also pp. 38–40). There is not actually much to see—it's a vast construction pit now—but the emptiness is giving way to activity. A new skyscraper is already rising high at 7 World Trade, and crews have already laid the cornerstone for the new Freedom Tower that will rise here. An information kiosk at the temporary PATH station, run by the Downtown Alliance, is a good place to orient yourself. The staff here is happy to supply you with information on the history of the World Trade Center, the rebuilding plans and the neighborhood at large.

Head back to Church Street and take it south for a few blocks to Wall Street, where you'll turn left. At the corner of Broadway and Wall Street stands **Trinity Church.** The first Trinity Church was the tallest structure in the city when it was built in 1697, but it was destroyed in the great fire that leveled much of downtown New York in 1776. A map inside the church, behind the last pews on the left, shows where Alexander Hamilton, Robert Fulton and others are buried in the church's historic graveyard.

Directly across Broadway at 1 Wall Street is the **Bank of New York,** with an eye-popping Art Deco lobby of red-and-gold mosaic.

Wall Street itself is a surprisingly narrow little lane, but it's lined with appropriately powerful neoclassical towers. The **New York Stock Exchange** is located at 20 Broad St., between Wall Street and Exchange Place. The exterior of this 1903 Beaux-Arts temple is pretty impressive, with massive Corinthian columns and an allegorical pediment sculpture titled "Integrity Protecting the Works of Man." (Insert your own Worldcom joke here.)

Diagonally across from the Exchange stands **Federal Hall National Memorial.** George Washington was sworn in as the first president of the United States on the steps of an earlier building on this site in 1789. Also at Federal Hall,

John Peter Zenger was acquitted of seditious libel in 1735, giving birth to the concept of freedom of the press. Exhibits inside illuminate the role of Lower Manhattan in the nation's early history.

Make your way back to Broadway and start heading south. This is the famous **"Canyon of Heroes,"** the setting for celebratory ticker-tape parades, which have been held throughout the past century to honor war heroes, astronauts and victorious Yankee squads and other New York teams. At no. 28 stands the **Museum of American Financial History,** which is worth a quick stop.

At the end of Broadway is a tiny green space, **Bowling Green Park,** which is said to be the very spot where Peter Minuit purchased Manhattan Island from a band of Indians for $24, in the very first New York real estate swindle on record. In colonial times, the park featured a gilded equestrian statue of King George III, but it was toppled by a mob in 1776 when the colonies were in revolt. Here you'll also see the famous "Charging Bull" statue, a symbol of Wall Street optimism (you might want to take your picture with it if you're feeling good about your portfolio).

Below Bowling Green Park is a gorgeous 1907 Beaux-Arts building designed by Cass Gilbert. Once the U.S. Customs House, it now houses the **National Museum of the American Indian,** a branch of the Smithsonian. The enormous sculptures out front were the work of Daniel Chester French; they represent Asia, America, Europe and Africa.

No. 1 Broadway is the building with blue awnings across the street. One entrance says "Cabin Class," and the other "First Class." Now a Citibank branch, this was where travelers of an earlier day booked passage on the United States Lines. The bank has preserved the hall as it was, a grand space befitting a great steamship company.

Now continue south into leafy **Battery Park,** the perfect place to relax and enjoy the breezes and the views, which extend out to the **Statue of Liberty,** holding her torch over New York Harbor. You can catch a ferry here if you'd like to sail out to the statue or to Ellis Island, which features riveting exhibits on the immigrant experience. Battery Park is the site of the damaged bronze sphere that once occupied the plaza between the World Trade Center towers; it now stands in the park as a temporary memorial to the victims of 9/11. Work has recently begun in the Battery Park Bosque, where a carousel, new walkways and a world-class ornamental garden are coming soon.

You can also opt to rest your weary feet by enjoying a picnic in the park, before mustering up the energy to visit the moving **Museum of Jewish Heritage—A Living Memorial to the Holocaust.** It stands just north of Battery Place, where the park meets the southern edge of the upscale but sterile residential neighborhood known as Battery Park City.

Greenwich Village

Greenwich Village long ago earned a reputation as a magnet for bohemians and intellectuals. Generations of artists and writers—Henry James and Edgar Allan

Poe, Jackson Pollack and e.e. cummings—gave the neighborhood its freewheeling identity, and radical thinkers from Upton Sinclair to John Reed have held forth in smoky Village cafes.

But it's been many years since starving artists were able to afford these rents. While the neighborhood does retain a definite live-and-let-live, left-of-center vibe, it's gone upscale these days. The really cutting-edge art scene has long since fled to Chelsea, the East Village, Brooklyn and Queens.

Nevertheless, the Village remains one of New York's most appealing neighborhoods, and an especially lovely place to stroll. Leafy streets, lined with Federal-style town houses and ivy-covered brownstones, meander at will, defying the symmetrical street grid pattern that brings order to the world above 14th Street. (Bring along a good map so you'll be able to wander without getting hopelessly lost.) Neighborhood residents remain loyal to the local organic bakery and the corner produce market. Funky craft stores, artsy boutiques and sidewalk cafes refuse to give way to Pottery Barns and Starbucks. It's a neighborhood on a very human scale, with small delights around every corner.

Start your stroll by taking the A, C or E train to Eighth Avenue and 14th Street, the Village's northern border. Head south along Eighth Avenue until you reach **Bleecker Street,** branching off toward your left. Now stroll along Bleecker, which will give you a good snapshot of the neighborhood. The three blocks between Bank Street and Charles Street offer terrific shopping, with a good concentration of antiques dealers, plus funky and affordable purses, jewelry, candles, cigars and more. You'll pass the chic **Marc Jacobs** boutique; **Les Pierre Antiques,** for upscale French Country pieces; **Rebel Rebel** and **Bleecker Bob's** for a great selection of used CDs; **Details,** for fun, colorful housewares and gifts; and **Condomania,** which sells a wider variety of condoms than you're likely to need during your stay in New York.

Bleecker intersects with **Christopher Street,** where you can veer off for more shopping. This is the heart of New York's gay community—the Gay Liberation Movement was born here during the famed Stonewall Rebellion of 1969—and many shops cater to a gay and lesbian clientele.

One block beyond Christopher is **Grove Street,** where you'll turn right. Walk one more block to the intersection of Grove and Bedford. At the corner stands a picturesque **wood-frame house;** sections of it date back to the early 19th century. Nearby, notice the house at **102 Bedford St.** with an odd chalet-style curved cornice. The very antithesis of gritty radical bohemia, Walt Disney himself once lived here. Continue along Grove Street, and peek into the charming **private courtyard** between nos. 10 and 12 Grove Street.

Now head a few steps south of Grove Street on Bedford Street. At no. 86 is the unheralded entrance to **Chumley's** (purposefully made unobtrusive to throw off the cops back in Prohibition days). This is one of New York's classic bars—definitely take a peek inside, as long as you can find the way in (take the steps right into the seemingly private courtyard, and don't be shy about asking for the bar's location if you can't find it). Chumley's has been a writer's hangout for decades, attracting patrons like Calvin Trillin, John Steinbeck, John Dos

Passos, Allen Ginsberg and many, many more. Pull up a chair near the fireplace and have a pint.

Grove Street dead-ends into Hudson Street near historic **St. Luke in the Fields** church, founded by Clement "'Twas the Night Before Christmas" Moore in 1822. Take Hudson Street one block south to **Barrow Street** and turn right. It's a splendid stroll along Barrow, which is lined with Federal-style and Italianate brownstones. Take Barrow for a couple of blocks to Washington Street, then turn left; take Washington one block to **Morton Street,** and turn left again. Morton is one of the most picturesque streets in the Village, lined with postcard-perfect brownstones.

Take Morton back two blocks to Hudson Street, make a right, then a left onto **St. Luke's Place,** which is lined with gingko trees and stately mid-19th-century Italianate town houses. At no. 6 is a gorgeous home once occupied by flamboyant New York mayor Jimmy Walker, a hard-partying public servant who was eventually forced to resign in disgrace. The brownstone at no. 10 was used for exterior shots of the Huxtable home in *The Cosby Show.* Theodore Dreiser, Marianne Moore and Sherwood Anderson all called this block home at one time or another.

Take St. Luke's back to Bedford Street and turn left. Just before you get to Commerce Street, be sure to notice **75 1/2 Bedford St.,** which a plaque proclaims to be the narrowest house in the Village (at 9 1/2 feet wide, it probably is). Edna St. Vincent Millay once lived here; later tenants included Cary Grant and John Barrymore.

Retrace your steps back south to Morton Street, and take Morton up to its terminus at Bleecker Street. Cross Bleecker and stroll along Cornelia Street. Cornelia ends at West 4th Street, which you'll take, heading east across Sixth Avenue. One block past Sixth Avenue is Macdougal Street, where you'll see the legendary **Provincetown Playhouse,** managed by Eugene O'Neill in the 1920's and site of the premieres for many of his plays. Bette Davis made her stage debut here. (If you need a break at this point, make a detour south along Macdougal to the corner of Bleecker Street, where you can snag an outdoor table at the atmospheric **Café Figaro** for a cappucino pick-me-up.)

At Macdougal and West 4th, you're at the southwest corner of **Washington Square Park.** It's not really much of a park at all, but rather the neighborhood's version of a town square. A triumphal (and newly renovated) arch designed by Stanford White presides over the park so majestically that you'd never guess this was once a lowly potter's field; in the early 19th century, felons met the hangman's noose on this spot in public executions at the Hanging Elm near Macdougal Street.

Despite Washington Square's seedy history, this area became a haven for the monied classes inhabiting the rarified world of Henry James and Edith Wharton. Stroll up the western edge of the park, and make a right onto **Washington Square North.** You can almost picture carriages arriving by the glow of gaslights for an elegant dinner party in this row of elegant and formal Greek Revival town houses, most of which date back to the 1830's.

At the northeast corner of the square, head north for one block along University Place. Turn left into **Washington Mews,** a charming cobblestone street lined with vine-covered two-story 19th-century buildings. These adorable houses are mostly converted stables and carriage houses, originally built to serve the wealthy residents of Washington Square North and now partly occupied by New York University. They're typical of the surprises hidden around every corner of this wonderful, historic neighborhood.

Midtown

Midtown is the heart of Manhattan, packed with architectural landmarks, the city's most popular retail shopping, hundreds of corporate headquarters and several of its top museums. This tour is a good overview for first-timers, since it encompasses many of Manhattan's top attractions.

Start your tour by taking the B, D, F, N, Q, R, V, 1, 2, 3 or 9 train to 34th Street. You have just been deposited at the gates of **Macy's,** the world's largest department store. It is worth seeing if you've never been before, but don't expect a civilized Harrods-style shopping experience. Especially in the holiday season, Macy's is migraine-inducing, with less-than-helpful service.

Head east along 34th Street, toward the **Empire State Building,** which soars skyward from the corner of 34th and Fifth. Completed in 1931, it is 102 stories of pure romance and Art Deco splendor. Visitors can take the elevators up to the 86th- and 102nd-floor observatories, where the views are marvelous. (Expect a long wait in line, though.)

Turn left and head north on Fifth Avenue. There's a **Yankees Clubhouse** store between 36th and 37th Streets; **Lord & Taylor,** an understated classic of a New York department store, stands at 39th Street. Just across the street is the former **Tiffany Building** (409 Fifth Ave.), designed in 1906 by Stanford White, who based it on a 16th-century Venetian palazzo.

At 42nd Street, you'll reach the magnificent main branch of the **New York Public Library,** a 1911 Beaux-Arts temple with rows of Corinthian columns. Two vigilant stone lions (christened Patience and Fortitude by Mayor Fiorello La Guardia) stand sentry at the entrance.

Take a detour east along 42nd Street for a look at **Grand Central Terminal,** Manhattan's famously bustling train station, where subways, underground shopping concourses, a food court and 48 sets of railroad tracks form one vast beehive of activity. Enter at 42nd Street and Vanderbilt Avenue. Walk down the entrance ramp, where you'll see the entrance to the main concourse. Take a look inside—it's a breathtaking space, with sweeping staircases and a vaulted ceiling soaring overhead, dotted with the constellations. Retrace your steps to the ramp on which you just entered; here you'll see some food counters for a quick bite, or you can take an escalator down to the food court, which offers an enormously varied selection. (But don't sit here if it's a nice day—we're headed off to a terrific picnic spot in just a minute.) Behind the escalator is a New York Transit Museum store, selling unique city souvenirs.

The Empire State Building

Now exit Grand Central, and backtrack along 42nd Street. When you reach Fifth Avenue, cross to the south side of 42nd Street, pausing for a moment in the crosswalk to look up and catch a perfect view of the gleaming spire of the **Chrysler Building,** another of New York's Art Deco masterpieces.

Keep heading west, past the library, to **Bryant Park,** a lovely green oasis in the heart of Midtown. Grab a chair and join the festive crowds of neighborhood workers who come here for their lunch breaks every day. (If you didn't already buy lunch at Grand Central, there are several places in Bryant Park itself to pick up a casual bite.)

After your lunch, continue up Fifth Avenue. Stretching from 48th to 50th Streets between Fifth and Sixth Avenues is **Rockefeller Center,** a magnificent complex of towering skyscrapers. Enter between 49th and 50th Streets, past Channel Gardens (and a branch of the Metropolitan Museum of Art gift shop) to the main plaza, which everyone recognizes as the home of the giant Rock Center Christmas tree and its petite skating rink, tucked under the golden statue of Prometheus. (The plaza's Rink Bar is a wonderful setting for an out-

door cocktail in summer, a cozy place to observe the twirling skaters in winter.)
Dominating the plaza is the soaring Art Deco GE Building; make sure to stop
inside and marvel at its beautiful lobby, adorned with murals by José-Maria
Sert. NBC's television studios are nearby (including the streetside set used for
the *Today* show). If you continue across to Sixth Avenue, you'll see **Radio City
Music Hall,** recently restored to all its original Deco splendor.

Return to Fifth Avenue. On the east side of Fifth, between 49th and 50th,
stand the chic confines of **Saks Fifth Avenue.** Across 50th Street rise the twin
Gothic spires of **St. Patrick's Cathedral,** seat of the Catholic Archdiocese of
New York. Peek inside to see the interior, where Zelda and F. Scott Fitzgerald
were married, and where funeral services were held for Robert Kennedy.

Continuing uptown, there's no shortage of shopping. At 51st Street, bargain
hunters will love **H&M** for trendy sportswear at jaw-droppingly low prices, and
Sephora, a stunning cosmetics emporium with offerings at all price levels.

Architecture buffs may want to detour east along 53rd Street to see **Lever
House** and Mies van der Rohe's **Seagram Building,** two prime examples of the
sleek, stark International style. At 55th and Madison (one block east of Fifth) is
Philip Johnson's pink granite **Sony Building** with Chippendale-style ornamentation at its roofline. Inside is the interactive **Wonder Lab** (free admission),
which offers the chance to try out the latest electronic gadgets from Sony.

Continue north on Fifth to 57th Street. This is one of the toniest intersections in New York, home to blue-chip **galleries,** a **Prada** boutique, **Bergdorf
Goodman** and the legendary **Tiffany's** (worth a browse even if you can't afford
its pricey baubles, always packaged in a signature blue box with a white ribbon).

At 59th Street, the **Plaza,** probably the world's most famous hotel, sits like
a giant wedding cake. Eloise had the run of the place in Kay Thompson's
beloved children's books, and it's been featured in movies from *North by Northwest* to *Home Alone 2*. Michael Douglas wed Catherine Zeta-Jones here in an
intimate little ceremony for 700 of their closest show-biz friends.

The tour will leave you at the corner of **Central Park.** This is one of the
park's loveliest sections, near the zoo and Wollman Rink. Buy a hot dog from
one of the street vendors and stake out a bench.

The Upper West Side

The Upper West Side is one of Manhattan's most prosperous neighborhoods,
but it lacks the stuffiness of the Upper East Side, that enclave of the super-rich
just across the park. Instead, this is home to bankers, lawyers, media types, rumpled intellectuals, yuppies pushing strollers and out-of-work actors walking their
dogs. It's a livable, convenient neighborhood, with a tiny dash of hip and a
decidedly liberal bent (hence its nickname, the People's Republic of the Upper
West Side).

Once upon a time, when most of Manhattan was concentrated way downtown, this was considered the country—rural farmland that was much too
remote for development. Obviously, development did come, originally led by

grand apartment buildings, many of which stand to this day. The neighborhood declined in the mid-20th century, as thousands of poor Hispanic immigrants settled here; these were the gang-ridden mean streets filmed in *West Side Story*. But gentrification began in the late 1960's, spurred by the construction of **Lincoln Center.** Patches of the neighborhood remained mired in poverty and crime well into the 1980's, but after a couple of stock-market booms, the entire West Side has now been thoroughly gentrified, with skyrocketing apartment prices. Residents bemoan the ever-widening presence of big-chain mega-stores (you can't throw a rock without hitting a Starbucks these days), but a few mom-and-pop stalwarts remain. This is a good walk if you'd like to see how New Yorkers really live outside the bustle of Midtown.

Start by taking the 1 or 9 train to the 86th Street station, and heading south down Broadway. If you've got kids in tow, you'll want to stop at the **Children's Museum of Manhattan,** on 83rd Street between Broadway and Amsterdam. The hands-on exhibits are so engaging that they make learning painless.

Continuing south down Broadway, you'll pass a few of the retail landmarks that define the neighborhood. Between 83rd and 82nd Streets is a **Barnes & Noble** superstore. West Siders railed against its presence (as West Siders are wont to do) when it arrived in the early 1990's, crushing the independent Shakespeare & Co. a block south, but it has won over locals with its massive selection and frequent appearances by high-profile authors. At 80th Street stands a West Side icon, **Zabar's.** This is one of the city's top gourmet stores, with a dizzying selection of cheeses, breads, prepared foods, salads and much more. It's a great place to stock up for a picnic in Central Park at the end of our tour. Just across the street is another great place to nosh: Pop into **H&H** and treat yourself to a bagel hot out of the oven.

Farther south, the massive **Apthorp** apartment building dominates an entire city block between 79th and 78th Streets. Take a peek inside the iron gates to envy the residents' private courtyard. At 74th Street, you'll see **Fairway,** another West Side institution, and the best place in town to buy fabulous produce at bargain prices.

A block farther south stands the grand **Ansonia Hotel,** a wedding-cake confection commanding an entire block between 74th and 73rd Streets. Originally opened in 1904 as a luxury residential hotel, the Ansonia offered its tenants a grand ballroom, a swimming pool, a theater and a system that sent messages swooshing in pneumatic tubes from room to room. Live seals cavorted in the fountain, and W. E. D. Stokes, the architect, kept a pet bear and chickens in the roof garden. Celebrities from Enrico Caruso to Babe Ruth have lived here, and the Chicago White Sox conspired here to throw the 1919 World Series.

Cross over to the east side of Broadway. Between 74th and 73rd Streets is the monumental **Apple Bank for Savings,** with a heavy limestone facade and intricate ironwork doors. Enter the building for a moment—it's a truly breathtaking interior, with a soaring vaulted ceiling inlaid with copper, intricate ironwork, and colorful inlaid marble floors.

Continue down to 72nd Street, where you might want to stop in at **Gray's Papaya** for the "recession special" (a hot dog and a papaya drink for $1.95). Take 72nd Street east, where you'll spot a branch of **Krispy Kreme** on the north side of the street (double-dare you to resist if the "Hot Doughnuts Now" sign is lit).

Now turn left on Columbus and wander uptown for several blocks, stopping at any boutique that catches your fancy. As you approach 77th Street, you'll see the grounds of the **American Museum of Natural History.** This is one of New York's top attractions, with a world-class collection of dinosaurs. Stop in if you have time, or continue up the Columbus Avenue side, and take the path through the museum lawn, passing the *New York Times* **time capsule** (established at the turn of the millennium and designed by Santiago Calatrava) at 79th Street. The path curves around the building at 81st Street. Up ahead you'll see the glorious **Rose Center for Earth and Space.** Even if you don't have time for the riveting Harrison Ford–narrated Space Show, you can admire the building, a stunning glass cube enclosing a glowing white globe.

At the corner of 81st Street and Central Park West rise the three cupola-topped towers of the **Beresford** (John McEnroe owns the northeast tower, Helen Gurley Brown occupies the southeast). Jerry Seinfeld also has a multimillion-dollar duplex here, and is currently building a private garage on 83rd Street with space for his collection of 20 Porsches—so he need not ever have a George Costanza–style meltdown over finding a parking spot.

Turn right down Central Park West, heading past the equestrian statue of Teddy Roosevelt outside the Natural History Museum. Below 77th Street, you'll pass the **New-York Historical Society,** a manageably sized museum with fascinating exhibits of the world's most unmanageable city.

Between 75th and 74th Streets stands the **San Remo,** another landmark apartment building designed by Emery Roth, architect of the Beresford. In the depths of the Depression, the projects fared poorly, and the two buildings were sold together for the total sum of $25,000 (a fee that would not buy you a broom closet in the San Remo today). Although Dustin Hoffman has given up his apartment, the building is still home to Steve Martin and Steven Spielberg.

At Central Park West and 72nd Street stands the brooding fortress-like hulk of the **Dakota** (so named because the developer's friends told him the site was so far north that it might as well be in Dakota territory). Though it's been home to an illustrious group of tenants over the years—Lauren Bacall, Boris Karloff, Leonard Bernstein, William Inge and many more—the Dakota will forever be associated with John Lennon, who was tragically gunned down outside its gates on 72nd Street. John's widow, Yoko Ono, still lives here.

It's only appropriate, after visiting the Dakota, to make a pilgrimage into Central Park across the way. Just inside the 72nd Street entrance is **Strawberry Fields,** a beautifully landscaped area dedicated to Lennon's memory. It's one of the loveliest, most tranquil spots in the park, and a perfect place to spread out your picnic and end your tour.

The Upper East Side

The Upper East Side is synonymous with old money; this is the land of blue-bloods and blue-haired ladies. That generalization doesn't hold true through-out the neighborhood, of course—the farther east you go from Central Park, the more affordable and down-to-earth things become. But for our purposes, we'll stay close to the park and take a look at the lifestyles of the rich and famous, the mansions of titans such as Vanderbilt, Carnegie and Whitney. Many of their homes are now museums, schools, charitable organizations or embassies; others have been subdivided into some of the most expensive apartments in the world.

Start by taking the 4, 5 or 6 train to 86th Street. Walk west along 86th Street till you reach Fifth Avenue. The giant **brick-and-limestone mansion** at the southeast corner was built in 1914, and was later purchased by Mrs. Cor-nelius Vanderbilt in 1944. The founder of the Vanderbilt fortune, Com-modore Cornelius Vanderbilt, was a notorious tightwad, but he left a bundle for generations of his descendants to build impressive homes.

Turn left and head down Fifth Avenue, toward the apartment building at no. 1040 that was the **home of Jackie Onassis.** Jackie loved living in the city, since New Yorkers take pride in playing it cool around celebrities; by blending into the scenery, she achieved a small measure of privacy here. Jackie O. was often spotted jogging around the Central Park reservoir nearby.

Continue strolling down Fifth, past the Metropolitan Museum of Art. At the southeast corner of 82nd Street stands the **former mansion of Benjamin Duke.** Born to a tobacco farming family in North Carolina, Duke and his younger brother, James, were founders of the American Tobacco Company and the principal benefactors of a little college that became Duke University. The Benjamin Dukes bought their place from a developer who built it on spec in 1901. They later sold it to his brother, James, who lived there until he built his own nearby. Members of the Duke family and their relatives, the Biddles, lived in the Benjamin Duke house until recently.

The French Gothic palace on the southeast corner of 79th Street, property of several millionaires at different times, belongs now to the **Ukrainian Insti-tute of America.** The onetime home of financier Payne Whitney (given to him as a wedding present by a doting uncle) between 78th and 79th Streets now serves as the French Embassy's cultural offices.

James Duke's place, modeled on a chateau in Bordeaux, rose on the north-east corner of 78th Street in 1912. A leading critic calls it "one of the most magnificent mansions in New York." Duke's widow and their daughter, Doris Duke, lived there until the late 1950's, when they gave it to New York Uni-versity. It is now **NYU's Graduate School of Art History.**

At 75th Street on the northeast corner, the **Commonwealth Fund** occupies the home of Edward Harkness, son of one of John D. Rockefeller's original partners in the Standard Oil Company. Edward Harkness built most of the undergraduate dorms at Harvard and Yale. The Commonwealth Fund, founded by his mother, devotes Harkness millions to health and medical research.

At 75th Street, you might take a detour east to Madison Avenue and the **Whitney Museum of American Art.** Even if you don't have the time for a full-fledged museum visit, this is a great place to rest and refuel; Sarabeth's at the Whitney stands head and shoulders above your average museum cafeteria. This stretch of Madison Avenue is also prime **gallery-hopping** territory.

On East 73rd Street between Fifth and Madison stands the house **Joseph Pulitzer** built—no. 11, the one with lots of columns—now subdivided by 13 less affluent tenants. Despite the luxury of this home, Pulitzer, German-born publisher of the *New York World* and the *St. Louis Post-Dispatch,* barely lived here, due to his extreme sensitivity to sound (a special soundproof room constructed here apparently didn't satisfy him).

Continuing down Fifth Avenue, you'll reach the mansion of coke and steel tycoon Henry Clay Frick, which stretches from 70th Street to 71st Street and encompasses a lovely courtyard and pool. Frick, once chairman of Carnegie Steel, was an avid collector of art, especially of the Italian Renaissance. The mansion was designed by the same architects who designed the New York Public Library, and planned from the start as both home and gallery. Frick left the house and the art to the city, and the **Frick Collection** is one of the real jewels of New York City's art scene.

Turn onto **East 70th Street** and stroll away from the park for a few blocks, continuing all the way to Lexington Avenue. This is one of the most elegant streets in Manhattan, lined with a row of stunningly beautiful town houses.

At the northeast corner of Park Avenue and 70th Street is the **Asia Society,** founded by John D. Rockefeller, Jr. in 1956 to foster better relations between America and Asia through culture and the arts. Its galleries are worth a look.

Walk south and look for **680 Park Ave.,** at the north corner of 68th Street. Designed by McKim, Mead & White, this neo-Federal town house was built for banker Percy Rivington Payne. It later became the Soviet Mission to the United Nations; Nikita Khrushchev stayed here while visiting the U.N.

Continue down to 66th Street, and turn right, heading back toward Central Park. At 3 East 66th St. was the **home of Ulysses S. Grant** from 1881 to 1885. Forced into bankruptcy after a scandal-ridden presidency and ravaged by cancer, Grant retired here to concentrate on penning his memoirs. After his death, his autobiography met with great critical acclaim and earned a tidy sum for his family.

The **Roosevelts' twin town house** is worth a final two-block walk from Fifth Avenue to 47–49 E. 65th St. It has just one front door. Inside the vestibule were separate entrances to FDR's domineering mother's quarters on the left, and her son's on the right. (Small wonder that Eleanor didn't like it.) The Roosevelts lived there in 1920–21 when FDR was convalescing from polio and stayed there whenever they were in the city. The house is now a student center for Hunter College, which is nearby on Park Avenue.

At Fifth Avenue and 61st Street stands **the Pierre,** one of Manhattan's poshest hotels and a member of the Four Seasons chain. Amid lavish trompe l'oeil murals, you can indulge in the pricey pleasure of afternoon tea in the Rotunda Lounge. The Café Pierre bar is an elegant spot for a cocktail.

GUIDED SIGHTSEEING TOURS

Boat, bus and other vehicular tours tend to have reasonably regular schedules, but some seasonal change can occur. Schedules, prices and meeting places for most of the walking tours listed here can vary wildly throughout the year, so call or check each company's Web site well in advance to avoid surprises.

Walking Tours

Adventure on a Shoestring (212) 265-2663. This group offers well-regarded and affordable 90-minute tours of New York's most interesting neighborhoods. Most outings focus on areas in Lower Manhattan, but tours of Astoria, Hoboken and Roosevelt Island are also available. Tours often include chats with members of the community, and some walks are followed by lunch at local ethnic restaurants. **Price:** $5 (meals not included).

Big Apple Greeter (212) 669-2896 *www.bigapplegreeter.org*. This terrific non-profit organization matches visitors with knowledgeable and enthusiastic local volunteers, who take pride in introducing their guests to New York's hidden secrets. You must call in advance to make a reservation, which gets you a very personal two- to four-hour visit in any of the five boroughs, designed just for you, your family or a small group of friends. It's a fantastic bargain, and a memorable way to get an insider's view of daily life in the city. **Price:** Free.

Big Onion Walking Tours (212) 439-1090 *www.bigonion.com*. Big Onion offers daily two-hour tours in summer (less frequently the rest of the year). Themes range from neighborhood tours and in-depth historical and ethnic surveys to special holiday and eating tours. All guides hold advanced degrees in American history, and are fonts of fun facts about New York. No reservations are required, although you should call ahead on the day of the tour to confirm the schedule; just meet at the designated starting point and bring cash. **Price:** $12 adults; $10 students and seniors; extra $4 for special culinary tours.

Central Park Conservancy (212) 360-2726 *www.centralparknyc.org*. The Central Park Conservancy sponsors one-hour tours that explore the history, ecology, design and simple beauty of Central Park. Routes vary, and some tours require registration. **Price:** Free.

Harlem Spirituals Gospel and Jazz Tours (212) 391-0900 *www.harlemspirituals.com*. Despite the name, Harlem Spirituals offers tours in every New York borough. But the Harlem tours are the real draw here, featuring everything from a Sunday gospel service (proper attire required) to Saturday-night soul food and jazz tours. Tours leave from the company's Midtown offices and include transportation to Harlem. **Prices:** $30–$95 adults; $22.50–$95 children. Prices vary with the tour option you pick, and the food or entertainment that's included.

Joyce Gold History Tours (212) 242-5762 *www.nyctours.com*. All of these highly recommended two- to three-hour tours are conducted by Joyce Gold herself. An instructor of history at NYU and author of several walking guides to New York City, Ms. Gold offers an extensive list of neighborhood tours that are heavy on history, with titles like "East Village—Culture and Counter-Culture" and "The New Meat Market—Butchers, Bakers and Art Scene Makers." No reservations are needed. **Price:** $12.

Municipal Art Society Tours (212) 935-3960 *www.mas.org*. The MAS program "Discover New York" sponsors a diverse selection of year-round tours of New York's neighborhoods, history and culture. Some tours, like "Cast in Iron: Manhole and Chute Covers," have companion lectures and slide shows. Some tours require reservations, so call ahead. **Prices:** Weekdays $12, weekends $15.

New York City Cultural Walking Tours (212) 979-2388 *www.nycwalk.com*. Alfred Pommer has been researching and conducting a wide array of tours for over 15 years. Featured walks include multi-ethnic heritage tours, as well as staples like the "Bohemian Walking Tour of Greenwich Village" and the unusual "Gargoyles in Manhattan." There is a different tour each month, March through December; meet on Sunday at 2 P.M. at the designated start of the tour. **Prices:** $10.

New York Talks and Walks (888) 377-4455 *www.newyorktalksandwalks.com*. Dr. Philip Schoenberg offers a multitude of seasonal, ethnic and historical tours, including the "Hidden Treasures of Chinatown" and the "Jewish Gangster Tour." Reservations are not required, but call ahead to confirm the schedule. **Prices:** Most tours $12–$15.

Radical Walking Tours (718) 492-0069 *www.he.net/~radtours*. These tours (most on Sundays) are led by historian Bruce Kayton. Walks explore significant sites in New York's history of political activism, with an emphasis on topics like civil rights, labor history and gay and lesbian liberation. No reservation required. **Price:** $10.

Rockefeller Center Tours (212) 664-3700 or (212) 664-7174 for reservations *www.rockefellercenter.com*. These 75-minute tours explore the history, art and architecture of Rockefeller Center, including Radio City, the GE Building, NBC Studios, the skating rink and much more. Meet at NBC Experience Store on Rockefeller Plaza at West 49th Street. Tours depart every hour from 10 A.M. to 5 P.M. Monday to Saturday, and until 4 P.M. on Sundays (indoor routes are used in bad weather). Reservations are recommended; no children under age six allowed. **Prices:** $10 adults; $8 seniors and children ages 6–16. $21 combination ticket also includes NBC Studios tour.

Savory Sojourns (212) 691-7314 *www.savorysojourns.com*. These tours can be expensive, but for your money you get a five- to six-hour eating tour of one of the city's neighborhoods, complete with market stops, cooking demonstrations, kitchen tours of acclaimed restaurants, food, beer and wine. This company is run by Addie Tomei (Marisa's mom). Reserve well in advance. **Prices:** $70–$155, including food.

Wall Street Walking Tour (212) 606-4064 *www.downtownny.com*. Every Thursday and Saturday at noon, the Downtown Alliance sponsors a free 90-

minute walking tour of Lower Manhattan. Meet on the steps of the U.S. Customs House at Bowling Green. Reservations are required for groups, but not individuals. **Price:** Free.

Wildman Steve Brill's Food and Ecology Tours (914) 835-2153 *www.wildmanstevebrill.com*. Steve Brill, once arrested for eating dandelions in Central Park, now offers four-hour tours of city parks teaching identification and applications of a variety of wild plants. Walkers are encouraged to bring bags and containers to carry home wild herbs, mushrooms and berries. Reserve at least 24 hours in advance. **Prices:** $10 adults; $5 children.

Cruises

Circle Line (212) 563-3200 *www.circleline42.com* or (212) 269-5755 *www.circlelinedowntown.com*. Tours leave from Pier 83 at the west end of 42nd St. and Pier 16 at the South Street Seaport. The three-hour "Full Island" cruise draws the biggest crowds, but you'll see just as many major sights on the shorter cruises. Stick with the one-hour "Liberty Cruise," the *Beast* and the *Shark* speedboat rides (great for kids!) or one of the themed trips. **Prices:** $18–$26 adults; $14–$20 seniors; $9–$13 children ages 12 and under.

New York Waterways (800) 533-3779 *www.nywaterway.com*. Tours depart from Pier 78 at the west end of 38th St. This is the Circle Line's biggest competitor, offering a similar variety of cruises on their new, clean boats. Besides the standard 90-minutes harbor cruises, they also run special baseball cruises to Yankee Stadium and a number of cruises to destinations up the Hudson. **Prices:** Harbor cruises $20–$25 adults; $10–$12 children; $17–$20 seniors.

Spirit Cruises (212) 727-2789 *www.spiritcruises.com*. Another catch-all cruise operator, offering a variety of packages that take in the major sights of New York's harbor and rivers, combined with decent entertainment and so-so food. Tours depart from Chelsea Piers on the Hudson at W. 23rd St. (A more upscale competitor is **World Yacht;** 212-630-8100; *www.worldyacht.com*.) **Prices:** $30–$85, depending on day and time of cruise.

Other Transportation
*(See also chapter **Sports & Recreation**, section "Biking.")*

Crypt Keeper Tours (888) 394-8633 or (212) 679-9777 *www.cryptkeepertours.com*. Visit sites of famous people's deaths (including John Lennon, Sid Vicious, Jackie Onassis, Andy Warhol and Typhoid Mary) in a vintage hearse. Reservations are required. **Price:** $45.

Liberty Helicopter Tours (212) 967-6464 *www.libertyhelicopters.com*. These are expensive and brief tours, but they do offer a unique perspective on the city. Trips tend to range from five to 20 minutes and take in most of the major sights, from the Statue of Liberty to Central Park. Reserve in advance. **Prices:** $56–$162.

NEW YORK CITY
SEASONAL EVENTS

Winter

The Nutcracker New York State Theater at Lincoln Center (212) 870-5570 *www.nycballet.com*. The New York City Ballet performs this holiday classic each year with students from the School of American Ballet.   *November–December*

Christmas Spectacular Radio City Music Hall, 1260 Sixth Ave. (at 50th St.) (212) 247-4777 *www.radiocity.com*. The Radio City Christmas Spectacular features the famed Rockettes in Santa hats, high-kicking alongside larger-than-life Nutcracker soldiers.   *November–early January*

Christmas Window Displays Along Fifth Avenue in Midtown, marvel at the intricate winter scenes in department store windows. (Lord & Taylor, Saks Fifth Avenue and Barney's are the most popular.) Check out the Cartier building wrapped for Christmas in an enormous red bow.   *December*

Christmas Tree Lighting Ceremony Rockefeller Center *www.rockefeller-center.com*. One of the tallest Christmas trees in the country is mounted in Rockefeller Center, where it is strung with five miles of lights and lit by a celebrity in a nationally televised ceremony that includes an ice-skating show and other entertainment.   *Early December*

Messiah Sing-Along Avery Fisher Hall, Lincoln Center (212) 333-5333 *www.lincolncenter.org*. The National Chorale Counsel organizes this sing-in of Handel's "Messiah" led by 20 conductors with an audience of up to 3,000, including four trained soloists to rescue the arias. No experience is necessary and lyrics sheets are provided. Amateurs, professionals, even high-school choirs participate.   *Mid-December*

New Year's Eve Ball Drop Times Square (212) 768-1560 *www.timessquare-bid.org*. It's not officially the New Year until the ball drops over Times Square. The new and improved ball is now adorned with a stunning 12,000 rhinestones and 180 75-watt bulbs. Arrive early, since the area is packed with revelers hours before midnight.

New Year's Eve Fireworks Central Park. Spectators gather at Tavern on the Green and other spots throughout the park for views of the annual fireworks display. Festivities begin at 11:30 P.M.

New York National Boat Show Jacob K. Javits Convention Center, 655 W. 34th St. (at 11th Ave.) (212) 216-2000 *www.discoverboating.com/newyork*. Enormous crowds show up each year to see 400 of the world's leading manufacturers show off the latest power-boats—from small craft to yachts—and marine accessories. Seminars on fishing and boating are also offered.
                                    Late December–early January

Winter Antiques Show Seventh Regiment Armory, Park Ave. (at 67th St.)
(718) 292-7392 *www.winterantiquesshow.com*. The city's premier antiques fair—
featuring collections ranging from ancient to Art Nouveau—is also a benefit for
East Side House Settlement.   *Late January*

Outsider Art Fair The Puck Building, 295 Lafayette St. (at Houston St.)
(212) 777-5218 *www.sanfordsmith.com*. This three-day event ($15 admission)
draws an international crowd of dealers, collectors and art lovers. Thirty-five
dealers exhibit self-taught, visionary and art brut pieces to crowds in the thousands. It's a good place for celebrity sightings and star-studded seminars.
                                                                   Late January

Chinese New Year For information, call the Chinese Cultural Center at (212)
334-3764. Five days of celebrating on and around Mott Street culminate in a
colorful procession of lions and dragons made from wood and silk that wind their
way through the narrow and festively decorated streets.
                                    Begins first full moon after January 21

Westminster Kennel Club Dog Show Madison Square Garden, Seventh
Ave. (at 33rd St.) (212) 465-6741 *www.westminsterkennelclub.org*. The nation's
most prestigious dog show features 3,000 pampered pooches that are pared down
to seven finalists and then a single winner of "Best in Show." About 30,000
spectators show up for the two-day event.   *Mid-February*

The Art Show Seventh Regiment Armory, Park Ave. (at 67th St.)
(212) 766-9200 *www.artdealers.org*. Sponsored by the Art Dealers Association
of America, this is New York's foremost art fair. Seventy of the nation's leading
galleries gather to exhibit works that span five centuries from 17th-century masters to contemporary artists in a range of media that includes painting, drawing,
print, sculpture, photography and video.   *Late February*

Spring

International Cat Show Madison Square Garden, Seventh Ave. (at 33rd
St.) (212) 465-6741. Hundreds of fabulous felines representing 40 breeds
compete for the Best of Show award with all the composure for which cats are
famous. After, you can shop for cat accessories at the cat supermarket or listen
to lectures on topics like cat acupuncture, massage and feline aerobics. *March*

Manhattan Antiques and Collectibles Triple Pier Expo 12th Ave.
(between 48th and 55th Sts.) (212) 255-0020 *www.stellashows.com*. Nine hundred dealers take over Piers 88, 90 and 92 along the Hudson River to sell everything from posters, toys, textiles, fashions and furniture to silver, porcelain, fine
china, paintings, jewelry and glassware. The selection is particularly strong in
mid-century modern collectibles and Americana.
        One weekend in March; one weekend in January; and two weekends in November

St. Patrick's Day Parade Fifth Ave. (from 44th to 86th St.) (212) 484-1222.
In one of the city's oldest annual events, 150,000 Irish Americans and other

revelers draped in green join the festivities along Fifth Avenue (starting at 11 A.M.) and fill the city's bars well into the night. You can find green beer, green bagels and virtually everything in the shape of shamrock, as New York goes Hibernian for a day. For best views of the parade, line up early.   *March 17*

International Asian Art Fair Seventh Regiment Armory, Park Ave. (at 67th St.) (212) 642-8572 *www.haughton.com*. Top dealers from around the world gather at the Armory to sell art from Southeast Asia and the Middle and Far East. Around 14,000 people come to browse and buy items that range anywhere from $200 to hundreds of thousands of dollars.   *Late March*

New Directors/New Films (212) 875-5610 *www.filmlinc.com*. This film festival, sponsored by MoMA and the Film Society of Lincoln Center, features works by emerging, overlooked and new directors. Such notables as Wim Wenders, Spike Lee and Steven Spielberg have screened films in past years.

Late March–early April

Ringling Bros. and Barnum & Bailey Circus Madison Square Garden, Seventh Avenue (at 33rd St.) (212) 465-6741 *www.ringling.com*. Kicking off its New York run each spring, the circus's lions, tigers and bears (and elephants) parade along 34th Street to Madison Square Garden at midnight on the night before the first performance. The spectacular procession of animals is a great way to get a free peek at "The Greatest Show on Earth."   *Late March–early May*

Whitney Biennial Whitney Museum of American Art, 945 Madison Ave. (at 75th St.) (212) 570-3600 *www.whitney.org*. Every two years (coming next in 2006), the Whitney presents a headline-grabbing exhibition of what it regards as the most influential contemporary American art, often highlighting works by innovative and vanguard artists.   *Late March–early June*

Easter Parade Fifth Avenue (44th-57th Sts.) (212) 484-1222. In a tradition dating back to the Civil War era, the Easter Parade is an informal procession of spectacularly bonneted strollers. Participants sport everything from classic bowlers to extravagantly flowering chapeaus. The best perch is the steps of St. Patrick's Cathedral, if you can get near it.   *Easter Sunday*

New York International Auto Show Jacob Javits Convention Center, 655 W. 34th St. (at 11th Ave.) (800) 282-3336 or (718) 746-5300 *www.autoshowny.com*. North America's first and largest auto show features hundreds of the newest cars and concepts and classics from automotive history.

Mid-April

New York Antiquarian Book Fair Seventh Regiment Armory, Park Ave. (at 67th St.) (212) 777-5218 *www.sanfordsmith.com*. About 180 international book dealers offer rare books, manuscripts, autographs, fine bindings, maps, modern firsts, illustrated books, children's books and more. Admission to the show is $15.   *Late April*

Macy's Flower Show 34th St. (at Broadway) (212) 494-5432
www.macys.com. With the arrival of spring, Macy's becomes a botanical paradise, displaying over 30,000 varieties of flowers, plants and trees from around the world.   *Starts Palm Sunday (Sunday before Easter)*

Japanese Cherry Blossom Festival Brooklyn Botanic Garden (718) 623-7333 *www.bbg.org*. To celebrate the blooming of the Garden's 200 cherry trees, this festival features classical Japanese dance performances accompanied by bamboo flutes and taiko drums. There is storytelling, as well as lessons in calligraphy, flower arranging, oriental brush painting, block painting and origami. Check the Web site for an update of the blossom status.   *Late April or early May*

TriBeCa Film Festival Venues throughout the neighborhood (866) 941-FEST *www.tribecafilmfestival.org*. The brainchild of Robert De Niro and producer Jane Rosenthal, this festival features dozens of screenings (usually including one major world premiere), free outdoor concerts and a family street fair. Buy tickets well in advance on the festival's Web site.   *Late April to early May*

Bike New York: The Great Five Boro Bike Tour (212) 932-BIKE *www.bikenewyork.org*. America's largest bicycling event draws 30,000 riders who traverse 42 miles (68k) and five boroughs. The tour starts in Battery Park with a sendoff by the mayor and ends with a ride across the Verrazano-Narrows Bridge to Staten Island. A post-ride festival and picnic given by sponsors features food, concessions and activities.   *Early May*

Ninth Avenue International Food Festival Ninth Ave. (37th-57th St.) (212) 581-7217. Hundreds of stalls are set up along Ninth Avenue for two days to serve every type of ethic food you can imagine—from Thai to Italian. Live music keeps things festive, and vendors sell plants, crafts and T-shirts while over a million people sample the gamut of New York's ethnic cuisines.   *Mid-May*

Bird Watching in Central Park Central Park *www.nycparks.org*. With 275 species sighted at last count, Central Park is one of the 14 best bird-watching places in North America. From parrots to bald eagles to the red-tailed hawks that nest along Fifth Avenue, all manner of birds show up for springtime in the park. Many of the more exotic species arrive en route from southern states, Mexico and even the tropical rain forests.   *May–June*

Fleet Week *U.S.S. Intrepid* Sea, Air and Space Museum (46th St. at 12th Ave.) (212) 245-0072 *www.uss-intrepid.com*. Fifteen to 20 battleships, aircraft carriers and other ships from the U.S. Navy and Coast Guard as well as foreign fleets sail up the Hudson, past the Statue of Liberty, and dock at Pier 86, where 10,000 uniformed personnel disembark so curious New Yorkers can explore their vessels for free. During the week there are also parachute drops and air displays that are sure to impress the kids.   *Late May*

Washington Square Outdoor Art Exhibition Washington Square Park (212) 982-6255. For nearly 70 years, the 20 blocks in and around the park have been transformed into an arts and crafts fairground on Memorial Day and continuing for the three following weekends. Around 600 exhibitors participate each day of the fair from noon until sundown.   *Starts Memorial Day*

Summer

Downtown NYC River to River Festival In venues throughout Lower Manhattan *www.rivertorivernyc.com* This summerlong festival encompasses 500 events (most of them free) in settings throughout Downtown, including Castle Clinton, the Winter Garden and South Street Seaport. Each year it kicks off with a big-name concert (such as Sheryl Crow or James Brown) in Battery Park. Check the Web site for a detailed calendar. Events include concerts, dance and theater performances, family fun days, food festivals, lectures, readings and much more. In September, River to River culminates with Evening Stars, a series that brings the world's most acclaimed dancers to Battery Park for several nights of free entertainment.   *June–September*

Metropolitan Opera Parks Concerts Various parks throughout the five boroughs (212) 362-6000 *www.metopera.org*. Each year the Met presents free performances of two operas in Central Park and other locations throughout the city. Bring a picnic and come early if you want to get a good view.   *June*

Bryant Park Free Summer Season Sixth Ave. (at 42nd St.) (212) 512-5700. Lunchtime concerts and performances are a favorite of Midtown workers throughout the summer. The free classic movies under the stars on Monday evenings have become a beloved New York tradition. Bring a blanket and a picnic and arrive early for some prime lawn space.   *June–August*

Celebrate Brooklyn! Performing Arts Festival Prospect Park Bandshell, 9th St. (at Prospect Park West), Park Slope (718) 855-7882 *www.briconline.org/celebrate*. Some 25 free outdoor performances in music, dance, film and theater are offered for nine weeks in Prospect Park. The city's longest-running free performing arts festival (a $3 donation is requested) attracts top-notch acts from around the country and the world. Check the Web site for a schedule of events; the 2004 schedule included performers like They Might Be Giants, Los Lobos, the Mark Morris Dance Project and many more.   *June–August*

Central Park SummerStage Rumsey Playfield, Central Park (at 72nd St.) (212) 360-2777 *www.summerstage.com*. Since its founding in 1986, SummerStage has presented over 500 free weekend afternoon concerts and performances for over 5 million people. Everyone from the latest pop stars to up-and-coming artists have graced the stage; the 2004 season featured an array of world music acts, plus headliners like Ben Folds, the Finn Brothers, Rufus Wainwright and G. Love & Special Sauce. A handful of benefit shows charge admission to help fund the program.   *June–August*

Puerto Rican Day Parade Fifth Avenue (44th to 86th Sts.) (718) 401-0404. With sizzling music, colorful floats and an enthusiastic crowd, this is one of New York's most festive parades.   *Second Sunday in June*

Belmont Stakes Belmont Race Track, Elmont, Long Island (516) 488-6000
www.nyracing.com/belmont. The final leg of the Triple Crown is a major event
on the horse-racing circuit.   *Sunday in early June*

Museum Mile Festival Various locations (212) 606-2296 *www.museum-
milefestival.org*. For one day in June, you can get into nine of the city's major
museums for free, enjoying live entertainment along Fifth Avenue
(82nd–104th Sts.) as you stroll from one to the other.   *Second Tuesday in June*

JVC Jazz Festival (212) 501-1390 *www.festivalproductions.net*. From small
clubs to Carnegie Hall and Lincoln Center, world-class jazz musicians and
lesser-known artists take to dozens of New York's stages for performances and
jam sessions.   *Mid- to late June*

Mermaid Parade Boardwalk at Coney Island (W. 10th–16th St., Brooklyn)
(718) 372-5159 *www.coneyisland.com*. To kick off the summer, hundreds of
mermaids, mermen, merchildren and other sea creatures march down the
boardwalk in a colorful display. Elaborate floats and outlandish costumes make
this one of the city's most unique parades.   *Saturday after summer solstice*

Lesbian and Gay Pride Week and March Fifth Ave. (from 52nd St. to
Christopher St.) (212) 807-7433 *www.nycpride.org*. Thousands take to the
streets to celebrate the birth of the gay liberation movement in the world's
largest gay pride parade. A week of events surrounds the flamboyant parade,
including a film festival, club events and parties throughout the city.   *Late June*

Restaurant Week *www.restaurantweek.com*. A prix-fixe lunch at over 100 of
the city's top restaurants is only $20.05 for a week in June. Check the Web site
for a list of participants; as soon as they're announced in mid- to late May,
reserve immediately—places fill up fast. Some restaurants continue the deal
throughout the summer.   *Late June*

Midsummer Night Swing Lincoln Center Plaza (212) 875-5766 *www.lincoln-
center.org*. Nothing compares to dancing under the stars with Lincoln Center's
famed fountain as a backdrop. Top dance bands play everything from swing to
salsa. Dance lessons (included in the price of admission) begin at 6:30 P.M. The
featured band goes on at 8 P.M. The dance floor can get dreadfully crowded, so
you might just listen in for free on the edge of the plaza.   *Late June–late July*

Lincoln Center Festival Lincoln Center (212) 875-5766
www.lincolncenter.org. This festival showcases dance, theater, music and opera
in and around Lincoln Center's several venues, with performances by the Center's regular companies and other artists from around the world. The festival also
offers special symposia about and inspired by the festival's performances.   *July*

New York Shakespeare Festival Delacorte Theater, Central Park (at 81st
St.) (212) 539-8750 *www.publictheater.org*. Sponsored by the Joseph Papp Public Theater, this is New York's quintessential summer event. Celebrity performers often headline these free outdoor performances. Tickets, available at the

Public Theater and the Delacorte Theater starting at 1 P.M. on the day of the performance, are tough to come by. *July–August*

Macy's Fourth of July Fireworks Spectacular Over the East River (212) 484-1222 *www.macys.com*. The FDR Drive is closed to traffic for a few hours so pedestrians can get a better look at the lavish 30-minute display launched from two points on the East River beginning at 9 P.M. *July 4*

New York Philharmonic Concerts in the Parks Various locations (212) 875-5656. The Philharmonic presents free evening concerts in parks throughout the city. *Late July–early August*

Mostly Mozart Avery Fisher Hall, Lincoln Center (212) 875-5030 *www.lincolncenter.org*. The Mostly Mozart Festival Orchestra—along with world-class soloists and guest performers—presents around 30 concerts in a four-week period each summer. *Late July–late August*

Harlem Week Throughout Harlem (212) 862-8477 *www.harlemdiscover.com*. The Taste of Harlem food festival, the Black Film Festival and a lively street fair along Fifth Avenue (125th–135th St.) are highlights, along with open houses, block parties, outdoor concerts and special events at area jazz clubs. *August*

Hong Kong Dragon Boat Festival The Lake at Flushing Meadows-Corona Park, Queens (718) 767-1776 *www.hkdbf-ny.org*. More than 80 teams from across the U.S. and Canada race traditional 39-foot boats decorated like Chinese dragons in a spectacular display. Admission is free. *Mid-August*

New York International Fringe Festival Venues throughout Downtown Manhattan (212) 279-4488 *www.fringenyc.org*. This festival—the 800-pound gorilla of offbeat theater and a kind of convention unto itself—takes over Downtown, with 200 companies from all over the world performing in more than 20 locations. That's more than 1,300 funky, experimental shows to choose from in a two-week span. *Mid- to late August*

Lincoln Center Out-of-Doors Lincoln Center (212) 875-5766 *www.lincolncenter.org*. Everything from classical music and dancing to children's puppet shows is featured in this series of free performances on the plazas of Lincoln Center. *August–September*

U.S. Open Tennis Championships USTA National Tennis Center, Flushing Meadows, Queens (718) 760-6200 or (866) OPEN-TIX *www.usopen.org*. This Grand Slam event is the premier U.S. tournament on the tour. Fans can pay top dollar for a seat at the showcased matches, or purchase grounds admission, which entitles them to wander from one early-round match to another; prices go up and the tournament progresses. Buy tickets well in advance; they go on sale in June. *Late August–Labor Day*

West Indian Day Carnival Eastern Parkway (Utica Ave.–Grand Army Plaza), Brooklyn (212) 484-1222, (718) 625-1515. A crowd of nearly 2 million revelers turns out to celebrate Caribbean culture in New York's biggest and most energetic parade. The parade of extravagant costumes and colorful floats caps a weekend of festivities beginning Friday evening with reggae, salsa and calypso at the Brooklyn Museum.   *Labor Day*

Autumn

Broadway on Broadway 43rd and Broadway (212) 768-1560 *www.timessquarebid.org*. For a couple of hours each year, Broadway is accessible to everyone. On a stage erected in the middle of Times Square, a free concert of highlights from the season's biggest shows features big stars and splashy production numbers.   *Mid-September*

Feast of San Gennaro Mulberry St. (Houston-Worth Sts.) (212) 768-9320 *www.sangennaro.org*. Since 1926, Little Italy's main drag, Mulberry Street, has been transformed into a fairground for 11 days each September. Three million people turn out each year for food, fun and music at this festival honoring the patron saint of Naples.   *Mid-September*

Atlantic Antic Atlantic Ave. (Flatbush Ave.–East River) (718) 875-8993. With music, food, arts and crafts, a children's circus and over 450 vendors, the Antic is one of Brooklyn's largest street fairs, drawing nearly 1 million people each year.   *Last Sunday in September*

New York Film Festival Lincoln Center (212) 875-5610 *www.filmlinc.com*. Approximately 20 independent, foreign and big-studio films are screened in a two-week run at Lincoln Center. Held annually since 1965, the festival has premiered films by directors such as Martin Scorsese, Jean-Luc Godard and Robert Altman.   *Late September–early October*

Columbus Day Parade Fifth Ave. (44th–86th Sts.) (212) 484-1222. Columbus may have landed far from New York on a Spanish ship, but he was born in Italy. That's enough for the city's Italian-Americans, who are front and center for this parade up Fifth Avenue.   *Columbus Day (second Monday in October)*

Halloween Parade Sixth Ave. (from Spring St. to 23rd St. or Union Square) *www.halloween-nyc.com*. Over 25,000 participants take to the streets of Greenwich Village for the most famous Halloween parade in the country. Join the crowd of elaborately costumed revelers or have nearly as much fun watching from the sidelines.   *October 31*

BAM Next Wave Festival Brooklyn Academy of Music (718) 636-4100 *www.bam.org*. BAM showcases experimental works by both established and lesser-known contemporary artists from around the world in music, theater and dance.   *October–December*

New York City Marathon (212) 860-4455 *www.nycmarathon.org*. This prestigious 26.2-mile race starts on the Staten Island side of the Verrazano-Narrows Bridge and finishes in Central Park as a crowd cheers on the 35,000 participants. Spectators line the streets all along the course, which hits each of the five boroughs.   *Last Sunday in October or first Sunday in November*

Michelle Agins/The New York Times

Macy's Thanksgiving Day Parade

Big Apple Circus Damrosch Park, Lincoln Center (212) 268-2500 *www.bigapplecircus.org*. With its local roots, intimate one-ring big top and kid-friendly mission, the Big Apple Circus has staked out its own ground between the glitz of the Ringling Brothers circus and the adults-only artistry of the Cirque du Soleil.   *November–January*

Macy's Parade Central Park West (at 77th St.) to Macy's (Broadway and 34th St.) (212) 494-2922 *www.macys.com*. From 9 A.M. to noon on Thanksgiving, a procession of floats and huge cartoon-character balloons marches down to Macy's in this children's favorite. Catch the inflating of the balloons the night before at Central Park West and 77th Street (6–11 P.M.).   *Thanksgiving Day*

Lower Manhattan

MANHATTAN NEIGHBORHOODS

Lower Manhattan

The difficulty of visiting **Ground Zero** is more than emotional and spiritual, though it is certainly that. After all, this is where 2,749 people died on Sept. 11, 2001.

The difficulty is also practical. There is no one place to take it all in, no public vantage that offers an all-encompassing panorama. But if you take the time to walk around the 14.6-acre excavation where the Twin Towers stood and venture a bit farther afield, if you filter out the crowds and let your heart grow still, you may begin to see a fathomless void where something vast and vital ought to be.

Begin in the 18th century. Behind the treetops of the churchyard across Church Street is the exquisite St. Paul's Chapel, one of the city's great landmarks. Within its walls, President George Washington worshiped when New York was the nation's capital. Here, workers from Ground Zero found solace, hot food, badly needed supplies and, in President Washington's own pew, care for their injured feet. The story is told in an exhibition, "Unwavering Spirit: Hope and Healing at Ground Zero," that should not be missed.

Though Church Street does not offer a good vista of Ground Zero, the viewing fence does contain informative historical panels and lists of the victims' names, set off in recessed bays. Between the bays is an 18-foot-high steel cruciform from 6 World Trade Center, the United States Custom House, that was found in the wreckage.

Outside the Century 21 store is a seven-year-old Heritage Trail marker—no one has presumed to take it down—that eerily refers to the Trade Center in the present tense. "Every weekday, 50,000 people come to work in 12 million square feet of office, hotel and commercial space," it says. "As many as 10,000 visitors in a single day ride the non-stop express elevators—from the lobby to the 107th floor in 82 seconds—to take in the spectacular views of the city and its surroundings."

On Liberty Street, you will pass 10 House, the recently rebuilt quarters of Engine Company 10 and Ladder Company 10, which lost three firefighters, two lieutenants and a retired captain. The rugged faces of all six men gaze out across Ground Zero from a bronze memorial plaque. A sign asks passersby to "remember that questions about 9/11 tend to bring back horrible memories for many firefighters."

Bad memories still have physical form on Liberty Street, where black netting shrouds the damaged 40-story Deutsche Bank building (the process of dismantling and clearing the structure will begin during the lifetime of this edition). The fantastic Gothic facade of 90 West Street, one block closer to the river, also sustained a grievous injury, but restoration is underway.

Liberty Street offers the best street-level overlook into Ground Zero. From here, you can see the multilevel remains of the 6 World Trade Center garage, where the Freedom Tower is to rise; the tracks and mezzanine of the reconstructed PATH commuter station; and the rising framework of the new 7 World Trade Center, now under construction, which replaces the third tower that fell on 9/11.

Cross the Liberty Street bridge to the World Financial Center. "From Recovery to Renewal," an exhibition in the Winter Garden by the Lower Manhattan Development Corporation, documents the planning of the new Trade Center site. Compare the two models showing the plan envisioned by Daniel Libeskind in 2003 and the design as it evolved.

Return to Ground Zero and the temporary World Trade Center PATH Station, which is entered through a winged canopy on Church Street. Within the station is the only structural remnant of the Trade Center that is open to the public: a 66-foot-long section of the original concourse, paved in tawny travertine. It can be found by following signs for the Chambers Street subway station.

The core of Ground Zero is best seen from the PATH station mezzanine, two levels below. It is well worth $1.50 to get beyond the turnstiles.

To orient yourself in Lower Manhattan, look for the astonishingly detailed, mural-sized aerial photograph of the trade center environs on the wall at the south end of the mezzanine. Next to it, in blue, is a corresponding street map.

At the north end are two placards, "Exchange Place Tunnels, 1907" and "Early H & M Railroad Cars." Standing at the column between them, looking down through a narrow gap in the translucent screen, you can make out a line of rusting steel squares set into the ground at regular intervals. These are the stub ends of the perimeter columns that once supported the north facade of 1 World Trade Center and are among the very few visible remnants of the Twin Towers that are still in place.

The first element of the new Freedom Tower is the granite cornerstone, laid July 4. You can see its rough-hewn side from the north end of the platform along Tracks 4 and 5.

If a PATH train happens to have its doors open, jump aboard for the four-minute ride to Exchange Place in Jersey City. This trip will give you a fleeting but awe-inspiring view of Ground Zero. In 35 seconds, you will see the inscribed side of the cornerstone. You may even be able to make out the words "enduring spirit of freedom." The 460-foot-long ramp will swing into view. Then it will seem as if the train is being swallowed into the parking garage, where the remaining columns are still color-coded yellow, red and blue.

Get off at Exchange Place, cross over to Track 1 and catch any inbound train, marked "WTC." As you re-enter Manhattan, you will feel the train slow before daylight breaks in. Next comes the screech of the wheels as they make a sharp turn into the station.

Jarring as it may be to your ears, it was a sweet sound on November 23, 2003, the morning the station reopened after more than two years of suspended service. It was the sound of Ground Zero coming back to life.

—*David Dunlap*

Subway: 1, 2, 3, 9 to Chambers St. or Park Pl.; 1, 9 to Rector St. or South Ferry; E to World Trade Center; N, R to Rector St. or Whitehall St.; 4, 5 to Wall St. or Bowling Green.

HIGHLIGHTS OF THE NEIGHBORHOOD

(For cruises in New York Harbor, see section "Guided Tours," earlier in this chapter.)

Battery Park Bordered by Battery Pl. and State St. at the southern tip of Manhattan. Wedged below the concrete canyons of the Financial District, windswept Battery Park is a lovely greenspace at the tip of Manhattan, offering sweeping vistas out to New York Harbor. A paved recreation path begins at the northwest border of the park, extending up the entire West Side of Manhattan, serving up gorgeous water views to joggers, bikers and in-line skaters. Built entirely on landfill, Battery Park is the site of **Castle Clinton National Monument** (212-344-7220), a circular fort designed in 1811 to protect against British invasion. Castle Clinton, now the setting for a series of free outdoor concerts in summer, is staffed by National Park Service rangers, and is the place to **buy ferry tickets for Ellis Island and the Statue of Liberty** *(see box)*. Battery Park is also the departure point for the **Staten Island Ferry** *(see listing below)*. Within the park stands Fritz Koenig's damaged bronze sphere, created as a symbol of world peace and once placed on the plaza between the Twin Towers. Recovered

Suzanne DeChillo/The New York Times

Brooklyn Bridge

from the World Trade Center site, it is damaged but still intact, and it was placed here on the six-month anniversary of the attacks as a **temporary memorial to the victims of 9/11.** A major facelift is underway at the Battery Park Bosque, which will soon boast a carousel, new walkways and a world-class ornamental garden with 100,000 flowering plants. **Subway:** N, R to Whitehall St.; 4, 5 to Bowling Green; 1, 9 to South Ferry.

Bowling Green Broadway and Whitehall Sts. This petite green triangle was Manhattan's first park, once used as a cattle market and later as a bowling lawn. A statue of King George III stood in the park until 1776, when an angry mob toppled it, railing against oppressive British rule. (The statue's remains were then melted down and turned into ammunition.) One statue that has survived here is the famous **"Charging Bull,"** a symbol of Wall Street optimism (although there's always the possibility that a mob of angry investors might take that one out, too). At the south end is the elegant U.S. Customs House, which houses the **National Museum of the American Indian** (*see listing below*). There are frequent lunchtime concerts on weekdays in summer. **Subway:** N, R to Whitehall St.; 4, 5 to Bowling Green; 1, 9 to South Ferry.

Brooklyn Bridge Manhattan entrance: Park Row at Centre St. Brooklyn entrance: Tillary St. at Adams St., or Washington St. near Sands St. One of the grandest and most potent symbols of New York City since the day it opened in 1883, the Brooklyn Bridge still provides the best free tourist activity in the whole city: walking across it toward the Manhattan skyline.

To start on the Brooklyn side, take the A or C train to Brooklyn's High Street station; exit and climb the three flights of stairs on Washington Street. You will be following in the steps of President Chester A. Arthur, who led the first group

Ruby Washington/ The New York Times

Wall Street

of pedestrians across. And you will thank John A. Roebling, who designed the
bridge in 1867 and put the elevated walkway in the center, above other traffic, so
pedestrians could "enjoy the beautiful views and the pure air."

From end to end, it is more than a mile (6,016 feet). The portion over the
East River soars 135 feet above the water.

But long before you thread through the massive keyholes of the bridge's
Gothic-arched towers (at the time they were built, the towers were taller than
anything on either shore, besides the Trinity Church spire), you will easily
understand why the bridge has loomed so large in the nation's imagination.

Over the years, it has loomed indeed. It has been painted by everyone from
George Bellows to Georgia O'Keeffe. Its glories have been sung in poetry and
prose by thousands, including Hart Crane, the poet who asked: "How could
mere toil align thy choiring strings!"   —*Randy Kennedy*

City Hall/City Hall Park & Environs Broadway and Chambers St. (212)
788-6865. Topped by a cupola that once offered commanding views of the
countryside, **City Hall** is now dwarfed by office towers. An amalgamation of
French Renaissance and Federal design, completed between 1802 and 1812, it
houses the offices of the mayor and the City Council. The steps outside are the
setting for official receptions in which the mayor bestows the key to the city on
winning teams and visiting dignitaries. The interior has a remarkable pair of
cantilevered stairs under a central rotunda.

City Hall presides over the lovely green lawns and manicured flower beds of
City Hall Park. Among the sights in and around the park are an entrance ramp
to the **Brooklyn Bridge** pedestrian walkway, the **Woolworth Building** and the
Municipal Building (*see separate listings for each of these attractions*).

The Italianate **Tweed Courthouse,** just north of City Hall, was the old New
York County Courthouse. It's a stunningly beautiful building—but then again it

should be, since William "Boss" Tweed ran up the construction bill from the budgeted $250,000 to $14 million in one of the biggest swindles in city history.

Across Chambers Street from the Tweed Courthouse stands the grandiose **Surrogates Court Hall of Records.** It boasts a sumptuous lobby with murals and an arched mosaic ceiling with an Egyptian motif. Whether or not citizens' records merited such splendor is another matter altogether, but the building itself is definitely worth a visit.

From here, take Elk Street up toward Duane Street, where you'll find the **African Burial Ground.** Some 20,000 African Americans were laid to rest here during the 18th century. The site was uncovered in 1991 during construction of the Federal office tower across the street.

Farther north along Centre Street are today's active court buildings. At 40 Centre Street is the **United States Courthouse,** a mid-1930's Classical Revival skyscraper topped with a golden pyramid. The **New York County Courthouse** moved to its current location at 60 Centre Street in 1927. This hexagonal, Roman classical building is a frequent backdrop for *Law & Order* and countless other television shows and films.
Subway: J, M, Z to Chambers St.; 4, 5, 6 to Brooklyn Bridge–City Hall; N, R to City Hall; 2, 3 to Park Pl..

Federal Hall National Memorial 26 Wall St. at Nassau St. (212) 825-6888 *www.nps.gov/feha.* Wall Street's version of the Parthenon, Federal Hall stands on the site of George Washington's inauguration as the nation's first president in 1789; a dignified statue of Washington towers over the front steps. It was also here that publisher John Peter Zenger stood trial in 1735 for seditious libel; his acquittal was the basis for the concept of freedom of the press. One of the finest Greek Revival buildings in the city, this former U.S. Customs House and early Federal Reserve branch was designed in 1834 and built in 1842. Behind its portico of severe Doric columns and five-foot walls, the building houses a museum of constitutional history. **Admission:** Free. **Hours:** Mon.–Fri. 9 A.M.–5 P.M. **Subway:** J, M, Z to Broad St.; 2, 3, 4, 5 to Wall St.

Federal Reserve Bank 33 Liberty Pl. (between Nassau and William Sts.) (212) 720-6130 *www.fednewyork.org/nycinfo.html.* Five stories below Liberty Street, the Federal Reserve's New York branch houses a substantial share of the world's gold reserves; its underground vaults store approximately $100 billion worth of gold ingots for some 60 countries. A government bank for banks, the Federal Reserve regulates U.S. currency, supervises commercial banks and has considerable impact on the economy through its influence on the money supply and interest rates. Its rusticated limestone building is reminiscent of a Florentine Renaissance palazzo. Reserve well in advance for **free hour-long tours,** offered five times daily on weekdays only. There's also an exhibit, created in collaboration with the American Numismatic Society, on "The History of Money." **Admission:** Free. **Hours:** Mon.–Fri. 10 A.M.–4 P.M.; you must make an appointment to visit (no walk-ins). **Subway:** 2, 3, 4, 5, J, M, Z to Fulton St.; A, C to Broadway–Nassau.

The Statue of Liberty & Ellis Island

These days, nothing more inspiring than the baggage-claim area at John F. Kennedy International Airport greets most visitors and immigrants to the United States. But a century ago, the exhilarating sight of the Statue of Liberty towering over the entrance to New York Harbor signaled to shiploads of travelers, both the bedraggled and the bejeweled, that they had reached the shores of a new land.

At Ellis Island, only paperwork was processed for first-class and second-class passengers; the passengers themselves were inspected on their ships and dispatched directly to Manhattan. But each day saw up to 5,000 poor and working-class immigrants, fresh from a two-week ocean voyage in steerage, herded inside and inspected for disease, deformities and destitution.

Inspired by the colossal monuments of Egypt and an outsized 19th-century French fascination with American egalitarian ideals, the Statue of Liberty still has the power to take your breath away, just as it thrilled the 12 million immigrants who passed it on their way to Ellis Island in the first decades of the 20th century.

Resolute and stern, the massive female figure, 151 feet high from her toes to the top of her torch of freedom, rests on a 150-foot-high pedestal at the tip of a tiny landscaped island in New York Bay. Gardens around the base offer a sumptuous view of the skyscrapers of Lower Manhattan.

The idea for a grand statue to celebrate friendship between France and the United States originated in 1865 around the Parisian dinner table of Edouard de Laboulaye, a scholar of the American Constitution. (A great-grandson of de Laboulaye spearheaded fundraising in France for restoration of the statue 100 years after it opened.) Alexis de Tocqueville, another admirer of American democracy, is said to have been a guest at the dinner. So was the sculptor who would design the statue, Frédéric-Auguste Bartholdi.

The Lower Manhattan skyline views are stunning from the skinny outdoor walkway around the base of the statue. It can be reached by an elevator, or up four flights of steps. Inside the pedestal, an informative museum shows the evolution of Bartholdi's vision of what the statue should look like, the engineering used to keep it stable in the tricky harbor winds, and the lasting impressions it made on generations of immigrants. A delightful collection of old Statue of Liberty kitsch, as opposed to the new collection in the gift shop downstairs, concludes the exhibit, demonstrating the monument's enduring role as both icon and huckster.

(**Important note:** Access to the interior of the Statue had been severely restricted after 9/11, but was relaxed in 2004. Although the crown remains off-limits, visitors can now enjoy panoramic vistas from an observation deck atop the 16-story-high pedestal, where a newly installed glass ceiling offer views up to the statue's crown. You still cannot climb the stairway up to the crown, however.)

At Ellis Island, renovations of the long-abandoned site have recreated the processing center as it looked in the first decades of the 20th century. Even if you do not trace your roots to an ancestor who arrived in the United States through Ellis Island, you may well feel a kinship with the 12 million anxious immigrants who shuffled through the echoing halls of this red-brick way station between 1892 and 1954 on their way to a new life in a new land. All through the impressively restored building, there are bigger-than-life sepia photos of the evocative faces that passed through Ellis Island to become symbols of the American experience. Among them: a young boy in a jauntily angled embroidered cap, his lips pursed as if he is trying to suppress a grin of pure exultation. Two Dutch brothers, each with a processing number pinned to his shirt and each with a determined gaze already directed far beyond New York Harbor. A pair of dignified young black women coming from Guadeloupe in 1911, both in ankle-length lace-trimmed dresses and tiny hats shaped like a handful of rose petals.

The main processing center is the only part of the original compound that is open to the public, but it is fascinating. Displays on its three floors use film, photos, turn-of-the-last-century posters and the voices of reminiscing immigrants to show a broader story of immigration. You hear immigrants tell their stories of adjustment, discrimination, poverty and success. You learn about the nativist movements that feared immigrants; a 1902 political cartoon shows them as the personification of "filth" and "disease." And you see how popular culture was enriched by immigrants—as in the old song, "Hello Wisconsin, Won't You Find My Yonnie Yonson?" At the Family History Center, visitors can look up the immigration records of anyone who arrived by way of Ellis Island up to 1924.   —*Susan Sachs*

For information, call (212) 363-3200, or (212) 269-5755 for ferry and ticket info. *www.nps.gov/stli, www.nps.gov/elis* and *www.statueoflibertyferry.com.*

Hours: First ferry departs Manhattan daily at 9:30 A.M., last ferry departs Manhattan at 3:30 P.M. Extended hours in summer, with last ferry at 6 P.M. **Admission:** Free. Round-trip Circle Line ferry tickets (with stops at both sights) $10 adults, $8 seniors, $4 children ages 4–12. Ferry departs from Manhattan's Battery Park; buy tickets in the park at Castle Clinton, by calling in advance or by ordering online.

James Esrin/The New York Times

Statue of Liberty

Fraunces Tavern Museum 54 Pearl St. (at Broad St.) (212) 425-1778 *www.frauncestavernmuseum.org*. The 18th-century Fraunces Tavern, now a small museum of American history, has been substantially rebuilt since it served as a watering hole for George Washington and the Sons of Liberty. The Long Room, where Washington made his farewell address to his Revolutionary War officers, is one of the several period rooms containing displays. The museum offers tours, lectures and performances coordinated with current exhibitions, as

well as special events on Washington's Birthday and Independence Day. Dining
in the restaurant at Fraunces Tavern (call 212-968-1776 for reservations) is a
great way to soak in the historic atmosphere. **Admission:** $3 adults; $2 students
and seniors; free for children under 6. **Hours:** Tues.–Wed. and Fri. 10 A.M.–5
P.M; Thu. 10 A.M.–7 P.M.; Sat 11 A.M.–5 P.M. **Subway:** N, R to Whitehall
St.; 2, 3 to Wall St.; 4, 5 to Bowling Green; J, M, Z to Broad St.

Irish Hunger Memorial Vesey St. and North End Ave. (in Battery Park City.
www.batteryparkcity.org/ihm.htm. Completed in 2002, the memorial commemorates the great Irish famine of 1845–52. Designed by sculptor Brian Tolle, the
memorial is a startlingly realistic quarter-acre replication of an Irish hillside,
complete with fallow potato furrows, stone walls, indigenous grasses and wildflowers and a real abandoned Irish fieldstone cottage. (The original materials
did not stand up well to a harsh winter on the Hudson, however, necessitating
a temporary closing and a major renovation in the spring of 2003. The memorial has since been restored and reopened.) The 96-by-170-foot field rests on a
giant concrete slab that is raised up and tilted on a huge wedge-shape base. It
slopes upward from street level to a height of 25 feet. A packed dirt path winds
up the slope, culminating in a hilltop with sweeping views of Ellis Island and
the Statue of Liberty.

The field is a walk-in relic of a distant time and place tenderly inserted into
the modern world. From its inception, the memorial was also intended to be a
reminder of world hunger. The plinth is lined with glass-covered bands of text
that mingle terse facts about the Irish famine with similarly disturbing statistics
about world hunger today, along with quotations from Irish poetry and songs. It
shows instances of suffering, prejudice and mismanagement so specific that they
can't help but reverberate into our own time.   *—Roberta Smith*

Municipal Building 1 Centre St. (at Chambers St.). This Beaux-Arts skyscraper—designed by McKim, Mead & White and completed in 1914—stands
guard over the approach to the Brooklyn Bridge and houses various city agencies. The entrance, which incorporates a Roman triumphal arch, boldly strad-
dles Chambers Street. Best known as the place where thousands of couples get
married every year, the Municipal Building is coincidentally crowned by a round,
colonnaded tower that resembles a wedding cake. Instead of two colossal newly-
weds, however, the top of the building houses a monumental gilt sculpture called
Civic Flame. **Subway:** J, M, Z to Chambers St.; 4, 5, 6 to Brooklyn Bridge.

Museum of American Financial History 28 Broadway (near Bowling
Green) (212) 908-4110 *www.financialhistory.org*. The small Smithsonian affiliate, housed on the site of Alexander Hamilton's law office and the former headquarters of John D. Rockefeller's Standard Oil Company, focuses on the history
of money. Displays include photos of historic Wall Street scenes, interactive
financial news terminals, actual ticker tape from the crash of 1929 and much
more. **Admission:** $2. **Hours:** Tue.–Sat. 10 A.M.–4 P.M. **Subway:** N, R to
Whitehall St.; 4, 5 to Bowling Green; 1, 9 to South Ferry; J, M, Z to Broad St.

Fred R. Conrad/The New York Times

New York Stock Exchange

Museum of Jewish Heritage—A Living Memorial to the Holocaust
18 First Pl., Battery Park City (at West St.) (212) 509-6130 *www.mjhnyc.org*.
This museum on the water's edge, beautifully designed by award-winning architect Kevin Roche, organizes its displays around three themes: Jewish Life a Century Ago, The War Against the Jews and Jewish Renewal. With thousands of
photographs, displays, artifacts and documentary films, the museum uses personal stories to place 20th-century Jewish history and the Holocaust in context.
New in 2003, the 82,000-square-foot Morganthau Wing includes multimedia
classrooms, a resource center for teachers, a performance space, gallery space for
special exhibits, a cafe and a new memorial garden designed by Andy Golswor-
thy. Its inaugural exhibit, running through December 2005, is "Ours to Fight
For: American Jews in the Second World War," which honors veterans by
telling their stories through video testimony, artifacts, letters and photographs.
Check the Web site for frequent concerts, lectures, films and performances.
Admission: $10 adults; $7 seniors; $5 students; children under 12 free. Free for
everyone Wed. 4–8 P.M. Admission to Garden of Stones always free. **Hours:**
Sun.–Tue. and Thu. 10 A.M.–5:45 P.M.; Wed. 10 A.M.–8 P.M.; Fri. and the eve
of Jewish holidays 10 A.M.–3 P.M. (till 5 P.M. on summer Fridays). **Subway:** 1,
9 to Rector St. or South Ferry; N, R to Whitehall; 4, 5 to Bowling Green.

National Museum of the American Indian, George Gustav Heye Center
1 Bowling Green (between Whitehall and State Sts.) (212) 514-3700
www.si.edu/nmai. This branch of the Smithsonian is located in the former U.S.
Customs House, a spectacular domed Beaux-Arts landmark designed by Cass
Gilbert at the foot of Broadway. The artifacts housed here span more than
10,000 years of history, representing virtually all tribes of the continental

Governors Island

In 1623, Holland's West India Company dispatched an expedition of 110 men, women and children aboard the sailing ship *New Netherland*. Their mission? To establish a base in America. They landed first at a place they called Nutten Island (its forest was thick with walnuts), which has been known for most of the last three centuries as Governors Island. It lies about one-half mile south of the Battery and just across Buttermilk Channel from Brooklyn. Peter Minuit led the settlers in 1624 to Lower Manhattan, where they established the colony of New Amsterdam—rechristened New York when the British wrested control from the Dutch in 1664. The colony's governors lived on Governors Island from 1708 on (hence the name).

Early in the Revolutionary War, a band of patriots overwhelmed the British garrison and fortified the island to protect the city, but the British recaptured the city in August and September 1776. The two forts that constitute the Governors Island National Monument—the star-shaped Fort Jay and the doughnut-shaped Castle Williams—were built between the Revolution and the War of 1812.

New York ceded the island to the federal government in 1800 as a strategic site for national defense. It played roles in the War of 1812, the Civil War and both World Wars, as a key army base until 1966 and then as the Coast Guard's largest base. The island was unoccupied after the Coast Guard left in 1997 until New York regained ownership in 2002.

The southern half of the island's 172 acres is landfill, extracted from tunnels dug for the first city subway 100 years ago. This section contains nondescript military housing and large open spaces that New Yorkers hope will become playing fields and a park. The northern 90 acres is a National Historic Landmark District. In addition to the two forts, it has neat rows of Victorian houses once occupied by ranking officers' families, a third fort facing Brooklyn, a chapel and Building 400, which could house an entire regiment. The Governor's House includes some elements of the British governors' home, but the structure mostly dates from 1805. The Admiral's House next door dates from 1840; it was the setting for a 1988 meeting between Ronald Reagan and Mikhail Gorbachev.

Wilbur Wright launched the first flight over water from Governors Island before circling the Statue of Liberty and returning. Military men in its past include a young lieutenant named Ulysses S. Grant, Gen. John J. Pershing, and Gen. Omar Bradley.

Governors Island opened to the public in 2003. A 99-minute tour, requiring 1.5 miles of walking outdoors, is led by National Park Service rangers (space is limited, and the tour schedule varies seasonally). For information, visit *www.nps.gov/gois* or call 212-514-8296. Tours are free; ferry fares are $5 adults, $3 children ages 5 to 12. Ferry tickets are sold at the South Street Seaport Museum ticket booth on Pier 16 beginning at 8:30 A.M. on the morning of the tour (first come, first served). You can reserve in advance for Saturday tours.

United States, Canada, Hawaii and Central and South America. **Admission:** Free. **Hours:** Daily 10 A.M.–5 P.M. (until 8 P.M. on Thu.). **Subway:** N, R to Whitehall St.; 4, 5 to Bowling Green; 1, 9 to South Ferry.

New York City Police Museum 100 Old Slip (at the East River, between Water and South Sts.) (212) 480-3100 *www.nycpolicemuseum.org*. This museum occupies the headquarters of the city's first police precinct, four blocks south of South Street Seaport. With interactive exhibits, computer simulations, vintage uniforms, weapons and antique badges, the museum presents a multifaceted view of the rigorous, clearly dangerous, at times political and often tedious life of a police officer. **Admission:** $5 adults; $3 seniors; $2 children ages 6–18. **Hours:** Tue.–Sat. 10 A.M.–5 P.M. **Subway:** 2, 3 to Wall St.; N, R to Whitehall St.

New York Stock Exchange 20 Broad St. (between Wall and Exchange Sts.) (212) 656-5168 *www.nyse.com*. On a good day—a day when the Dow is soaring—you can almost smell the money in the air outside the Stock Exchange. This is the nerve center of the global financial markets. The Exchange once offered tours, but due to heightened security after 9/11, it remains closed to visitors as of this writing. Call ahead or check the Web site to find out the latest status. **Subway:** J, M, Z to Broad St.; 2, 3, 4, 5 to Wall St.

New York Unearthed Rear side of 17 State St. (opposite Battery Park between Pearl and Whitehall Sts.) (212) 748-8628. The South Street Seaport Museum's urban archaelogy museum and laboratory preserves thousands of artifacts from New York City's past. Currently, the museum is featuring artifacts from digs in the notorious Five Points (*Gangs of New York*) neighborhood. **Admission:** Free. **Hours:** Mon.–Fri. noon–5 P.M. **Subway:** 1, 9 to South Ferry; 4, 5 to Bowling Green; N, R to Whitehall.

St. Paul's Chapel 211 Broadway (between Fulton and Vesey Sts.) (212) 602-0800, or (212) 602-0747 for concert info *www.saintpaulschapel.org*. New York City's oldest church building, St. Paul's served uptown parishioners of Trinity Church as the colonial city expanded northward, and is still considered a satellite of Trinity. Completed in 1766, the church is a New York brownstone version of London's St. Martin-in-the-Fields. George Washington worshipped here on the day of his inauguration and during the 18 months that New York was the nation's capital. The leafy graveyard behind the church preserves a parcel of the 18th-century countryside. Despite its proximity to the World Trade Center, the chapel miraculously survived 9/11 unscathed, and in the months of recovery and cleanup, it served as a place of refuge for the rescue workers. An exhibit commemorating the Ground Zero ministry is open Monday to Saturday 10 A.M. to 6 P.M., Sundays 9 A.M. to 4 P.M. In conjunction with Trinity Church, St. Paul's offers a well-attended lunchtime concert series on Mondays at 1 P.M. (the exhibit closes during performances). Services are held Monday to Saturday at 12:30 P.M., Sundays at 8 A.M. **Subway:** 2, 3 to Park Pl.; 1, 9 to Chambers St. or Rector St.; N, R to Cortlandt St.

Shrine of St. Elizabeth Ann Seton 7 State St. (between Whitehall and Pearl Sts.) (212) 269-6865. This 1793 Federal-style building is dedicated to Elizabeth Ann Seton, the first American-born Catholic saint. Seton, who founded the American Sisters of Charity, the first order of nuns in the United States, lived here from 1801 to 1803. The building is one of the few surviving mansions in Lower Manhattan. The adjoining church was built at the same time. **Subway:** N, R to Whitehall St.

Skyscraper Museum 39 Battery Place (at the southern tip of Battery Park City) (212) 968-1961. *www.skyscraper.org.* Finally installed in its permanent home, which opened in 2004 against the panorama of the Downtown skyline, this compact museum aims to explore the history of the high-rise. On display here through summer 2006 is a World Trade Center model that was built more than 30 years ago by Yamasaki & Associates, architects of the Twin Towers. The silvery towers in this model stand 6.8 feet tall, large enough to convey—even at a 1:200 scale—something of the three-dimensional impact of the Trade Center. **Admission:** $5 adults; $2.50 seniors and students. **Hours:** Wed.–Sun. noon–6 P.M. **Subway:** 4, 5 to Bowling Green; 1, 9 to Rector St. or South Ferry.

South Street Seaport Encompassing 11 blocks just south of the Brooklyn Bridge. (Visitors Center on Pier 16 at the foot of Fulton St.) (212) 748-8600 *www.southstreetseaport.com* or *www.southstseaport.org.* Before Ellis Island opened in 1892, immigrants entered America through the South Street docks. This historic link to our past has been restored over 11 blocks just south of the Brooklyn Bridge. For more than a century this was the nation's busiest port, a thriving dockland of warehouses and markets, sailing ships and fishing boats, and the foreign-born filled with hope. Steamships made it obsolete in the late 1800's, when new and larger piers opened on the Hudson.

This jewel of a neighborhood has been brought back in recent years to evoke a great age in the city's past, its cobbled streets free of all but foot traffic, its piers lined with historic ships and open to wind and water. Alas, the redevelopment has made the Seaport into a theme-park shopping mall, especially Pier 17, packed with bland restaurants and retail chains just like those back home.

But don't overlook the genuine history here. Street-level storefronts have all been restored to the style of the mid- and late 1800's; J. Crew's plaque tells you it was built in 1880 for a grocery, then converted to a hotel for "single men" at the docks. At the Water Street entrance to the Seaport is the **Titanic Memorial Lighthouse,** built in 1913 to commemorate the fate of that "unsinkable" ship. In the **Bowne & Co.** print shop two doors down Water Street, they still set type by hand and print on hand presses as when the company began in 1775; you can order cards and letterheads or purchase their printed cards and gifts.

On Fulton Street between South and Front Streets is **Schermerhorn Row,** seven early-19th-century Georgian and Federal buildings once used as warehouses. Upstairs is a galaxy of new galleries with changing displays and a permanent "World Port New York" exhibit spread through virtually the entire space. (Admission to the South Street Seaport Museum is $8 for adults, $6 for students and seniors, $4 for children ages 5–12. Hours are 10 A.M. to 5 P.M. daily.) Moored nearby are a half-dozen historic vessels, including the **Peking,** launched in 1911 and one of the largest sailing ships ever built.

Tickets to board the ships are sold at the Visitors Center. Harbor sails are offered in summer aboard the 1885 schooner **Pioneer** (call 212-748-8786 for advance reservations). Tickets for commercial boat cruises are sold at an adjacent booth. The Lower Manhattan **TKTS booth,** at the corner of John and Front Streets, has half-price tickets for Broadway and Off-Broadway shows, with shorter waiting lines than its sister booth in Times Square.

The South Street Seaport Museum runs tours ($12) of the historic **Fulton Fish Market** at 6 A.M. on the first and third Wednesdays every month, April to October, rain or shine. Reservations are required; call 212-748-8786. The **Market Grill** across the street and around the corner on Peck Slip opens when the market does; you can pull up a chair and have your breakfast alongside the fishmongers.

There are frequent festivals, concerts and other events at the Seaport, many of them free (check both Web sites for details). And the decks around Pier 17 offer wonderful water views anytime.

Subway: J, M, Z, 2, 3, 4, 5 to Fulton St.; A, C to Broadway–Nassau.

Staten Island Ferry southeast end of Battery Park (718) 815-2628 *www.ci.nyc.ny.us/html/dot.* A ride on the Staten Island Ferry is unquestionably one of the best deals in town—it's absolutely free. It leaves Manhattan's Battery Park (a short walk from the 1/9 stop at South Ferry, the N/R stop at Whitehall or the 4/5 station at Bowling Green) and deposits passengers at St. George, Staten Island.

The ferry is a lifeline to the city for many Staten Islanders; some 30,000 people ride it each midweek day. But it also provides as romantic a journey as the city can offer. The ferry operates 24 hours a day—every 15 minutes during rush hours, every 30 minutes the rest of the day and evening, and once an hour at night. To truly appreciate the grandeur of New York, ride the ferry at sunrise, starting with the 25-minute trip from Manhattan to Staten Island and then reversing the journey on the next boat back. At dawn, the first rays of the sun strike the glass towers of Lower Manhattan, while off to the left, the Statue of Liberty's torch still burns bright in the vanishing darkness.   —*Clyde Haberman*

Trinity Church and Museum Broadway (at Wall St.) (212) 602-0800 or (212) 602-0747 for concert info *www.trinitywallstreet.org.* At the foot of Wall Street stands Trinity Church, once the tallest structure in Manhattan. The first Episcopal church in New York, the parish was chartered in 1697 (after two earlier churches on this site were destroyed by fire). This Gothic-style church was built in 1846 by Richard Upjohn—complete with flying buttresses, vaulted ceilings and doors modeled after Ghiberti's Gates of Paradise in Florence. Many prominent New Yorkers, including Alexander Hamilton, Robert Fulton and William Bradford, are buried in the graveyard next to the church. The church features a small museum, and offers a free tour daily at 2 P.M. Trinity also hosts an acclaimed lunchtime concert series of chamber and orchestral music. Services are held Monday to Friday at noon, Sundays at 9 and 11:15 A.M. **Subway:** 4, 5 to Wall St.

Woolworth Building 233 Broadway (at Park Pl., opposite City Hall Park). View this dramatic structure from a distance far enough to take in the Gothic flourishes of intricately carved buttresses capped by a summit that sits like a medieval castle 792 feet above lower Broadway. The building is truly from another era, when corporate barons like F.W. Woolworth, of five-and-dime fame, battled for skyscraper supremacy. Designed by the celebrated architect Cass Gilbert, the Woolworth Building was the tallest skyscraper until the Chrysler Building (and countless others subsequently) conquered it in 1930. It remains a standout among the more contemporary glass-and-steel boxes of the nearby Financial District. Somewhere inside are a swimming pool and a storeroom of Gothic ornaments to replace the ones adorning the exterior. The only area open for casual visitors is the lobby, a sight itself to behold, with its murals and marble splendor. Peer up into the vaulted ceilings of tiled mosaics, and check out the carved figures under the crossbeams. (That's Cass Gilbert holding a model of the building, and Frank Woolworth counting nickels and dimes.)

—Randy Archibold

Subway: 2, 3 to Park Pl.; N, R to City Hall.

World Financial Center and Winter Garden 1 World Financial Center (between Albany and Liberty Sts.) (212) 945-0505 *www.worldfinancialcenter.com.* Built on landfill along the Hudson River, this commercial development includes office towers, shops, restaurants, gallery space, a yacht harbor and the Winter Garden. A sleek, modern complex (one wag called it "Dallas without the parking"), the World Financial Center was damaged on 9/11, but has been repaired and reopened to corporate tenants. The Winter Garden, a spectacular glass-vaulted public space complete with 40-foot-tall palm trees, was ravaged, but looks better than ever after a painstaking restoration. This grand space is frequently the setting for free concerts, dance performances and cultural events. Outside, a promenade circles the yacht harbor, offering benches and an outdoor plaza for summer concerts. **Subway:** N, R to Cortlandt St.; 1, 2, 3, 9 to Chambers St.

Recommended Neighborhood Restaurants

*(See chapter **Restaurants** for reviews.)*

		$25 & Under	
Shore			SEAFOOD
Bayard's	☆☆	$ $ $	NEW AMERICAN
Delmonico's	☆	$ $ $	ITALIAN/NEW AMERICAN
Les Halles Downtown	☆	$ $ $	FRENCH

Chinatown

Geography, New York style: China shares a border with Italy, and has for more than a century. The boundary is fluid, to be sure, and Chinatown's expansion in recent years across the traditional demarcation line of Canal Street has whittled Little Italy down to Tiny Italy. The area has Vietnamese, Cambodian and Hispanic communities, too, and some traces of a once-vibrant Jewish culture. But since 1965, the Chinese population has exploded; this is now the largest Chinese community in the Western Hemisphere and one of the most densely populated sections of the city.

This is a self-sufficient community, with a large population of non-English speakers, and many residents never leave the neighborhood (many of them toil in sweatshops, manufacturing clothing). On narrow streets, fishmongers and greengrocers spill onto the sidewalks. Exotic shops offer teas and Chinese herbs. In late January or early February, the **Chinese New Year** is marked by a raucous street festival.

To the outsider searching for the perfect spring roll, Chinatown may seem changeless. Yet along with the infusion of Hong Kong capital has come a shift in the economic center from Mott Street to **the Bowery** and **East Broadway,** while the traditional dominance of immigrants from China's Guangdong Province is being ceded to those from Fujian.

There are hundreds of restaurants in the area focusing on Chinese regional cuisines. After dinner or dim sum, try the **Chinatown Ice Cream Factory** (65 Bayard St. between Mott and Elizabeth Sts.) for a scoop of green-tea ice cream.

The **Pearl River Mart,** at Canal Street and Broadway, carries a huge selection of Chinese imports—dishes, traditional costumes and decorations, housewares and food. Along with smaller import shops, most Chinatown streets (particularly **Canal Street**) are lined with little storefronts and sidewalk stands selling everything from cheap electronics and batteries to Rolex knockoffs and discount luggage.

Just south of the Manhattan Bridge entrance (at Bowery and Canal St.) past Confucius Plaza, one of the area's newer housing developments, is **Chatham Square.** Here the Kimlau Arch honors Chinese soldiers killed in American wars. Where Catherine Street meets East Broadway is the **Republic National Bank,** the quintessential Chinatown building designed with the flourishes of a pagoda.

Subway: J, M, N, Q, R, W, Z, 6 to Canal St.; F to East Broadway.

HIGHLIGHTS OF THE NEIGHBORHOOD

Columbus Park Mulberry St. at Bayard St. This mostly concrete plaza in the heart of Chinatown seems like a lush oasis when you enter it from some of the narrowest and most congested streets in the city. The park's benches and stone chess tables are usually occupied, from dawn to dusk, by elderly Chinese women and

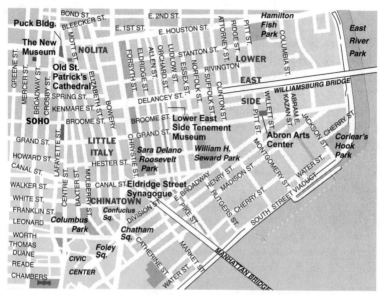

Chinatown/Little Italy/Lower East Side

men playing cards and mah-jongg. The park is located on the site of the Mulberry Bend, an infamous tenement slum of the 1800's, terrorized by gangs like the Plug Uglies and the Dead Rabbits. The buildings were torn down at the urging of the reformer Jacob Riis, who wrote a scathing report on the area's disgraceful condition. Now, as he dreamed, the neighborhood has a safe and welcoming place to play and congregate.

Museum of the Chinese in the Americas 70 Mulberry St. (at Bayard St.) (212) 619-4785 *www.moca-nyc.org*. This institution is dedicated to preserving and interpreting the history of the Chinese people in the Western hemisphere. Located on the second floor of a century-old school building, it offers educational and community programs and facilities for research on Chinese and Asian-American studies. On summer weekends, the museum offers neighborhood walking tours (call 212-619-4785 to reserve). **Admission:** $3; $2 students and seniors; free for children under age 12. **Hours:** Tue.–Sun. noon–5 P.M.

Recommended Neighborhood Restaurants

(*See chapter* **Restaurants** *for reviews.*)

Goody's	$25 & Under	CHINESE
Congee	$25 & Under	CHINESE
Joe's Ginger	$25 & Under	CHINESE
Joe's Shanghai	$25 & Under	CHINESE
New York Noodle Town	$25 & Under	CHINESE
Nha Trang	$25 & Under	VIETNAMESE

The Lower East Side

The Lower East Side has always been a testament to New York's diversity. Since the mid-19th century, it has been the gateway to America for countless generations of immigrants. Waves of families from Eastern Europe, Italy, Ireland, Germany, and, more recently, China, Puerto Rico and the Dominican Republic, have passed through here. For many decades, it was a landscape of poverty; Lower East Side tenements were the first home for new immigrants struggling to make a living in factories and sweatshops.

As recently as the 1980's, this was a crime-ridden area with drug dealers on every corner. But the last two decades have brought amazing change to the neighborhood. The Lower East Side has become a hangout for hipsters, a thriving center for art, fashion and nightlife. This is where dingy old New York meets cutting-edge chic, and the result is a fascinating, edgy neighborhood with an abundance of raw energy. It's still grungy, still rough around the edges—nothing has been totally sanitized here. The current Lower East Side story is a mix of the old, the new and the resurrected.

Though most of the neighborhood's traditional Jewish businesses have disappeared, the Lower East Side of the past and present converge everywhere. Signs in Yiddish alternate with signs in Chinese or Spanish; sleek cafes and lounges beckon the young and the hip.

Delancey Street bisects the area, beyond which residents are largely Hispanic, with a strong showing of younger newcomers. This thoroughfare offers mostly discount goods and cheap knock-offs, and an occasional shaved-ice snow cone vendor. Ratner's, a beloved neighborhood institution serving Jewish dairy food since 1905, has given way to the **Lansky Lounge,** an old speakeasy turned swank supper club.

Rivington Street, one block north of Delancey, is dotted with Puerto Rican and Dominican businesses and is home to **ABC No Rio,** one of several area cultural centers. It's also home to **Streit's Matzos,** one of the premier suppliers of matzo and other Jewish staples for over 75 years.

Clinton Street, especially between Stanton and Rivington Streets, is lined with an interesting assortment of upscale restaurants. The Lower East Side was once considered too out-of-the-way for a serious restaurant, until celebrity chef Wylie Dufresne became a neighborhood pioneer. The dining scene has never looked back since.

Just west of Rivington is the **Orchard Street Bargain District** (*see chapter* **Shopping**), where peddlers with pushcarts once crowded the streets. Shoppers still come to the area for discount leather goods, luggage and clothing.

Orchard and Ludlow Streets are home to some of the hottest boutiques and a slew of chic cafes, bars and lounges (*see chapter* **Nightlife**). A few paces away are some of the Lower East Side's classic eateries. **Katz's Delicatessen,** an area artifact, still carves pastrami and corned beef by hand. (It's a hoot to see this classic old-time deli invaded by pierced and tattooed club kids in the wee hours.) In the kitschy Borscht Belt party atmosphere of **Sammy's Roumanian,** the enormous garlic-rubbed beef tenderloins and the bowls of schmaltz (ren-

dered chicken fat) on every table are a nostalgic paean to the days before cho-
lesterol consciousness. A new resident of 87 Orchard St. is **Guss' Pickles,**
which was a fixture on Essex Street for more than 90 years. Stop in and buy a
few pickles from their massive barrels. (The neighborhood once supported
about 80 pickle shops!) Also don't miss **Russ and Daughters** for smoked fish
and other deli specialties, and **Yonah Shimmel,** supplying noshers with knishes
since 1910. Next door is the lyrical brick facade of **Landmark's Sunshine Cinema,** a modern art-film multiplex with stadium-style seating, a beautiful renovation of a century-old showplace for Yiddish vaudeville and films.

Subway: F to Delancey St.; F, V to Second Ave.; J, M, Z to Essex St.

HIGHLIGHTS OF THE NEIGHBORHOOD

ABC No Rio 156 Rivington St. (between Clinton and Suffolk Sts.) (212) 254-
3697 *www.abcnorio.org.* This cultural center supports both art and political
activism. It sponsors everything from poetry readings and world music performances to political discussions, film screenings and art exhibitions.

Eldridge Street Synagogue 12 Eldridge St. (between Canal and Division Sts.)
(212) 219-0888 *www.eldridgestreet.org.* Even in a state of disrepair, the Eldridge
Street Synagogue's intricate carved facade and stained-glass windows stand out
amid the tenements. Built in the late 1800's by immigrants from Eastern
Europe, it was the first large-scale Orthodox synagogue in New York. It is being
restored under the stewardship of the Eldridge Street Project, which offers tours
of the building (Sun 11 A.M.–4 P.M., Tue. and Thu. 11:30 A.M.–2:30 P.M.; $5
adults, $3 students and seniors) plus lectures and educational programs like
rugelach baking lessons and genealogy workshops.

Henry Street Settlement—Abrons Arts Center 466 Grand St. (at Pitt St.)
(212) 766-9200 *www.henrystreet.org.* In its century or so of existence, the
Henry Street Settlement has presented a multitude of cultural and community-
related activities—including opera, music, dance, theater, talks and workshops.
The hub of the Settlement, which occupies a row of handsome Greek Revival
town houses, is the Abrons Arts Center. Most performances take place in the
350-seat Harry De Jur Playhouse, a national historic landmark. There is also a
smaller theater, a recital hall, an outdoor amphitheater, classrooms, studios and
art galleries.

Lower East Side Tenement Museum 90 Orchard St. (at Broome St.) (212)
431-0233 *www.tenement.org.* If a museum is meant to teach us who we are and
where we've come from, then a glimpse into this dingy time capsule may be
more meaningful than a visit to the Louvre or the Met. Thousands of new
arrivals, hailing from 25 different nations, found their first home in America at
97 Orchard St., a five-story tenement that illuminates the story of the great
waves of immigration of the late 19th and early 20th centuries. Several apartments have been faithfully restored to their exact lived-in condition, and tour
guides recount the true stories of their former occupants in fascinating detail.

The only way to see the museum is by joining an hour-long guided tour; there are two main themed options, both of them fascinating. On weekends, you can also choose the 45-minute **Confino Family Apartment tour,** an interactive living-history program in which kids can touch artifacts, try on period clothes and dance to the music on the wind-up victrola. The museum also sponsors neighborhood walking tours on many weekends.

Each apartment tour is limited to 15 visitors, so buy your tickets at least two days in advance through Ticketweb at (800) 965-4827 or *www.ticketweb.com.* **Admission:** $12 adults; $10 students and seniors. Confino Apartment $11 adults, $9 seniors and students. **Hours:** Visitor Center daily 11 A.M.–5:30 P.M. Tenement tours depart every 40 minutes Tue.–Fri. 1– 4:45 P.M.; Sat.–Sun every half-hour 11 A.M.–5 P.M. (check the schedule, as times vary for tours with different themes). Confino Apartment tour Sat.–Sun hourly noon–3 P.M.

Williamsburg Bridge Delancey St. and the East River. The Williamsburg Bridge was born of a dare. Could Leffert Lefferts Buck, the city's chief engineer, build a bridge that was longer than the Brooklyn Bridge in half the time and with less money? He could and he did. When it opened in 1903, the Williamsburg was the world's longest suspension bridge at 7,308 feet, with a main span of 1,600 feet (five feet bigger than the Brooklyn Bridge, thank you very much). At a cost of $24,188,090, it came in $906,487 under its rival. And it was built in seven years; the Brooklyn took 13. (*See also the* Williamsburg *section, near the end of this chapter.*)

Selected Restaurants and Food Shops

Katz's Delicatessen, 205 E. Houston St. (at Ludlow St.) (212) 254-2246.

Russ and Daughters, 179 E. Houston St. (between Orchard and Allen Sts.) (212) 475-4880.

Sammy's Roumanian, 157 Chrystie St. (between Delancey and Houston Sts.) (212) 673-0330.

Streit's Matzos, 150 Rivington St. (at Suffolk St.) (212) 475-7000.

Yonah Shimmel Knishes, 175 E. Houston St. (between Eldridge and Forsythe Sts.) (212) 477-2858.

Recommended Neighborhood Restaurants
(*See chapter* **Restaurants** *for reviews.*)

aKa Café	$25 & Under	FUSION
Alias	$25 & Under	NEW AMERICAN
Crudo	$25 & Under	SPANISH
Petrosino	$25 & Under	ITALIAN
71 Clinton Fresh Food	☆☆ $$	BISTRO/NEW AMERICAN
WD-50	☆☆ $$$	NEW AMERICAN

Little Italy/Nolita

Historically, Little Italy was a family neighborhood, home to several waves of immigrants who settled in its five- and six-story tenement buildings. Some of them moved up and out, but others turned into the gray-haired grandmothers who still sit out on the stoops in pleasant weather.

The Italians moved in during the 1850's. In the first half of the 20th century, nearly everyone was of Italian descent. Since the late 1960's, when the United States opened its doors to Chinese immigrants, Chinatown has been creeping northward, crossing over its traditional Canal Street boundary. Although many Italian restaurants and stores remain, much of Little Italy proper—the blocks between Canal and Kenmare Streets—has the feel of Chinatown.

Mulberry Street is the real Italian heart of the neighborhood. It's lined with dozens of Italian restaurants and sidewalk cafés serving such specialties as coal-oven pizza and chocolate cannoli. **Ferrara** (195 Grand St.) has been producing traditional Italian desserts for 110 years. Try **Puglia** (189 Hester St.) for a unique, family-style dining experience. **Mare Chiaro** (176 1/2 Mulberry St.), with its Sinatra photos and authentic feel, is the place to go for a drink (*see chapter* **Nightlife**). For a taste of the area's Mafia past, go to the former site of **Umberto's Clam House** (149 Mulberry St.), where mobster Joey Gallo was gunned down in 1972. A couple of blocks north was the **Ravenite Social Club** (247 Mulberry St.), now a boutique, which served as the late John Gotti's unofficial headquarters until he was arrested there in 1990.

The big annual event is the **Feast of San Gennaro,** which starts the Thursday after Labor Day. For 10 days, several streets are closed to traffic, and the area becomes one giant colorful street festival, with rides, music and lots of food.

Old St. Patrick's Cathedral on Prince Street (at Mulberry St.) was founded by Irish immigrants in 1809. The cathedral became a parish church in 1879 when it was eclipsed by the new St. Patrick's Cathedral on Fifth Avenue. The old church was the childhood parish of Martin Scorsese and served as a backdrop for several movies, including two in Francis Ford Coppola's *Godfather* trilogy.

Nolita (which stands for **N**orth of **Li**ttle **Ita**ly) is the extension of Little Italy north to Houston Street. A young crowd of artists, professionals and hipsters has recast this neighborhood in the decidedly upscale mold of nearby SoHo. A host of sophisticated boutiques (many of them selling pricey shoes and handbags), galleries, cafes and nightclubs have sprouted in once-vacant storefronts (*see also chapters* **Shopping** *and* **Nightlife**). The heart of the action here is along **Elizabeth Street,** especially between Houston and Spring Streets.

Subway: F, S, V to Broadway–Lafayette St.; N, R to Prince St.; 6 to Spring St.

Recommended Neighborhood Restaurants
(*See chapter* **Restaurants** *for reviews.*)

Funky Broome	$25 & Under	CHINESE
Lombardi's	$25 & Under	PIZZA
Capitale	☆ ☆ $ $ $	ITALIAN

TriBeCa

TriBeCa doesn't have the street life of its trendy neighbor, SoHo. It's hard to tell which of the many cast-iron loft buildings have apartments tucked inside and which are commercial spaces. But its quiet demeanor is misleading, for there's an interesting array of galleries, retail stores and acclaimed restaurants mixed in with the residential buildings that occupy this patch of Downtown (bounded to the north by Canal Street, to the east by Broadway, to the south by Chambers Street and to the west by the Hudson River).

TriBeCa was a bustling commercial and manufacturing center in the 19th century. Since the neighborhood was near the river and several shipping piers, wealthy merchants built warehouses there to hold agricultural goods, including spices, nuts and coffee. Factories and warehouses dominated the neighborhood well into the 20th century, but most were abandoned by 1970. That's when artists began trickling in, transforming space in many empty lofts into studios, galleries and living quarters.

Savvy real estate developers came up with the name TriBeCa, from **Tri**angle **Be**low **Ca**nal Street. By the early 80's, the neighborhood was drawing investment bankers who liked its proximity to Wall Street, celebrities who liked its relative privacy, and anyone else who could afford the vast loft apartments whose values were shooting up.

A well-known landmark is the **Odeon,** the sleek and cavernous restaurant that played a leading role in *Bright Lights, Big City,* Jay McInerny's novel about the hedonistic nightlife of young New Yorkers in the 80's. TriBeCa is also home to a handful of hip restaurants owned by Robert De Niro and Drew Nieporent, including **Nobu,** for creative, adventurous Japanese cuisine; and **TriBeCa Grill,** a bustling spot offering contemporary American food and great stargazing.

Miramax has its headquarters here, as does neighborhood resident De Niro, who opened the **TriBeCa Film Center** at 375 Greenwich St. More recently, De Niro and producer Jane Rosenthal created the **TriBeCa Film Festival** to welcome the world back to Downtown after 9/11 and to publicize the creative spirit and resilience of the neighborhood.

Reade Street between Broadway and Church has some fine examples of the marble and cast-iron buildings that the neighborhood is known for, as does **Duane Street** between Church and West Broadway. Franklin, White and Walker Streets are also good places to check out the local architecture. **Subway:** A, C, 1, 2, 3, 9 to Chambers St.; A, C, E, 1, 9 to Canal St.; 1, 9 to Franklin St.

Recommended Neighborhood Restaurants

(See chapter **Restaurants** *for reviews.)*

Lunchbox Food Company	$25 & Under		DINER/AMERICAN
Bouley	☆ ☆ ☆ ☆	$ $ $ $	FRENCH
Chanterelle	☆ ☆ ☆	$ $ $ $	FRENCH
Danube	☆ ☆ ☆	$ $ $ $	EAST EUROPEAN/GERMAN
Layla	☆ ☆	$ $ $	MIDDLE EASTERN

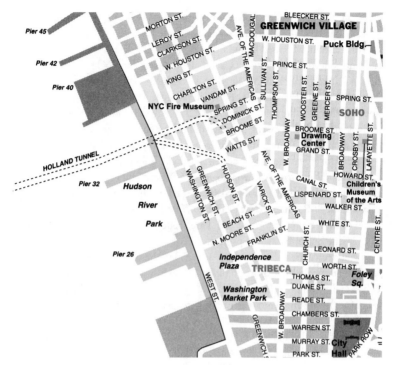

TriBeCa/SoHo

Next Door Nobu	☆☆☆	$ $ $ $	JAPANESE
Nobu	☆☆☆	$ $ $ $	JAPANESE
Odeon	☆☆	$ $	BISTRO/NEW AMERICAN
Salaam Bombay	☆☆	$ $	INDIAN
66	☆☆	$ $ $	CHINESE
Tribeca Grill	☆☆	$ $ $	NEW AMERICAN

SoHo

Art and commerce coexist in SoHo (for **S**outh of **Ho**uston St.) more fiercely, perhaps, than anywhere else in New York City, yet still haven't driven each other out. (Artists who can't afford million-dollar lofts are a different matter.) There is impromptu art, like the fetchingly arranged baskets of unbelievably yellow tomatoes at **Dean & DeLuca** *(see chapter* **Shopping***)* or the plumage of an elegant woman stepping down restaurant row on West Broadway. And then there is the more institutional art: the **galleries** that have colonized the neighborhood ever since four prominent uptown dealers, Leo Castelli, Ileana Sonnabend, John Weber and Andre Emmerick settled in the big loft building at 420 West Broadway in 1971 *(see section* "Galleries" *in chapter* **The Arts***)*.

The arrival of the big-four dealers signalled the transformation of a once-gritty warehouse neighborhood populated, often illegally, by penniless artists. Today it's a chic scene, with limousines idling outside stores where a deceptively minimalist esthetic—lots of space, little merchandise—tempts new-money patrons. Many working artists have moved on to Chelsea.

Mr. Castelli, who used to put artists on a payroll whether they produced or not, introduced Andy Warhol's Campbell's Soup cans to SoHo. The neighborhood went on to nurture the wiggly post-graffiti art of Keith Haring and Jean Michel Basquiat. Mary Boone, a Castelli protégée who promoted Julian Schnabel and David Salle, has since moved her gallery north of 58th Street, where she was arrested for handing out nine-millimeter cartridges to visitors the way coffee shops offer mints. (She might've gotten away with it downtown.)

In SoHo, almost nothing lacks elegant style, from the ornate brackets at upscale hardware store **Anthropologie** (375 West Broadway), to the handmade note papers at **Kate's Paperie** (561 Broadway), to the french fries with lemony mayonnaise at **Balthazar** (80 Spring St.). Trendy clothing and accessory designers like **Anna Sui** (113 Greene St.), **kate spade** (454 Broome St.) and **Agnes B.** (79 Greene St.) also have shops here.

Cheap rents are a thing of the past in SoHo these days, gone with the sweatshops that once occupied the 26 blocks of the historic cast-iron district (once called Hell's Hundred Acres, because of the frequent fires fueled by cloth and chemicals). The anonymous artist homesteaders have been replaced by celebrity denizens.

Would they, let alone the original artists, have discovered SoHo without its architecture? From the magical **Puck Building** (295 Lafayette St.), with its gilded homage to A Midsummer Night's Dream on East Houston, to the **Haughwout Building** (488–492 Broadway), to the **Marble House** (southern edge of Mercer and Canal), the area is filled with distinctive buildings. The most famous, of course, are the post–Civil War cast-iron buildings, their Italianate elegance belying their seminal role as the grandfather of prefab architecture, the Sears catalog of building design, with owners choosing a Doric capital from column A and a Corinthian from column B. The bottle-glass sidewalks once allowed sunlight to illuminate the storage vaults below. Some streets are still paved with Belgian brick (not cobblestone) brought over as ship's ballast.

For children, a cast-iron tour can be almost as much fun as the **New York City Fire Museum**, with its collection of old firefighting equipment. Just buy a pack of cheap magnets; they'll help you tell the authentic cast-iron facades from the ringers.   —Anemona Hartocollis

Subway: F, S, V to Broadway–Lafayette St.; N, R to Prince St.; C, E, 6 to Spring St. or Bleecker St.

HIGHLIGHTS OF THE NEIGHBORHOOD

(For the **Drawing Center** and coverage of the galleries, see chapter **The Arts.** For the **Children's Museum of the Arts,** see chapter **New York for Children.**)

New York City Fire Museum 278 Spring St. (between Hudson and Varick Sts.) (212) 691-1303 www.nycfiremuseum.org. Located in a 1904 firehouse, the New York City Fire Museum traces the history of New York's Bravest from the

1600's to the present. What is best about the Fire Museum is the Americana—in one case, a stuffed dog, the heroic companion of firemen who could not bear to part with him, a street mutt all heart. Just as wonderful is the red and gold beauty of the old fire engines, their ornate brass gleaming. An exhibit of photographs records the nation's most serious fires, including New York's Triangle Shirtwaist fire of 1911 and the Chicago fire of 1871. Real firefighters are often on hand to share stories and fire-safety tips. This is a good place to buy authorized FDNY logo gear. **Admission:** $4 adults; $2 seniors and students; $1 children under age 12. **Hours:** Tue.–Sat. 10 A.M.–5 P.M., Sun 10 A.M.–4 P.M.

Recommended Neighborhood Restaurants

(See chapter **Restaurants** for reviews.)

Jean Claude	$25 & Under		BISTRO/FRENCH
Soho Steak	$25 & Under		BISTRO/STEAK
Balthazar	☆☆	$ $	BISTRO/FRENCH
Fiamma Osteria	☆☆☆	$ $ $	ITALIAN
Honmura An	☆☆☆	$ $ $	JAPANESE/NOODLES
Kittichai	☆☆	$ $	THAI

NoHo

It's easy to forget that NoHo, wedged between the West Village, the East Village and SoHo, is a neighborhood in its own right (New Yorkers have been known to debate whether or not it even exists). But while it shares many qualities with its better-known neighbors, NoHo—which stretches from Houston Street to Astor Place, and from Mercer Street to the Bowery—has its own quirky history.

Some of the city's blue-blood families, including the Astors and the Vanderbilts, were drawn to the neighborhood in the 1830's. They lived in the Greek Revival town houses known collectively as **Colonnade Row** (Lafayette St. between Astor Pl. and Great Jones St.). Only four of the nine mansions remain, and although the city has designated them landmarks, they are in shabby shape.

One of the old mansions houses the **Astor Place Theater** (434 Lafayette St.) where the ever-popular performance troupe called Blue Man Group has been putting on a wacky show involving Twinkies, paint and marshmallows since 1991. But NoHo's most venerable performance venue is the **Joseph Papp Public Theater** (425 Lafayette St.). The grand Italian Renaissance-style building originally belonged to John Jacob Astor, the city's first multimillionaire and one of the area's most famous residents. He donated the building to New York in 1854, and it became the city's first free public library. The building was set to be demolished in the 1960's, but at the last minute it was renovated and reopened by Joseph Papp, founder of the New York Shakespeare Festival. There are six theaters inside, and altogether they seat more than 2,500 people. Hair and A Chorus Line opened there, and the theater now stages about 25 productions a year.

The city designated much of NoHo a historic district in 1999, after a three-

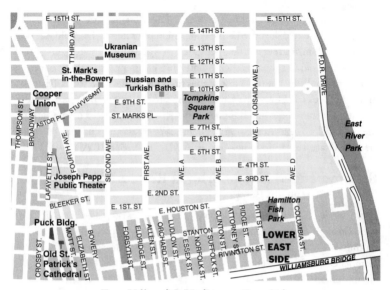

East Village/NoHo/Lower East Side

year crusade by residents to preserve the largely intact rows of 19th-century loft buildings scattered throughout the neighborhood. The buildings, with facades of marble, cast iron, limestone and terra-cotta, once housed retail stores topped by manufacturing spaces or warehouses.

Artists began moving into the area in the early 1970's, trickling north from SoHo in search of cheaper rents. They adopted the name NoHo—for **North** of **Houston**—and in 1976 got the city to rezone the neighborhood similarly to SoHo, allowing artists to live and work in the same space.

NoHo has no park, school or library, but trendy bars and restaurants abound. One popular dinner spot is the **Time Café** (380 Lafayette St.), in an 1888 building designed by Henry J. Hardenburgh, architect of the Plaza Hotel and the Dakota apartment house on Central Park West. In the basement is **Fez,** a neo-Moroccan lounge with Persian rugs, plenty of couches and performances that range from folk music to poetry readings.   —*Abby Goodnough*

Subway: F, S, V to Broadway–Lafayette St.; 6 to Bleecker St.

HIGHLIGHT OF THE NEIGHBORHOOD

Merchant's House Museum 29 E. 4th St. (between Lafayette St. and Bowery) (212) 777-1089 *www.merchantshouse.com*. If you get a charge out of browsing through *Architectural Digest,* you'll enjoy this small museum, housed in a Greek Revival town house. It provides a historically accurate glimpse of the lifestyle of an affluent 19th-century family, with original furnishings and exhibitions related to the period. Ask the staff for their self-guided neighborhood walking tour; guided neighborhood tours are sometimes offered on weekends, weather permitting. **Admission:** $6 adults; $4 students and seniors; free for children under 12. **Hours:** Thu.–Fri. 1–5 P.M., Sat.–Mon. noon–5 P.M.plus guided tours Sat.–Sun.

The East Village

The East Village has always been a place for bold statements. It was here, at **Cooper Union,** in what is now the city's oldest auditorium, that Abraham Lincoln delivered the fiery anti-slavery speech that helped him win the Republican nomination in 1860. It was on St. Marks Place that Leon Trotsky started talking up revolution before joining one in Russia. And it was in the smoky music clubs around the Bowery, most notably **CBGB** (*see chapter* **Nightlife**), many decades later, that punk got its deafening start.

These days, skyrocketing rents and sleek new cocktail lounges have have arrived. But the East Village—stretching from the East River to the Bowery, and from 14th Street to Houston Street—has not lost the rough edges it acquired back in the early 1960's, when radicals, musicians, artists and hippies flocked here, having been priced out of Greenwich Village. Stroll, for example, past the **Hell's Angels'** headquarters on East 3rd Street. Most of the members are middle-aged now, but the plaque near the door still offers this youthful advice: "When in doubt, knock 'em out." Or drop in for a beer at the oldest bar in New York, **McSorley's** (E. 7th St. near Third Ave.), which looks as if no one has mopped the floor since the first mugs were filled there in 1854 (or 1862, depending on whose version of New York bar history you believe).

There are also still a few traces left of the neighborhood's multi-ethnic past. Beginning after World War II, the East Village became the center of the city's Ukrainian community, as immigrants fleeing Soviet oppression joined others who had settled in the neighborhood around the turn of the last century. On Second Avenue you can still spot old men reading *Svoboda,* the Ukrainian-American newspaper. You can also grab a blintz or a bowl of borscht at **Veselka,** an honest-to-goodness Ukrainian diner at the corner of 9th Street.

Practically all evidence has disappeared of the days when a stretch of Second Avenue was known as the Jewish Rialto, the Broadway of Yiddish theater. But a quick side trip on East 10th Street takes you to the **Russian and Turkish Baths,** a cavernous, tiled throwback to a time when the neighborhood was filled with "shvitzes" (Yiddish slang for sweat or steambath).

Little India (E. 6th St. between First and Second Aves.) offers a cluster of cramped Indian restaurants with nearly identical menus and décor. These are great places to stop for a cheap tasty meal. For dessert, grab a cannoli at **Veniero's** (342 E. 11th St.) or **De Roberti's** (176 First Ave.) around the corner. These turn-of-the-century shops are two of the city's oldest Italian pasticcerias.

The best example of the East Village's bohemian credentials can be found on **St. Marks Place,** which—despite the presence of a Gap and a Subway sandwich shop—still manages to attract nightly crowds of the heavily pierced and the colorfully coifed to its used-record stores, bars and cafes. The street is not quite as scrappy as it used to be: If you decide you'd like a tattoo, you can get one while sipping a cappuccino.

St. Marks dead-ends at another of the neighborhood's raucous landmarks, **Tompkins Square Park,** where riots erupted back in 1988 when the police moved in to impose a curfew. Three years later, the police cleared out an encampment of homeless people and self-styled anarchists and closed the park for extensive renovations and clean-up. Today the park has a much more manicured appearance, and the only shouting tends to come from the chess tables, where speed players shout to throw off their opponents' concentration.

The easternmost part of the East Village, from Avenues A to Avenue D, was known until only a decade ago mostly for its abundance of drug dealers and crime. But this area—called **Alphabet City**—has been undoubtedly the most changed by the neighborhood's rapid gentrification. On the same corner where heroin sales were once the main commercial activity, upscale bakeries are doing a brisk business in blackberry scones. Buildings once called tenements now offer $1,500-a-month, closet-sized studios with high-speed Internet connections. So what about all the radicals, musicians and artists who came to the neighborhood in search of lower rents? They're searching elsewhere.

—*Randy Kennedy*

Subway: F to Second Ave. or Broadway–Lafayette St.; 6 to Astor Pl. or Bleecker St.; N, R to 8th St.; L, N, Q, R, W, 4, 5, 6 to Union Sq.

HIGHLIGHTS OF THE NEIGHBORHOOD

Cooper Union 30 Cooper Square, E. 8th St. and Fourth Ave. (212) 254-6300 *www.cooper.edu*. Housed in the city's first steel-frame building, Cooper Union was New York's first free nonsectarian college, founded in 1859 by Peter Cooper, the industrialist who built the first U.S. locomotive. Cooper wanted to offer students the technical education that he himself had never received and to create a center for open discussion. The school's Great Hall is just that. Inaugurated in 1859 by Mark Twain, it served as the site for Lincoln's "right makes might" speech in 1860. Today you can still attend lectures and concerts there. In the triangle south of the building is a statue of Peter Cooper by Augustus Saint-Gaudens. The gallery features exhibitions of fine art, architecture and graphic design. Very competetive, the school offers college degrees in engineering, architecture and the graphic arts—and tuition is still free.

Grace Church 802 Broadway (at 10th St.) (212) 254-2000. This Gothic-style Episcopalian church, built in 1846, was designed by James Renwick, who later achieved fame as the architect of St. Patrick's Cathedral. Later in the century, a marble spire was added to the white limestone church, as were several adjacent Gothic Revival buildings.

Nuyorican Poets Cafe 236 E. 3rd St. (between Aves. B and C) (212) 505-8183 *www.nuyorican.org*. Since the 1970's, the Nuyorican Poets Cafe has been in the vanguard of the neighborhood's alternative culture. A product of the black and Latino liberation movements, the café was a pioneer in offering spoken-word poetry slams. The slams, contests in which the audience judges poets in game-show fashion, still take place in the high-ceilinged space, as do featured reader nights, Latin big-band music blowouts and occasional theater productions and film screenings.

Russian and Turkish Baths 268 E. 10th St. (between First Ave. and Ave. A) (212) 473-8806 *www.russianturkishbaths.com*. There is nothing particularly remote or serene about these baths, housed in a timeworn tenement. But a visit there offers a voyage to an era when the neighborhood bustled with peddlers and Yiddish-speaking immigrants. Before the arrival of sushi and $10 martinis, a dozen or so public bathhouses were basic amenities for people deprived of indoor plumbing. Today, only the 10th Street Baths remain. Aside from the addition of a juice bar—which still serves borscht and blintzes—little seems to have changed at what regulars still call "the shvitz," a temple to the art of sweating. And most of the clientele is refreshingly oblivious to the latest fitness fads. No need for advance reservations—you can sign up for a massage when you arrive. **Admission:** $25 for day pass. **Hours:** Mon.–Tue. and Thu.–Fri. 11 A.M.–10 P.M., Sat 7:30 A.M.–10 P.M. (coed); Wed. 9 A.M.–2 P.M. (women only) and 2–10 P.M. (coed); Sun 7:30 A.M.–2 P.M. (men only) and 2–10 P.M. (coed).

St. Marks Church in the Bowery 131 E. 10th St. (between Second and Third Aves.) (212) 674-6377 *www.saintmarkschurch.org*. Tilted on a true east-west axis, this Episcopal church sits on land that was the farm of New Amsterdam's Governor Peter Stuyvesant. A Federal-style fieldstone building completed in 1799, Manhattan's second-oldest church (after St. Paul's Chapel) was later outfitted with a Greek Revival steeple and a cast-iron portico. Following a devastating fire in 1978, the interior was restructured into a versatile open space that functions as a venue for the performing arts as well as religious services. In addition to its ongoing Poetry Project, the progressive East Village church sponsors music, dance and frequent lectures and seminars. Stuyvesant and his wife are buried under the church.

Ukrainian Museum 203 Second Ave. (between 12th and 13th Sts.) (212) 228-0110 *www.ukrainianmuseum.org*. The East Village is home to a small but thriving Ukrainian population. The Ukrainian Museum houses permanent and changing exhibitions of folk art, fine art, photos, documents, coins, stamps, textiles, costumes, Easter eggs and rare books. The museum's programming is temporarily limited, pending a move to a new, larger facility at 222 E. 6th St. **Admission:** $3 adults; $2 students and seniors. **Hours:** Wed.–Sun. 1–5 P.M.

Recommended Neighborhood Restaurants

(See chapter **Restaurants** *for reviews.)*

Acquario	$25 & Under	MEDITERRANEAN
First	$25 & Under	NEW AMERICAN
Frank	$25 & Under	ITALIAN
Habib's Place	$25 & Under	MIDDLE EASTERN
Holy Basil	$25 & Under	THAI
Le Tableau	$25 & Under	MEDITERRANEAN
Mermaid Inn	$25 & Under	SEAFOOD
Soba-Ya	$25 & Under	JAPANESE/NOODLES
Bambou	☆ ☆	$ $ $	CARIBBEAN
industry(food)	☆	$ $ $	NEW AMERICAN

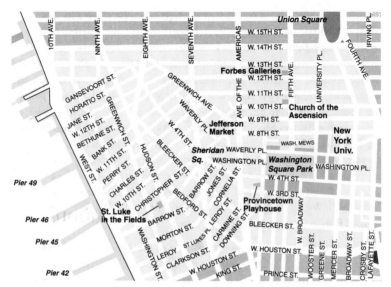

GreenwichVillage/West Village

Greenwich Village

Back in the earliest days of New York City, the Village was full of rolling farm-land and winding country lanes. Wealthy New Yorkers would arrive for short holidays, seeking to escape the congestion of Lower Manhattan.

But the Village evolved into something decidedly less bucolic and serene. For generations, this was where radicals, writers, artists and intellectuals lived the bohemian life, starving for the sake of their art in tiny garrets and debating politics and philosophy in smoky cafés. Here you'd find Dylan Thomas hoisting a few pints, Eugene O'Neill scribbling away at his latest play or John Reed furi-ously denouncing the bourgeois.

Throughout the 1960's, the Village was a hotbed of counterculture, com-plete with beatnik poets, bongo drummers and druggy musicians. After a police raid of the **Stonewall Inn** (an incarnation still stands on Christopher Street) in 1969, a group of gay men, tired of being harassed and closeted, staged an upris-ing that ignited the gay liberation movement. To this day, the Village is a stronghold of gay and lesbian culture.

The neighborhood has become too expensive to be considered truly bohemian anymore (it's home to a bevy of celebrities like Gwenyth Paltrow, Sarah Jessica Parker, Michael Stipe, James Gandolfini and Christy Turlington), but it's still got a funky charm and an anything-goes sensibility. Parking yourself at an outdoor cafe for a couple of hours of people-watching (perhaps at **Café Reggio,** at 119 Macdougal St.) is endlessly entertaining. Street life in the Village is always unpre-dictable, always flamboyant.

The shady, tree-lined streets of the Village are populated with lovely brownstones and town houses, not with towering high-rises. It's one of the most intriguing shopping areas in the city; on the same block, you can find high-priced antiques and used records, sleek designer fashions and vintage clothing, the latest kitchen gadgets and temporary tattoos.

A handful of landmark clubs with steep cover charges maintain the Village's longtime reputation as a hotbed of great jazz; today they're outnumbered by clubs featuring rock, blues and alternative sounds. Add into this mix a huge array of restaurants, neighborhood pubs and sleek cocktail lounges, and you've got a rollicking nightlife scene.

Subway: A, C, E, F to W. 4th St.–Washington Sq.; A, C, E, F, V, 1, 2, 3, 9 to 14th St.; 1, 9 to Christopher St.

HIGHLIGHTS OF THE NEIGHBORHOOD

Church of St. Luke in the Fields 487 Hudson St. (between Grove and Christopher Sts.) (212) 924-0562 *www.stlukeinthefields.org*. "'Twas the night before Christmas," the opening line of Clement Clarke Moore's famous Yuletide poem, has special meaning for parishioners at this enchanting Federal-style landmark church. Moore was a founding warden of the church, which was built in 1822 as a satellite of Trinity Church. Strolling through the delightful gardens behind St. Luke in the Fields adds to the sense of being in a remote village. In 1981, a devastating fire (the second in the church's history) destroyed the structure, and it was restored to capture its original simplicity. The church is extremely active in neighborhood life and maintains a high musical profile. The St. Luke's Chamber Ensemble was born here, and the West Village Chorale regularly performs.

Church of the Ascension Fifth Ave. and 10th St. (212) 254-8620 *www.ascensionnyc.org*. Richard Upjohn's legacy to New York City includes several wonderful churches, among them the Church of the Ascension. Completed in 1841, the church was the first built on Fifth Avenue, which was then an unpaved track ending in a wooden fence at 23rd Street. A Gothic Revival-style brownstone structure, the church relates closely to Upjohn's earlier (and better-known) Trinity Church in Lower Manhattan. The beautiful interior is famous for its John LaFarge mural and stained-glass windows, and exquisite marble statuary by Louis Saint-Gaudens. The extraordinary Voices of Ascension, a professional choir and orchestra, presents some of the finest choral concerts in town.

Forbes Magazine Galleries 60 Fifth Ave. (at 12th St.) (212) 206-5548. Malcolm Forbes, millionaire publisher, collected glamorous friends, bejeweled Fabergé eggs, toy soldiers, toy boats, old Monopoly games, autographs and presidential papers. Except for the glamorous friends, it's all here, tastefully exhibited on the ground floor of the *Forbes* magazine building. **Admission:** Free. **Hours:** Tue.–Wed. and Fri.–Sat. 10 A.M.–4 P.M.

New York Public Library—Jefferson Market Library 425 Sixth Ave. (between Ninth and 10th Sts.) (212) 243-4334. You can't miss this eyeful of bright red stone and ornate pinnacles, towers, carvings and stained-glass windows, all topped off with a clock tower that still keeps perfect time. These days it houses a branch of the New York Public Library, but it was originally built in 1877 as a courthouse, on the site of a public meat-and-produce market. The courthouse was part of a complex including a firehouse and a jail, which stood in the area now occupied by a lush community garden.

New York University Information Center, 40 Washington Sq. South (at Wooster St.) (212) 998-4636 *www.nyu.edu*. Sometimes it seems as if everywhere you turn in Greenwich Village, you see a violet flag on a building telling you that you are looking at another part of New York University's sprawl. Washington Square Park is the de facto center of the campus, surrounded by university offices, student centers, dorms and libraries. Founded in 1831, NYU hosts some 17,000 undergraduate and 18,000 graduate students, and boasts the nation's largest open-stack library. The university sponsors performances at several of its auditoriums, including the Loewe Auditorium, the NYU Theater and the Loeb Student Center.

75 1/2 Bedford Street (at Commerce St.). Only 9.5 feet wide and dating from 1893, this house is said to be the narrowest in the city. Edna St. Vincent Millay, Margaret Mead, William Steig and Cary Grant all lived in this tiny place at one time or another. Around the corner at 38 Commerce Street you can also visit the **Cherry Lane Theater,** opened by Millay and friends in 1924 in an old barn and still in operation.

Washington Mews Fifth Ave., between Washington Sq. North and E. 8th St. This private street of two-story houses in Greenwich Village once functioned as stables and service quarters for the residents of the Greek Revival row houses along Washington Square North. These 19th-century structures were converted into private residences during the early 1900's, and were leased to New York University in 1949. Today, some of the buildings contain NYU offices, but this cobblestone street maintains its quiet charm.

Washington Square Park W. 4th St. (at Macdougal St.) (212) 387-7676. Washington Square Park brings together downtown's diverse population. Musicians jam near the central fountain as skateboarders jump park benches. Students from nearby NYU lounge or shoot films; gay and straight singles swap canine tales as their dogs frolic and children swing in the fenced playground. The southwestern corner is also the proving ground for the city's most serious chess players. The park's identifying landmark is Stanford White's large marble arch, constructed in 1895 to commemorate George Washington's inauguration. In the early part of the 20th century, the artists Marcel Duchamp and John Sloan climbed onto the arch to declare the secession of the neighborhood from the United States. A generation earlier, Henry James had named a novel for the square. But as a public gathering place, the park also has its dark history, having served in the early 19th century as a graveyard and the site of public hangings. You would be excused for thinking it's haunted, as the gallows tree remains standing and many of the graves were left undisturbed when the park was established in 1827.

Recommended Neighborhood Restaurants

*(See chapter **Restaurants** for reviews.)*

Bar Pitti	$25 & Under		ITALIAN
Crispo	$25 & Under		ITALIAN
Da Andrea	$25 & Under		ITALIAN
Fish	$25 & Under		SEAFOOD
Do Hwa	$25 & Under		KOREAN
Gonzo	$25 & Under		PIZZA/ITALIAN
Le Gigot	$25 & Under		FRENCH
Marumi	$25 & Under		JAPANESE/SUSHI
Mexicana Mama	$25 & Under		MEXICAN
Moustache	$25 & Under		MIDDLE EASTERN
Paradou	$25 & Under		FRENCH/SANDWICHES
Pearl Oyster Bar	$25 & Under		SEAFOOD
Babbo	☆☆☆	$ $ $ $	ITALIAN
Blue Hill	☆☆	$ $ $	FRENCH
Gotham Bar and Grill	☆☆☆	$ $ $ $	NEW AMERICAN
Jarnac	☆	$ $ $	FRENCH
Jefferson	☆☆	$ $ $	NEW AMERICAN/ASIAN
Sumile	☆☆	$ $ $	JAPANESE FUSION
Surya	☆☆	$ $	INDIAN

Sara Krulwich/The New York Times

Washington Square Park

The Meatpacking District

Perhaps no other neighborhood in New York has seen a more startling change in the last five years than the Meatpacking District, the cobblestoned, three-block-deep neighborhood below 14th Street at the Hudson River. Already home to a gaggle of trendy nightspots dating to the late 1990's, the area has been positively flooded in recent years by high-end restaurants, boutique hotels and roped-off lounges (and the clientele that loves them). Limousines crowd the streets and sidewalks almost every night, as do the hot-dog vendors and pedicab drivers more commonly associated with Times Square.

As its popularity has increased, the neighborhood—once a shadowy sanctum of transvestite prostitutes, leather bars and full-service poultry and beef providers —has become a kind of an Epcot Center of alcoholic fun, with everything from ersatz France (Pastis) and ersatz Goa (Spice Market) to ersatz Miami (the Hotel Gansevoort) and ersatz London (Soho House). On any given night, the Meat-packing District feels like a mobbed, boozy and tragically hip theme park.

All of this has come, of course, with a decline in its native character. Instead of being a place where anything goes, it is a place where everyone goes. For all the trendy overkill, the Meatpacking District is still home to some of best, and most exciting, nightlife in the city, as well as a gaggle of one-of-a-kind boutiques and restaurants.

Much of the neighborhood's early development was on 14th Street, where stalwart fashion emporiums like **Stella McCartney** and **Jeffrey's** are found, as are perennial hot spots like **Lotus, Markt** and **Son Cubano.** In recent years the action has also shifted south, to the crossroads of Little West 12th Street, Gan-sevoort Street and Greenwich Street, home to **Pastis,** the popular French bistro, where taxis idle seven or eight deep on a Friday night, and ladies' skirts run from short to criminal pretty much year-round.

Of the new restaurants, perhaps the most hyped is **Spice Market,** celebrity chef Jean-Georges Vongerichten's two-level Eastern bistro on West 13th Street, serving multistar Asian food upstairs and $15 cocktails downstairs. Lines usually run out the door, as they do at **Vento,** another newcomer on Hudson Street, which serves Italian food on its first two floors and $300 bottles of vodka in its hoity-toity basement lounge. Just above Spice Market is **Soho House,** the nomi-nally private six-floor hotel with a celebrity-friendly bar and a rooftop pool. Also angling for the hipster dollar is the new South Beach-inspired **Hotel Gansevoort,** which also features a rooftop pool and bar with fantastic views and pricey drinks.

West 13th Street is still home to a couple of gritty survivors: **Hogs and Heifers** and the **Hog Pit,** sister country-and-western bars where binge drinking is heavily encouraged and where ladies are known to dance on the bar and shed their brasseries. (It's also, not surprisingly, where many of the remaining meat-packers do their early morning business.) Little West 12th is perhaps the least developed street (for now), though it does boast the dance club **Cielo,** where the music is loud and the doormen snooty, as well as **One,** a nightclub with a scant-ily-clad 20-something clientele.

The neighborhood's southern border is Gansevoort Street, home to **Florent,** the pleasant 24-hour diner and neighborhood trailblazer (it opened in 1986),

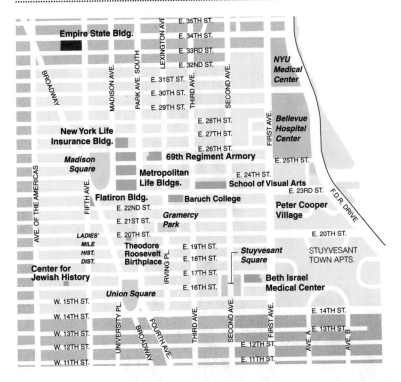

Flatiron/Union Square/ Gramercy Park

plus restaurant/lounges like **Meet, Rhone** and **Macelleria.** The street's most distinctive establishments are **PM,** a wildly popular nightclub/tapas bar where a half dozen doormen guard its gates, and **Hell,** a mixed gay and straight bar that keeps the old neighborhood's vibe alive. It's a little trendy, a little grungy and a little sexy, but more than anything, it's inclusive—and that's a lot more than can be said for many of the newly minted places with velvet ropes.   —*Jesse McKinley*

The Flatiron District/Union Square/Gramercy Park

The neighborhoods that make up the broad swath of Manhattan between Sixth Avenue and the East River, from 14th to 27th Streets, contain some of the best-preserved historic districts and landmarks in the city, as well as a host of chic spots for shopping, dining and nightlife. The area is dotted with little emerald oases—five parks whose importance far exceeds their acreage.

Madison Square (Fifth Ave. and 23rd St.) was once home to a depot of the New York and Harlem Rail Road and two earlier incarnations of Madison Square Garden. It offers a front-row view of two quintessential New York buildings: the **Flatiron Building** (175 Fifth Ave.) and the **Metropolitan Life Insurance Building** (1 Madison Ave.), whose 1909 tower with its four-faced clock and lantern is

The Flatiron Building

still intact despite substantial renovations. Also in the area are the exquisite **Appellate Division Courthouse** (27 Madison Ave.), the headquarters of the **New York Life Insurance Company** since 1928 (51 Madison Ave.). The Flatiron District earned the nickname "Silicon Alley" in the heyday of the dot-com firms once based here, but few of the companies have survived.

   Union Square (14th–17th Sts. and Broadway) was once a rallying place for the Labor movement, but it got its name as the union of the Bloomingdale Road (now Broadway) and the Bowery Road (now Fourth Ave.). By turns the province of aristocrats, anarchists and addicts, it has in recent decades felt more like a village green, thanks to its wonderful farmers' market (*see section* "Food Markets" *in chapter* **Shopping**). In the past decade, an array of trendy restaurants has sprung up along the edges of the square, along with a Barnes & Noble superstore and a Virgin Megastore.

Between Madison Square and Union Square from Broadway to Sixth Avenue is **Ladies' Mile**, the post–Civil War shopping district that was the former home of Lord & Taylor (901 Broadway) and B. Altman & Co. (615–629 Sixth Ave.) until department stores began to migrate uptown in the early decades of the 20th century. The buildings that once housed the dry-goods emporiums of the Gilded Age have been restored to retail life as home furnishing stores, like **ABC Carpet and Home** on Broadway and **Bed, Bath & Beyond** on Sixth Avenue. This area is a hotbed for upscale restaurants; Park Avenue South, in particular, is a veritable Restaurant Row.

Gramercy Park (Lexington Ave. and 21st St.), a fenced and locked enclave (only residents who live directly on its perimeter are given keys), remains one of the most genteel squares in urban America, as it has been since 1831. One of the city's earliest high-rise apartment buildings stands on the park's southeast corner, while several town houses with ornate wrought iron porches endure on the western side. At 15 Gramercy Park South stands the elegant headquarters of the **National Arts Club** (212-477-2389; *www.nationalartsclub.org*), which promotes American art by awarding prizes and scholarships. The club's headquarters is a Gramercy Park brownstone, which Calvert Vaux (Frederick Law Olmsted's partner in the design of Central Park) renovated in a Victorian Gothic style for Gov. Samuel J. Tilden. The neighborhood around the park is home to celebrity denizens like Mike Piazza, Uma Thurman and Ethan Hawke, and Winona Ryder.

Nearby is the **69th Regiment Armory** (68 Lexington Ave.), which hosted the celebrated 1913 "Armory Show" that introduced America to modern art and continues to host various arts and antiques shows. Also in the area are several prominent nightspots, like **Irving Plaza** (*see chapter* **Nightlife**).

Subway: L, N, R, Q, W, 4, 5, 6 to Union Sq.; N, R, 6 to 23rd St. or 28th St.

HIGHLIGHTS OF THE NEIGHBORHOOD

Center for Jewish History 15 W. 16th St. (between Fifth and Sixth Aves.) (212) 294-8301 *www.cjh.org*. The Center for Jewish History is an enormous complex dedicated to exploring Jewish history, art, culture and literature. Its main exhibition space, the Yeshiva University Museum (*www.yumuseum.org*), features a variety of displays, including a sculpture garden and a collection of Judaica confiscated by the Nazis. Additional resources include a Reading Room, a genealogy institute, national archives of the Jewish people in America and scholarly research institutes. There's also an auditorium that features regular films, lectures and performances; a kosher cafe; a bookstore; and a children's discovery room. **Admission:** Yeshiva University Museum: $6 adults; $4 students and seniors; free to other facilities. **Hours:** Yeshiva University Museum: Sun. and Tue.–Thu. 11 A.M.–5 P.M. Reading Room and Geneaology Institute:

Mon.–Thu. 9:30 A.M.–4:30 P.M. Gallery spaces: Mon.–Thu. 9 A.M.–5 P.M., Fri. 9 A.M.–2 P.M., Sun. 11 A.M.–5 P.M.

Flatiron Building 175 Fifth Ave. (at 23rd St.). Originally known as the Fuller Building, the Flatiron Building took its nickname from its shape—an odd triangular design devised to fit on this peculiar plot of land (it's only 6 feet across at its narrowest end). The architect, Daniel H. Burnham, designed this early skyscraper, built in 1902, by overlaying an Italian Renaissance terra-cotta facade on a modern steel frame. The tall, wedge-shaped office building looks like a ship sailing uptown. Today the surrounding neighborhood has taken on the building's name.

Museum of Sex 233 Fifth Ave. (at 27th St.) (212) 689-6337 *www.museumof-sex.com* or *www.mosex.com*. Now this is truly astonishing. A claim is afoot in New York City that men and women were having sex as long ago as the 1910's, and maybe even further back than that. This is hard to believe. Everybody knows that sex was invented in the 1960's. But suddenly new evidence is being put forth to smash old assumptions.

A rather graphic stag film said to have been made around 1915 leaves little doubt that some people had figured out a thing or two even then. Photographs, posters and writings from the 19th century are equally disheartening for anyone who put full faith in the 60's. It is possible that sex was already lurking in the wings, and not just between men and women. Apparently, the love that dared not speak its name found a way to make itself heard once in a while.

The bearer of these illusion-shattering tidings is the Museum of Sex, which puts on a sober face. With an admission charge of $14.50, you can't exactly accuse it of offering cheap thrills. "It's primarily anthropological and social research, as opposed to erotic art," said Daniel Gluck, the museum's founder. That may be. But there are also films and photographs likely to make some people reach for their smelling salts. Still, a society that has no problem putting Anna Nicole Smith on television seems unlikely to lose much sleep over a sex museum. There could even be a series of such museums, one for each of the seven deadly sins. Lust is taken care of. Why not a Museum of Avarice? A splendid location would be the building at 9 West 57th Street, where Tyco International has its offices. I had some thoughts for a Museum of Sloth, but took a nap and forgot to write them down.   —*Clyde Haberman*

Admission: $14.50 adults; $13.50 students and seniors. $1.50 service charge for purchasing advance tickets online or by phone. Recommended for mature audiences only. **Hours:** Sun.–Fri. 11 A.M.–6:30 P.M. (last ticket sold at 5:45 P.M.), Sat 11 A.M.–8 P.M. (last ticket sold at 7:15 P.M.).

School of Visual Arts Museum 209 E. 23rd St. (between Third and Fourth Aves.) (212) 592-2144 *www.schoolofvisualarts.edu*. The School of Visual Arts trains students as professional graphic and fine artists. Its museum features changing exhibitions by students and established artists; in the past, it has featured works by Willem de Kooning, Keith Haring and Roy Liechtenstein. Most of the work is contemporary, but shows span an array of mediums including illustration, fine art, sculpture, animation and photography. The school hosts film, music and lecture events throughout the year, and there are three additional on-campus galleries for student exhibits.

Theodore Roosevelt Birthplace 28 E. 20th St. (between Park Ave. South and Broadway) (212) 260-1616 *www.nps.gov/thrb*. This brownstone, which includes period rooms restored to their appearance from 1865 and 1872, is a reconstruction of the four-story house where Theodore Roosevelt was born and lived until he was 14. During much of his childhood, Roosevelt was confined to the house with a variety of illnesses, including chronic asthma. There are 250,000 objects in the permanent collection, including T.R.'s christening gown and the stuffed teddy bears that take his name. The site, which can only be seen on a guided tour, boasts the largest collection of the president's memorabilia anywhere, and is one of the more fascinating hidden gems of the National Park system. Displays from the permanent collection change regularly, and the museum hosts concerts and lectures throughout the year. **Admission:** $3 adults; free for children under 16. **Hours:** Tue.–Sat. 9 A.M.–5 P.M. Tours leave on the hour, with the last tour at 4 P.M.

Recommended Neighborhood Restaurants
(*See chapter* **Restaurants** *for reviews.*)

Bar Jamón	$25 & Under		SPANISH
Havana Central	$25 & Under		CUBAN/PAN-LATIN
Mandler's	$25 & Under		SANDWICHES
Blue Water Grill	☆	$ $	SEAFOOD
Bolo	☆ ☆ ☆	$ $ $ $	SPANISH
Casa Mono	☆ ☆	$ $ $	TAPAS
Eleven Madison Park	☆ ☆	$ $ $	NEW AMERICAN
Gramercy Tavern	☆ ☆ ☆	$ $ $ $	NEW AMERICAN
I Trulli	☆ ☆	$ $ $	ITALIAN
Mesa Grill	☆ ☆	$ $ $ $	SOUTHWESTERN
Patria	☆ ☆ ☆	$ $ $	LATIN AMERICAN
Sueños	☆	$ $	MEXICAN
Tabla	☆ ☆ ☆	$ $ $ $	PAN ASIAN
Veritas	☆ ☆ ☆	$ $ $ $	NEW AMERICAN

Chelsea

The formerly gritty neighborhood of Chelsea is best known these days for its vibrant gay and lesbian community, a sprawling riverside sports complex and an astonishing concentration of **art galleries** (some 170 in all, mostly concentrated in the 20's between 10th and 11th Aves.).

Chelsea stretches from Sixth Avenue to the Hudson River, roughly between West 14th and West 28th Streets. Its eastern end, along Sixth Avenue, is

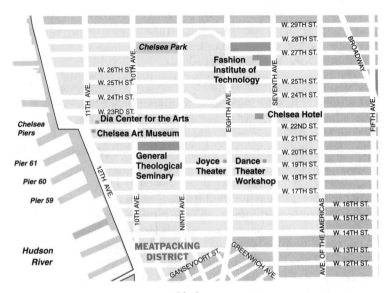

Chelsea

increasingly dominated by big-box stores like **Bed, Bath & Beyond** and **Old Navy.** For an outdoor shopping alternative, try the weekend flea market at the corner of Sixth Avenue and West 26th Street. It's a fun place to troll for kitschy treasures, although true bargain hunters will scoff at the prices. Also nearby is the flower district (around 27th St. and Sixth Ave.).

For more breathing room, wander over to the residential cross streets between Seventh and 10th Avenues, where 19th-century brownstones proliferate and river breezes often take wanderers by surprise. West 20th, 21st and 22nd Streets between Eighth and 10th Avenues are especially winsome blocks, perfect for strolling. **Cushman Row** (408–18 W. 20th St., between Ninth and 10th Aves.) contains some particularly notable Greek Revival row houses (1839–40). One landmark worth glimpsing is the **General Theological Seminary,** whose ivy-covered, Gothic-style buildings occupy the block between Ninth and 10th Avenues, from 20th to 21st Street.

Eighth Avenue in Chelsea is another heavily trafficked retail strip, where quirky boutiques mix with restaurants whose tables spill onto the sidewalks in the warmer months. There are also many bars and clubs catering to the area's large gay community *(see chapter* **Nightlife***)*. At Chelsea's southwestern fringe, its border blur into New York's trendiest nightlife playground, the Meatpacking District *(see separate neighborhood section, earlier in this chapter)*. The new **Maritime Hotel** on Ninth Avenue and 16th Street draws a hip crowd, with clubs and bars on three floors (and many annoyed neighbors complaining about the noise).

One of Chelsea's most lively thoroughfares is West 23rd Street, whose best-known landmark is probably the **Chelsea Hotel** (222 W. 23rd St. between Seventh and Eighth Aves.). In the past it was a beloved, if verging on decrepit, way station for artists, poets and rock musicians—everyone from Eugene O'Neill and Thomas Wolfe to Lenny Bruce and Sid Vicious have stayed here. Renovations have removed a good deal of the outright seediness, since a nearby crop of new moderately priced boutique hotels is providing stiff competition. If you're hungry, grab a glazed doughnut from the **Krispy Kreme** shop down the block.

Fitness fanatics would say that no tour of Chelsea is complete without a stop at the **Chelsea Piers** sports complex, which occupies four piers on the Hudson River from 17th to 23rd Street (*see chapter* **Sports & Recreation**). There are ice and roller skating rinks, a health club, a fieldhouse for soccer and other sports, batting cages, a driving range and a bowling alley.

For those not inclined to exert themselves, Chelsea Piers also has benches on which to loaf an afternoon away, with views across the river to Jersey City and, if you linger long enough, the setting sun. —*Abby Goodnough*

Subway: C, E, F, V, 1, 9 to 23rd St.

HIGHLIGHTS OF THE NEIGHBORHOOD

(*For the* **Dia Center for the Arts,** *the* **Chelsea Art Museum** *and the temporary location of the* **New Museum of Contemporary Art,** *the* **Joyce Theater, The Kitchen** *and coverage of the gallery scene, see chapter* **The Arts.** *For* **Chelsea Piers,** *see box in chapter* **Sports & Recreation.**)

Fashion Institute of Technology Seventh Ave. and 27th St. (212) 217-5779 *www.fitnyc.suny.edu.* The alma mater of superstars like Calvin Klein and Norma Kamali, the Fashion Institute of Technology (FIT) is the training ground for many of the players, and even more of the workers, in New York's garment industry. The maze of buildings that makes up the campus occupies a full block. You'll notice a proliferation of fashion-forward students in the neighborhood sporting their own exotic designs. The museum at FIT (free admission; open Tue.–Fri. noon–8 P.M., Sat. 10 A.M.–5 P.M.) boasts one of the world's largest collections of costumes, textiles and accessories of dress from the 18th to the 20th century, and it presents inventive fashion-related exhibitions.

Recommended Neighborhood Restaurants

(*See chapter* **Restaurants** *for reviews.*)

El Cid	$25 & Under		SPANISH
Grand Sichuan	$25 & Under		CHINESE
Gus's Figs Bistro & Bar	$25 & Under		MEDITERRANEAN
Le Zie 2000	$25 & Under		ITALIAN
O Mai	$25 & Under		VIETNAMESE
Royal Siam	$25 & Under		THAI
Amuse	☆☆	$ $	NEW AMERICAN
Chelsea Bistro & Bar	☆☆	$ $ $	BISTRO/FRENCH
Frank's	☆	$ $ $	STEAKHOUSE
Le Madri	☆☆	$ $ $	ITALIAN
The Red Cat	☆	$ $	NEW AMERICAN

Murray Hill

When the British landed in 1776 near importer Robert Murray's country estate (which stood near where E. 37th St. crosses Park Ave.), Murray's wife and daughters are said to have invited British General Sir William Howe to tea, a respite that diverted Howe's forces long enough to allow George Washington's exhausted American troops to escape to Harlem.

The core of old Murray Hill—which stretches along the middle to upper 30's between Madison and Third Avenues—includes landmarks like the **Pierpont Morgan Library** and the renovated carriage houses of **Sniffen Court** (150–158 E. 36th St.). Side streets are lined with diplomatic missions, social and cultural clubs and mid-range hotels.

Murray Hill residents have long been wary of commercial development. When Benjamin Altman opened what was among the first luxury department stores on Fifth Avenue and 34th Street in 1906, he disguised it as an Italian palazzo in an effort to allay those fears. The landmark B. Altman & Co. building now houses the Public Library's high-tech **Science, Industry and Business Library** (188 Madison Ave. at 34th St.), the **Graduate Center of the City University of New York** (365 Fifth Ave. at 34th St.) and **Oxford University Press.** The west side of Fifth Avenue bustles with small retail stores, while a number of Asian, Indian and Middle Eastern restaurants line Third Avenue. On the northern edge of Murray Hill is **Tudor City,** completed in 1928, a middle-class "city within a city."

Anchoring the area on the south is the picturesque **Church of the Transfiguration** on 29th Street (between Madison and Fifth Aves.). It earned a place in the hearts of actors in 1870 when the minister at a nearby church refused to bury actor George Holland, and suggested instead "the little church around the corner."

Subway: 6 to 33rd St.; S, 4, 5, 6, 7 to Grand Central.

HIGHLIGHT OF THE NEIGHBORHOOD

The Pierpont Morgan Library 29 E. 36th St. (at Madison Ave.) (212) 685-0610 *www.morganlibrary.org*. The world's most powerful financier in his day, J. P. Morgan started collecting medieval and Renaissance manuscripts, rare books and English and American manuscripts in 1890. Within a decade, he needed an entire building to house his growing collection. Designed by Charles McKim and completed in 1906, the neoclassical building that houses the library opened to the public in 1924, serving as both a museum and a center for scholarly research. The Morgan owns drawings by Dürer, Blake and Degas; the country's largest collection of Rembrandt etchings; 1,300 manuscripts; and a working draft of the U.S. Constitution. The library's literary holdings include illuminated manuscripts, three copies of the Gutenberg Bible, letters by Jane Austen, Charles Dickens's manuscript of *A Christmas Carol* and Henry David Thoreau's journals. Musical texts include handwritten works by Bach, Mozart, Schubert and Stravinsky. *Note:* The library is undergoing a major renovation and will be closed to the public until early 2006.

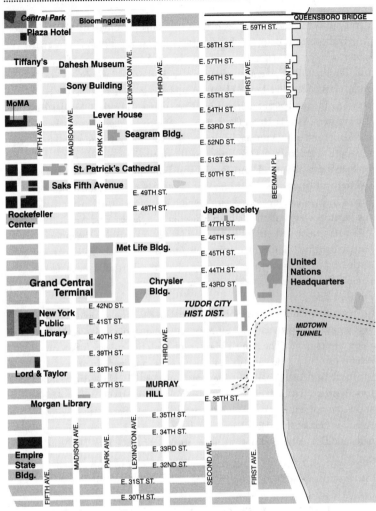

Midtown East/Murray Hill

Recommended Neighborhood Restaurants

(See chapter **Restaurants** for reviews.)

Da Ciro	$25 & Under		ITALIAN
Wu Liang Ye	$25 & Under		CHINESE
Asia de Cuba	☆	$ $ $	ASIAN/LATIN
Atelier	☆ ☆ ☆	$ $ $ $	FRENCH
BLT Steak	☆ ☆	$ $ $	STEAK/AMERICAN
Hangawi	☆ ☆	$ $	KOREAN/VEGETARIAN

Midtown East

From its posh designer boutiques filled with European jet setters to the diplomatic polyglot that is the **United Nations,** Midtown East is one of New York

City's most cosmopolitan areas and one of its largest business districts. Its sky-scrapers host many corporate headquarters that are filled each day by commuters who pass through the cavernous Beaux-Arts concourse of **Grand Central Terminal.** Park Avenue and other neighborhood thoroughfares are lined with "glass boxes" like **Lever House,** completed in 1952 (390 Park Ave. between 53rd and 54th Sts.); and Art Deco marvels like the **Chrysler Building,** the **Waldorf-Astoria Hotel** (Park Ave. at 49th St.), a favorite stopover for U.S. presidents and other visiting dignitaries, and the ornate **Chanin Building,** on the southwest corner of 42nd Street and Lexington Avenue.

Saks Fifth Avenue, Henri Bendel and **Takashimaya** are only a few of the stylish retail landmarks in the area (*see chapter* **Shopping***)*. Neighborhood streets and avenues are dotted with grand hotels and cultural institutions like the **Japan Society** and the **Dahesh Museum** (*see chapter* **The Arts***)*.

At rush hour, pedestrians and drivers battle for control of the asphalt. It is hard to imagine Midtown East ever being the tranquil place it once was when turtles thrived near the quiet cove from which the **Turtle Bay** area takes its name. The most serene spots left are the affluent cul-de-sacs of **Beekman and Sutton Places.**

Second Avenue between 43rd and 53rd Streets is the commercial hub of Turtle Bay, lined with shops, businesses and a variety of clubby steakhouses and elegant restaurants. The **Amish Market,** on 45th Street just off Second Avenue, stocks a wide variety of produce, cheese and specialty items.

Turtle Bay's most charming side-street enclave is **Turtle Bay Gardens Historic District,** a stretch of 10 town houses on the north side of East 48th Street and 10 on the south side of East 49th Street between Second and Third Avenues. Gardens residents have included Katharine Hepburn, Stephen Sondheim and E.B. White, who wrote about the neighborhood for *The New Yorker*.

Subway: S, 4, 5, 6, 7 to Grand Central; E, N, R, V, W to Fifth Ave. or Lexington Ave.; 6 to 51st St.; 4, 5, 6 to 59th St.

HIGHLIGHTS OF THE NEIGHBORHOOD

(*For the* **Dahesh Museum** and the **Whitney Museum of Art at Altria,**
see chapter **The Arts.***)*

Chrysler Building 405 Lexington Ave. (between 42nd and 43rd Sts.) (212) 682-3070. In late 1929, New Yorkers gawked as the Chrysler Building emerged from its construction scaffolding. The brilliant steel ornaments and spire were unlike anything else in New York, and at 1,046 feet, 4.75 inches high, it was the tallest building in the world.

Kenneth Murchison, an architect and critic of the time, admired the steel crown and "the astonishing plays of light which nature alone can furnish." While other buildings had been put up with distinctive spires, they were all in traditional materials: copper, terra-cotta, iron, stone, brick. But on the Chrysler Building, the entire upper section above the 61st floor—and much of the ornamentation below—is gleaming chrome-nickel steel, which reflects sunlight with dazzling brilliance.

The Seagram Building

From a distance, the Chrysler Building seems like near kin to the Empire State Building, which took away its height record in 1931. But unlike the Empire State, which was proudly hailed by one of its architects as a building where "hand work was done away with," the Chrysler Building is like a giant craft project. The metal is generally soldered or crimped—all by hand—and the thick, wavy solder lines and the irregular bends all betray individual craftsmanship. The broad surfaces of

Park Avenue and 20th-Century Architecture

To a surprising number of architects and city-lovers, the so-called Park Avenue Corridor is the architectural heart of the 20th century. The corridor is the crystallization of the New York myth, the soaring city of work and ambition, where the sky is the limit and dreams are fulfilled. It symbolizes New York's displacement of Paris as the century's most vibrant City of Light.

The corridor contains several individual buildings of distinction from the 1950's to 60's, including the **Seagram Building** (*disscussed in detail below*), **Lever House**, **500 Park Avenue** and the **Chase Building** (originally the Union Carbide Building), the last three designed by the New York firm Skidmore, Owings & Merrill, and Philip Johnson's Russell Sage Foundation (originally Asia House). James Ingo Freed's **Park Tower**, completed in 1981, is a somber late addition to the group, while Frank Lloyd Wright's 1958 **Mercedes-Benz Showroom** (originally Jaguar) offers a quirky footnote to the ramp of the Guggenheim Museum's rotunda.

But much of the corridor's power lies in the aggregate, in the mix of lesser buildings with well-known landmarks. At the century's outset, long before the first curtain wall was actually hung, architects used to dream about the gleaming cities that glass would enable them to build. Here, the dream was realized.

The term International Style was coined by Philip Johnson and Henry Russell Hitchcock for an exhibition in 1932 at the Museum of Modern Art. In the postwar decades, the International Style became shorthand for the steel and glass towers like the Seagram Building, the supreme example of the genre, designed by Mies van der Rohe and Philip Johnson in 1957–58.

Mies described his own aesthetic as one of "almost nothing," a paring down of form to the discreet articulation of construction and enclosure. Walls were reduced to the transparent membrane of the glass curtain wall. Structure was expressed on the exterior by the application of nonstructural I-beams. This approach exemplified the architect's belief that less is more. It enlarged the artistic significance of proportion, scale, quality of materials and refinement of detail.

Not long ago, it was said that these buildings represented a rejection of history. In fact, the International Style was grounded in 19th-century historicism: the view that each epoch should produce a distinctive architectural style.

In the early 1960's, the International Style was a symbol of urban sophistication in many Hollywood movies, as accurate a barometer as we have of popular desires. In *Breakfast at Tiffany's*, *The Best of Everything* and even several Doris Day comedies, the glass tower epitomized worldly aspiration and success. In the reflections of the crystal canyon, the world of external reality merges with the subjective realm of ambition, fantasy and desire.

No design in recent years has given firmer shape to this idea than Christian de Portzamparc's **LVMH Tower** at 19–21 East 57th Street. Described by Mr. Portzamparc as an homage to the city of glass, the 23-story tower features a faceted glass skin that unfolds like a crystal flower. While the tower can't possibly be mistaken for an International Style skyscraper, LVMH responds to the context of the mythical New York where modernity took root. And it is the first blossom that this root has sent forth in many years.

Seagram Building and Plaza 375 Park Ave. (between 52nd and 53rd Sts.) (212) 572-7000. For much of the past thousand years, the pendulum of Western architectural taste has swung between two esthetic poles: Gothic and classical, they eventually came to be called. Because it fuses elements of both positions in a supremely elegant whole, the Seagram Building is my choice as the millennium's most important building.

The 38-story Manhattan office tower was designed in 1958 by Ludwig Mies van der Rohe in association with Philip Johnson and is the most refined version of the modern glass skyscraper. It faces Park Avenue across a broad plaza of pink Vermont granite, bordered on either side by reflecting pools and ledges of verd antique marble. The tower itself is a steel-framed structure wrapped in a curtain wall of pink-gray glass. Spandrels, mullions and I-beams, used to modulate the surface of the glass skin, are made of bronze. The walls and elevator banks are lined with travertine.

Mies once defined architecture as the will of an epoch translated into space. For architects of his generation, this meant reckoning with the reality of the industrial age and the transforming power of machine technology. But it also meant overcoming the war of the styles, which had fragmented architecture into battling ideological camps.

In the Seagram Building, the classical elements are more obvious: the symmetry of its massing on the raised plaza; the tripartite division of the tower into base, shaft and capital; the rhythmic regularity of its columns and bays; the antique associations borne by bronze.

The building's Gothicism is subtler. It is evident in the tower's soaring 516 feet, the lightness and transparency of the curtain wall, the vertical emphasis conveyed by the I-beams attached to the glass skin and the cruciform plan of the tall shaft and the lower rear extension. Indeed, the Gothic cathedral was the prelude to the whole of modern glass architecture.

Today we recognize that Gothic and classical represent more than two architectural styles. They stand for two views of the world, neurologists have determined, that correspond to functions located in the left and right sides of the brain. The classical is rational, logical, analytic. The Gothic is intuitive, exploratory, synthetic. In hindsight, we recognize, too, that there's little to be gained by embracing one side at the other's expense. The business of civilization is to hold opposites together. That goal, often reached through conflict, has been rendered here by Mies with a serenity unsurpassed in modern times.

—Herbert Muschamp

metal, almost all stamped to form on the site, are wavy and bumpy, like giant pieces of hand-finished silver jewelry.

Just as surprising is the section just below the spire. So solid-looking from the outside, this part has no occupants and only intermittent flooring; only a few of the triangular openings have glazing. Inside, the wind rushes through what seems like a high, thin gazebo-shell of steel, at striking variance with the otherwise modernistic solidity of this continually fascinating building.   —*Christopher Gray*

Citicorp Center 153 E. 53rd St. (between Lexington and Third Aves.). The wedge-shaped spire of Citicorp Center, designed by Hugh Stubbins and Emery Roth, was designed to hold penthouse apartments, but residential zoning was denied. The aluminum and glass tower is headquarters for Citigroup, but it also has commercial, retail, mass-transit and even religious functions. The 915-foot building, supported entirely by four massive pillars, hovers over a sunken plaza that connects a multilayered shopping mall, a subway crossroads and a church. The starkly modernist St. Peter's holds Sunday jazz vespers and weekday concerts.

French Institute and Florence Gould Hall 55 E. 59th St. (between Park and Madison Aves.) (212) 355-6100 *www.fiaf.org*. The French Institute/Alliance Française offers language courses as well as a variety of cultural events with French themes. Florence Gould Hall offers films, concerts and dance, while the smaller Tinker Auditorium holds lectures, receptions and cabaret performances.

Grand Central Terminal 42nd St. at Park Ave. *www.grandcentralterminal.com*. On its physical merits alone, Grand Central Terminal is one of New York's great treasures. Its main concourse is an immense, bustling space with a blue-green ceiling painted to resemble a starlit sky. But Grand Central is vastly important also as a historical and political symbol, for it lies at the heart of court decisions affirming the city's right to protect its architectural heritage. Opened in 1913, the Beaux-Arts monument was threatened in the 1960's by developers who planned to demolish the concourse and build office towers all around it. Preservationists took their case to court and to the public, with high-profile assistance from Jacqueline Kennedy Onassis. They won. In 1978, the United States Supreme Court ruled that the city had a right to protect Grand Central—and, by extension, other landmarks—from destruction. After falling into disrepair, the station got an expensive cleanup in the 1990's that restored much of its original grandeur. Above all, Grand Central remains what it has always been: one of the world's busiest train stations, with half a million people passing through it each day.
                                                                —*Clyde Haberman*

Additional notes on Grand Central: MetroNorth trains serve suburban New York, Connecticut, upstate New York and points west; several subway lines converge here. There's also the **Grand Central Market** for gourmet goods, and an extensive downstairs food court. More formal dining choices include **Michael Jordan's,** for fine steaks and a great view of the twinkling stars in the constellations on the stunning sky ceiling, and the landmark **Oyster Bar,** for a wide variety of fresh seafood. The **Municipal Arts Society** (212-935-3960; *www.mas.org*) conducts tours of the building ($10), departing from the information booth in

Fred R. Conrad/The New York Times

Grand Central Terminal

the main concourse every Wednesday at 12:30 P.M. The **Grand Central Partnership** (212-697-1245) offers its own free tours on Fridays at 12:30 P.M.; meet outside the station in front of the Whitney Museum at Altria. Grand Central's exterior facade is currently undergoing a major cleaning and restoration; as it emerges, the building is looking brighter and fresher than it has in decades.

Japan Society 333 E. 47th St. (between First and Second Aves.) (212) 832-1155 www.japansociety.org. The Japan Society brings New Yorkers a wonderful blend of the traditional and the contemporary in Japanese culture. Events include regular film series and live kabuki theater. Art exhibitions (such as "Shomei Tomatsu: Skin of the Nation," which features works from one of Japan's most noted photographers, scheduled from late September 2004 to early January 2005) are mounted in elegant galleries. The society also offers language lessons at all levels. **Admission:** $5 adults; $3 students and seniors; free for children age 16 and under. **Hours:** Galleries: Tue.–Fri. 11 A.M.–6 P.M.; Sat.–Sun. 11 A.M.–5 P.M.

Lever House 390 Park Ave. (between 53rd and 54th Sts.) This sleek glass box, designed between 1949 and 1951 by architect Gordon Bunshaft of Skidmore, Owings & Merrill, is a landmark of high modernism and the International Style. The elegant Lever House pioneered the use of thin "glass curtain walls,"

Chester Higgins, Jr./The New York Times

The United Nations

an innovation that became commonplace in future skyscrapers, and its blue-green glass and stainless steel positively gleam (which is only fitting for a building housing a soap and detergent company). The base is a horizontal slab, a single-story mezzanine supported by columns and offering a public pedestrian way underneath. In late 2003, the new Lever House restaurant opened, attracting an upscale crowd with its sleek design.

MetLife Building 200 Park Ave. (between 43rd and 45th Sts.) (212) 922-9100. Pan Am's former headquarters was the world's largest commercial office building when it was completed in 1963, and its mammoth bulk effectively blocked the vista up and down Park Avenue. A team that included Emery Roth and Sons, Pietro Belluschi and Walter Gropius used concrete curtain walls to frame the building's structure. The lobby doubles as a concourse leading to Grand Central. In the 1980's, Metropolitan Life Insurance bought the building from the financially troubled airline, and the MetLife logo supplanted Pan Am's globe as a landmark of Manhattan's skyline.

St. Patrick's Cathedral Fifth Ave. (at 50th St.) (212) 753-2261 *www.ny-archdiocese.org/pastoral*. St. Pat's is the Roman Catholic cathedral for the Archdiocese of New York, which covers Manhattan, the Bronx, Staten Island and several upstate counties, and is generally recognized as a center of Catholic life in America. Its design, by James Renwick, was based on the great cathedral in Cologne, Germany. The nave was opened in 1877, almost 20 years after the start of construction; the 330-foot twin spires were completed in 1888. At the time it stood on the northern edge of the city, visible from miles around. Architectural purists deride its mixed forms and the lack of flying buttresses, but it is a grand and elaborate statement nonetheless, surrounded now by city skyscrapers.

A magnificent rose window over the central portal measures 26 feet in diameter. The cathedral's 70 stained-glass windows were crafted in studios in

Chartres and Nantes in France, Birmingham, England and Boston—and not finally completed until the 1930's. The 14 stations of the cross were carved in Holland. The Pietà is three times larger than the Michelangelo masterpiece in St. Peter's in Rome, and there are three organs.

United Nations First Ave. at 42nd St. (Visitors Entrance at First Ave. and 46th St.) (212) 963-8687, ext. 1 for tour info. *www.un.org*. Literally in a world of its own, United Nations headquarters and its grounds occupy a strip of international territory on the edge of Manhattan, running between First Avenue and the East River from 42nd to 48th Street. The site was donated to the U.N. in 1946, a year after the organization's birth, by John D. Rockefeller, Jr. Designed by an international team of architects, including Le Corbusier, three connected buildings—the boxy Dag Hammarskjold Library, the glass-walled Secretariat tower and the low-slung General Assembly—dominate the site. Erected between 1947 and 1953, they frame a central fountain crowned with a 21-foot-high bronze sculpture, *Single Form* by Barbara Hepworth, dedicated to the memory of Hammarskjold, the only Secretary General to have been killed in office (on a peace mission to the Congo in 1961).

Daily public tours take in the most famous indoor chambers, including the Security Council and General Assembly halls. An eclectic collection of artwork donated by many countries is scattered throughout corridors and lounges. In the basement, shops sell jewelry and handicrafts from around the world, international books for adults and children and souvenirs of the U.N. itself. There are also outdoor attractions, especially when the weather is warm. Visitors stop to see the colorful array of flags from 188 nations flying along First Avenue or to enjoy walking on the riverside promenade and through the quiet formal gardens that form a two-block oasis of serenity north of the 46th Street visitors' entrance. The gardens form a backdrop for several other monumental sculptures dedicated to the ideal of peace among nations.   —*Barbara Crossette*

Additional notes on the U.N.: Visitors can enjoy lunch on weekdays in the Delegates' Dining Room. Advance reservations are required; call (212) 963-7625. Be sure to bring a photo I.D., dress nicely (jackets required for men; no jeans or sneakers) and be prepared for a security check before the elevator attendant takes you up. Lunch buffets are $22. **Tours:** $10.50 adults; $8 seniors; $7 students; $6 children ages 5–14. No children under age 5. **Hours:** Mon.–Fri. 9:30 A.M.–4:45 P.M., Sat.–Sun. 10 A.M.–4:30 P.M. (no weekend tours Jan.–Feb.). Tours in English leave approximately every 30 min., and take 45–60 min. Schedules may be limited during special events.

Recommended Neighborhood Restaurants
(See chapter Restaurants for reviews.)

Jubilee	$25 & Under		FRENCH
Katsu-Hama	$25 & Under		JAPANESE
Meltemi	$25 & Under		GREEK/SEAFOOD
Amma	☆☆	$$$	INDIAN
Brasserie	☆☆	$$$	BISTRO/FRENCH

Chola	☆☆	$ $	INDIAN
Felidia	☆☆☆	$ $ $ $	NORTHERN ITALIAN
Fifty Seven Fifty Seven	☆☆☆	$ $ $ $	AMERICAN
The Four Seasons	☆☆☆	$ $ $ $	NEW AMERICAN
Guastavino's	☆☆	$ $ $ $	ENGLISH/FRENCH
Heartbeat	☆☆	$ $	NEW AMERICAN
Il Valentino	☆☆	$ $	ITALIAN
Kuruma Zushi	☆☆☆	$ $ $ $	JAPANESE
La Grenouille	☆☆☆	$ $ $ $	FRENCH
Le Colonial	☆☆	$ $	VIETNAMESE
L'Impero	☆☆☆	$ $ $	ITALIAN
March	☆☆☆	$ $ $ $	NEW AMERICAN
Oceana	☆☆☆	$ $ $ $	SEAFOOD
Patroon	☆☆☆	$ $ $ $	NEW AMERICAN
Shun Lee Palace	☆☆	$ $ $ $	CHINESE
Smith & Wollensky	☆☆	$ $ $ $	STEAKHOUSE
Solera	☆☆	$ $ $ $	SPANISH
Sushi Yasuda	☆☆☆	$ $ $ $	JAPANESE/SUSHI
Zarela	☆☆	$ $	MEXICAN/TEX-MEX

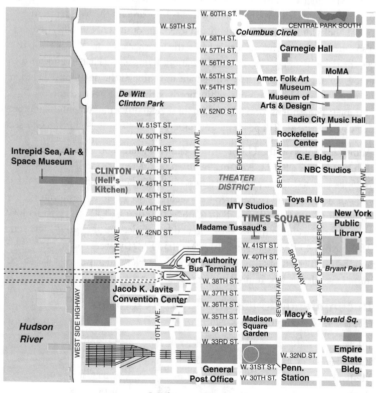

Midtown West

Midtown West

There is probably more to see and do in Midtown in the West 30's, 40's and 50's than anywhere else in the city—not least the sizzling wattage of the newly booming Times Square. Long touted as "the crossroads of the world," it is fast becoming America's carnival midway. Shaking off its seedy past and ridding itself of porn theaters, this neighborhood has become family-friendly. Amid the famous swirl of neon signs and the glitz of Broadway theaters, it has sprouted attractions like theme restaurants, high-tech arcades and even a branch of London's silly **Madame Tussaud's Wax Museum.** Everything is supersized, including the massive **Virgin Megastore** and a flagship branch of **Toys R Us.**

But Midtown is also the tonier gleam of **Rockefeller Center,** the breathtaking pinnacle of the **Empire State Building,** the vigilant marble lions guarding the Fifth Avenue entrance to the **New York Public Library** and the sleek new galleries of the reconfigured **Museum of Modern Art.**

If you're a fan of the *Today* show or *Good Morning America*, see them live and full-size through the plate glass of their **street-level studios**—in Rockefeller Center and Times Square, respectively. (For tickets to other TV shows, see the box later in this section.) **MTV** has studios behind glass in Times Square, too, not so easy to view because they are on the second floor; to find them, listen for squealing teeny-boppers. For headier music, there's **Carnegie Hall** on 57th Street (*see chapter* **The Arts**). For a corned beef sandwich that feeds two, there's the **Carnegie Deli** just two blocks away.

Broadway and Seventh Avenue in the 30's have been the main arteries of the **Garment District** for more than 100 years, home to the warehouses and workshops of the fashion industry.

The biggest attraction for most visitors is **Broadway theater.** The epicenter of the Theater District is at Broadway and 42nd Street; dozens of theaters line Broadway and its side streets in the 40's. (*See chapter* **The Arts** *for details on finding out what's playing and how to get tickets.*)

West of the Theater District is a residential neighborhood famed as **Hell's Kitchen,** the rough-and-tumble home of immigrant Irish in the second half of the 19th century—former Senator Daniel Patrick Moynihan once lived there. Greeks, Eastern Europeans, Puerto Ricans and other groups moved in later. The p.c. name for the area now is **Clinton** (for DeWitt, not Bill) and its residents are young professionals, theater people and remnants of the old immigrant groups. **Restaurant Row** (46th St. between Eighth and Ninth Aves.) is a long block of restaurants side-by-side, all packed with theatergoers before curtain time—and half-empty after 8 P.M. A host of affordable ethnic restaurants and bars lines Ninth Avenue.

Subway: A, B, C, D, E, F, N, Q, R, S, V, W, 1, 2, 3, 9 to 34th St.; A, B, C, D, E, F, N, Q, R, S, V, W, 1, 2, 3, 7, 9 to 42nd St.; B, D, F, S, V to 47th-50th St.–Rockefeller Center; N, R, W to 49th St.; 1, 9, C, E, to 50th St.; F, N, R, Q, S, W to 57th St.; A, B, C, D, 1, 9 to 59th St.

Nancy Siesel/The New York Times

New York Public Library

HIGHLIGHTS OF THE NEIGHBORHOOD

(*For the* **Museum of Modern Art,** *the* **American Folk Art Museum,** *the* **International Center of Photography** *and the* **Museum of Art and Design,** *see chapter* **The Arts.** *For* **Carnegie Hall** *and full coverage of Broadway theater, see section* "The Performing Arts" *in chapter* **The Arts.** *For* **Madison Square Garden,** *see chapter* **Sports & Recreation.** *For cruises departing from the West Side piers, see section* "Guided Tours," *near the beginning of this chapter.*)

Bryant Park Sixth Ave. (stretching from 40th to 42nd Sts.) *www.bryantpark.org.* On warm weekdays, Midtown workers descend on Bryant Park to shed ties and high heels for some lunchtime relaxation. They arrange the park's folding chairs to log onto the wireless network or gossip, or stretch out on the luxurious lawn for catnaps. Regulars play chess near a statue honoring the park's namesake, William Cullen Bryant, longtime editor of the *New York Post* and an early advocate of radical ideas such as abolition and public parks. At the rear of the New York Public Library, there's the lovely **Bryant Park Grill** (212-840-6500), offering upscale bistro food and summertime alfresco dining. More informal and affordable choices for dining include the **Bryant Park Pub, Il Forno Toscano** for pizza and of course the ubiquitous **Starbucks.** Dotting the park are statues commemorating literary figures ranging from Goethe to Gertrude Stein, making the park a great place to read a chapter before heading back to the office. So it was only appropriate that the park restored its "Reading Room" program in the summer of 2003. Reviving a Depression-era tradition, the park offers a free summer public lending library (weather permitting) from 11 A.M. to 5 P.M. Probably the best time to go, though, is on Monday nights in the summer, when HBO presents free movie classics on a huge screen.

Empire State Building 350 Fifth Ave. (between 33rd and 34th Sts.) (212) 736-3100 *www.esbnyc.com*. Known as the "Empty State" after it was completed in 1931, the Empire State Building remained half-rented during the Depression. Nevertheless, it is one of New York's great icons. Designed by Shreve, Lamb and Harmon, the Empire State was constructed at breakneck speed on the former site of the original Waldorf-Astoria Hotel. This glorious Art Deco tower won a three-way competition with the Chrysler Building and 40 Wall Street to become the world's tallest skyscraper, a title it kept for more than half a century. After the destruction of the World Trade Center, the Empire State is once again the tallest building in the city, and New Yorkers hold it a little more dearly in their hearts. The spire, immortalized as King Kong's perch, was designed—but used only once—as a mooring mast for dirigibles; it is floodlit at night, adding a glamorous note to the skyline. Visitors can ascend the elevators to **observation decks** on the 86th and 102nd floors, where the panoramic views are breathtaking. **Admission:** $12 adults, $11 seniors and children ages 12–17, $7 children ages 6–11. Ticket lines can be brutal, but you can avoid them by ordering online (with a $2-per-ticket service charge). **Hours:** Observatory daily 9:30 A.M.–midnight. Last elevators ascend at 11:15 P.M.

General Post Office 421 Eighth Ave. (between 32nd and 33rd Sts.) (212) 330-3601. When you're running to get your tax return postmarked before midnight on April 15, the main post office's staircase feels as monumental as it looks. The facility is open 24 hours a day. Built in 1914 and designed by McKim, Mead and White as a complement to the first Pennsylvania Station—a landmark that was demolished in the 1960's—the Classical Revival building stretches across two city blocks. The post office motto is spelled out above a parade of imposing Corinthian columns: "Neither snow nor rain nor heat nor gloom of night stays these couriers from the swift completion of their appointed rounds." Plans are now being developed to turn a large part of the building into a new train station to replace the current, uninspiring incarnation of Penn Station.

Jacob K. Javits Convention Center 655 W. 34th St. (between 11th and 12th Aves.) (212) 216-2000 *www.javitscenter.com*. The convention complex, boasting over 17 acres of floor space, was designed by the architectural firm of I. M. Pei. The New York International Auto Show, held here each April, draws more than one million visitors.

Madame Tussaud's New York 234 W. 42nd St. (between Seventh and Eighth Aves.) (212) 512-9600 *www.nycwax.com*. The competition is tough, but Madame Tussaud's gets our vote as the most overpriced tourist trap in town. But if you've got 28 bucks to burn and an hour to kill, help yourself to a overdose of kitsch. You'll see hundreds of incredibly lifelike wax figures, with an emphasis on celebs like J.Lo, John Travolta, Michael Jordan, Robin Williams and the Rock, and you can photograph your entourage cavorting with them. **Admission:** $28 adults, $25 seniors over age 60, $22 children ages 4–12; free for children age 3 and under. **Hours:** Daily 10 A.M.–8 P.M. (until 10 P.M. on weekends). May close early to host occasional special events.

Museum of Television and Radio 25 W. 52nd St. (between Fifth and Sixth Aves.) (212) 621-6600 or (212) 621-6800 *www.mtr.org*. Don't expect to find the same kind of displays and exhibits that you'd find in other museums here. The real treasure here is the incredible archive, a collection of thousands of classic TV episodes, commericals and specials. The theaters offer special screenings, but most visitors opt to sign out tapes of their favorite programs, which they can screen at private consoles (you can request up to four shows in one sitting). **Admission:** $10 adults; $8 students and seniors; $5 children under age 14. **Hours:** Tue.–Sun. noon–6 P.M. (until 8 P.M. Thu.).

New York Public Library Fifth Ave. and 42nd St. (212) 661-7220, or (212) 869-8089 for info on exhibits and events. *www.nypl.org*. One of the world's greatest libraries, this two-block-long Beaux-Arts palace of books has long been thought of as the main branch of the New York Public Library system, which includes 85 branches in the Bronx, Manhattan and Staten Island. But the building is actually the biggest of the system's four research libraries, formally known as the Humanities and Social Sciences Library. No books are allowed to leave the building. Its 15 million items, from rare illuminated manuscripts to pulp fiction to Cherokee literature, may be checked out and read in the library.

It is a place where leafing through a book takes on a whole new meaning. The Main Reading Room on the third floor stretches the length of a football field. Beneath its soaring ceiling murals of bright blue skies and clouds, readers can plug in a laptop, peruse a newspaper or just daydream.

Anyone can ask for a book to be fetched from seven floors of stacks underneath the room or two more floors concealed under the lawn of Bryant Park next door. There are about 132 miles of shelves in the stacks, not open to the public. (In order to maintain the proper hush, tourists are encouraged to take scheduled tours of the Reading Room.)

The library came along relatively late in the city's history—it is just 100 years old. A little-known architecture firm, Carrere and Hastings, won a competition to build what was then the largest marble structure ever attempted in the country.

And the famous marble lions? They have stood guard at the Fifth Avenue entrance since the beginning of Mayor Fiorello La Guardia's administration. He dubbed the one to the south Patience and the one to the north—you guessed it—Fortitude.   —*Randy Kennedy*

Radio City Music Hall 1260 Sixth Ave. (at 50th St.) (212) 247-4777 *www.radiocity.com*. Radio City Music Hall is Manhattan's version of a natural wonder. It's our Rainbow Arch, our Old Faithful, our Niagara Falls. After a $70 million restoration in 1999, the great hall's awesome beauty can be seen once again in the genius of its original conception.

Completed in 1932, the Music Hall is a tribute to the Rockefeller family's spirit of culturally progressive enterprise. Like Rockefeller Center, which surrounds it in Midtown, the theater countered the Great Depression with a great infusion of hope in the city's future. Radio City! Live from Radio City!

Always seen as a place for families, the Music Hall opened at a time when

Fred R. Conrad/The New York Times

Radio City Music Hall

family entertainment might include ballet, symphony and opera, along with comedy, popular song, acrobatics and the Rockettes. The vaudeville mix was recognizably of the radio age, when folks gathered round the Bakelite console to hear their favorite shows. The Music Hall gave them tunes and great visuals besides.

Three New York architectural firms are credited with the design of the theater. These firms brought to harmonious realization the unlikely alliance between the patrician Rockefellers and the plebeian Samuel L. Rothafel, known as Roxy, an impresario of movie palaces for the masses.

The entrance and ticket lobby are lodged on the ground floor of an office tower that gives little sign of the grandiose space inside, but the box offices anticipate the amplitude within. From here we proceed to a grand ocean liner of a space, the Grand Foyer, one of the world's great Art Deco interiors, its length and height amplified by mirrors of gold-backed glass.

Entering the auditorium, we find ourselves on the deck of the ocean liner, gazing out to sea, precisely the image Roxy Rothafel wanted his architects to capture for his new 6,000-seat show palace. In time the showman's wish was conveyed to the young Edward Durell Stone, a draftsman in one of the three architectural firms responsible for the design. In later life, Stone made his mark with Manhattan buildings like the Museum of Modern Art and the General Motors Building. At age 30, Stone found himself designing the most stupendous arch this side of Rome.

The auditorium's formal power is derived from the plain, unadorned half-circle of the proscenium, and from the projection of that shape from the front to the rear of the house. Like a dome, the design eliminates both walls and ceiling. This is why the auditorium is psychologically so overwhelming. No matter where you sit, you have the sensation of tumbling through the sky.

For design historians, the Music Hall is forever linked to Donald Deskey, responsible for the theater's iconic Art Deco interiors. Plate-glass vanity tables,

If You'd Like to Be Part of the Studio Audience . . .

Many TV shows are taped in New York live (and eager) audience. Unfortunately, tickets are tough to get, even if you plan months in advance. If all else fails, you can always join the crowds outside the *Today* show's glass-walled studio on the southwest corner of 49th Street and Rockefeller Plaza. Tapings are Monday to Friday from 7 to 10 A.M.

For info on more show tapings, check *www.nycvisit.com* (click on "Visitors," then "Things to Do").

The Daily Show With Jon Stewart Taped Mon.–Thu. at 5:45 P.M. at 513 W. 54th St. No one under 18. Call (212) 586-2477 weeks in advance, or stop by Mon.-Thurs. 10:30 A.M.–4 P.M. to ask about cancellations.

Late Night With Conan O'Brien Tapings are Tues.–Fri. at 5:30 P.M. No one under 16 admitted. Arrive at 4:45 P.M. at the 49th Street entrance to 30 Rockefeller Plaza. Reserve months in advance by calling (212) 664-3056. Standby tickets are available at 9 A.M. outside the studio; line up early.

The Late Show with David Letterman Tapings are Mon.–Wed. at 5:30 P.M., and Thu. at 5:30 and 8 P.M. No one under 18 admitted. Send a postcard request a year in advance (two tickets max; one request only, or all will be disregarded), to Late Show Tickets, Ed Sullivan Theater, 1697 Broadway, New York, NY 10019. You can also register at *www.cbs.com/latenight/lateshow* to be notified of tickets that may become available for specific dates in the next 3 months.

Live With Regis and Kelly Tapings are Mon.–Fri. at 9 A.M. at ABC Studios at Columbus Avenue and West 67th Street. No one under 10 admitted. Send your postcard requesting up to four tickets at least a full year in advance to Live! Tickets, Ansonia Station, P.O. Box 230777, New York, NY 10023-0777 (212) 456-3054. Standby tickets are often available; arrive at the studio by 7 A.M.

Saturday Night Live Tapings are Sat. at 11:30 P.M. (arrival time 10 P.M.). No one under 16. Tickets are so hot that written requests are only accepted in the month of August, with lotteries held throughout the year. Call (212) 664-4000 for details. Standby tickets for the show and the dress rehearsal are given out at 9 A.M. on the day of taping outside 30 Rockefeller Plaza, on the 49th Street side of the building (first-come, first-served; one ticket per person).

The View Mon.–Fri., 11 A.M. No one under 18 admitted. Send ticket requests by postcard to The View, Tickets, 320 W. 66th St., New York, NY 10023 or go online at *www.abc.go.com/theview*. Requests should be made four to six months in advance.

metal tube chairs, mohair sofas, round mirrors, balustrades, light fixtures, theater seats: these are some of the classic pieces Deskey created for the Hall.

—*Herbert Muschamp*

Additional notes on Radio City: One-hour guided tours of the building are offered daily, approximately every half hour from 11 A.M. to 3 P.M. You can order tour tickets online or call (212) 307-7171. Prices are $17 adults, $14 for seniors, $10 for children under age 10.

Rockefeller Center Between 48th and 52nd Sts., Fifth to Seventh Aves. (212) 332-6868 *www.rockefellercenter.com*. This soaring 18-building complex of monumental architecture in the heart of Manhattan includes some of New York's best-known skyscrapers and landmarks, including the Art Deco splendor of **Radio City Music Hall** *(see listing above)*. The brainchild of John D. Rockefeller, the complex incorporates office buildings, stores, theaters and open space.
The central sunken plaza is magically transformed into the focal point of the city's holiday festivities each winter, as skaters twirl and glide on the ice of the tiny **Rink at Rockefeller Center** (212-332-7654; *see also chapter* **Sports & Recreation**), under the massive **Rockefeller Center Christmas tree** and the watchful eye of Paul Manship's golden statue of **Prometheus.** In any season, the plaza is an impressive sight, ringed by the flags of all United Nations member countries, and the new **Rink Bar** offers a lovely setting for an alfresco cocktail in summer. The 70-story **G.E. Building** soars overhead; step into its lobby to inspect the murals by José Maria Sert. Paul Goldberger once called this space "a setting for a 1930's movie about corporate power, pulsing with the energy of capitalism both real and romantic."

Rockefeller Center was the largest privately sponsored real estate venture ever undertaken in New York City when construction began in 1929. Originally it was to include a new Metropolitan Opera House, those plans were scrapped after the stock market crash that October. Mr. Rockefeller then reconceived the project as an entirely commercial complex. Rockefeller Center is home to over 100 works of art, all chosen along one theme: "The Progress of Man." One of the most notable pieces, "Atlas" (Lee Laurie, 1937) stands in front of the International Building (630 Fifth Ave.). There are also wonderful facade sculptures, including "News" (Isamu Noguchi, 1940). An impressively dynamic stainless steel relief adorns the old **Associated Press Building,** at 50 Rockefeller Plaza, depicting five news reporters.

NBC's New York studios are scattered throughout the complex; *Saturday Night Live* and *Late Night with Conan O'Brien* are among the shows filmed here *(see the box in this section for details on obtaining tickets)*. Each weekday morning brings crowds who've come to stand outside the glass studios of the *Today* show; in summer, the show sponsors free outdoor concerts each Friday morning. The **NBC Experience Store** offers silly interactive features and a store full of logo merchandise and DVDs (of course). The store is the departure point for behind-the-scenes **NBC Studio Tours** (reservations are recommended; call 212-664-7174). Tours depart every 30 minutes (or more frequently in peak seasons) Monday to Saturday 8:30 A.M. to 5:30 P.M., Sundays 9:30 A.M. to 4:30

The New York Times

The G.E. Building at Rockefeller Center

P.M. Prices are a whopping $17.75 for adults, $15.25 for seniors and children ages 6–16; no children under age 6 allowed.

Tours of the entire Rockefeller Center complex, focusing on its art, architecture and history, also leave from the NBC Experience Store hourly (Mon.–Sat. 10 A.M.–5 P.M., Sun. 10 A.M.–4 P.M.). Reservations are recommended; call (212) 664-7174. The hour-and-fifteen-minute tours are $10 adults, $8 seniors and children ages 6-16 (no children under age 6).

Times Square Broadway and Seventh Ave., from 42nd to 47th Sts. *www.timessquarebid.org.* New Yorkers insist on calling it the Crossroads of the World. Of course, New Yorkers like to think of their city as the center of the cosmos, let alone the planet. But this time, their penchant for overstatement happens to be fact.

Times Square is, without a doubt, the most recognized intersection on the planet, never more so than on **New Year's Eve,** when hundreds of thousands of people jam the square and tens of millions more watch on television as a glittering ball slowly descends, ticking off the final seconds of the dying year. By now, some may well believe that there would not be a new year without this communal gathering in the heart of New York.

It wasn't always like that. At the turn of the last century, the area was a humble place called Long Acre Square. The name was changed in 1904 when *The New York Times* moved there; the cachet of the Times Square name attracted people to the surrounding blocks, and the square became a neighborhood. For decades to come, Times Square would provide the country with some of its most enduring images. For moviegoers, it took only an overhead shot of the neon-bathed square for them to know they were entering a world of sophistication.

Decay set in with the Great Depression. By the 1970's, Times Square had become synonymous with sleazy arcades and tawdry sex shows. Historic theaters and hotels were sacrificed for office space. Even the *Times* was gone by then, having moved around the corner, its old building's terra-cotta facade replaced with faceless white marble.

But the 90's brought rebirth, with porno houses giving way to Disney shows. At first, some found the new attractions too sanitized, but few truly mourned the passing of the dope dealers and pimps.

With the arrival of the new millennium, the transformation of Times Square is nearly complete. It has become a center of finance and media, dominated by glass-enclosed studios for ABC and MTV, and by soaring buildings that are the headquarters for Reuters and the Condé Nast publishing empire. Outdoor television screens, high-tech lighting and fast-paced graphics give new dimension to the stretch of Broadway known as the Great White Way.

As ever, there is no better place to people-watch. Street performers, gawking tourists, get-out-of-my-way New Yorkers and occasional street hustlers—they are all here. There are also about 600 businesses and organizations here; 21.8 million square feet of commercial space, with much more space under construction; one-quarter of all New York City hotel rooms; 28 million day-trippers; some 178 restaurants; 44 movie theaters, bars and clubs; and 39 landmarked Broadway theaters. And believe it or not, thousands of people actually live in the Times Square area; 258,000 folks go to work there every day.

Times Square is still evolving. Yet some things don't change. It remains the place to gather, whether to watch a televised news event or protest a war or celebrate a national triumph. It is far more than a neighborhood. It is America's town square.   —*Clyde Haberman*

U.S.S. Intrepid **Sea-Air-Space Museum** Pier 86, 46th St. at 12th Ave. (212) 245-0072 *www.intrepidmuseum.org*. Launched in 1943 and decommissioned in 1974, the *Intrepid* once housed more than 100 aircraft and a crew of over 3,000. This aircraft carrier was deployed in World War II, the Korean and Vietnam Wars and served as a recovery vessel for NASA capsules. There are jets and prop planes on the flight and hangar decks, and exhibits relating to the ship's history and undersea exploration. A flight simulator recreates the feeling of being inside an F-18 fighter during the Persian Gulf war. The open-air flight deck allows access to the navigation bridge and wheelhouse, and close examination of planes, helicopters and gun galleries. The destroyer *Edison* and the submarine *Growler* lie alongside. All three vessels are open to visitors, but the 900-foot *Intrepid*, which occupies an area greater than a Midtown block, is the most impressive. The interactive exhibit called "All Hands on Deck" allows kids to get a first-person experience of how things work on a real Navy warship. Admission includes a free film called "Intrepid Wings," shown continuously throughout the day. **Admission:** $14.50 adults; $10.50 students, seniors and veterans; $9.50 children ages 6–17; $2.50 children ages 2–5; children under 2 free. Active-duty U.S. military personnel free. **Hours:** Apr.–Sept. Mon.–Fri. 10 A.M.–5 P.M., Sat.–Sun. 10 A.M.–6 P.M.; Oct.–Mar. Tue.–Sun. 10 A.M.–5 P.M. (closed Mon.). Last admission 1 hr. before closing.

Recommended Neighborhood Restaurants

(See chapter **Restaurants** *for reviews.)*

Carnegie Deli	$25 & Under		DELI
Havana NY	$25 & Under		LATIN AMERICAN
Topaz Thai	$25 & Under		THAI
Wu Liang Ye	$25 & Under		CHINESE
Acqua Pazza	☆	$ $ $	ITALIAN/SEAFOOD
Aquavit	☆ ☆ ☆	$ $ $ $	SCANDINAVIAN
Chez Josephine	☆ ☆	$ $ $	BISTRO/FRENCH
Cho Dang Gol	☆ ☆	$ $ $	KOREAN
Churrascaria Plataforma	☆ ☆	$ $ $	BRAZILIAN
Estiatorio Milos	☆ ☆	$ $ $ $	GREEK/SEAFOOD
Firebird	☆ ☆	$ $ $	RUSSIAN
Kai	☆ ☆	$ $ $ $	JAPANESE
Kang Suh	☆ ☆	$ $	KOREAN
Le Bernardin	☆ ☆ ☆ ☆	$ $ $ $	FRENCH/SEAFOOD
Molyvos	☆ ☆	$ $ $	GREEK
Petrossian	☆ ☆	$ $ $ $	RUSSIAN
San Domenico	☆ ☆ ☆	$ $ $ $	ITALIAN
Sea Grill	☆ ☆	$ $ $	SEAFOOD
"21" Club	☆ ☆	$ $ $ $	NEW AMERICAN

The Upper East Side

From the stately homes and manicured flower beds along **Park Avenue** to the art galleries and pricey boutiques on **Madison Avenue,** the Upper East Side has all the trappings of power and privilege. Walk along Park or its side streets on a weekday morning and you're likely to see professional dog walkers being tugged along in a tangle of pedigree poodles, or uniformed children traipsing off to Spence, Chapin and other exclusive private schools.

Historically, the Upper East Side has been an old-money enclave, home to some of the nation's wealthiest corporate titans and robber barons. But the Upper East Side has a more diverse population than its reputation suggests, especially on the far eastern side of the neighborhood. On Lexington Avenue, institutions such as **Bloomingdale's, Hunter College** and the **92nd Street Y** lure shoppers, students and culture lovers from across the city. Farther east, middle-class families and young professionals who've snagged rent-stabilized apartments fill the high-rise apartments that sprouted up after World War II.

This area boasts some of the best-known cultural institutions in the world. Museum Mile, along Fifth Avenue, is home to the **Metropolitan Museum of Art,** the **Solomon R. Guggenheim Museum,** the **Jewish Museum,** the **Museum of the City of New York** and **El Museo del Barrio.** The Frick and Carnegie mansions house the **Frick Collection** and the **Cooper-Hewitt National Design Museum,** respectively (*see chapter* **The Arts** *for full listings of all these museums*). The mansions are two remnants of Millionaire's Row, where European-style grand residences overlooking Central Park were built in the early 1900's by super-rich industrialists competing to outdo each other. Several institutions dedicated to world societies and cultures are also located here including the **Asia Society** and the **China Institute in America.**

Farther south is the **Seventh Regiment Armory** (Park Ave. and 66th St.), an 1879 medieval-style building that became the model for armories throughout the country. With its Tiffany interiors and enormous drill room, the armory hosts frequent art and antiques shows. Also at the southern end of the neighborhood are several private clubs that are housed in historic buildings. Worth seeing are the **Metropolitan Club** (1–11 E. 60th St.; designed by Stanford White in the 1890's), the **Knickerbocker Club** (2 E. 62nd St.) and the **Lotos Club** (5 E. 66th St.).

In **Yorkville** (70th-96th St., east of Lexington Ave.), the Old World flavor of this once German and Hungarian (also Irish and Czech) enclave is fading. There are remnants such as **Schaller and Weber** (1654 Second Ave. between 85th and 86th Sts.), which has been selling authentic German sausage and other specialties since 1937. For the most part, the old groceries and bakeries have been replaced by a more youthful spirit found in the cafes along Second and Third Avenues and bars that fill with exuberant drinkers on weekends. Joggers and inline-skaters take to the **East River esplanade** and **Carl Schurz Park** outside **Gracie Mansion,** the mayor's official residence.

Across the East River, just minutes away by aerial tram, lies tranquil **Roo-**

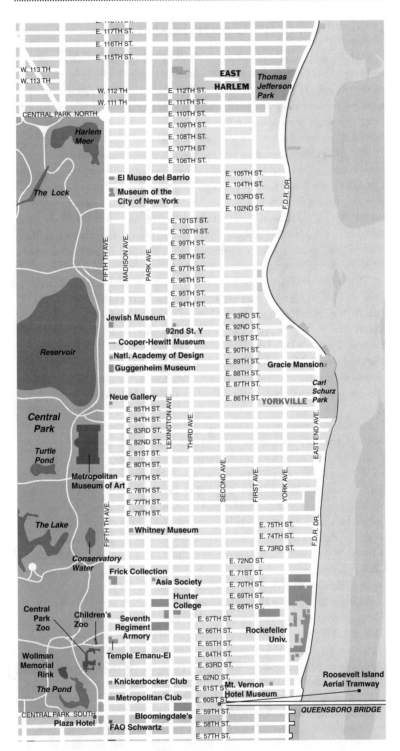

Upper East Side

sevelt Island, the site of a prison, an almshouse and an insane asylum from the early 1800's through the early 1900's. Today, the island is a mixed-income residential community that offers an escape from Manhattan's frenzy. At East 61st Street and Second Avenue, you can take a quick tram ride over the East River to enjoy wonderful Manhattan skyline views from this tiny island.

Subway: 4 (express), 5 (express) and 6 (local) make stops along Lexington Ave. from 59th St. to 125th St.

HIGHLIGHTS OF THE NEIGHBORHOOD
(For the **Metropolitan Museum of Art,** *the* **Guggenheim,** *the* **Frick Collection,** *the* **Whitney,** *the* **Cooper-Hewitt National Design Museum, El Museo del Barrio** *and* **Neue Gallery New York,** *see chapter* **The Arts.***)*

Asia Society 725 Park Ave. (between 70th and 71st Sts.) (212) 517-ASIA *www.asiasociety.org.* The Asia Society was founded by John D. Rockefeller III to introduce Americans to the cultures of Asia and the Pacific. Scholarly symposia, films, public programs and publications have long been central to its mission, with an emphasis on the arts. Today its elegant galleries feature changing exhibitions for connoisseurs as well as for the general public. The elegant AsiaStore has a lovely selection of Asian-inspired books, gifts and home furnishings. **Admission:** $7 adults; $5 students and seniors; free for children under 16. **Hours:** Galleries Tue.–Sun. 11 A.M.–6 P.M. (till 9 P.M. on Fri.).

Carl Schurz Park East End Ave. at 84th St. (212) 360-1311. Named after a newspaper editor and reform politician, Carl Schurz Park is the site of **Gracie Mansion,** the mayor's official residence. (Billionaire Mayor Bloomberg prefers his own plush Upper East Side digs, and has declined the invitation to move in.) Stretching along the East River, the park is also one of the city's quietest. Benches line a relaxing promenade that offers views of tugboats, Hell's Gate Bridge and the Roosevelt Island lighthouse. To the delight of loungers, the brick paths make the park a terrible place for in-line skating. The park has a basketball court and children's playground.

China Institute in America 125 E. 65th St. (between Park and Lexington Aves.) (212) 744-8181 *www.chinainstitute.org.* The China Institute offers classes in Chinese languages, arts and calligraphy; hosts lectures, films and discussions; and stages art shows in its galleries. Courses for children are also available. **Admission:** $5 adults; $3 students and seniors; free for children under age 12; free for everyone Tue. and Thu. 6–8 P.M. **Hours:** Galleries Mon.–Sat. 10 A.M.–5 P.M. (till 8 P.M. Tue. and Thu.); closed Sun.

Goethe-Institut/German Cultural Center 1014 Fifth Ave. (between 82nd and 83rd Sts.) (212) 439-8700 *www.goethe.org/uk/ney/.* This institute, funded by the German government, promotes German language and culture abroad by sponsoring lectures and art exhibitions. Occupying a Beaux-Arts limestone town house, the institute also collaborates with other organizations around the city in presenting film series and music performances. The organization operates a lending and reference library, and offers language courses through NYU's Deutsches Haus. **Hours:** Mon.–Fri. 10 A.M.–5 P.M. (till 8 P.M. Tue. and Thu.).

Jewish Museum 1109 Fifth Ave. (at 92nd St.) (212) 423-3200 *www.thejewishmuseum.org*. Located on Museum Mile in a Gothic chateau built in 1908, the Jewish Museum is dedicated to exploring Jewish identity, from artworks by Marc Chagall to video archives preserving the Jewish comedy of television's golden age. The two-floor permanent exhibit is the intriguing "Culture and Continuity: The Jewish Journey," which explores 4,000 years of history through archeological treasures, ceremonial objects, art and interactive media. Running from mid-April to mid-August 2005 is a special exhibit on the multifaceted career of Maurice Sendak, exploring his Jewish identity and the creation of his latest work, an opera entitled "Brundibar" in collaboration with Tony Kushner. The museum also hosts film screenings, lectures, panel discussions, concerts and family programs. Newly opened in September 2004 is an interactive children's exhibit called "Our Great Garden: Nurturing Planet Earth," inspired by the Jewish concept of "Tikkun Olam" (Hebrew for "repairing the world").
Admission: $10 adults; $7.50 students and seniors; free for children under 12; Thu. 5–8 P.M., pay what you wish. **Hours:** Sun. 11 A.M.–8 P.M.; Mon.–Wed. 11 A.M.–5:45 P.M.; Thu. 11 A.M.–9 P.M.; Fri. 11 A.M.–5 P.M. Closed Sat. and Jewish holidays.

Mount Vernon Hotel Museum and Garden 421 E. 61st St. (between First and York Aves.) (212) 838-6878. *www.mountvernonhotelmuseum.org*. This small museum sits within earshot of the FDR Drive and in the shadow the Queensboro Bridge, so it's hard to imagine that people once flocked here for a peaceful escape from the hustle and bustle of downtown. But after a docent has led you through the museum's nine richly appointed period rooms and you're relaxing on a stone bench in the 18th-century-style gardens, it seems more plausible. In the 1830's, wealthy New Yorkers would retreat to what was then called the Mount Vernon Hotel for the weekend. The Federal-style structure, built in 1799, is the only remaining building of its kind in Manhattan. Abigail Adams Smith, daughter of President John Adams, originally commissioned it as part of a planned 23-acre estate modeled after Mount Vernon, though her project was never completed. **Admission:** $5 adults; $4 students and seniors; free for children under 12. **Hours:** Tue.–Sun. 11 A.M.–4 P.M. (last tour at 3:30 P.M.). Closed Aug. and some holidays.

Museum of the City of New York 1220 Fifth Ave. (between 103rd and 104th Sts.) (212) 534-1672 *www.mcny.org*. Created in 1923 to collect and preserve the history of the city, the museum's intimate galleries are filled with a rich trove of artifacts from the 19th and 20th centuries, including period rooms, furniture, silver, theater costumes, prints, photographs and rare manuscripts. Its collections trace the development of the modern city and its people, from the skating ponds portrayed in Currier & Ives prints to the skyscrapers photographed by Berenice Abbott. Visitors can count on exhibits about the history of Broadway theater and American decorative arts. Kids will be drawn to the historic fire pumps and a gallery of toys and dolls. **Admission:** $7 adults; $4 students, children and seniors. **Hours:** Wed.–Sun. 10 A.M.–5 P.M. Closed Mon. and open only for group tours on Tue.

Temple Emanu-El 1 E. 65th St. (at Fifth Ave.) (212) 744-1400 *www.emanuel-nyc.org.* Temple Emanu-El is home to what is said to be the largest Jewish congregation in the world. The impressive limestone Moorish-Romanesque structure was completed in 1929 on the site of an Astor mansion. In size and beauty it rivals some of Europe's cathedrals. The sanctuary, which seats 2,500, has an extraordinary bronze ark in the shape of a Torah and is decorated with marvelous mosaics by Hildreth Meiere. The temple regularly hosts concerts and lectures. **Hours:** Open to visitors daily 10 A.M.–5 P.M. Services held Sun.–Thu. at 5:30 P.M., Fri at 5:15 P.M., Sat. at 10:30 A.M. Free tours after Sat. services.

Recommended Neighborhood Restaurants
(See chapter **Restaurants** *for reviews.)*

Ajisai	$25 & Under		JAPANESE/SUSHI
Bandol	$25 & Under		FRENCH
Bistro Le Steak	$25 & Under		BISTRO/STEAK
Congee Village	$25 & Under		CHINESE
Heidelberg	$25 & Under		GERMAN
Luca	$25 & Under		ITALIAN
Pig Heaven	$25 & Under		CHINESE
The Sultan	$25 & Under		TURKISH
Uskudar	$25 & Under		TURKISH
Café Boulud	☆☆☆	$$$$	FRENCH
Cafe Sabarsky	☆☆	$$	AUSTRO-HUNGARIAN
Centolire	☆☆	$$$	ITALIAN
Circus	☆☆	$$$	BRAZILIAN
Daniel	☆☆☆☆	$$$$	FRENCH
David Burke & Donatella	☆☆	$$$$	FUSION
Geisha	☆	$$$	JAPANESE
Hacienda de Argentina	☆	$$$	ARGENTINE
Jo Jo	☆☆☆	$$$	FRENCH
Maya	☆☆	$$$	MEXICAN/TEX-MEX
92	☆	$$	NEW AMERICAN
Paola's	☆☆	$$	ITALIAN
Payard Pâtisserie	☆☆	$$$	BISTRO/FRENCH

Central Park

It happens every spring. New Yorkers by the thousands stream into Central Park (*www.centralparknyc.org* for information on the park, special events, sport and walking tours) to revel in the glory of the new forsythia and cherry blossoms. There, they are again reminded that the park is the city's common ground, the democratic village green where people of all backgrounds and enthusiasms come to pursue their separate pleasures, for the most part congenially.

In a single 843-acre rectangle, there are more or less permanent and overlapping communities of folk dancers, horseback riders, bird watchers, storytellers, dog walkers, nannies, chess fans, volleyball players, softball leagues, joggers, cyclists, tennis players, ice skaters, soccer teams, ultimate Frisbee devotees and pint-size fishermen.

There is a racially polychromed assortment of roller skaters who shimmy to a disco beat around a macadam oval northeast of the Sheep Meadow, and there is a separate set of in-line skaters who slalom through rows of soda bottles. There are pétanque devotees who play a French version of the Italian game of boccie on a hardscrabble patch of ground, and there are lawn bowlers, in mandatory whites, who play on a manicured court. There is even a weekly lakeside gathering of fans of a guitar-playing folk singer, David Ippolito.

All these communities coexist in a park that celebrated its 150th birthday in 2003, now in what many believe is its best shape in at least half a century.

Before Frederick Law Olmsted and Calvert Vaux, the park's designers, came along, large urban parks were virtually nonexistent. Most large American parks were playgrounds for the aristocracy, for hunting or grazing deer, but Olmsted and Vaux wanted a people's park. Even if modern minds might find their rationale patronizing, they laid out footpaths beside the carriage roads so poorer people could use the gentry as a refining influence. Today, people seem to recognize one another's rights because they essentially share the same reason for coming to the park.

While their origins almost 25 years ago were rather spontaneous, the dance skaters have become so institutionalized that they have an association, publish a newsletter and charge dues of $15 a year. Still, at their oval, lawyers and bike messengers; the rich and the subsidized; black, white, Hispanic and Asian mingle seemingly without effort.

Most groups that start haphazardly eventually get the Parks Department's blessing with a dedicated ground and permit. For more than 30 years, the folk dancers have been doing Balkan, Israeli and other circle dances on Sundays on a plaza near Belvedere Castle. The 30-team Broadway Show League, where you might see *The Lion King* defeat *The Producers* in softball, has been at the Heckscher ball fields for 50 years. The Model Yacht Club, made up mostly of men who still like playing with small boats (although ones that cost more than $1,000), has its own house at Conservatory Water.

The pétanque enthusiasts, most of them workers in the city's French restaurants, have no court or permit. But 30 years ago, they simply staked out a shaded plot of earth southwest of the Heckscher ball fields, choosing it precisely because it was rutted and offered challenging plays.

The two dozen regulars include a maître d'hôtel of La Grenouille, the captains at Le Perigord and René Pujol and the bartender at Pierre au Tunnel. After four hours of afternoon play they usually adjourn to Tout Va Bien for glasses of Ricard.

Michael Touchard, who is younger and works as a bartender at Tout Va Bien, says he particularly likes playing in Central Park because it seems a far more welcoming place than, say, the Bois de Boulogne, the park's equivalent in Paris. "In Central Park you have everybody, from the rich who walk their dogs to average Joes," he said. "You have a guy who is a busboy and a guy who owns four restaurants, and they all play together."

Central Park is for the birds, the bird-watchers might insist. And it would be hard to argue, seeing the single-mindedness with which they go about spotting the more than 200 species that pass through Central Park on their way to more exotic ports of call.

On a recent morning, 16 bird-watchers with dangling binoculars gathered at Fifth Avenue and ambled into the Ramble, one of the world's great migratory way stations. Their leader was Sarah Elliott, a red-crested sparrow of a woman who has been leading paying tours of the park's bird life for 25 years.

She pointed out the scraggly nest of a red-tailed hawk tenderly patched together above a stone decoration on the top floor of a regal Fifth Avenue building. Deeper into the park, the birdwatchers spied a red-bellied woodpecker, a great egret, a white-throated sparrow, a red-winged blackbird, a cardinal, a downy woodpecker, a barn swallow, a rough-winged swallow and a double-crested cormorant. The bird-watchers are drawn by the astonishment of "a sighting," gasping at the anomaly of a great egret in Turtle Pond. But they also simply enjoy the serenity of the woodlands and hidden meadows.

"There are so many different villages," said George van der Ploeg, a bird-watcher. "It's like New York City, with a Greek section in Queens, Asians in Flushing, the South Americans and Russians in Brooklyn. In a way the park is a mirror of the city itself." —*Joseph Berger*

Transportation: West side of park: A, B, C, D, 1, 9 to 59th St.-Columbus Circle or any B/C subway stop or M10 bus stop between 59th and 110th Sts. East side of park: N, R, W to Fifth Ave. at 59th St.; any 4, 5, 6 subway or M1, 2, 3, 4 bus stop between 59th and 110th Sts.

PARK ATTRACTIONS

The Arsenal 64th St. and Fifth Ave. Originally built in 1848, the Arsenal is one of only two buildings in Central Park that stood here before the park existed. This imposing structure resembles a medieval castle, with many architectural and artistic touches added over the years inside and out. It's worth visiting for its Depression-era murals and art exhibits focused on New York or Central Park. It also houses Olmsted and Vaux's original "Greensward Plan" for the park. This landmark building is now the headquarters of New York City's Dept. of Parks and Recreation and the Central Park Wildlife Conservation Center.

Arthur Ross Pinetum Mid-park, 84th–86th Sts. This collection of 20 species of pine tree (plus elms and oaks) is the largest collection of evergreens in Central Park. Walking tours of the Pinetum are available starting at nearby Belvedere Castle, including a popular seasonal tour in early December. Birdwatchers also come here to spot owls in the pines, and there is a small playground that finds more use as a quiet picnic spot.

Balto East Drive at 66th St. This is one of the most sought-out sites in the park, and is the only park statue commemorating an animal. Balto was a heroic Siberian husky who braved a blizzard to bring diptheria antitoxin to Nome, Alaska; he was also the subject of a popular animated film. Created by Frederick George Richard Roth in 1925, Balto sports a golden back and snout, the patina and outer layer of bronze rubbed off by fingers, noses and backsides of thousands of worshipful children.

Belvedere Castle Mid-park at 79th St. (212) 772-0210. This impressive Victorian structure, perched atop the highest natural point in the park, was occupied by the U.S. Weather Bureau from 1919 to the early 1960's. The site now offers good views of the park as well as excellent bird-watching. It also houses the **Henry Luce Nature Observatory,** which introduces the plants and animals of the park through interactive exhibits. The observatory also loans out backpacks with information and binoculars to help budding young scientists study the nearby Ramble or Turtle Pond (available Tue.–Sun. 10 A.M.–5 P.M.).

Bethesda Terrace and Fountain Mid-park at 72nd St. The split-level Terrace, decorated with detailed carvings of plants and animals, is one of the most popular areas of the park, affording gorgeous views of the Mall, the Lake, the Ramble, and all the human activity around the plaza. Bethesda Fountain itself, possibly the most-photographed monument in Central Park, commemorates the opening the Croton Aqueduct in 1842. It was the only sculpture called for in the original park plan, and its creator, Emma Stebbins, was the first woman to receive a commission to produce a major piece of public art in the city.

The Carousel 65th St. Transverse and Central Drive (212) 879-0244. This is one of the largest merry-go-rounds in America, with 58 hard-carved horses and two chariots. Built in 1908 by the firm of Stein and Goldstein, respected carvers from Brooklyn, it was rescued from Coney Island by the Parks Department. Today the quaint building and calliope music draw over 250,000 riders per year. Rides are $1. **Hours:** Apr.–Nov. daily 10 A.M.–6 P.M. (winter, open only on weekends, weather permitting, closing at 4:30 P.M.).

Central Park Drive This six-mile road circling the park has a lane set aside for bikers, joggers and in-line skaters. The best time to use it is when the park is closed to traffic: Monday to Friday 10 A.M. to 3 P.M. and 7 to 10 P.M., and

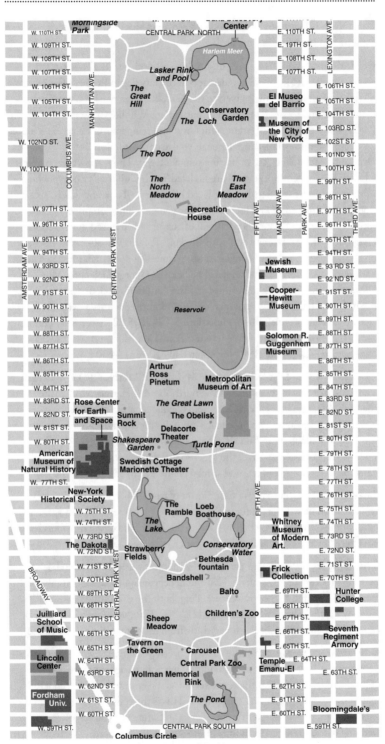

Central Park

from 7 P.M. Friday to 6 A.M. Monday. Keep alert, since this lane gets heavy use from high-speed athletes on wheels.

Central Park Wildlife Center East Side, 63rd-66th Sts. (212) 861-6030 *www.centralparkzoo.com*. The oldest zoo in the city began in the 1860's as a menagerie to house animals given to the park, but has since been renovated many times and rechristened as the Central Park Wildlife Conservation Center. Divided into three zones (Arctic, rain forest and temperate), the center features animals in naturalistic settings (though you've got to admit those poor polar bears don't seem happy on sweltering summer days). The emphasis on public education is evident in the newly remodeled **Tisch Children's Zoo,** in which interactive nature exhibits have replaced kitschy storybook characters. Admission to the children's zoo is included in the general admission price, but make sure you bring along an extra pocketful of quarters for the feed dispensers. Kids love to feed the goats, cows and potbellied pig. Parents will also want to check on sea lion, polar bear and penguin feeding times—all of which provide a fascinating spectacle for kids and adults. The beloved **George Delacorte Musical Clock,** between the Wildlife Center and the Children's Zoo, draws crowds on the hour and half-hour when a menagerie of motorized animals twirl around the clock to nursery-rhyme tunes. **Admission:** $6 adults; $1.25 seniors; $1 children ages 3–12; children under 3, free. **Hours:** Apr.–Oct. Mon.–Fri. 10 A.M.–5 P.M., Sat.–Sun. 10 A.M.–5:30 P.M. Nov.–Mar. daily 10 A.M.–4:30 P.M.

Charles A. Dana Discovery Center Mid-park at 110th St. (212) 860-1370. Central Park's newest building, on the north shore of Harlem Meer at the top of the park, offers general park information, conducts nature classes, showcases community projects and art, and loans out poles for catch-and-release fishing in the Meer (available Tue.–Sun. 10 A.M.–4 P.M. from Apr.–Oct.). A deck outside the Center looks out over the Meer to the south, and an outdoor plaza, bordered by trees, hosts concerts and special public events throughout the year.

Chess and Checkers House East Side at 65th St. This is the park's largest and most ornate wooden summer house. Playing pieces for the 24 indoor and outdoor tables here can be borrowed from the Dairy, and children's chess lessons are offered by the Central Park Conservancy in the summer.

The Concert Ground Mid-park, 69th–72nd Sts. Music, theater, and dance performances are occasionally held at the neoclassical limestone **Naumberg Bandshell.** Behind the shady Wisteria Pergola to the east of the bandshell, Rumsey Playfield hosts **SummerStage** (212-360-2756; *www.summerstage.org*), a series of free summer concerts (everything from rock and folk to world music).

Conservatory Garden East Side, 104th–106th Sts. One of Central Park's best-kept secrets, these six acres of horticultural magnificence are tucked away behind wrought-iron gates that once served as the entrance to the Vanderbilt mansion at Fifth Avenue and 58th Street. This is the only formal garden in the park, with three very different sub-gardens (on Saturdays, you can often see wedding parties piling in for formal photographs). To the north is a French-style garden, with concentric rings of flowers around a central fountain. There are massive displays of tulips in the spring, chrysanthemums in the fall, and white roses in the summer. The central area is done in an Italian style, with a carefully tended central lawn and a simple fountain. The southern portion of the garden was created in an English style and is perhaps the most popular of the three because of its statuary fountain featuring characters from *The Secret Garden*.

Conservatory Water East Side, 72nd–75th Sts. The name of this popular pond comes from the conservatory, or greenhouse, that was meant to be built nearby. Most park patrons know it as the boat pond, because of the numerous model ships floating in it on most good days. The **Kerbs Memorial Boathouse,** on the east side of the pond, rents out boats and sells refreshments beside a large patio. Summer brings storytelling sessions near the **statue of Hans Christian Andersen** to the west of the pond; children love to climb on the **Alice in Wonderland** statue to the north.

The Andersen statue is also the best vantage point for one of the park's most remarkable wildlife dramas. For years, a pair of red-tailed hawks have been nesting on the 12th-floor ledge of a building just across from the pond (at Fifth Ave. and 74th St.). One most weekends, hawk watchers bring in telescopes and offer all passersby close-up views of the nest.

The Dairy East Side at 65th St. (212) 794-6564. During 19th-century "milk scandals" and diphtheria outbreaks, this Swiss-Gothic hybrid cottage served as a distribution center for fresh milk brought in from farms outside New York. It now serves as Central Park's **Visitor Information Center and Recreation Building.** The Dairy houses exhibits and information about the park, including an excellent flip map documenting the changes wrought on the landscape during park construction, as well as before-and-after photographs of the area. **Hours:** Tues.–Sun. 10 A.M.–5 P.M. (closes 4 P.M. in winter).

Delacorte Theatre Mid-park at 80th St. (SW corner of Great Lawn) (212) 539-8655. For over 30 years, the Delacorte has offered free **Shakespeare in the Park** performances in July and August (212-539-8750 or *www.publictheater.org* for information). With Belvedere Castle looming nearby, the Turtle Pond to the east, and the Great Lawn across a path to the north, a star-studded evening of theater in Central Park can be unforgettable. New Yorkers and tourists line up for hours to get tickets, which are distributed at 1 P.M. the day of the performance (limit two per person). Tickets are also available from the Joseph Papp Public Theater at 425 Lafayette Street, near Astor Place.

The Great Lawn Mid-park, 79th–86th Sts. Today the Lawn is one of the most popular areas of the park, but until 1934 this was the site of the Croton Reservoir. When the city's water supply changed, the reservoir became obsolete. It was filled in with rubble from city construction to become the Great Lawn, a pond and two playgrounds. These 13 acres of grass, with eight softball fields, are used for all manner of private and public functions; they look terrific after a massive restoration project in the late 1990's. The Great Lawn has been the site of some of New York's largest outdoor events, including Paul Simon's 1991 concert and Pope John Paul II's 1995 Mass (which drew 600,000 and 350,000 people, respectively); it also plays host to annual summer concerts by the Metropolitan Opera and the New York Philharmonic. All this use takes its toll, however, so the rules here are strict these days: no dogs, no bicycles, permits required for ball games. It is open only when the Keeper of the Great Lawn feels the lawn can handle public use. Despite pleas from activists who recognized Central Park's role as the "village green" of New York, demonstrators were denied permission to gather here during the Republican National Convention in 2004.

Harlem Meer East Side, 106th–110th Sts. A walking tour of the 11-acre Meer (Dutch for "small sea") takes in an impressive array of plants and wildlife, including some impressive oak, beech and gingko trees. The formerly fenced-off edge of the Meer has been restored to a more natural state, including a small sandy beach near the Charles A. Dana Discovery Center. At the southeast corner of the Meer, follow some steps to the water, where you will find yourself completely surrounded by flowers, with a private view of the water.

The Jacqueline Kennedy Onassis Reservoir Mid-park, 85th–96th Sts. Until 1991, this 106-acre body of water still provided water to parts of Manhattan and the Bronx; now three huge tunnels bring water from upstate New York, but the Reservoir remains a good spot for jogging, bird-watching and observing the city skyline. The New York Road Runners Club (which organizes the New York City Marathon) holds weekly races on the 1.58-mile track, which is especially beautiful when the cherry trees bloom in the spring. Also worth a look are three elegant cast-iron pedestrian bridges that span the Bridle Trail, and three Vaux-designed gatehouses containing water-treatment equipment.

The Lake Mid-park, 71st–78th St. After the Reservoir, this is the largest body of water in Central Park. Its meandering shoreline offers many sights and attractions, from the wisteria arbor in the south and **Bow Bridge,** the beautiful span in the center of the Lake, to the ornate Ladies' Pavilion on its northwest shore. Some of these sights may be best viewed from one of the rowboats available for rental at the **Loeb Boathouse** *(see below)*, at the northeastern edge of the Lake.

Lasker Rink and Pool Mid-park, 108th–109th St. (212) 534-7639. Located just below the scenic Harlem Meer, the Lasker Rink is open for ice skating during the winter season ($4 for adults, $2 for children under age 12; skate rentals are available). In summer, this is Central Park's only swimming pool (admission is free; open daily 11 A.M.–2:45 P.M. and 4–6:45 P.M.). Swimmers must wear a swimsuit (no denim shorts or T-shirts). Lockers are available, but bring your own lock.

Lawn Sports Center West Side at 69th St. (north of Sheep Meadow). Visitors can play croquet or lawn bowling on two tiny lawns from May 1st to October 1st. The New York Croquet Club (212-369-7949) offers free clinics on Tuesday nights and tournaments on weekends; the New York Lawn Bowling club (212-289-3245) also offers free lessons and regular club games.

Loeb Boathouse East Side, 74th–75th Sts. The original Vaux-designed wooden building burned down long ago, but the current Loeb Boathouse has become a hub of park activity. The restaurant, **Park View at the Boathouse** (212-517-2233), is a romantic, two-star favorite; there's also a more affordable and casual cafeteria-style option. Energetic visitors can **rent bicycles** (choose from three-speed, 10-speed or tandems, from $10 to $15 an hour; you must leave a driver's license, credit card or passport as a deposit) and **rowboats** ($10 for the first hour, $30 cash deposit is required; reservations accepted; available daily March–Oct. only, 10 A.M.–5 P.M.). Those in search of more relaxation can take a ride in a genuine Venetian **gondola** ($30 per half hour; summer only, Mon.–Fri. 5–9 P.M., Sat.–Sun. 2–9 P.M.). Bird-watchers come here to enter their sightings in the **Bird Register,** a large notebook stored in the Boathouse. And the Conservancy has installed a small wildflower garden, meant to attract butterflies, to the west of the Boathouse entrance.

The Mall (Literary Walk) Mid-park, 69th–72nd Sts. Four long rows of American elms, often the first park stop for spring warblers, form a cathedral-like canopy over the Mall. This grand promenade is one of only two formal elements remaining from Olmsted and Vaux's original park design (the other is Bethesda Fountain), and it contains many of the park's best-known sculptures. Among them are William Shakespeare, Robert Burns, Victor Herbert, Beethoven and Christopher Columbus. At the southern end of the walk is a tribute to Frederick Law Olmsted—a memorial flower garden surrounded by American elms.

Merchants' Gate and Maine Monument Southeast park entrance (Columbus Circle). Most of the original entrances to the park were dedicated to different professions, and Olmsted and Vaux insisted on very modest designs for the gates. Over time, however, the city added striking military monuments to the entrances along Central Park South, including this massive pylon commemorating the sinking of the battleship *Maine* in 1898. The monument honors the Americans killed in the Spanish-American War, and was partially funded with pennies and nickels collected from schoolchildren after the war.

Naturalists' Walk West Side, 77th–81st Sts. This landscape was restored with the nearby American Museum of Natural History in mind: a dramatic variety of flowers, plants and trees have been introduced to this area, attracting birds and butterflies and making it a natural destination after exploring the museum's Hall of Biodiversity and other exhibits.

The North Meadow Mid-Park, 97th–102nd Sts. This is the largest grassy space in Central Park, divided only by 12 fields for baseball, softball and soccer. Inside the landmark **North Meadow Recreation Center,** the Conservancy offers a wide range of programs for children, from computer-based education to more physical activities. Any visitor with a photo ID can borrow one of the Center's Field Day kits, containing items like balls, Frisbees and jump ropes.

The Obelisk (Cleopatra's Needle) East Side at 81st St. This 3,500-year-old stone obelisk was erected behind the Metropolitan Museum on January 22, 1881, after being uprooted from the city of Heliopolis, making a tumultuous ocean crossing, and crawling through the streets of Manhattan for four months. It remains the oldest man-made object in the park. Each corner is supported by a massive bronze replica of a sea crab—the originals of which are in the Met's Sackler Wing.

The Pond Southeast corner of the park. Once an area of foul swampland, this is now one of the most attractive parts of Central Park, newly renovated and well shielded from street noise by trees and rocks. The small fenced-in area here is the Hallett Nature Sanctuary—four acres of park left untended, creating a haven for animals (like woodchucks, rabbits and raccoons) and plants (including Black Cherry trees and many wildflowers).

The Pool West Side, 100th–103rd Sts. This body of water is a romantic place, sheltered by weeping willows and an impressive assortment of other tree species. A small peninsula on the south shore is a good spot for duck feeding or for viewing the Pool's foliage.

The Ramble Mid-park, 73rd–79th Sts. It's hard to believe that this 38-acre sprawl of pathways, streams, cliffs and trees is entirely man-made—meticulously designed by Frederick Law Olmsted and carved out of a natural hillside. This may be the easiest place to get lost in Central Park, so bring along a map. But the opportunity to lose yourself and escape from the crush of city life has also made it one of the most popular destinations in the park, a fact that has led to an ongoing need for restoration. This is also one of the best sites for bird-watching in the country, ranked among the top 15 by the Audubon Society. Over 200 different species of birds have been seen here; the best time for birding is during spring and fall migration (Apr.–May and Sept.–Oct.).

The Ravine Mid-park, 102nd–106th Sts. Stretching from the southern end of Lasker Rink to the Pool just above West 100th St., the Ravine is a peaceful destination filled with wildflowers, bird-watching trails, and odd and beautiful bridges. One of the most impressive of these is Huddlestone Arch, a careful assemblage of rough boulders fitted together without any mortar or other binding material.

Shakespeare Garden West Side, 79th–80th Sts. Once an extension of the Ramble, this area was dedicated to Shakespeare on the tricentennial of his death in 1916. This meandering, four-acre garden showcases about half of the 200 plants mentioned in the Bard's works, including a mulberry tree said to be grown from a cutting from Shakespeare's mother's garden. Bronze plaques provide the quotations relevant to each plant.

Sheep Meadow Mid-park, 66th–69th Sts. This 15-acre meadow was an actual grazing field for sheep until the 1930's, when the sheep were shipped out and their building became the Tavern on the Green restaurant. In the 1960's and 70's the field suffered severe damage from sporting activities, concerts and hip-

Fred R. Conrad/The New York Times

Central Park

pie be-ins. But since the 1980's, the Park Conservancy has exercised strict control over meadow visitors. On warm summer days, this rolling lawn still attracts thousands of walkers, sunbathers and people-watchers. Radios, team sports and dogs are prohibited, but often show up anyway. Just outside the northern fence is Lilac Walk, lined with 23 varieties of lilac. The Meadow is open mid-April to mid-October, dawn to dusk in fair weather.

Strawberry Fields West Side, 72nd St. The landscaping of this area was made possible by Yoko Ono, who presented it to the city in memory of John Lennon, who was murdered outside the nearby Dakota apartment house in 1980. There is an incredible variety of plants and trees, all donated by countries around the world, forming a "Garden of Peace." The most evocative touch is a gift from the city of Naples, Italy: a mosaic with the word "Imagine" at its center.

Summit Rock West Side, 81st–85th Sts. At 137.5 feet, this is the highest point in Central Park. An ampitheater overlooks the south and east slopes, and a path leads up the southern slope to a beautiful green lawn that affords good views of the park and the Upper West Side. This and adjacent areas of Central Park were home to 5,000 New Yorkers before the city purchased the land and began park construction. At the time, there were nearly a thousand buildings on the land, including factories and churches. Seneca Village occupied this territory in the mid-1800's; this was one of the best-known African-American communities in New York, composed mostly of free black land-owning families.

Swedish Cottage Marionette Theater West Side at 79th St. (212) 988-9093. This replica of a 19th-century Swedish schoolhouse seats 100 children and features central air-conditioning and a state-of-the-art stage. Puppet shows, often classics like *Peter Pan*, are staged at 10:30 A.M. and noon Tuesday through Friday, 1 P.M. on Saturdays (no Saturday shows in July or August). The season runs from early November through mid-August; advance reservations are required. **Prices:** $6 adults; $5 children.

Turtle Pond Mid-park, 79th–80th Sts. When the old Croton Reservoir was filled in with construction debris in the 1930's, becoming the Great Lawn, the southern end became Belvedere Lake. It quickly attracted a wide range of aquatic life and the site was rechristened in honor of some of its more popular inhabitants in 1987. A 1997 renovation altered the pond's shoreline, added new plants and introduced Turtle Island, a new habitat for the turtles and birds that make their home here. A dock and nature blind offer great views of the pond and its denizens sunning themselves on dead tree trunks.

Wollman Memorial Skating Rink East Side at 62nd St. (212) 439-6900 *www.wollmanskatingrink.com*. The 33,000-square-foot Wollman Rink offers a spacious ice-skating area and an unparalleled view of the Duck Pond framed by landmark buildings like the Plaza Hotel. During the summer of 2003, the rink was transformed into Victorian Gardens, an old-fashioned family fun park filled with rides, games and attractions (admission $14 for children, $9 for adults; open mid-May to mid-Sept., Mon.-Fri. 11 A.M.–7 P.M., Sat.–Sun. 10 A.M.–8 P.M.). Winter ice skating runs $8.50 for adults ($11 on weekends), $4.25 for children ($4.50 on weekends); private lessons and hockey leagues are available. Skate rental is $4.75. (During winter, the rink is open Mon.–Tue. 10 A.M.–2:30 P.M., Wed.–Thu. 10 A.M.–10 P.M., Fri–Sat. 10 A.M.–11 P.M., Sun. 10 A.M.–9 P.M.).

SPORTS IN CENTRAL PARK
(See also chapter **Sports & Recreation.***)*

Baseball/Softball: The **North Meadow** has baseball diamonds. The **Great Lawn** has seven softball fields; five more are at the **Heckscher Ballfields.** Arsenal West (16 W. 61st St.) is the place to go for permits, or call (212) 408-0226. Permits are expensive, and are usually snatched up well in advance by organized leagues, but you might find a pickup game on the Great Lawn.

Biking: Stick to the roads: park security may confiscate your bike if you ride on walkways or trails. Rental bikes are available near **Loeb Boathouse,** at 74th St. and the East Drive *(see listing above)*. The **Central Park Drive** loop is 6 miles; this road is closed to cars 10 A.M.–4 P.M., and then again 7 P.M.–dusk. Even when vehicular traffic is permitted, there is a multi-use lane for runners, bikers and in-line skaters.

Boating: Rowboats and gondolas can be rented at the **Loeb Boathouse** *(see listing above)*.

Fishing: The **Dana Discovery Center** *(see listing above)* loans out poles and bait for catch-and-release fishing; fishing in the Lake is permitted, but may become more restricted in the future following the poisoning of some birds.

Horseback Riding: Horse rentals and riding lessons are available at the **Claremont Riding Academy** at 175 W. 89th St.; call (212) 724-5100 for information. The park's bridle path runs around the Reservoir and northern quadrant of the park, and down the west side to 60th St.

Ice Skating: Available November through March at **Wollman** (212-439-6900) and **Lasker** (212-534-7639) rinks *(see listings above for more information)*.

In-line Skating: The park drives are popular with skaters, but some prefer the area at the north end of the Mall and the driveway to the west of the Mall.

Running: There are designated running lanes on all park drives, and the entire road is closed to automobile traffic between 10 A.M. and 4 P.M. and after 7 P.M. on weekdays, and from 7 P.M. Friday to 6 A.M. Monday.

Swimming: Swimming is forbidden in all open bodies of water in the park, but Lasker Rink (212-534-7639) becomes a free swimming pool in July and August.

Tennis: The **tennis center** to the northwest of the Reservoir houses 30 courts; permits are required most of the time and are available at the Arsenal. Call (212) 360-8131 for details.

The Upper West Side

The Upper West Side begins at **Columbus Circle,** where the lofty but sterile new **AOL Time Warner Center** has transformed a once-seedy area with a bevy of upscale boutiques and restaurants (shoppers now flock here from all over the city for the exquisite produce available at the Whole Foods flagship store). The neighborhood extends all the way uptown to **Columbia University.** In between these two landmarks is a rectangle four miles long and one mile wide, home to more latte-drinking, stroller-pushing NPR listeners than you can shake a stick at.

But the Upper West Side's reputation as a haven for rumpled intellectuals, writers, activists and actors is becoming a thing of the past. It's still one of the nation's most liberal neighborhoods, but the middle class is being squeezed out as property values soar. Increasing numbers of yuppie lawyers and bankers have moved in, and dozens of mom-and-pop businesses have been shuttered as a wave of national chains and big-box retailers robs this once-funky neighborhood of its personality. The presence of **Lincoln Center,** the **Beacon Theater,** and a handful of small neighborhood stages ensure that genuine culture will always have a foothold here, but the Upper West Side is beginning to feel more and more like the Upper East Side, with all of its rough edges thoroughly smoothed out by gentrification. It's still one of the most livable, convenient and family-friendly neighborhoods in the city—lucky residents can always find respite from the urban bustle on the grassy lawns of Central Park and Riverside Park.

The Upper West Side was farmland until well after the Civil War—the city, such as it was, covered only the lower third of the island of Manhattan. Before the proud apartment buildings began marching up Central Park West, Central Park's 843 acres were penciled off as a big green rectangle— "the grand-daddy of all American landscaped parks," an American Institute of Architects guide called it. But Frederick Law Olmsted, principal designer of the park, did not want New Yorkers to think of the park as architecture. "What we want to gain is tranquility and rest to the mind," he said. The park is full of places where one can gain both. (*See* "Central Park" *earlier in this chapter.*)

From there, you can see the **Dakota,** an apartment building so spacious that Leonard Bernstein had no trouble fitting two grand pianos into his living room. The Dakota was also home to John Lennon, who was brutally murdered just outside the archway that leads to the building's elegant courtyard. His widow, Yoko Ono, still lives in the Dakota, only a short walk from **Strawberry Fields,** an area inside the park honoring his memory.

Up Central Park West, past the twin-towered **San Remo** apartments, are the museums. The **New-York Historical Society** has kept the hyphen that the rest of the city dropped more than a century ago. Next door is the **American Museum of Natural History.** The oldest section of the museum was designed by Calvert Vaux, Olmsted's collaborator on the design of the park just across the street. The museum's newest addition is the sleek glass box that encloses the Hayden Planetarium in the **Rose Center for Earth and Space.** Three blocks west is Broadway; the stretch between 74th and 80th Streets is a food shopper's paradise, with markets like **Fairway, Citarella** and **Zabar's.**

Three stops beyond 96th Street on the No. 1 local is **Columbia University.** The campus was laid out by Charles Follen McKim, a partner in McKim, Mead & White, the legendary firm that satisfied the city's lust for carefully proportioned neoclassical creations at the beginning of the 20th century. The newest building on the Columbia campus is an $85 million student center, a gleaming glass box that opened in 1999, completing McKim's master plan.

Subway: 1 (local), 2 (express), 3 (express), 9 (local) make stops along Broadway from 59th St. to 96th St. (1, 9 continue uptown on the West Side); B, C make stops along Central Park West.

HIGHLIGHTS OF THE NEIGHBORHOOD

(*See* chapter **The Arts** *for information on* **Lincoln Center,** *the* **Miriam and Ira D. Wallach Art Gallery** *and the* **Nicholas Roerich Museum.**)

American Museum of Natural History Central Park West and 79th St. (212) 769-5100 or (212) 769-5200 to order tickets in advance *www.amnh.org.* Holden Caulfield reported in *The Catcher in the Rye* that he loved this huge, hushed museum because "everything always stayed right where it was."

But over the last several years, the Natural History Museum—the largest of its kind in the world, with about three-quarters of a million square feet of public exhibition space—has actually moved a lot of things around. There's a high-tech **IMAX theater** offering a rotating selection of features on a giant screen.

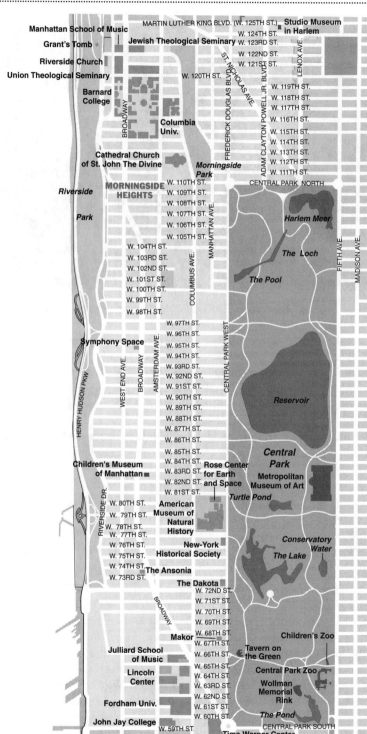

MARTIN LUTHER KING BLVD. (W. 125TH ST.)

Manhattan School of Music

Grant's Tomb

Riverside Church

Union Theological Seminary

Barnard College

Columbia Univ.

Cathedral Church of St. John The Divine

Jewish Theological Seminary

Studio Museum in Harlem

W. 124TH ST.
W. 123RD ST.
W. 122ND ST.
W. 121ST ST.
W. 120TH ST.
W. 119TH ST.
W. 118TH ST.
W. 117TH ST.
W. 116TH ST.
W. 115TH ST.
W. 114TH ST.
W. 113TH ST.
W. 112TH ST.
W. 111TH ST.

BROADWAY

ST. NICHOLAS AVE.

FREDERICK DOUGLAS BLVD.

ADAM CLAYTON POWELL JR. BLVD.

LENOX AVE.

Morningside Park

CENTRAL PARK NORTH

MORNINGSIDE HEIGHTS

Riverside

Park

W. 110TH ST.
W. 109TH ST.
W. 108TH ST.
W. 107TH ST.
W. 106TH ST.
W. 105TH ST.

Harlem Meer

The Loch

The Pool

MANHATTAN AVE.

W. 104TH ST.
W. 103RD ST.
W. 102ND ST.
W. 101ST ST.
W. 100TH ST.
W. 99TH ST.
W. 98TH ST.

COLUMBUS AVE.

W. 97TH ST.
W. 96TH ST.
W. 95TH ST.
W. 94TH ST.
W. 93RD ST.
W. 92ND ST.
W. 91ST ST.
W. 90TH ST.
W. 89TH ST.
W. 88TH ST.
W. 87TH ST.
W. 86TH ST.
W. 85TH ST.
W. 84TH ST.
W. 83RD ST.
W. 82ND ST.
W. 81ST ST.

Symphony Space

WEST END AVE.

BROADWAY

AMSTERDAM AVE.

CENTRAL PARK WEST

FIFTH AVE.

MADISON AVE.

Reservoir

Children's Museum of Manhattan

Rose Center for Earth and Space

Metropolitan Museum of Art

Central Park

Turtle Pond

RIVERSIDE DR.

HENRY HUDSON PKW

W. 80TH ST.
W. 79TH ST.
W. 78TH ST.
W. 77TH ST.
W. 76TH ST.
W. 75TH ST.
W. 74TH ST.
W. 73RD ST.

American Museum of Natural History

New-York Historical Society

The Ansonia

Conservatory Water

The Lake

The Dakota

W. 72ND ST.
W. 71ST ST.
W. 70TH ST.
W. 69TH ST.
W. 68TH ST.
W. 67TH ST.
W. 66TH ST.
W. 65TH ST.
W. 64TH ST.
W. 63RD ST.
W. 62ND ST.
W. 61ST ST.
W. 60TH ST.
W. 59TH ST.

BROADWAY

Makor

Julliard School of Music

Lincoln Center

Fordham Univ.

John Jay College

Children's Zoo

Tavern on the Green

Central Park Zoo

Wollman Memorial Rink

The Pond

CENTRAL PARK SOUTH

Time Warner Center

Upper West Side/Morningside Heights

D. Finnin/AMNH

Hall of Ocean Life, American Museum of Natural History

The world-famous **dinosaur halls** were expanded and spruced up in the late 1990's, and the fossils themselves were rearranged to conform with new anthropological research. The towering Tyrannosaurus Rex was completely reshaped into a low stalking pose with its tail in the air. The Barosaurus, probably the first thing you will see when you walk in, still towers; at five stories, it is the world's tallest free-standing dinosaur exhibit.

In 2000, the museum opened the **Rose Center for Earth and Space,** which encloses the rebuilt Hayden Planetarium, now the most technologically advanced planetarium in the world. The Rose Center includes a recreation of the birth of the universe in the Big Bang Theater, and a dazzling variety of exhibits relating to Mother Earth and outer space *(see full listing below)*.

But if you get tired of flash, the museum still has many reliable standbys to remind you of its origins. There's Akeley Hall, with its silent herds of stuffed elephants; the famous Star of India sapphire, the world's largest; and the 15.5-ton meteorite in the main Hall of the Universe.   *—Randy Kennedy*

Additional notes on the Natural History Museum: In spring 2003, the museum unveiled a $25 million renovation of its **Hall of Ocean Life.** You enter the hall, appropriately enough, from a gallery devoted to the diversity of life. There on the mezzanine level you come face-to-face with the museum's beloved 94-foot blue whale, who has been given a fresh paint job, and, like New Yorkers of a certain age, a bit of cosmetic surgery. The entire hall is enhanced by high-definition video projections and computer stations. (Want to hear a whale sing? To know how gills work? It's all there, at the touch of a computer screen.)

On the main floor, at the bottom of the staircase, is a huge television screen that continuously shows a six-minute orientation film about the Earth's oceans.

At the opposite end of the hall is a two-story diorama of a coral reef with 40 tons of real coral from the Bahamas. Surrounding the main floor are 14 restored dioramas that encompass detailed models of more than 750 sea creatures, nearly all completely new. The mezzanine has eight new dioramas, each one a porthole onto a particular marine habitat. *—John Noble Wilford*

Admission (includes entry to Rose Center for Earth and Space): $12 adults; $9 students and seniors; $7 children ages 2–12. Museum admission plus IMAX movie or special exhibition, $19 adults, $14 students and seniors, $11 children ages 2–12. Museum admission plus Space Show at Rose Center, $22 adults, $16.50 seniors and students, $13 children ages 2–12. Museum admission plus unlimited special exhibitions, Space Shows and IMAX screenings $29 adults, $22 students and seniors, $18 children ages 2–12. Advance tickets may be purchased online or at (212) 769-5200 for Space Shows and IMAX movies. **Hours:** Daily 10 A.M.–5:45 P.M.

The Ansonia 2109 Broadway (between 73rd and 74th Sts.) The thick, soundproof walls of the Ansonia have long harbored musicians. Enrico Caruso and Igor Stravinsky once lived upstairs in the Beaux-Arts apartment building, which dates from 1904, and Bette Midler launched her career singing downstairs in the Continental Baths, a gay spa that doubled as a cabaret in the 1970's. In more recent years, the building has been the site of fierce battles between the landlord and rent-regulated tenants, some of whom operate music rehearsal studios in their apartments. A confection of balconies, turrets and dormer windows, the restored 17-story facade gives its block of upper Broadway the look of a Parisian boulevard exaggerated on a New York scale.

Cathedral Church of St. John the Divine 1047 Amsterdam Ave. (212) 316-7540, or (212) 932-7347 for tour info. *www.stjohndivine.org.* The clerics at the Cathedral Church of St. John the Divine like to call it a medieval cathedral for New York City, not just in architectural style but in spirit and commitment. The cathedral is the seat of the Episcopal Diocese of New York; its bishop once said it combines all the life and struggle of the city. Peacocks strut across the bucolic 13-acre grounds. Artists in residence haunt the basement vaults, rehearsing their pieces, then perform them in the eclectic splendor of the Gothic, Romanesque and Byzantine sanctuary. The cathedral tends to New York's forgotten homeless, and holds memorial services for many of the city's most famous citizens. About the only time you might see an elephant on Amsterdam Avenue is early fall, when St. John's clergy bless animals large and small in honor of St. Francis.

Neighborhood residents have affectionately nicknamed the cathedral, with its soaring Gothic arches, two luminous rose windows and carved stone figures, St. John the Unfinished. When its cornerstone was laid in 1892, on the site of a former orphan asylum, it was envisioned as a great acropolis on a hill, the rocky schist of upper Manhattan. Indeed, it is second in size only to St. Peter's Basilica in Rome, with more floor area than Notre Dame and Chartres combined, and still growing, mainly upward. Construction ceased during the iron and steel shortages of World War II. During the civil rights struggles of the late 1960's, the Diocese hesitated to lavish money on a building in an area filled with poverty, and dedicated itself to good works instead. Work has slowly resumed.

On the vertiginous vertical tour, you can peer down from the crossway more than 100 feet above the floor—the real excitement of the cathedral for visiting schoolchildren. A guided tour through the interior helps uncover details from the whimsical (the prayer bay dedicated to sports) to the sobering (the bay dedicated to the healing arts, now dominated by a memorial to those who have suffered and died from AIDS). Among the profusion of icons, both sacred and mundane, are an ostrich egg, a symbol of meditation, donated by P.L. Travers, the author of *Mary Poppins*, and a prominently displayed pair of menorahs donated by Adolph Ochs, former publisher of *The New York Times*. The bronze lights in front were salvaged from the demolished Penn Station. The bronze doors were fabricated in Paris by Ferdinand Barbedienne, who also cast the Statue of Liberty. Emerging miraculously unscathed (except for damage to its gift shop) from a frightening fire in December 2001, St. John's is truly, as its founders hoped, a house of prayer for all nations.   —*Anemona Hartocollis*

Tours: $3; vertical tour $10 (temporarily suspended due to fire repairs). **Hours:** Mon.–Sat. 7 A.M.–6 P.M., Sun 7 A.M.–7 P.M. Tours offered Tue.–Sat. at 11 A.M., Sun at 1 P.M. Check the Web site for schedule of services.

Columbia University 116th St. and Broadway (212) 854-1754 *www.columbia.edu.* Built on the site of a former insane asylum, Columbia University's main campus represents one of the most balanced expressions of Beaux-Arts urban design in America. Chartered as King's College before the American Revolution, New York's Ivy League university moved from Madison Avenue and 49th Street to Morningside Heights at the turn of the last century. McKim, Mead & White designed a symmetrical quadrangle of Italian Renaissance-style buildings around the classical Low Library, whose monumental stone staircase has become a favorite warm-weather hangout for students. As Columbia expanded into a major research university, it overflowed its original four-block plan, creating tensions with the surrounding community. A stage for beatniks in the 1950's and student protests during the Vietnam War, Columbia has in recent years become a quieter place, both politically and culturally. Despite gentrification moving up the Upper West Side, the university's neighborhood—with its academic bookstores and antiquated coffee shops—maintains a certain detachment from the rest of the city. (*See chapter* **The Arts** *for Columbia University's* **Miriam and Ira Wallach Art Gallery.**)

The Dakota 1 W. 72nd St. (at Central Park West) Located far uptown amid largely vacant lots when it was completed in 1884, the Dakota was so named because the developer's friends told him it was as remote as the Dakota Territory. An early luxury building in an era when rich New Yorkers had only just begun to move from town houses into apartments, the Dakota came equipped with steam-pumped elevators and ceilings that soar as high as 15 feet. In addition to John Lennon, who was fatally shot here in 1980, the building has housed a flock of arts and entertainment figures, including Leonard Bernstein and Lauren Bacall, and provided the setting for *Rosemary's Baby*. With its steeply gabled roof and massive structures—features that Henry J. Hardenbergh, the architect, deployed in his later design for the Plaza Hotel—the Dakota stands like a fortress guarding the 72nd Street entrance to Central Park.

Grant's Tomb Riverside Dr. at 122nd St. (212) 666-1640 *www.nps.gov/gegr*. Everybody's heard the old joke and everybody knows that the tomb contains the remains of Ulysses S. Grant, the great Civil War general and perhaps not-so-great 18th president. But many are unaware that next to him, in a matching sarcophagus of red granite, lies his wife, Julia Dent Grant. Grant, who died in 1885, had wanted to be buried at West Point, but his wife would not have been allowed to join him there. Thus he became the only president buried in New York City, in a neoclassical granite monument overlooking the Hudson.

For decades after its dedication in 1897, the tomb was among the most celebrated buildings in the country. Time dimmed its popularity. Over the years, the memorial deteriorated into a graffiti-scarred drug hangout, until finally in the 1990's the National Park Service gave it a much deserved face-lift.

Admission is free, and visitors are few. That is good news for anyone interested in a tranquil refuge, embodying Grant's epitaph, chiseled above the entrance: "Let us have peace."   —*Clyde Haberman*

Morningside Park Morningside Ave. (at 110th St.) (212) 360-1311. Morningside Park was built in 1887 atop the cliffs just to the east of the site, now occupied by Barnard College, where the Battle of Harlem Heights was fought in 1776. (A later battle over Columbia University's plans to build a gym in the park led to the student demonstrations and takeover of the campus in 1968.) The thin 31-acre park, which lies between Harlem and the Columbia campus, includes a concourse at the top of a tall stone wall built along Morningside Drive. The promontories on the concourse offer commanding views of spirited basketball and handball games in the courts below.

New-York Historical Society 2 W. 77th St. (at Central Park West) (212) 873-3400 *www.nyhistory.org*. New York City's oldest museum in continuous operation, the society is an important institution for the study and preservation of the city's history and culture. The society's art collection includes landscape paintings by major artists from the Hudson River School, 135 Tiffany lamps and one of the largest collections of miniature portraits in the country. The building also houses a highly regarded print collection with thousands of photographs, architectural drawings and ephemera (available by appointment only) and a research library with over two million manuscripts, 10,000 maps, and hundreds of photographs, prints and other materials. From mid-November 2004 to mid-February 2005, the museum will host two special exhibits: one, called "Tunnel Visions," celebrates the 100th anniversary of the busiest subway system in the world. The second, called "History Made Here," celebrates the museum's own 200th anniversary with displays of some its most extraordinary acquisitions, including

The Rose Center for Earth and Space

Washington's camp cot from Valley Forge, the only known portrait of Peter Stuyvesant and an original copy of the Declaration of Independence. **Admission:** $10 adults; $5 students and seniors; free for children 12 and under. **Hours:** Tue.–Sun. 10 A.M.–6 P.M. Closed Mon.

Riverside Church Riverside Drive and 120th St. (Claremont Ave. and 121st St.) (212) 870-6700 *www.theriversidechurchny.org.* Built in 1930 and modeled after the cathedral in Chartres, France, this mammoth Gothic-style church has magnificent stonework and stained-glass windows. The church's nearly 400-foot tower has an observation deck affording spectacular views of the city and the Palisades across the Hudson. At $1 to ascend, it's a true bargain. Aside from vistas of the landscape, there are unique views inside of the peregrine falcons that have taken up residence, as well as a close-up look at the innards of the famous carillon, a gift of the Rockefeller family. (It has 74 bells—one weighing 20 tons—making it the world's largest.) You can hear it played every Sunday at 3 P.M. The church also sponsors a host of arts programs, including family festivals, theater, music and dance (check the Web site for a schedule of offerings).

Riverside Park Running along the Hudson River, 72nd–158th Sts. Frederick Law Olmsted designed this lovely narrow ribbon of parkway along the Hudson River. From Riverside Drive, the landscape terraces down steeply in three levels to a manmade shoreline and promenade, constructed between

1937 and 1941 by Robert Moses. At the 72nd Street entrance stands a monument to Eleanor Roosevelt, dedicated in 1996. Make your way north to the 79th Street Boat Basin, where houseboats, yachts and pleasure craft bob in the Hudson. The **Boat Basin Café** is a wonderful spot for enjoying a beer and a burger on a sunny afternoon. The park's main promenade is a wonderful stroll that takes you past sylvan lawns, luxuriant community gardens and towering elm trees, offering waterfront vistas along the way and free public tennis courts at the end of the path. Riverside Park is never quite as congested as Central Park, affording West Siders the chance to enjoy bike paths, imaginative playgrounds, dog runs, baseball and soccer fields, basketball courts, outdoor chess tables, tennis courts and skateboarding courses. Grant's Tomb is at 122nd Street and Riverside Drive *(see listing above)*.

Rose Center for Earth and Space 79th St. and Central Park West (212) 769-5100 *www.amnh.org/rose*. The $210 million Rose Center for Earth and Space opened in 2000, offering visitors a virtual journey through time, space and the mysteries of the cosmos. The 333,500-square-foot, seven-floor facility includes the new Hayden Planetarium, the Cullman Hall of the Universe and the Gottesman Hall of Planet Earth. The Hayden Planetarium contains the Space Theater and the Big Bang Theater, featuring narrated visual and audio effects simulating how the universe began. The Cullman Hall of the Universe is a 7,000-square-foot permanent exhibition hall on the bottom level of the Rose Center, divided into four zones that illustrate the processes that led to the creation of the planets, stars, galaxies and universe.

The domed **Space Theater** offers spectacular virtual rides through the universe, with the help of a supercomputer, a state-of-the-art Zeiss star projector, an advanced laser system, a gigantic database and, of course, the hemispheric Space Theater itself, a marvelous celestial playhouse. Two **Space Shows** are offered: "The Search for Life: Are We Alone?" narrated by Harrison Ford, and "Passport to the Universe," narrated by Tom Hanks.

The sky show occupies the upper half of the center's 87-foot diameter sphere; the lower half is devoted to a very brief light and sound show depicting the Big Bang. Between the upper and lower levels of the Rose Center is a spiral walkway with a splendid gallery of 220 astronomical photographs.

The spiral ramp itself is one of many devices incorporated in the Rose Center to impart a sense of scale—in particular, an appreciation of the staggering dimensions of the universe. The length of the walkway, nearly 100 yards, represents a span of about 13 billion years, at the end of which is a single hair, the thickness of which represents the duration of human history. Some of the most interesting photographs along the walkway show the results of gravitational lensing, an effect not explained until we reach a little enclosure called the Black Hole Theater on the lowest level of the center, which gives viewers the flavor of relativity theory, of the genius of Einstein and of the bizarre distortions enormous masses cause in nearby space-time.

On the first Friday evening of every month, the Rose Center hosts Starry Nights, an evening of live jazz, featuring tapas and a wine bar.

Admission: Entrance (with no Space Show) is included with admission to the American Museum of Natural History (*see listing above*), which is $12 adults; $9 students and seniors; $7 children ages 2–12. Museum admission plus Space Show, $22 adults, $16.50 seniors and students, $13 children ages 2–12. Museum admission plus unlimited special exhibitions, Space Shows and IMAX screenings $29 adults, $22 students and seniors, $18 children ages 2–12. Advance tickets may be purchased online or at (212) 769-5200 for Space Shows and IMAX movies. **Hours:** Daily 10 A.M.–5:45 P.M. Space shows run throughout the day Sun.–Thu. 10:30 A.M.–4:30 P.M., Fri 10:30 A.M.–7:30 P.M.

Recommended Neighborhood Restaurants

(*See chapter* **Restaurants** *for reviews.*)

Celeste	$25 & Under		PIZZA/ITALIAN
Gabriela's	$25 & Under		MEXICAN
Isola	$25 & Under		ITALIAN
Josie's	$25 & Under		NEW AMERICAN
Luzia's	$25 & Under		PORTUGUESE
Metsovo	$25 & Under		GREEK
Mughlai	$25 & Under		INDIAN
Turkuaz	$25 & Under		TURKISH/MIDDLE EASTERN
Calle Ocho	☆	$ $	PAN-LATIN
'Cesca	☆ ☆	$ $ $	ITALIAN
Compass	☆	$ $ $	AMERICAN
Gabriel's	☆ ☆	$ $ $	ITALIAN
Jean Georges	☆ ☆ ☆ ☆	$ $ $ $	NEW AMERICAN
Nice Matin	☆ ☆	$ $	FRENCH
Ouest	☆ ☆	$ $ $	NEW AMERICAN
Picholine	☆ ☆ ☆	$ $ $ $	MEDITERRANEAN/FRENCH
Ruby Foo's	☆ ☆	$ $	PAN-ASIAN

Harlem

The Harlem Renaissance of the 1920's brought the world the likes of Langston Hughes, Countee Cullen, Dorothy West and Zora Neale Hurston. The Harlem renaissance now under way is bringing the community the likes of the Gap, Starbucks and . . . Bill Clinton. It is an economic blooming as sure as the literary one of generations ago. And visitors will find plenty to satisfy their interest in both.

Harlem emerged in the 18th century as an upper Manhattan getaway for wealthy downtowners, who gave way to a succession of immigrants—Jews, Irish and, in the early 1900's, blacks, who turned it into the capital of black America. Its exact boundaries are disputed; geography and emotion don't always mix. But Harlem's history and legend indisputably resonate today, particularly among black Americans. In its heydey in the 1920's and 30's, jazz and blues luminaries such as Ella Fitzgerald and Duke Ellington played long into the night at places like the Savoy and Cotton Club, now long gone. Langston Hughes gave poetry readings at the Harlem YMCA, one of the early cultural centers, and 125th Street bustled with the energy of any village main street.

Eventually, with the flight of the middle class and the scourge of drugs and crime, Harlem slid into a decay from which it is only now emerging. The middle and upper classes are moving back into its elegant brownstones and newer housing, and the neighborhood once again is growing into a popular tourist destination. The decision by Mr. Clinton to locate his post-presidential offices on the 14th floor of 55 West 125th St. was seen by many in the community as an affirmation of Harlem's rebirth.

Popular new restaurants such as **Bayou, Jimmy's Uptown, the Sugar Shack** and **Amy Ruth's** draw a racially mixed clientele, joining legendary mainstays like **Charles' Southern Style Kitchen,** offering what many consider the best soul food in the city. The **Lenox Lounge,** more than a half-century old and recently renovated, offers jazz, along with more intimate settings like **St. Nick's Pub** *(see chapter* **Nightlife***)*.

All the change suits many residents just fine, but it has irked others who scoff at the rising rents and worry that gentrification will diminish Harlem's status as the capital of black America.

The most popular destination remains **125th Street,** the thriving main shopping strip. The **Apollo Theater** (212-531-5305 for the box office; *www.apollotheater.com*) is the old-time showplace where Billie Holiday, Aretha Franklin, Count Basie, Lauryn Hill and many others graced the stage—and many more aspiring stars got the "hook" for disappointing feisty audiences during the Apollo's raucous Amateur Nights (a tradition that continues to this day).

Famous places such as the Audubon Ballroom, where Malcolm X was assassinated in 1965, have disappeared. But many cultural and historic spots remain. **The Schomburg Center for Research on Black Culture, the Studio Museum in Harlem** *(see chapter* **The Arts***)* and the **National Black Theater** (212-722-3800) all have deep roots in the community and offer frequent exhibitions and shows that testify to the importance of black culture.

New development on 125th Street includes a 285,000-square-foot shopping mall called **Harlem U.S.A.,** a nine-screen cinema, Old Navy, a branch of the New York Sports Club and the **Hue-Man Experience Bookstore and Cafe,** the largest African-American-owned bookstore in the country.

The new development has not reached much into nearby East Harlem, though **El Museo del Barrio,** on Fifth Avenue at 104th Street *(see chapter* **The Arts***)*, is worth the trek for a look at the Hispanic culture that defines East Harlem.   —*Randy Archibold*

Subway: A, B, C, D, 2, 3 to 125th St.; B, C, 2, 3 to 135th St.; A, B, C, D, 3 to 145th St.

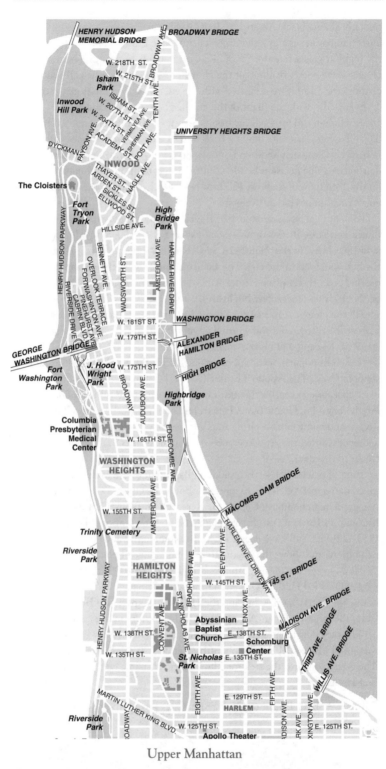

Upper Manhattan

HIGHLIGHTS OF THE NEIGHBORHOOD
(*For the* **Studio Museum in Harlem,** *see chapter* **The Arts.**)

Abyssinian Baptist Church 132 Odell Clark Pl. (W. 138th St., between Adam Clayton Powell and Malcolm X Blvds.) (212) 862-7474 *www.abyssinian.org*. The Abysinnian Baptist Church has become such a popular attraction that it has had to turn away tourists on Easter. Known for its rousing gospel choir, this 1923 Gothic church was home for many years to rousing sermons by Adam Clayton Powell, the charismatic preacher and congressman. A memorial room displays artifacts from his life. Visit during Sunday services (at 9 A.M. and 11 A.M.) if you can, and afterward head over for a soul food lunch at Sylvia's nearby. (The church asks that if you attend services, you stay for the entire one-an-a-half- to two-hour duration, and refrain from taking photos or video.)

Hamilton Grange National Memorial 287 Convent Ave. (between. 141st and 142nd Sts.) (212) 283-5154 *www.nps.gov/hagr*. Alexander Hamilton—George Washington's aide during the Revolutionary War, then a member of Congress, co-author of the Federalist Papers and first U.S. Secretary of the Treasury—commissioned architect John McComb Jr. to design a Federal-style country home on a sprawling 32-acre estate in upper Manhattan. This house was completed in 1802 and named "The Grange" after the Hamilton family's ancestral home in Scotland, but served as his home for only two years. On July 11, 1804, Hamilton was fatally wounded in a duel with his political rival Aaron Burr. Rangers offer hourly guided tours. **Admission:** Free. **Hours:** Fri.–Sun. 9 A.M.–5 P.M.

Schomburg Center for Research on Black Culture 515 Malcolm X Blvd. (at 135th St.) (212) 491-2200 *www.nypl.org* (click on "Research Libraries"). The Schomburg Center's holdings are built on the personal collection of Arturo Alfonso Schomburg, a black Puerto Rican scholar and bibliophile who died in Brooklyn in 1938. Schomburg's materials went to the New York Public Library, and over the decades, the collection has grown to include more than five million items—books, manuscripts, art objects, audio, video and even sheet music—documenting the history and culture of people of African descent throughout the world. Call ahead to make an appointment to view the art and artifacts collection.

Recommended Neighborhood Restaurants
(*See chapter* **Restaurants** *for reviews.*)

Bayou	$25 & Under	CAJUN/SOUTHERN
El Fogon	$25 & Under	SPANISH
Gumbo Cafe	$25 & Under	NEW ORLEANS
Emily's	$25 & Under	SOUTHERN
Sylvia's	$25 & Under	SOUTHERN

Washington Heights/Inwood

Dominican immigrants are only the latest arrivals in Washington Heights, an area that has been the first stop for many new Americans. In the early 1900's, the Irish poured into the area, especially to Inwood. In the period around World War II, a large contingent of German Jews—including a young Henry Kissinger—made a home in the northern section near Fort Tryon Park.

Before the surge of immigration, Washington Heights was a rural retreat where the wealthy had country estates. It was spaciousness that first attracted two major institutions: **Columbia-Presbyterian Hospital,** which opened in 1928, and **Yeshiva University,** which came in 1929. Other landmarks include **the Cloisters,** the Metropolitan Museum of Art's showcase for medieval art, which sits atop a hill in **Fort Tryon Park** as an oasis of tranquility amid a noisy city. Long gone is the Polo Grounds, the former home of the baseball and football Giants, which overlooked the Harlem River at 157th Street.

At Manhattan Island's northernmost tip, Inwood lies between the Harlem River and Inwood Hill Park, where the borough's last stands of primeval forest remain. This neighborhood's newest arrivals are young professionals seeking affordable apartments in the Art Deco apartment buildings. On the banks of the Harlem River near Broadway, another dream lives on at Baker Field, where Columbia University's football team continues its often quixotic quest for glory.

Subway: A, C, 1, 9 make stops from 168th St.–Washington Heights uptown into Inwood.

HIGHLIGHTS OF THE NEIGHBORHOOD

The Cloisters Fort Tryon Park (near 190th St.) (212) 923-3700 *www.metmuseum.org.* Set atop a hill in Fort Tryon Park, with stunning views of the Hudson River, the Cloisters houses much of the Metropolitan Museum of Art's extensive collection of medieval art. Surrounded by lovely gardens planted according to horticultural information found in medieval treatises and poetry, it's a wonderful place to escape from the bustle of the city. The complex encompasses a 12th-century chapter house, five cloisters from medieval monasteries and a Romanesque chapel (which occasionally hosts concerts). The collection features 5,000 works on art from medieval Europe, including rare illuminated manuscripts, stained glass, sculpture and the priceless series of Unicorn Tapestries, woven around 1500. The museum offers free highlights tours Tuesday through Friday at 3 P.M., Sundays at noon. There are also regular garden tours offered in the spring and fall, and concerts of medieval music held in the 12th-century Spanish chapel. **Admission:** Included in same-day admission to the Met, or $12 adults; $7 students and seniors; free for children under 12. **Hours:** Tue.–Sun. 9:30 A.M.–5:15 P.M. (closes at 4:45 P.M. Nov.–Feb.). **Directions:** A to 190th St., then a 10-min. walk along Margaret Corbin Dr. (or take the M4 bus 1 stop from the subway station to the Cloisters).

Fort Tryon Park 741 Fort Washington Ave. (at 193rd St.) (212) 360-1311. Best known as the site of the Metropolitan Museum's **Cloisters** *(see separate list-*

The George Washington Bridge

ing above), Fort Tryon Park encompasses Manhattan's highest point. For years, the park languished in a sad state, its stairways crumbling and its magnicifent vistas blocked by overgrown vines and unpruned trees. Only the old-timers, like the Jewish immigrants who had arrived from Germany and Russia in the 1930's, knew about the 10-acre English-style heather garden, with its 500 species of plants. The garden, designed by Frederick Law Olmsted Jr. and John Charles Olmsted, had once formed a grand promenade up to a stone terrace shaded by lindens. Winding stone staircases and eight miles of paths led gracefully through the 67 acres of the park and to the Cloisters at its north end.

The park, with its startling views of the Palisades, was the dream of John D. Rockefeller Jr., who bought the property in 1917. A decade later, he hired the Olmsteds to build a park there and a landscape worthy of the Cloisters, which the Metropolitan Museum of Art was going to construct out of bits and pieces of five medieval monasteries and chapels from France and Spain, backed by Rockefeller. In 1935, Rockefeller gave the entire park to New York City.

Since the 1980's, the Greenacre Foundation, founded by Rockefeller's granddaughter, has paid for pruning 3,000 trees in the park and planting 5,000 more. The city has poured about $20 million into improvements.

The gardeners' first mandate was clearing the Norway maples and the shrubs that were obscuring the river views and sightlines, or shading out other plants. After cutting 100 Norway maples, which seed themselves and grow fast, and pruning out overgrown yews to reveal pathways, the gardeners planted dogwood and Franklinia, magnolia and viburnum. Now, standing on Linden Terrace, you can see across the river to the blue-gray Palisades, and to the south, the George Washington Bridge.

There are still millions of dollars to raise for maintenance and restoration. But the payback will be deep. First, there is that staggering view, from a lofty 250 feet above the river. Then there is the history, so palpable atop the rocks. On Nov. 16, 1776, some 2,800 scrappy American soldiers held this ridge for a few bloody hours, before 14,400 British and Hessian troops took Fort Tryon Hill and occupied the upper end of Manhattan, where they stayed until the Revolutionary War ended in 1783. Margaret Corbin Circle at the south entrance to the park, where yellow violas bloom, is named after the young woman who leapt to replace her husband, John Corbin, after he was killed at his cannon by a Hessian bullet.   —*Anne Raver*

George Washington Bridge Fort Washington Ave. at 178th St. The longest suspension bridge in the world when it opened in 1931, the George Washington Bridge remains New York City's only bridge across the Hudson. The bridge's towers were supposed to be sheathed in granite; as a result of the Depression, however, the steelwork was left exposed. They are now illuminated at night. With the postwar rise in automobile traffic, a lower level was added in 1962. Le Corbusier, the French proponent of modernist architecture, called the steel-cabled structure the most beautiful bridge in the world. "It is blessed. It is the only seat of grace in the disordered city," he said. A pedestrian and bike lane is set off from traffic.

Highbridge Park overlooking the East River between Amsterdam Ave. and the Harlem River Drive in Upper Manhattan. (212) 691-9510. Highbridge Park, designed in 1888 by Samuel Parsons Jr. and Calvert Vaux, begins in a thin spit called Coogan's Bluff that rises abruptly at West 155th Street and Edgecombe Avenue. In the swamps below, abutting the Harlem River, were the Polo Grounds, once home to the baseball and football Giants (kids who didn't have the price of admission could perch on the bluff and see part of the field). The southern zone of the park, stretching roughly 20 blocks uptown to the grand old High Bridge itself, was long impassable. But in 1997 the Parks Department began the arduous work of opening a trail along the route of the buried Croton Aqueduct. Three bridges—the Washington, the Hamilton and the pedestrian High Bridge—traverse the midpoint of the park within seven blocks. Rather than being a fatal incursion, the spans with their warren of access ramps lend to this stretch of park beneath them an extra dimension of drama.

Hispanic Society of America Broadway at 155th St. (212) 926-2234 *www.hispanicsociety.org*. The Hispanic Society of America, in its atmospheric shabby-genteel Beaux-Arts setting on Audubon Terrace, is one of New York's hidden treasures. It's filled with fabulous paintings by El Greco, Goya and Velázquez, as well as fine examples of decorative arts, sculpture and textiles. There are some amazing pieces, like a breathtaking 10th-century Hispano-Mooresque ivory box; the only comparable pieces of this kind locally are a few precious examples in the Met's collection. The Society also maintains a 250,000-volume research library (open to the public with photo ID) on all aspects of history and culture in Spain, Portugal, Latin America and the Philippines, as well as an extensive collection of rare books. **Admission:** Free. **Hours:** Museum and library Tue.–Sat. 10 A.M.–4:30 P.M.; museum only Sun 1–4 P.M.

Inwood Hill Park Seaman Ave. at 207th St. (212) 304-2381. The most dramatic approach to the park is from the north, along 218th Street, a five-minute walk from the 215th Street subway station on the No. 1 line. You'll come upon a vista unlike any other in Manhattan. To the north, on your right, is the Harlem River on its final leg before joining the Hudson in the swirl of Spuyten Duyvil. The sheer cliff on the far side, threaded at its base by Metro North tracks, defines Marble Hill, its heights studded with ungainly apartment buildings. Straight ahead is a tidal lagoon (bordered by swamp grasses, it is the only accessible salt marsh in Manhattan and a magnet for water birds). Off to the left are low rolling athletic fields where soccer is the favored sport. Straight ahead, Inwood Hill itself juts into Spuyten Duyvil, which is spanned by the Henry Hudson Bridge to the Bronx with its steel gridwork. Beyond that is the low-slung Amtrak bridge, part of the shoreline route to Albany. The final piece of this tableau is the noble New Jersey Palisades, looming up a mile away across the Hudson. Before heading into the forest, stop first at the park's ecology center on the lagoon. You can pick up a map and a schedule of tours (including canoe expeditions) led by urban park rangers year round.

Morris-Jumel Mansion 65 Jumel Terrace (at 160th St. and Edgecombe Ave.) (212) 923-8008 *www.morrisjumel.org*. In the midst of an urban neighborhood scenically situated on a high bluff, a delightful enclave suddenly opens up. In its center is a columned, white, two-story house, all peaks and gables, in a verdant acre-and-a-half setting of greenery. The Georgian-Federal mansion was built in the 1760's as a summer home by Roger Morris, a Tory who left during the Revolution. George Washington made it his headquarters in 1776 as his troops were being driven from the city. During that retreat, he made the troops bite back in the Battle of Harlem Heights, in July 1776, when the British actually gave ground to the Americans. The mansion's name also recognizes a later occupant, Stephen Jumel, a wine merchant whose widow, Eliza, married Aaron Burr in the front parlor in 1833. The mansion's eight rooms are furnished in old-style elegance with 1,000 artifacts dating between 1740 and 1860 (including a fine collection of Chippendale and French and American Empire-style furniture pieces). **Admission:** $3 adults; $2 students and seniors; free for children age 12 and under. **Hours:** Wed.–Sun. 10 A.M.–4 P.M. Closed Mon.–Tue.

Trinity Cemetery Amsterdam Ave. (at W. 153rd St.) (212) 368-1600 *www.trinitywallstreet.org/cemetery.html*. Spread across a sloping hillside, Trinity Cemetery was opened in 1843 after a series of epidemics left the congrega-

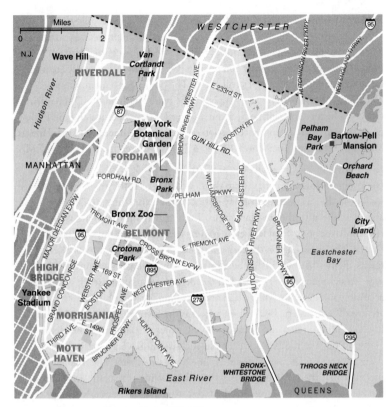

The Bronx

tion's Wall Street churchyard dangerously overcrowded. Many of New York's most prominent citizens ended up on this rocky promontory, which overlooks the Hudson River and the Palisades. As soon as you pass through the tall, wrought-iron gates on West 153rd Street, the roar of Broadway is eclipsed by the cawing of ravens. A century-old canopy of ash and oak trees keeps the grassy knolls and manicured walkways appropriately shady and peaceful. Trinity's monuments are richly varied in material, form and symbolism. Look for broken columns (died in the prime of life), sheaves of wheat (lived to a ripe old age), polished spheres and shrouded urns (symbols of the soul). There are Gothic-style marble mausoleums, towering steles of brownstone and simple slabs that conceal spacious subterranean vaults. Among those buried at Trinity are John Jacob Astor, the fur trader turned real estate tycoon, who was the wealthiest man in the United States on his death in 1848; John James Audubon, the naturalist and former owner of this farmstead; and Clement Clarke Moore, who wrote "A Visit From St. Nicholas."

Recommended Neighborhood Restaurants

El Presidente	$25 & Under	CARIBBEAN/PAN-LATIN
Republi'K	$25 & Under	PAN-LATIN

THE BOROUGHS

THE BRONX

"The Bronx is up" in more ways than one. Geographically, this is the northern-most part of the city and the only borough attached to the U.S. mainland. More important is the Bronx's rise from the ashes of the burning buildings and crime-ridden streets of the 1970's. With a sparkling cleanup of much of the Bronx River, the city's only true freshwater river, and new housing in what residents would like to call Downtown Bronx instead of the nasty South Bronx, renewed vibrancy and pride have come to the borough that was a collection of rural vil-lages in the 1890's, before being annexed into the expanding city. Throughout the early decades of the 20th century, the Bronx was mainly populated by waves of Irish and German immigrants seeking the open, green space of the borough, made accessible by the growth of the subway system. Early Bronxites could watch D.W. Griffith making movies in a local studio, and some spent their sum-mers living in tents on a rocky shoreline, where Robert Moses later hauled in sand for Orchard Beach in the 1930's.

Perhaps best known as the home of the **Bronx Zoo** and **Yankee Stadium,** the Bronx also features the green spaces of the **New York Botanical Garden, Van Cortlandt and Pelham Bay Parks,** as well as **Wave Hill** in Riverdale. **City Island** is a virtual New England village.

The Bronx is home to several colleges and universities: **Fordham University** and **Manhattan College; Bronx Community College,** once the uptown campus of NYU, with its Hall of Fame for Great Americans; and **Lehman College,** for-merly Hunter College.

Many visitors to the Bronx travel to **Woodlawn Cemetery** to view its grandiose mausoleums and especially the grave of Herman Melville (the man at the gate is happy to tell you where to find it). Those more interested in the liv-ing go to **Arthur Avenue** in the Belmont section of the borough. There they find excellent food shopping and lively Italian dining just down the street from the zoo and opposite Fordham University's Rose Hill campus.

How did the Bronx get its name? Yes, the Bronx River flows through the borough, but the name probably goes back to the early Dutch settlers of the city that was originally called New Amsterdam. The first Dutch inhabitants of the area were Dutch farmer Jonas Bronck and his family, who owned a 500-acre farm near what is now Morrisania. According to legend people would say they were going to visit "the Broncks," thereby establishing the use of the definite article in the borough's name, the only one of the five with that distinction.

A good way to explore the borough's top attractions is by taking the free **Bronx Tour Trolley,** which provides a convenient weekend link from the Ford-ham Plaza Metro-North station to the Bronx Zoo, the New York Botanical Gar-den, and Arthur Avenue at 187th Street. For a schedule and more information on the entire borough, visit **www.ilovethebronx.com** or call (718) 430-1808.

The Bronx Zoo

Sprawling over 265 acres, with paths winding through lush greenery shaded by canopies of trees, the Bronx Zoo has more than 7,000 animals of over 700 species, enough to make any skeptic marvel at nature's prolific creativity. There are the exotic: cassowaries (flightless birds capable of killing a person with their toenails); Mongolian wild horses, completely extinct in the wild; a 24-foot-long reticulated python; black-necked swans. And there are the routine but lovable: massive, placid elephants; vanilla-colored polar bears; docile zebras.

The zoo has contrived all sorts of settings to let nature do its thing, and let you watch. The "World of Darkness," for example, takes you through a darkened building so you can see how nocturnal animals behave—bats spread their wings, a gopher snake resolutely devours a mouse (conveniently delivered by a zookeeper). And some of the outdoor settings are lovely, such as the steep, grassy hill that is home to gelada baboons and nubian ibex, with their baroquely curled horns.

The zoo brings not just the wild, but the world, to the city. JungleWorld recreates four Asian habitats, including a mangrove forest stocked with bear cats, black leopards and the Asian small-clawed otter. The Bengali Express Monorail crosses the Bronx River to take you on a leisurely, photo-friendly journey though Wild Asia. There are antelopes, wild cattle with their white-stockinged feet, Asian elephants and the Indian rhinoceros (the largest land animal on earth).

One of the zoo's highlights is the Congo Gorilla Forest, a green playland for African rain-forest animals, with 11 waterfalls, 55 artificial rain-forest trees, misting machines and even jungle sounds. The animals range from tiny,

Don Hogan Charles/The New York Times

scampering colobus monkeys to massive, lolling silverbacks. Some of the gorillas are lazy, some bawdy, some familially inclined, but all are fascinating to watch.

The gorilla exhibit includes a film on their threatened habitats, which is in keeping with the larger mission of the Wildlife Conservation Society: to preserve species and habitats around the world. The conservation message is ubiquitous and effective. The diversity of species on display generates amazement—but also alarm, given the number that are on the edge of extinction.

In keeping with this theme, the Bronx Zoo added Tiger Mountain in 2003 This spectacular three-acre exhibit recreates the natural habitat of the Siberian tiger with an open viewing shelter that allows dramatic close encounters with these massive, graceful cats. These extraordinary creatures, too, are in grave peril—only 5,000 remain in the wild.

Throughout the park, of course, are ample opportunities to consume food, drink and souvenirs. A day at the zoo will not necessarily come cheap, given the extra charges for the Children's Zoo, the Bengali Express Monorail and the Congo Gorilla exhibit.

The crowds can be overwhelming as well, sometimes giving the zoo the feel of an amusement park. Be prepared, for example, to wait 45 minutes or more for Congo Gorilla Forest on a summer weekend.

But those gripes aside, it is a remarkably pleasant way to spend a day, not least because you get to see New Yorkers in nature themselves—for once, unhurried, and perhaps only mildly more aggressive than many of the animals they are contemplating. —*Amy Waldman*

Fordham Rd. and Bronx River Pkwy. (718) 367-1010 *www.bronxzoo.com.* **Admission:** $11 adults; $8 seniors and children ages 2–12. Extra fees for special exhibits: Congo Gorilla Forest, Children's Zoo, Butterfly Zone and Bengali Express Monorail $3 each; Skyfari Aerial Tramway and Zoo Shuttle $2 each (shuttle is free for seniors); camel rides $5. Pay-one-price ticket (covers six special exhibit entries or rides, excluding camel rides) $20 adults, $16 seniors and children ages 2–12; currently sold in May–Oct. only. Holiday Lights (evenings, Nov. 26–Jan. 2) $6. All-day parking $7. **Hours:** Mon.–Fri. 10 A.M.–5 P.M.; Sat.–Sun. and holidays 10 A.M.–5:30 P.M. Hours abbreviated in winter. **Services:** Baby stroller rental; wheelchairs available by reservation at (718) 220-5188. Extensive educational programs available. Check the Web site for helpful logistical tips. **Directions:** By subway, 2 to Pelham Pkwy., or 2, 5 to E. Tremont Ave./W. Farm Square. See Web site for detailed walking directions from subway station. Or take Liberty Lines' BxM11 express bus, which makes various stops on Madison Ave. and will take you directly to the zoo for $4 (no MetroCards accepted; call (718) 652-8400 or visit www.libertylines.com/express.htm for details.

HIGHLIGHTS OF THE BRONX
(*For* **Yankee Stadium,** *see chapter* **Sports & Recreation.**)

Bartow-Pell Mansion Museum 895 Shore Rd. (718) 885-1461 *www.bartow-pellmansionmuseum.org.* A 150-year-old Federal-style mansion with formal gardens, the Bartow-Pell house is all but hidden in foliage off the heavily traveled road to Orchard Beach. The neo-classical stone mansion has a magnificent Greek Revival interior complete with an elegant freestanding elliptical staircase. The 19th-century Empire decor is an example of the finest quality found in New York homes at that time. The house sits on property purchased from the Indians by Thomas Pell in 1654, in a nine-acre setting that preserves with its original surroundings. **Admission:** $2.50 adults; $1.25 seniors and students; free for children under 12. **Hours:** Wed. and Sat.–Sun. noon–4 P.M.; call in advance for tours. **Subway:** 6 subway to Pelham Bay Park (about a mile from the station).

Bronx Museum of the Arts 1040 Grand Concourse (at 165th St.) (718) 681-6000 *www.bxma.org.* This museum focuses on 20th-century and contemporary art, particularly by Bronx artists or artists related in some way to the borough. Known for its high-quality, well-curated exhibitions, it's one of the many well-kept secrets in the Bronx. The permanent collection includes a strong collection of work by artists of African, Asian and Latin-American ancestry. The museum's Performance Lab is a new alternative space for film and the performing arts. **Admission:** $5 adults; $3 seniors and students; free for children under 12. Free for everyone on Wed. **Hours:** Wed. noon–9 P.M., Thu.–Sun. noon–6 P.M. **Subway:** D, B, or 4 to 161st St.; or D to 167th St.–Grand Concourse.

City Island Just off the northeastern edge of the Bronx, City Island is a year-round virtual village of some 4,000 permanent residents, with one main drag, many boatyards and marinas, several newish condominium colonies and a serious concentration of seafood restaurants (including the ever-popular **Lobster Box,** 718-885-1952). It's a quiet enclave for much of the year, though it's bustling in summer. A mile and a half long and no more than half a mile wide, the island blends the forlorn mystery of a Hopper dreamscape with a cheerful blue-collar brawn and flashes of intriguing wealth. **Le Refuge Inn** on City Island (718-885-2478) is a charming French provincial bed-and-breakfast with an acclaimed restaurant and a series of Sunday string-quartet concerts. At the **Boat Livery,** 663 City Island Ave. (718-885-1843), you can rent a small motorboat for the day to explore City Island and nearby High Island. **Directions:** 6 train to Pelham Bay Park, then take the Bx 29 bus.

Edgar Allan Poe Cottage 2640 Grand Concourse (at Kingsbridge Rd.) (718) 881-8900. Edgar Allan Poe moved to this cottage in Kingsbridge, the Bronx, from Manhattan in 1846, hoping that the country air would help his wife recover from tuberculosis. For three years, he lived in the tiny house, where he wrote "Annabel Lee." Three period rooms—a kitchen, parlor and bedroom—are filled with furniture from the 1840's, including Poe's own rocking chair and bed plus the bed where his wife died not long after the move. At the museum you can watch a 20-minute film on Poe's life and the house's history. A small gallery houses paintings, photographs and drawings from the 1840's. **Admission:** $2. **Hours:** Sat 10 A.M.–4 P.M., Sun 1–5 P.M. Tours by appt. Wed.–Fri. Closed mid-Dec. to mid-Jan. **Subway:** C, D, 4 to Kingsbridge Rd.

Hall of Fame for Great Americans University Ave. at W. 181st St. (718) 289-5162. This landmark institution was founded in 1900 as part of the uptown campus of New York University (now Bronx Community College). The main attraction here is the 630-foot open-air Colonnade, honoring Americans who have played a significant role in the nation's history—authors, inventors, statesmen, artists, military leaders and many more. **Admission:** Free. **Hours:** Daily 10 A.M.–5 P.M. **Subway:** 4 to Burnside Ave.

New York Botanical Garden Opposite the Bronx Zoo, Bronx River Pkwy. at Fordham Rd. (718) 817-8700 *www.nybg.org*. This elegant, expansive garden was created in the 1890's, inspired by the success of the Royal Botanic Garden at Kew, England. The lush grounds feature 48 different garden and plant collections, including thousands of shrubs and trees, plus day lilies, herbs, magnolias, roses, tulips, orchids and many more. Fifty acres of virgin forest have been preserved to show New York's original landscape before any settlers arrived. The Bronx River flows through the site, next to a stone mill dating from 1840.

The garden runs hands-on discovery, craft and gardening activities for everyone on weekends. There are special events throughout the year, such as a holiday model train show and the **Everett Children's Adventure Garden,** with attractions like topiary bunnies, outdoor mazes and interactive features. In spring 2004, the garden opened a new Visitor Pavilion, with a cafe, retail shop, plant shop, ticketing center, information desk, restrooms and orientation displays.

It's worth the small extra charge to visit the spectacular **Enid A. Haupt Conservatory,** a beautiful Victorian greenhouse featuring rain forest and desert ecosystems and dazzling seasonal displays.

Admission: Grounds only, $6 adults ($5 for Bronx residents), $3 seniors, $2 students with ID, $1 children ages 2–12. Entry to grounds free all day Wed., and Sat. 10 A.M.–noon. (Separate admission to Conservatory and Children's Adventure Garden. Tram and golf cart tours available at additional fee.) Combination Ticket (including admission to grounds, plus Conservatory, Children's Adventure Garden and narrated tram tour) $13 adults, $11 seniors and students, $5 children ages 2-12. Onsite parking $5. **Hours:** Grounds and Conservatory, Apr. –Oct. Tue.–Sun 10 A.M.–6 P.M., Nov.–Mar. Tue.–Sun. 10 A.M.–5 P.M. Also open Mon. holidays. Children's Adventure Garden open same hours on weekends, more limited on weekdays. **Directions:** Metro-North train from Grand Central to Botanical Garden.

Van Cortlandt Park Broadway and W. 240th St. (at Birchhall Ave.) (718) 430-1890. Frederick Van Cortlandt's stone mansion, built in 1748 and today

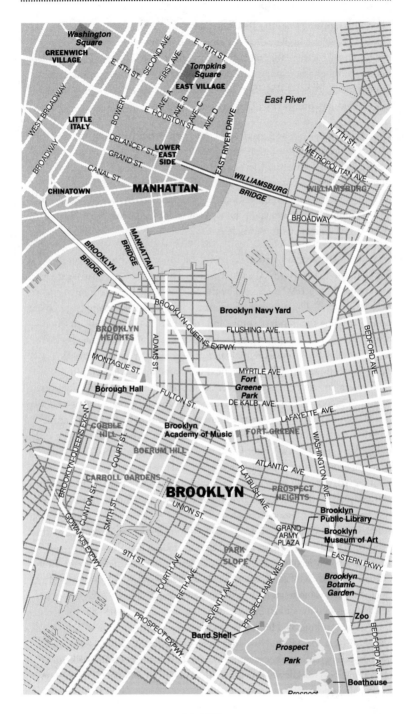

Brooklyn

the Bronx's oldest building, served as Revolutionary War headquarters for both George Washington and a British general. In the late 19th century, the Van Cortlandt family donated the house and the surrounding 1,146 acres to the city. The park's southern portion houses the **Van Cortlandt House Museum,** a lake, a golf course and playing fields for soccer, cricket, rugby, baseball and hurling. Meanwhile, the northern end of the park remains largely pastoral; along with a nationally renowned cross-country track, it features nature trails that wind through a 100-year-old hardwood forest populated by foxes, raccoons and pheasant. **Subway:** 1, 9 to 242nd St.–Van Cortlandt Park.

Wave Hill 675 W. 252nd St. (at Independence Ave., near Palisade Ave.) (718) 549-3200 *www.wavehill.org.* This was once a private estate, comprising an 1843 stone mansion (which once hosted Teddy Roosevelt, Mark Twain and Arturo Toscanini) and 28 bucolic acres overlooking the Hudson. Now a center for the arts and environmental studies, Wave Hill is a lovely place to walk along wooded paths or through carefully tended gardens and greenhouses. It's a magical setting for concerts, literary readings and art exhibitions—so lovely that it's a favorite spot for weddings. A new visitor center opened in 2004. **Admission:** $4 adults, $2 seniors and students; free for children under 6. Free in winter, and on Sat. mornings and all day Tue. in summer. **Hours:** Spring–summer Tue.–Sun. 9 A.M.–5:30 P.M. (till 9 P.M. on Wed. and in June–July). Fall–winter Tue.–Sun. 9 A.M.–4:30 P.M. Greenhouses open 10 A.M.–noon and 1–4 P.M. **Directions:** Metro-North from Grand Central to Riverdale, walk five blocks (uphill).

BROOKLYN

If you're not a native, all you might know about Brooklyn is this: The Brooklyn Bridge is at one end, Coney Island is at the other, and the Dodgers used to play ball somewhere in between. Historically, though, Brooklyn has given more to the world than Jackie Robinson and Nathan's Famous hot dogs—for one thing, it has always nourished all types of artistic voices, from Walt Whitman to Spike Lee. The borough is home to millions who are drawn to New York but find Manhattan life too hectic or too expensive.

The original town of Breuckelen was chartered by the Dutch West India Company in 1646 and incorporated into Kings County in 1683. Under British occupation during the Revolutionary War, and site of the war's largest battle, Kings County continued to grow, reaching a population of over 4,500 by 1800. By then, more than 25 percent of the county's residents were black slaves.

Brooklyn was incorporated by New York state as a village in 1816 and as a city in 1834. During the Civil War, Brooklyn found itself at the center of the abolitionist movement in America. The area was home to some of the first black landowners in America, as well as one of the first towns (Weeksville) settled by freed slaves.

At the start of the war, Brooklyn ranked as the third largest city in the U.S., and its dynamic population and proximity to New York had already sparked a major cultural renaissance. In 1855, a Brooklyn resident named Walt Whitman

The Brooklyn Academy of Music

It's the oldest performing arts center in the United States, yet the Brooklyn Academy of Music (BAM) is synonymous with the avant-garde. The neighborhood around BAM, **Fort Greene,** is a low-key, multicultural community with interesting shops and restaurants along Fulton Street.

BAM Opera House The main building houses the main stage, which is the BAM Opera House. Seating 2,109, it hosts programs like the innovative **Next Wave Festival,** which brings the best in new music, dance, opera and theater to New York each fall (festival regulars include Laurie Anderson, Philip Glass and Robert Wilson). Other annual Opera House performers include the Brooklyn Philharmonic and BAM Opera.

BAM Harvey Theater Built in 1904 as a legitimate theater and later used to show movies, the Harvey Theater (once named the Majestic) was abandoned in 1968 and lay dark until its renovation in 1987. But don't be fooled by the term "renovation": The building's shell, with exposed brick, crumbling paint, chipped friezes and exposed ducts, was deliberately left more or less intact. The theater has 900 seats and practically no obstructed views. BAM uses it to stage dance, jazz, theater and opera.

BAM Rose Cinemas Also housed in the main BAM building, the Rose Cinemas shows first-run independent and foreign films in four theaters with fine sightlines and good-size screens. One of those screens is devoted exclusively to classic American and foreign films, documentaries, retrospectives and special festivals.

BAMcafé A good place for food and drinks before and after BAM performances. The café also hosts BAMcafé Live every Thursday, Friday and Saturday night, featuring a wide range of musical and spoken-word performances (no cover, $10 food and drink minimum).

30 Lafayette Ave. (off Flatbush Ave.), Brooklyn (718) 636-4100 *www.bam.org* Tickets are available at the box office or through TicketMaster. **Subway:** 2, 3, 4, 5, M, N, Q, R, W to Pacific St./Atlantic Ave.

published *Leaves of Grass*; the next decade saw the creation of the Philharmonic Society of Brooklyn, the Brooklyn Academy of Music and the National Association of Baseball Players—the first such centralized organization in the country. In 1867, Olmsted and Vaux completed work on **Prospect Park,** which rivals Central Park in its beauty and the genius of its design and execution. **Eastern Parkway,** another of the duo's designs, opened a year later, becoming the nation's first six-lane parkway.

The second major wave of immigrants began to arrive from eastern and southern Europe around 1880; the increased labor force helped Brooklyn to become the country's fourth largest producer of manufactured goods. In 1883 the magnificent **Brooklyn Bridge** opened a vital link to Manhattan; it was soon followed by an elevated railroad and electric trolley service. Brooklynites fought hard for years to retain the city's identity and political independence, but in 1898, a close vote finally consolidated Brooklyn into Greater New York City. Brooklyn entered the 20th century as a borough of New York, with a population of over one million.

The **Williamsburg** and **Manhattan bridges** (as well as the IRT, New York's first subway line) made the Manhattan–Brooklyn commute even easier. The "Great Migration" of African-Americans to Brooklyn began around 1915, adding to the steady influx of European immigrants. By 1930, half of the borough's residents were foreign born, and a substantial percentage were African-American—but the Depression was tough on these immigrants and poor families from the rural South, and some of Brooklyn's beautiful neighborhoods turned into slums.

Lately, things are looking up. Business is growing again in the downtown Brooklyn area, especially the business district around **Borough Hall** and the **MetroTech Center.** Extensive plans have been announced for new office towers, a stunning new performing-arts public library from acclaimed Mexican architect Enrique Norten and a home for the Theater for a New Audience, to be designed by Frank Gehry and Hugh Hardy. The **Brooklyn Academy of Music** consistently draws cutting-edge artists and crowds from Manhattan. Many young artists, writers and musicians, priced out of Manhattan, have put down roots in Fort Greene, the neighborhood surrounding BAM, creating an entirely new cultural hub where new talent can develop and thrive. The **Brooklyn Bridge Park** is transforming old shipping piers into much-needed green space along the waterfront. **Williamsburg** is hipper and hotter than any gallery scene in Manhattan. And as Manhattan rents creep skyward, more young professionals are drifting across the river, bringing new life (and money) to old neighborhoods, and making areas like **Brooklyn Heights** and **Park Slope** some of the more desirable addresses in New York. Brooklyn's population of nearly 2.5 million makes it (unofficially, of course) the fourth-largest city in the United States, and it seems poised for many more changes in the century ahead.

Brooklyn Heights/Cobble Hill/ Carroll Gardens

In 1965, **Brooklyn Heights** was designated the city's first historic district, assuring protection for brick-and-brownstone row houses on streets that have been little altered since the Civil War. The area is now one of Brooklyn's most desirable (and expensive) residential areas, and remains a popular destination for architecture lovers. Its serene, leafy streets are lined with lovely brownstones and other gracious town houses. **Montague Street,** the neighborhood's main commercial drag, is lined with shops, chain stores and restaurants.

Brooklyn Heights has played host to some impressive literary figures over the years, including Walt Whitman, who wrote *Leaves of Grass* while living here. Truman Capote, Arthur Miller and W.H. Auden all lived here for a time, and Thomas Wolfe completed *You Can't Go Home Again* in a house on Montague Terrace. Today, Norman Mailer lives in one of the elegant brownstones on Columbia Heights.

One of the best reasons to visit, however, has to be the **Brooklyn Heights Promenade**. Stretching from Montague to Middagh Street, it offers striking views of the Lower Manhattan skyline and the Brooklyn Bridge. Lined by the lush gardens of picturesque town houses and offering inviting benches, the walkway draws joggers, families and—at night—romancing couples. The view of Manhattan is startling: You're far enough away to take it all in, but close enough that the buildings still loom large. If you lean over the railing a bit, you'll realize that the peaceful esplanade juts over the Brooklyn-Queens Expressway.

The best ending to a visit here is a stroll back across the **Brooklyn Bridge** (*See the section on* Lower Manhattan *earlier in this chapter*). The footpath is accessible from Cadman Plaza Park, and the trip toward Manhattan offers the best views and photo opportunities.

If you want to venture a little deeper into Brooklyn, head south to the quiet neighborhood of **Cobble Hill,** most of which is part of a New York City Historic District. In the 1930's, Thomas Wolfe lived here on Verandah Place. Jenny Jerome, the mother of Winston Churchill, was born on Amity Street in 1854. And Louis Comfort Tiffany in 1917 designed the windows, high altar and other appointments of the **Christ Episcopal Church** at 326 Clinton St., a Greek Revival structure built in 1842.

Restaurants and specialty food shops dot **Atlantic Avenue,** offering Middle Eastern delicacies, particularly from Egypt, Yemen and Morocco. The **Sahadi Importing Company** at no. 187 offers a fascinating selection of dried fruits, spices, olives and much more. Atlantic Avenue is also well known for its antiques stores.

Carroll Gardens, slightly farther south, has long had a strong Italian-American flavor that is still very much in evidence. **Court Street,** the area's commercial district, has a high density of Italian restaurants and pizzerias. The **Carroll Gardens Historic District** contains more than 160 buildings, including houses on President and Carroll Streets between Smith and Hoyt Streets, mostly brownstones erected between 1869 and 1884. **Smith Street** has a nice concentration of restaurants, cafés, bars and hip boutiques.

Subway: Brooklyn Heights: 2, 3 to Clark St. or Borough Hall; 4, 5 Borough Hall; N, R, to Court St. Cobble Hill: 2, 3, 4, 5 to Nevins St. Carroll Gardens: F to Carroll St. or Bergen St.

HIGHLIGHTS OF THE AREA

Borough Hall Court St. (at Joralemon St.) (718) 875-4047. This historic 1848 building won a Municipal Art Society award after its renovation around 1990. The plaza between Borough Hall and the nearby Supreme Court is the site of a large greenmarket on Fridays and Saturdays, and is a popular spot for rollerbladers and local office workers on their lunch breaks. Tours of the building are available on Tuesdays.

Brooklyn Historical Society 128 Pierrepont St. (between Clinton and Montague Sts.) (718) 222-4111 *www.brooklynhistory.org*. Founded in 1863 as the Long Island Historical Society, the society has long housed the world's most extensive collection of Brooklyn artifacts in its landmark building. Its holdings range from fine paintings and sculpture to an outstanding collection of ephemera on the late, lamented Brooklyn Dodgers. After a major renovation, the society's landmark building reopened in 2004 and launched a new core exhibit, "Brooklyn Works: 400 Years of Making a Living in Brooklyn," which explores the history, impact and resilience of Brooklyn's workforce. The society also offers free neighborhood guides, and a series of informative Brooklyn walking tours (usually $15 adults, $12 seniors and students, $5 children). Call ahead for admission and open hours for the museum collection; details had not yet been set at press time.

New York Transit Museum Boerum Pl. and Schermerhorn St. (718) 694-5100 *www.mta.info/mta/museum*. This small but fascinating museum, housed in an authentic old subway station, offers a glimpse into New York's past through multimedia exhibits and authentic artifacts. Some of the old turnstiles are made of wood and ask for just five cents; the subway cars include magnificent wooden carriages from the early 1900's, with big windows and narrow wicker benches. And the kids can touch and play with nearly everything—you can even sit in a motorman's seat and operate a signal tower. **Admission:** $5 adults, $3 seniors and children ages 3–17. **Hours:** Tue.–Fri. 10 A.M.–4 P.M., Sat.–Sun. noon–5 P.M. Closed Mon. and holidays.

Plymouth Church of the Pilgrims 75 Hicks St. (near Henry St.) (718) 624-4743. From the pulpit at this historic church, pastor Henry Ward Beecher, one of the 19th century's most passionate abolitionists, delivered thundering sermons denouncing the evils of slavery. (Beecher's sister, Harriet Beecher Stowe, also took up the cause as the author of *Uncle Tom's Cabin*.) The church itself was sometimes referred to as the Grand Central Terminal of the Underground Railroad. Abraham Lincoln once worshipped here. Plymouth Church features windows designed by Louis Comfort Tiffany.

Park Slope and Vicinity

At the turn of the century, Park Slope was one of the wealthiest neighborhoods in the country. But by the 1920's, mansions were being razed to make room for apartment houses, and brownstones were going out of fashion. By the end of World War II, many buildings had been carved up into low-income rooming houses. Through the 50's, middle-class families fled to the suburbs and urban decay set in. But in the early 60's, a few adventurous pioneers, recognizing a real estate bargain, arrived to renovate and restore fading brownstones and eventually reverse the area's precipitous decline.

Park Slope has been on the rise ever since; today it's known as an enclave for families and young professionals. A stroll down **Eighth Avenue** takes you past some of the finest brownstones in New York; start near Grand Army Plaza at the historic **Montauk Club** (at Eighth Ave. and Lincoln Pl.), and follow Eighth Avenue south, exploring the homes on President Street, Carroll Street and Montgomery Place.

In few other parts of Brooklyn does the past so enrich the present. The **Soldiers' and Sailors' Memorial** at **Grand Army Plaza,** a grand arch with a crowning statue (by Frederick MacMonnies) of Victory in her horse-drawn chariot, is modeled after the Arc de Triomphe. The arch is the gateway to Prospect Park, whose main entrance on the Plaza was designed by McKim, Mead and White. Gorgeous **Prospect Park** (*see section below*) on the neighborhood's eastern edge is thronged on weekends. And every Labor Day weekend, the massive **West Indian-American Day Parade** rolls along nearby Eastern Parkway, the first six-lane parkway in the world (*see section* "New York City Seasonal Events" *earlier in this chapter*).

With its handsome brownstone row houses, and thriving Seventh and Fifth Avenue shops and restaurants, Park Slope is one of the city's most vibrant neighborhoods. Its proximity to the park, the **Brooklyn Public Library,** the **Brooklyn Museum** and the **Brooklyn Botanic Garden** adds to its desirability, as does easy subway access to Manhattan. Rents and property values have been climbing ever upward, pushing many of the area's younger and less affluent residents into nearby **Prospect Heights**, a neighborhood that's beginning to blossom.

Residents invariably speak of neighborhood's sense of community. Park Slope is a kid-friendly place, where shopkeepers know their customers by name and people stop in the street to chat. The population mix is racially diverse, with a sizable lesbian and gay community.

A good way to explore the area's top attractions is the free **Heart of Brooklyn Trolley,** which operates on Saturdays, Sundays and holidays, noon to 6 P.M., throughout the year. It leaves from the Wollman Rink on the hour and makes stops throughout Prospect Park, as well as near the Brooklyn Public Library, Brooklyn Museum, Prospect Park Zoo and Brooklyn Botanic Garden. This hour-long ride is a great way to see the sights in and around the park, including historic Grand Army Plaza. A connection to the Brooklyn Children's Museum Trolley is also available. Visit *www.prospectpark.org* for more details (click on "General Info," then click "Getting Around/Trolley").

Subway: F to Seventh Ave. or to Prospect Park–15th St.; Q to Seventh Ave. or to Prospect Park; 2, 3 to Grand Army Plaza; R to Union or 9th St.

HIGHLIGHTS OF THE AREA
(For the **Brooklyn Children's Museum,** *see chapter* **New York for Children.** *See also the* **Prospect Park** *section immediately below.)*

Brooklyn Botanic Garden 1000 Washington Ave. (at Eastern Parkway) (718) 622-4433 *www.bbg.org.* In this stunningly beautiful and tranquil setting, you can forget you're anywhere near a city. The best time to visit the garden is late March through mid-May, when the cherry trees flower in all their glory.

But there's plenty more to see year-round. Wander through the famous collection of bonsai trees or steam yourself in a fern grotto in the Warm Temperate Pavilion. Admire a great reproduction of a Kyoto temple or visit the orchids in the Aquatic House.

In all, more than 12,000 kinds of plants from around the world fill the intricate, multilevel gardens and the interiors of soaring greenhouses in the Steinhardt Conservatory. And you might catch a wedding party spilling out of the glass-and-steel Palm House, the conservatory's Victorian centerpiece.

It's hard to imagine that the whole 52-acre spread was, in the late 1800's, mostly an ash dump. By the mid-1920's, the bonsai collection had already begun and the famous rose garden was being built. In the garden now, you can find a hybrid tea rose named for Audrey Hepburn and another variety called Elizabeth Taylor. In 1955, the Fragrance Garden was built, the first in the country to be designed for the vision-impaired. By the late 1970's, the garden was even granted its own patent—for developing the first yellow magnolia.

—Randy Kennedy

Admission: $5 adults; $3 students with ID and seniors (free for seniors on Fri.); free for children under 16. Free for everyone all day Tue., Sat. 10 A.M.–noon, and weekdays from mid-Nov. to mid-Mar. Art & Garden tickets, including same-day admission to the Brooklyn Museum of Art, $9.50 adults, $5 seniors and students (not available during cherry-blossom season). **Hours:** Grounds Tue.–Fri. 8 A.M.–6 P.M.; Sat.–Sun. 10 A.M.–6 P.M. (grounds close at 4:30 P.M. Oct.–Mar.). Conservatory, visitor center and gift shop Tue.–Sun. 10 A.M.–5:30 P.M. (closing at 4 P.M. Oct.–Mar.). Closed Mon. and holidays. **Subway:** Q to Prospect Park; 2, 3 to Eastern Parkway.

Brooklyn Museum 200 Eastern Parkway (at Washington Ave.) (718) 638-5000 *www.brooklynart.org*. As Brooklyn's population skyrocketed in the 19th century, the Brooklyn Museum grew from a library for apprentices into a full-fledged museum with an encyclopedic scope. Its monumental Beaux-Arts building, designed by McKim, Mead and White in 1893, is just one pavilion of a larger plan that was never completed. Having divested its science and natural history exhibits in the 1930's, the museum now concentrates on the fine arts. It is one of the largest art museums in the country. In 2004, the museum unveiled a renovation that includes a sleek glass-and-steel entrance flanked by a plaza and fountains.

The museum has an impressive track record for presenting blockbuster exhibitions (such as "Sensation," which famously drew the wrath of then-Mayor Giuliani) and smaller, highly innovative shows (on topics such as the relationship between hip-hop and fashion).

The **Egyptian art collection** is one of the finest in the world. In spring 2003, the museum christened newly designed galleries to display hundreds of additional Egyptian pieces, including elaborate cosmetic containers; alabaster, wood, ivory, faience, and gold jewelry; Dynasty XXV reliefs of the major deities; and the renowned Brooklyn Black Head of the Ptolemaic Period. Another section contains a thematic exhibition entitled "Temples, Tombs, and the Egyptian Universe." Its highlights include exquisitely decorated sarcophagi, coffins, mummy cases, a wrapped 2,600-year-old human mummy, and a portion of the Theban tomb of an important 8th-century B.C. vizier.

But the museum ranges far afield from ancient Egypt to explore a wide range of cultures—from Asia to colonial America. Highlights include a Gilbert Stuart portrait of George Washington and an array of sculptures by Rodin. There are also 28 period rooms featuring American decorative arts. In the Beaux Arts Court, a long-term installation titled "About Time: 700 Years of European Painting" organizes selections from the museum's collection of European paintings around the painters' depiction of time; featured artists include Bonnard, Cézanne, Degas, Ghirlandaio, Goya and Monet. And in the recently refurbished Hall of the Americas, another long-term exhibit, called "Living Legacies: The Arts of the Americas," includes selections from the museum's world-renowned collection of indigenous art from North, Central and South America.

In addition to its many educational programs, the museum's **First Saturday** program draws thousands of visitors on the first Saturday of each month, who come to enjoy free admission and an array of live entertainment.

Admission: $6 adults; $3 students and seniors; free for children under 12. **Hours:** Wed.–Fri. 10 A.M.–5 P.M.; Sat.–Sun. 11 A.M.–6 P.M. (open until 11 P.M. first Sat. of each month, with free admission, cash bar and live music from 5 P.M.). Closed Mon.–Tue. **Subway:** 2, 3 to Eastern Parkway/Brooklyn Museum.

Grand Army Plaza Intersection of Prospect Park West, Flatbush Ave. and Eastern Pkwy. This triumphal arch commemorates the soldiers and sailors who fought for the Union Army during the Civil War (which interrupted the construction of the park). The arch was designed by John H. Duncan, the designer of Grant's Tomb, and sculpted by Frederick William MacMonnies. Art exhibits and tours are held in the spring and fall. (Call 718-965-8999 for information on seeing the top of the arch.) Nearby Bailey Fountain is the site of the second-largest greenmarket in New York, after Union Square.

Prospect Park

As a destination in itself or as a starting point for exploring Brooklyn's artistic and cultural treasures, Prospect Park (718-965-8951, or 718-965-8999 for events information; *www.prospectpark.org*) is well worth the trip from Manhattan. This 526-acre arrowhead-shaped enclosure is considered by many to be the crowning achievement of Olmsted and Vaux, who designed Central Park a decade earlier. It's easy to combine a stroll in the park with a visit to the nearby **Brooklyn Museum of Art, Brooklyn Botanic Garden** and **Brooklyn Public Library,** or an exploration of **Park Slope,** one of Brooklyn's most beautiful neighborhoods, which lies just outside the park across Prospect Park West. (The free **Heart of Brooklyn Trolley** runs between all these sights, plus various stops in Prospect Park itself, on Saturdays, Sundays and holidays, noon to 6 P.M., throughout the year. It leaves from the Wollman Rink on the hour.)

The park itself has many formal attractions, starting with its grand main gateway: the 72-foot-tall **Memorial Arch in Grand Army Plaza** with its bronze sculptures honoring the soldiers and sailors of the Union forces in the Civil War. The park offers **Wollman Rink** for skating and **Lefferts Homestead,** a historic Dutch farmhouse with a children's museum. There's **a zoo, a carousel** and many fine examples of architecture from the late 19th and early 20th centuries, such as the whimsical **Oriental Pavilion** and neighboring formal garden. And don't miss the elegant Italian-style **boathouse** with its romantic setting along the **Lullwater,** a fingerlike extension of Prospect Lake, and its view of the graceful, arched **Lullwater Bridge,** designed by McKim, Mead & White. At the lake, people feed ducks, fish for striped bass or pedal a boat into one of the many small inlets that make this body of water feel much larger than its 60 acres.

For more information on the park, including its tennis center and skating rink, see chapter **Sports and Recreation.**

Parking: Available at Wollman Rink, Bartel-Pritchard Circle, Litchfield Villa and the Picnic House. **Subway:** 2, 3 to Grand Army Plaza; F, Q to Seventh Ave.

SITES OF INTEREST IN PROSPECT PARK

The Boathouse/Audubon Center near the Lincoln Rd. entrance (off Ocean Ave.) (718) 287-3400 *www.prospectparkaudubon.org.* A graceful 1905 Beaux-Arts structure set on the Lullwater, the Boathouse is a lovely and historic structure. It recently emerged from a major five-year renovation, reincarnated as the first urban Audubon Center in America. It offers free bird-watching tours, maps, nature trails, educational programming for all ages, interactive exhibits and electric boat rides on the Lullwater ($5 ages 13 and up, $3 for ages 3–12). It's a good place to pick up visitor information and get yourself oriented. This is also the site of the Songbird Café, offering sandwiches, salads, coffee, snacks and weekend breakfast.

Lefferts Homestead Children's Historic House Museum Flatbush Ave. and Empire Blvd. (in Prospect Park) (718) 789-2822. Peter Lefferts was an affluent farmer, a delegate to the New York State Constitutional Convention in 1788 and head of the largest slaveholding family in Kings County. One of the few surviving Dutch-American farmhouses in Brooklyn, the homestead, which couples Dutch colonial architecture with federal details, was built in 1783 to replace the earlier family home, destroyed by fire in the Battle of Long Island in 1776. The period rooms reflect daily life in the 1820's, with changing exhibitions detailing the concerns of the day, including slave emancipation and the opening of the Erie Canal. The museum has a strong educational focus, offering tours, sheep-shearing, storytelling and numerous family events. **Admission:** Free. **Hours:** Thu.–Sun. noon–6 P.M. (closes at 5 P.M. in spring and fall; open weekends only noon–4 P.M. in winter).

The Long Meadow off Prospect Park West, 15th to Union St. This 90-acre expanse of grass stretches nearly a mile down the west side of Prospect Park, and may be the most visited and familiar site in the park. Many of the park's six million annual visitors end up here at some point to play ball, fly kites or just lie on the grass. The Metropolitan Opera also performs in the meadow once each June, and the New York Philharmonic Orchestra plays one evening concert each July, complete with fireworks.

Playgrounds The Prospect Park Alliance has directed extensive playground renovations over the last decade, making the park's major play areas safer and more entertaining for kids. There are six playgrounds around the perimeter of the park, including the **Tot Spot** (at the Garfield Pl. entrance), which is designed specifically for the three-and-under set. The **Imagination Playground** (Ocean Ave. entrance) features safe, modern play equipment, as well as a water-spouting dragon and a storytelling area with an array of statues of characters from the books of Brooklyn-born author Ezra Jack Keats. **Harmony Playground** (near the bandshell at Prospect Park West between 9th and 11th Sts.) features whimsical water motifs. In addition to the playgrounds highlighted above, there are renovated playgrounds near the Lincoln Rd., 3rd St. and Vanderbilt St. park entrances.

Prospect Lake Southeast edge of the park. Swimming is prohibited in this 60-acre lake, but it hosts all kinds of other activities throughout the year. Visitors are welcome to fish on a catch-and-release basis, and each July kids 14 and under can compete in the annual Macy's Fishing Contest (same-day registration is available for individuals). **Pedal boats** are also available for rental at the Wollman Center and Rink for $12.50 per hour plus a $10 refundable deposit (718-282-7789; rentals early May–Sept. Thu.–Sun. and holidays noon–5 P.M. or till 6 P.M. July through Labor Day).

Prospect Park Band Shell 9th St. and Prospect Park West (718) 855-7882. With state-of-the-art sound and lighting systems, this amphitheater on the edge of Park Slope is one of the city's most pleasant outdoor venues for summer concerts. It's the home of the eclectic **Celebrate Brooklyn!** series, featuring world music, readings, children's shows, rock and folk music and occasional opera and classical performances. Check *www.briconline.org/celebrate* or *www.prospect-park.org* for a schedule of events.

Prospect Park Carousel Enter at Empire Blvd. and Flatbush Ave. (718) 965-6512. This is one of only 12 remaining carousels designed by renowned carver Charles Carmel. The carousel (operating Thu.–Sun. and holidays noon–6 P.M.; closes at 5 P.M. in spring and fall; closed in winter) features 51 magnificent horses and an assortment of other animals. Rides are $1.

Prospect Park Zoo 450 Flatbush Ave., Brooklyn (718) 399-7339 *www.wcs.org*. It isn't as grand and comprehensive as its counterpart in the Bronx, but this 19-acre park is still a charming small zoo, complete with critters like wallabies, prarie dogs and baboons. **Admission:** $5 adults; $1.25 seniors; $1 children ages 3–12; free for children under 3. **Hours:** Apr.–Oct. Mon.–Fri. 10 A.M.–5 P.M., Sat.–Sun. and holidays 10 A.M.–5:30 P.M. Abbreviated hours in winter. **Subway:** Q to Prospect Park.

ACTIVITIES IN PROSPECT PARK

Baseball: Permits are required to play baseball or softball on the **9th Street ball-fields** at the southwest end of the Long Meadow. Call (718) 965-8943 for permits or (718) 965-8969 for more information on playing ball in Prospect Park.

Bicycling: During periods when autos are permitted, cycling is permitted only on designated bicycle lanes; the entire park drive is available at other times.

Birding: The **Urban Park Rangers** (718-438-0100) and the **Brooklyn Bird Watchers Club** (718-875-1151) run bird-watching tours in the park. See also the listing above for the **Boathouse,** which is home to a brand-new **Audubon Center** (718-287-3400).

Festivals: Prospect Park festival information is available at (718) 965-8999 and on the sandwich boards at Park entrances. One of the largest events is the **Celebrate Brooklyn! Performing Arts Festival,** running annually from June through August at the Bandshell. Most shows carry a $3 suggested donation. Check *www.briconline.org/celebrate* or *www.prospectpark.org* for a schedule of performances; the 2004 festival featured Los Lobos, Burning Spear, the Brooklyn Philharmonic, the Mark Morris Dance Group, They Might Be Giants and an African music festival.

Horseback Riding: Prospect Park's bridle path runs from Park Circle to the end of the Long Meadow. Contact **Kensington Stables** for horse rental information (718-972-4588).

Nature Walks: Guides and maps for self-guided walking tours are available at the Prospect Park Alliance office in Litchfield Villa, at the Wollman Rink and at the Audubon Center in the Boathouse, where a number of nature trails begin.

Running: There's a 3.35-mile running lane along Park Drive and miles of pathways through wooded hills and open spaces.

Williamsburg

No great poem has been written to the Williamsburg Bridge like Hart Crane's ode to the Brooklyn Bridge, and no one has ever tried to sell the Williamsburg to an out-of-town sucker. Yet in its long life as a workhorse, the Williamsburg Bridge, which celebrated its 100th birthday in 2003, has carved out its own distinct identity. It was the Williamsburg Bridge that opened Brooklyn to the proletarian Jewish and Italian immigrants who had been crowded into the ghettoes of the Lower East Side, reshaping the face of Brooklyn.

These immigrants crossed the new bridge from their swarming tenements, moving into other tenements that might have had the small but precious advantage of a bathroom inside the apartment or a back alley instead of an air shaft. They took jobs along Williamsburg's waterfront, which was chockablock with refineries, foundries and warehouses. Yet the bridge, with its walkway to Delancey Street, allowed them to stay in touch with the relatives they left behind in Manhattan without the expense of a ferry.

The comedian Mel Brooks, born Melvin Kaminsky, grew up on Williamsburg's teeming South Third Street during the Depression. The bridge connected him to the glamorous world uptown. It was over the bridge that Mr. Brooks's Uncle Joe took him in his cab to see his first Broadway show, *Anything Goes*.

In the 1940's and 1950's, the bridge and its subway line opened Brooklyn to another set of newcomers—Puerto Ricans straight from the island or from crowded Manhattan—and in more recent years, the bridge has transported a group of aesthetic refugees, bohemian artists fleeing the day-tripper buzz of the East Village across the East River.

In serving as this gateway, the bridge created some of New York's most flavorful neighborhoods. There are the streets filled with Yiddish-speaking Hasidim branching off clamorous Lee Avenue, the awning-shaded row houses and indolent cannoli cafés in the Italian enclave to the north, the domino players and Technicolor murals of the Puerto Rican Southside, the garage-art galleries of the bohemian quarter along Bedford Avenue.

The stately Brooklyn Bridge preceded the Williamsburg by 20 years. But it was not exactly an immigrant pathway because it connected Wall Street and City Hall with the somewhat elite Brooklyn Heights. When the Williamsburg was built, it was the world's largest suspension bridge—7,308 feet long, with a main span of 1,600 feet. Built for horse and carriage, it soon carried trucks and subway trains.

Williamsburg was then largely Irish and German. The **Peter Luger Steak House** opened as a German establishment in 1887. Betty Smith sketched the neighborhood's poor Irish warren in her autobiographical novel, *A Tree Grows in Brooklyn*. Within 10 years of the bridge's opening, the neighborhood's population had doubled to 250,000, and the better-off Irish and Germans began leaving. And as many Jews moved out to Queens or the suburbs, the only Jews left in Williamsburg seemed to be Hasidim.

Melting-pot encounters, partly created by the bridge, have clearly reshaped the 128,000 people who now live in Williamsburg. They have brought conflicts, like those between the Hasidim and the Latinos over scarce housing. Old-timers are wary of the cell-phone-toting hipsters who prowl the bars and art galleries along Bedford Avenue. But the melting pot undeniably brings many pleasures.

—*Joseph Berger*

Subway: L train to Bedford Ave. or Lorimer St.; G to Metropolitan Ave.

HIGHLIGHTS OF THE NEIGHBORHOOD

*(For the **Williamsburg Bridge**, see "Lower East Side" earlier in this chapter.)*

McCarren Park Northern end of Bedford Ave. (between N. 12th St. and Leonard Ave.). The park is a spiffier spot these days after undergoing some long-overdue repairs. From spring through fall, this is a great place to take in the local scene: Older Polish couples dance to live polka music; Latino families play fierce games of soccer and volleyball and stage huge, festive barbecues; twentysomethings sunbathe or play Frisbee; and Hasidic men toss around baseballs.

Metropolitan Pool and Bathhouse 261 Bedford Ave. (718) 599-5707. This historic site was reopened in 1997 after a major renovation. The 1922 building, which includes a 30-by-75-foot public city swimming pool, a glass enclosure, two new locker rooms, a community room and a fitness area, was originally designed by Henry Bacon, architect of Washington's Lincoln Memorial.

Art in Williamsburg

In the past decade, Williamsburg has sprouted a cluster of **art galleries,** with the largest concentration on Bedford Avenue and its surrounding side streets. The art here tends to be more fresh and daring (and sometimes more raw and amateurish) than what you'd find in the more established Manhattan galleries. The art scene has drawn a hip and very young crowd to Williamsburg and created a new industrial-chic vibe. This is only a very small sampling of Williamsburg's galleries; visit *www.freewilliamsburg.com* and click on "Galleries" for a detailed alphabetical listing, complete with current exhibitions.

Aquatic Creations 99 N. 10th St. (between Wythe and Berry Aves.) (718) 302-9080. The name gives away the twist at this warehouse-style gallery: Yep, there are live mini-sharks and other fish swimming in small tanks beside the art. And they're for sale, too, right along with the cutting-edge art.

Galapagos 70 N. 6th St. (between Wythe and Kent Aves.) (718) 782-5188 *www.galapagosartspace.com*. This Williamsburg bar and arts center is hard to find but worth the hunt for its seductive front-entrance reflecting pool, expansive cathedral-like interior (brilliantly spotlit with candles on the walls) and a stark, minimalist bar ringed with tables. Ocularis is Galapagos's screening room, which seats about 100 people and offers regular Sunday films. In addition to movies and art exhibits, look for dance and theater performances in a 125-seat back room. Opens after 6 P.M. every night (to 2 A.M. on weeknights, to 4 A.M. on weekends).

Pierogi 2000 177 N. 9th St. (at Bedford Ave.) (718) 599-2144. *www.pierogi2000.com*. Joe Amrhein, one of the neighborhood's artistic pioneers, decided to promote the work of Williamsburg artists by filling a flat file with their drawing portfolios, creating a remarkably efficient and mobile way to let interested parties see the work of hundreds of artists. Mr. Amrhein mounts two ambitious solo shows highlighting neighborhood arts each month.

Roebling Hall 390 Wythe Ave. (at S. 4th St.) (718) 599-5352 *www.brooklynart.com*. Joel Beck and Christian Viveros-Fauné stage cutting-edge alternative shows at one of Williamsburg's hottest galleries.

Sideshow Gallery 319 Bedford Ave. (between S. 2nd and S. 3rd Sts.) (718) 486-8180 *www.sideshowgallery.com*. Richard Timperio, an artist who has lived in Williamsburg since 1979, founded this innovative gallery as a place where artists could share their ideas. He has been known to hang paintings on the exterior walls, and to host readings, dance performances and the Sideshow Bass Choir, a monthly collaboration of stand-up bass players. Open noon to 6 P.M. Monday to Friday.

Coney Island

A seemingly endless stretch of sand, a boardwalk offering every imaginable variety of fast food, water-squirt games, a roller-coaster that defines the term death-defying, a Ferris wheel you can see from miles away at night, carnival music, the world's best hot dog, cheap beer—no wonder Coney Island became the most famous beach in America back in 1920s and 1930s, attracting some 15 million visitors a year in its heyday.

But Coney Island has gone through some tough decades since then. For many years it was written off as a filthy, crime-ridden place. More recently, however, Coney Island has gotten a shot in the arm, as a glorious little ballpark has sparked the beginnings of an economic renewal. There are still clusters of empty storefronts along Surf Avenue and few new jobs have been generated, but hopeful signs abound and a new development corporation has been formed. Hordes of magenta-haired hipsters poured in for a recent alternative rock festival, and thousands of working-class families come from across the city to taste a little bit of that old carnival magic. For these visitors, Coney Island has slowly become what it once was: a wonderland by the sea, just a subway ride away from the stifling heat of the city, packed with whimsy that can be found nowhere else but on this oddball peninsula.

It's a fascinating journey to the far reaches of Brooklyn. In summer, families still pack the sands and the Boardwalk, and the lighthearted fun in the sun captures the essence of Coney Island's heyday. In the off-season, there's a haunting, evocative quality to the shuttered remnants of New York's most beloved beachscape. The Boardwalk stretches from the community of Brighton Beach through Coney Island to Sea Gate, a strip that has known better and worse days. At the turn of the century, the eastern end was a high-society preserve, with oceanfront luxury hotels, restaurants, theaters and a racetrack. But anti-gambling sentiment closed the track in 1910, and by 1920, all the hotels were gone. To the west, more popular attractions developed, including the great amusement parks of Dreamland, Luna Park and George C. Tilyou's Steeplechase.

The arrival of the subway in 1920 created what was known as "a poor people's paradise"; soon hundreds of thousands of working-class New Yorkers were spending weekends at the beach. Decline set in during the social dislocations of the 1960's. Changing populations and a series of fires in the flimsily built fun parks brought decaying buildings, poverty and crime. In more recent years, Russian and Ukrainian immigrants have established a thriving beachhead in the area.

For decades, Coney Island seemed a ghost of its former self, but now a whole new generation has discovered the pleasures of a Nathan's hot dog, the thrills of the **Wonder Wheel** and the performing dolphins of the **New York Aquarium.** Baseball recently returned to Brooklyn in a gorgeous little field of dreams on Surf Avenue, with a view of the beach and the Boardwalk from the grandstand. The **Cyclones** (*www.brooklyncyclones.com*), a Mets minor-league affiliate, arrived in 2001 to much enthusiasm from Brooklynites, many of whom had never recovered from the departure of the Dodgers nearly a half century ago (*see chapter* **Sports & Recreation**). Although a full-fledged Coney Island renais-

Cyclone Roller Coaster at Coney Island

sance has not entirely materialized, the opening of **Keyspan Park** promises further economic growth and an influx of new energy and hope.

After you exit the subway, head straight for Coney Island's legendary **Boardwalk,** which is the hub of all the action. If it's a nice day, bring a beach towel and relax on the sands. Otherwise, just stroll along the 2.5 miles of oceanfront, stopping for a circus sideshow, a ride on the Ferris wheel or a bite of saltwater taffy. At West 17th Street, **Steeplechase Pier** allows you to walk 1,000 feet out over the Atlantic as the waves lap beneath you. Here you can gaze out to sea, claim a bench for a picnic or watch the fishermen hook herring.

The Boardwalk also offers a nostalgic bird's-eye view of some of the most evocative remnants of Coney Island's glory days, which faded decades ago. At West 17th Street, the old 250-foot-high **Parachute Jump** looks remarkably intact. Originally a ride at the 1939–40 New York World's Fair, it was moved here in 1941. The Boardwalk is also the setting for the flamboyant **Mermaid Parade,** held annually on the first Saturday after the summer solstice (*see section* "Seasonal Events" *earlier in this chapter*).

Check out *www.coneyisland.com* for an overview of the neighborhood and its current events, and *www.brightonbeach.com* for an intriguing history of the Russian immigrant community that lives nearby.

Subway: F, N, Q, W to Coney Island—Stillwell Ave. (about an hour from Manhattan).

HIGHLIGHTS OF THE NEIGHBORHOOD

Astroland Amusement Park 1000 Surf Ave. (718) 372-0275 *www.astroland.com*. This small amusement park has been a Coney Island tradition for 40 years. It has a host of thrill rides, including a water flume, bumper cars and a tilt-a-whirl, and more. Kids will like the tamer rides scaled just to their size. But Astroland is best known as the home of the **Cyclone,** a rickety wooden dandy of a roller-coaster that's been scaring the living daylights out of its shrieking riders for decades. **Admission:** $17.99 for unlimited rides during a specified period of several hours ($21.99 with the Cyclone included), or pay per ride at $2–$5 each. Cyclone is $5, with re-rides at $4. Kiddie rides $2 each, or 10 for $17. **Hours:** Spring and Sept. weekends only, from noon till closing (which depends on crowds and weather). Mid-June to Labor Day daily noon–midnight.

B & B Carousel Surf Ave. at W. 10th St. Its painted steeds were carved around 1920 in the renowned workshop of Marcus Illions, a Polish immigrant who established the fancifully flamboyant Coney Island style of carousel horses. The beautiful Gebruder organ still cranks out classic carousel tunes while the ride is spinning. Unlike many other attractions, the carousel (with its misspelled sign) operates year-round.

Coney Island Museum 1208 Surf Ave. (at W. 12th St.) (718) 372-5159. This small museum is stocked with mementos from the great pay-one-price amusement centers, like Luna Park, Dreamland and Steeplechase, that once ruled the shore. Chief among the antic artifacts are a fun-house mirror, an original wicker Boardwalk Rolling Chair and one of the wooden Steeplechase Horses. The museum has a video loop of rare Coney Island film clips, which includes a bizarre 1904 film of an elephant being electrocuted, a stunt apparently engineered by Thomas Edison to persuade the public that the electric chair would be the most humane form of capital punishment. **Admission:** 99¢. **Hours:** Sat.–Sun. noon–sundown.

Deno's Wonder Wheel Park 1025 Boardwalk (at W. 12th St.) (718) 372-2592 *www.wonderwheel.com.* This amusement park features 25 rides (including the legendary **Wonder Wheel** Ferris wheel, and a slew of kiddie rides), plus two arcades and live entertainment. **Admission:** $18 for 5 adult rides (or 10 kiddie rides), or pay per ride ($4–$5 per ride, or $2 per kiddie ride). **Hours:** Memorial Day–Labor Day daily 11 A.M.–midnight. Apr.–May and Sept.–Oct. weekends only, noon–9 P.M.

New York Aquarium for Wildlife Conservation Surf Ave. and W. 8th St., Brooklyn (718) 265-FISH *www.nyaquarium.com.* Located on a strip of coastline between Coney Island and Brighton Beach, the aquarium is worth the long schlep from Manhattan. With more than 300 species of marine life and an impressive collection of marine mammals, it features narrated feedings, underwater viewing areas and up-close animal encounters. Check out sea lion and dolphin performances in the Aquatheater, as well as the hands-on Discovery Center and the brand-new Alien Stingers exhibit of jellyfish. **Admission:** $11 adults; $7 children ages 2–12 and seniors; children under 2 free. Children under 18 must be accompanied by an adult. Parking $7. **Hours:** Summer Mon.–Fri. 10 A.M.–6 P.M.; Sat.–Sun. and holidays 10 A.M.–7 P.M. Spring and fall, closes at

5 P.M. on weekdays, 5:30 P.M. on weekends. Winter, closes at 4:30 P.M. every day. **Subway:** F, Q to W. 8th St.; take pedestrian bridge to aquarium.

Sideshows by the Seashore Surf Ave. and W. 12th St. Step right up, folks! And leave your political correctness behind. This is a traditional 10-in-1 circus sideshow, complete with "human curiosities" like Koko the Killer Clown, The Painproof Rubber Girl and assorted other fire eaters, sword swallowers and snake charmers. The theater, which seats 99 spectators, was originally **Childs' Restaurant,** a magnificent dining palace that featured singing waiters when it opened back in 1923. (In the 1950's and 60's, it was Dave Rosen's Wonderland Circus Sideshow, which featured sideshow legends such as Jojo the Dogfaced Boy.) Performances run continuously on weekends, depending on the crowds and the weather. **Admission:** $5 adults, $3 children under 12.

Recommended Brooklyn Restaurants

Brooklyn Heights
(*See the chapter* **Restaurants in New York City** *for key to symbols.*)

Grimaldi's $$ PIZZA
19 Old Fulton St. (between Front and Water Sts.)   (718) 858-4300
This stellar pizzeria in the shadow of the Brooklyn Bridge makes classic, coal-oven New York pizza. Crusts are thin and crisp in the center, blackened and blistered around the dense and bready edges. The mozzarella is fresh, the tomato sauce is fragrant and homemade, and Sinatra croons in the background. Expect a long, long wait. **Price range:** Pies $15 and up. Cash only.

Kapadokya $25 & Under   TURKISH
142 Montague St. (near Henry St.)   (718) 875-2211
From the flowers strewn on the stairway leading to the dining room to the belly dancers, Kapadokya tries hard to make everybody feel welcome. Waiters wear traditional Turkish costumes, and the dining room is bedecked with colorful Turkish lanterns. To anyone experienced with the grilled meats, savory stews and pungent dips that are Turkish touchstones, Kapadokya will demonstrate that it does the familiar well. Cold dips are the essential starters. Entrees are cooked with care. **Price range:** Entrees $11.50–$20.

River Café   ☆☆ $$$$ NEW AMERICAN
1 Water St. (at the Brooklyn Bridge, near Old Fulton St.)   (718) 522-5200
With waterside seating, a spectacular view of downtown Manhattan, soft light-ing, heaps of flowers and live piano music, it's a contender for New York City's most romantic restaurant. Such a view might have made the food irrelevant, but this has been a seminal restaurant in the annals of New American food. The menu is excellent and innovative; brunch is a special pleasure (as is the whimsical chocolate dessert shaped like the Brooklyn Bridge). **Note:** Jackets are required for men. **Price range:** Dinner is prix fixe only: $78 for three courses, $95 for six-course tasting menu.

Cobble Hill, Boerum Hill, Carroll Gardens, Red Hook

Alma $25 & Under   MEXICAN
187 Columbia St. (near Sackett St.)   (718) 643-5400

From Alma, Manhattan appears like a stage backdrop. It's difficult to grasp how such a good restaurant could be in such an odd place, amid a strip that includes a shipyard and a live poultry market on the edge of Carroll Gardens. It's a lovely setting in summer, when you can sip a margarita on the deck and enjoy views of the Manhattan skyline. Everything on the menu is recommendable. The cooking is thoughtful and precise, with distinctive splashes of spice and brilliant sauces. **Price range:** Entrees $11–$17.

Banania Café $25 & Under   FRENCH
241 Smith St. (between Butler and Douglass Sts.)   (718) 237-9100

Banania, named for a French children's drink, has an enticing menu of reasonably priced bistro dishes with Asian and Middle Eastern touches. Calamari rings, for example, are dusted with cumin, roasted and served with carrot purée, a happy match of power and pungency. It's a simple spot with nice romantic touches like candlelit tables, copper wainscoting and wine racks. **Price range:** Entrees $12–$15. Cash only.

Chestnut $25 & Under   BISTRO
271 Smith Street (at Degraw St.), Carroll Gardens   (718) 243-0049

All the materials in this small, attractive dining room convey a sense of the natural. Without a doubt, the best dish on the menu is a rectangular pillow of pork loin stuffed with sausage and served with tangy collard greens, forceful flavors that are gutsy and satisfying. Gamy duck, with a thin layer of rich fat and skin, also aces the flavor test, and its sides of crisp rice croquettes and quince with Indian spices, tasting more of curry than fruit, are fascinating. **Price range:** Entrees, $15-$19.

Ferdinando's Focacceria $25 & Under   ITALIAN
151 Union St. (between Columbia Pl. and Hicks St.)   (718) 855-1545

They filmed *Moonstruck* on this street, and you can see why. Ferdinando's is a throwback to turn-of-the-century Brooklyn, before Ebbets Field had even been built. The menu offers old Sicilian dishes, like chickpea-flour fritters; vasteddi, a focaccia made with calf's spleen; and pasta topped with sardines canned by the owner. Closed Sun. **Price range:** Entrees $10–$13. Cash only.

Hope & Anchor $25 & Under   DINER/AMERICAN
347 Van Brunt St. (near Wolcott St.)   (718) 237-0276

Deep in Red Hook, where you can smell the salt off New York Bay, is the Hope & Anchor, a real neighborhood restaurant. It's a standard-issue diner breakfast spot—eggs served all day—and a purveyor of lunchtime sandwiches to local artists, homesteaders and layabouts. It's also an art-world dinner spot, serving luxe tuna steaks on the cheap, as well as wings and burgers. Closed Mon. **Price range:** Entrees $5–$14.

Joya $ THAI

215 Court St. (near Warren St.)   (718) 222-3484

This large room with an industrial décor manages to feel warm. That's probably because it's so often packed with a lively crowd of area residents eating cheap but above-average Thai food and drinking cocktails along to the sounds of a resident DJ. The back deck is a great option for a summer evening, though you may have to wait. **Price range:** Entrees $8–$15. Cash only.

Pacifico $25 & Under   MEXICAN

269 Pacific Street (Smith Street), Boerum Hill   (718) 935-9090

Pacifico's interior looks like a boozy, dimly lighted hangout of Frida Kahlo and friends, with a long tiled bar and murals; the menu culls inspiration from across the Mexican map. It is conducive to sharing, with platters of flavorful pork ribs glazed with smoky chipotle, and meaty chicken wings chargrilled with garlicky chimichurri. The inexpensive Taco Stand section of the menu includes succulent pulled pork carnitas, braised in Coca-Cola and cooked in a pizza oven. The guiltiest pleasure is a chicken entree, deep-fried in a cushiony beer-battered crust that is reminiscent of sweet-and-sour Chinese breading. **Price range:** Entrees, $6-$13.

Patois $25 & Under   BISTRO/FRENCH

255 Smith St. (between Douglass and Degraw Sts.)   (718) 855-1535

This small storefront restaurant offers rich, gutsy bistro fare that can range from authentically French tripe stew—a mellow, wonderful dish, if not destined for popularity—to apricot pork medallions and a nicely done roast chicken with tomato herb polenta. There's lovely garden seating in summer. Closed Mon. **Price range:** Entrees $13–$17.

Pier 116 $25 & Under   SEAFOOD

116 Smith Street (at Dean St.), Boerum Hill   (718) 260-8900

Pier 116 has a bright dining room and bar to complement its backyard beer garden, which feels like a picnic. The restaurant excels at fried seafood: its fried clams are almost perfect, with a nutlike clammy flavor, and the oysters yield a delicate crunch before practically melting in the mouth. The big surprise is the Pop-Tart ice cream sandwich, exactly the sort of trashy, inelegant inspiration that the environment requires. **Price range:** Entrees, $8-$18.

Robin des Bois (a.k.a. Sherwood Cafe) $$ BISTRO/FRENCH

195 Smith St. (between Warren and Baltic Sts.)   (718) 596-1609

Have a seat at one of the kitschy mid-century tables inside or, even better, in the absolutely delightful back garden for tasty, reasonably priced bistro fare. The atmosphere is lively, the staff is both French and friendly, and the croque monsieur is delicious. Sherwood's a great place to eat or just sip a reasonably priced glass of wine, and if you're in the mood to shop, the place doubles as an antique store with everything for sale down to the retro light fixtures. **Price range:** Entrees $8–$19.

Sam's $25 & Under   BISTRO/NEW AMERICAN
391 Henry St. (at Warren St.), Cobble Hill   (718) 625-8150
By day Sam's is a tiny coffee shop, offering simple breakfasts and sandwiches to
passing students and workers. By night it turns into a modest but winning bistro
with a small but changing menu of homey dishes; friendly, personalized service
and a bring-your-own-bottle policy. Main courses receive minimal effort at pre-
sentation but the food tastes really good: chunks of tender pork require no more
than a simple sauce of pan juices with red wine and a side of creamy mashed
potatoes, and monkfish is grilled just enough to bring out its characteristic
meaty flavor while remaining light and delicate. **Price range:** Entrees, $12-$15.

360 $25 & Under   FRENCH
360 Van Brunt St. (at Wolcott St.), Red Hook   (718) 246-0360
The menu here is small but changes nightly, with several à la carte items that
can be swapped in and out. The food is intensely seasonal, like a chilled corn
soup that captures perfectly its late-summer sweetness and yet is never one
dimensional. Perhaps best of all is a dish of tiny, feathery spaetzle, blended with
bits of braised chicken and Chinese chives. What is great are the unexpected
moments, when crepes of bananas and stewed plums go so perfectly in a chocolate sauce that you cannot help trying to sop up every last drop. **Price range:**
Entrees, $20 prix fixe, reservations required.

Tuk Tuk $25 & Under   THAI
204 Smith St. (near Butler St.)   (718) 222-5598
Tuk Tuk offers the clear, bright and balanced flavors for which Thailand is
known. While the kitchen is aiming for more authentic Thai flavors than the
usual tamed and sweetened New York versions, the narrow, minimalist dining
room, with its long brick wall, handsome hanging lights and bleached wood
floor, fits right into the Smith Street lineup of casually appealing restaurants.
Price range: Entrees $6–$16. Cash only.

Fort Greene & vicinity

Cambodian Cuisine $25 & Under   CAMBODIAN
87 S. Elliott Pl. (between Fulton St. and Lafayette Ave.)   (718) 858-3262
A great place to try the exotic flavors of Cambodia, though there's no décor to
speak of and service can be gruff. In the signature dish, chicken *ahmok,* chicken
breast is marinated in coconut milk, lemongrass, galangal and kaffir lime and
steamed until it achieves a soft, pudding-like texture. **Price range:** Entrees
$3.50–$14.95.

Ici   ☆ $$ BISTRO
246 Dekalb Ave. (at Vanderbilt Ave.), Fort Greene   (718) 789-2778
Ici is a sweet restaurant full of unpretentious pleasures. The menu is brief and
features quality ingredients like grass-fed beef, organic poultry and produce from
nearby farms. The handiwork behind some dishes is as simple as a sauté pan,

butter and a few accents and herbs. With its lovely backyard garden surrounded by a white picket fence, Ici has the intentions and soul of a neighborhood bistro, not a destination restaurant, although it turns out to be a very pleasant destination. **Price range:** Entrees $12-$17.

Junior's $$ DINER

386 Flatbush Ave. (at DeKalb Ave.)   (718) 852-5257

There's a full menu of meat, fish and pan-ethnic dishes, but the real house specials are the superb cheese blintzes (minus strawberry sauce), hefty egg dishes, corned beef or tongue sandwiches—and the gloriously creamy but firm cheesecake that made the place world-famous. **Price range:** Entrees $6–$10.

Locanda Vini & Olii $25 & Under   ITALIAN

129 Gates Ave. (between Cambridge Pl. and Grand Ave.)   (718) 622-9202

This mom-and-pop trattoria was a pharmacy for 130 years. The woodwork has been lovingly restored, and many old features have been left intact. But Locanda's menu is full of surprising dishes. Superb choices abound among the pastas, especially the *maltagliati*, fat strands of carrot-colored pasta in a light ricotta sauce with soft fava beans, diced prosciutto and plenty of sage. Closed Mon. **Price range:** Entrees $6.75–$18.50.

Park Slope & Prospect Heights

Al di la $25 & Under   ITALIAN

248 Fifth Ave (at Carroll St.)   (718) 783-4555

The food at Al di la is soulful and gutsy, with profound flavors. This neighborhood restaurant serves on bare wooden tables, but the chef coaxes deep flavors out of simple dishes. All the pastas and risottos are wonderful, and the wine list is full of hard-to-find Italian treasures. The wait can be long on weekends, and no reservations are accepted. But the owners have recently opened a wine bar around the corner to help pass the time. **Price range:** Entrees $9–$17.

Biscuit $25 & Under   SOUTHERN/BARBECUE

367 Flatbush Ave. (near Sterling Pl.)   (718) 398-2227

Biscuit, a no-nonsense barbecue storefront, serves fried chicken, ribs and pulled-meat sandwiches to a mostly takeout crowd. There's the scent of smoke and grease in the air, squeeze-bottles of hot sauce, plastic utensils, and a few tables. The double-fried chicken is a golden, shining mess of a thing, with the soft meat falling off the bone. **Price range:** Entrees $6–13.

Bistro St. Mark's $25 & Under   BISTRO

76 St. Mark's Ave. (between Flatbush and Sixth Aves.)   (718) 857-8600

Bistro St. Mark's blends so inconspicuously with its surroundings that you might walk by. But a look at the menu provokes a double take, because this is no simple bistro fare. Try the glistening mackerel tartar topped with a luscious smidgen of caviar and dressed in capers and a bracing sauce gribiche, or the moist and delicious skate wing, dusted with ground walnuts. **Price range:** Entrees $14–$19.

Blue Ribbon $$ NEW AMERICAN
280 Fifth Ave. (at First St.)   (718) 840-0404
The Brooklyn outpost of the Blue Ribbon empire feels like many things at once.
It's part saloon, part oyster bar, part bistro and part diner. The extensive menu
hops from raw bar and clam stew to hummus and hamburgers. This is home
cooking, no matter where home happens to be. The staff is exceptional, and the
bar is friendly and comfortable, making this a great place to stop in for a drink.
Price range: Entrees $9–$25.

Blue Ribbon Sushi   ☆ $$ JAPANESE
278 Fifth Ave. (near 1st St.)   (718) 840-0408
Blue Ribbon Sushi brings a hip, downtown sensibility from Manhattan but
tones it down and loosens it up for local consumption. The dining room, with
its beamed ceilings and dark wooden window slats, is visually soothing. The
menu is extensive and varied, supplemented by a daily list of specials. One
could live happily on the specials and the sushi. **Price range:** Sushi and sashimi
$2.50–$5 a piece; sushi rolls $3.50–$16.75; entrees $14.50–$27.50.

Coco Roco $25 & Under   LATIN AMERICAN
392 Fifth Ave. (near 6th St.)   (718) 965-3376
This bright, pleasant restaurant offers some of the best Peruvian food in New
York. The menu ranges from tender, delicious ceviches from Peru's coast to
Andean dishes that have been enjoyed since the days of the Incan empire.
Roast chicken is excellent, and desserts like rice pudding and lucuma ice cream,
made with a Peruvian fruit, are wonderful. **Price range:** Entrees $8.95–$16.95.

Cocotte $25 & Under   FRENCH/BISTRO
337 Fifth Ave. (at 4th St.)   (718) 832-6848
At Cocotte you'll find buffed brick walls and rough-hewn artificial beams; dark
wood is everywhere. Ingredients run to foie gras, lobster, peekytoe crab meat
and New Zealand rib-eye prepared in ways that are regionally French or at any
rate French-ish. There is great value to be found in a plate of delicious oven-
roasted chicken served with smoky garlic mashed potatoes and vegetables
cooked in the juice of the bird. **Price range:** Entrees $13–$21.

Kombit $25 & Under   HAITIAN
279 Flatbush Ave. (at Prospect Pl.), Prospect Heights   (718) 399-2000
This sophisticated alternative to casual Haitian joints has the look of upscale
dining but the soul of a family hangout. The food is homey and affordable, and
those new to Haitian food could not ask for a better introduction. Kombit's
kitchen coaxes flavor out of root vegetables, perfumes dishes with whiffs of nutmeg and clove and excels in fried seafood, which comes with the sinus-clearing
piklis. Escovitch (the Caribbean version of escabeche)—an entire fish, fried
crisp and drizzled with spicy vinegar—yields juicy pieces of forcefully flavored
meat beneath the skin. **Price range:** Entrees, $7-$16.

Tom's Restaurant $ DINER

782 Washington Ave. (at Sterling Pl.) (718) 636-9738

Around the corner from the Brooklyn Museum is Tom's, a 70-year-old Brooklyn institution offering terrific diner fare at ludicrously low prices. With a classic diner menu (they still serve cherry lime rickeys) and the warmest atmosphere (and kitschiest décor) in town, Tom's alone is worth a trip to Prospect Heights. Closes daily at 4 P.M. Closed Sun. **Price range:** Entrees $5 and up.

Williamsburg

Diner $25 & Under DINER

85 Broadway (at Berry St.) (718) 486-3077

Diner brings the diner idea up to date, offering the sort of everyday food that appeals to the local artsy crowd. The basics are fine, and other dishes can be superb, like skirt steak, perfectly cooked whole trout, black bean soup and eggs scrambled with grilled trout. The atmosphere is bustling and funky. **Price range:** Entrees $6.50–$15.

DuMont $25 & Under NEW AMERICAN

432 Union Ave. (near Metropolitan Ave.) (718) 486-7717

DuMont, just east of the grimy shadows cast by the Brooklyn-Queens Expressway, is a warm and pleasant refuge for young couples, old neighborhood hands, even the occasional visitor. It serves a simple menu of six items, accompanied by daily chalkboard specials. For entrees, there is no sense in avoiding that fragrant "yardbird" chicken, served in its crackling gold skin, with succulent meat tinctured with garlic and olive oil. Smart money goes with the buttery burger. **Price range:** Entrees $8.25–$18.

Khao Sarn $25 & Under THAI

311 Bedford Ave. (at S. 2nd St.) (718) 963-1238

Khao Sarn is a sweet and simple place. Judging by its plywood benches, strewn with soft pillows, the rough-hewn counter and the paper menus that double as takeout flyers. It's a low-budget operation and that is part of its charm. The food is low-key, spicy but not fiery, delicately balanced between hot, sour, salty and sweet, rather than overtly assertive. Soups are superb, especially the tom yum, spicy, full of shrimp and gloriously sour yet fresh. Curries are likewise deftly prepared. Price range: Entrees $5.50–$12.95. Cash only.

Peter Luger ☆☆☆ $ $ $ $ STEAKHOUSE

178 Broadway (at Driggs Ave.) (718) 387-7400

Peter Luger serves no lobsters, takes no major credit cards, lacks a great wine list and looks like a simple beer hall. Service, though professional and often humorous, can sometimes be brusque. So why is it packed night and day, seven days a week? Simple: Peter Luger has the best steaks in New York City. The family that runs the restaurant buys fresh shortloins and dry-ages them on the premises. An occasional diner will choose the thick and powerfully delicious lamb chops, or the nicely done salmon. And even side dishes have their moments. But the steak's the thing here, and they serve just one cut: an enormous porterhouse charred to perfection over intense heat. **Price range:** Avg. price for three courses $60. Cash only.

Plan Eat Thailand   **$25 & Under**   THAI
133 N. 7th St. (between Bedford and Berry Sts.)   (718) 599-5758
This unusual, much-applauded Thai restaurant has its ups and downs, but more often than not, it comes through with just-fine sushi and spicy, meticulously prepared Thai dishes like ground-pork salad, sautéed bean curd and striped bass with crunchy greens. Huge crowds pack into the post-industrial space, partying with two bars and a DJ. **Price range:** Entrees $4.75–$12.95. Cash only.

Relish   **$25 & Under**   NEW AMERICAN/DINER
225 Wythe Ave. (at N. 3rd St.)   (718) 963-4546
Relish is a sleek diner of gleaming, embossed stainless steel. The chef is clearly at home in the modern vernacular, and his menu is rarely pretentious and often winning. You might raise an eyebrow at ordering foie gras in a diner, but this version is quite good. Among the main courses, juicy, flavorful chicken and fresh waffles are served with a mound of garlic-imbued kale. **Price range:** Entrees $11–$17.

Coney Island

Gargiulo's   **$$$**   ITALIAN
2911 W. 15th St. (between Surf and Mermaid Aves.)   (718) 266-4891
In business since 1907 and at this location since 1928, Gargiulo's is a longtime favorite, especially for subtle, freshly prepared Neapolitan specialties. You won't go wrong with roasted peppers, fried calamari with a delicate tomato sauce dip, baked clams, mussels in tomato broth, all of the southern pastas and lobster oreganato (here called *racanati*). **Price range:** Entrees $8.50–$24.

Nathan's Famous   **$**   FAST FOOD
1310 Surf Ave. (between Stillwell Ave. and W. 16th St.)   (718) 946-2202
Famous indeed is this 1916 original, opened to compete with the long-gone Feltman's, where Charles Feltman, a German immigrant, is believed to have invented the hot dog by slipping a frankfurter into a long, heated roll. One of his waiters, Nathan Handwerker, spun off his own version, and the rest is hot-dog history. It is said that these juicy all-beef franks are still made according to the meat and spice recipes developed by Nathan and his wife, Ida.

Totonno Pizzeria   **$$**   PIZZA
1524 Neptune Ave. (between W. 15th and W. 16th Sts.)   (718) 372-8606.
Just three blocks off the Boardwalk, in the heart of what's left of Coney Island's Little Italy, this is a highly touted 74-year-old pizzeria, more interesting for its history than for its pizzas, which can be fine or fair.

Brooklyn Nightlife

Brooklyn Heights, Cobble Hill, Boerum Hill & Carroll Gardens

Boat 175 Smith St (between Warren and Wyckoff Sts.) (718) 254-0607. This neighborhood joint has a friendly, attentive staff and a laid-back clientele. There's plenty of seating, with cafe-style tables in front, a long wooden bar and the lounge at the rear. Boat may just have the hippest jukebox in the area.

Brooklyn Inn 138 Bergen St. (at Hoyt St.) (718) 625-9741. Believed to have opened in 1868, the Brooklyn Inn is a regal, historic bar where the residents of Boerum Hill still gather over pints of beer. There's no sign out front, adding to the bar's mystique. The high ceilings, woodwork and stained-glass panels are impressive.

Gowanus Yacht Club 323 Smith St. (at President St.) No phone. The tongue-in-cheek name lends a false air of formality this utterly laid-back spot. The beer garden's décor was clearly a result of two-stop shopping — that which couldn't be found at a thrift store was supplemented with plywood from Home Depot. Cans of Pabst Blue Ribbon are $2. It's the ultimate local's hangout.

Last Exit 136 Atlantic Ave. (between Henry and Clinton Sts.) (718) 222-9198. With its brick walls, red track-lighting, vintage couches, art on the walls and a full house of young, laid-back hipster types, you might think you're in the East Village. But the lack of attitude will tell you otherwise.

Pete's Waterfront Ale House 155 Atlantic Ave. (between Clinton and Henry Sts.) (718) 522-3794. Pete's is a classic, amiable neighborhood bar. Neither too divey nor too formal, it's all about decent beer in a nice, well-ventilated space that offers a kid- and dog-friendly environment.

Quench 282 Smith St. (at Sackett St.) (718) 875-1500. Behind its sleek, frosted-glass exterior, Quench—a highlight on the Smith Street scene—exudes an air of unpretentious sophistication. Illuminated orbs hang from the ceiling, while the rich wood floor and bar give the place a relaxed elegance.

Vegas 135 Smith St. (at Dean St.) (718) 875-8308. A 2003 addition to the Smith Street strip, Vegas offers a pool table, a good jukebox, and a DJ on Friday nights in a spacious, comfortable room with high tin ceilings and couches in the back. Friendly bartenders host a mixed crowd.

Fort Greene

Frank's Lounge 660 Fulton St. (at S. Elliott Pl.). (718) 625-9339. This old-school lounge is a Fort Greene gem. With Christmas lights, red vinyl seats and three-inch stucco spikes hanging from the ceiling over the bar, Frank's is a kitsch-lover's dream. Check local listings for DJs and other events both in the lounge and in the loft upstairs.

Park Slope & Prospect Heights

(See also section "Gay & Lesbian" in chapter **Nightlife***. For* **South Paw** *see "Popular Music Venues" in chapter* **Nightlife***.)*

Freddy's 485 Dean St. (at Sixth Ave.) (718) 622-7035. With a neighborhood feel, cheap drinks and backroom pool table, Freddy's is the ultimate dive. Everyone is welcome here; the crowd is a mix of older regulars, younger locals and everything in between. Look for occasional live music.

The Gate 321 Fifth Ave. (at 3rd St.) (718) 768-4329. The Gate is a textbook example of low-key charm, from the attractive, distressed wood benches and tables to the amiable Irish bartender. There are dozens of microbrews to sample, along with a nice selection of single-malt scotches.

Great Lakes 284 Fifth Ave. (at 1st St.) (718) 499-3710. On a busy Friday night, Great Lakes seems to have been transplanted straight from Manhattan. It's dimly lit and filled with hipsters listening to the mostly indie rock jukebox. Also check out **Buttermilk** (577 Fifth Ave.), Great Lakes' sister bar in the south Slope.

Loki 304 Fifth Ave. (at 2nd St.) (718) 965-9600. Dark and cavernous, with something for everyone, Loki's front room is dominated by a long bar lined with candles. The middle space is its rumpus room, with a pool table, jukebox and a dart board. Tucked behind a cascade of heavy, red-velvet curtains, is a back room filled with a lavish, haphazard assortment of plush couches. And finally, there's a pleasant garden in the back in which to enjoy a drink in warmer months.

O'Connor's 39 Fifth Ave. (between Bergen and Dean Sts.) (718) 783-9721. Although O'Connor's might look scary from the outside, it's actually a delightful neighborhood bar where a mix of Park Slope residents socializes with ease. A second-generation Irish bar that was a speakeasy during Prohibition, O'Connor's is beer- and smoke-worn, with rickety old wooden booths.

Williamsburg

(For **Northsix, Luxx** *and* **Warsaw***, see "Popular Music Venues" in chapter* **Nightlife***. For* **Galapagos***, see "Art in Williamsburg" earlier in this chapter.)*

The Abbey 536 Driggs Ave. (between N. 7th and N. 8th Sts.) (718) 599-4400. Take refuge in the monastic intimacy of the Abbey. Exposed brick and a red felt pool table exude warmth, while torch-like wall candles dripping big blobs of wax enhance the medieval feel. Within, talkative, dressed-down twenty-somethings cluster in booths, perch on stools, and circle the pinball machine.

Enid's 560 Manhattan Ave. (at Driggs Ave.) (718) 349-3859. This spot has struck the perfect formula for hipster cachet. Once a raw loft space, Enid's has been transformed into a comfortable SoHo-style living room, complete with amber lighting and just the right hints of a suburban rec room (including plastic-covered couches and the "Revenge from Mars" pinball machine).

Iona 180 Grand St. (between Bedford and Driggs Aves.) (718) 384-5008. Housed in a mid-19th-century Williamsburg building, Iona has all the hallmarks of a classic Irish pub: a worn mahogany bar, creaking floors, plank tables, and soft lighting. This lived-in ambiance has made it a favorite for young locals.

Mug's Ale House 125 Bedford Ave. (between N. 10th and N. 11th Sts.) (718) 384-8494. The name of this traditional bar and grill derives from the beer steins strung along the top of wall—they range from a simple glass to a monstrous, elaborate German tankard. Though it has a full bar, Mug's is, of course, all about beer, with over 20 varieties on tap for $3 to $5 a pint.

Pete's Candy Store 709 Lorimer St. (between Frost and Richardson Sts.) (718) 302-3770. As its name suggests, Pete's Candy Store is full of treats. The small, comfortable space is at once eclectic and traditional, a cross between a hip bar and a genuine sweets shop. Its appeal is in the details: tables covered in Japanese newspaper, a menu of various "toasted sandwiches," plastic chickens roosting in a bale of hay in the storefront window.

Sweet Water Tavern 105 N. 6th St. (between Berry and Wythe Sts.) (718) 963-0608. The steamed-up windows on the facade of this longtime Williamsburg joint seem to advertise a wanton world behind the glass. People hang out at the bar, mill around the pool table or crowd into the small back room, where you'll find a jukebox heavy on punk and metal tunes, a pinball machine and a wall full of playfully obnoxious graffiti.

Teddy's 96 Berry St. (at N. 8th St.) (718) 384-9787. Teddy's is a homey tavern, where mouthwatering pub fare, drinks and good spirits are served up nightly. The ornate, dark wood furnishings don't just look old: They once inhabited a brewery that opened this space in the 1890's. Performers appear every other Thursday; on Saturday nights, DJ's are featured.

Union Pool 484 Union Ave. (at Meeker Ave.) (718) 609-0484. This joint — a former pool-supply store, hence the name — is a mere two stops on the L from Manhattan, and feels like it. The crowd is distinctly Williamsburg, with a smattering of rock-a-billy types rubbing elbows with working stiffs and scruffy artists, while the surroundings are classy and comfortable. An attractive finishing touch is the bar's retro refrigerator, which displays a wide selection of chilled bottled beers and picture-perfect whole limes, lemons and oranges.

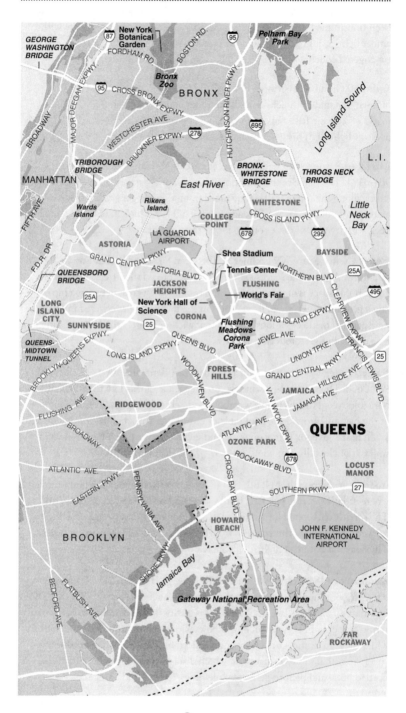

Queens

QUEENS

There's more to Queens than two airports and Archie Bunker. Ethnically diverse and mostly residential, it is the second most populous borough (after Brooklyn), with over 2 million residents. But it is far and away the largest in terms of geography, occupying one-third of the city's total area.

Its neighborhoods are still identified by the original names they bore as villages before being merged into New York City in 1898—Flushing, Jamaica, Astoria (named for John Jacob Astor), Little Neck (where the clams got their name), the Rockaways (with their gorgeous Atlantic Ocean beaches) and the upper-class enclaves of Forest Hills and Douglaston. Industry is concentrated in Long Island City, which faces Manhattan across the East River, and in nearby neighborhoods such as Steinway (where William Steinway once made pianos and his heirs still do) and Astoria (where Gloria Swanson, Rudolph Valentino and the Marx Brothers made movies in the Kaufman Astoria studios, still the largest film-and-TV studios in the East).

Queens was mostly farmland until the Queensboro Bridge linked it to Manhattan in 1909. Today the borough is heavily populated by first- and second-generation immigrants. There are more than 100,000 Chinese and Koreans in Flushing. An Indian community thrives in Jackson Heights. There's a heavy concentration of Greeks in Astoria, Irish in Sunnyside and Latinos in Elmhurst. To see for yourself, take "the international express"—the No. 7 subway line from Times Square (once famously derided for the diversity of its ridership by noted social critic and redneck relief pitcher John Rocker). A 15- to 30-minute ride from Midtown Manhattan will deposit you at Queens landmarks like Shea Stadium, the U.S. National Tennis Center and the New York Hall of Science.

Astoria/Long Island City

Although Astoria has long been known as a Greek neighborhood, the area is home to large numbers of Italian, Brazilian, Indian and Korean residents. You can get a taste of its incredible ethnic diversity by spending a sunny afternoon visiting an authentic beer garden. The **Bohemian Hall and Beer Garden,** at 29-19 24th Ave. (718-274-4925; *www.bohemianhall.com*), was built in 1910, when hundreds of beer gardens dotted the city, serving immigrant Czechs and Slovaks. The beer is plentiful and the food—goulash, kielbasa, bread dumplings—is just right for the setting.

Once written off as just a wind-swept industrial district along the East River, perhaps worth visiting for its great Greek diners, Astoria and Long Island city are now becoming known as an exciting destination for art. Long Island City really hit the big time when MoMA temporarily relocated here while its Midtown location underwent a major renovation. MoMA has now bid farewell to Queens and returned to Manhattan, but its impact lives on. The neighborhood's artistic reputation continues to grow, with many artists flocking here to work in affordable studio space.

HIGHLIGHTS OF THE AREA

American Museum of the Moving Image 35th Ave. at 36th St., Astoria
(718) 784-0077 *www.ammi.org*. Before Hollywood drew much of the film industry west, Long Island City was the heart of American film production. Now,
appropriately, it is the location of this museum devoted to the art, history, technology and social impact of film and television. The exhibits here skillfully
demonstrate the science of moving images with demonstrations of film editing,
animation, special effects and other processes. There's also a fascinating collection of memorabilia and sets from familiar movies and television shows. The
museum also offers screenings of avant-garde films. **Admission:** $10 adults;
$7.50 students and seniors; $5 children ages 5–18; free for children under 5.
Hours: Wed.–Thu. 11 A.M.–5 P.M., Fri. 11 A.M.–7:30 P.M., Sat.–Sun. 11
A.M.–6 P.M. Screenings Fri. at 7:30 P.M., Sat.–Sun. afternoons and evenings.
Check the Web site for the latest schedule. **Subway:** R, V (or G on weekends)
to Steinway St.

Fisher Landau Center for Art 38-27 30th St., Long Island City (718) 937-
0727 *www.flcart.org*. Ask anyone in Queens where to find it, and more than
likely you'll draw a blank stare. Yet it houses more than 1,000 paintings in an
elegantly reworked parachute-harness factory (designed by Max Gordon, architect of the ultracool Saatchi Gallery in London). This once-private preserve
was open by appointment only until it established regular public hours in 2003.
It focuses on works by artists from the 1960's to now, among them Jasper Johns,
Ed Ruscha, Robert Rauchenberg, Kiki Smith, Ellsworth Kelly, Susan Rothen-
berg, Cy Twombly and Andy Warhol. **Admission:** Free. **Hours:** Thu.–Mon.
noon–5 P.M. Closed Tue.–Wed. **Subway:** N (or W on weekends) to 39th
Ave./Beebe.

Gantry Plaza State Park 49th Ave. on the East River (718) 786-6385. With
the Manhattan skyline as a backdrop and gorgeous light bouncing off the
river, Gantry Plaza's site itself is magnificent. The park takes its name from
two giant, hulking structures of blackened iron on the site, which used to lift
freight trains onto river barges. The gantries are as powerful as the triumphal
arches and classical monuments built by the City Beautiful Movement a century ago. So is the brick power station, with its quartet of de Chirico stacks,
that looms nearby. Visitors are greeted by a circular area that encloses a fog
fountain, a shallow cauldron of seething mist that cools the air in summer.
Beyond is a large, hemispherical plaza for performances.

The plaza connects to two of four piers that project into the river. Each is
different in length, shape and furnishings. One has a circular lunch bar, with
stools and awning. Another, the Star Gazing Pier, is outfitted with overscaled
wooden chaises. On the Fishing Pier, there's a large, free-form table complete
with running water, for dressing the catch of the day. But the best thing about
the piers is the views they afford of each other and the people using them. Or
you can proceed along one of the paths that lead away from the plaza's southern
edge. The widest path, paved with stone, defines the water's edge in a series of

graceful, serpentine arcs. A second path, lined with gravel, takes you on an inland ramble, through vegetation and stone blocks clustered in crystalline formations. The overall effect is of a Cubist rock garden. **Subway:** 7 to Vernon Blvd.

—Herbert Muschamp

Isamu Noguchi Garden Museum 32–37 Vernon Blvd. (at 33rd Rd.), Long Island City (718) 204-7088 *www.noguchi.org*. It's not immediately apparent that the Noguchi Museum has just emerged from a two-and-a-half-year, $13.5 million renovation. The floors are distressed concrete; the original wood ceilings are intact; and the tranquil sculpture garden is shaded by a mature Katsura tree.

The museum's spirit is a reflection of Isamu Noguchi (1904–88), the Japanese-American sculptor who melded Modernism with Japanese aesthetics. Although he is perhaps best known for what he called his Akari light sculptures (hanging lamps), his work encompassed many disciplines: he designed sets for the choreographers Martha Graham, Merce Cunningham and George Balanchine; he created public sculptures, sculpture parks and sculpture gardens both here and abroad; and he designed furniture for Knoll and the Herman Miller Company.

Visitors can go into the galleries, where all of Noguchi's abstract sculptures are where he had originally placed them, or into the sculpture garden. In keeping with Japanese tradition, the museum has no coat room, the signs are discreet, and no guards hover about, a plan that allows viewers to have an intimate relationship with the art.

Another part of the renovation involved relocating and expanding the museum's current design shop and its café, whose tin roof has been painstakingly restored. The shop offers a wide range of products, from Noguchi's Akari lamps and furniture designs to other designers' mid-century furniture and design objects like teacups and tools for stone carving. **Admission:** $5 adults; $2.50 students and seniors. **Hours:** Wed.–Fri. 10 A.M.–5 P.M.; Sat.–Sun. 11 A.M.–6 P.M. Closed Mon.–Tue. **Subway:** N, W to Broadway (in Queens). Walk ten blocks down Broadway towards the Manhattan skyline and the East River. Turn left onto Vernon Blvd. (not onto 11th St.; walk past the Socrates Sculpture Park offices). Museum is 2 blocks farther on the left at 33rd Rd.

Museum for African Art 36–01 43rd Ave. (3rd floor), Long Island City, Queens (212) 966-1313 *www.africanart.org*. The Museum for African Art mounts provocative changing exhibitions on the rich and varied artistic heritage of African art, which include historical surveys in addition to contemporary works. In 2002, the collection moved to this temporary facility in Queens; it will remain here until its new home on Museum Mile is completed sometime in 2005. **Admission:** $6 adults; $3 students, seniors and children. Free 10–11 A.M. on Mon., Thu. and Fri. **Hours:** Mon. and Thu.–Fri. 10 A.M.–5 P.M., Sat.–Sun. 11 A.M.–6 P.M. Closed Tue.–Wed. **Subway:** 7 to 33rd St./Queens.

P.S. 1 Contemporary Art Center 22–25 Jackson Ave. (at 46th Ave. and 46th Rd.), Long Island City (718) 784-2084 *www.ps1.org*. P.S. 1's outer-borough location is an apt metaphor for its focus on marginal artists and art that isn't often exhibited in more traditional museums. It occupies a Romanesque Revival school building, built from 1893 to 1906. Renovated by Frederick Fisher, it features a dramatic front entry, a two-story project space for large-scale exhibitions and a 20,000-square-foot outdoor courtyard that serves as a sculpture garden. An affiliate of MoMA, P.S.1 does not exhibit a permanent collection, but rotates many long-term, site-specific installations throughout its 125,000 square feet of gallery space by artists including James Turrell, Pipilotti Rist, Richard Serra, Lucio Pozzi, Julian Schnabel and Richard Artschwager. The museum also offers outstanding educational and family programs. On summer Saturdays, P.S. 1 hosts an outdoor music series called Warm Up ($8 admission), featuring everything from techno beats to hip-hop and Latin-tinged electronica. **Admission:** $5 adults; $2 students and seniors. Free on Sat. noon–2 P.M. **Hours:** Thu.–Mon. noon–6 P.M. Closed Tue.–Wed. **Subway:** E, V to 23rd St./Ely Ave.; 7 to 45th Rd./Court House Sq.; G to 21st St./Van Alst. or Court Sq.

The Queensboro Bridge (59th Street Bridge). Silhouetted against a darkening sky, this elaborate expanse linking Queens and Manhattan looks like a work of crochet. Walking across on the south side, a look through the lacy structure reveals an incredible panorama of Midtown skyscrapers. From the north walk, you will see river currents rushing over rocks, and get a good close-up view of Roosevelt Island and the little red Roosevelt Island tram that ferries residents to and from Manhattan.

Socrates Sculpture Park Broadway and Vernon Blvd., Long Island City (718) 956-1819 *www.socratessculpturepark.org*. This 4.5-acre jewel on the banks of the East River in Long Island City was once a shipyard, then for 20 years an illegal dump site. Through the efforts of sculptor Mark di Suvero, the site was converted in the mid-1980's to an outdoor sculpture park featuring semi-annual exhibitions of public sculpture in a variety of media. Among the sculptures are subtle and pleasing artistic touches: winding paths, marble benches, and stones carved to resemble a child's letter blocks. In summer, the park hosts music and dance performances, plus screenings of international films—all set against the spectacular backdrop of the Manhattan skyline. **Admission:** Free. **Hours:** Daily 10 A.M.–sunset. **Subway:** N, W to Broadway, then walk 8 blocks toward the East River.

AREA RESTAURANTS

Chips $25 & Under   MEXICAN
42-15 Queens Blvd., Long Island City   (718) 786-1800
This petite Mexican shoebox features hot-pink tablecloths, hand-painted chairs, sombrero light fixtures and bright colors everywhere. **Price range:** $10–$15 per person for lunch.

Christos Hasapo-Taverna $25 & Under   GREEK/STEAK
41–08 23rd Ave. (at 41st St.), Astoria   (718) 726-5195
Richly flavored steaks and chops dominate the menu at this cheerful, handsome Greek steakhouse, and on some nights, more traditional fare like piglet and baby lamb, is turned on the rotisserie. **Price range:** Entrees $20–$26.

Churrascaria Girassol $25 & Under   BRAZILIAN
33-18 28th Ave., Astoria   (718) 545-8250
With juicy, salt-edged steaks, rich sauces mellowed with palm oil and the
prospect of unlimited meat courses, Girassol is a little bit of paradise for carnivores. **Price range:** Entrees $12–$18.

Dazies $25 & Under   ITALIAN
39-41 Queens Blvd., Long Island City   (718) 786-7013
With its dark wood, piano music and plush linens, this classic Italian restaurant
is a favorite formal choice. It has a welcoming, gracious atmosphere and uncommon competence in the kitchen. **Price range:** About $30–$40 per person for
two-course lunch.

Elias Corner $25 & Under   GREEK/SEAFOOD
24–02 31st St. (at 24th Ave.), Astoria   (718) 932-1510
This bright, raucous Greek seafood specialist offers no menus. Regulars know to
check the glass display case in front to select the freshest-looking fish. Go in the
off hours, before the crowd arrives. **Price range:** Entrees $14–$19. Cash only.

Tournesol $25 & Under   BISTRO/FRENCH
50-12 Vernon Blvd., Long Island City   (718) 472-4355
Like a flower poking through the gritty concrete near the mouth of the Midtown Tunnel, Tournesol is a spray of brightness. The dining room is pleasant,
and the chef displays a sure hand with Tournesol's small selection of bistro
dishes. **Price range:** Entrees $13–$19. American Express or cash only.

Uncle George's $25 & Under   GREEK
33–19 Broadway, Astoria   (718) 626-0593
A cross between a giant 24/7 diner and a boisterous family restaurant, Uncle
George's is an Astoria Greek classic. Portions are big, service is speedy and the
menu offers every kind of Greek dish, but it's fair to say that the draw isn't the
décor. **Price range:** Entrees $7–$15. Cash only.

Water's Edge   ☆☆ $$$$ NEW AMERICAN
44th Dr. at the East River, Long Island City   (718) 482-0033
From Manhattan, you reach the Water's Edge by taking a free ferry ride from
34th Street and the East River. The restaurant sits on a barge in the river, offering a magnificent ship captain's view of Midtown. The menu falls squarely in the
mainstream, with trendy Asian touches and newly familiar ingredients. **Price
range:** Prix-fixe lunch $29; dinner entrees $22–$34; prix-fixe dinners $55 or $70.

Flushing Meadows — Corona Park

Immortalized as the "Valley of the Ashes" in F. Scott Fitzgerald's *The Great
Gatsby,* these former marshes were filled in long ago and became a park in 1939,
when the site hosted the New York World's Fair. (It did so again in 1964.)
There's something for everyone at the park: You can catch a Mets game at **Shea
Stadium,** or play on the same courts that host the U.S. Open at the **U.S.T.A.**

National Tennis Center (*see chapter* Sports & Recreation). You can also marvel at the 12-story-high Unisphere, visit the New York Hall of Science to marvel at the collection of American spacecraft (*see chapter* New York for Children) or walk around a scale model of New York at the Queens Museum—all of which were first built for the '64 fair.

HIGHLIGHTS OF THE NEIGHBORHOOD

(*For* Shea Stadium *and* USTA National Tennis Center, *see chapter* Sports & Recreation. *For* New York Hall of Science *and the* Queens Zoo, *see chapter* New York for Children.)

Bowne House 37–01 Bowne St. (between 37th and 38th Aves.), Flushing (718) 359-0528 *www.bownehouse.org*. One of the city's oldest and most historic homes, this farmhouse was built by John Bowne in 1661. He lived there and used it as New Amsterdam's first indoor Quaker meeting place, in defiance of Governor Peter Stuyvesant's ban on the sect. Nine generations of Bownes lived here while a bustling Flushing neighborhood grew up around them. The house, a fine example of vernacular Dutch-English architecture, features restored rooms that are complete with period furniture and pewterware. At press time, the house was closed to visitors for a renovation; call ahead to see if it has reopened by the time you visit. Subway: 7 to Main St.–Flushing.

Flushing Town Hall 137–35 Northern Blvd. at Linden Pl. (718) 463-7700. This two-story brick Romanesque Revival building served as Flushing's town hall until 1900, when the village was incorporated into New York City. Constructed in 1862 on what are believed to have been the Matinecock Indians' burial grounds, it is a veritable encyclopedia of American history. It served as a militia depot during the Civil War, a forum for speeches by Ulysses S. Grant and Teddy Roosevelt, a performance space for P.T. Barnum and Mark Twain, as well as a traffic court, jail, opera house, ballroom, police precinct and even a dinner theater. The Flushing Council on Culture and the Arts maintains three galleries here with rotating art exhibits; there's also a visitors center and café, plus occasional jazz concerts and other cultural events. Hours: Mon.–Fri. 10 A.M.–5 P.M., Sat.–Sun. noon–5 P.M. Subway: 7 to Main St.–Flushing.

Louis Armstrong's House 34-56 107th St., Corona (718) 478-8274 *www.satchmo.net*. Louis and his wife, Lucille, lived here from 1943 until they died. The house was built in 1910, and remains today just as Lucille left it when she passed away in 1983. After a major restoration, it opened to the public for tours in 2003. Admission: $8 adults; $6 seniors and students. Hours: Tues.–Fri. 10 A.M.–5 P.M.; Sat.–Sun. noon–5 P.M. Subway: 7 to 103rd St./Corona Plaza.

Queens Museum of Art New York City Bldg. (111th St. and 49th Ave., next to the Unisphere), Flushing Meadows/Corona Park. (718) 592-9700 *www.queensmuseum.org*. If you come to the Queens Museum just to see the Panorama, an immense model of New York City, it would be well worth the trip. Originally built for the 1964 World's Fair, the model replicates in

painstaking detail the geography, buildings, bridges and roads of all five boroughs at a scale of 1,200 to 1. The world's largest scale model, it fills a room
the size of two basketball courts. The museum is housed in one of the few
remaining buildings of the 1939 World's Fair (it was also home to the United
Nations General Assembly from 1946 to 1952). In addition to exhibiting
contemporary art, the museum has an impressive collection of World's Fair
memorabilia, an assortment of Tiffany lamps and a sculpture hall. **Admission:** $5 adults; $2.50 students and seniors; free for children under 5. **Hours:**
Wed.–Fri. 10 A.M.–5 P.M.; Sat.–Sun. noon–5 P.M. Closed Mon.–Tue. Mid-
July to Labor Day Wed.–Sun. 1–8 P.M. only **Subway:** 7 to Willets
Point/Shea Stadium. Exit on the park side, not the stadium side; follow the
yellow signs for the 10-min. walk to the museum.

AREA RESTAURANTS

East Buffet & Restaurant $25 & Under   CHINESE
42-07 Main St., Flushing   (718) 353-6333
This huge, glossy eating hall seats 400 people in the buffet hall and 350 in
another room for sit-down service. Three islands in the center of the buffet area
hold more than 30 dim-sum selections, a dozen soups, 40 dishes served cold and
another 40 served hot. **Price range:** Dinner $20–$25.

Joe's Shanghai   ☆☆ $ CHINESE
136–21 37th Ave. (near Main St.), Flushing   (718) 539-3838
Joe's signature dish, "steamed buns," is alone worth the trip. The buns are wonderful soup dumplings that hold a lusty blend of pork or crab meat in a richly
flavored broth. Among entrees, try the tea-smoked duck and braised pork shoulder in brown sauce. **Price range:** Entrees $10 and up. Cash only.

Master Grill $25 & Under   BRAZILIAN
34–09 College Point Blvd., Flushing   (718) 762-0300
Possibly the most elaborate Brazilian rodizio in the city: Master Grill feels like
an enormous banquet hall, with seating for 1,000 and a samba band playing full
tilt. It's all great fun if you're in the mood. **Price range:** All you can eat $21.95.

New Lok Kee $25 & Under   CHINESE
36-50 Main St. (near 37th Ave.), Flushing   (718) 762-6048
After fire destroyed Chinatown's Sun Lok Kee, it reopened as New Lok Kee in
Flushing. Its tradition of informal excellence is cooked into every meal. **Price
range:** Entrees $6–$16.

Pearson's Texas Barbecue $25 & Under   BARBECUE
71–04 35th Ave., Jackson Heights   (718) 779-7715
The only pit barbecue restaurant in New York City. In the rear, burnished slabs
of pork ribs glisten behind a counter next to piles of plump sausages and chickens turned almost chestnut by smoke. The glory of Pearson's is its brisket. **Price
range:** Sandwiches $6.95; barbecue by the pound $5–$15. Cash only.

Shanghai Tang $25 & Under   CHINESE
135–20 40th Rd., Flushing   (718) 661-4234
This bright, handsome restaurant, one of the best Chinese places in Flushing,
serves many excellent Shanghai specialties. Service is unusually friendly and
helpful. **Price range:** Entrees $8–$16.

Spicy and Tasty $25 & Under   CHINESE
39–07 Prince St., Flushing   (718) 359-1601
Sichuan cuisine is known for spiciness, and Spicy and Tasty does not stint on
the chilies. Living dangerously is rewarded in classic dishes like double-cooked
pork, a savory, salty, spicy combination that strikes all the Sichuan chords. **Price
range:** Entrees, $7–$17.

Other Attractions in Queens

Gateway National Recreation Area (718) 354-4606 *www.nps.gov/gate*. This
26,000-acre recreation area extends through three city boroughs and into
northern New Jersey. It encompasses a series of beautiful beaches along the
Atlantic shoreline, including popular **Riis Park** (which has parking, restrooms,
showers, recreational fields, picnic tables and food vendors). Throughout the
preserve, you can explore decommissioned military sites, walk nature trails, enjoy
water sports, cycle along bike paths and much much more.

One section of the NRA, the **Jamaica Bay Wildlife Refuge** (718-318-4340),
near Kennedy Airport, spans an area almost the size of Manhattan and offers a
visitors center. Thousands of birds—including geese and ducks—stop here during their migration north and south along the Atlantic flyway. (The best time
to visit is in the spring or fall, when birds fill the skies.) Over 300 species of
birds and 65 species of butterflies have been found on the 9,000-acre preserve.
Diverse habitats include salt marshland, upland fields, woods, ponds and an
open expanse of bays and islands. **Admission:** No entrance fees, but Riis Park
and Sandy Hook beaches have parking fees. There's a $25 fee for an annual
fishing permit. **Subway:** A, S to Broad Channel.

Queens County Farm Museum 73–50 Little Neck Pkwy. at Union Tpke.,
Floral Park (718) 347-3276 *www.queensfarm.org*. This 47-acre, 200-year-old
farm became such an anomaly that the city decided to turn it into a museum.
But it's not what you'd expect. To this day it continues as a working farm with
planted fields, orchards and livestock. The historic 1770's home features period
rooms and changing exhibitions on the history of agriculture. Special events
include agricultural and craft fairs, apple festivals and antique car shows, as well
as quilting, candle-making and other craft demonstrations and courses. A seasonal farmstand sells fresh produce, and a greenhouse offers the chance to buy
house and garden plants. **Admission:** Free. **Hours:** Mon.–Fri. 9 A.M.–5 P.M.
(outdoor visits only); Sat.–Sun. 10 A.M.–5 P.M. (farmhouse tours available,
plus hayrides in good weather). **Directions:** E, F to Kew Gardens, then take the
Q 46 bus to Little Neck Pkwy.

Staten Island

STATEN ISLAND

Disdainful Manhattanites usually dismiss Staten Island out of hand. But this borough is a wonderful place to explore—and to some, it's so out, it's in. There are great little museums, three centuries of American architecture, historic military sites, extensive gardens and lots of programs for children. Nature lovers can meander through 7,500 acres of lush protected parkland and along miles of uncrowded beaches, or discover wetlands that are ripe for canoeing and communing with herons and cormorants.

Staten Island can seem surprisingly big to first-time visitors, so a car can be an advantage. But even if you don't drive here, the borough is well served by public transportation, starting with the **Staten Island Ferry** (*see listing in the* Lower Manhattan *section, near the beginning of this chapter*). The Staten Island Railroad and many bus routes ply the borough, and there's efficient express bus service from Manhattan (all of these services take MetroCards).

The ferry is still the best way to get to Staten Island. It's absolutely free. Riding one of those big orange boats at sunset on a summer evening is like a mini-cruise and almost as restorative.

Boats leave from South Ferry in Manhattan and dock in St. George, the county seat and transportation hub. A short walk form the ferry dock is the **Richmond County Bank Ballpark,** home to the **Staten Island Yankees** (*www.siyanks.com*), the Bronx Bombers' minor-league affiliate. Since the first ball was thrown out in 2001, the Baby Bombers have drawn huge crowds, as much for the sport as for the stadium's sweeping views of New York Harbor.

Another new landmark for St. George is the brand-new **National Lighthouse Museum**. Housed in what was most recently a Coast Guard base adjacent to the ferry terminal, it explores the science and lore of lighthouses.

The **Staten Island Institute of Arts and Sciences,** the borough's main museum, is just a three-block walk from the ferry terminal. Its holdings include everything from bugs and botanicals to paintings and decorative objects. Look for surprise gems such as paintings by the Staten Island native Jasper Cropsey, or works by Chagall, Warhol, Toulouse-Lautrec, Piranesi or Dürer.

The **Newhouse Center for Contemporary Art,** just a 10- to 15-minute ride west along Richmond Terrace by car, bus or bike, is the main exhibition space at the borough's best-known art and performance site, the 83-acre **Snug Harbor Cultural Center.** Opened 200 years ago as a haven "for aged, decrepit and worn-out sailors"—or Snugs, as the retired seamen were called—Snug Harbor is a collection of 28 buildings in the Greek Revival, Italianate and Beaux-Arts styles, all of which are slowly being spruced up. There's an 1892 music hall that is just a year younger than Carnegie Hall and the John A. Noble Maritime Collection, housed in a three-story 1844 Greek Revival structure.

You could spend a whole day at Snug Harbor, which offers an escape for every taste and age. If nature is what you crave, amble into the **Chinese Scholar's Garden** to be instantly transported to China's Suzhou province, and maybe to serenity. The crown jewel of the **Staten Island Botanical Garden,** the Scholar's Garden was created by 40 artisans from China and is the only garden of its kind in the United States.

Youngsters visiting Staten Island probably won't care about the deeper meaning of Moon Gates and mandalas, but they might go for the Botanical Garden's mazes. Through a clutch of screaming peacocks is the **Connie Gretz Secret Garden,** complete with circuitous paths, hedges and a turreted castle. Inspired by Frances Hodgson Burnett's book, it's a good place for the little ones to let loose.

And then there's always the **Carousel-for-All-Children** in Willowbrook Park, about 10 minutes by car. Its 51 old-fashioned wooden animals, hand-carved and hand-painted, revolve on a structure decorated with scenes of Staten Island. (*See chapter* **New York for Children** *for the* Staten Island Children's Museum *and the* Staten Island Zoo.)

A flood of development since the 1964 opening of the **Verrazano-Narrows Bridge** has robbed the island of much of its charm and character. But scattered among the new houses and overly elaborate lawn ornaments are some unusual attractions that add to the borough's appeal.

The **Jacques Marchais Museum of Tibetan Art,** on Lighthouse Hill in the middle of the island, has a wonderful, intimate garden. Climbing the hill is a bit daunting, but the surprise of finding a replica Himalayan monastery tucked in the trees soon makes you forget your fatigue. The collection of Tibetan artifacts inside was praised for its authenticity by the Dalai Lama, who visited in 1991.

Mandolin Brothers, a bustling little shop-cum-museum close to the zoo, is one of the world's foremost dealers in new and vintage guitars and other fretted instruments. The shop has been responsible for bringing some unlikely tourists to Staten Island: Joni Mitchell, for one, who immortalized the shop in a song.

Historic Richmond Town, a village of 27 structures, offers not Disney-style reproductions but restorations of actual Staten Island buildings, some local and others moved to the 100-acre site from other island communities. The oldest is the red 17th-century Voorlezer's house, which is the oldest known school in the United States. The collection of 18th-century Dutch Colonial farmhouses and workshops and a 19th-century country church are interesting for their insight into long-ago community and family life. The **County Fair** here, with its pig races and do-wop concerts, is an end-of-summer tradition.

At the **Conference House,** 15 minutes by bike from the Oakwood train station, you can begin to trace Staten Island's role in international politics. It was here in September 1776, with 32,000 British troops and Hessian mercenaries billeted among the island's 3,000 residents, that Lord Admiral Richard Howe met with Ben Franklin, John Adams and Edward Rutledge in a failed attempt to hammer out the finer points of the country's independence. The Conference House is in Tottenville, the end of the train line and Staten Island's southernmost tip. An unusual mix of Victorian houses and cottages, old mansions, odd urban and industrial ruins, beaches and tranquil wooded areas make this area a popular cycling destination.

The area also has lots of little green pockets, most of them too dense for cycling but great for hikes. The Urban Park Rangers offer canoeing lessons at **Wolfe's Pond Park,** but those with their own canoes or kayaks can discover how unusual the **William T. Davis Wildlife Refuge** is. Part of the 2,800-acre **Greenbelt,** a collection of six Staten Island parks and nature preserves, it has a network of navigable creeks whose grasses and banks are a habitat for native wildlife and temporary quarters for many migratory birds. It also provides a bird's-eye view of the old Fresh Kills Landfill.

For those interested in things military, **Battery Weed,** a multitiered fortress, is a short bus or bike ride from the ferry. It is one of the oldest forts in the nation and one of only three examples of its kind ever built. The site, **Fort Wadsworth,** visible from the Verrazano-Narrows Bridge as you cross from Brooklyn, is the oldest continuously staffed military post in the United States.

The 19th century might be considered Staten Island's Golden Age, when the island appealed even to international political exiles. The Italian patriot Giuseppe Garibaldi forged the plan for his country's independence in the home of Antonio Meucci, said to be the true inventor of the telephone. At the **Garibaldi-Meucci Museum,** between the ferry and Fort Wadsworth, you can see some of the first telephones and assorted Garibaldi memorabilia.

In the 19th century, life was madcap for the privileged classes on Staten

Island, a playground for families like the Vanderbilts and the Cunards. You can see the busy life of the borough's comfortably wealthy as it was captured on film by one of their own, Alice Austen, at her family's home, now a museum. Austen was one of the first American women to take up photography. Her vine-covered cottage, **Clear Comfort,** serves as a museum of the Victorian lifestyle as well as a photo gallery   —*Claire Wilson*

Getting There: By **subway and ferry,** take the 1, 9 to South Ferry; the 4, 5 to Bowling Green; or the N, R to Whitehall Street. Walk to the ferry terminal, and take the Staten Island Ferry (free) to St. George.

From Manhattan, there are 30 **express buses** (1X, 9X, 10X, for example) that go to various Staten Island destinations. For info, call (718) 330-1234.

By car from Manhattan, take either the Brooklyn Bridge or the Brooklyn Battery Tunnel to Route 278, then head for the Verrazano-Narrows Bridge (toll is $8 from Brooklyn, no toll back to Brooklyn). This takes you to the Staten Island Expressway. From New Jersey, there are three bridges: from the Bayonne Bridge, Route 440 takes you to Route 278; from I-95, the Goethals Bridge takes you to Route 278; from the Outerbridge Crossing, Route 440 takes you to the West Shore Expressway and then to Route 278.

ATTRACTIONS

(For the **Staten Island Ferry,** *see section "Lower Manhattan" earlier in this chapter. For the* **Staten Island Children's Museum** *and* **Staten Island Zoo,** *see chapter* **New York for Children.** *For the* **Staten Island Yankees,** *see chapter* **Sports & Recreation.** *See the introduction above for more details about the sights listed below.)*

Alice Austen House 2 Hylan Blvd., Rosebank (718) 816-4506 *http://aliceausten.org.* **Admission:** $2 adults; free for children under 6. **Hours:** Thu.–Sun. noon–5 P.M. Closed Jan.–Feb. **Bus:** S-51 from ferry terminal.

Carousel-for-All-Children Willowbrook Park, 1 Eaton Pl., Willowbrook (718) 477-0605 **Tickets:** $1 a ride. **Hours:** Spring–fall daily 11 A.M.–5:45 P.M. **Bus:** S-62 to the park's gate on Victory Blvd.

Conference House waterfront at end of Hylan Blvd., Tottenville (718) 984-0415 *www.theconferencehouse.org.* **Admission:** $3 adults; $2 seniors and children. **Hours:** Fri.–Sun. 1–4 P.M. Closed mid-Dec. to Mar. **Bus:** S-78 to Craig Ave.

Fort Wadsworth and Battery Weed Bay St. at Hylan Blvd. (718) 354-4500 *www.nps.gov/gate.* Added to the sprawling Gateway National Recreation Area in 1995, Fort Wadsworth was a linchpin to the defense of New York Harbor for nearly two centuries. Park rangers lead walks and tours highlighting both its history and its shoreline environment. **Admission:** Free. **Hours:** Visitor Center (offering exhibits, tours and a short film on the history of New York's harbor defenses) Wed.–Sun. 10 A.M.–5 P.M. **Bus:** S51 to Von Briesen Park.

Garibaldi-Meucci Museum 420 Tompkins Avenue, Rosebank (718) 442-1608 *www.garibaldimeuccimuseum.org.* **Admission:** $3. **Hours:** Tue.–Sun. 1–5 P.M. **Bus:** S52, S78 or S79.

Historic Richmond Town 441 Clarke Ave., Richmond (718) 351-1611
www.historicrichmondtown.org. Staten Island's answer to Colonial Williamsburg
is this a living-history complex of 27 buildings set on 100 acres; costumed actors
give visitors a glimpse into everyday colonial life. Interpreter-led tours are conducted daily at 2:30 P.M. on weekdays, and at 2 and 3:30 P.M. on weekends.
Admission: $5 adults; $4 seniors; $3.50 children ages 5–17; free for children
under 5. **Hours:** July–Aug., Wed.–Sat. 10 A.M.–5 P.M., Sun. 1–5 P.M.
Sept.–June, Wed.–Sun 1–5 P.M. (closed Sun.–Mon.). **Bus:** S-74 from ferry terminal to Richmond Rd. and St. Patrick's Pl.

Mandolin Brothers 629 Forest Ave., West Brighton (718) 981-3226
www.mandoweb.com. **Hours:** Mon.–Sat. 10 A.M.–6 P.M. **Bus:** S-48 to Forest
and Pelton Aves.

Jacques Marchais Museum of Tibetan Art 338 Lighthouse Ave., Richmond
(718) 987-3500 *www.tibetanmuseum.com*. This hilltop museum is designed to
resemble a Himalayan Temple, with art, ritual objects and musical instruments.
Admission: $5 adults; $3 students and seniors; $2 children under 12. **Hours:**
Wed.–Sun. 1–5 P.M.

National Lighthouse Museum 1 Lighthouse Plaza, St. George (718) 556-
1681 *www.lighthousemuseum.org*. Tours Wed. and Sat. at 11 A.M. and 1, 2 and 3
P.M.; Sun. at 1, 2 and 3 P.M. Reservations required. **Admission:** $2. **Directions:**
Walk from ferry.

Staten Island Institute of Arts and Sciences 75 Stuyvesant Pl., St. George
(718) 727-1135 *www.siiasmuseum.org*. The oldest cultural organization on
Staten Island, the museum offers interactive children's programs as well as art
and natural science exhibits featuring more than 500,000 entomological specimens, 25,000 plant specimens, and shells and archaeological objects. The general collections include ethnographic art, paintings, sculpture, crafts, prints and
drawings, including a portion of the Kress Collection of the Italian Renaissance.
You'll also find historic collections of 19th- and 20th-century American costumes and 18th- to 20th-century American, European and Asian furniture and
decorative arts. **Admission:** $2.50 adults; $1.50 seniors and children. **Hours:**
Tue.–Sat. 9 A.M.–5 P.M.; Sun. 1–5 P.M. **Directions:** Walk from ferry.

Snug Harbor Cultural Center 1000 Richmond Terrace, Livingston (718)
448-2500, or (718) 815-SNUG for tickets to events *www.snug-harbor.org*. Snug
Harbor's 26 architecturally impressive buildings are now home to art galleries,
performance spaces, cultural and educational institutions, all set on 86 acres of
wetlands, woods and botanical gardens. The complex includes the **Newhouse
Center for Contemporary Art** (admission $2 adults, $1 seniors, free for children under 10; open Tue.–Sun. 10 A.M.–5 P.M.) and the **John Noble Maritime
Collection** (718-447-6490; *www.noblemaritime.org*; admission $3, $2 seniors
and students; open Thu.–Sun. 1–5 P.M.). There's also the **Staten Island Botanical Garden** (718-273-8200; *www.sibg.org*; admission charges and hours for various parts vary), which encompasses the **Chinese Scholar's Garden** (described

above), and the **Staten Island Children's Museum** (718-273-2060; admission $5; open Tue.–Sun. noon–5 P.M., with an 11 A.M. opening time in summer). **Bus:** From the ferry terminal, head to Ramp D and take the S-40 bus. Snug Harbor is less than 2 miles away.

Verrazano-Narrows Bridge With a main span of 4,260 feet, this is the longest suspension bridge in the United States and the second longest in the world. Still, the Verrazano plays second fiddle to the Brooklyn Bridge. It lacks its elder sibling's pedestrian walkway, its close-up views of Manhattan and its romantic history. But there's no denying the Verrazano's grandeur, with a total length (including the approaches) of over two-and-a-half miles.

The Verrazano-Narrows opened to traffic in 1964. It is the youngest span in New York, but it is literally and figuratively linked to the past. The name comes from Giovanni da Verrazano, the first European to sail into New York Harbor, and the ends of the bridge lie in the historic guardians of the harbor: Brooklyn's Fort Hamilton and Staten Island's Fort Wadsworth. Today, the bridge is the only direct link between Brooklyn and Staten Island, and it offers the shortest route between Long Island and the Middle Atlantic states.

AREA RESTAURANTS

Aesop's Tables 1233 Bay St., Rosebank (718) 720-2005. Among the best, with a garden out back.

Adobe Blues 63 Lafayette Ave., New Brighton (718) 720-2583. Casual Mexican, not far from St. George.

American Grill 420 Forest Ave., West Brighton (718) 442-4742. Good bet for American fare.

Cargo Café 120 Bay St., St. George (718) 876-0539. Much better than it looks. Great fries, and a five-minute walk from the ferry.

Denino's Pizzeria Tavern 524 Port Richmond Ave., Port Richmond (718) 442-9401. Thin-crust pizza and a big line to get in. Try the white pizza.

Killmeyer's Old Bavarian Inn 4254 Arthur Kill Rd., Charleston (718) 984-1202. German food, a great old bar and a beer garden out back.

Ralph's Ice Cream Store 501 Port Richmond Ave., Port Richmond (718) 273-3675. The authority—in the whole city, not just the borough—on Italian ice.

The Arts

New York is a whirlwind of creativity, the center of the nation's artistic life. Its galleries and stages feature the best and the brightest from all over the world. The sheer number of artistic possibilities can be overwhelming. If you love painting, you can visit five world-class museums, or go gallery hopping in hopes of discovering new talent. Music lovers can find performances from some of the world's top performers any night of the week. And it goes without saying that New York offers the best in American theater, from big, brassy Broadway musicals to experimental dramas. Whatever your artistic interests, New York won't disappoint.

ART MUSEUMS AND GALLERIES

New York City has dozens of museums and hundreds of art galleries. Even for the most committed art lover, it's a dizzying array of choices. First-time visitors might focus on the Metropolitan Museum of Art, which in itself is overwhelming in its scope. Another big name is the Museum of Modern Art, which is reopening in its newly expanded and renovated Midtown home. MoMA has a peerless collection of 20th-century works and frequently stages blockbuster shows.

When it comes to contemporary art, MoMA isn't the only game in town. There's also the Guggenheim, the even more cutting-edge New Museum of Contemporary Art and P.S. 1, MoMA's more experimental sibling. Those interested in American art will be drawn to the Whitney, and classicists may branch out beyond the Met to explore the Brooklyn Museum (see "Brooklyn" *in chapter* **Exploring New York**), or smaller gems, such as the Frick.

Gallery-goers will find a cluster of blue-chip galleries on the East Side, around 57th Street and Madison Avenue. SoHo made its splash in the art world long ago, and has transformed itself from a daring new outpost of art into a more upscale neighborhood dotted with established, high-toned galleries. Chelsea (especially West Chelsea) boasts the hippest, most dynamic collection of galleries in Manhattan; it has blossomed from a funky frontier into a mature force in the contemporary art world. Harlem, too, has attracted a host of new artists as the neighborhood has gentrified. Out in Brooklyn, Williamsburg and Dumbo (Down Under the Manhattan Bridge Overpass) are bursting with creativity, with a much younger, lighter focus and a raw edge.

There's something for every taste, so see what piques your interest and plan your itinerary (consult the **Exploring New York** chapter to see what other sights are nearby). New York's art world doesn't sit still, so there's always something new to see, even for locals who spend a lifetime trying to take it all in.

Major Art Museums

Museum Mile

The Met, being one of the world's premier art museums, is naturally the hub of art in the city. It's also the anchor of Museum Mile, the city's catchphrase for a stretch of Fifth Avenue on the Upper East Side of Manhattan that also encompasses the Frick Collection, the Guggenheim Museum, the National Academy of Design, the Jewish Museum, Neue Gallery New York, and several other institutions that encapsulate the artistic diversity of New York.

A visit to **the Met** should include checking out the European paintings, the Near Eastern and Egyptian rooms, and the Greek and Roman galleries, which include the coffered, skylit, barrel-vaulted gallery beside the Great Hall at the entrance to the museum (one of the city's most splendid public spaces). If you can't bear the inevitable crowds at the special exhibitions and in the Impressionist galleries, you can seek out less-trammeled quarters. Examples include the Astor Court; a scholar's garden in the Chinese galleries; the rooms of musical instruments, of arms and armor and of American pioneer and colonial-era furniture, which are so obscure that you almost feel like a pioneer yourself for going to see them.

Another must on Museum Mile, the **Frick Collection,** is almost everyone's favorite small museum. The Frick building itself, a mansion designed in 1913 by Thomas Hastings, the architect of the New York Public Library, was once a lavish private home. Picture for picture (Bellini, Holbein, Rembrandt, Vermeer, Fragonard—the list goes on), the quality of the collection is unsurpassed in America.

Farther up Museum Mile, tourists ogle Frank Lloyd Wright's spiral **Guggenheim** often without bothering about the art in it, although the permanent collection, which includes the Justin K. Thannhauser Collection, is, after the Modern's collection, the top overview of art from the first half of the 20th century regularly available in the city. The Guggenheim is embarking on a major restoration aimed at repairing and freshening Wright's landmark building.

The **Jewish Museum** (*see the* "Upper East Side" *section of chapter* **Exploring New York**) is the best institution of its kind in the country, complementing its collection of objects relating to the history of Judaism with a strong exhibition program that emphasizes modern and contemporary art.

The **Whitney Museum of American Art,** a block off Fifth, on Madison Avenue, isn't technically on Museum Mile but should be on the itinerary, too. It has permanent galleries where visitors can see the Hoppers and Calders they expect to find there, and a lively program of changing exhibitions.

Savvy visitors along Museum Mile might also see the less-heralded stops at the north end of Fifth. One of the best choices is **El Museo del Barrio,** a museum of the art and culture of Latin America and the city's expanding Latino community. Like the Studio Museum in Harlem, El Museo del Barrio was founded during the late 1960's in a period of upheaval, when artists of many backgrounds clamored for places to show their work. MoMA, with its stress on high European modernism and big-name postwar Americans, wasn't paying them enough attention, so they came up with the idea of community-based institutions. The result was a new breadth of collections and exhibitions—and renewed debate, as these young museums themselves turned into established institutions and faced criticism from within their own diversifying communities.

New York, they demonstrated, rejects the status quo, whatever it may be, and its museums reflect this fact. To travel along Museum Mile from Frick's mansion to El Museo del Barrio is to see a fraction of what's going on in art, but it's to go a long distance toward understanding the essential nature of a place where culture, like the rest of life, never stands still.

—*Michael Kimmelman*

Metropolitan Museum of Art   UPPER EAST SIDE
Fifth Ave. at 82nd St. (212) 535-7710   *www.metmuseum.org*
The Met is a national treasure, one of the world's great museums. The collection as a whole is simply outstanding. From ancient Greek vases and statuary to canvasses by Monet, Jasper Johns and Ellsworth Kelly, its variety is breathtaking.

This magnificent museum boasts more than two million works of art—paintings, sculpture, decorative arts, artifacts from ancient cultures, arms and armor, elegant clothing and musical instruments. There are 53 galleries devoted solely to European painters, and another maze is devoted to Americans.
(*See the* "Washington Heights/Inwood" *section in chapter* **Exploring New York** *for details on* **the Cloisters,** *the Met's uptown showcase for medieval art.*)

NAVIGATING THE MET
Since the Met is so vast, it's smart to draw up a game plan before you plunge in. Unfortunately, the Met doesn't make it easy to find your way around. A very general floor plan of the whole museum is offered at the information desks as you enter the main lobby (available in several languages). There are two detailed maps for European paintings and sculpture, none for other collections.

Some galleries are numbered, but many aren't. As you enter a gallery, you may see numbers on your right and on your left; as a general rule, the one on your right is the one you are entering.

Best bet: The Met's Web site (*www.metmuseum.org*) is excellent. Things that are hard to find in the museum itself are easy to find online, including daily schedules of tours and gallery talks, the exact location of the painting you're looking for, and everything else you might want to know before you visit.

Once you're at the museum, ask any uniformed guard to help you find your way. They are walking, talking catalogs, and they're happy to help.

Each of the Met's departments is a museum in itself. It would take more than an afternoon to fully explore the holdings of any one section. Wandering through the galleries, you'll stumble onto some wonderful surprises—perhaps a living room designed by Frank Lloyd Wright in the American Wing or violins made by Nicolo Amati and his student Antonio Stradivari in the 17th century. But you may get more from your visit by picking some objects or areas ahead of time, and searching them out. Or take a "highlights" tour to see what interests you and then go back and give it more time yourself.

New and Noteworthy in 2004-2005: Among the many special exhibitions on this year's calendar are **"Klee: His Years at the Bauhaus,"** running from October 8, 2004 to February 20, 2005, and featuring 30 works created by the painter Paul Klee when he taught at the Bauhaus in the 1920's.

A major retrospective of the drawings of **Peter Paul Rubens**, running from January 15 to April 3, 2005, will unite more than 100 of the Flemish master's drawings, many of them on loan from major European collections.

Another highly anticipated event, scheduled for March 8 through May 30, 2005, is **"Diane Arbus Revelations,"** the first major retrospective of this photographer in 30 years.

Running through February 2005 is **"Art Deco Paris,"** an exhibition of furniture, jewelry, bookbinding, lacquer and costumes representing the height of Parisian design in the 1920's.

Check *www.metmuseum.org* for a more extensive calendar of events, including a full slate of concerts and lectures.

More than 100 paintings, sculptures, drawings, and prints by some of the most prominent artists of the 20th century have been donated to the Met by the Pierre and Maria-Gaetana Matisse Foundation. Works by Henri Matisse, Balthus, Chagall, Derain, Dubuffet, Magritte, Giacometti and Miró are part of the new **Pierre and Maria-Gaetana Matisse Collection,** which made its debut in 2004. Selections from this collection will be exhibited in rotation.

Through June 2005, the Met is displaying a number of **medieval masterworks** on loan from the Morgan Library while that facility is being renovated.

Main Floor   As you enter the main lobby, the **Egyptian Art** collections and the **Temple of Dendur** are to your right, **Greek and Roman Art** to your left.

At the entrance to the Egyptian section, kids can walk right into a spooky tomb. The Met's own archeological explorations are responsible for more than half of the collection, which extends chronologically through 40 galleries. The Temple of Dendur was a gift from Egypt in recognition of U.S. aid in saving ancient monuments from the rising waters of the Nile behind the Aswan Dam.

The Greek and Roman works encompass a full range of classical art, from jewelry and pottery to sculpture and painting, with prize examples of Greek vases and Roman portrait busts. A famously fusty cafeteria and restaurant used to lie just beyond these galleries, but they were closed in 2003, and this space, with its grand columns, will soon be transformed into a Roman sculpture court as part of a multimillion-dollar renovation of the Greek and Roman galleries. Someday it will display treasures like a restored sixth-century B.C. bronze-and-ivory Etruscan chariot.

Straight through the main lobby from the entrance, passing to either side of the main stairway, you will find **Medieval Art** and a large spread of **European Sculpture and Decorative Arts.** This is one of the museum's largest collections. One of its gems is an ornate 15th-century *studiolo*—it means "little study"— with walls of inlaid woodwork that look three-dimensional but are actually flat.

Metropolitan Museum of Art

Fred R. Conrad/The New York Times

There are only two such rooms in the world, this one and another in the ducal palace in Urbino, Italy.

The **Petrie Court Cafe** (at the western edge of the European Sculpture Court) offers sit-down meals; its glass wall faces Cleopatra's Needle in Central Park. (For faster, more affordable meals, head down one flight of stairs to the cafeteria.)

Continuing straight ahead from the main entrance to the back of the museum, don't miss the eclectic **Robert Lehman Collection** of Impressionists and Old Masters, paintings and drawings, and pieces of decorative art. The gallery space, on two floors, is designed to evoke Lehman's own stately home on East 54th Street in Manhattan. Highlights include an "Annunciation" by Botticelli; a Rembrandt sketch of Leonardo's "Last Supper"; a Leonardo sketch of "A Bear Walking"; paintings by Rembrandt, El Greco, Goya, Renoir, Seurat and van Gogh; and some impressive pieces of Renaissance earthenware and Venetian glass.

The southern flank of the first floor houses the **Arts of Africa, Oceania and the Americas,** an enormous collection donated to the Met by Nelson Rockefeller, featuring royal decorative art from the Court of Benin in Nigeria, and the world's most comprehensive collection of gold objects from the Americas.

Next you'll see a series of galleries of **20th-century art** on two floors in the southwest corner of the building. This is where to find Jasper Johns, Picasso, Braque, Modigliani, O'Keeffe and Pollock.

In the northern flank of the first floor is the stunning **Arms and Armor** collection, as well as the **Temple of Dendur.** Another knockout at the same end of the museum is a grand wrap-around panorama of the palace and gardens at Versailles, from the early 1800's. Standing in the center of this large chamber, you can imagine you are there on the palace steps. And while you are at the north end of the building, check out the Met's collection of classic baseball cards, exhibited in the hallway behind Dendur on the way to Versailles.

The Arms and Armor collection is unique among American museums, with elegantly etched armor and weaponry ranging from the fourth century B.C. to the 19th century A.D., and from ancient Egypt and Islam to the Americas. The Japanese pieces are generally regarded as the finest anywhere outside Japan.

The **American Wing,** on two floors, is a magnet for tourists and New Yorkers alike. Everyone will recognize the epic "George Washington Crossing the Delaware," 21 feet wide, painted in Düsseldorf some 75 years after the fact by Emanuel Leutze. Note also the surrounding display of that particular gallery (no. 223). It has been arranged to resemble the museums of a century ago, crammed full of art, with three, four or five paintings hung one above the other.

This wing also houses familiar Washington portraits by Gilbert Stuart and Charles Willson Peale, as well as John Singer Sargent's "Madame X," Frederic Church's "Heart of the Andes," Alfred Bierstadt's "Rocky Mountains: Lander's Peak," paintings by Winslow Homer, James McNeill Whistler and Mary Cassatt, and sculptures by Frederic Remington and John Quincy Adams Ward.

Extraordinary features of the wing include **25 period rooms,** furnished and decorated just as they were in years and centuries past, plus a stunning collection of **stained glass,** much of it by Louis Comfort Tiffany.

Second Floor   On the balcony overlooking the main entrance in the Great Hall, the Met has placed some 60 objects from its extensive **Islamic collection,** including a seventh-century bronze ewer from Iran, an exquisite carved-ivory plaque from 10th-century Spain and important illuminated manuscript pages. The display will reside here while the museum is renovating its Islamic galleries.

Straight ahead at the top of the central stairway from the lobby, push through a pair of glass doors and enter the wonderful world of **European Paintings.** This is one of the two collections for which there are detailed maps if you ask for them at the information desk in the lobby. The works here are the Old Masters—starting with three enormous paintings by Tiepolo in the first gallery, past a remarkable diptych of "The Crucifixion" and "The Last Judgment" by Jan van Eyck, to Bruegel, Rubens, El Greco, Raphael, Titian, Tintoretto, Vermeer, Rembrandt, Hals, Gainsborough, Velázquez, Fragonard, Goya and still more.

These galleries are not to be confused with **Nineteenth-Century European Paintings and Sculpture**—the second collection for which there is a detailed map. Reach this area by turning left at the top of the central stairs and walking through a long gallery hall of etchings and photographs. Don't hurry. The etchings are the works of great artists; they illustrate how an artist sketches out ideas for later paintings—whole scenes, or a torso, or maybe just an elbow or a nose.

In the 19th-century galleries you will find the popular works of the **Impressionists,** but first a large expanse of Rodin's sculptured marbles. Inside are the young Claude Monet's vibrantly colorful "Garden at Sainte-Adresse," daring for its time; a Cézanne still-life once owned by Monet; Edouard Manet's peaceful "Boating"; van Gogh's "Cypresses"; and room after room featuring Bonnard, Degas, Rousseau, Daumier, Toulouse-Lautrec, Renoir and more.

Adjacent to these galleries, to the west, you'll find the second-floor space of the **20th-Century Art** collection, and on the Fifth Avenue side to the east, the currently closed galleries of **Islamic Art.** Some of the pieces from the Islamic collection have been integrated into the **Ancient Near Eastern Art** gallery found here, which spans nearly 9,000 years and ranges geographically from Mesopotamia to the Indian subcontinent. The long Fifth Avenue side of the second floor proceeds from the Near East section at the southern end, through the balcony over the lobby to a half-dozen sectors of **Asian Art—Chinese, Japanese, Korean, South Asian and Southeast Asian**—at the northern end. The Asian collections are reputed to be the largest and most comprehensive in the West; they're best known for their Chinese calligraphy, folding screens and other decorative objects from Japan, sculpture from Southeast Asia and paintings from the Himalayan kingdoms. Here, too, is the serene **Chinese Scholar's Garden** called Astor Court, behind a wall with a round entryway symbolizing a full moon.

Close by are the upper floor of the **American Wing** and the **Musical Instruments** collection, where you will find a piano made by the instrument's inventor, Bartolomeo Cristofori; two guitars owned and used by Andres Segovia; and all sorts of rare horns, harps and other music makers from distant lands and times.

Ground Floor Entering the museum through the street-level door to the south of the outside steps, or through the parking garage, there is an information desk where you'll pay your admission fee, a splendid model of the Acropolis, and a coat check (where the line moves faster than in the main lobby). The museum library is down here, too. A large, sleek **cafeteria** opened here in 2003.

The galleries of the **Costume Institute** are also on the ground floor, but they are entered from above, by stairs or an elevator from the main floor in the middle of Egyptian Art. A little hard to find, the institute is a small three-gallery treasure. Fashions dating from the 18th century and to the present are exhibited on mannequins in glass showcases with informative descriptions, and shows are organized around themes and particular designers.

Sculpture Garden Finally, weather permiting, take yourself up to the rooftop **Sculpture Garden,** not only for the sculpture but for an aerial view of Central Park. The **café** here is a nice place to take a break.

Admission: Suggested prices are $12 for adults or $7 for students and seniors (you are permitted to pay less); children under 12 are free with an adult. You can order tickets in advance at www.ticketweb.com, although this entails an extra service fee. **Hours:** Fri.–Sat. 9:30 A.M.–9 P.M.; Sun. and Tue.–Thu. 9:30 A.M.–5:30 P.M. Closed Mon. **Special programs:** Check the museum's online calendar for guided tours, gallery talks, lectures, films, concerts, workshops and family activities; most are free with museum admission. The Great Hall Balcony Bar (2nd floor) is open Fri. –Sat. evenings, with live music 4–8:30 P.M. Cocktails and light fare are also served in the Roof Garden Cafe, with views over Manhattan, as weather permits from May to late fall. **Subway:** 4, 5, 6 to 86th St.

The Solomon R. Guggenheim Museum

Solomon R. Guggenheim Museum   UPPER EAST SIDE

1071 Fifth Ave. (at 89th St.) (212) 423-3500   *www.guggenheim.org*

Long before it was completed in 1959, the Guggenheim—the strange round building in a city full of square boxes—was already suffering darts from critics. It was
called everything from a washtub to an indigestible hot-cross bun. Robert Moses,
the city's irascible master builder, said it looked like an inverted oatmeal dish.

But the museum's creator, Frank Lloyd Wright, called it nothing less than
"the liberation of painting by architecture." And on the first Sunday it opened,
10,000 people lined up to get in for 50 cents a head. (Only 6,000 made it; bribes
offered to guards did not work.)

The landmarked museum, considered by some to be Wright's masterpiece,
was expanded with a controversial 10-story annex in 1992. Along with one of
the world's largest Kandinsky collections, it has works by many major 20th-cen-
tury artists—Brancusi, Calder, Chagall, Delaunay, Klee, Joan Miró and Picasso.
The building itself is, of course, a major attraction. And worth the trip, despite
its admission charge, which is one of the highest in the city.

Instead of moving from room to room, as in other museums, you take the
elevator to the top, 92 feet up, then soak up the art as you descend a gently
sloping circular ramp, glancing across the sweeping rotunda at other art lovers
winding their way around you.   —*Randy Kennedy*

Note for 2005: After 45 years, the Guggenheim will undergo a major facelift.
While it has good bones, it is, like many Wright buildings, plagued with cracks,
leaks and corroding surfaces. The museum will remain open during the restoration, which is expected to take two years. In addition to removing nine coats of
paint to properly fix the building's cracking surface, the project includes repair-

The Guggenheim as Architecture

Frank Lloyd Wright's Guggenheim has always been like an explosion on Fifth Avenue. It is strident, it is loud, it defers not a whit to anything around it. It breaks every rule. It is so astonishing as a piece of architecture, of course, that it makes you feel that rules hardly matter. But the very way in which Wright's building breaks the rules of urban design becomes its own rule: the way it clashes with its surroundings is the way the Guggenheim communicates its architectural essence.

It has been a commonplace since this building opened in 1959 to speak of it as inhospitable to paintings, to talk of the long spiral ramp and slanted walls as Wright's way of forcing painting to be subservient to architecture. While this complaint has always been exaggerated—Wright's space can work wonderfully for the display of large Color Field abstractions, Calder mobiles, Pop Art and other postwar works—there is no question that the architecture fights the art a lot of the time. The building usually ends up in the foreground of one's consciousness, no matter what the paintings.

The rush of joy that Wright's great rotunda brings has always been worth its limitations as a gallery. There aren't a lot of cathedrals in New York—never mind that, there isn't a lot of architecture anywhere that is capable of making the heart beat faster, that so fills you with the sense that the making of enclosure can be an act of opening up, a discovery of noble possibilities. It is a wonderful paradox to find, in the act of enclosing, revelation. There is nowhere else in New York where the passion of architecture is more clearly there, set more directly in front of us for all to see and understand.

The north side addition, built in 1992, contains double-height galleries, which gave the Guggenheim the ability to display large contemporary canvases for the first time. While the galleries are not ideal display spaces—they are a bit narrow, and the elevator core intrudes partway into them—they are more versatile than anything the museum had before. If the Guggenheim's roles as a museum and as a piece of architecture have always been somewhat at odds, the addition at least partly resolved them.

—*Paul Goldberger*

ing the sidewalk, with its metallic rings set into concrete. Inside the building, the terrazzo floor in the main rotunda will also be restored, and the climate and security systems updated.

Coming in 2004–2005: Opening in October 2004 and running through mid-February 2005 is **"The Aztec Empire,"** featuring more than 450 works (sculpture, jewelry, musical instruments, ceremonial artifacts and much more) drawn from major collections in the United States and Mexico, including many pieces never before seen outside Mexico. From February 10 through May 8, 2005, watch for **"Cézanne: The Dawn of Modern Art,"** a major exhibition tracing the influence of Cézanne on the succeeding generation of 20th-century artists.

Admission: $15 adults; $10 students and seniors; free for children 12 and under.
You can order tickets in advance at www.ticketweb.com; this can help you avoid
standing in line, but also entails an extra service fee. **Hours:** Sat.–Wed. 10
A.M.–5:45 P.M.; Fri. 10 A.M.–8 P.M. Closed Thu. **Special programs:** Check the
Web site for a schedule of guided tours, lectures, films, workshops and family
activities. Tours are free, but other programs require a fee and advance registration. **Subway:** 4, 5, 6 to 86th St.

Frick Collection   UPPER EAST SIDE

1 E. 70th St. (between Fifth and Madison Aves.) (212) 288-0700 *www.frick.org*
This stately Upper East Side mansion, completed in 1914, offers a fascinating
glimpse into New York's Gilded Age. Each lavishly furnished room has been
preserved much as it was during the heyday of its owner, Henry Clay Frick
(1849–1919), a railroad and steel baron. Frick amassed an extraordinary personal art collection (not to mention an array of 18th-century French furniture,
Chinese porcelain vases and Italian bronzes). Start by viewing the video that's
screened every half hour in the Music Room, and consider taking the free audio
guide to the permanent collection that's included with your admission fee.

The galleries are intimate and serene; care is taken to offer appropriate
lighting and a quiet atmosphere, allowing the art to shine. Highlights of the
permanent collection include Bellini's "Saint Francis in Ecstasy," della
Francesca's "St. John the Evangelist," van Eyck's "Virgin With Child, With
Saints and Donor," Vermeer's "Officer and Laughing Girl," Holbein's "Sir
Thomas More and Thomas Cromwell," Rembrandt's "Self-Portrait," and
Stuart's "George Washington."

Admission: $12 adults; $8 seniors over age 62; $5 students. No children under
age 10; ages 10–16 must be accompanied by an adult. **Hours:** Tue.–Sat. 10
A.M.–6 P.M.; Sun. 1–6 P.M. Closed Mon. **Special programs:** Frequent free lectures and classical and chamber-music concerts; check the Web site for details.
Subway: 6 to 68th St.

Whitney Museum of American Art   UPPER EAST SIDE

945 Madison Ave. (at 75th St.) (212) 570-3676 or (800) 944-8639

www.whitney.org

Founded in 1914 by Gertrude Vanderbilt Whitney—mostly as a response to a
snub from the Met, which refused donation of the original 500-work collection—the Whitney opened in 1931 in three adjoining Greenwich Village
brownstones. Today its home is a hulking Madison Avenue building designed by
Bauhaus icon Marcel Breuer.

The Whitney takes a dynamic and uninhibited approach to 20th-century
and contemporary American art; it's a more freewheeling and controversial collection that what you'll find at MoMA. Two entire floors showcase highlights of
the comprehensive permanent collection, which features seminal works by
Louise Nevelson, Claes Oldenburg, Reginald Marsh, Jasper Johns and Georgia
O'Keeffe—not to mention the entire artistic estate of Edward Hopper. Most visitors are enchanted by Alexander Calder's charming "Calder's Circus," an intricate installation that recreates an entire miniature Big Top performance.

Every two years (and coming up in the spring of 2006), the Whitney stages the **Biennial,** a much-hyped and often-controversial exhibition that surveys the cutting edge of contemporary American art.

Sarabeth's at the Whitney is a huge cut above the typical museum cafeteria; it's a lovely place to take a lunch break.

(*See* "Other Art Museums" *below, for details on the* **Whitney Museum of Art at Altria,** *the museum's small corporate-funded offshoot opposite Grand Central.*)

Admission: $12 adults; $9.50 students with ID and seniors over age 62; free for children under 12. Fri. 6–9 P.M., pay as you wish. You can order tickets in advance at www.ticketweb.com or over the phone; this can help you avoid standing in line, but also entails an extra service fee. **Hours:** Wed.–Thu. and Sat. –Sun. 11 A.M.–6 P.M.; Fri. 1–9 P.M. Closed Mon. and Tue. **Special programs:** Check the Web site for details on lectures, seminars, family activities, concerts, films and workshops. **Subway:** 6 to 77th St.

MoMA   MIDTOWN WEST
11 West 53rd St. (between Ave. of the Americas and Fifth Ave.)
(212) 708-9400   *www.moma.org*

After an ambitious renovation, MoMA returns to Manhattan in November 2004. (MoMA's Queens facility closed at the end of September 2004, and will be converted into a study and storage center.) The museum boasts one of the world's greatest collections of paintings and sculpture from the late nineteenth century to the present, including landmark works from Picasso, Monet, van Gogh, Hopper, Warhol, Kahlo and many more.

The spectacular new midtown structure, designed by Yoshio Taniguchi, nearly doubles the size of the original museum, offering dramatically expanded space for exhibitions and programming. A new six-story gallery building now showcases the permanent collection and temporary exhibitions, with massive column-free spaces that will accommodate the display of oversized works. The painting and sculpture galleries on the fourth and fifth floors are the heart of the permanent collection. Each of these galleries is now devoted to a period, a movement, an artist or a group of artists, offering new approaches to understanding the development of modern art.

Taniguchi restored Philip Johnson's original, larger 1953 design for the Abby Aldrich Rockefeller Sculpture Garden, re-establishing the southern terrace as an elegant outdoor patio for the Museum's new restaurant. On the lower level, two theaters have been refurbished with the latest surround-sound and digital projection to accommodate the museum's acclaimed film-and-media program (including the return of the annual New Directors/New Film series held in conjunction with the Film Society of Lincoln Center, presenting two dozen new features by emerging directors from around the world).

Among the major exhibitions planned for 2005 are **"Michael Wesely: Open Shutter at the Museum of Modern Art,"** a unique photographic project inspired by the museum's reconstruction. Beginning in 2001, Wesely installed specially designed cameras around the museum; his exposures are a striking chronicle of the contruction project's evolution. **"Groundswell: Contructing the Contemporary Landscape,"** running from February 25 to May 16, 2005, will present 20 designed landscape projects selected for their outstanding design, environmental sensitivity, materials and contexts. **"Thomas Demand,"** running from March 1 through May 30, 2005, is the first major U.S. exhibit of the work of this German photographer, widely regarded as one of leading artists of his generation. **"Pioneering Modern Painting: Cézanne and Pissarro 1865-1885,"** scheduled for June 24 through September 12, 2005, is a major exhibition of more than 80 paintings and drawings that present the work of Paul Cézanne and Camille Pissarro in the context of their 20-year artistic relationship.

Admission: $12 adults; $8.50 seniors and students with ID; free for children under 16 accompanied by an adult. Fri. 4–7:45 P.M. pay as you wish. **Hours:** Sat.–Mon. and Thu. 10 A.M.–5 P.M.; Fri. 10 A.M.–7:45 P.M. Closed Tue.–Wed. Note that the midtown branch had not reopened as of press time. Call ahead to confirm hours and admission charges, which are subject to change. **Subway:** E, F to Fifth Ave.; B, D, F, Q to 47th-50th Sts./Rockefeller Center. *(See the* "Queens" *section in chapter* **Exploring New York** *for MoMA's cutting-edge affiliate, P.S.1.)*

Other Art Museums

(For other types of museums and historic houses, many containing art collections, see chapter **Exploring New York.***)*

American Folk Art Museum MIDTOWN WEST 45 W. 53rd St. (between Fifth and Sixth Aves.) (212) 265-1040 *www.folkartmuseum.org.* This small gem of a museum is worth a visit not only for its fascinating look at the American folk-art tradition, but also for its stunning gallery space—a state-of-the-art facility that won glowing reviews for architects Tod Williams and Billie Tsien. This wonderful building finally gives the museum a presence in the city's cultural scene that had long eluded it. The collection offers a glimpse into America's shared national experiences and the diversity of its heritage, with items such as weathervanes, textiles, flags, quilts, sculpture, 18th- and 19th-century portraits and more. The museum also mounts provocative shows of "outsider art," or "untrained art." Don't miss the wonderful gift shop. **Admission:** $9 adults; $7 students and seniors; free for children under 12; free for everyone Fri. 5:30–7:30 P.M. **Hours:** Wed.–Sun. 10:30 A.M.–5:30 P.M.; Fri. 10:30 A.M.–7:30 P.M. Closed Mon. and Tue. **Subway:** E, V to Fifth Ave.; B, D, F, Q, V to 47th–50th Sts./Rockefeller Center. The museum has an annex, the **Eva and Morris Feld Gallery,** in its old location at 2 Lincoln Square, across from Lincoln Center; admission is free.

Chelsea Art Museum CHELSEA 556 W. 22nd St. (at 11th Ave.) (212) 255-0719 *www.chelseaartmuseum.org.* The Chelsea Art Museum focuses on contemporary abstract art, with an emphasis on the school known as "L'Informel" (a movement similar to abstract expressionism). The three-story, red brick building—once a factory producing Christmas ornaments—has large windows with views of the Hudson River and abundant natural light. The collection features European abstract artists of the Informel group, especially Jean Miotte, plus American abstract artists and sculptors. The ground floor currently houses temporary exhibition space for the New Museum of Contemporary Art. **Admission:** $5 adults; $2 students and seniors; free for children under 12. **Hours:** Tue.–Sat. 10 A.M.–6 P.M. (until 8 P.M. Thu.). **Subway:** C, E, 1, 9 to 23rd St.

The Cloisters WASHINGTON HEIGHTS/INWOOD Fort Tryon Park (212) 923-3700 *www.metmuseum.org*. Perched on a cliff overlooking the Hudson in the northernmost reaches of Manhattan, this is the Metropolitan Museum's satellite branch, an extraordinary collection of art and architecture from medieval Europe. *(See full listing in* "Washington Heights/Inwood" *section of chapter* **Exploring New York**.*)*

Cooper-Hewitt National Design Museum UPPER EAST SIDE 2 E. 91st St. (at Fifth Ave.) (212) 849-8300 *http://ndm.si.edu*. Peter Cooper would have been proud. The small museum he envisioned more than 100 years ago to support Cooper Union's instruction in the applied arts developed into what is now the country's best place to view and study design. In 1897, Cooper's granddaughters opened a museum modeled after Paris's Musée des Arts Décoratifs in the Cooper Union Building. The museum has amassed a collection encompassing objects as diverse as radiators, gloves and 18th-century French furniture, all of them showcasing the beauty and utility of fine design. Part of the Smithsonian Institution since 1969, it later moved to Andrew Carnegie's Fifth Avenue mansion. Recent shows have focused on everything from Alexander Calder's designs for everyday objects to architects' plans for doghouses. **Admission:** $10 adults; $7 students and seniors; free for children under 12. **Hours:** Tue.–Thu. 10 A.M.–5 P.M.; Fri. 10 A.M.–9 P.M.; Sat. 10 A.M.–6 P.M.; Sun. noon–6 P.M. Closed Mon. **Subway:** 4, 5, 6 to 86th St. or 96th St.

Dahesh Museum MIDTOWN EAST 580 Madison Ave. (between 56th and 57th Sts.) (212) 759-0606 *www.daheshmuseum.org*. The Dahesh Museum's mission is collecting, preserving, exhibiting and interpreting 19th- and 20th-century European academic art. Modern art was founded in opposition to academic art, which was subsequently dismissed for over a century. As the word "academic" became derogatory, once-influential artists and teachers such as William-Adolphe Bouguereau, Jean-Léon Gérome and Alexandre Cabanel were derided as reactionaries. More recent scholarship has taken a less ideological view, and the Dahesh allows the most popular art of its time to be seen on its own terms. **Admission:** $9 adults; $4 students and seniors; free for children under 12. **Hours:** Tue.–Sun. 11 A.M.–6 P.M. Closed Mon. **Subway:** 4, 5, 6 to 59th St.; E, N, R, V, W to Fifth Ave./59th St.

Dia Center for the Arts CHELSEA 545 and 548 W. 22nd St. (between 10th and 11th Aves.) (212) 989-5566 *www.diacenter.org*. The Dia Center provides exhibition space for large-scale works—particularly earth works and minimalist sculpture—that conventional museums have trouble accommodating. It is closed for renovation until 2006, although it will continue to present lecture series. In 2003, the museum opened a critically acclaimed new affiliate upstate in Beacon, New York, on the banks of the Hudson.

Drawing Center SOHO 35 Wooster St. (between Broome and Grand Sts.)
(212) 219-2166 *www.drawingcenter.org*. This small nonprofit museum is dedicated to drawings, loosely defined as original works on paper. Past exhibits have
included wall drawings, monoprints and computer-generated drawings. In addition to its four or five annual group shows, usually featuring emerging artists, the
center mounts historical and special exhibitions, such as the working drawings
of Ellsworth Kelly. Across the street is the Drawing Room, an annex dedicated
to site-specific projects by individual artists. The gallery sponsors the Tuesday-
night "Line Reading" series ($5), which features prominent authors exploring
the relationship between literature and the visual arts. **Admission:** Free.
Hours: Tue.–Fri. 10 A.M.–6 P.M.; Sat. 11 A.M.–6 P.M. **Subway:** J, M, N, Q, R,
W, Z, 1, 6, 9 to Canal St.

El Museo del Barrio UPPER EAST SIDE 1230 Fifth Ave. (at 104th St.) (212) 831-
7272 *www.elmuseo.org*. Located in Central Park's Heckscher Building,
El Museo was founded by a group of Puerto Rican educators, artists and
activists in 1969 to serve the Puerto Rican community in nearby Spanish
Harlem. Its mission has since expanded in response to the growth of New
York's Latino population—particularly the Mexican, Central and South
American, and Caribbean communities. The collection ranges from pre-
Columbian artifacts to contemporary videos to a splendid installation of Puerto
Rican religious figures called *santos*. **Admission:** $7 adults; $5 students and
seniors; free for children under 12. **Hours:** Wed.–Sun. 11 A.M.–5 P.M. (open to
8 P.M. on Thu.) **Subway:** 6 to 103rd St.

International Center of Photography MIDTOWN WEST 1133 Sixth Ave. (at
43rd St.) (212) 857-0000 *www.icp.org*. Sleek galleries feature the ICP's intriguing permanent collection and a host of frequently changing temporary exhibitions. The museum's scope encompasses everything from fashion photography
to photojournalism, including the complete works of Robert Capa, the founder's
brother. In addition to hosting lectures, films and gallery tours, ICP offers an
extensive roster of continuing-education courses. **Admission:** $10 adults; $7
seniors and students. **Hours:** Tue.–Thu. 10 A.M.–5 P.M.; Fri. 10 A.M.–8 P.M.;
Sat.–Sun. 10 A.M.–6 P.M. Closed Mon. **Subway:** B, D, F, V to 42nd St.

Miriam and Ira D. Wallach Art Gallery UPPER WEST SIDE Columbia University, Schermerhorn Hall, 1190 Amsterdam Ave. (near 118th St.)
(212) 854-7288 *www.columbia.edu/cu/wallach*. This facility serves Columbia as
a resource for teaching and study, and a public exhibition space. Since its cura-
tors are often graduate students and faculty from the art history department,
the gallery's exhibitions tend to be well researched and often have titles that
require two sentences and a colon. They are nevertheless treasure troves, presenting issues, methods and art not often seen elsewhere. **Admission:** Free.
Hours: Wed.–Sat. 1–5 P.M. **Subway:** 1, 9 to 116th St.

Museum of Arts & Design MIDTOWN WEST 40 W. 53rd St. (between Fifth and
Sixth Aves.) (212) 956-3535 *www.americancraftmuseum.org*. The American
Craft Museum has been rechristened as the Museum of Arts & Design, to

emphasize its mission of celebrating objects that transcend the boundaries between art, craft and design. The collection, on three floors of exhibition space, ranges from utilitarian objects with a strong aesthetic focus to sculptural pieces with a barely conceivable utility. The exhibits tend to be carefully designed and thematic, exploring a single craft, material or artist. Don't miss the lovely gift shop. **Admission:** $9 adults; $6 seniors and students; free for children under 12. Thu. 6–8 P.M., pay as you wish. **Hours:** Daily 10 A.M.–6 P.M. (until 8 P.M. on Thu.). **Subway:** E, V to Fifth Ave.; N, R to 49th St.

National Academy of Design UPPER EAST SIDE 1083 Fifth Ave. (between 89th and 90th Sts.) (212) 369-4880 *www.nationalacademy.org*. Occupying a grand Beaux-Arts town house on Museum Mile, this institution aims to uphold the academic tradition by sponsoring a fine arts school and a professional organization for artists. In addition to hosting the nation's oldest juried show, rotating temporary exhibits, and frequent lectures and discussions with artists, the museum has a large permanent collection of 19th- and 20th-century American art. Its holdings range from the landscapes of the Hudson River School to masterworks of Fauvism, abstraction and magic-realism. **Admission:** $10 adults; $5 students and seniors. **Hours:** Wed.–Thu. noon–5 P.M., Fri.–Sun 11 A.M.–6 P.M. Closed Mon.–Tue. **Subway:** 4, 5, 6 to 86th St.

Neue Gallery New York UPPER EAST SIDE 1048 Fifth Ave. (at 86th St.) (212) 628-6200 *www.neuegallery.org*. Focusing on the art of Germany and Austria, this collection of painting, sculpture and decorative arts features works by Gustav Klimt, Max Beckmann, Erich Heckel and others. Special programming includes chamber music, cabaret performances, lectures and film. The museum's Café Sabarsky is a lovely place to indulge in a traditional Viennese meal, including superb, authentic pastry *mit schlag* (with real whipped cream). **Admission:** $10 adults; $7 students and seniors. No children under age 12; ages 12–16 must be accompanied by an adult. **Hours:** Sat.–Mon. 11 A.M.–6 P.M., Fri. 11 A.M.–9 P.M. Closed Tue.–Thu. **Subway:** 4, 5, 6 to 86th St.

New Museum of Contemporary Art CHELSEA 556 West 22nd St. (212) 219-1222 *www.newmuseum.org*. The New Museum is abandoning its former location in SoHo for a specular new building on the Lower East Side. Until that facility opens in 2006, the museum will operate from this temporary exhibition space on the ground floor of the Chelsea Art Museum. The New Museum lives on the cutting edge of the art world; it's built a reputation for controversial exhibitions, edgy programs as well as a mixed critical reception. The focus is global, with works in a wide range of media, and the curation is provocative. So it's no surprise that the museum's new home would be an innovative design from avant-garde Tokyo-based architects Sejima + Nishizawa/SANAA. **Admission:** $6 adults; $3 seniors and students; free for ages 18 and under; half-price Thu. 6–8 P.M. **Hours:** Tue.–Wed. and Fri.–Sun. noon–6 P.M.; Thu. noon–8 P.M. Closed Mon. **Subway:** F, S, V to Broadway–Lafayette St.; C, E, N, R to Prince St.; 6 to Spring St. or Bleecker St.

Nicholas Roerich Museum UPPER WEST SIDE 319 W. 107th St. (between Broadway and Riverside Dr.) (212) 864-7752 *www.roerich.org*. Nicholas Roerich, the Russian-American star of this one-man museum, was a true Renaissance man, involved in a vast range of artistic, philosophical and spiritual pursuits. He worked with Stravinsky to design sets and costumes, studied Russian archaeology, wrote, painted and traveled extensively. The museum features a permanent collection of Roerich's works and personal memorabilia, including numerous paintings inspired by his interest in Buddhism and the Tibetan highlands, and regularly hosts concerts and poetry readings. **Admission:** Free. **Hours:** Tues.–Sun. 2–5 P.M. **Subway:** 1, 9 to 110th St.

Studio Museum in Harlem 144 W. 125th St. (between Lenox Ave. and Adam Clayton Powell Blvd.) (212) 864-4500 *www.studiomuseuminharlem.org*. Dedicated to African-American art, as well as work from Africa and throughout the diaspora, the Studio Museum features works by Romare Bearden, Elizabeth Catlett, Jacob Lawrence and Norman Lewis, and the James Van Der Zee photographic archives. The museum has undergone an extensive renovation in the last couple of years, adding a new gallery space, an auditorium, workshop space, a reading room and a cafe. **Admission:** $7 adults; $3 students and seniors; free for children under 12. **Hours:** Sun. and Wed.–Fri. noon–6 P.M.; Sat. 10 A.M.–6 P.M. Closed Mon.–Tue. **Subway:** 2, 3 to 125th St.

Whitney Museum of American Art at Altria MIDTOWN EAST 120 Park Ave. (at 42nd St.) (917) 663-2453. The headquarters of Altria, across the street from Grand Central Terminal, houses a Midtown exhibition space for the Whitney Museum. The Sculpture Court accommodates large sculptures that the museum cannot, while the gallery primarily shows contemporary painting and smaller sculptures. **Admission:** Free. **Hours:** Gallery Mon–Fri. 11 A.M.–6 P.M. (Thu. until 7:30 P.M.). Sculpture Court Mon.–Sat. 7:30 A.M.–9:30 P.M.; Sun. 11 A.M.–7 P.M. **Subway:** 4, 5, 6, 7, S to 42nd St.

Art in the Outer Boroughs

Most Manhattanites are convinced that their island borough is the center of the universe, artistically speaking (and in every other way, too, but that's another story). But despite Manhattan's dominance, there's a flourishing cultural life in the outer boroughs. Outer-borough attractions are covered in detail in the **Exploring New York** chapter, but a number of highlights deserve special mention here.

Queens has been quietly evolving for years as a locale for artists and museums, a process that got a major jump-start when MoMA temporarily relocated to Long Island City, Queens, while its Midtown quarters were renovated. MoMA QNS closed in September 2004, but its impact is likely to remain. MoMA's more cutting-edge affiliate, **P.S. 1** (*www.ps1.org*), located at 22-25 Jackson Ave., Long Island City, remains as a major presence in Queens. P.S. 1 is devoted solely to contemporary arts, with frequently changing exhibits and an acclaimed studio program. Also worth a visit on a nice day is the funky **Socrates Sculpture Park** (*www.socratessculpturepark.org*), where an array of large-scale outdoor sculpture enjoys an East River setting at Broadway and Vernon Boulevard.

Long Island City is also home to the **Isamu Noguchi Garden Museum** (*www.noguchi.org*), which displays a wonderful collection of works from this acclaimed Japanese-American sculptor. The facility has just emerged from a two-and-a-half-year renovation, and it's a miraculous aesthetic oasis in the midst of a gritty industrial area.

In the same section of Long Island City, the **Fisher Landau Center for Art** (*www.flca.org*) recently opened to the public, featuring a noteworthy collection of more than 1,000 contemporary paintings.

In Astoria, Queens, exhibits at the **American Museum of the Moving Image** (*www.ammi.org*) offer a fascinating glimpse into the art of filmmaking—supplemented, of course, by frequent screenings, lectures and panel discussions.

In Flushing Meadows/Corona Park, the **Queens Museum of Art** (*www.queensmuse.org*) boasts a wide array of holdings, including a fascinating scale model of New York City created for the 1939 World's Fair and a large collection of Tiffany glass.

Brooklyn also boasts a thriving arts scene. **Williamsburg** is bursting with galleries and art installations, with a focus on edgy young artists. A stroll along Bedford Avenue, the neighborhood's main drag, will give you a good snapshot of Williamsburg's personality.

The **Brooklyn Museum** (*www.brooklynmuseum.org*) is an outstanding museum, well worth a trip from Manhattan. Its temporary exhibitions are often blockbusters, and its permanent collection is wide-ranging, encompassing ancient Egyptian artifacts (in fabulous new galleries), plus European and American painting and sculpture, extensive Asian and African galleries, and dozens of period rooms displaying the decorative arts.

The prestigious **Brooklyn Academy of Music** (*www.bam.org*) is the oldest performing arts center in the nation; its inventive programming draws huge crowds and has given its neighborhood, Fort Greene, an interesting, funky personality.

Up in the Bronx, art lovers might check out the sophisticated, well-curated exhibitions at the **Bronx Museum of the Arts** (*www.bxma.org*), which concentrates on contemporary works, and offers an performance space for experimental, socially relevant programming.

Art Galleries

There are probably more art galleries with active exhibition schedules in New York than anywhere else—far too many to list them all here. But the names and brief descriptions of the dealers below represent a hearty sampling. From paintings to ceramics, from photography and film to Conceptual art, from small decorative objects to massive installations, their exhibitions make up an art menu unequalled in range and variety.

The criteria for the listed galleries are that they hold regular exhibitions and they are open to the public during normal viewing hours (generally from 10

A.M. to 6 P.M. five days a week, closed Sundays and Mondays). But it's always smart to call first, or check the Friday *New York Times* for art listings. Other resources for gallery-goers include the "Cue" section of *New York* magazine (*www.nymetro.com*); *The New Yorker*'s "Goings on about Town" section (*www.newyorker.com*); and sites such as *www.galleryguide.org*.

SoHo

ACE Gallery 275 Hudson St. (at Dominick St.) (212) 255-5599. A sharp contemporary sensibility prevails in this gallery, which aims at museum-quality exhibitions. It does not have a regular roster of artists, but the range is from Abstract Expressionism to present-day work, from "old masters" like Sam Francis and Robert Rauschenberg to the young sculptor Tara Donovan, who uses everyday materials in dense Minimalist sculptures. So eclectic is the menu that even the fashion designer Issey Miyake has shown here.

Howard Greenberg 120 Wooster St., 2nd Fl. (between Prince and Spring Sts.) (212) 334-0010. With one of the biggest inventories in the trade, this gallery focuses on classic 20th-century European and American photography. It handles the estates of such icons as Ruth Orkin, Roman Vishniac, James Van Der Zee, Andre Kertesz and Edward Steichen, and represents well-known contemporaries like William Klein, Sarah Moon, Bill Owens, Ralph Gibson, Gordon Parks, Arnold Newman and the Japanese photographer Kenro Izu. Theme shows have dealt with American car culture, the New York subway and civil rights, among other topics.

Nolan/Eckman 560 Broadway (at Prince St.) (212) 925-6190. This small, intimate and easy gallery specializes in works on paper by contemporary American and German artists. Shows range from the outrageous, no-holds-barred polemics of the cartoony Peter Saul and the whimsical drawings of Carroll Dunham to the musings of German stars like Gerhard Richter, Martin Kippenberger and Sigmar Polke.

Phyllis Kind Gallery 136 Greene St. (between Prince and Houston Sts.) (212) 925-1200. The quirky, the odd and the offbeat are to be found at this SoHo gallery, whose offerings run from far-out folk art like the garrulous paintings of the preacher Howard Finster to the wacky renderings of Chicago School painters like Jim Nutt. The gallery's lively Chicago sensibility reveals its start in the Second City.

Ronald Feldman Fine Arts 31 Mercer St. (212) 226-3232. With a reputation for handling "difficult art," this long-established dealer was the first American to exhibit far-out contemporary Russians, particularly the now-noted team of Komar and Melamid (whose subversive works were smuggled out of their country). Known for its diversity, the gallery also presents the work of political artists, like Leon Golub and Nancy Chunn, and those of a scientific persuasion like Shusaku Arakawa, Todd Siler and the computer conceptualist Carl Fudge. The witty conceptual filmmaker and photographer Elinor Antin also stars here, as does the painter Ida Applebroog.

Chelsea

Barbara Gladstone Gallery 515 W. 24th St. (between 10th and 11th Aves.) (212) 206-9300. An émigré from SoHo (where it opened in the early 1980's), this gallery represents all areas of the visual arts, with the emphasis on Conceptual, installation, video and photographic work. The rhapsodic filmmaker Matthew Barney is one of its stars, along with painter Anish Kapoor, painter/photographer Richard Prince, photographer Shirin Neshat, German installation artists Gregor Schneider and Thomas Hirschhorn, Italian Conceptual artists Mario and Marisa Merz, and German sculptor Stephen Balkenhol.

Cheim and Read 547 W. 25th St. (between 10th and 11th Aves.) (212) 242-7727. One of the most wide-ranging galleries in Chelsea, this spacious ground-floor showcase handles a variety of contemporary painters, sculptors, photographers, video and installation artists of different generations. The gallery emphasizes art with strong psychological themes, like that of sculptor Louise Bourgeois, as well as work devoted to the language of painting, like the abstractions of Richmond Burton. Other high-profile artists represented by the gallery are painters Joan Mitchell, Louise Fishman, Pat Steir, Donald Baechlar and Juan Uslé; sculptor Lynda Benglis; photographers William Eggleston, Robert Mapplethorpe, Adam Fuss and Jack Pierson; and installation artist Jenny Holzer.

Feigen Contemporary 535 W. 20th St. (between 10th and 11th Aves.) (212) 929-0500. The newest branch of the veteran Richard L. Feigen Gallery, which in its uptown headquarters focuses on old masters, Feigen Contemporary represents emerging, mid-career and established contemporary artists, ranging from James Rosenquist and the late Ray Johnson to the young video artist Jeremy Blake.

Leslie Tonkonow Artworks + Projects 535 W. 22nd St. (between 10th and 11th Aves.) (212) 255-8450. The roster of this young gallery emphasizes photographers from all over the world, among them the Korean Nikki S. Lee, the Japanese Tokihiro Sato and the American Peter Campus. But a recent move into larger quarters allows the showing of other kinds of visual artists, too, such as sculptor Beverly Semmes. The dealer's eye for lively talent makes the gallery a cool stop on the Chelsea trail.

Matthew Marks Gallery 523 W. 24th St., 522 W. 22nd St., and 529 W. 21st St. (all between 10th and 11th Aves.) (212) 243-0200. It takes not one but three spacious galleries in Chelsea to display the work of the 20-odd artists on Matthew Marks's superstar roster of contemporaries. Look for works by old masters like the sculptor Ellsworth Kelly, the English figure painter Lucian Freud and the estate of the Abstract Expressionist Willem deKooning, or seek out the very contemporary abstract painters Terry Winters and Brice Marden, the quirky sculptor Robert Gober and photographers Nan Goldin and Andreas Gursky.

MetroPictures 519 W. 24th St. (between 10th and 11th Aves.) (212) 206-7100. Receptive to the new and far-out, this gallery, which opened in SoHo in 1980 but now occupies a vast Chelsea space, carries on with a group of contemporaries that have become more established over the years. They include painter, sculptor and filmmaker Robert Longo; installation artists Tony Oursler and Mike Kelley; and Fred Wilson, who represented the United States at the 2003 Venice Biennale; and photographers Cindy Sherman and Louise Lawlor.

Paula Cooper 534 W. 21st St. and 521 W. 21st St. (both between 10th and 11th Aves.) (212) 255-1105. Founded in 1968, this gallery was one of the very first to open in SoHo, establishing early on an agenda focused on (but not limited to) Conceptual and Minimalist sculpture. Sol LeWitt, Carl Andre, Donald Judd, Robert Grosvenor and Dan Flavin were among early exhibitors, but the gallery also has different breeds of artists in its stable, among them painters Jennifer Bartlett and Michael Hurson; sculptors Mark di Suvero, Robert Wilson, Claes Oldenburg and Coosje Van Bruggen.

Sonnabend Gallery 536 W. 22nd St. (between 10th and 11th Aves.) (212) 627-1018. Noted for introducing 60's proto Pop pioneers like Rauschenberg and Johns to Europe, Illeana Sonnabend came to New York in 1970 and has assembled a stable of internationally known contemporary European and American painters, sculptors, photographers and installation artists. Some of its current stars are the English conceptualists Gilbert and George, kitsch-loving sculptor Jeff Koons, assemblagists Ashley Bickerton and Haim Steinbach from the East Village "Neo-Geo" movement of the mid-1980's, German photographers Bernd and Hilla Becher and site sculptors Anne and Patrick Poirier.

Midtown and Uptown

Adelson Galleries, Inc. The Mark Hotel, 25 E. 77th St., 3rd floor (212) 439-6800. The gallery specializes in American paintings of the late 19th and early 20th centuries, including the work of John Singer Sargent, Mary Cassatt, Childe Hassam, Maurice Prendergast, Thomas Wilmer Dewing and George Bellows. Recent theme shows have included European landscapes by Sargent and a mini-retrospective of the work of Childe Hassam, as well as shows of prints by Cassatt and Bellows.

C & M Arts 45 E. 78th St. (between Park and Madison Aves.) (212) 861-0020. Distinguished presentations of European and American masters—from Impressionists through Matisse, Picasso, deKooning, Jackson Pollock and Joseph Cornell—are at home in this discriminating gallery, quartered in what was once a luxurious town house. The gallery does relatively few shows, but high standards prevail.

Edwynn Houk 745 Fifth Ave. (at 57th St.) (212) 750-7070. Specializing in masters of 20th-century photography, with an emphasis on the 1920's and 30's as well as the work of contemporary Americans, this elegantly understated gallery has a cavernous space in which to show them. It represents the estates of Brassai, Dorothea Lange, Brett Weston, Ilse Bing and Bill Brandt, among others, and is the exclusive representative for such American contemporaries as Elliott Erwitt, Sally Mann, Lynn Davis and Andrea Modica.

Gagosian 980 Madison Ave. (at 76th St.) (212) 744-2313; 555 W. 24th St. (between 10th and 11th Sts.) (212) 741-1111. Big-name contemporaries as well as the works of Pop artists light up the big spaces of this two-location gallery. Large-scale installations by Richard Serra, Mark di Suvero, Damien Hirst and others appear in the huge Chelsea branch; the Madison Avenue gallery handles more conventional-size works. Works by the sculptors Maya Lin and Elyn Zimmerman and the painters Ed Ruscha, Francesco Clemente, Anselm Kiefer, Cy Twombly, Andy Warhol and David Smith are also on the roster.

Galerie St. Etienne 24 W. 57th St. (between Fifth and Sixth Aves.) (212) 245-6734. Austrian and German Expressionism from the turn of the last century through the 1920's are the house specialties at this gallery, along with the work of American folk artists. Founded in 1939 by Dr. Otto Kallir, St. Etienne was the first to show Grandma Moses. The gallery introduced major Expressionists like Gustav Klimt, Oskar Kokoschka and Egon Schiele to the United States, and deals with other Austrian and German modernists, including Kaethe Kollwitz, Lovis Corinth and Paula Modersohn-Becker. Its stable of classic American folk painters includes John Kane, Morris Hirshfield and Horace Pippin.

Garth Clark 24 W. 57th St. (between Fifth and Sixth Aves.) (212) 246-2205. Also Garth Clark Project Space, 45-46 21st St., Long Island City, Queens (718)706-2491. This small but serious showcase for 20th-century ceramics handles a mix of artists spanning the century. Some come from the ceramics world, like George Ohr, Beatrice Wood and Ron Nagle; others, better known as painters or sculptors, have turned their hands to ceramics, among them Lucio Fontana, Sir Anthony Caro, Joan Miró and Louise Nevelson. The gallery in Queens, opened in September, 2002, focuses on ceramics that are more sculptural and a bit more on the edge.

Hirschl & Adler; Hirschl & Adler Modern 21 E. 70th St. (at Madison Ave.) (212) 535-8810. American and European paintings, watercolors, drawings and sculpture from the 18th through the early 20th century are the province of this active gallery, along with American prints of all periods and American decorative arts from 1810 to 1910. Established in 1952, it occupies a handsome landmark town house that is also home to a contemporary arm that deals with European and American art from post–World War II to the present.

Joan T. Washburn 20 W. 57th St. (between Fifth and Sixth Aves.) (212) 397-6780. American art from World War I to the present is the territory staked out by this long-established gallery, which handles the estates of the painters Jackson Pollock and Myron Stout, Louise Nevelson's sculpture and drawings from the 1930's and 40's, and David Smith's paintings from the same period. Its contemporary stable includes the sculptors Jack Youngerman and Gwynn Murrill and the painter Richard Baker.

Kennedy Galleries 730 Fifth Ave. (at 56th St.) (212) 541-9600. Now celebrating its 127th year, Kennedy is one of the oldest dealers in American art. In its plush, carpeted quarters, it shows paintings from an inventory that runs from the 18th to the 20th century, including the Hudson River School, American Impressionism, Social Realism and Modernism. On the 20th-century side, it exclusively handles the estates of Charles Burchfield and Rockwell Kent, and regularly exhibits the work of American classics like George Bellows, John Sloan, Stuart Davis, Charles Demuth, John Marin and Walt Kuhn.

Knoedler & Company 19 E. 70th St. (between Fifth and Madison Aves.) (212) 794-0550. The oldest art gallery in New York, Knoedler goes back to 1846, when its French founder immigrated to America. It became a leading international dealer in European and American art and in 1930 scored a coup by buying 21 masterpieces from the Hermitage in St. Petersburg for the American acquisitor Andrew Mellon. Always a champion of contemporary artists as well, it shows works today by Helen Frankenthaler, Milton Avery, Adolph Gottlieb, Richard Pousette-Dart and other established talents.

Marian Goodman 24 W. 57th St. (between Fifth and Sixth Aves.) (212) 977-7160. An international repertory distinguishes this long-established gallery, a quiet but important presence on the art scene that has recently added significantly to its space. To its schedule of shows by prominent European and American Conceptual artists such as Gerhard Richter and John Baldessari, members of the socially conscious Italian Arte Povera group, along with the Conceptual artists Lawrence Weiner and Dan Graham, it has been adding newer names, among them German photographer Thomas Struth, Italian sculptor Maurizio Cattelan and the French filmmaker Pierre Huyghe, who also makes sculpture for social spaces.

Marlborough 40 W. 57th St. (between Fifth and Sixth Aves.) (212) 541-4900 and **Marlborough Chelsea** 211 W. 19th St. (between Seventh and Eighth Aves.) (212) 463-8634. The emphasis in the spacious uptown branch of this gallery is on contemporary artists with established reputations. Larry Rivers, Marisol, Red Grooms and the Colombian sculptor-painter Fernando Botero are regular exhibitors at Marlborough's glossy uptown headquarters. A graphics division there shows 19th- through 20th-century work, with occasional historical shows; the roomy Chelsea branch specializes in the work of such contemporary sculptors as Anthony Caro, Magdalena Abakanowicz, Kenneth Snelson, Tom Otterness and Beverly Pepper.

Mary Boone 745 Fifth Ave. (at 58th St.) (212) 752-2929; and in Chelsea, 541 W. 21st St. (between 10th and 11th Aves.). Not so cutting-edge as it once was, this trendy, highly publicized gallery, a launching pad for rockets like Julian Schnabel and David Salle, is still going strong. The gallery continues to represent some of the older talents from its roster in the 1970's and 80's, such as painters Salle, Bill Jensen, Ross Bleckner, Eric Fishchl and Barbara Kruger, and it continues to be a showcase for younger artists, among them Leonardo Drew, Damian Loeb, Karin Davie and Will Cotton. The gallery recently opened additional space in Chelsea for large-scale works and installations.

Michael Rosenfeld 24 W. 57th St. (between Fifth and Sixth Aves.) (212) 247-0082. Specializing in American art from 1910 to 1970, the gallery has mounted "movement" shows of early American abstraction and Abstract Expressionism; it also handles the estates of the Surrealist Alfonso Ossorio and the abstractionist Burgoyne Diller, and the work of contemporaries such as Charles Seliger, Martha Madigan and Betye Saar. The gallery is particularly receptive to the work of minority artists, and has mounted a number of shows of African-American art.

PaceWildenstein 32 E. 57th St. (between Fifth and Sixth Aves.) (212) 421-3292 and 534 W. 25th St. (212) 929-7000; Pace MacGill 32 E. 57th St. (between Fifth and Sixth Aves.). Beautifully mounted shows in cool, elegant settings are the rule at PaceWildenstein, originally founded as the Pace Gallery in the 1960's. Not a hotbed of new talent, it's the place to see the work of contemporary "Old Masters," such as Mark Rothko, Ad Reinhardt, Louise Nevelson and the satirist Saul Steinberg, as well as living icons Julian Schnabel, Chuck Close and Alex Katz. Pace MacGill, in the same building, shows 20th-century American photography; the Chelsea branch of PaceWildenstein adds more space for larger-scale sculpture and installations.

Salander-O'Reilly Galleries 20 E. 79th St. (at Madison Ave.) (212) 879-6606. With one of the most ambitious rosters in the art world, this gallery in an impressive town house shows a broad range of American and European painting and sculpture from the Renaissance to the 20th century. It has mounted more than 300 exhibitions, from works by the 17th-century Italian sculptor Gianlorenzo Bernini and the 19th-century English painter John Constable to the American modernist Alfred Maurer and the late abstractionist Stanley Boxer. It represents the estates of Stuart Davis, Gaston Lachaise, Gerald Murphy, Elaine deKooning, Paul Georges, Louisa Matthiasdottir and Elie Nadelman, as well as the work of living artists such as Paul Georges, Don Gummer, Graham Nickson, John Dubrow and Michael Steiner.

Tibor de Nagy 724 Fifth Ave. (212) 262-5050. Established in 1950, this gallery specializes in painterly representation, ranging from names like the landscapist Jane Freilicher to Susanna Coffey, who only does her own self-portraits. Even quirkier talents on the roster include Trevor Winkfield, Joe Brainard, Donald Evans and Shirley Jaffe. The gallery also shows the work of artists from the recent past, among them the photographer-filmmaker-painter Rudy Burckhardt and the painters Fairfield Porter, Edwin Dickinson and Joan Mitchell.

Zabriskie 41 E. 57th St. (between Fifth and Sixth Aves.) (212) 752-1223. Opened in 1955, the Zabriskie Gallery is known for its strong emphasis on American Modernism, Dada and Surrealism, showing works in all media. It is also a stronghold of modern and contemporary French and American photography, from the Frenchman Eugène Atget to the American Nicholas Nixon. The gallery represents the estates of the sculptors Richard Stankiewicz and William Zorach as well as the work of contemporary painters such as Pat Adams and Shirley Goldfarb. Group shows of important movements and periods as well as of emerging contemporary artists are also part of the fare.

—Grace Glueck

THE PERFORMING ARTS
Theater in New York

Broadway, as a word, still has an enchanted sound to the stagestruck, summoning an impossibly glamorous neighborhood of palatial theaters, stars of incandescent wattage and plays and musicals of unmatchable wit and polish. That, anyway, is the myth. In reality, such a Broadway—and by Broadway, one means an area of roughly 40 square blocks around Times Square in Midtown Manhattan—hasn't existed, if it ever did, for at least some 30 years and probably longer. Broadway more than ever is a state of mind, albeit a state within the city of New York. As a piece of nomenclature, it has never been exact, since most "Broadway" theaters are found on other streets. And if you can stretch your imagination—and your legs—to encompass at least a few hundred more blocks, you'll discover that something very much like the Broadway that was still exists. You just can't find it all in one place, any more than all of the city's multistar restaurants are within an oyster shell's throw of one another.

Finding what meets your tastes may require a little more research than it might have in, say, the 1930's. What is produced in the official Broadway area is still what gets the most attention nationally. The plays put on there have bigger budgets and usually bigger names, with ticket prices to match. What it seldom offers is much in the way of originality or daring. Investing in a Broadway production is a high-risk gamble, and producers are accordingly cautious. That is why the neighborhood is dominated by revivals, shows based on successful movies and British imports perfumed with class and flowery reviews from abroad. With the cleaning up and slicking up of Times Square in the 1990's, there has also arisen a new crop of shows directly targeted at tourists, trading on brand-name familiarity, most notably those of Disney, whose *Lion King* (admittedly, a brilliantly rethought stage production of a cartoon movie) may well outlive us all.

The climate of caution has only grown in the wake of 9/11. Theatergoers, especially from outside the city, are less likely to buy tickets far ahead these days, shrinking the kitty of advance sales. And producers are less willing than they were in the 1990's to keep shows open in the face of unfriendly reviews, hoping that a critically unloved production will find an audience on its own.

It's true that in the last couple of years, ticket revenues for Broadway shows have shown healthy increases. But the estimates for attendance were actually down substantially. This seeming discrepancy between sales and attendance figures is easily accounted for by the unpleasant fact of sharply rising ticket prices. Good orchestra seats for a hit musical are now likely to cost you around $100 (and as much as five times that if you go through one of the premium ticket services). The good news is that if you're willing to spend that money, last-minute tickets are now easier to come by, as are discounted seats at the TKTS booth in Times Square (*see below*).

There's still plenty to get excited about on Broadway. Revivals of dramas in recent seasons have been of an exceptionally high level. Conventional book musicals have largely tended to be lost or leaden, though every so often there is the blessed exception of a *Producers, Hairspray* or *Wicked*. What's encouraging is the ways in which some surprisingly venturesome directors have been willing to extend the parameters of what a Broadway musical can be, as with Twyla Tharp's exhilarating narrative dance show *Movin' Out*.

But cutting edge, or even nicking-edge, is definitely not an attribute of Midtown Manhattan theater. When a production with a cool quotient shows up on Broadway (*Avenue Q*), you can safely assume that it started life in some other neighborhood. The same can be said for plays of any topical weight. Since 1970, the overwhelming majority of Pulitzer Prizes for drama have gone to non-Broadway productions.

Finding what's hot **Off-Broadway** and in the increasingly less marginalized realm known as **Off-Off-Broadway** can take you as far from Midtown as Brooklyn or as close as Theater Row—the stretch of 42nd Street west of Eighth Avenue, where antiseptic, mall-like complexes of theaters are springing up like synthetic toadstools. The estimable **Signature Company,** which devotes a full season to examining the work of one American playwright, has established permanent headquarters just a script's throw from the Hudson River. There's no strict rule of thumb for conducting your search: a theater, after all, is judged by what is on its stage, and that changes constantly.

In the glitzy block of 42nd Street between Seventh and Eighth Avenues, where a McDonald's has the most glamorous marquee, there is a charming and innovative theater for children, the restored little jewel box called the **New Victory** (*see chapter* **New York for Children**) right next door to the goliath **Ford Performing Arts Center.** If you're looking for literate, polished plays in thoroughly professional productions, there are several institutional theaters that have become bywords for just that: the **Manhattan Theater Club** (which now has a permanent presence on Broadway at the Biltmore), the **Roundabout Theater Company, Lincoln Center, Playwrights Horizons** and the **Joseph Papp Public Theater,** which has experienced a revitalizing surge of creative energy in the past several years.

There are also younger, smaller companies that have already established a track record for putting on works that get people talking. These include the **Vineyard Theater,** off Union Square (birthplace of everything from Pulitzer winner Edward Albee's *Three Tall Women* to the grownup puppet musical *Avenue Q*), the **New York Theater Workshop** on 4th Street in the East Village (the cradle of the now-fabled rock opera *Rent* and Tony Kushner's prescient drama of Afghanistan, *Homebody/Kabul*), and the **Drama Dept.** on Barrow Street, filled with some of the most vital young theater talents in the city.

If your tastes lean more toward the truly experimental—that is, without such conventions as plot and easily understood characters—there remains a host of fertile outlets for such work, mostly located south of 14th Street, from the legendary **La MaMa** on 4th Street in the East Village to the **HERE** performing arts complex on Sixth Avenue in SoHo. Two mighty bastions of the avant-garde remain indomitably in place and abidingly influential: Richard Foreman's **Ontological-Hysteric Theater** and the **Wooster Group,** both of which have hardcore cult followings, making tickets to their productions tough to come by.

For theatergoers with an international palate, there is the annual **Lincoln Center Festival,** which in recent years has brought major works from Ireland, South Africa and Eastern Europe. And just across the river from Manhattan is the **Brooklyn Academy of Music** (*see section* "Brooklyn" *in chapter* **Exploring New York**), unquestionably the city's most ambitious and adventurous importer of theater, regularly bringing in productions from titanic directors such as Peter Brook and Ingmar Bergman. Indeed, some of the most electric theater seen in New York of late has been at the Academy. Even those who consider Brooklyn a foreign country must concede that it's closer than Stockholm.

— *Ben Brantley*

Practical Matters

Broadway theater has become increasingly pricey (*The Producers* was first to break the $100 barrier, and other shows have not been shy about following in its footsteps). And squeezing into the cramped seats in the older theaters is actually less comfortable than flying coach class. But those things cease to matter when the lights go down and the curtain goes up. You are in the right place.

There are dozens of "Broadway" theaters, and even more Off-Broadway and Off-Off-Broadway. Off- and Off-Off- are less expensive than Broadway, and the theatrical quality can be superior, but the comfort level is no better.

To find out what's playing and where, the fullest **listings** are in *Time Out New York, The New Yorker* and *The New York Times* (listings every day, but more on Friday and Sunday; *www.nytimes.com*).

If you want to see a popular show like *The Lion King,* order your tickets by phone or online months in advance. Broadway theaters do not sell tickets over the phone, though some Off- and Off-Off-Broadway theaters do.

Tickets to most shows are available through **TicketMaster** (212-307-7171; *www.ticketmaster.com*) and **Tele-Charge** (212-239-6200; *www.telecharge.com*). Both of these services tack on outrageous service charges, but if you've got your heart set on a particular show, it may be worth it to you.

American Express Gold Card Events (800-448-TIKS; *www.americanexpress.com/gce*) is often able to offer hard-to-get tickets to cardholders at full price.

Several good Web sites offer up-to-date listings and discount offers to those who register. It's worth checking **www.playbill.com, www.broadway.com** and **www.theatermania.com.**

If you're not trying to see a specific smash hit and you're willing to wait until you arrive in New York to purchase tickets, you have several options. Before you try anything else, call the box office directly to determine availability; if there are tickets to be had, you can drop by the theater in person.

The best-known strategy for bargain hunters is standing on line at the half-price **TKTS booth** (*www.tdf.org*) in Times Square, at Broadway and 47th Street. It's open 3 to 8 P.M. for evening shows (10 A.M.–2 P.M. for Wed. and Sat. matinees, from 11 A.M. to 3 P.M. on Sun. for matinees and 3 P.M. to 7 P.M. for evening performances). Tickets for that day's performances are usually offered at half price (a few are reduced only 25 percent), with a $3 per ticket service charge. Boards outside the ticket windows list available shows; you won't see the latest blockbuster listed, but there are plenty of Broadway and Off-Broadway options. No credit cards are accepted; bring cash or traveler's checks. Come early and be prepared for a long wait. If you're willing to gamble, the line is relatively painless toward the end of the day, and you may even get lucky by scoring seats that have been released as curtain time approaches.

There's also a **downtown branch of TKTS** in the South Street Seaport at the corner of John and Front Streets (by subway: 1, 2, 4, 5, J, Z, M to Fulton Street; A, C to Broadway/Nassau Street). It's open Monday to Saturday 11 A.M. to 6 P.M.; lines are usually much shorter here. At this location only, matinee tickets are sold the day before the show. Do not buy tickets from scalpers hovering around the TKTS lines. They offer deeper discounts, but you run the risk that the tickets are counterfeit and the theater will turn you away. (The same is true of hawkers around the theaters themselves.)

Another option is the **Hit Show Club,** 630 Ninth Ave., Rm. 808 (between 44th and 45th Sts.; 212-581-4211; *www.hitshowclub.com*; open Mon.–Fri. 9 A.M.–4 P.M.; subway: A, C, E to 42nd St.). When you walk in, you'll see a rack with discount coupons for some dozen shows. The choice is smaller than same-day tickets at TKTS, but there is a big advantage: You can use these coupons to buy tickets in advance. Another advantage: You don't have to stand on a long line outside in foul weather. (As an unexpected bonus, the lobby of the club's landmarked building is a gorgeous Art Deco interior.) Take your coupon to the theater, present it, and if the box office has what you want, they'll sell you one or two tickets at the discounted price (they may also sell to you over the phone, asking you to supply the Hit Show Club discount code). Most Hit Show Club discounts are about 40 percent, with no extra service charge. (You may also see Hit Show and other discount coupons in hotel lobbies and beside the cash register in some restaurants. Not all discounts are the same, so read the fine print carefully.) Hit Show coupons are also distributed at the **NYC & Company Visitor Information Center,** 810 Seventh Avenue at 53rd Street.

Classical Music

Musical life in New York begins but by no means ends with two big institutions. Carnegie Hall and Lincoln Center generate concerts of every size and description and have halls big and small in which to stage them. Next to these giants is a ring of smaller organizations; they organize chamber music, new music ensembles and recitals. Though traditionally the season stretches from September until well into June, it's now possible to find worthwhile events in August as well as November.

Surrounding these major islands of activity is an ocean of free enterprise, and it is this mass of self-generated events and cottage industries that gives New York its energy. Experimental music groups, amateur choirs with big agendas, small opera companies doing new or esoteric repertory, self-financed and self-promoted debut performances fill downtown lofts and uptown churches in profusion. The quality will vary as much as the material, but the level of ambition is always high.

Carnegie Hall (*see below for full listing*) has no resident orchestras or ensembles; it is a presenter, gathering the best orchestras, singers and recitalists from around the world and fitting them into subscription series. Sign up for a season-long list, or choose individual events. In the main hall (seating 2,800) expect the Vienna and Berlin Philharmonics every year, as well as the orchestras of Cleveland, Philadelphia, Boston and Chicago. The Pittsburgh and Montreal Symphonies and many others will drop in, too, and there will be both familiar and exotic symphonic visitors from Europe and the East.

Within Carnegie Hall is a little gem called **Weill Recital Hall,** which hosts chamber music series, musical theater in concert, song recitals by good artists and debut recitals by talented young professionals selected by Carnegie Hall in conjunction with several European concert halls.

Lincoln Center's Avery Fisher Hall (soon to be renovated) is Carnegie's equivalent in size and seating capacity, if not beauty. It produces series in the same way as well, but with a difference. For Fisher is also the home of the New York Philharmonic. The smaller Alice Tully Hall next door houses the Chamber Music Society of Lincoln Center. The Philharmonic is at work steadily through the season, either under its music director Lorin Maazel or guest conductors. Weekly programs are generally repeated three to four times, often with Friday morning performances for those less easy with nightlife in the city. (*See the box* "Lincoln Center" *in this chapter for full listings.*)

The Chamber Music Society is a permanent ensemble of 10 to 20 performers. They mix and match their instruments and skills to make all possible combinations. Sextets with bassoon are no problem, but conventional quartets and trios turn up as well. The Society's programs are usually repeated only once.

Also in the Lincoln Center complex, the **Juilliard School** is eager to put its best students before the public and sponsors a number of in-house competitions with major public recitals as rewards. Go to the box office at the school in Lincoln Center for schedules and tickets. Most performances are free (*see below for full listing*).

Indeed, the students of Juilliard and their companion schools, **Mannes** and **Manhattan** (*see below*), often blur the distinction between amateur and professional. All three schools teem with concerts and operas at which the public is welcome, usually for free. Opera productions at the Juilliard Theater (one of the city's best spaces) are often on a par if not superior to the professional efforts of companies in other cities. Manhattan regularly puts on skillful versions of out-of-the-way 20th-century operas, and Mannes has recently been in the midst of an extensive Handel project.

Although New York is often criticized for having only one major orchestra, the accusation is deceptive. Floating groups like the estimable Orchestra of St. Luke's have their own seasons. The New York Chamber Symphony and the conductorless Orpheus are well rated, and the American Symphony Orchestra is making strides as well. Under Robert Spano, the Brooklyn Philharmonic is giving some of the most interesting orchestra programs in town. The group performs at the **Brooklyn Academy of Music** (*see box in the* "Brooklyn" *section of* *chapter* **Exploring New York**), a quick and easy subway ride across the East River from Manhattan.

Smaller venues are remarkably active. The **Miller Theater at Columbia University** has become the hotbed of choice for the serious new-music crowd. **Merkin Concert Hall** is plain to look at but night after night provides a place for every kind of music, new and old, provocative and conservative. The **Florence Gould Theater** and the **Kaye Playhouse** join the **92nd Street Y** as East Side presenters. **The Kitchen** downtown near the Hudson River is a clearinghouse for musical and theatrical experiment where electronic instruments and new sounds are the norm. The **World Music Institute** brings in ethnic performers from Tibet, Africa or, for that matter, down the street.

Summer is becoming busy, although Carnegie Hall usually closes in August. In June and July, the **Lincoln Center Festival** brings operas, orchestra concerts and interesting exotica. It uses its own halls and a few others nearby. There's also the vastly popular **Mostly Mozart Festival,** which divides its frequent summer-long programs between Avery Fisher and Alice Tully Halls.

A lot of summer entertainment is free: the Met giving concert versions of operas in the parks of the five boroughs, the New York Philharmonic doing much the same, and Lincoln Center's Damrosch Park offering concert brass bands, choruses and mostly lighthearted fare.   —*Bernard Holland*

Classical Music Centers

Below is a brief list of places that offer concerts on a regular basis. Serious music lovers should check the listings every Sunday in *The New York Times* "Arts & Leisure" section.

Bargemusic BROOKLYN Fulton Ferry Landing (between Water and River Sts.) (718) 624-4061 *www.bargemusic.org*. One of the city's most unusual venues is this refurbished barge, now a floating chamber music space where artists can perform in an informal atmosphere and actually enjoy making music. Moored in the East River under the Brooklyn Bridge, with the Manhattan skyline providing a breathtaking backdrop, Bargemusic is a cozy, wood-paneled room that seats about 125 people on folding chairs. Year-round, the finest chamber music performers play concerts of the highest caliber. It's a magical spot, well worth the trip to Brooklyn Heights and the occasionally choppy waters. Advance reservations are necessary, as performances sell out. Tickets are usually $35 ($25 for students, $30 for seniors on Thursday). **Subway:** A, C to High St.; 2, 3 to Clark St.

Carnegie Hall MIDTOWN WEST Seventh Ave. and 57th St. (212) 247-7800 *www.carnegiehall.org*. From the time it opened in 1891 (with Tchaikovsky conducting the inaugural concert), the 2,804-seat landmark has been synonymous with the greatest musicians of the 20th century, from Arturo Toscanini, Marian Anderson and Vladimir Horowitz to Ella Fitzgerald, Frank Sinatra and the Beatles.

Carnegie's acoustics are legendary. Once you get past the claustrophobic lobby, you're in for a visual and sonic treat. On the walls are photos and letters from famous composers, singers, instrumentalists and conductors. The seats are plush

Lincoln Center

With controversial architecture, but indisputably stunning cultural offerings, Lincoln Center is a great stop on any visitor's itinerary, with a full schedule featuring everything from opera to ballet to film to jazz.

Renovation plans for Lincoln Center are underway; the first phase is a redesign of West 65th Street, the complex's main artery. Eventually, all the buildings that house the center's 12 constituent groups—including the Metropolitan Opera, the New York City Ballet and the New York Philharmonic—are to receive upgrades ranging from new travertine for the plaza to an improved Avery Fisher Hall.

Although the World Trade Center site promises to become another cultural anchor, for now Lincoln Center remains the hub of the city's cultural life and one of the nation's most prestigious stages.   *—Robin Pogrebin*

Broadway (W. 62nd–66th St.) (212) 546-2656 *www.lincolncenter.org.* **Subway:** 1, 9 to 66th St.; A, B, C, D to 59th St.

Alice Tully Hall (212) 875-5050. With 1,096 seats, this is a wonderfully intimate stage for chamber music and recitals, as well as small-scale opera and orchestral concerts. Jazz and avant-garde artists play here, and there's even an occasional appearance by a pop star or two. This is the regular stage for the **Chamber Music Society of Lincoln Center** (*www.chambermusicsociety.org*), which often performs with superstar guest artists. Alice Tully Hall is due for a thorough renovation under Lincoln Center's redevelopment plan.

Avery Fisher Hall (212) 875-5030. Its acoustics may be a frequent subject of debate, but this 2,738-seat hall is one of the city's premier concert venues and home to the internationally acclaimed **New York Philharmonic,** led by Lorin Maazel. Avery Fisher also hosts the world's top visiting orchestras, instrumentalists and chamber groups, as well as pop and jazz performers.

Jazz at Lincoln Center (212) 258-9800 *www.jazzatlincolncenter.com.* In October 2004, Jazz at Lincoln Center moved "off-campus" to its own home in the glitzy new Time Warner Center at Columbus Circle. The complex, designed by Rafael Viñoly and called Frederick P. Rose Hall, has three performance stages: the 1,100- to 1,220-seat Rose Theater, which can also accommodate opera, dance, theater, film and orchestral performances; the 300- to 600-seat Allen Room, with a glass wall overlooking a spectacular view of Central Park; and the 140-seat Dizzy's Club Coca-Cola for smaller concerts and special events.

Library for the Performing Arts at Lincoln Center/Dorothy and Lewis B. Cullman Center (212) 870-1630. This branch of the New York Public Library is a treasure trove of invaluable materials, boasting the largest reference, archival and circulating arts-related collection in the world.

Lincoln Center Theater (212) 362-7600. Lincoln Center presents first-rate theater on two stages: the **Vivian Beaumont**, a large, modern Broadway stage, and the more intimate **Mitzi E. Newhouse Theater,** which presents Off-Broadway productions. Check *www.lct.org* for details.

Metropolitan Opera House (212) 362-6000. Dominating Lincoln Center's plaza is the world's largest opera house. Five enormous glass arches overwhelm the eye. Behind them hang Marc Chagall's spectacular murals, "The Triumph of Music" on the south wall and "The Sources of Music" on the north.

Inside the 3,900-seat house, the sweeping staircase ushers you into a glittering world of red velvet, gold leaf and gaudy crystal chandeliers that rise up to the ceiling at the beginning of each performance. Even in the nosebleed sections, the sound is good, so it's not necessary to spend $170 or more for orchestra seats. Standing-room tickets are about $15, but they sell out fast.

Technically, the Met is a director's dream, equipped with a slew of mechanical wonders: four huge stages with elevators and revolving platforms, and a computerized lighting system. Every seat has a "Met Titles" screen, providing simultaneous translation. The orchestra pit accommodates more than 100 top-notch musicians under the artistic direction of James Levine.

In addition to hosting the world-renowned **Metropolitan Opera** (*www.metopera.org*), the opera house is also the home of **American Ballet Theater** (*www.abt.org*) in May, June and early July.

New York State Theater (212) 870-5570. It may not be as posh as its sister opera house across the plaza, but in some ways, the New York State Theater is the more interesting building. Designed by Philip Johnson, the 2,800-seat home for the **New York City Ballet** (*www.nycballet.com*) and the **New York City Opera** (*www.nycopera.com*) boasts a grand, four-story foyer, flanked by two marvelous white marble Elie Nadelman sculptures and surrounded by balconies. The seats are comfortable, the sightlines good.

Walter Reade Theater (212) 875-5600. This is Lincoln Center's venue for film, with a widely varied calendar of independent and foreign films. Check *www.filmlinc.com* for schedules, including details on the **New York Film Festival.**

Seasonal Events: Check *www.lincolncenter.org* for details. In summer, the **Lincoln Center Festival** draws an incredible array of performing artists from around the globe; the always-festive **Midsummer Night's Swing** brings would-be Freds and Gingers to the plaza for dancing to swing and salsa; **Mostly Mozart** is an August concert series of crowd pleasers; and **Lincoln Center Out-of-Doors** presents an array of free performances. (The Metropolitan Opera and the New York Philharmonic also stage free summer concerts in each borough's parks.) Autumn brings the **New York Film Festival.** *The Nutcracker* is a traditional holiday event, as is a special gala performance on **New Year's Eve.**

and the gilded décor is ravishing. Even if a performance does not live up to your expectations, a visit to Carnegie always does.

During intermission, instead of squeezing into the lobby or the Café Carnegie, stop by the Rose Museum on the First Tier level, where interesting music-related exhibits give you a taste of the hall's illustrious history. On the same level are another cafe, the Rohatyn Room and a gift shop. But beware: The shop is even more claustrophobic than the lobby.

In addition to the main 2,804-seat **Isaac Stern Auditorium,** there's also the more intimate 268-seat **Weill Recital Hall.** In 2003, Carnegie Hall christened the 650-seat **Zankel Concert Hall,** an underground space that was a movie theater for decades. **Subway:** B, N, Q, R to 57th St.

Juilliard School—Juilliard Theater UPPER WEST SIDE 60 Lincoln Center Plaza (Broadway at 65th St.) (212) 769-7406, or (212) 721-6500 for Centercharge *www.juilliard.edu.* The Juilliard School is one of the world's leading music conservatories; its alumni include some of the world's best-known performers. The main auditorium, the Juilliard Theater, is as impressive as the students who regularly appear on its stage. A steeply raked 933-seat hall with comfortable seats, superior acoustics and excellent sightlines, it is most often used for opera and orchestral concerts, although chamber music, jazz, drama and dance are no strangers here. This is also one of the city's best bargains: many performances are free. Others have relatively modest ticket prices, usually under $25. Check the Web site for the frequently changing calendar of events (there are usually no performances in summer). **Subway:** 1, 9 to 66th St.

Kosciuszko Foundation UPPER EAST SIDE 15 E. 65th St. (between Madison and Fifth Aves.) (212) 734-2130 *www.kosciuszkofoundation.org.* On the second floor of the Kosciuszko Foundation's splendid three-story limestone town house, just off Central Park, is one of the loveliest recital spaces in town. An elegant wood-paneled parlor at the top of a red-carpeted spiral staircase, the room doubles as a gallery for 19th- and 20th-century Polish art. The Foundation, founded in 1925, is a center for Polish culture and education, so naturally the focus of its excellent concert series is on Polish music and musicians. It also sponsors films screening, lectures and other events. **Subway:** 6 to 68th St.; N, R to Fifth Ave.

Manhattan School of Music UPPER WEST SIDE 122 Claremont Ave. (at Broadway and 122nd St.) (917) 493-4428 *www.msmnyc.edu.* One of the country's premier conservatories, the Manhattan School of Music is bustling with all sorts of performances, from student, faculty and professional recitals and chamber music to opera, jazz and musical theater. The quality is usually high and the price of admission is often free (or less than $20). The two principal spaces are Borden Auditorium, a long, narrow 1,000-seat hall with decent if not wonderful sound, and upstairs, the intimate, 380-seat Hubbard Recital Hall. **Subway:** 1, 9 to 125th St.

Mannes College of Music UPPER WEST SIDE 150 W. 85th St. (between Amsterdam and Columbus Aves.) (212) 580-0210 *www.mannes.edu.* Mannes is the third big-name music school, along with Juilliard and the Manhattan School of Music, on Manhattan's West Side. It presents hundreds of high-quality performances from September to May, from chamber music to grand opera and beyond. Its two auditoriums—the 200-seat Concert Hall and the 60-seat Goldmark Auditorium, used mainly for recitals—are adequate if not luxurious. (For larger-scale events, Mannes often uses the nearby Symphony Space; see listing in "Other Arts Venues," below.) Tickets are usually free or very inexpensive. **Subway:** 1, 9, B, C to 86th St.

Merkin Concert Hall UPPER WEST SIDE 129 W. 67th St. (between Broadway and Amsterdam Ave.) (212) 501-3330 *www.elainekaufmancenter.org.* This intimate 457-seat hall is an attractive space with superior acoustics, making it a favorite for chamber ensembles, recitalists and even mid-size orchestras and choral groups. A number of popular series are held here, including "New Sounds Live," which focuses on avant-garde, jazz or ethnic music. Merkin is part of the Elaine Kaufman Cultural Center, which means that many programs here highlight Jewish roots and culture. **Subway:** 1, 9 to 66th St.

Metropolitan Museum of Art—Grace Rainey Rogers Auditorium UPPER EAST SIDE 1000 Fifth Ave. (between 81st and 82nd Sts.) (212) 570-3949 *www.metmuseum.org* (click on "concerts and lectures"). The Met's excellent 708-seat hall, acoustically one of the best in town, is well suited for recitals and chamber music. One of its secrets is the warm-toned African korina wood paneling, a highly reflective material that helps magnify sound. Many of the world's prominent performers appreciate the merits of this hall, which is why you may find the Juilliard and Guarneri String Quartets, the Beaux-Arts Trio and other big-name artists gracing the stage in its September-to-June season. There are also occasional jazz concerts, and many of the museum's popular lectures take place here. Concerts are also presented in other locations around the museum— check the Web site for times and locations. **Subway:** 4, 5, 6 to 86th St.

Opera

Opera in New York means, first and foremost, the **Metropolitan Opera** at Lincoln Center. Sometimes it seems that opera in the whole world means, first and foremost, the Metropolitan Opera. The company essentially deserves its iconic status. Leading international singers regularly perform there; indeed, a Metropolitan Opera debut is still a benchmark of a singer's career. In more than 25 years as artistic director, James Levine has built the Met orchestra into one of the finest anywhere. The musicians know they are good and play with palpable pride and confidence. The 3,900-seat opera house, which opened in 1966, is looking a bit tattered these days, but the sound in the auditorium remains marvelous, and, if anything, the sound up in the cheaper balcony and family circle seats is better than that in the pricey orchestra section. (*See the box* "Lincoln Center" *earlier in this chapter for full listing.*)

Which brings up price. The Met is expensive, to the tune of $170 to $315

The Metropolitan Opera

for the best seats to each season's top performance. But putting on international-level opera is an expensive enterprise. It's mostly worth it. Yes, there are off-nights at the Met, and ill-conceived productions, and automatic-pilot performances of the most popular bread-and-butter operas. And sometimes second-string casts fall too far below the level of the name singers who open a production and garner the original reviews. Still, company officials assert that, night after night, the Met presents opera on a more consistently high level than any other company, and they are right.

A newcomer to opera or a visitor from out of town will be tempted to go to the crowd-pleasers, such as *La Boheme, Tosca* and *Aida.* These are good shows. But it would be wise to check out reviews and select something special, for the Met at its best is exhilarating. In recent seasons, for example, the presentations of Tchaikovsky's *Queen of Spades,* Mozart's *Marriage of Figaro,* Strauss's *Ariadne auf Naxos*, Wagner's *Meistersinger* and Berg's *Wozzeck* have been exceptionally produced and splendidly sung.

By the way, the Met's official guided tour is one of the best-kept secrets in New York. It's fascinating to go backstage and see the rotating stage, the set shops, the rehearsal spaces. The costume builders also demonstrate how they must adapt outfits to singers with enormously varying sizes and shapes.

Across the plaza from the Met, in the New York State Theater, is the **New York City Opera,** and the biggest frustration of this enterprising company is its location (there was talk that the company would someday move to the new World Trade Center site, but it was not among the cultural institutions selected to relocate there). The mission of the company under its current leader, Paul Kellogg, is to create an identity that is distinct from its neighbor's. Why do what the Met can do better? So City Opera may not offer world-famous singers in the standard repertory, but it can offer young, eager artists who look and act like the characters they portray. Moreover, the City Opera tends to be more daring about repertory than the Met. The company regularly offers Baroque operas by Handel, neglected 20th-century works like Strauss's *Intermezzo,* Britten's *Paul Bunyan* (an entrancing production), and Carlisle Floyd's *Of Mice and Men* (a riveting musical and dramatic experience).

Ticket prices for City Opera are much more affordable than those at the Met, as well (as little as $12, with prices topping out at $115). All this has made the company attractive to younger, hipper audiences.

The company's goal of distinguishing itself from the Met would be easier, however, if it performed in a different facility in a different neighborhood. With over 2,700 seats, the New York State Theater is somewhat too big for the type of involving musical theater experience the City Opera works have to offer. And the acoustics of the auditorium are far from ideal, though the company is currently experimenting with an electronic sound-enhancement system for the space, a move that has agitated many traditionalists but been largely unnoticed by most attendees. All in all, City Opera is not just a cheaper alternative to the Met, but an interesting company in its own right.

There are many other smaller opera companies in the city, organizations that typically present two or three productions per season. **DiCapo Opera** is a scrappy company that performs in an appealing modest-sized theater on East 76th Street, and presents classics and occasionally contemporary works in effective productions with, by and large, talented young casts.

For 50 years, the **Amato Opera** has been a mom-and-pop outfit on a tight budget with a loyal following, presenting popular operas in a theater on the Bowery that gives new meaning to the term "intimate drama."

The **Bronx Opera** usually presents just two productions per year (check local listings), in English translation, on two consecutive weekends, first at the Lehman Center in the Bronx, then at John Jay College Theater in Manhattan.

The **Juilliard Opera Center** is not, as its name implies, a company of students from the Juilliard School, but a training institute that offers singers in leading roles who are on the brink of, or already engaged in, professional careers. Students fill out the smaller roles and provide the orchestra and chorus. But Juilliard students are more accomplished than many professionals, and the Opera Center productions are often excellent. The **Manhattan School of Music** also presents some worthwhile productions in its commodious theater on Broadway and 122nd Street, for example, an important recent revival of Ned Rorem's stirring operatic adaptation of Strindberg's *Miss Julie*. Opera at the **Mannes College of Music** on West 85th Street is also worth checking out.

The estimable **L'Opera Français de New York** presents stylish, semi-staged performances of French operas, often rarities, at Alice Tully Hall in Lincoln Center, although just two a year (check local listings). They are always first-rate.

If you can do without sets and costumes entirely, the **Opera Orchestra of New York** (*www.oony.org*), directed by the conductor Eve Queler, is a must. Ms. Queler seeks out inexplicably neglected operas and presents them in concert performances at Carnegie Hall with strong casts, sometimes including major singers. In recent seasons Renée Fleming, Ruth Ann Swenson and Vesselina Kasarova, to cite just some illustrious artists, have scored triumphs with the Opera Orchestra. Ms. Queler's work reminds us that opera is, at its core, music, and can work quite effectively without its theatrical trimmings. *(See section* "Classical Music Centers" *earlier in this chapter for more information on venues.)*   —Anthony Tommasini

Amato Opera Theater 319 Bowery (between 2nd and Bleecker Sts.) (212) 228-8200 *www.amato.org*. Intimate venue, affordable tickets and innovative programming for children. **Subway:** F, V to Second Ave.; 6 to Bleecker St.

DiCapo Opera Theater 184 E. 76th St. (between Lexington and Third Aves.) (212) 288-9438 *www.dicapo.com*. **Subway:** 6 to 77th St.

Juilliard Opera Center—Juilliard Theater 60 Lincoln Center Plaza (Columbus Ave. and 64th St.) (212) 799-5000 *www.juilliard.edu*. **Subway:** 1, 9 to 66th St.; A, B, C, D to 59th St.

Metropolitan Opera House—Lincoln Center Columbus Ave. and 64th St. (212) 362-6000 *www.metopera.org*. You can beat the high cost of tickets by paying for standing room. Standing room tickets are usually $15–$20; they go on sale at the box office on Saturday at 10 A.M. for the entire week that follows (lines start early). Student tickets are available for $25–$35 for selected performances. In summer, the Met also stages free performances in the city's parks. Guided tours are offered October through June at 3:30 P.M. on weekdays and 10:30 A.M. on Sundays for $10 adults, $5 students. Call (212) 769-7020 to reserve. **Subway:** 1, 9 to 66th St.

Regina Opera Company Regina Hall, 65th St. and Twelfth Ave., Brooklyn. (718) 232-3555 *www.reginaopera.org*. Performances at 7 P.M. Saturday and 4 P.M. Sunday. General admission (at door) $15. **Subway:** D to 62nd St.; N to Fort Hamilton Parkway.

New York State Theater—Lincoln Center 20 Lincoln Center Plaza (Columbus Ave. and 63rd St.) (212) 870-5570 *www.nycopera.com*. **Subway:** 1, 9 to 66th St.; A, B, C, D to 59th St.

Dance

Ballet, modern dance, jazz dance, tap dance and folk groups: As the dance capital of the world, New York plays host to them all. Troupes from abroad and resident companies perform throughout the year.

The New York City Ballet and American Ballet Theater, the country's top classical troupes, have regular seasons. Founded in 1948 by the Russian-born choreographer George Balanchine and his American patron, Lincoln Kirstein, the **New York City Ballet** (*www.nycballet.com*) remains faithful to Balanchine's view of dance for dance's sake. One-act plotless works, not story ballets, are the norm. The focus on the company's two late resident geniuses, Balanchine and Jerome Robbins, makes for high art. New works by Peter Martins, the current director, continue the emphasis on distinguished composers. The company has a winter season (including five weeks of *The Nutcracker*) and a spring season at Lincoln Center's **New York State Theater** (*see the box* "Lincoln Center" *earlier in this chapter*).

American Ballet Theater (*www.abt.org*), founded in 1939, is more eclectic. Its reputation stems from its ballets in different styles and an ability to attract great dancers. Male virtuosity has been dazzling. The company tends to stage 19th-century classics and other three-act story ballets during its May and June stint at the **Metropolitan Opera House** (*see the box* "Lincoln Center"). In the fall, a brief season at **City Center** concentrates on one-act works, including premieres by contemporary choreographers such as Twyla Tharp.

New York has a variety of theaters and performing spaces that are hospitable to dance. For raw cutting-edge, the loftlike spaces of **The Kitchen** (*see section* "Other Arts Venues" *later in this chapter*), the **Dance Theater Workshop,** and **St. Mark's Church** are a must (*see below*). Many a newcomer, including Mark Morris, had a start in these well-attended nonproscenium theaters.

Brooklyn Academy of Music (BAM)   BROOKLYN
30 Lafayette Ave. (off Flatbush Ave.) (718) 636-4100 *www.bam.org*. Autumn's **Next Wave Festival** makes BAM the mecca for trendy and serious audiences (sometimes the two overlap). Experimental dance is at the heart of the festival. Piña Bausch, Germany's iconoclastic choreographer, and Sankai Juku, a group working in Japan's post-Hiroshima Butoh style, are staples of the series. Leading American experimental choreographers associated with the Next Wave and BAM are more unpredictable and include Trisha Brown, Bill T. Jones, Meredith Monk, Lucinda Childs and Mark Morris (whose company is headquartered in a newly constructed dance center adjacent to BAM). **Subway:** M, N, Q, R, W, 2, 3, 4, 5 to Atlantic Ave./Pacific St.

City Center of Music and Drama   MIDTOWN WEST
131 W. 55th St. (between Sixth and Seventh Aves.) (212) 581-1212 *www.city-center.org*. The **Paul Taylor Dance Company** performs in the spring and the **Alvin Ailey American Dance Theater** is usually here in December. Both are highly popular modern-dance companies with brilliant dancers. Taylor's choreography ranges in mood from light to dark and his mastery is unquestioned.

Ailey died in 1989 but his troupe, inspired by African-American heritage, has brought the dancing to an even more exciting level. The company's signature work is *Revelations*, a masterpiece that Ailey set to spirituals.

City Center offers a diverse schedule (one that might feature comedy or the Gilbert and Sullivan players), but it frequently hosts other world-renowned dance companies as well, including the **Dance Theater of Harlem,** the **Martha Graham Dance Company,** and the **Merce Cunningham Dance Company.** Subway: B, D, E to Seventh Ave.; F, N, Q, R, W to 57th St.

Joyce Theater   CHELSEA

175 Eighth Ave. (between 18th and 19th Sts.) (212) 242-0800 *www.joyce.org.* The choreographer Eliot Feld reinvented this former movie house as a theater for dance and a home for his ballet company, now called Ballet Tech. Feld's quirky ballets for young dancers have a loyal following and can be seen in the spring and in a brief season in December. In January, this 500-seat Art Deco theater produces the "Altogether Different" series, featuring small experimental troupes. A wide range of modern dance predominates during the year. The popular Pilobolus troupe appears in July. The Joyce has a satellite branch, the **Joyce SoHo** (*see listing below*). The Joyce was selected as one of the cultural institutions that will eventually relocate to the redeveloped World Trade Center site in a few years. **Subway:** A, C, E to 14th St.; 1, 9 to 18th St.

Metropolitan Opera House   UPPER WEST SIDE

Lincoln Center, Columbus Ave. and 64th St. (212) 362-6000 *www.lincolncenter.org.* In July, the Met is the way station for major ballet companies from abroad. You might see Russia's Kirov Ballet and Bolshoi Ballet, the Royal Ballet from England or the Paris Opera Ballet. Also in July, the Lincoln Center Festival stages dance performances in the Met, the New York State Theater and the Center's smaller theaters. (*See the box* "Lincoln Center" *earlier in this chapter.*) **Subway:** 1, 9 to 66th St.   —*Anna Kisselgoff*

Other Dance Theaters and Studios

Dance Theater Workshop—Bessie Schonberg Theater 219 W. 19th St. (between Seventh and Eighth Aves.) (212) 924-0077 *www.dtw.org.* The DTW boasts perhaps the most technologically sophisticated dance theater space in the nation; new technology enables artists to work with video and dance in innovative ways. Passersby can watch rehearsals through floor-to-ceiling windows. The lineup is varied and even funky, with generally affordable ticket prices. **Subway:** 1, 9 to 18th St.

Isadora Duncan Foundation Studio 141 W. 26th St., 3rd Fl. (between Sixth and Seventh Aves.) (212) 691-5040 *www.isadoraduncan.org.* This small, attractive studio seats about 50 for its occasional shows of classic Duncan works (often performed by the all-female Lori Belilove & Company) and dances from contemporary choreographers. **Subway:** F, V, 1, 9 to 23rd St.

Joyce SoHo 155 Mercer St. (between Houston and Prince Sts.) (212) 431-9233 *www.joyce.org.* The Joyce SoHo provides a place for new choreographers to showcase their work before they venture on to larger performance spaces. With 75 free-standing seats, the comfortable loft-like space (created from a former firehouse) has a very open feel. Thanks to the lack of columns, every seat in the house is a good one. **Subway:** F, S, V to Broadway-Lafayette St.; N, R to Prince St.

Movement Research at the Judson Church 55 Washington Sq. South (212) 477-0351 *www.movementresearch.org.* Since the 1960's, this former house of worship has hosted performances of bold and eclectic new works by dance and performance artists. Movement Research continues the tradition with a free Monday-night series (doors open at 7:45 P.M.; arrive early). **Subway:** A, C, E, F, S, V to W. 4th St.

Mulberry Street Theater 70 Mulberry St. (at Bayard St.) (212) 349-0126 *www.htchendance.org.* A former public school was transformed into Chinatown's only performance space, with two dance studios and a black-box theater. It is home to H.T. Chen and Dancers, a company that infuses technically vigorous American modern dance with Chinese inflections. Mulberry also hosts other programs, including "Newsteps," a showcase for emerging choreographers. **Subway:** J, M, N, Q, R, W, Z, 6 to Canal St.

St. Mark's Church in the Bowery 131 E. 10th St. (at Second Ave.) (212) 674-8112 *www.danspaceproject.org.* Following a devastating fire in 1978, the interior of the city's second-oldest church was restructured into a versatile open space that hosts performing arts (especially dance) and religious services. Danspace Project performances are daring and experimental. **Subway:** 6 to Astor Pl.

Other Arts Venues: A Mixed Bag

Many of New York's performance spaces host a wide variety of offerings. Although **Carnegie Hall** is listed under "Classical Music," its season might include anything from opera to jazz to stand-up comedy. And **Lincoln Center's** array of theaters and performance spaces play host to theater, opera, classical and chamber music, jazz, film—you name it. See also the **Exploring New York** chapter for details on **Radio City Music Hall,** where the offerings tend to be more pop and glitz than classical—but the Art Deco setting is magical.

Brooklyn Academy of Music 30 Lafayette Ave. (off Flatbush Ave.) (718) 636-4100 *www.bam.org.* BAM is Brooklyn's answer to Lincoln Center, but with an emphasis on the contemporary and the cutting-edge. BAM hosts innovative programming, including theater, dance, music, performance art and more. Independent films are regularly screened at **BAM Rose Cinemas,** and BAM's **Next Wave Festival,** held in the fall, is a major event on the city's cultural calendar. *(See* "Brooklyn" *in chapter* **Exploring New York** *for details.)* **Subway:** M, N, Q, R, W, 2, 3, 4, 5 to Atlantic Ave./Pacific St.

Columbia University—Miller Theater 2960 Broadway (at 116th St.) (212) 854-7799 *www.millertheater.com.* Columbia has a state-of-the-art theater that brings innovative music and dance, as well as theater, poetry readings and lectures, to Morningside Heights. **Subway:** 1, 9 to 116th St.

The Kitchen 512 W. 19th St. (between 10th and 11th Aves.) (212) 255-5793
www.thekitchen.org. The careers of avant-garde luminaries such as composer
Philip Glass and performance artist Laurie Anderson began at The Kitchen.
Today the theater continues to present emerging and innovative artists in dance,
theater, film and everything in between. Tickets are quite affordable. **Subway:** A,
C, E to 14th St.; L to Eighth Ave.

La MaMa ETC 74A E. 4th St. (between Second Ave. and Bowery) (212) 254-
6468 *www.lamama.org*. La MaMa's four stages showcase a diverse and sometimes bizarre program of avant-garde theater, dance and performance art from
American and international troupes. **Subway:** F, V to Second Ave.

Makor 35 W. 67th St. (between Central Park West and Broadway) (212) 601-
1000 *www.makor.org*. Makor is a Jewish community arts center (affilated with
the 92nd Street Y; see below) that's made a splash with its innovative and
avant-garde events, whether it's acid jazz or Jewish/Latino hip-hop. A twenty-
and thirtysomething crowd of hip intellectuals flocks to this intimate setting to
take in music, film, gallery shows, comedy, lectures, readings, seminars and
more. Tickets are generally inexpensive. **Subway:** 1, 9 to 66th St.

92nd Street Y Tisch Center for the Arts 1395 Lexington Ave. (at E. 92nd St.)
(212) 996-1100 or (212) 415-5500 *www.92ndsty.org*. This is no ordinary
YMHA—it's a center for the performing arts, offering an array of top-flight entertainment and cultural programming. New Yorkers come here for the chance to
see world-class performers in an intimate setting, or to hear leading writers and
intellectuals engage in thought-provoking panel discussions. You might catch big-
name classical and jazz performers, chamber music, an evening of cabaret, a lecture from a Nobel Prize winner, a documentary film screening, modern dance or a
literary reading. Tickets are a bargain given the quality of the offerings—usually
under $35 for live performances, and much less for films and lectures. **Subway:** 4,
5, 6 to 86th St.; 6 to 96th St.

Symphony Space 2537 Broadway (at 95th St.) (212) 864-1414 or (212) 864-
5400 *www.symphonyspace.org*. Symphony Space emerged from a major renovation in 2002, with a revamped main stage hosting music and dance performances,
a new cafe (which hosts book-club discussions), and a revitalization of the **Thalia
Theater,** which screens classic and independent films and serves as a smaller aux-
iliary performance space. Regular events include an annual Bloomsday marathon
reading of Joyce's *Ulysses,* performances by the New York Gilbert and Sullivan
Players and the "Wall to Wall" series of 12-hour marathon performances celebrating individual composers or choreographers. **Subway:** 1, 2, 3 to 96th St.

Town Hall 123 W. 43rd St. (between Sixth and Seventh Aves.) (212) 840-2824
www.the-townhall-nyc.org. This landmark theater hosts theater, dance, music, lectures, pop and world music, comedy—you name it. The offerings range from live tapings of *A Prairie Home Companion* to performances by international symphonies,
Broadway stars and chamber-music companies. **Subway:** B, D, F, N, Q, R, S, V, W, 1,
2, 3, 7, 9 to 42nd St.

FILM

So many movies are shown throughout the city in a single evening that it's important to learn a few essentials. For starters, tickets to most standard theaters are now around $10.50, and if you buy your tickets in advance through **Moviefone** at (212) 777-3456 or *www.moviefone.com*, an additional $1 per ticket will be charged to your credit card. Moviefone and a similar service, **www.fandango.com,** handle most major theaters; their service charge is often the price you have to pay to beat the crowds and get into a new release or a showing on Friday or Saturday evenings. If you're going to a popular recent release, show up at least 30 minutes before showtime to get a good seat (even if you've ordered tickets in advance). Local papers, including *The New York Times*, list times and locations.

Serious movie buffs will want to visit the **American Museum of the Moving Image** *(see section* "Queens" *in chapter* **Exploring New York***)*.

Movie Theaters of Note

Angelika Film Center 18 W. Houston St. (at Mercer St.) (212) 995-2000 *www.angelikafilmcenter.com*. One of New York's favorite venues for independent and foreign films is this six-screen theater on the border of SoHo and Greenwich Village. In addition to the concession stand, the theater's loftlike lobby cafe serves higher than standard fare to match its higher prices. Buy tickets in advance, as shows can sell out quickly. **Subway:** F, S, V to Broadway-Lafayette St.; N, R to Prince St.

Anthology Film Archives 32 Second Ave. (at 2nd St.) (212) 505-5181 *www.anthologyfilmarchives.org*. It's no surprise that this theater has a wealth of unusual material to offer, since it began in 1970 as a museum dedicated to avant-garde cinema. The films shown here are often unknown, but you're likely to find the best of the genre. Check listings for documentaries and early works from better-known directors as well as the chance to catch a classic on the big screen. Tickets are available only at the box office. **Subway:** F, V to Second Ave.

Film Forum 209 W. Houston St. (between Sixth Ave. and Varick St.) (212) 727-8110 *www.filmforum.com*. Film buffs throughout the city know this charming three-screen theater consistently provides some of the best cinema New York offers, ranging from recent documentaries to silent films. Tickets often sell out quickly, especially on weekends; you can buy them online. **Subway:** 1, 9 to Houston St.; C, E to Spring St.

Lincoln Plaza Cinemas 1886 Broadway (at 62nd St.) (212) 757-2280. This modest six-screen theater on the cusp of the Upper West Side may be the best place to see foreign and independent movies uptown. Don't expect to find Snow Caps or Raisinettes at the concession stand—you're more likely to overpay for a smoked salmon sandwich. **Subway:** A, B, C, D, 1, 9 to 59th St.

Sony IMAX at Lincoln Center 1992 Broadway at 68th St. (212) 336-5000. At the top of the casino-style four-story monolithic movie theater on the Upper

West Side is a massive IMAX theater. The size and scope of the screen is tremendous, and the seats are arranged on an alarmingly steep angle. The films range from enhanced Discovery Channel material to supersized showings of features like *Titanic* or *Star Wars: The Phantom Menace*. **Subway:** 1, 9 to 66th St.

Walter Reade Theater 70 Lincoln Center Plaza (at Columbus Avenue) (212) 875-5600. This spacious, state-of-the-art theater in the heart of the Lincoln Center complex screens a diverse lineup: Jewish cinema, films celebrating human rights, Iranian cinema and a "dance on camera" series. Also common are retrospectives of particular actors and directors, films by up-and-coming Independent American directors and silent movies accompanied by a live orchestra.

The best way to keep up with what's going on is via the **Film Society of Lincoln Center** Web site (*www.filmlinc.com*). Inside, the atmosphere is spacious and the single screen is large. The 268 plush, comfortable seats are set on a sloping floor, which ensures that there's not a bad seat in the house. Tickets sell out quickly. **Subway:** 1, 9 to 66th St.

The Ziegfeld 141 W. 54th St. (at Sixth Ave.) (212) 765-7600. One of the few older movie theaters left in New York that hasn't been renovated into a multiplex, this Midtown classic with a bright red décor boasts an enormous screen and seating for nearly 1,200 people. It's the perfect place to see the latest special-effects epic or a singalong revival of *The Wizard of Oz*. **Subway:** B, D, E to Seventh Ave.; F, N, R, Q, W to 57th St.

Film Festivals

The **New York Film Festival** is easily the biggest and most famous of New York's film celebrations. Held annually in late September or early October, the festival screens around 20 independent, foreign and big-studio films in a two-week run at Lincoln Center. Buy tickets early—especially for the much-anticipated film that opens the event. Check *www.filmlinc.com* for schedules and ticketing details, or call (212) 875-5601.

Another festival of note, **New Directors/New Films,** is held each March and co-sponsored by the Film Society of Lincoln Center and the Museum of Modern Art. For the past three decades the New Directors/New Films festival has offered first glimpses at the work of directors as talented and varied as John Sayles, Steven Spielberg, Peter Greenaway and Whit Stillman. Check *www.filmlinc.com* for this year's lineup, and plan to buy tickets well in advance.

Conceived as a way to support the revitalization of Lower Manhattan after 9/11 and to reinforce New York's image as a major filmmaking center, the **TriBeCa Film Festival** was launched in 2002. Staged by Robert De Niro and producer Jane Rosenthal, it has become an annual event around the beginning of May, complete with dozens of screenings (including a major world premiere), plus concerts and a family-oriented street fair. For the 2005 schedule, check *www.tribecafilmfestival.org*.

Shopping in New York

Welcome to New York City, shoppers—you're in the big leagues now. A Big Apple shopping spree affords endless possibilities, from world-famous department stores to a seemingly infinite variety of boutiques. Special finds can be had at every price, whether you spend $10 or $10,000. Everything you've heard is true: You can buy anything here—and it's a lot more fun than surfing the Net.

MIDTOWN & UPTOWN SHOPPING

Shopping in Manhattan above 34th Street is a little like ascending a Himalayan peak. The foot of the mountain is dense and rich with store growth, but there is a lot of undesirable vegetation. Ascend to the lofty heights of the peak and the views are spectacular, but the expenses are so steep that it might make your blood thin.

The trailhead for the expedition is **Herald Square,** home to **Macy's,** the world's largest department store. Navigating Macy's, which takes up an entire city block, is neither easy nor particularly satisfying. Your best bet is to stick to the subterranean floors, where bargains are abundant.

Move up Broadway from 34th and come smack into the heart of the **Garment District**—not particularly inviting to casual shoppers, but a paradise for do-it-yourself fashionistas. Every fabric, button, feather or bit of leather trim ever imagined is available here. Shops tend to specialize in one niche or another, so if a particular shop doesn't have what you want, ask the proprietor to direct you to a store that will.

Continue walking north up Broadway and emerge at the recently cleansed and sanitized **Times Square.** The goods news is that the triple-X pornography is gone; the bad news is that there is mostly schlock in its place. But for those who cannot leave the city without a Yankees cap or a Statue of Liberty headpiece made of green Styrofoam, this is the place. **Toys "R" Us** has opened a flagship store (they claim it's the world's largest toy store) at Broadway and 44th Street, complete with its own full-scale Ferris wheel. On the opposite corner, **MTV** has its own sleek boutique brimming with tiny "Real World" Ts and irony, while **Swatch** has opened a bright new megastore at carrying their full line of fun watches a block to the north on the southeast corner of Broadway and 45th Street. The vibrant, multisensory **Virgin Megastore** continues to dazzle crowds and dominate its own full neon block in the heart of the square. Nearby, 42nd Street between Seventh and Eighth Avenues has been transformed into a neon-bright shopping arcade, complete with such mall standards as a Hello Kitty boutique.

Style mavens with something a little classier in mind should make a quick break east, and start strolling up Fifth Avenue. As the famous sites of St. Patrick's Cathedral and Rockefeller Center loom ahead, **Saks Fifth Avenue,** the venerable clothier to the ladies who lunch, will appear on the right.

Fifth Avenue from 50th Street to Central Park is one of the richest shopping corridors in the world (surpassed only in recent years by Madison Avenue). As you parade up the designer-clad avenue—which has been democratized of late by super-boutiques from accessible retailers such as **Banana Republic** and **H&M**—don't miss one of the more unique offerings. Whatever you think of the clothes, the **Versace** store at 52nd Street is worth a quick stop. Remodeled to look like an 18th-century palazzo, it comes complete with a marble facade, a sweeping serpentine staircase and elaborate mosaics.

As Fifth Avenue meets Central Park, it suddenly morphs from a commercial hub into a fancy residential boulevard. For years, **F.A.O. Schwartz** presided over the corner of 59th and Fifth as a landmark institution for children of all ages. It was a huge city-block-long wonderland full of life-sized stuffed elephants, pint-sized Porsches and other amazing playthings. But at press time, the store stood empty after its parent company filed for bankruptcy protection in 2004. (The Wal-Marts and Targets of the world have not been kind to specialty toy stores.) The current word is that the store will be reopened and remodeled with an updated look at feel, but details are currently scarce.

Go east one block and yet another Gold Coast emerges. It seems that every upscale merchant on the planet has a store on Madison Avenue between 57th and 72nd Streets. The boulevard continues its platinum march through the 70's and 80's, where it becomes a haven of luxury home décor shops.

Most shops along Madison specialize in sumptuous merchandise—every design house under the sun has a shop along this gold-plated stretch. It's all here, from the clean modern lines of **Calvin Klein** and **Donna Karan** to the sleek confidence of **Carolina Herrera;** from the preppy-luxe of **Michael Kors** to the knowing girlishness of **Chloé;** from the lush elegance of **Emanuel Ungaro** to freshly streamlined **Valentino** and the youthful Italian glam of **Gianfranco Ferré** and **Roberto Cavalli.** High-end jewelers such as fashion-forward **David Yurman** bring sparkle to the avenue. **BCBG Max Azria** adds a welcome dash of feminine sophistication, while Parisian designer **Sonia Rykiel** offers sultry sensuality for women with the runway figure for it. No designer says romance like **Morgane le Fay,** whose cutting edge yet oh-so-romantic ballgowns would make Cinderella blush. You'll find a different kind of new romanticism at **Jean-Paul Gaultier,** Madonna's old favorite, who continues to make waves on the runway. Old favorites like **Burberry,** whose hot new multistory boutique dominates 57th Street just off Madison Avenue, and **Christian Dior** prove that even the classics can dominate the cutting edge. Nestled between the household names are such best-kept secrets as **Pilar Rossi,** which features dramatically styled yet timeless women's business and evening wear in stunning hues and easy-flowing fabrics.

It's worth strolling the blocks even if you don't intend to buy, as the windows can be particularly entertaining. Worth seeking out is U.K. import **Nicole**

Farhi's showcase on 60th Street off Madison. It is a wide-open loft space, with clean lines, a muted palette and clothes ranging from simple cotton separates to orange leather shirt-coats, plus a stunning collection of distressed leather and globally influenced furniture and homewares on the subterranean level. The other Madison must is **Barneys New York,** a dizzying display that's a must stop on any Manhattan-style shopping spree.

Once a serious shoppers' wasteland, the Upper West Side now has some decent shops these days. While it's definitely gone upscale, it's still not rarefied designer-label territory like the Upper East Side. The major development in 2004 was the debut of the **Time Warner Center** at Columbus Circle (at the intersection of Broadway and Eighth Ave, between 58th and 60th Sts.), a massive modern structure with a pair of reflective glass towers that soar more than 80 floors skyward. Its enormity and bravado instantly made it one of Manhattan's most famous buildings. Among its many features is a multilevel shopping arcade (*www.shopsatcolumbuscircle.com*). Purveyors of fine goods include clothiers **Thomas Pink, Hugo Boss, Joseph Abboud, A/X Armani Exchange, J. Crew, Eileen Fisher** and **Stuart Weitzman;** makeup central **Sephora; Tourneau** for watches; **Williams Sonoma,** a clearinghouse of pretty kitchen gadgets and housewares; and a huge **Borders Books.** The pièce de résistance is a gigantic flagship branch of **Whole Foods,** where food-obsessed New Yorkers can cruise the aisles in search of top-quality gourmet delicacies.

Moving north a few blocks on Broadway, a **Bed, Bath & Beyond** was slated to open in late 2004 across from Lincoln Center, offering affordable towels, sheets and other household gear. A new **Barney's New York Co-op** store, all cool fashion and cutting-edge fun, also opened in the fall of 2004, just a block from the incomparable **Fairway** food store at 74th Street. Fairway may not be as aesthetically pleasing as Whole Foods, but its fresh produce and dizzying cheese selection take a backseat to no one—and its prices are much more reasonable than its new neighbor's. (Next door to Fairway is **Citarella,** for top-quality steaks and fish; farther up Broadway at 80th Street is **Zabar's,** another fantastic stop for foodies. This incredible cluster of gourmet shops makes the Upper West Side the best neighborhood in New York for food shopping.) Beyond its excellent gourmet shops, however, the Upper West Side shopping scene is increasingly dominated by mega-retailers and national chains, making it convenient for locals but not terribly interesting for shoppers in search of something special.

—*Leslie Kaufman*

Garment District

Subway: A, B, C, D, E, F, N, R, S, Q, V, W, 1, 2, 3, 7, 9 to 42nd St.

Daytona Trimmings 251 W. 39th St. (between Seventh & Eighth Aves.) (212) 354-1713. Every possible kind of adornment, all excellently priced.

Hyman Hendler & Sons 67 W. 38th St. (at Sixth Ave.) (212) 840-8393 *www.hymanhendler.com*. The last word in ribbons; Martha Stewart's a fan.

Paron Fabrics Annex 206 W. 40th St. (between Seventh and Eighth Aves.)

(212) 768-3266 *www.paronfabrics.com*. The city's best outlet for quality fabrics, often at a substantial discount.

Fifth & Madison Avenues
(See also "Jewelry" later in this chapter.)

Subway: E, N, R, V, W to Fifth Ave.; 4, 5, 6 to nearest cross street.

Ann Taylor 645 Madison Ave. (at 60th St.) (212) 832-2010 *www.anntaylor.com*. The gorgeous multistory flagship, carrying all lines, including career wear, petites, shoes, and fragrance.

Banana Republic 626 Fifth Ave. (at 50th St., Rockefeller Center) (212) 974-2350 *www.bananarepublic.com*. The elegant three-floor flagship emporium, carrying all clothing and fragrances.

BCBG Max Azria 770 Madison Ave. (at 66th St.) (212) 717-4225 *www.bcbg.com*

Burberry 9 E. 57th St. (between Fifth and Madison Aves.) (212) 371-5010 *www.burberry.com*

Calvin Klein 654 Madison Ave. (at 60th St.) (212) 292-9000

Chanel 15 E. 57th St. (between Fifth and Madison Aves.) (212) 355-5050 *www.chanel.com*

Carolina Herrera 954 Madison Ave. (at 75th St.) (212) 249-6552 *www.carolinaherrera.com*

Chloé 850 Madison Ave. (at 70th St.) (212) 717-8220 *www.chloe.com*

Christian Dior 17 E. 57th St. (between Fifth and Madison Aves.) (212) 207-8848 *www.dior.com*

David Yurman 729 Madison Ave. (at 64th St.) (212) 752-4255 *www.davidyurman.com*

Donna Karan 819 Madison Ave. (between 68th and 69th Sts.) (212) 861-1001 *www.donnakaran.com*. **DKNY** 655 Madison Ave. (at 60th St.) (212) 223-DKNY *www.dkny.com*.

Emanuel Ungaro 792 Madison Ave. (at 67th St.) (212) 249-4090 *www.ungaro.com*

Gianfranco Ferré 870 Madison Ave. (at 71st St.) (212) 717-5430 *www.gianfrancoferre.com*

Giorgio Armani 760 Madison Ave. (at 65th St.) (212) 988-9191 *www.giorgioarmani.com*. **Emporio Armani** 601 Madison Ave. (at 57th St.) (212) 317-0800 *www.emporioarmani.com*

Givenchy 710 Madison Ave. (at 63rd St.) (212) 688-4338 *www.givenchy.com*

Gucci 685 Fifth Ave. (at 54th St.) (212) 826-2600 *www.gucci.com*

Hermès 691 Madison Ave. (at 62nd St.) (212) 751-3181 *www.hermes.com*

H&M 640 Fifth Ave. (at 51st St.) (212) 489-0390 *www.hm.com*

Jean-Paul Gaultier 759 Madison Ave. (beteen 65th and 66th Sts.) (212) 249-0235 *www.jeanpaul-gaultier.com* and *www.galeriegaultier.com*

Michael Kors 974 Madison Ave. (at 76th St.) (212) 452-4685

Nicole Farhi 10 E. 60th St. (between Fifth and Madison Aves.) (212) 223-8811

Pilar Rossi 784 Madison Ave. (between 66th and 67th Sts.) (212) 288-2469

Prada 724 Fifth Ave. (between 56th and 57th Sts.) (212) 664-0010 *www.prada.com*. Other location: 841 Madison Ave. (at 70th St.) (212) 327-4200

Ralph Lauren 867 Madison Ave. (at 72nd St.) (212) 606-2100 *www.polo.com*

Roberto Cavalli 711 Madison Ave. (between 63rd and 64th Sts.) (212) 755-7722 *www.robertocavalli.it*

Sonia Rykiel 849 Madison Ave. (at 70th St.) (212) 396-3060 *www.soniarykiel.com*

Valentino 747 Madison Ave. (at 65th St.) (212) 772-6969 *www.valentino.it*

Versace 647 Fifth Ave. (between 51st and 52nd Sts.) (212) 317-0224 *www.versace.com*. Other location: 815 Madison Ave. (between 68th and 69th Sts.) (212) 744-6868

Upper West Side
(See also "Food Markets" *later in this chapter.)*

Subway: 1, 9 to 59th St., 66th St., 72nd St., 79th St. or 86th St. Or 2, 3 to 72nd St.

Barneys New York Co-op 2147 Broadway (between 75th and 76th Sts.) (212) 450-8624 *www.barneys.com*

Citarella 2135 Broadway (at 75th St.) (212) 874-0383 *www.citarella.com*

Fairway 2127 Broadway (at 74th St.) (212) 595-1888 *www.fairway-market.com*

Time Warner Center Columbus Circle *www.shopsatcolumbuscircle.com*

Whole Foods In the Time Warner Center (212) 823-9600 *www.wholefoods.com*

Zabar's 2245 Broadway (at 80th St.) (212) 496-1234 *www.zabars.com*

DEPARTMENT STORES

Barneys New York 660 Madison Ave. (at 61st St.) (212) 826-8900 or (212) 945-1600 *www.barneys.com*. **Barneys New York Co-Op**, 236 W. 18th St. (between Seventh and Eighth Aves.) (212) 593-7800; and a new location at 2147 Broadway (between 75th and 76th Sts.) (212) 450-8624. Barneys continues to be the last word in what is hip and chic. The beautiful store offers cutting-edge fashion, accessories, cosmetics and wearable designs from up-and-coming visionaries, both international and homegrown. The tabletop department is a dazzler. Fashionistas usually go straight for the shoe section to pick up sharp, sexy heels. The two Barneys Co-Op stores offer casual-chic fashions, from Daryl K jeans to Juicy Couture tees, with the Broadway store also carrying a few more upscale designers like Prada Sport and Mui Mui. Fabulous twice-a-year warehouse sales are held at 255 West 17th Street (between Seventh and Eighth Aves.). The summer sale generally runs from late August until Labor Day, the winter sale in February or March. **Subway:** 4, 5, 6 to 59th St.

Bergdorf Goodman 754 Fifth Ave. (at 58th St.) (212) 753-7300. **Bergdorf Goodman Man,** 745 Fifth Ave. (at 58th St.). Visit Bergdorf's for a whiff of old New York glamour. This purveyor of sophistication dresses both ladies who lunch and the Park Avenue junior socialites following in their footsteps. An ultra-refined, almost exclusive atmosphere sets the stage for haute couture fashions of Badgley Mischka, Carolina Herrera, Dolce and Gabbana and other upscale designers. The elegant emporium is particularly excellent in high-end housewares, handbags, jewelry and shoes. **Subway:** E, N, R, V, W to Fifth Ave.

Bloomingdale's 1000 Third Ave. (at 59th St.) (212) 705-2000 *www.bloomingdales.com.* Many New Yorkers are devoted to Bloomie's for everything from beaded cocktail dresses to bridal registries. This massive square-block store attracts a diverse clientele, from trust-fund teens to stylish professionals and savvy tourists, all of whom exit with arms full of "big brown bags." The upscale selection is a step above Macy's in quality and sophistication, but more egalitarian and affordable than Saks. Great for shoes, coats, cosmetics and homewares, the store also boasts a huge men's department for the fashion-conscious who demand a stylish cut. Men's and women's selections run the gamut from reliable basics to sexy international couture threads. Regular weekend sales happen about once a month. Bloomingdale's has expanded its empire to 504 Broadway in SoHo, with an apparel store geared to young shoppers. **Subway:** 4, 5, 6 to 59th St.

Century 21 22 Cortlandt St. (between Church St. and Broadway) (212) 227-9092 *www.c21stores.com.* This discount department store extraordinaire was heavily damaged on 9/11, but reopened its doors in March 2002. Shopping pros come to sift through deeply discounted designer goods. Menswear is on the first floor, and the second floor is famous for the chaotic but bargain-rich shoe department, where the goods include Prada and Kenneth Cole at low, low prices. For the real shopaholic, the third floor is the place to be, with end-of-season steals on designer goods from the likes of Gucci, Urchin, Prada and Tocca. If you've got the patience, a worthwhile find is inevitable. Weekday lunch hours and Saturdays can be a frenetic crush. **Subway:** R, W to Cortlandt St.

Henri Bendel 712 Fifth Ave. (at 56th St.) (212) 247-1100. The signature brown-and-white striped Bendel bags alone are reason enough to buy something in this jewel box of a store. One of Manhattan's prettiest stores, Bendel's offers an excellent selection of both sophisticated and funky designer threads and accessories. The first floor greets you with counters of Bobbi Brown, MAC and Trish McEvoy cosmetics. A circular staircase winds up through the entire town-house-style store, serving as its grand focal point and enabling you to spot a silk scarf on the third floor that will go perfectly with that cashmere twin set you're holding on the second. The hat department is a delight in any season. Although Bendel's does not carry menswear or shoes, it's an essential stop on any Fifth Avenue shopping jaunt. Hairstylist to the stars **Garren New York** (212-841-9400) keeps a chic salon on the third floor. **Subway:** 4, 5, 6 to 59th St.; E, N, R, V, W to Fifth Ave.

Lord & Taylor 424 Fifth Ave. (between 38th and 39th Sts.) (212) 391-3344 *www.lordandtaylor.com*. A few blocks from Macy's, Lord & Taylor offers reasonable prices, regular sales, excellent offerings for petites, quality mid-priced lines and some big-name designers. Although not exactly poised at the fashion forefront, Lord & Taylor is wearing a decidedly sophisticated mein these days. It also offers New York's most relaxing and service-oriented shopping experience. Shoppers browse mostly for dresses, bags and work suits; think conservative, tasteful American classics, plus a dash of new American style. Midtown workers come in droves to buy hosiery on their lunch breaks, especially during the first-rate sales. **Subway:** B, D, F, V, S, 4, 5, 6, 7 to 42nd St.

Macy's 151 W. 34th St. (between Broadway and Seventh Ave.) (212) 695-4400 *www.macys.com*. The world's largest department store, and the historic heart of New York shopping. Don't expect a glamorous shopping experience, however; the store is perpetually in need of a good sorting out and feels chaotic at any time of day. The mammoth, always-crowded store is particularly well known for its storewide one-day sales (midweek, usually Wednesdays) and great Cellar bargains on essentials for the home. The extensive first-floor cosmetics department offers all major brands, and the coat, bathing suit, hosiery, and shoe sections are exceptionally large. The fourth-floor junior department packs a dense array of trendy gear targeted at the quintessential American teen. You'll find a jewel of a Metropolitan Museum of Art gift boutique, one of the store's few saving graces, on the mezzanine level. Try to visit during the annual Flower Show, a two-week event that marks the launch of Spring. **Subway:** B, D, F, N, R, Q, V, W, 1, 2, 3, 9 to 34th St.

Saks Fifth Avenue 611 Fifth Ave. (between 49th and 50th Sts.) (212) 753-4000 *www.saksfifthavenue.com*. Poised in a coveted location across from Rockefeller Center, Saks is a city landmark for sophistication, style and selection. Saks has served an upscale crowd for almost a century with the best and most extensive designer shoe and cosmetics departments in the city, plus expansive, well-organized apparel and accessories departments. The lingerie department is also exquisite. Most high-end labels for both women and men are on hand—including Bagley Mischka, Gaultier, Lina Beday, TSE and Vera Wang—but you'll also find many upscale basics. If you visit during the holidays, get in line to see the exquisitely decorated store windows. **Subway:** B, D, F, V to 47th-50th St.–Rockefeller Center; E, N, R, V, W to Fifth Ave.

DOWNTOWN SHOPPING

The premier shopping district of downtown Manhattan is the square mile known as SoHo (Houston to Grand Street, from Broadway to Sixth Avenue). This jumble of cobblestone streets and industrial-era loft buildings grew to prominence two decades ago as an artists' paradise—a place where an aspiring painter or sculptor could grab 6,000 square feet of raw space in crowded Manhattan for next to nothing.

The creative community has largely been driven out by soaring real estate values, but the cavernous spaces they once inhabited have been converted to galleries and fabulous stores, both familiar names and one-of-a-kind boutiques. Everything from vinyl platform boots to minimalist beige bed linens is available in this richly varied shopping district. But fair warning: Everything costs top dollar. In fact, like the Fifth and Madison Avenue corridors, SoHo is also couture territory, but with a downtown, left-of-center, rock-and-roll twist: Expect to find a world atlas's worth of artsy international designer names like **Anna Sui, Marc Jacobs, Helmut Lang, Vivienne Tam, Jill Stuart** and **Yohji Yamamoto,** plus an increasing number of hipped-up outlets of uptown retailers such as **Louis Vuitton** and **Prada,** including Prada's **Miu Miu** boutique, funkier and flouncier than the streamlined original, and **Philosophy di Alberta Ferretti,** featuring the Italian designer's more playful, (somewhat) less expensive line of sexy womenswear. Best-kept secret designers and stars of tomorrow that occupy SoHo storefronts include **Marianne Novobatzky,** whose elegant evening sheaths and timeless suiting are at once retro-inspired and fashion-forward.

Other better-than-garden-variety, less-than-couture-priced merchants include **Otto Tootsie Plohound,** which offers the latest in platform footwear in a setting more like a dance club than a shoe store. **Anthropologie** has a whimsical selection of velvet slip dresses, antiqued candlesticks and wicker furniture to go with its exotic-tinged, mod-attic décor, while Italian import **Replay General Store** has managed to transform all-American work-a-day denim into a fashion-forward statement. Home design wears futuristic at **Property,** gets a sculptural modern look in the hot pottery of **Jonathan Adler,** and brings high style into the bathroom at **Waterworks.**

Just east of SoHo is **Nolita,** which has evolved into a chic shopping scene in the last few years. The unique boutiques along Mott, Mulberry and Elizabeth Streets are pricey but wonderful, leaning toward up-and-coming clothing, jewelry and accessories designers, plus modern home-design shops. If you have a passion for headwear, do not miss milliner **Kelly Christy,** who can frequently be found outside her shop, sipping coffee with friends, while French handbag designer **Jamin Puech** is a standout for romantic French-sewn totes.

The **East Village,** especially along 9th Street east of Second Avenue, and **NoHo** around Bond Street, have become another bastion of young designers styling one-of-a-kind wear, much of it quite affordable. Just a few blocks away, on 4th Street, you'll find another hat designer who's hot, hot, hot: **Eugenia Kim,** whose sexy, spunky toppers have tressed such style-setting songbirds as Janet Jackson, Alicia Keys and Jennifer Lopez; Nicole Kidman even wore a sweeping straw style in the pages of *Vogue*.

Above 14th Street, Broadway from Union Square north has become a corridor of home decorating stores. The essential stop here is **ABC Carpet & Home,** an eclectic, expensive bazaar of luxuriant clutter, from quality furnishings to international carpets to luxury linens.

Fashionistas looking for the newest frontier should head to the Meatpacking District. There's fabulous **Jeffrey New York** (think pony skin belts and fur-lined stiletto heels) plus a multiplying crop of modernist design boutiques selling everything from lingerie and designer eyewear to sneakers and sculpture, particularly along Gansevoort and Washington Streets and on 14th Street between Ninth and Tenth Avenues. It's bizarre to see these fancy little boutiques, all perfect and polished and brimming with pricey things, just steps from the industrial meatpacking wholesalers that still do business here, occasionally splattering pig guts, cow ears and squiggly pieces of who knows what on the sidewalk (seriously, watch your step).   *—Leslie Kaufman*

(See also "Specialty Stores" later in this chapter for recommendations on outstanding shops throughout the downtown area. See "Clothing" for **Jeffrey New York** *and* "Gifts & Homewares" *for* **ABC Carpet & Home.***)*

SoHo & Nolita

Subway: B, D, F, V to Broadway–Lafayette St.; N, R, W to Prince St.; 6, C, E to Spring St.

Anna Sui 113 Greene St. (between Prince and Spring Sts.) (212) 941-8406 *www.annasui.com* or *www.annasuibeauty.com*

Anthropologie 375 West Broadway (between Spring and Broome Sts.) (212) 343-7070 *www.anthropologie.com*

Bloomingdale's 505 Broadway (between Spring and Broome Sts.) (212) 729-5900 *www.bloomingdales.com*

Eugenia Kim 203 E. 4th St. (between Aves. A and B) (212) 673-9787 *www.eugeniakim.com*

Helmut Lang 80 Greene St. (between Spring and Broome Sts.) (212) 334-1014 *www.helmutlang.com*. **Helmut Lang Parfums** 81 Greene St. (between Spring and Broome Sts.) (212) 334-3921.

Jamin Puech 252 Mott St. (between Houston and Prince Sts.) (212) 334-9730 *www.jamin-puech.com*

Jill Stuart 100 Greene St. (between Prince and Spring Sts.) (212) 343-2300 *www.jillstuart.com*

Jonathan Adler 47 Greene St. (between Broome and Grand Sts.) (212) 941-8950 *www.jonathanadler.com*

Kelly Christy 235 Elizabeth St. (between Houston and Prince Sts.) (212) 965-0686 *www.kellychristyhats.com*

Louis Vuitton 116 Greene St. (between Prince and Spring Sts.) (212) 274-9090 *www.vuitton.com*

Marc Jacobs 163 Mercer St. (between Houston and Prince Sts.) (212) 343-1490 *www.marcjacobs.com*

Marianne Novobatzky 65 Mercer St. (between Spring and Broome Sts.) (212) 431-4120

Miu Miu 100 Prince St. (between Mercer and Greene Sts.) (212) 334-5156

Otto Tootsie Plohound 413 West Broadway (between Prince and Spring Sts.) (212) 925-8931

Philosophy di Alberta Ferretti 452 West Broadway (between Houston and Prince Sts.) (212) 460-5500 *www.philosophy.it*

Prada 575 Broadway (at Prince St.) (212) 334-8888

Property 14 Wooster St. (between Grand and Canal Sts.) (917) 237-0123 *www.propertyfurniture.com*

Replay General Store 109 Prince St. (at Greene St.) (212) 673-6300 *www.replay.it*

Vivienne Tam 99 Greene St. (between Prince and Spring Sts.) (212) 966-2398 *www.viviennetam.com*

Waterworks 469 Broome St. (at Greene St.) (212) 966-0605 *www.waterworks.com*

Yohji Yamamoto 103 Grand St. (at Mercer St.) (212) 966-9066 *www.yohjiyamamoto.co.jp*

BARGAIN SHOPPING

Bargains, bargains, come and get your bargains!

The **Diamond District** (W. 47th St. between Fifth and Sixth Aves.) is the place to go for deals on diamonds, precious gems, gold and other fine jewelry. The block is lined with dealers, most of whom are Hasidic Jews for whom diamonds are the family business. You can get an emerald ring for one-fifth the price of a similar ring at Tiffany's—but you have to know what you're doing. Prepare in advance by reading up on the kinds of gems or jewelry you're interested in, perhaps visiting some high-end jewelers in your area who can point out the qualities to look for in fine jewelry. You might also check out *www.47th-street.com*, which has some frank and useful tips that will help you avoid pitfalls, plus a full list of reputable dealers. Once you arrive in the Diamond District, be sure to comparison shop. Virtually all stores are open only weekdays, usually from 10 A.M. to 5 P.M. or so.

It's not as tough to find real bargains in clothes, but you still have to know where to go. Generally speaking, stay off Madison Avenue. Instead, try stores like **Daffy's** ("Clothing Bargains for Millionaires") or **Century 21.** They're both badly organized, with a slightly neurotic atmosphere, but persevere.

And take a subway (F train to Delancey St.) to **Orchard Street,** in the heart of the Lower East Side. Hipster boutiques are spreading through this historic bargain district like wildfire, but there are still plenty of deals to be had. People say the bargains are only pseudo-bargains, but check out **Ben Freedman,** an old-world cheapie paradise with sidewalk racks that feature $5 leather belts and $6 ties. Don't miss the string of leather shops; **Grace Bags** for designer knockoff handbags of surprisingly decent quality, some for as little as $10; **Fine & Klein** or **Altman's Luggage** for brand-name luggage at a discount; and **Joe's Fabrics** for a kaleidoscope of linens, velvets, silks and damasks. The secret on Orchard Street is haggling: Don't be afraid. You don't have to be a pro. Just try walking out and see what happens. Think of what you want to pay, and keep repeating it on your way to the door. You'll probably get what you want. But don't play the game if you're not serious, or you'll end up with some angry merchants! Stop in first at the **Lower East Side Visitor Center** (261 Broome St. between Orchard and Allen Sts., 866-224-0206 or 212-226-9010, *www.lowereastsideny.com*) to pick up a pamphlet-sized shopping guide (you can also find a full list of neighborhood shops online).

Chinatown's **Canal Street** is a blast to stroll if you're looking for inexpensive backpacks, cheap leather belts or exotic souvenirs, both in permanent storefronts and fleeting street sellers. Stroll east from the intersection of Canal and Broadway for the best bounty, and bargain as you go. Skip the bootleg CDs, videos and DVDs, though—you will be disappointed.

If you're in town just before—or better—just after Christmas, or in mid-summer, check out the sales in the world's best boutiques and department stores. Open the paper once you arrive and start researching; the sales in the finest stores usually appear in the first couple of pages. Even on sale, the prices won't be cheap at stores like Hermès and Henri Bendel, but you won't find merchandise of this quality anywhere else, including the so-called premium outlet malls.

The other secret of New York City bargains is the **sample sale,** in which last season's designer merchandise is offered at a fraction of the price. These sales go on throughout the year. To give you an idea, take the Echo Scarf sample sale: Silk scarves that normally sell for between $60 and $90 can be found in cardboard boxes labeled $5, $10 and $15. The best places to hunt them down is in the "Check Out" section of the weekly *Time Out New York*; *New York* magazine's New York Metro Web site (*www.nymetro.com*; click on "Fashion & Shopping"), which updates its sale picks daily; and online at NYSale (*www.nysale.com*), your other best source to locate the hottest sales. When you hit a sample sale, avoid the lunch-hour crowds, bring cash, and don't expect much in the way of dressing rooms, so know your size or be ready to be creative (no returns).

Syms is the most famous of the men's discount clothiers, but they actually cater to women with careerwear, too; unfortunately, the shopping experience at these no-frills stores is discounted, too. The Flatiron District is lined with familiar discount names like **T.J. Maxx, Filene's Basement** and **Bed, Bath & Beyond.** Some say that the merchandise in these stores is picked especially for chic Manhattan shoppers and is better than what comes to the suburbs.

Manhattan fashionistas in the know often skip the more famous discount names in favor of the aptly named **Find Outlet,** a pair of discount boutiques boasting persistently stylish finds—think sample sale with a fixed address. Sign up online at *www.findoutlet.com* to receive exclusive advance notification of in-store promotions and special arrivals.

While you're in the neighborhood, check out the thrift shops just around the corner. The **Housing Works Thrift Shop** is a gem for men's and women's designer hand-me-downs, shoes and, best of all, furniture, with items like a great-looking oval Biedermaier table for $200. Another delightful-to-browse stop is the **City Opera Thrift Shop,** offering up one of the best selected and displayed secondhand selections in town.

And if you're in town on a weekend, don't forget the indoor and outdoor **flea markets** that operate all year round on and near the corner of Sixth Avenue and West 26th Street *(see "Flea Markets" later in this chapter).*   *—Tracie Rozhon*

(See "Vintage, Thrift & Resale" *in the* "Clothing" *section for* **Housing Works Thrift Shop**, **Salvation Army** *and other stores for used clothing and housewares.)*

Diamond District
Subway: B, D, F, V to 47th-50th St.–Rockefeller Center.

M Khordipour Enterprises 10 W. 47th St. (between Fifth and Sixth Aves.) (212) 869-2198 *www.estatediamondjewelry.com*

Peachtree Jewelers Inc. 580 Fifth Ave. (between 47th and 48th Sts.) (212) 398-1758

Unusual Wedding Rings In the National Jewelers Exchange, 4 W. 47th St., booth 86 (800) 877-3874 or (212) 944-1713 *www.unusualweddingrings.com*. Beautifully designed, top-quality wedding sets in gold and platinum at below-market prices.

Orchard Street Bargain District
Subway: F to Delancey St.; J, M, Z to Essex St.

Altman Luggage 135 Orchard St. (between Delancey and Rivington Sts.) (800) 372-3377 or (212) 254-7275 *www.altmanluggage.com*.

Arivel Fashions 150 Orchard St. (between Rivington and Stanton Sts.) (212) 673-8992 *www.arivel.com*. For furs, shearlings and leather goods.

Ben Freedman 137 Orchard St. (between Delancey and Rivington Sts.) (212) 674-0854

Fine & Klein 119 Orchard St. (near Delancey St.) (212) 674-6720

Grace Bags 190 Orchard St. (between Houston and Stanton Sts.) (212) 228-6118

Joe's Fabrics Warehouse 102 Orchard St. (at Delancey St.) (212) 674-7089

Klein's of Monticello 105 Orchard St. (at Delancey St.) (212) 966-1453. High-quality womenswear.

Rita's Leather Fair 176 Orchard St. (at Houston St.) (212) 533-2756.

Discount Clothing
(For **Century 21,** *see* "Department Stores" *earlier in this chapter.)*

Burlington Coat Factory Burlington Coat Factory 707 Sixth Ave. (at 23rd St.) (212) 229-1300 *www.coat.com*. More than just coats—men's, women's and children's wear, plus housewares and luggage. **Subway:** F, V to 23rd St.

Canal Jean Co. 718 Broadway (between Washington and Waverly Sts.) (212) 226-3663 *www.canaljean.com*. Cheapie jeans and T's for the MTV crowd. **Subway**: N, R, W to 8th St.

Daffy's 111 Fifth Ave. (at 18th St.) (212) 529-4477 *www.daffys.com*. Other locations: 1311 Broadway (at 34th St.) (212) 736-4477; 1775 Broadway (at 57th St.) (212) 294-7444; Madison Ave. and 44th St. (212) 557-4422; 462 Broadway (at Grand St.), SoHo (212) 334-7444. Check Web site for additional locations. **Subway:** L, N, Q, R, W, 4, 5, 6 to 14th St.

Filene's Basement 620 Sixth Ave. (at 18th St.) (212) 620-3100 *www.filenes.com*. **Subway:** F, V to 14th St. Other location: Broadway at 79th St. (212) 873-8000. Subway: 1, 9 to 79th St.

Find Outlet 361 W. 17th St. (between Eighth and Ninth Aves.) (212) 243-3177 *www.findoutlet.com*. **Subway:** 1, 9 to 18th St. Other location: 229 Mott St. (between Prince and Spring Sts.) (212) 226-5167 **Subway:** 6 to Spring St.

Loehmann's 101 Seventh Ave. (at 16th St.) (212) 352-0856 *www.loehmanns.com*. The place for designer fashions at a discount. **Subway:** 1, 2, 3, 9 to 14th St.

Saint Laurie Merchant Tailors 22 W. 32nd St. (between Fifth Ave. and Broadway), 5th Fl. (212) 643-1916 *www.saintlaurie.com*. **Subway:** F, V, B, D, Q, R, N, W to 34th St.; 6 to 33rd St.

T.J. Maxx 620 Sixth Ave. (between 18th and 19th Sts.) (212) 229-0875 *www.tjmaxx.com*. **Subway:** F, V to 14th St.

Syms 400 Park Ave. (at 54th St.) (212) 317-8200 *www.syms.com*. Discount career wear for men and women. **Subway:** 6 to 51st St. Other location: 42 Trinity Pl. (between Rector St. and Battery Park) (212) 797-1199. **Subway:** 1, 9, R, W to Rector St.

ANTIQUES

New York is the largest center for antiques and collectibles in the world, a giant bazaar stocked with period furniture, china, glassware, textiles, books, jewelry and toys from just about anywhere on earth. Collectors are either ecstatic by the sheer abundance of antiques, or frustrated by the high prices and the difficulty of finding exactly what they seek—be it a 19th-century weather vane, a Ming vase, an 18th-century desk from Versailles, a 1930's Mickey Mouse toy or a baseball signed by Babe Ruth.

Collectors with limited time, plan ahead. If you're a serious shopper, put together an itinerary, and let the dealers you're interested in know beforehand about the type of pieces you wish to see. Dealers are busy, especially such world-class dealers as **James J. Lally,** a specialist in Chinese art. They travel as much as some of their clients do in order to present scholarly exhibitions with catalogues in their museum-style galleries.

Browsers who are not in the market for a specific piece but prefer to browse can do well in a few select neighborhoods—most notably on the Upper East Side, along East 59th, 60th and 61st Streets around Second Avenue, and along Madison Avenue in the 70's. Lafayette Street north and south of Houston Street is a good hunting ground for 20th-century finds.

New York is host to about 60 antiques fairs each year. Dealers come from throughout the world to participate in fairs, the most notable of which take place in the Park Avenue and Lexington Avenue armories. The **Asian Art Fair,** a spring event (*www.haughton.com*), is often described as the best of the art and antiques shows in Manhattan. The preeminent dealer in Asian art, Robert H. Ellsworth, explained its success, saying, "Even if you spent a year going around the world, you would never be able to see all the fine Asian art exhibited here." At the **Triple Pier Antiques Show,** held in the passenger ship terminals on the Hudson River in March and November (212-246-5450), more than 600 dealers sell goods spanning the centuries and collectors' budgets. The same organizer hosts a busy calendar of seasonal and specialty shows throughout the year, including the Modern Show in autumn and the Gramercy Garden Antiques Show in spring; check *www.stellashows.com* for dates of these and other fine shows.

Antiques and collectibles are also sold year-round at flea markets, the most enduring of which is held on weekends at a parking lot on Sixth Avenue at 26th Street (*see* "Flea Markets" *later in this chapter*).   —*Rita Reif*

Barry Friedman Ltd. 32 E. 67th St. (between Park and Madison Aves.) (212) 794-8950. *www.barryfriedmanltd.com*. Art Deco and Art Noveau Viennese furniture and decorations, plus avant-garde art. **Subway:** 6 to 68th St.

Chisholm Gallery 56 W. 22nd St. (between Fifth and Sixth Aves.), 2nd floor (212) 243-8834 *www.vintagepostersnyc.com*. A century of collectible-quality advertising posters from around the globe. **Subway:** F, V to 14th St.

City Barn Antiques 269 Lafayette St. (at Prince St.) (212) 941-5757 *www.citybarnantiques.com*. One of the nation's premier specialists in mid-20th-century Heywood Wakefield furnishings. **Subway:** N, R, W to Prince St.

Didier Aaron 32 E. 67th St. (between Park and Madison Aves.) (212) 988-5248 *www.didieraaron.com*. Prominent Parisian dealer in French 17th- and 18th-century palace-quality furniture, objects and art. **Subway:** 6 to 68th St.

Doyle & Doyle 189 Orchard St. (between Houston and Stanton Sts.) (212) 677-9991 *www.doyledoyle.com*. Fine estate and antique jewelry, including Georgian, Victorian, Edwardian, Art Deco and Art Nouveau pieces, in a jewel box of a store. **Subway:** F, V to Second Ave..; J, M, Z to Essex St.

Evergreen Antiques 1249 Third Ave. (at 72nd St.) 212-744-5664 *www.evergreenantiques.com*. Mostly 19th-century Northern European and Scandinavian furniture in the neoclassical, Biedermaier and Empire styles. **Subway:** 6 to 68th St.

Guéridon 359 Lafayette St. (between Bleecker and Bond Sts.) (212) 677-7740. *www.gueridon.com*. French mid-century modern furnishings and accents. **Subway:** 6 to Bleecker St.; B, D, F, V to Broadway–Lafayette St.

J.J. Lally & Co. 41 E. 57th St. (at Madison Ave.), 14th floor (212) 371-3380. Chinese art and antiques. **Subway:** 4, 5, 6 to 59th St.; N, R, W to Fifth Ave.

Kentshire Galleries 37 E. 12th St. (between University Pl. and Broadway) (212) 673-6644. *www.kentshire.com*. Large gallery dedicated to 18th- and 19th-century English antiques, ranging from jewelry and tabletop items to formal furnishings. **Subway:** L, N, R, Q, W, 4, 5, 6 to 14th St.

Manhattan Art & Antiques Center 1050 Second Ave. (between 55th and 56th Sts.) (212) 355-4400 *www.the-maac.com*. Three-floor antiques center housing more than 100 dealers. Genres run the gamut from antiquities to fine early 20th-century collectibles. **Subway:** 4, 5, 6 to 59th St.

R 82 Franklin St. (between Church St. and Broadway) (212)343-7979 *www.r20thcentury.com*. A premier source for mid-century modern legacy design. The emphasis is on Scandinavian furnishings and accessories, but you'll also find pieces from such wide-ranging masters as Henry Bertoia, Gio Ponti and the Eamses. **Subway:** 1, 9 to Franklin St.

Skyscraper 237 E. 60th St. (between Second and Third Aves.) (212) 588-0644 *www.skyscraperny.com*. High-quality Art Deco and streamline furniture and collectibles. **Subway:** N, R, W to Lexington Ave. Other location: Deco Deluxe II, 1038 Lexington Ave. (at 74th St.) (212) 249-5066. **Subway:** 6 to 77th St.

WaterMoon Gallery 110 Duane St. (between Broadway and Church St.) (212) 925-5556. Fine Chinese and Tibetan antique furniture, Tibetan carpets, and Chinese porcelain and ceramics from the Neolithic era to the Ming Dynasty, plus an extensive selection of Chinese and Miao textiles and contemporary artwork by young Chinese artists. **Subway:** A, C to Chambers St.; R, W to City Hall.

AUCTIONS

Despite the price-fixing scandals that rocked the world's biggest houses in recent years, Manhattan's world-renowned auction houses continue to provide lavish forums for those who can afford to indulge their passions for collecting. If you are interested in buying, be sure to attend the sale preview and study the catalog for price estimates before you raise your paddle and bid. For those not in the market, simply watching the ceremonious sale can be fascinating. Check local publications such as *The New York Times* and *Time Out New York*, as well as the auctions' own Web sites, for dates and events.

Christie's 20 Rockefeller Plaza (49th St. between Fifth and Sixth Aves.) (212) 636-2000 or (212) 636-2010 *www.christies.com*. Items that have graced the block at this two-century-old British institution include everything from Matisse and da Vinci canvases to the Academy Award Bette Davis won for *Jezebel*. This house also boasts departments for wine, cars, coins and sports memorabilia. **Subway:** B, D, F, V to 47th-50th Sts.–Rockefeller Center.

Sotheby's 1334 York Ave. (between 71st and 72nd Sts.) (212) 606-7000 *www.sothebys.com*. From its humble beginnings in 1744 as a London book dealer, this house has grown into one of the world's most esteemed auction houses with branches all over the map. Auctions run the gamut, from the sale of van Gogh's "Irises" to Jacqueline Kennedy Onassis's estate. **Subway:** 6 to 68th St.

Guernsey's 108 E. 73rd St. (between Park and Lexington Aves.) (212) 794-2280 *www.guernseys.com*. One of New York's smaller auction houses, this institution is an esteemed source for modern collections, from artwork of the Soviet Union to rock-and-roll memorabilia. **Subway:** 6 to 77th St.

Swann Auction Galleries 104 E. 25th St. (between Park and Lexington Aves.) (212) 254-4710 *www.swanngalleries.com*. This specialized house devotes itself to rare books and the visual arts, including photos, vintage posters, autographs, maps and atlases, drawings and the like. **Subway:** 6 to 23rd St.

Tepper Galleries 110 E. 25th St. (between Park and Lexington Aves.) (212) 677-5300 *www.teppergalleries.com*. To simply say that estates are sold off here doesn't do justice to the fine pieces that pass through this house. Offerings include antique furniture, fine silver, jewelry, carpets and fine artworks. **Subway:** 6 to 23rd St.

SPECIALTY STORES
Beauty & Spa
Bath & Beauty

C.O. Bigelow 414 Sixth Ave. (between 8th and 9th Sts.) (212) 533-2700 *www.bigelowchemists.com*. This West Village spot offers a quirky mix of quality products, from the hard-to-find Biotherm skincare line to practical pillboxes. Perfect your hair with Knotty Girl Drama Queen Marshmallow moisture balance shampoo, or give your daily regimen an international touch with a 2,000-bristle Elgydium toothbrush from France. **Subway:** B, C, D, E, F, V to W. 4th St.

Face Stockholm 110 Prince St. (at Greene St.) (212) 966-9110 *www.facestockholm.com*. Other locations: In the Time Warner Center at Columbus Circle (212) 823-9415; 226 Columbus Ave. (at 70th St.) (212) 769-1420; 1263 Madison Ave. (between 90th and 91st St.) (212) 987-1411. As if lighting ceremonial candles, faithful customers stand before rows of lipsticks, glitter and nail polish, testing the wide array of hip shades. A perfect buy is one of FACE's sleek custom-filled compacts with miniature applicator. **Subway:** N, R, W to Prince St.

Fresh 57 Spring St. (between Lafayette and Mulberry Sts.) (212) 925-0099 *www.fresh.com*. Other location: Bleecker St. (between Perry and W. 11th St.) (917) 408-1850. This Boston-based line excels at bath and body treats that come in delicious scents—cocoa, lychee, lemon, milk, honey, soy, rose—that are almost good enough to eat. Soaps are individually wrapped and tied with wire and stone, making perfect gifts to go. **Subway:** 6 to Spring St.

Jo Malone 949 Broadway (between 22nd and 23rd Sts.) (212) 673-2220 *www.jomalone.com*. The North American flagship of London's favorite perfumery is located in the Flatiron Building. All products boast Jo Malone's gorgeous snow-white, black-trimmed packaging, a perfect statement of the line's elegant simplicity. Malone's philosophy is that one can find the perfect personal scent by experimenting with her 10 original fragrances, so enjoy the sniffing. The line is carried in Bergdorf's and now also available in the SoHo Bloomingdale's. **Subway:** N, R to 23rd St.

Kiehl's 109 Third Ave. (between 13th and 14th Sts.) (212) 677-3171 *www.kiehls.com*. Long lines at this venerable beauty landmark allow you to spot more products to add to your basket. Models and athletes alike are devotees of such classics as the Ultra Facial Moisturizer, Creme with Silk Groom for glossy hair and Lip Balm #1, a ubiquitous item in many city bags. Stay calm as the knowledgeable staff rewards you with more exceptional product samples, all in Kiehl's plain-wrap bottles. Saks boasts a well-stocked Kiehl's counter, too. **Subway:** L, N, R, Q, W, 4, 5, 6 to 14th St.

Lafco New York 285 Lafayette St. (between Prince and Houston Sts.) (800) 362-3677or (212) 925-0001 *www.lafcony.com*. This sleek and sprawling store is the proud purveyor of the cult favorite Santa Maria Novella bath products. These beautifully packaged soaps by the famous Italian monastery are home accents in themselves. **Subway:** 1, 9 to Canal St.

L'Occitane 92 Prince St. (between Broadway and Mercer St.) (212) 219-3310 *www.loccitane.com*. Other locations: 198 Columbus Ave. (at 69th St.) (212) 362-5146; 510 Madison Ave. (between 52nd and 53rd Sts.) (212) 826-5020. This Provençal import is a bath lovers' dream. The luxuriant hand cream is an epiphany. The most popular product is the 100 percent shea butter; extracted from the fruit of the African shea tree, it works wonders on skin, lips and hair and is an excellent treat for expectant mothers. Candles, shampoos, moisturizing soaps and fragrances are among the offerings. **Subway:** N, R, W to Prince St.; 6 to Spring St.

M.A.C. 113 Spring St. (between Mercer and Greene Sts.) (212) 334-4641 *www.maccosmetics.com*. Other locations: 14 Christopher St. (at Gay St.) (212) 243-4150; 1 E. 22nd St. (between Broadway and Fifth Ave.) (212)677-6611. M.A.C. cosmetics raise the roof with bold colors, sleek black packaging, and spokesdivas like Lil' Kim, k.d. lang and RuPaul. It's hard to resist sassy lipsticks; a purchase of one of M.A.C.'s signature Viva Glam lipsticks is also a donation to AIDS research. **Subway:** N, R, W to Prince St.; 6 to Spring St.

9 Bond Street 9 Bond St. (between Broadway and Lafayette St.) (212) 228-1732. Other locations: 897 Madison Ave. (between 72nd and 73rd Sts.) (212) 794-4480; 680 Madison Ave. (between 61st and 62nd Sts.) (212) 838-2780. A custom-made fragrance by this two-century-old French perfumer—which has designed signature scents for Audrey Hepburn and Grace Kelly—is a grand splurge. You may have to be a real princess to afford it, but what wonderful company you'll be in. **Subway:** 6 to Bleecker St.

Sephora 1500 Broadway (between 43rd and 44th Sts.) (212) 944-6789 *www.sephora.com*. Other locations: 555 Broadway (between Prince and Spring Sts.) (212)625-1309; 2103 Broadway (between 73rd and 74th Sts.) (212) 362-

1500; 119 Fifth Ave. (at East 19th St.) (212) 674-3570; check Web site for additional locations. Sephora's black-and-white-striped columns support a dazzling beauty superstore. Gloved staff guide customers through aisles of Stila, Hard Candy, Clarins and other impressive international brands from A to Z, including its own bath line. Create your own scent at the perfume bar. **Subway:** E, V to Fifth Ave.

Shu Uemura 121 Greene St. (between Prince and Houston Sts.) (212) 979-5500 *www.shuuemura.com*. Well-lit workstations help customers identify a complexion-perfect hue from among the powders and blushes of this elegant Japanese line. With a selection of over 100 brushes, this is a great place to pick up basic makeup tools. For the perfect wink, buy the popular eyelash curler and a chic set of come-hither lashes. **Subway:** B, D, F, V to Broadway–Lafayette St.; N, R, W to Prince St.

Zitomer 969 Madison Ave. (between 75th and 76th Sts.) (212) 737-4480 *www.zitomer.com*. Probably the only pharmacy in town with a doorman, the five-decade-old Zitomer is the upscale bath, beauty and health resource for Upper East Siders, featuring such bare necessities as Clarin's sunscreen and Chanel moisturizers. **Subway:** 6 to 77th St.

Day Spas

Acqua Beauty Bar 7 E. 14th St. (between Fifth Ave. and Union Sq. West) (212) 620-4329 *www.acquabeautybar.com*. This trendy choice draws a hipper-than-thou crowd with chic designer style and first-class treatments, including sublime pedicures. A number of Eastern facial and massage techniques are available, including invigorating Chinese Tui Na, yoga-like Thai massage, and the sensual 90-minute Indonesian Ritual of Beauty body treatment. **Subway:** L, N, R, Q, W, 4, 5, 6 to 14th St.

Ajune 1294 Third Ave. (between 74th and 75th Sts.) (877) 99-AJUNE or (212) 628-0044 *www.ajune.com*. This Zen-elegant oasis offers first-rate facials and body treatments that balance aesthetic and clinical care. Serious gravity-defiers include botox and collagen injections, but the Ajun glow facial, which includes full facial analysis and relaxing shoulder massage, will be restorative enough for most. Body treatments run the gamut from hydrotherapy to endermologie; the sweet ginger massage comes out the winner. **Subway:** 6 to 77th St.

Avon Centre Salon & Spa Trump Tower, 725 Fifth Ave. (between 56th and 57th Sts.) (888) 577-AVON or (212) 755-AVON *www.avonsalonandspa.com*. This chic uptowner is home to colorist-to-the-stars Brad Johns, king of the buttery blondes, and eyebrow doyenne Eliza Petrescu, the woman who revolutionized shaping and tweezing. Spa treatments run the gamut from mud wraps and collagen facials to cellulite-reducing endermologie and one-on-one yoga sessions. Expensive, but worth it. **Subway:** N, R, W to Fifth Ave.

Bliss 568 Broadway (between Houston and Prince Sts.), 2nd Fl. (212) 219-8970 *www.blissworld.com*. Other location: 19 E. 57th St. (between Fifth and

Madison Aves.), 3rd Fl. (212) 219-8970. The Big Apple's favorite day spa is housed in a stylish loft space with a funky downtown look and buckets of *Sex and the City* attitude. There's no arguing with the top-notch facials and massages. Book as far in advance as possible. **Subway:** N, R to Prince St.

Body Central 99 University Pl. (at 12th St.), 5th Fl. (212) 677-5633 *www.bodycentralnyc.com*. This simple, soothing spa emphasizes the healing power of massage therapy. Body Central is the domain of Dr. JoAnn Weinrib, whose focus is chiropractic care, including massage for stress and pain relief to improve circulation and enhance immune function, a wonderous sinus and allergy treatment, and a jaw-release massage famous for relieving persistent jaw clenchers and teeth grinders. Dr. Weinrib also offers nutrition counseling, while other experts offer facials, body wraps, anti-aging coaching and pre- and post-natal treatments. Don't expect plush robes or fancy waiting room, but you'll be hard-pressed to find a more complete wellness center in the city. **Subway:** F, L, N, Q, R, V, W, 4, 5, 6 to 14th St.

Carapan Urban Spa 5 W. 16th St. (between Fifth and Sixth Aves.) (212) 633-6220 *www.carapan.com*. This candlelit, Native American-inspired spa is an original oasis of tranquility in the urban jungle. Eastern and Western techniques are combined in the relaxing spa treatments, which run the gamut from aromatherapy facials to reiki to sports massage, and the romantic space is a true delight. Book ahead if you want sauna time. The signature product collection Plateau is stellar. **Subway:** F, L, N, Q, R, V, W, 4, 5, 6 to 14th St.

Ella Baché Spa 8 W. 36th St. (between Fifth and Sixth Aves.), 8th Fl. (212) 279-8562 *www.ellabache.com*. Women in the know have celebrated the arrival of this Parisian skin care haven on New World shores. The spa is intimate and delightful, the signature products are first-rate, and the noninvasive imported therapies—from massages to facials to body polishes to waxing—are administered with a supremely gentle touch. **Subway:** B, D, F, N, Q, R, S, V, W to 34th St.

Paul Lebrecque 171 E. 65th St. (at Third Ave.) (212) 988-7816 *www.paullebrecque.com*. Other location: Reebok Sports Club/NY, 160 Columbus Ave. (at 67th St.) (212) 988-7816. All manner of spa treatments are available, but first-class facials—from relaxing aromatherapy and oxygen treatments to medical peels—are the specialty. A great source for salon services (the E. 65th St. store provides excellent services for men as well as women, using separate floors for each), including hair and nail care; traditional barber services include an expert straight-razor shave. **Subway:** 6 to 68th St.

Stone Spa 125 Fourth Ave. (between 12th and 13th Sts.) (212) 254-3045 *www.stonespa.com*. This gorgeous, distinctly downtown spa isn't for everybody—but hot stone massage simply doesn't get better. All of the sublimely relaxing treatments incorporate soothing hot stones in some capacity (even the marvelous Jurlique facials), the therapists are all first-rate and the soundtrack tends more toward ethereal world music than the new-age standard. The Gemstone Facial will have you feeling like a sparkling jewel. The location is Zen gorgeous. **Subway:** F, V to 14th St.

Bookstores

New York is Book City. While the big chains' discount prices and huge inventories have driven some independents out of business, the Big Apple still shines with first-rate neighborhood and special-subject bookstores.

Major Chains

Barnes & Noble 33 E. 17th St. (at Union Sq.) (212) 253-0810 *www.bn.com.* Other locations: 105 Fifth Ave. (at 18th St.) (212) 807-0099; 1972 Broadway (at 66th St.) (212) 595-6859; 4 Astor Pl. (between Broadway and Lafayette St.) (212) 420-1322; check for more locations. Barnes & Noble is Manhattan's biggest book retailer, with supersized stores located throughout the city. In addition to huge selections of current and backlist titles in every genre, you'll find extensive magazine racks, plus cafes in most locations. (The original Fifth Ave. and 18th St. store has been selling books since 1863, so you can't get a latte there. Its selection is heavy on academic texts.) A chock-full events calendar includes best-selling authors reading from their latest. B&N events are advertised in *The New York Times* and *Time Out New York.* **Subway:** L, N, R, Q, W, 4, 5, 6 to 14th St.

Borders Books & Music 461 Park Ave. (at 57th St.) (212) 980-6785 *www.bordersstores.com.* Other locations: 576 Second Ave. (at 32nd St.) (212) 685-3947; 100 Broadway (at Wall St.) (212) 964-1988; Time Warner Center, 2nd floor, at Columbus Circle (212) 823-9775. New York's second-biggest book chain is this well-stocked retailer, which averages 150,000 book and titles per store. (The Park Avenue location is substantially larger than the Second Avenue one; all four feature cafes.) Borders has a stronger emphasis on music and video than Barnes & Noble (videos and DVDs are carried in all branches). Call or check the Web site for music, book signings, author readings and other events. **Subway:** 4, 5, 6 to 59th St.

Independent Bookstores

Coliseum Books 11 W. 42nd St. (west of Fifth Ave.) *www.coliseumbooks.com* (212) 803-5890. Manhattan celebrated in 2003 when the city's favorite browse-and-buy bookstore reopened its doors after being shuttered by prohibitive rents in 2002. The new location, across from the New York Public Library, is smaller than the old store, but has nearly as many titles on display (almost 100,000), as well as the majority of the original top-notch staff. The emphasis is on quality fiction, but Coliseum has answers in every category. An adjacent cafe and a full slate of readings, art exhibits, and book signings make this a great destination. **Subway:** S, 4, 5, 6, 7 to 42nd St.

Posman Books 9 Grand Central Terminal (Vanderbilt Ave. and 42nd St.) (212) 983-1111 *www.posmanbooks.com.* This pleasant shop on the main level at Grand Central offers a high-quality selection of general-interest fiction and nonfiction as well as gift books, making it an ideal stop for readers on the go. **Subway:** S, 4, 5, 6, 7 to 42nd St.

Rizzoli 31 W. 57th St. (between Fifth and Sixth Aves.) (212) 759-2424 *www.rizzoliusa.com*. This sophisticated bookstore has a strong emphasis on art books, but it also makes a very browsable general-interest shop with an opinionated and helpful staff. **Subway:** N, R, F to 57th St.

Shakespeare & Co. 939 Lexington Ave. (at 69th St.) (212) 570-0201 *www.shakeandco.com*. Other locations: 137 E. 23rd St. (at Lexington Ave.) (212) 505-2021; 716 Broadway (at Washington Pl.) (212) 529-1330; 1 Whitehall St. (between Bridge and Stone Sts.) (212) 742-7025; check for more locations. The emphasis at these comfortable, unpretentious neighborhood bookstores is on quality fiction, with a good selection of small-press titles in the mix. A New York favorite. **Subway:** 6 to 68th St.

St. Marks Bookshop 31 Third Ave. (at 9th St.) (212) 260-7853 *www.stmarksbookshop.com*. This winning East Villager is a prime haunt for left-of-center readers. The well-chosen and nicely displayed selection runs the gamut from avant-garde poetry and alternative fiction to Eastern philosophy and glossy photography books with an esoteric bent. **Subway:** 6 to Astor Pl.

Three Lives & Company 154 W. 10th St. (at Waverly Pl.) (212) 741-2069 *www.threelives.com*. This ultra-charming West Village landmark—*New York* magazine's 2002 winner for Best Independent Bookstore— is a real find for those who truly delight in reading, especially fiction, biography and memoirs. Author readings are a big part of the mix. **Subway:** 1, 9 to Christopher St.

Out-of-Print, Used and Rare Books

Argosy Book Store 116 E. 59th St. (between Park and Lexington Aves.) (212) 753-4455 *www.argosybooks.com*. This wonderful, wood-paneled septuagenarian bookshop overflows with antiquarian, rare and well-cared-for used books—77,000 of them, to be exact—plus antique prints, maps and autographs. Prices run from $5 to $5,000. The bargain table out front can be a treasure trove. **Subway:** 4, 5, 6 to 59th St.

Bauman Rare Books 535 Madison Ave. (between 54th and 55th Sts.) (212) 751-0011; smaller gallery at the Waldorf=Astoria, 301 Park Ave. (at 49th St.) (212) 759-8300 *www.baumanrarebooks.com*. Bauman, one of the best-respected rare-book dealers in the nation, has two Big Apple galleries rife with museum-quality titles. The place to go if you're on the hunt for a rare first edition; many are signed. Bring a well-padded wallet. **Subway:** 4, 5, 6 to 59th St.

Bookleaves 304 W. 4th St. (near Bank St.) (212) 924-5638. This cozy nook is everything a local used-book store should be. **Subway:** 1, 9 to Christopher St.

Housing Works Used Books Cafe 126 Crosby St. (at Houston St.) (212) 334-3324 *www.housingworksubc.com*. This warm and wonderful wood-paneled, library-like store is the perfect antidote for chain-store rebels who nevertheless appreciate a good latte while perusing the stacks. The high-quality, all-used selection boasts upwards of 45,000 titles, and is particularly strong on coffee-table books and review copies. All profits go to not-for-profit Housing Works, which provides housing and services to homeless New Yorkers living with HIV and AIDS. **Subway:** B, D, F, V to Broadway–Lafayette St.; 6 to Bleecker St.

JN Bartfield Fine Books 30 W. 57th St. (between Fifth and Sixth Aves.), 3rd Fl. (212) 245-8890 *www.bartfield.com*. Good, pricey selection of rare and antiquarian books, focusing on fine bindings. **Subway:** N, R, W to Fifth Ave.

Skyline Books & Records 13 W. 18th St. (near Fifth Ave.) (212) 759-5463 *www.skylinebooks.com*. A well-chosen selection of used reads as well as jazz and blues records. **Subway:** F, L, N, R, Q, V, W, 4, 5, 6 to 14th St.

The Strand 828 Broadway (at 12th St.) (212) 473-1452 *www.strandbooks.com*. Annex, 95 Fulton St. (between William and Gold Sts.) (212) 732-6070. This epic new and used-book emporium—which claims to have "eight miles of books"—is heaven for used-book hounds. You could get lost in the monolithic stacks and omnipresent crowds, but patience and time are guaranteed to turn up a stack of must-haves in any category. A good selection of new books at greatly reduced prices is usually on hand at the smaller Fulton Street annex. **Subway:** L, N, R, Q, W, 4, 5, 6 to 14th St.

Ursus Books & Prints Carlyle Hotel, 981 Madison Ave. (between 76th and 77th Sts.), 2nd Fl.. (212) 772-8787 *www.ursusbooks.com*. Other location: 132 W. 21st St. (between Sixth and Seventh Aves.) (212) 627-5370. Like Bauman (listed earlier in this section), another stop for well-funded collectors looking for first-rate rarities. Ursus stocks art in its print department as well. **Subway:** 6 to 77th St.

SPECIALTY BOOKSTORES

Art & Architecture

Urban Center Books Villard Houses, 457 Madison Ave. (at 51st St.) (212) 935-3592 *www.urbancenterbooks.com*. The store for both serious students and avid fans of architecture, design and urban planning. **Subway:** 6 to 51st St.

Biography

Biography Bookshop 400 Bleecker St. (at 11th St.) (212) 807-8655. The most comprehensive selection for readers fascinated with the lives of others. A small nonbiography section has diversified the shelves in recent years. **Subway:** A, C, E to 14th St.; L to Eighth Ave.

Children

(*See also* "Toys" *later in this chapter.*)

Books of Wonder 16 W. 18th St. (west of Fifth Ave.) (212) 989-3270 *www.booksofwonder.com*. The city's oldest and largest independent children's bookstore. Book talks and readings are a regular feature; every Sunday at noon is storytime. **Subway:** F, L, N,Q, R, V, W, 4, 5, 6 to 14th St.

Scholastic Store 557 Broadway (between Prince and Spring Sts.) (212) 343-6166 *www.scholastic.com/sohostore*. This mammoth store sells the full line of products—books, toys, software and more—from children's publisher Scholastic. Your prime source for everything Harry Potter. A full calendar of in-store events keeps kids busy. **Subway:** R, W to Prince St.

Comics

Cosmic Comics 10 E. 23rd St. (between Broadway and Madison Aves.), 2nd Fl. (212) 460-5322 *www.cosmiccomics.com*. **Subway:** 6, N, R, W to 23rd St.

Forbidden Planet 840 Broadway (at 13th St.) (212) 473-1576 *www.fpnyc.com*. The city's largest collection of science fiction, fantasy, comics and graphic-illustration books, plus games and toys. **Subway:** L, N, Q, R, W, 4, 5, 6 to 14th St.

St. Marks Comics 11 St. Marks Pl. (between Second and Third Aves.) (212) 598-9439. St. Marks boasts a huge merchandise collection and the city's largest back-issue archive. **Subway:** 6 to Astor Pl.

Cooking & Gourmet

Bonnie Slotnick Cookbooks 163 W. 10th St. (at Seventh Ave.) (212) 989-8962. This cozy Village shop is the prime source for out-of-print and antiquarian cookbooks. **Subway:** 1, 9 to Christopher St.

Kitchen Arts & Letters 1435 Lexington Ave. (between 93rd and 94th Sts.) (212) 876-5550. Food lovers from professional chefs to take-out gourmets will relish the vast collection of more than 10,000 cookbooks here, including rare, hard-to-find, out-of-print and French-language titles. A browser's delight. **Subway:** 6 to 96th St.

Gay & Lesbian/Gender Subjects

Bluestockings Women's Bookstore & Cafe 172 Allen St. (south of Houston St.) (212) 777-6028 *www.bluestockings.com*. With a wide and well-varied selection, a friendly staff, and a busy calendar of events and workshops, this feminist bookstore caters to the literary needs and wants of women, both straight and gay. **Subway:** F, V to Second Ave.

Creative Visions Books 548 Hudson St. (between Charles and Perry Sts.) (212) 645-7573 *www.creativevisionsbooks.com*. An excellent resource and meeting place for gays and lesbians. **Subway:** 1, 9 to Christopher St.

Oscar Wilde Bookshop 15 Christopher St. (at Gay St., between Sixth and Seventh Aves.) (212) 255-8097 *www.oscarwildebooks.com*. This literary landmark was the world's very first bookstore catering to the gay and lesbian community, and it's still going strong; the selection runs the gamut from vintage to cutting-edge. **Subway:** 1, 9 to Christopher St.

History

Chartwell Booksellers Park Avenue Plaza, 55 E. 52nd St. (between Park and Madison Aves.) (212) 308-0643 *www.churchill-books.com*. Who knew an entire store could focus solely on books by, about, and with contributions from Winston Churchill and still pay the rent? A fascinating collection for rare-book collectors and history buffs. **Subway:** 6 to 51st. St.

The Liberation Bookstore 421 Lenox Ave. (at 131st St.) (212) 281-4615. This legendary bookstore dedicated to Africa and the African diaspora is under the threat of closure, so call first. **Subway:** 2, 3 to 135th St.

The Military Bookman 29 E. 93rd St. (at Madison Ave.) (212) 348-1280 *www.militarybookman.com.* The prime stop for books on military, naval and aviation history, with a focus on out-of-print and rare titles. **Subway:** 6 to 96th St.

Revolution Books 9 W. 19th St. (between Fifth and Sixth Aves.) (212) 691-3345. For the diehard Marxist who refuses to give up the fight, this utilitarian store is for you. **Subway:** F, V to 14th St.

Mystery
Armchair detectives will love these three shops, all stocked from floor to ceiling with both new and used mysteries, including out-of-print titles and rare signed editions.

Murder Ink 2486 Broadway (between 92nd and 93rd Sts.) (212) 362-8905 *www.murderink.com.* **Subway:** 1, 2, 3, 9 to 96th St.

The Mysterious Bookshop 129 W. 56th St. (between Sixth and Seventh Aves.) (212) 765-0900 *www.mysteriousbookshop.com.* **Subway:** N, R, Q, W to 57th St.; B, D, E to Seventh Ave.

Partners & Crime 44 Greenwich Ave. (between Sixth and Seventh Aves., at Charles St.) (212) 243-0440 *www.crimepays.com.* **Subway:** 1, 9 to Christopher St.

Religion
Christian Publications 315 W. 43rd St. (between Eighth and Ninth Aves.) (212) 582-4311 *www.christianpub.com.* New York's largest Christian bookstore also stocks music and videos. **Subway:** A, C, E to 42nd St.

J. Levine Books and Judaica 5 W. 30th St. (at Fifth Ave.) (212) 695-6888 *www.levinejudaica.com.* More than a bookstore—a full resource center for Judaica. **Subway:** B, D, F, N, Q, R, V, W to 34th St.; 6 to 33rd St.

Theater
Drama Book Shop 250 W. 40th St. (east of the Port Authority Bus Terminal) (800) 322-0595 or (212) 944-0595 *www.dramabookshop.com.* The resource for books on the arts of stage and screen, including scripts and screenplays, scene and monologue books, biographies and more. **Subway:** A, C, E, N, Q, R, S, 1,2, 3, 9 to 42nd St.

Richard Stoddard Performing Arts Books 43 E. 10th St., Ste. 6D (212) 598-9421 *www.richardstoddard.com.* Specialists in out-of-print performing arts books. Phone or e-mail your request, or make an appointment to shop. **Subway:** L, N, Q, R, W, 4, 5, 6 to 14th St.

Travel

Complete Traveller 199 Madison Ave. (at 35th St.) (212) 685-9007
www.completetravellerbooks.com. This unique bookstore is largely dedicated to
antiquarian travel literature, travelogues and travel guides, as well as a good
selection of modern first editions. **Subway:** 6 to 33rd St.

Hagstrom Map & Travel Center 51 W. 43rd St. (between Fifth and Sixth
Aves.) (212) 398-1222 *www.hagstrommap.com*. Other location: 125 Maiden
Lane (between Pearl and Water Sts.) (212) 785-5343. The top publisher of city
maps runs two excellent shops dedicated to cartography and travel. **Subway:** B,
D, F, V to 42nd St.

Traveler's Choice 2 Wooster St. (between Grand and Canal Sts.) (212) 941-
1535. This good general-interest travel store also features travelogues and
guides. **Subway:** J, M, N, R, Q, W, Z, 6 to Canal St.

Wellness & Eastern Teachings

East-West Books 78 Fifth Ave. (between 13th and 14th Sts.) (212) 243-5994.
The shelves are stocked with books that bring Eastern philosophy, healing religion and literature to the West. **Subway:** F, L, N, R, Q, V, W, 4, 5, 6 to 14th St.

New York Open Center 83 Spring St. (between Broadway and Crosby St.)
(212) 219-2527 *www.opencenter.org*. This center for holistic learning also features a small but well-stocked bookshop. **Subway:** 6 to Spring St.

Quest Bookshop 240 E. 53rd St. (between Second and Third Aves.) (212)
758-5521 *www.questbookshop.org*. This petite shop stocks titles ranging from
Astrology to Zoroastrianism. **Subway:** 6 to 51st St.

Cameras & Electronics

With the terrific buys available on the Web these days, New York isn't the discount electronics mecca it once was. Unless you've done your homework, stay
out of the shady electronics stores that line Broadway near Times Square. Also
avoid the stretch along Canal Street near East Broadway, where the hawkers
will surely take advantage of your good nature given a chance.

If you are in the market for a cordless phone or VCR and don't feel like
venturing downtown to **J&R** *(below)*, East 86th Street between Second and
Third Avenues is uptown's **Electric Avenue,** with **Circuit City** (232-240 E.
86th St., 212-734-1694, *www.circuitcity.com*) at the heart of the boulevard. In
Chelsea, you'll find a value-packed location of suburban electronics favorite
Best Buy (60 W. 23rd St. near Sixth Ave., 212-366-1373, *www.bestbuy.com*).

B&H Photo-Video—Pro-Audio 420 Ninth Ave. (at 34th St.) (800) 606-
6969 or (212) 444-6615 *www.bhphotovideo.com*. Many professional photographers wouldn't consider going anywhere else. This superstore sells everything
an amateur or pro could want, from an impressive selection of cameras to dark-
room equipment. Video equipment, lighting, pro audio and telescopes also fill

the cavernous space, as does a decent selection of used merchandise. **Subway:** A, C, E to 34th St.

J&R Music/Computer World 23 Park Row (between Beekman and Ann Sts., across from City Hall Park) (800) 806-1115 or (212) 238-9000 *www.jr.com.* New York's premier electronics store shines for both its extensive range of merchandise and its reasonable prices. Just about anything that plugs in or uses a battery can be found here, from travel irons to PDAs, cameras to iBooks. The Web site is a terrific resource for comparing the various features available in different brands; do a little surfing before you buy, since service can be a bit rushed. Great prices on CDs and DVDs, too. **Subway:** 4, 5, 6 to Brooklyn Bridge; R to City Hall.

Olden Camera & Lens Co. 1265 Broadway (between 31st and 32nd Sts.) (212) 725-1234. This Herald Square standard carries a full timeline of photography equipment, from the most technologically advanced to used Super 8s. Prices are equally diverse. **Subway:** B, D, F, N, Q, R, V, W to 34th St.

Sony Style 550 Madison Ave. (between 55th and 56th Sts.) (212) 833-8000 *www.sonystyle.com.* Your source for Sony products, from PlayStations and Vaios to fully integrated home entertainment systems. You'll pay full price, but the store is fun, attractive and user-friendly. **Subway:** E, V to Fifth Ave.

Clothing

Below are just a few standouts from a monster crop of clothing stores in Manhattan. If you're in the market for couture wear, the big-name designers will probably have one or more boutiques on Fifth Avenue in the 50's, on Madison Avenue or in SoHo. (*See* "Midtown & Uptown Shopping" *and* "Downtown Shopping" *earlier in this chapter for addresses. The city's stellar department and discount stores are also listed earlier in this chapter.*)

Men's & Women's

Harley Davidson of New York, NY 686 Lexington Ave. (between 56th and 57th Sts.) (212) 355-3003 *www.harleydavidson.com.* Hog heaven for city dwellers. No rides to buy, but everything else Harley is on hand, from leather and T's to logo barware and accessories, to Harleywear for the little ones. **Subway:** 4, 5, 6 to 59th St.

H&M 640 Fifth Ave. (between 51st and 52nd Sts.) (212) 489-0390 *www.hm.com.* Other locations: 1328 Broadway (at 34th St.) (646) 473-1165; 435 7th Ave. (at 34th St.) (212) 643-6955; 558 Broadway (between Prince and Spring Sts.) (212) 343-2722. Fashion-forward wearables for men, women and kids at low, low prices from Swedish discounter Hennes & Mauritz. The youthful looks won't outlast the season—but when it's $7 for a tiny T, who cares? Accessories are so cheap they're almost free. **Subway:** E, F, V to Fifth Ave.

Jeffrey New York 449 W. 14th St. (between Ninth and 10th Aves.) (212) 206-1272. If you consider yourself a big-league fashionista, then a trip to this cutting-edge fashion mecca in the booming Meatpacking District is sure to satisfy. Jeffrey dresses style-conscious women and men that demand chic from the hottest designers, including talented upstarts like Tuleh and Veronica Branquinho. The shoe department is a standout, sharpened by the likes of Jimmy Choo and Christian Louboutin, as is the tiny but selective cosmetics counter. **Subway:** A, C, E to 14th St.; L to Eighth Ave.

Kenneth Cole 610 Fifth Ave. (at 49th St.) (212) 373-5800 *www.kencole.com* This two-story flagship carries Kenneth Cole's complete lines of modern, casually glamorous clothing and footwear for men and women, including his affordable Reaction line. Stylish outerwear and accessories add the finishing touches. **Subway:** B, D, F, V to 47th–50th Sts.–Rockefeller Center.

Lucky Brand Jeans 38 Greene St. (at Grand St.) (212) 625-0707 *www.luckybrandjeans.com*. Other locations: 172 Fifth Ave. (at 22nd St.) (917) 606-1418; 151 Third Ave. (at 67th St.) (646) 422-1192; 216 Columbus Ave. (at 70th St.) (212) 579-1760. America's hippest name in denim operates four stylish and well-stocked city stores. **Subway:** A, C, E, J, M,N, R, Q, W, Z, 6 to Canal St.

Patricia Field In the Hotel Venus, 382 W. Broadway (between Spring and Broome Sts.) (212) 966-4066 *www.patriciafield.com*. A favorite for two decades for her fresh and funky fashion, Pat Field hit the big time a few years back when she became the woman behind the wardrobe at *Sex and the City*. Expect eye-popping club clothes and ultra-urban designer wear for attention-grabbing men and women. **Subway:** 6 to Astor Pl.

Seize sur Vingt 243 Elizabeth St. (between Houston and Prince Sts.) (212) 343-0476 *www.16sur20.com*. Made-to-measure businesswear with downtown flair is the stock in trade at this marvelous Nolita shop. Bespoke suits come in clean, slim, contemporary lines for both men and women. Divine Egyptian cotton shirts are both custom-tailored and pre-sized for men and women; sweaters and accessories are part of the picture now, too. **Subway:** B, D, F, V to Broadway–Lafayette St.; N, R, W to Prince St.

Shanghai Tang 714 Madison Ave. (between 63rd and 64th Sts.) (212) 888-0111 *www.shanghaitang.com*. Expect stylish, witty and boldly hued takes on Chinese classics—Mandarin-collared shirts, form-fitting "Suzie Wong" chengosam dresses, glorious lounging pajamas for both men and women—from this elegant Hong Kong clothier and imperial tailor, which occupies a serene tri-floor boutique. Super-elegant home accessories, too. **Subway:** E, N, R, V, W to Fifth Ave.; 4, 5, 6 to 59th St.

Thomas Pink 520 Madison Ave. (at 53rd St.) (212) 838-1928 *www.thomaspink.co.uk*. Other locations: 1155 Sixth Ave. (near 44th St.) (212) 840-9663; and in the Time Warner Center at Columbus Circle (212) 823-9650. This legendary British shirt maker has taken the Big Apple by storm with its beautifully cut, classically crafted button-downs (all made from finest quality twofold pure cotton poplin) in bold colors and patterns that add a dramatic twist to tradition. Men's ties come in dame-catching jewel tones. **Subway:** E, V to Fifth Ave.

Turnbull & Asser 42 E. 57th St. (between Madison and Park Aves.) (212) 752-5700 *www.turnbullandasser.com*. This London import, the first name in made-to-measure shirting for men and women, now offers the same faultless service and first-class style in the Big Apple. Styles are thoroughly traditional, but never boring—which is why the world's most well-dressed men throughout history, from Winston Churchill to James Bond, don't shop anywhere else. Classic suiting and a vibrant silk tie collection could transform any Gap guy into a real dandy. **Subway:** E, V to Fifth Ave.

Women's Only

Women looking for up-and-coming designers selling unique but wearable fashions at affordable prices will do well to browse East 9th Street between Second Avenue and Avenue A, where stars include **Jill Anderson** (331 E. 9th St., 212-253-1747, *www.jillanderson.com*), who unites a retro-reminiscent sensibility and the clean lines of modernism in her distinctly feminine, trend-proof and utterly stylish clothing. Another stunner on the block is **Selia Yang** (328 E. 9th St., 212-254-9073, *wwwseliayang.com*), who specializes in breathtaking special-occasion sheath dresses, including beaded and bridal versions, while **Mark Montano** (434 E. 9th St., 212-505-0325, *www.markmontano.com*) defines retro glamour with Jackie O-inspired fashions.

Nolita is another excellent neighborhood for fresh fashion looks. Check out **Mayle** (242 Elizabeth St. between Houston and Prince Sts., 212-625-0406), whose vintage-inspired looks have even made a few famous fans; and **Tracy Feith,** 209 Mulberry St., between Spring and Kenmare Sts., 212-334-3097), for funky, flirty, fashion-forward looks.

Diane von Furstenberg—The Shop 385 W. 12th St. (near Washington St.) (646) 486-4800 *www.dvf.com*. The Me Decade's favorite designer gets serious props for understanding the fashion-forward value of a Meatpacking District location. Her slim, clingy, 70's look is back in style in a big way. **Subway:** A, C, E to 14th St.

Eileen Fisher 395 West Broadway (between Spring and Broome Sts.) (212) 431-4567 *www.eileenfisher.com*. Other locations: 166 Fifth Ave. (between 21st and 22nd Sts.) (212) 924-4777; 1039 Madison Ave. (at 79th St.) (212) 879-7799; 314 E. 9th St. (between First and Second Aves.) (212) 529-5715; in the Time Warner Center at Columbus Circle, 2nd floor (212) 823-9575; check for more locations. Eileen Fisher's gorgeous clothing is for stylish, grown-up women who prefer season-transcending cuts that bespeak ease and movement over trendy look-at-me wear. The lines may be simple, but the fabrics—from crinkly silks to cashmere—rich textures and colors are stunning. The West Broadway flagship carries the full line, including petites and women's sizes, while the narrow 9th Street store is great for bargain hunters. **Subway:** N, R, W to Prince St.; C, E to Spring St.

Kirna Zabête 96 Greene St. (between Prince and Spring Sts.) (212) 941-9656 *www.kirnazabete.com*. Kirna Zabête is every stylish girl's favorite SoHo shop, thanks to 5,000 square feet of racks full of ultra-chic wearables from such hard-to-find designers as Alice Roi, Elisa Jiminez and Balenciaga; delightful accessories and home accents that surpass the SoHo standard; and fab mod décor that even includes a couple of iMacs to entertain significant others of the male persuasion who are far less enchanted than you are. **Subway:** B, D, F, V to Broadway–Lafayette St.; N, R, W to Prince St.; C, E to Spring St.

Makola 1045 Madison Ave. (between 79th and 80th Sts.) (212) 772-2272. This serene boutique specializes in classic mid-century dresses—the kind Grace Kelly wore so well—reinvented for the 21st-century woman. Jackets wear wide collars, tops are tailored, and skirts almost always flair. The fabrics are universally gorgeous. Prices are high, but so is the timeless quality. **Subway:** 6 to 77th St.

Stella McCartney 429 W. 14th St. (between Ninth Ave. and Washington St.) (212) 255-1556 *www.stellamccartney.com*. After causing a tidal wave in the fashion world with her revitalization of Chloë, Sir Paul's designer daughter has struck out with her own haute-couture label with even greater success. Stella is a girl's girl who loves corsets and cashmere, soft ruffles and sexy sensuality. But don't expect throwaway styles here—Stella trained with Bond Street's greatest traditional tailors, so fine construction is at the heart of all her work. The store is as pretty and coy as the clothes are. **Subway:** A, C, E, to 14th St.; L to Eighth Ave.

Men's Only

No well-dressed man should pass up a morning at **Bergdorf Goodman Man,** followed by an afternoon atelier run to **Barneys New York.** *(See* "Department Stores" *earlier in this chapter.)*

Saint Laurie Merchant Tailors 22 W. 32nd St. (between Fifth Ave. and Broadway) (212) 643-1916 *www.saintlaurie.com*. The place to treat yourself to a made-to-measure suit or jacket. Visiting the fifth-floor showroom is a joy; tables are lined with bolts of fine wools and tweeds to browse, each tagged with the prices for a suit or sport coat. You can choose both your fabric and your style—fitted, like an Italian count, or baggy like a Boston Brahmin. Their 3D Laser Body Scanner gets accurate image and body measurements, so the fit will be perfect. Prices run $1,000 and up for a suit, around $700 for a blazer; they do custom shirts, too. **Subway:** B, D, F, N, Q, R, V, W to 34th St.

Children's

Bebe Thompson 1216 Lexington Ave. (between 82nd and 83rd Sts.) (212) 249-4740. The atmosphere here is exclusive and the prices high, but it's worth visiting for the very best in delightful, well-crafted imported European wear for infants and children up to size 16. **Subway:** 4, 5, 6 to 86th St.

Bu & the Duck 106 Franklin St. (between Church St. and West Broadway) (212) 431-9226 *www.buandtheduck.com*. Owner and designer Susan Lane really likes kids—and understands them. Gone are pastels and the cartoony farm animals. Instead, Lang's vintage-inspired clothing and shoes are bold and interesting, practical and playful. A real gem. **Subway:** 1, 9 to Franklin St.

Lilliput/Lilliput SoHo Kids 240 & 265 Lafayette St. (between Spring and Prince Sts.) (212) 965-9567 or (212) 965-9201 *www.lilliputsoho.com*. These sibling shops offer an enjoyably eclectic selection of wear-a-day apparel for babies and youngsters for parents who'd rather not outfit their kids in uniform Gap or Oshkosh B'Gosh. Prices on some imported labels can soar, but most are reasonable. Shoes, accessories and toys are also in the mix. **Subway:** 6 to Spring St.; N, R, W to Prince St.

Peanutbutter & Jane 617 Hudson St. (between W. 12th and Jane Sts.) (212) 620-7952. This fun store for teenagers as well as younger kids stocks clothes and accessories that brim with the imagination of youth and funky West Village style. The eclectic mix ranges from girlish party dresses to leather skirts. **Subway:** A, C, E to 14th St.; L to Eighth Ave.

Zitomer 969 Madison Ave. (at 76th Sts.) (212) 737-4480 *www.zitomer.com*. This chic Upper West Side apothecary (see "Beauty" earlier in this chapter) is also well known for its high-quality selection of baby and children's clothing, especially designer-label party and flower-girl dresses, plus little-man clothing from labels like Calvin Klein. **Subway:** 6 to 77th St.

Vintage, Thrift & Resale

Allan & Suzi 416 Amsterdam Ave. (at 80th St.) (212) 724-7445 *www.allanandsuzi.net*. This terrific boutique is often overlooked by thrifty shoppers who can't see beyond the Superfly-meets–Dance Fever windows. That's just fine—there's more one-of-a-kind finds for the rest of us. Most of the collection is a thoughtfully selected and well-organized 20th-century fashion timeline, from gently worn bell-bottoms to pristine couture gowns worn once and cast aside. **Subway:** 1, 9 to 79th St.

City Opera Thrift Shop 222 E. 23rd St. (between Second and Third Aves.) (212) 684-5344. This culture center offshoot is one of the city's most delightful-to-browse secondhand boutiques. Bounty runs the gamut from mid-century modern furniture to vintage couture to collectible posters. Prices aren't always low, but with finds like this, why quibble? **Subway:** 6 to 23rd St.

Foley & Corinna 108 Stanton St. (between Essex and Ludlow Sts.) (212) 529-2338 *www.foleyandcorinna.com*. This warm and wonderful Lower East Side boutique specializes in hand-picked vintage finds, creative restructurings of vintage pieces (such as old T's wearing new beaded trim), and vintage-inspired new designs. Think Stella McCartney style at less-than-couture prices. **Subway:** F to Delancey St.; F, V to Second Ave.; J, M, Z to Essex St.

Housing Works Thrift Shop 143 W. 17th St. (between Sixth and Seventh Aves.) (212) 366-0820 *www.housingworks.org*. Other locations: 157 E. 23rd St. (between Lexington and Third Aves.) (212) 529-5955; 202 E. 77th St. (at Third Ave.) (212) 772-8461; 306 Columbus Ave. (between 74th and 75th Sts.) (212) 579-7566. Fashionable clothing, accessories, books, housewares, furniture and more. The wares are almost always excellent quality, and the proceeds benefit people living with HIV and AIDS. **Subway:** F, V, 1, 2, 3, 9 to 14th St.

Ina 21 Prince St. (between Mott and Elizabeth Sts.) (212) 334-9048 *www.inanyc.com*. Other locations: 101 Thompson St. (between Prince and Spring Sts.) (212) 941-4757; 208 East 73rd St. (between Second and Third Aves.) (212) 249-0014. A gorgeous designer consignment boutique specializing in vintage and current fashions for men and women, often from the world's top couture houses. Shoes and accessories add to the gently worn glory. **Subway:** N, R, W to Prince St.; 6 to Spring St.

Michael's 1041 Madison Ave. (between 79th and 80th Sts.), 2nd Fl. (212) 737-7273 *www.michaelsconsignment.com*. This elegant consignment boutique boasts top-shelf designer wear in like-new condition—but for a fraction of the original prices. Don't expect dated styles—society dames shed this season's Chloé, Chanel and Manolos faster than you'd think. The Bridal Salon is a savvy gal's dream come true. **Subway:** 6 to 77th St.

Resurrection 217 Mott St. (between Prince and Spring Sts.) (212) 625-1374 *www.resurrectionvintage.com*. Vintage pieces carry like-new price tags here, but the designer threads are chosen with an artist's eye. It's the coolest, most pristine collection of retro-wear in the city. Expect an emphasis on the 1960's and 70's, with such designer names as Pucci and Halston peppering the racks. **Subway:** N, R, W to Prince St.; 6 to Spring St.

Screaming Mimi's 382 Lafayette St. (between 4th and Great Jones Sts.) (212) 677-6464 *www.screamingmimis.com*. Laura Wills's legendary store boasts a top-notch collection of vintage threads, all at reasonable prices. Every piece is something special, whether it's a vivid floral design stamped onto an A-line mini-dress or a perfect vintage suit from the 40's. Housewares, bags, shoes, lingerie, even vintage New York souvenirs are on hand, all prettily displayed. **Subway:** 6 to Bleecker St.

Tokio 7 64 E. 7th St. (between First and Second Aves.) (212) 353-8443 *www.tokio7.com*. Here's a funky designer consignment shop for the downtown set, featuring gently used couture from labels like Anna Sui, Helmut Lang and Vivienne Westwood. **Subway:** 6 to Astor Pl.

Eyewear

Morgenthal Frederics 699 Madison Ave. (between 62nd and 63rd Sts.) (212) 838-3090 *www.morgenthalfredericsny.com*. Other locations: 944 Madison Ave. (between 74th and 75th Sts.) (212) 744-9444; 399 W. Broadway (at Spring St.) (212) 966-0099; Bergdorf Goodman, 754 Fifth Ave. (at 58th St.), main floor

(212) 872-2526. The place to go for the finest—and most expensive—frames in town. The styles are so original and sophisticated that they dress such famous faces as Renee Zellweger and Jack Nicholson. **Subway:** 4, 5, 6 to 59th St.

Oliver Peoples 755 Madison Ave. (between 65th and 66th Sts.) (212) 585-3433 *www.oliverpeoples.com*. Other location: 366 W. Broadway (near Broome St.) (212) 925-5400. These sleek white-on-white boutiques are a favorite for fashion-forward frames. **Subway:** 6 to 68th St.

Robert Marc 400 Madison Ave. (at 47th St.) (212) 319-2900 *www.robert-marc.com*. Call for other locations. Retro-cool styles, including the latest in hornrims and Robert Marc's own beautiful and beautifully made lines. Also good for antique wire frames in top-notch shape. **Subway:** 6 to 51st St.

Flea Markets

Manhattan's flea markets offer wonderful opportunities for bargain hunters in search of antiques and collectibles. Whether your grail is pristine Lustreware, vintage velvet Elvis paintings or old opera 78s, you have a good shot at finding what you want at the **Annex Antiques Fair and Flea Market** (212-243-5343, *www.annexantiques.citysearch.com*), the city's biggest and best outdoor flea market, held in a series of adjoining parking lots on Sixth Avenue between 25th and 26th Streets every Saturday and Sunday year-round. You can expect top-quality finds in furnishings, clothing and jewelry. Once you're done, head over to **The Garage**, (112 W. 25th St., between Sixth and Seventh Aves.; 212-647-0707), the city's largest indoor market, brought to life every Saturday and Sunday.

    Greenflea (212-721-0900) operates two markets: on Greenwich Street at 11th Street on Saturdays, and at I.S. 44 on Columbus Avenue at 77th Street on Sundays. Serious flea fans swear by these events, where you can find anything from used records and vintage jewelry to farm-fresh veggies and discount pet supplies.

Food Markets

Agata & Valentina 1505 First Ave. (at 79th St.) (212) 452-0690. Focused on the foods of Sicily, with a great selection of olives, oils, and Italian meats and cheeses. The prepared foods surpass the gourmet-market standard. It's pricey, but the quality and service are peerless. **Subway:** 6 to 77th St.

Barney Greengrass 541 Amsterdam Ave. (between 86th and 87th Sts.) (212) 724-4707 *www.barneygreengrass.com*. The self-proclaimed "Sturgeon King" has been a fixture on the Upper West Side since 1929, selling caviar, smoked fish and herring. The sturgeon is exquisitely moist and thin, as is the smoked salmon. The excellent whitefish salad, borscht and chicken livers can be carried out or eaten in the lively diner. **Subway:** 1, 9 to 86th St.

Chelsea Market 88 10th Ave. (between 15th and 16th Sts.) (212) 243-5678 *www.chelseamarket.com*. This huge, brick-walled ex-cracker factory overflows with wonderful purveyors of gourmet goods, from bakers (**Amy's Bread,** 212-

462-4338; **Fat Witch Bakery,** 212-807-1335) to butchers (**Frank's Butcher Shop,** 212-242-1234) to professional kitchenware hawkers (**Bowery Kitchen Supplies,** 212-376-4982)—and much, much more. You can lunch at several small restaurants inside and outside the concourse. **Subway:** A, C, E to 14th St.; L to Eighth Ave.

Citarella 2135 Broadway (at 75th St.) (212) 874-0383 *www.citarella.com*. Other locations: 1313 Third Ave. (at 75th St.) (212) 874-0383; 424 Sixth Ave. (at 9th St.) (212) 874-0383. The city's best seafood market is bright and well organized and the prepared foods are first-rate. Choice and service like this comes at a high price, however. **Citarella To Go** (Sixth Ave. at 49th St.) makes a great lunch stop in the Rockefeller Center area; an adjacent full-service restaurant wins solid reviews. **Subway:** 1, 9 to 79th St.

Dean & Deluca 560 Broadway (at Prince St.) (212) 431-1691; 1150 Madison Ave. (at 85th St.) (212) 717-0800 *www.dean-deluca.com*. Prices are stratospheric, but this gorgeous SoHo grocer is New York's best. A mecca for well-heeled foodies, Dean & Deluca offers picture-perfect produce and dazzling selections of pâtés, cheeses, meats, fish, baked goods and prepared foods, all handsomely displayed and knowledgeably attended. A small selection of fine cookware and cookbooks is nestled in back. **Subway:** N, R, W to Prince St.

Eli's Vinegar Factory 431 E. 91st St. (near York Ave.) (212) 987-0885 *www.elizabar.com*. **Eli's Manhattan** 1411 Third Ave. (between 80th and 81st Sts.) (212) 717-8100. To rival his uncles on Broadway (see Zabar's below), Eli Zabar turned an old vinegar factory into a gourmet market overflowing with top-quality produce, cheese, meat, fish, prepared foods, fresh flowers, baked goods and Eli's tasty breads, as well as wines and housewares. Prices—even for tomatoes grown in the rooftop greenhouse—are not unreasonable. Brunch is served on weekends. Eli's Manhattan offers virtually the same products and services, as well as a restaurant and cafe. **Subway:** 4, 5, 6 to 86th St.

Fairway 2127 Broadway (at 74th St.) (212) 595-1888. Other location: 2328 12th Ave. (at 132nd St. and the Hudson River) (212) 234-3883 *www.fairwaymarket.com*. You can't beat Fairway's two uptown stores for low prices, no-frills shopping and a huge selection of everything—olive oils, sauces, condiments, meat, fresh fish, bread, produce and groceries. Both feature enormous produce sections with some of the best organic fruits and vegetables in the city. The choice and quality of cheeses surpasses that of much fancier shops. **Subway:** 1, 2, 3, 9 to 72nd St.

Grace's Marketplace 1237 Third Ave. (at 71st St.) (212) 737-0600 *www.gracesmarketplace.com*. Grace Balducci's uptown market offers fine service, stunning displays of produce, wonderful baked goods and cheeses, quality smoked and fresh meats and fish, fresh pastas, whole-bean coffee and everything else worth wanting in a gourmet grocery. Sandwiches are excellent and fairly priced. **Subway:** 6 to 68th St.

Grand Central Market Grand Central Terminal, Lexington Ave. (between 42nd and 44th Sts.) *www.grandcentralterminal.com*. The crown jewel of Grand Central's glorious renovation is this spiffy gourmet food mart, where the array of first-rate vendors include **Koglin German Hams** for quality cold cuts and meats; **Zaro's Bread Market and Bakery** for fresh breads; **Pescatore Seafood Company** for a first-quality range of fresh catches; **Murray's Cheese** for a large selection of cheeses from all over Europe and the U.S.; and much, much more. The most elegant place in Midtown to pick up a takeout or ready-to-cook dinner. **Subway:** S, 4, 5, 6, 7 to 42nd St.

Kam Man Food Products 200 Canal St. (between Mott and Mulberry Sts.) (212) 571-0330 *www.kammanfood.com*. This market is New York's largest Asian grocer. Kam Man specializes in fresh and bulk foods, including barbecued meats, fresh water chestnuts, fresh and dried fish, pickled vegetables, dozens of soy and hoisin sauces, a broad selection of fresh vegetables and specialties from Vietnam and Thailand. The language barrier can be formidable. **Subway:** J, M, N, Q, R, W, Z, 6 to Canal St.

Russ & Daughters 179 E. Houston St. (between Allen and Orchard Sts.) (800) RUSS-229 or (212) 475-4880 *www.russanddaughters.com*. The Lower East Side's premier Jewish gourmet market has been supplying smoked fish, cream cheese and sturdy, old-fashioned bagels (made at nearby Kossar's bakery) to loyal shoppers since 1914. Prices are lower than in most uptown stores, even for the divine caviar. **Subway:** F, V to Second Ave.

Union Square Greenmarket E. 17th St. and Broadway (212) 788-7476. The city's premier greenmarket is held alfresco year-round at Union Square (Mon., Wed., Fri., Sat., 8 A.M.–6 P.M.), with the biggest markets on Saturday and Wednesday. You might discover diminutive Japanese turnips and baby Chinese cabbages, fresh baked goods, exotic fresh flowers and more. Everything is fresh, lots of organics are on hand, and prices tend to be low. More important, this is the real New York: diverse, friendly and enthusiastic. **Subway:** L, N, Q, R, W, 4, 5, 6 to 14th St.

Whole Foods In the Time Warner Center at Columbus Circle (Eighth Avenue and 59th St.) (212) 823-9600 *www.wholefoods.com*. This nearly 60,000-square-foot market is Manhattan's largest. At its splashy debut in February 2004, lines snaked up the escalators as hordes of New Yorkers clamored for their first peek at this mecca of fine food. Only in food-obsessed New York is the opening of a highfalutin grocery store the talk of the town. And it's true that Whole Foods—which prides itself on featuring organic products and meat and poultry raised without hormones or other additives—isn't your average corner store. There are aisles of beautifully displayed groceries, fresh produce, dairy, baked goods, butcher counters and seafood along with a huge spread of prepared foods. Before you check out at one of the 40 registers, hit the 248-seat foodcourt-style café with goodies from the sushi bar, brick-oven pizza counter, chocolate counter, bakery, salad bars or soup station (not to mention the hot-food bars, which are brimming over with everything from Indian to Latin and

Pan-Asian specialties). There's also a wine shop on premises. **Subway:** 1, 9, A, B, C & D to 59th St.

Zabar's 2245 Broadway (at 80th St.) (800) 697-6301 or (212) 496-1234 *www.zabars.com*. Visiting this West Side institution is like dropping into a scene from a Woody Allen movie. It's particularly well known for its smoked fish and herring counter, where you can sample the goods before your smoked nova is sliced paper-thin. Other delights include hundreds of cheeses, condiments, breads, cold cuts and pâtés, kosher foods and an array of prepared foods, including divine rice and tapioca puddings (no greens, though). Service is fast and efficient. Bargain housewares fill the second floor, and a corner cafe features hot foods and sandwiches. **Subway:** 1, 9 to 79th St.

Ethnic Markets
*(See also **Kam Man Food, Agata & Valentina, Barney Greengrass** and **Russ & Daughters**, above.)*

African: West African Grocery 535 Ninth Ave. (between 39th and 40th Sts.) (212) 695-6215. **Subway:** A, C, E to 42nd St.

English: Myers of Keswick 634 Hudson St. (between Jane and Horatio Sts.) (212) 691-4194 *www.myersofkeswick.com*. **Subway:** A, C, E to 14th St.; L to Eighth Ave.

German: Schaller & Weber 1654 Second Ave. (between 85th and 86th Sts.) (212) 879-3047 *www.schallerweber.com*. **Subway:** 4, 5, 6 to 86th St.

Indian: Foods of India 121 Lexington Ave. (between 28th and 29th Sts.) (212) 683-4419. **Subway:** 6 to 28th St.

Japanese: Katagiri & Co. 224 E. 59th St. (between Second and Third Aves.) (212) 755-3566 or (212) 838-5453 (gift store) *www.katagiri.com*. **Subway:** 4, 5, 6 to 59th St.

Minamoto Kitchoan, 608 Fifth Ave. (at 49th St.) (212) 489-3747 *www.kitchoan.com* Traditional Japanese cakes (wagashi) displayed in a Tiffany-worthy boutique. **Subway:** B, D, F, V to 47th-50th Sts.–Rockefeller Center.

Korean: Han Arum Market 25 W. 32nd St. (between Broadway and Fifth Ave.) (212) 695-3283. **Subway:** B, D, F, N, Q, R, V, W to 34th St.

Latin American: Mosaico 175 Madison Ave. (between 33rd and 34th Sts.) (212) 213-4700. Restaurant and grocer. **Subway:** 6 to 33rd St.

Mexican: Kitchen Market 218 Eighth Ave. (at 21st St.) (888) HOT-4433 or (212) 243-4433 *www.kitchenmarket.com*. A prime stop for chiles, spices and hot sauces; first-rate prepared foods, too. **Subway:** C, E to 23rd St.

Middle Eastern/International: Kalustyan's 123 Lexington Ave. (between 28th and 29th Sts.) (212) 685-3451 *www.kalustyans.com*. Excellent selection of spices and beans, plus a globe-trotting selection of gourmet foods, from Bangladesh to the West Indies. **Subway:** 6 to 28th St.

Polish: Kurowycky Meat Products 124 First Ave. (between 7th St. and St. Marks Pl.) (212) 477-0344. **Subway:** 6 to Astor Pl.

Gifts & Homewares

New York is such a home-design mecca that the list of shops below barely scratches the surface. Shoppers looking for one-of-a-kind home décor can't go wrong exploring Madison Avenue in the 80's for luxury goods with a European flair. SoHo and Nolita are best for offbeat and international looks.

The West Village is a delight for browsers. The leafy, town-house-lined streets run the style gamut. Boutiques range from **The Lively Set** (33 Bedford St. between Downing and Carmine Sts., 212-807-8417), a charming shop overflowing with collectible-quality home and garden accents from days past, to **Flight 001** (96 Greenwich Ave. near 12th St., 212-691-1001, *www.flight001.com*), for the grooviest travel-related goods, both chic and practical. And be sure to check out modern **Mxyplyzyk** (123-125 Greenwich Ave. at 13th St., 212-989-4300, *www.mxyplyzyk.com*), a fun-filled shop offering high-design housewares, arty toys for grown-ups and the like, all at affordable prices.

Additionally, the far East 50's have blossomed into a home-design mecca. The biggest name here is the **Terence Conran Shop,** London's high-design twist on IKEA-style home décor, located in the **Bridgemarket complex**—worth a look in itself for its stunning architecture (407 E. 59th St. at First Ave., 212-755-9079, *www.conran.com*). Joining Sir Terence in the area are upscale boutiques such as **Extraordinary*** (251 E. 57th St. between Second and Third Aves., 212-223-9151), a warm and wonderful gallery that displays affordable home accents handcrafted around the world, from Japanese lacquer coasters to horn-carved dishes from Madagascar; and Mary Vinson's ultra-elegant **Royal Hut** (328 E. 59th St. between First and Second Aves., 212-207-3027; *www.royalhut.com*), offers stunning cross-cultural furnishings and textiles from, or inspired by, Africa and Asia. Also consider **Bacarrat** and **Tiffany & Co.** for crystal and silver, Fifth Avenue (*see* "Jewelry" *later in this chapter*).

ABC Carpet & Home 881 and 888 Broadway (at E. 19th St.) (212) 473-3000 *www.abchome.com*. Two landmark buildings house the city's crown jewel of home shopping, with six floors abundantly stocked with luxury home furnishings and wares. The first floor indulges shoppers with eclectic tastes in home accessories, from baby Tiffany lamps to bead-fringed cashmere pillows. On other floors you will find a wide-ranging mix that includes Indonesian wooden chests, flat screen TVs, mid-century modern office chairs, luxury linens, imported fabrics on the bolt and much, much more. And of course, there are the rugs—a whole building, in fact, dedicated to helping you find that perfect gabbeh to place beneath your feet. **Subway:** L, N, Q, R, W, 4, 5, 6 to 14th St.–Union Square.

The Apartment 101 Crosby St. (between Prince and Spring Sts.) (212) 219-3066 *www.theapt.com*. In this super-groovy showroom, outfitted like a real New York apartment, you can browse and buy the clever modern goods on display in every room, from the bed to the slippers half-hidden underneath. Beyond the pop value, the goods are first-rate. Tours are by appointment only, so be sure to call first. **Subway:** N, R, W to Prince St.; 6 to Spring St.

Apartment 48 48 W. 17th St. (between Fifth and Sixth Aves.) (212) 807-1391 *www.apartment48.com*. Apartment 48 takes The Apartment concept *(above)* one step further, expanding the design spectrum from antique to sleek—and cozying it up substantially in the process. **Subway:** F, L, N, Q, R,V, W, 4, 5, 6 to 14th St.

Avventura 463 Amsterdam Ave. (at 82nd St.) (212) 769-2510 *www.forthatspecialgift.com*. This stunning Upper West Sider is two stores in one: One side is stocked with eye-catching art glass from the best Italian artisans, while the other boasts beautifully displayed Italian table settings and serveware. Prices are high, as is the quality. **Subway:** 1, 9 to 79th St.

Chelsea Garden Center 499 Tenth Ave. (between 37th and 38th Sts.) (212) 727-7100 *www.chelseagardencenter.com*. This outdoor open space is a haven of green in the concrete jungle. The marvelous store sells everything from bonsai-scale cacti to fountains and full sets of garden furniture, plus all the essentials for city gardening and gorgeous garden-inspired gifts. **Subway:** A, C, E to 42nd St.

Dune 88 Franklin St. (between Broadway and Church Sts.) (212) 925-6171 *www.dune-ny.com*. Dune designs and manufactures (in its own Brooklyn factory) some of the most thrilling and multifunctional contemporary furniture on the market, by some of today's most inspired designers. Each piece is custom-built to order, so you can choose fabric and finish, and even modify measurements as you wish. Expensive, but well worth it for a destined-to-be-classic modern piece. **Subway:** 1, 9 to Franklin St.

Homer 939 Madison Ave. (between 74th and 75th Sts.) (212) 744-7705 *www.homerdesign.com*. Create the perfect Hamptons-modern look at designer-to-the-stars Richard Mishaan's home design showcase. The joyous mix—legacy pieces, Mishaan's own furnishings, and accessories from today's most thrilling designers—sings with artful inspiration and vibrant color. **Subway:** 6 to 77th St.

Karkula 68 Gansevoort St. (between Washington and Greenwich Sts.) (212) 645-2216 *www.karkula.com*. Funky form tends to prevail over function in many of the post-modern shops that have come on strong in the area. Not so here, a stunning space overflowing with the finest in clean, contemporary design, from furniture to lighting to tableware, much of it industrial-chic and created by Brooklyn-based designers. **Subway:** A, C, E to 14th St.; L to Eighth Ave.

Leekan Designs 93 Mercer St. (between Spring and Broome Sts.) (212) 226-7226 *www.leekandesigns.com*. Come to this SoHo boutique for affordable gifts, textiles and housewares from Asia, Oceania and Africa, from Moroccan table linens to handwoven sisal baskets to Japanese lanterns—and much, much more. **Subway:** N, R, W to Prince St.; C, E to Spring St.

MoMA Design Store 44 W. 53rd St. (between Fifth and Sixth Aves.) (212) 767-1050 *www.momastore.org*. Other location: 81 Spring St. (at Crosby St.) (646) 613-1367. The best museum shop in the city is operated by the Museum of Modern Art. The sleek and innovative goodies range from clever toys and desktop accessories to licensed reproductions of Alvar Aalto free-form vases, Eames chairs and the like. The newer SoHo location is even bigger and better. **Subway:** E, V to Fifth Ave.

Moss 146-150 Greene St. (between Houston and Prince Sts.) (212) 226-2190 *www.mossonline.com.* Murray Moss has created an industrial design museum of the highest order. Homewares, mostly of European design, are displayed in glass cases as if they were priceless art; in reality, many of the items are homeware basics, like staplers, glassware and kitchen knives—albeit the most perfectly realized examples in existence. Bathroom fixtures and a contract division are part of the thoroughly modern mix. **Subway:** N, R, W to Prince St.

Pearl River 477 Broadway (between Broome and Grand Sts.) (212) 431-4770 *www.pearlriver.com.* This department store is Chinatown's top stop for exotic souvenirs, from paper lanterns to mandarin-collared silk pajamas to Hong Kong action videos. Everything's super-cheap. **Subway:** J, M, N, Q, R, W, Z, 6 to Canal St.

Steuben 667 Madison Ave. (between 60th and 61st Sts.) (212) 752-1441 *www.steuben.com.* This glittering gallery—one of Midtown's most breathtaking shops—is the flagship store for America's premier manufacturer of fine glass and crystal. **Subway:** N, R, W to Fifth Ave.

Takashimaya 693 Fifth Ave. (between 54th and 55th Sts.) (212) 350-0100. This is Zen shopping, exquisite and spare. This Japan-goes-French country store beckons customers to browse with an air of tranquility after escaping the sensory overload of Fifth Avenue. Takashimaya specializes in high-end household gifts for people with an eye for design, from subtly fragranced soaps to delicate beaded floral barrettes. Exotic flowers and elegant garden essentials fill the first floor, while the upper floors offer home, bath and fashion accessories both luxe and minimalist. **Subway:** E, V to Fifth Ave.

TransLuxe 10 Greene St. (north of Canal St.) (212) 925-5863. This tiny shop is a hidden gem. Sandra Santos crafts elegant one-of-a-kind lampshades and hanging lamps in elegant and fluid shapes using vintage and exotic fabrics. Choose from the ready-to-wear selection, or have her design and craft your own original inspiration. **Subway:** J, M, N, Q, R, W, Z, 6 to Canal St.

Jewelry

All of the biggest names in diamonds, gold and platinum have dazzling boutiques on Fifth Avenue in the 50's, often with a second location on Madison Avenue. Witness **Bulgari** (*www.bulgari.com*), whose bold, flashy Italian jewels can be had at 730 Fifth Avenue at 57th Street (212-315-9000), and 783 Madison Avenue between 66th and 67th Streets (212-717-2300); and **Cartier** (*www.cartier.com*), whose luxe French designs are available at 653 Fifth Avenue at 52nd Street (212-753-0111) and 828 Madison Avenue at 69th Street (212-472-6400). Fifth Avenue is also home to the timelessly glamorous wedding sets of **Harry Winston** (718 Fifth Ave. at 56th St., 212-245-2000), considered "King of the Diamonds"; and **Van Cleef & Arpels** (744 Fifth Ave. at 57th St., 212-644-9500, *www.vancleef.com*), with its movie-star glamorous jewels. The crystal, gold and silver of **Baccarat** (625 Madison Ave. at 59th St., 212-826-4100, *www.baccarat.fr*) are surprisingly modern, while the first name in estate jewelry and Oscar baubles is **Fred Leighton** (773 Madison Ave. at 66th St., 212-288-1872).

Those looking for cutting-edge styles and lower prices will do well to browse Nolita, where the fashion-forward jewelry designers include **Me & Ro** (241 Elizabeth St. between Prince and Houston Sts., 917-237-9215, *www.meandro-jewelry.com*), whose beautiful contemporary designs—many with Near East inspirations that lend them a gypsy feel—appeared on Drew, Cameron and Lucy in *Charlie's Angels 2*. **Push** (240 Mulberry St. between Prince and Spring Sts.; 212-965-9699, *www.pushnewyork.com*), showcases Karen Karch's rough-hewn, nature-inspired, gem-studded jewelry; it's classic with a modern edge. **Jill Platner** (113 Crosby St. between Houston and Prince Sts., 212-324-1298, *www.jillplatner.com*) showcases her own marvelous aboriginal-inspired silver collars and bracelets, many strung on brightly colored Goretex, lending her pieces a wonderfully contrary modern accent.

For antique pieces, browse the stalls at the **Manhattan Art & Antiques Center,** where a number of dealers specialize in collectible jewelry of yore, or visit **Doyle & Doyle** (*see* "Antiques" *earlier in this chapter*). Additionally, hardcore hunters might want to seek out street vendor **Olivia Garay,** who sells vintage jewelry, both cheap and couture chic, at her own open-air tables at the corner of Third Avenue and 70th Street. And don't forget to check out the **Diamond District** if you're in the market for a nice rock or custom-designed piece at a bargain price (*see* "Bargain Shopping" *earlier in this chapter*).

Fortunoff 681 Fifth Ave. (between 53rd and 54th Sts.) (212) 758-6660 *www.fortunoff.com*. Known for fine merchandise and competitive prices, Fortunoff boasts one of the city's largest selections of fine jewelry, and an impressive selection of silver and other bridal registry staples. Stone cuts and designs stick close to the classics, but the discount prices are very attractive. **Subway:** E, V to Fifth Ave.

H. Stern 645 Fifth Ave. (between 51st and 52nd Sts.) (212) 688-0300. Other location: 301 Park Ave. (between 49th and 50th Sts., in the Waldorf=Astoria) (212) 753-5595. This elegant Brazilian company specializes in high-end contemporary designs, with many pieces at the affordable end of the spectrum. Some of the pieces are crafted with unusual semiprecious stones. The store is streamline gorgeous. **Subway:** E, V to Fifth Ave.

Mikimoto 730 Fifth Ave. (between 56th and 57th Sts.) (212) 457-4600 *www.mikimotoamerica.com*. This beautiful Japanese shop is known exclusively for high-luster cultured pearls. While countless perfect strands come from Mikimoto's own farms, you can also find some of New York's most respectable South Sea and fresh-water varieties. **Subway:** E, N, R, V, W to Fifth Ave.

Reinstein/Ross 29 E. 73rd St. (between Fifth and Madison Aves.) (212) 772-1901 *www.reinsteinross.com*. Other location: 122 Prince St. (between Greene and Wooster Sts.) (212) 226-4513. This fine jeweler has been a huge hit with young brides in search of wedding sets with an exotic look. Expect matte finishes, rich-hued high-karat gold, intricate detailing and unusual gems. **Subway:** 6 to 77th St.

Stuart Moore 128 Prince St. (at Wooster St.) (212) 941-1023 *www.stuart-moore.com*. This futuristic jewel box is the place to come for the sleekest, most ultra-modern designs around in fine jewelry, including wedding sets. **Subway:** N, R, W to Prince St.

Tiffany & Co. 727 Fifth Ave. (at 57th St.) (212) 755-8000 *www.tiffany.com*. Long before Holly Golightly gazed into its jewel-bedecked windows, Tiffany's was firmly established as one of the world's premier jewelers. The collection is remarkable, ranging from affordable silver pieces in signature Tiffany designs to nature-inspired and jewel-studded baubles soaring into the thousands. The collection is elegantly displayed on multiple floors; don't be shy about just stopping into browse—everybody else does. The fine china, sterling silver and crystal are also magnificent. Small pieces—money clips, key chains and the like—for less than $100 let even shoppers with limited budgets depart with a signature blue box in tow. **Subway:** E, N, R, V, W to Fifth Ave.

Tourneau 12 E. 57th St. (between Fifth and Madison Aves.) (212) 758-7300 *www.tourneau.com*. Other locations: 500 Madison Ave. (at 52nd St.) (212) 758-6098; 200 W. 34th St. (at Seventh Ave.) (212) 563-6880; and in the Time Warner Center at Columbus Circle (212) 823-9425. The city's finest collection of watches is available at Tourneau, particularly at the large 57th Street location, Tourneau Time Machine, where brands range from Swiss Army to Rolex. **Subway:** E, N, R, V, W to Fifth Ave.

Leather, Handbags & Luggage

(*See* "Midtown & Uptown Shopping" *in this chapter for details on top designers, many of whom*—**Gucci**, **Prada**, **Kenneth Cole** *and others—make gorgeous handbags and leather goods. Check out the Lower East Side for discount bags and luggage; see* "Bargain Shopping" *earlier in this chapter.*)

Bottega Veneta 635 Madison Ave. (between 59th and 60th Sts.) (212) 371-5511 *www.bottegaveneta.com*. This Gucci offshoot specializes in fine woven leather and other chic handbags—with shoes and coats (and designer price tags) to match. **Subway:** 4, 5, 6 to 59th St; N, R, W to Lexington Ave.

Coach 595 Madison Ave. (at 57th St.) (212) 754-0041 *www.coach.com*. Other location: 342 Madison Ave. (at 44th St.) (212) 599-4777; 2321 Broadway (at 84th St.) (212) 799-1624; check for other locations. Known for butter-soft leather and classic handbag designs, Coach has hipped up its high-quality everyday lines of late, adding vivid colors, 21st-century fabrics, and fashion-forward backpacks, purses, organizers, jackets, and other super-cool accessories.

The Madison and 57th location shines as a tri-level showcase for the full line. **Subway:** 4, 5, 6 to 59th St.; N, R, W to Fifth Ave.

Greenwood Leather Goods & Gifts 263 Bleecker St. (between Sixth and Seventh Aves.) (212) 366-0825. While Original Leather (below) is your best Greenwich Village source for leather coats and pants, this tidy shop is the top stop for leather handbags, wallets, backpacks, luggage and the like from quality manufacturers like Frye and Latico. The selection is excellent, and prices are very reasonable. **Subway:** 1, 9 to Houston St.

Jutta Neumann 158 Allen St. (between Stanton and Rivington Sts.) (212) 982-7048 *www.juttaneumann-newyork.com*. German-born leather worker Jutta Neumann has crafted her own bold, brightly hued line of handbags, backpacks, wallets and sandals. The slides and strappy sandals are particularly stunning. **Subway:** F, V to Second Ave.

kate spade 454 Broome St. (at Mercer St.) (212) 274-1991 *www.katespade.com*. Everybody knows about handbag and accessories maven Kate Spade by now; her cute rectangular totes are carried by stylish, *Sex and the City*–watching gals around the world. Here you'll find the whole super-chic collection, which has expanded to include accessories, pajamas, shoes, stationery and a travel line large enough to justify its own store, **kate spade travel** (59 Thompson St. between Spring and Broome Sts., 212-965-8654). **Subway:** N, R, W to Prince St.

Louis Vuitton 116 Greene St. (between Spring and Prince Sts.) (212) 274-9090 *www.vuitton.com*. Other location: 1 E. 57th St. (at Fifth Ave.) (212) 758-8877. The most instantly recognizable designer leather goods and luggage on the planet is the perpetually chic Vuitton line. The empire has expanded to include bold fashions, shoes, outerwear and even travel guides over the years, but the unmistakably monogrammed bags—from totes to steamer trunks—are the heart of the matter. **Subway:** N, R, W to Prince St.

Manhattan Portage Factory Store 333 E. 9th St. (between First and Second Aves.) (212) 995-5490 *www.manhattanportage.com*. Loved for their durable, colorful, made-in-New York messenger bags finished with a red skyline logo, Manhattan Portage is also the place to go for hip one-shoulder backpacks and DJ bags. **Subway:** 6 to Astor Pl.

Original Leather Store 171 W. 4th St. (between Sixth and Seventh Aves.) (212) 675-2303 *www.originalleather.com*. Other locations: 256 Columbus Ave. (at 72nd St.) (212) 595-7051; 301 West Broadway (between Canal and Greene Sts.) (212) 226-4557. Greenwich Village is well known for its collection of leather houses hawking outerwear at discount prices, but Original Leather boasts the best selection, usually without the hard sell that's so common in this district. **Subway:** A, B, C, D, E, F, V to W. 4th St.

Rafe New York 1 Bleecker St. (at Bowery) (800) 486-9544 *www.rafe.com*. By taking classic shapes and imbuing them with color, wit and exotic twists, Rafe ("rah-fee") Totengco is crafting the most gorgeous designer handbags in the city. The collection is a thrill to browse, from smooth-finish, contrast-stiched leather to bamboo, willow, pandanus and exotic fabrics. Beading and embroidery sometimes add elegant and playful accents. **Subway:** 6 to Bleecker St.

T. Anthony Ltd. 445 Park Ave. (at 56th St.) (212) 750-9797 *www.tanthony.com*. This luxury luggage company crafts bold-hued, contrast-stiched leather pieces that are practical, eye-catching and classic. This is luggage built to last—and remain stylish—for a lifetime. No wonder Marilyn Monroe was a fan. Wonderfully classic handbags and accessories, too. **Subway:** 4, 5, 6 to 59th St.

Music

Greenwich Village is a record-hunting bonanza just north of Houston Street, mainly along Bleecker and West 3rd Streets. Between Sixth and Seventh Avenues, the highlights include legendary **Bleecker Bob's Golden Oldies** (118 W. 3rd St. between Macdougal St. and Sixth Ave., 212-475-9677, *www.bleeckerbobs.com*), a dirty hole of a store that's nevertheless a prime source for vinyl collectors; **Bleecker St. Records** (239 Bleecker St. near Carmine St., 212-255-7899), a real standout for its clean and well-organized selection of CDs and vinyl, which offers everything from blues, folk and golden oldies to 70's punk and current rock; **Vinylmania** (60 Carmine St., between Bedford St. and Seventh Ave. S., 212-924-7223, *www.vinylmania.com*), a prime stop for DJs as well as hip-hop, classic funk and current dance music fans. East of Sixth Avenue, **Generation Records** (210 Thompson St. between Bleecker and W. 3rd Sts., 212-254-1100), is a bright and well-organized store specializing in hardcore sounds upstairs, with one of the city's best used CD departments downstairs; and **Rebel Rebel** (319 Bleecker St. between Christopher and Grove Sts., 212-989-0770), the place for U.K. imports from glam to alt-pop to techno.

In the East Village, St. Marks Place between Second and Third Avenues is another prime hunting ground, especially for used CDs; the lineup of shops seems to be ever-changing, but you'll always find bargain-basement prices. A standout is **Mondo Kim's** (6 St. Marks Pl.; 212-598-9985; *www.kimsvideo.com*), for anything weird on CD, DVD and video; and **Joe's 13** (13 St. Marks Pl., 212-477-4376), an orderly shop boasting standout collections in rock, metal, country, blues, jazz and folk. Around the corner is **Wowsville** (125 Second Ave., 646-654-0935, *www.wowsville.net*), a hoot of a shop specializing in 60's psychedelia, Ramones-era punk, psychobilly and other underground sounds on vinyl, CD and video. Around the corner on Third Avenue is **Norman's Sound & Vision** (67 Cooper Sq., 212-473-6610), a tidy, well-stocked store with a straightforward selection of new and used CDs.

If you're in the market for musical instruments, West 48th Street between Sixth and Seventh Avenues is your neighborhood. The block's big kahuna is **Sam Ash** (160 W. 48th St., 212-719-2299, *www.samashmusic.com*), hawking everything from pro-DJ turntable systems to Les Pauls and Flying V's to the latest in accordions.

Academy Records & CDs 12 W. 18th St. (between Fifth and Sixth Aves.) (212) 242-3000 *www.academy-records.com*. Other location: 77 E. 10th St. (between Third and Fourth Aves.) (212) 780-9166. This tidy, relaxed shop is the prime city stop for used classical, opera, jazz and soundtrack LPs and CDs, plus video and DVDs. The East 10th Street location specializes in jazz, pop vocal, and genre vinyl. **Subway:** F, L, N, Q, R, V, W, 4, 5, 6 to 14th St.

Colony Music Center 1619 Broadway (at 49th St.) (212) 265-2050 *www.colonymusic.com*. Housed in the legendary Brill Building—the Tin Pan Alley of the 50's and 60's—this emporium of nostalgia doesn't offer any bargains, but it does have an excellent selection of vintage vinyl and CD reissues of classic and contemporary pop and Broadway cast recordings. A wide range of sheet music is also on hand, especially for the latest top-40 hits and Broadway scores. **Subway:** N, R to 49th St.

Footlight Records 113 E. 12th St. (between Third and Fourth Aves.) (212) 533-1572 *www.footlight.com*. Serious aficionados of cast recordings, big band, pop vocalist and spoken-word collectibles should skip Colony and head straight for this collectors' favorite. **Subway:** L, N, Q, R, W, 4, 5, 6 to 14th St.

Jazz Record Center 236 W. 26th St. (between Seventh and Eighth Aves.), room 804 (212) 675-4480 *www.jazzrecordcenter.com*. Here you'll find New York's best selection of jazz on vinyl and CD, including a phenomenal choice of rare and out-of-print records. **Subway:** C, E, 1, 9 to 23rd St.

Joseph Patelson Music House 160 W. 56th St. (between Sixth and Seventh Aves.) (212) 582-5840 *www.patelson.com*. Where better to house the city's finest collection of classical sheet music—some 47,000 titles—than behind Carnegie Hall? The collection features both common and unusual scores and sheet music, as well as metronomes and pitch pipes. **Subway:** F, N, R, Q, W to 57th St.; B, D, E to Seventh Ave.

Other Music 15 E. 4th St. (between Broadway and Lafayette St.) (212) 477-8150 *www.othermusic.com*. This super-cool store spans the globe and expands your mind with otherworldly sounds. This is the place for the most esoteric new releases, including out-there electronica, avant-garde and Japan-only releases, plus cult classics (MC5, Holy Modal Rounders), groove and free jazz, and 70's Krautrockers. **Subway:** 6 to Bleecker St.

Stern's Music 71 Warren St. (at West Broadway) (212) 964-5455 *www.sternsmusic.com*. This tri-continental cubby (with outposts in London and São Paulo) is a prime source for world music, especially African and Brazilian. **Subway:** 1, 2, 3, 9 to Chambers St.

Tower Records 692 Broadway (at 4th St.) (212) 505-1500 *www.towerrecords.com*. Other location: 1961 Broadway (at 66th St.) (212) 799-2500. The nation's best chain music retailer has a veritable compound surrounding the Greenwich Village on East 4th Street between Broadway and Lafayette, where you'll not only find the mainstream retail outlet (including Tower's first-rate classical department) but also **Tower Books** (20 E. 4th St., at Lafayette St., 212-505-1166). **Subway:** 6 to Bleecker St.; B, D, F, V to Broadway–Lafayette St.

Virgin Megastore 1540 Broadway (at 45th St.) (212) 921-1020 *www.virgin-mega.com*. Other location: 52 E. 14th St. (212) 598-4666. Richard Branson's rollicking entertainment complex—complete with a huge CD collection, listening posts, an extensive video and DVD department, a small but eclectic bookstore and a cafe, as well as a multiplex movie theater—is a Times Square attraction unto itself. The CD selection is excellent, new releases are usually on sale, and celebrity appearances are common. **Subway:** N, Q, R, S, W, 1, 2, 3, 7, 9 to 42nd St.

Shoes

New York has an endless supply of shoe retailers. Madison Avenue is the place to be if you're willing to pay top dollar for the biggest names. Look for **Timberland** (709 Madison Ave. at 63rd St., 212-754-0436, *www.timberland.com*), smart sophisticates **Cole Haan** (667 Madison Ave. at 61st St., 212-421-8440, *www.colehaan.com*) and **Bally of Switzerland** (628 Madison Ave. at 59th St., 212-751-9082, *www.bally.com*), and stiletto mavens **Stuart Weitzman** (625 Madison Ave. at 59th St., 212-750-2555, *www.stuartweitzman.com*) and **Sergio Rossi** (772 Madison Ave. at 66th St., 212-327-4288, *www.sergiorossi.it*).

SoHo and adjacent Nolita are tops for shoe fanatics looking for top quality with a twist, be it from **Camper** (125 Prince St. at Wooster St., 212-358-1841, *www.camper.com*), offering runway-hot updates on the classic bowling shoe and other smart-comfy styles; funky, punky, youth-minded **John Fluevog** (250 Mulberry St. at Prince St., 212-431-4484, *www.fluevog.com*); **Hogan** (134 Spring St. between Greene and Wooster Sts., 212-343-7905), whose grown-up styles are comfortably preppy-chic; and strappy, sexy **Sigerson Morrison** (28 Prince St. between Mott and Elizabeth Sts., 212-219-3893). The stores on Broadway between 8th and Canal Streets offer styles that emphasize affordability and comfort.

For the latest trendy footwear at affordable prices, stroll 8th Street between Fifth and Sixth Avenues in Greenwich Village and newly cutting-edge Orchard Street in the Lower East Side, where you'll find such outposts of hip as **alife** (178 Orchard St. south of Houston St., 646-654-0628).

The major department stores also have sizable shoe departments offering a sampling of famous labels, from casual to couture. Another great place to shop for shoes is in stylish clothing boutiques that carry their own lines, such as the **Kenneth Cole** flagship store or **Jeffrey New York** (*see* "Department Stores" *and* "Clothing.") Also see "Leather, Handbags & Luggage," as many of the retail outlets—including **Jutta Neumann, kate spade** and **Coach**—also carry their own shoe lines. For athletic shoes, you can't beat **Niketown** or **Modell's** (*see* "Sporting Goods" *later in this chapter*).

Arche 10 Astor Pl. (between Broadway and Lafayette St.). (212) 529-4808 *www.arche-shoes.com*. Other location: 128 W. 57th St. (between Sixth and Seventh Aves.) (212) 262-5488; check for more locations. Women's casual shoes don't get more comfortable than these French-made sandals and slip-ons, which come in a rainbow of soft nubucks that feel like suede but wear beautifully. **Subway:** 6 to Astor Pl.

Harry's Shoes 2299 Broadway (at 83rd St.) (866) 4-HARRYS or (212) 874-2035 *www.harrys-shoes.com*. If you prefer comfort and quality over flashy couture labels, head to Harry's for the biggest and best selection of shoes for the entire family. You name it, Harry's has it: comfort brands like Rockport, Mephisto, Ecco, Clark's and Dansko; weekend footwear by New Balance, Birkenstock and Teva; as well as kids favorites Keds and Stride Rite. **Subway:** 1, 9 to 86th St. You can compare prices and styles at nearby **Tip Top Shoes** (155 W. 72nd St. between Broadway and Columbus Ave., 212-787-4960 or 800-WALKING, *www.tiptopshoes.com*), which carries a similar, comfort-minded selection.

Jimmy Choo 645 Fifth Ave. (entrance on 51st St.) (212) 593-0800 *www.jimmychoo.com*. These seductive designs unite bold finishes and come-hither allure with the very best materials and workmanship. The sexy women's line is what Jimmy Choo is about, but the eye-catching men's line is worth a look, too. **Subway:** E, V to Fifth Ave.

John Lobb 680 Madison Ave. (between 61st and 62nd Sts.) (212) 888-9797 *www.johnlobb.com*. This royal shoemaker peddles its handmade English shoes for men, heralded for both their comfort and timeless style, in this classic storefront. Despite the pedigree, the collection includes a surprisingly terrific collection of classic and contemporary styles. Loafers don't come more gorgeous than this. **Subway:** 4, 5, 6 to 59th St.

Manolo Blahnik 31 W. 54th St. (between Fifth and Sixth Aves.) (212) 582–3007. The first name in ultra-sexy, ultra-luxury pumps and mules for women who firmly believe that it's better to look good than to feel good. Manolo's sultry signatures are pointy toes, narrow stiletto heels and platinum-card pricing. **Subway:** E, V to Fifth Ave.

Stapleton Shoe Company 68 Trinity Pl. (at Rector St.). (212) 964-6329. The place for deep discounts on designer men's shoes bearing such top-quality labels as Bally, Johnston & Murphy, and Timberland. **Subway:** N, R to Rector St.

Tod's 650 Madison Ave. (between 59th and 60th St.) (212) 644-5945 *www.tods.com*. This famous-name bag- and shoemaker hawks the most stylish moccasins in town, particularly the women's styles. The branded handbags come in a supple selection of warm-hued leathers, too. **Subway:** 4, 5, 6 to 59th St.

Unisa 701 Madison Ave. (between 62nd and 63rd Sts.) (212) 753-7474 *www.unisa.com*. Eye-catching women's shoe designs at affordable (generally less than $100) prices—and in a stylish boutique to boot. Summer styles bridge playful and practical. **Subway:** 4, 5, 6 to 59th St.

Varda 147 Spring St. (between West Broadway and Wooster St.) (212) 941-4990. Other locations: 786 Madison Ave. (between 66th and 67th Sts.) (212) 472-7552; 2080 Broadway (near 72nd St.) (212) 873-6910. These gorgeous styles in soft and supple Italian leather are the Manolo equivalent for the mid-priced and more practical woman. Varda's shoes are not only beautifully crafted, but they'll last—and remain in style—for years to come. **Subway:** C, E to Spring St.; N, R, W to Prince St.

Via Spiga 692 Madison Ave. (between 62nd and 63rd Sts.) (212) 871-9955 *www.viaspiga.com*. Other location: 390 West Broadway (between Spring and Broome Sts.) The best-kept secret weapon for fashionistas who want stylish and well-made heels for less than $200. Some of-the-moment men's styles, too. **Subway:** 4, 5, 6 at 59th St.

Walter Steiger 417 Park Ave. (at 55th St.) (212) 826-7171 *www.walter-steiger.com*. Stylish footwear for uptown women, from sexy retro-inspired heels to comfort walkers to high-style wedges. Shoes often surpass the $300 mark, but the quality is very high, and the styles will outlive the latest trend. **Subway:** 4, 5, 6 to 59th St.

Sporting Goods

Bicycle Habitat 244 Lafayette St. (between Prince and Spring Sts.) (212) 431-3315 *www.bicyclehabitat.com*. Downtown's most highly regarded bike shop is this friendly SoHo cubby, featuring wheels from Trek and Specialized, plus Mercian custom road frames, rentals and repairs. **Subway:** 6 to Spring St.; N, R, W to Prince St.

Bicycle Renaissance 430 Columbus Ave. (at 81st St.) (212) 724-2350 *www.bicyclerenaissance.com*. Selling everything from the newest mountain and racing models to custom bikes built by in-house professionals, this friendly and well-regarded shop also offers repair services. **Subway:** 1, 9 to 79th St.

Eastern Mountain Sports 591 Broadway (south of Houston St.) (212) 966-8730 *www.ems.com*. Other location: 20 W. 61st St. (at Broadway) (212) 397-4860. If you're planning a camping trip, learning to kayak or just want the best insect repellent for a Central Park picnic, EMS can meet your needs. They sell several top labels as well as their own sturdy brand of outdoor wear and gear. **Subway:** B, D, F, V to Broadway–Lafayette St.; 6 to Bleecker St.

Mets Clubhouse Shop 143 E. 54th St. (between Lexington and Third Aves.) (212) 888-7508 *www.mets.com*. Stop in for amazin' goods galore—baseball caps, T-shirts, posters, Piazza jerseys, '69 Miracle Mets memorabilia and much more. Fans can also score tickets. **Subway:** E, V to Lexington Ave., 6 to 51st St.

Modell's 1293 Broadway (at 34th St.) (212) 244-4544 *www.modells.com*. Other location: 51 E. 42nd St. (between Vanderbilt and Madison Aves.) (212) 661-4242; check for more locations. Family-owned and -operated since 1889, Modell's can't be beat for athletic wear and sporting goods. The range of brand names runs the gamut and prices are fair. **Subway:** 1, 2, 3, 9 to 34th St.

NBA Store 666 Fifth Ave. (at 52nd St.) (212) 515-NBA1 *www.nbastore.com* This tri-level mega-store is a high-tech multimedia celebration of pro-basketball, both NBA and WNBA. Star-studded events are frequent. **Subway:** E, V to Fifth Ave.

Niketown 6 E. 57th St. (between Fifth and Madison Aves.) (212) 891-6453 *www.niketown.com*. This high-design five-story advertorial for all things Nike carries the full line, all stunningly displayed. You'll pay full retail prices, but the shopping experience is first-class. **Subway:** N, R, W to Fifth Ave.

Paragon Sports 867 Broadway (at 18th St.) (212) 255-8036 *www.paragon-sports.com*. This sprawling shop covers all the bases, from racquet sports and golf to ice skating and sailing. Equipment is top of the line and prices can be steep, but sales are gold mines. **Subway:** L, N, Q, R, W, 4, 5, 6 to 14th St.

Patagonia 101 Wooster St. (between Prince and Spring Sts.) (212) 343-1776 *www.patagonia.com*. Other location: 426 Columbus Ave. (between 80th and 81st Sts.) (917) 441-0011. The first name in eco-friendly fleece and other nature-minded sports and adventure wear for men, women and kids (no gear, though). **Subway:** N, R, W to Prince St.; 6 to Spring St.

Scandinavian Ski & Sports Shop 40 W. 57th St. (between Fifth and Sixth Aves.) (212) 757-8524 *www.skishop.com*. Come to this cozy Midtown nook before you hit the slopes to meet all your ski and board needs, from boots, goggles, parkas and poles to high-end après-ski wear. **Subway:** N, R, W to Fifth Ave.

Yankees Clubhouse Shop 245 W. 42nd St. (between Seventh and Eighth Aves.) (212) 768-9555 *www.yankees.com*. Check for more locations. The Big Apple's favorite home team has its own mini-chain of boutiques where you can pick up everything from logo jerseys to home-game tickets. **Subway:** A, C, E, N, Q, R, S, W, 1, 2, 3, 7, 9 to 42nd St.

Stationery & Paper Goods

Dempsey & Carroll 110 E. 57th St. (between Park and Lexington Aves.) (212) 486-7526. Personal stationers since 1878, this elegant and serene little shop specializes in gorgeous notecards and stationery that are yours for customization (which takes four to six weeks). Despite the pedigree and traditional style of the shop, styles include striking Asian designs and lots of warm colors, plus plenty of choices for traditionalists. Friendly, somewhat formal service. **Subway:** 4, 5, 6 to 59th St.

Jamie Ostrow 54 W. 24th St. (between Fifth and Sixth Aves.) (212) 734-8890. There's no better stop in town for custom stationery, business cards and invitations if you're in the market for bold fonts and contemporary looks. **Subway:** 1, 9, C, E to 23rd St.

Kate's Paperie 561 Broadway (between Prince and Spring Sts.) (212) 941-9816 *www.katespaperie.com*. Other locations: 8 W. 13th St. (between Fifth and

Sixth Aves.) (212) 633-0570; 140 W. 57th St. (between Sixth and Seventh
Aves.) (212) 459-0700; 1282 Third Ave. (between 73rd and 74th Sts.) (212)
396-3670. For stationery with a twist, eye-catching invitations for your next
get-together or wrap that will make your gifts really pop, come to Kate's, the
best paper store in New York. The large selection also features beautifully bound
journals and albums, fountain pens, and more. **Subway:** N, R, W to Prince St.

Papivore 233 Elizabeth St. (north of Prince St.) (212) 334-4330 *www.papi-
vore.com*. This fragrant, candlelit shop sells the simple, delicate stationery of
Parisian papermaker Marie-Papier. Think simple lines and soft sherbet hues.
Custom cards and invites, too. **Subway:** N, R, W to Prince St.; 6 to Spring St.

Rebecca Moss 510 Madison Ave. (at 53rd St.) (212) 832-7671 *www.rebecca-
moss.com*. This top-notch stylo shop makes Oprah's favorite pens. Excellent for
first-quality ballpoints and fountain pens, from affordable to collectible.
Subway: E, V to 53rd St.

Toys

Alphaville 226 W. Houston St. (between Varick St. and Sixth Ave.) (212)
675-6850 *www.alphaville.com*. Specializing in vintage toys from the 1950's to
the 70's, this gallery-like shop is entirely for grown-ups who are nostalgic kids at
heart. The collection includes items like Mr. Potato Heads and classic Paint-by-
Numbers sets, and there's a strong emphasis on TV-themed and outer-space
toys. **Subway:** 1, 9 to Houston St.

American Girl Place 609 Fifth Ave. (at 49th St.) (877) AG-PLACE
www.americangirlplace.com. Girls across America ages 3 through 13 are obsessed
with American Girl history-themed dolls and their accompanying wardrobes,
books and accessories. This 42,500-square-foot store also boasts a cafe and the
American Girl Theater, which stages the original American Girl Revue. **Subway:** B, D, F, V to 47th-50th Sts.–Rockefeller Center.

Big City Kites 1210 Lexington Ave. (at 82nd St.) (888) 476-KITE or (212)
472-2623 *www.bigcitykites.com*. This entire store is a loving ode to kites.
Choices range from delicate, artful tissue-paper creations to utilitarian plastic
varieties that can withstand the learning curve of first-time fliers. The wonderful staff also offers repair services. **Subway:** 4, 5, 6 to 86th St.

Classic Toys 218 Sullivan St. (between Bleecker and 3rd Sts.) (212) 674-4434
www.classictoysnyc.com. Both kids and collectors love this toy store for its wide
range of old and new toys, from die-cast trucks and Matchbox cars to the latest
modern playthings. More than a century's worth of toy soldiers are on display, as is
a fascinating collection of antique toys. **Subway:** A, B, C, D, E, F, V to W. 4th St.

Dinosaur Hill 306 E. 9th St. (east of Second Ave.) (212) 473-5850
www.dinosaurhill.com. Toys from around the world can be found in this tiny,
fanciful East Village space: old-fashioned American wooden blocks, Latin

American masks, marbles, puppets, crafts and much more, as well as a good selection of children's literature. **Subway:** 6 to Astor Pl.

Toys "R" Us 1514 Broadway (at 44th St.) (646) 366-8800 or (800) 869-7787 *www.toysrus.com* Other location: 24-32 Union Sq. (212) 674-8697. With its own working Ferris wheel in the atrium, the Times Square flagship is mighty impressive. In fact, the bright, beautifully organized store is impressive through and through, thanks to a comprehensive and well-ordered selection includes the city's cuddliest selection of stuffed animals. **Subway:** N, Q, R, S, W, 1, 2, 3, 9 to 42nd St.

Wine Shops

New York has a world-class selection of wine shops. Standouts include **Sherry-Lehmann,** regularly lauded as among the best wine shops in the world; **Morrell & Company,** boasting a sumptuous wine bar and cafe in the adjacent storefront; **Chelsea Wine Vault at Chelsea Market;** and, on the Upper West Side, **67 Wines & Spirits, Gotham Wines & Liquors, Beacon Wines & Spirits** and **Acker, Merrall & Condit.** These are full-service shops where the clerks are knowledgeable and always ready to rescue the clueless—provided it's not during a busy Saturday morning or in the middle of the frantic holiday season.

Bargain hunters often head to **Garnet Wines & Liquors, Best Cellars, Crossroads Wine & Liquor** and **Astor Wines & Spirits.** The atmosphere in these shops, particularly Garnet, can be hectic, so savvy customers try to know what they want before they push open the doors. If business is slow, which it rarely is, the staff can be most helpful. And prices can be appealingly low.

New York has its specialists, too. When they run short on Romanee-Conti, Burgundy and Rhône lovers head for the **Burgundy Wine Company** in the West Village, where you usually have to ring the bell and wines are often selected from an order book rather than samples on the very tiny floor.

Looking for a special Barolo or a little-known Chianti? Take a trip to the **Italian Wine Merchants.** Some of New York's best-known restaurateurs, Mario Batali and Lydia Bastianich, are partners in this first-class shop. Devotees of rare old Bordeaux know they are likely to find what they want at **Royal Wine Merchants.**   —*Frank Prial*

Acker, Merrall & Condit 160 W. 72nd St. (between Broadway and Columbus Ave. (212) 787-1700 *www.ackerstore.com.* **Subway:** 1, 2, 3, 9 to 72nd St.

Astor Wines & Spirits 12 Astor Pl. (at Lafayette St.) (212) 674-7500 *www.astorwines.com.* **Subway:** 6 to Astor Pl.

Beacon Wines & Spirits 2120 Broadway (at 74th St.) (212) 877-0020 *www.beaconwines.com.* **Subway:** 1, 2, 3, 9 to 72nd St.

Best Cellars 1291 Lexington Ave. (between 86th and 87th Sts.) (212) 426-4200 *www.bestcellars.com.* **Subway:** 4, 5, 6 to 86th St.

Burgundy Wine Company 143 W. 26th St. (between Sixth and Seventh

Aves.) (212) 691-9092 *www.burgundywinecompany.com*. **Subway:** A, C, E, 1, 2,3, 9 to 14th St.; L to Eighth Ave.

Chelsea Wine Vault Chelsea Market, 75 Ninth Ave. (between 15th and 16th Sts.) (212) 462-4244 *www.chelseawinevault.com*. **Subway:** A, C, E to 14th St.; L to Eighth Ave.

Crossroads Wine & Liquor 55 W. 14th St. (between Fifth and Sixth Aves.) (212) 924-3060. **Subway:** F, V to 14th St.

Garnet Wines & Liquors 929 Lexington Ave. (between 68th and 69th Sts.) (212) 772-3211 *www.garnetwine.com*. **Subway:** 6 to 68th St.

Gotham Wines & Liquors 2515 Broadway (between 93rd and 94th Sts.) (212) 932-0990 *www.gothamwines.com*. **Subway:** 1,2,3 & 9 to 96th St.

Italian Wine Merchants 108 E. 16th St. (between Union Square East and Irving Pl.) (212) 473-2323 *www.italianwinemerchant.com*. **Subway:** L, N, Q, R, W, 4, 5, 6 to 14th St.

Morrell & Company 1 Rockefeller Plaza (at 49th St.) (212) 981-1106 *www.morrellwine.com*. **Subway:** B, D, F, V to 47th-50th St.–Rockefeller Center.

Royal Wine Merchants 25 Waterside Plaza (at the East River near 23rd St.) (212) 689-4855 *www.royalwinemerchants.com*. **Subway:** 6 to 23rd St.

Sherry-Lehmann 679 Madison Ave. (between 61st and 62nd Sts.) (212) 838-7500 *www.sherry-lehmann.com*. **Subway:** N, R, W to Fifth Ave.; 4, 5, 6 to 59th St.

67 Wines & Spirits 179 Columbus Ave. (at 67th St.) (888) 671-6767 or (212) 724-6767 *www.67wine.com*. **Subway:** 1, 9 to 66th St.

New York for Children

At first glace, New York may not seem like a kid-friendly place. After all, it's all concrete and steel, with a cultural life geared strictly to grown-ups. But in reality, the city is a magical place for young visitors. This chapter will highlight the city's top attractions for the under-12 set, from museums to puppet shows and playgrounds.

Moms and dads should also consult the **Exploring New York** chapter, which covers many other sights that will be a hit with kids. Look there for details on the **American Museum of Natural History,** where the magnificent hall of dinosaurs provides New York's answer to Jurassic Park. A blockbuster space show inspires budding astronauts at the adjacent **Rose Center for Earth and Space. Times Square** has an array of family-friendly shops, arcades, theaters and gimmicks. Youngsters will also love a **Circle Line cruise** (especially the Beast speedboat tour), the **Statue of Liberty,** the **New York City Fire Museum,** the *Intrepid* **Sea-Air-Space Museum** and the **Empire State Building.**

Also covered in the **Exploring New York** chapter are outer-borough attractions that will appeal to children, including Brooklyn's **Coney Island** amusement park, beach and boardwalk; and the **New York Aquarium,** where children can get nose to nose with sharks and handle crabs and starfish in a "touch tank." The **Bronx Zoo** is a world-class wildlife park—and a guaranteed kid-pleaser. Kids may also enjoy taking the **Staten Island ferry;** from the ferry landing, you can walk to the **Staten Island Institute of Arts and Sciences,** which has an enormous insect collection.

Most of New York's major museums and cultural institutions have programs geared to families and young people *(see* "Museums for Children" *later in this chapter).*

(For children's bookstores, clothing stores and toy stores, see chapter **Shopping in New York.** *For great places to play and burn off excess energy, see chapter* **Sports & Recreation.***)*

Six Great Places for Kids

New Victory Theater   MIDTOWN WEST
209 W. 42nd St. (between Seventh and Eighth Aves.) (646) 223-3020 or (646) 223-3065 for VicTeens. *www.newvictory.org.* If you think of children's theater as marionettes, fairy tales and clowns, you have obviously never visited the New Victory. This is not to say that its productions never use these elements, but if they do, the marionettes are likely to be life-size, the fairy tales sometimes grim (as well as Grimm), and the clowns more like Bill Irwin than the Three Stooges. Opened in 1995 as part of the redevelopment of Times Square, the New Victory is Broadway's first theater for families, and it is deter-

mined never to condescend to its audiences. Its season (October to June) includes the best productions worldwide, from extravaganzas like Montreal's Cirque Eloize to inventive productions like the Young Vic's *Sleeping Beauty*, which takes up the plot after the "happily ever after." Generally geared to children 6 and older, the New Victory also offers Vic Teens, a program in which teenage patrons can see certain shows and then mingle with the cast and creators. This is intelligent and creative children's theater, with family-friendly prices ($10–$30, with 30 percent discounts for members). The theater is right across from *The Lion King* on 42nd Street.
Subway: A, C, E, N, Q, R, S, W, 1, 2, 3, 7, 9 to 42nd St.

Theatreworks/USA   CHELSEA
787 Seventh Ave. (between 51st and 52nd Sts.) (800) 497-5007 for box office *www.theatreworksusa.org*. You don't have to fork over your money to Disney to take your children to a memorable musical that will send them (and you) home humming. Theatreworks/USA is America's largest nonprofit theater for young audiences. The company tours throughout the nation, but its home base is in New York, where there's a regular slate of performances at the Auditorium at Equitable Tower. Theatreworks' musicals and drama not only provide children ages 4 and older with an introduction to the theater—they offer insights into history that are so entertaining that the kids may not realize how much they're learning. In the last several years, Theatreworks has illustrated a number of important chapters in the growth of the United States, with plays such as *Gold Rush; Young Tom Edison; The Color of Justice* (about Thurgood Marshall and *Brown v. Topeka*); and *Paul Robeson, All-American*. It has also brought literary favorites to the stage, such as *Ramona Quimby; Charlotte's Web; A Christmas Carol; Sarah, Plain and Tall; Island of the Blue Dolphins*; and *The Lion, the Witch and the Wardrobe*. The season of hour-long shows plays on weekends, November to April. Tickets are $25 (or $18 if you buy 10 or more throughout the season); look for special free productions every summer. The best works are repeated season to season, but they never get old. **Subway:** 1, 2, 9 to 50th St.; N, R to 49th St.

Children's Museum of Manhattan   UPPER WEST SIDE
212 W. 83rd St. (between Amsterdam Ave. and Broadway) (212) 721-1234 *www.CMOM.org*. Few children's museums offer what adults might consider real art: paintings, sculptures, photographs and installations that could just as easily be found in a SoHo gallery. But the Children's Museum of Manhattan broke new ground with its 2002-2003 exhibition called "Art Inside Out," in which artists Elizabeth Murray, William Wegman and Fred Wilson created environments and displays designed to introduce children to contemporary art.

This combination of fun and learning is typical of the museum, which is unusual for both the breadth of its offerings and the wide age range it serves. One of its exhibitions, "Wordplay," includes places for infants to crawl, gaze at mobiles and push buttons as their parents learn about the role of language in their babies' lives. Literacy, in fact, is one of the museum's passions; many of its exhibits are devoted to the works of beloved children's authors. Running through September 2005 is an imaginative, colorful exhibit called "Oh, Seuss! Off to Great Places," which features dozens of activity areas ranging from playground simple to marvels of digital technology

Conveniently located on the Upper West Side, the museum is just a few minutes' walk from Central Park, and a stone's throw from an array of family-friendly restaurants. Look for art and music classes; the Sussman Environmental Center, an outdoor oasis for learning about urban ecology; and a digital design workshop where children can create their own inventions with the help of computers. Currently in the midst of a major expansion, the museum will someday offer a renovated performance theater and a glass-enclosed rooftop garden. **Admission:** $7 adults and children; $4 seniors; children under age 1 free. Strollers must be checked. **Hours:** Wed.–Sun.10 A.M.–5 P.M. (also open Tue. in summer). **Subway:** 1, 9 to 86th St.

Brooklyn Children's Museum   BROOKLYN

145 Brooklyn Ave. (at St. Mark's Ave.) (718) 735-4400 *www.bchildmus.org.* City chauvinists wouldn't be surprised to learn that the world's first children's museum is in New York. They might be shocked, however, to learn that it's in Crown Heights, Brooklyn. This museum, which celebrated its centennial in 1999, pioneered the hands-on approach characteristic of contemporary children's exhibitions as early as 1904, when it began taking the objects on display out of their glass cases. That's still the philosophy at the museum, which invites children to pluck at musical instruments, handle insect models or try on shoes. The Brooklyn Children's Museum has more than 27,000 objects, ranging from an elephant skeleton to Queen Elizabeth II coronation dolls. Totally Tots, a gallery specially geared to toddlers under age 5, offers the Baby Patch, a giant artificial bird's nest; Play Pond, a series of small pools for dabbling, pouring and handling marine objects; and Kids Quarry, a wall with foam rocks for building. The museum also has a greenhouse, where children can "adopt a plant" and handle earthworms. In the Animal Outpost, children can observe species like frogs and double-crested basilisks while learning about their life cycles through displays that include animal skeletons and a microscope. The museum is currently embarking on a $39 million expansion that will double its space. The new facility, designed by Rafael Vinoly, is scheduled to open in 2006. **Admission:** $4; free for children under age 1. **Hours:** Sept.–Jun. Wed.–Fri. 2–5 P.M., Sat.–Sun. 11 A.M.–6 P.M. Jul.–Aug. Tue.–Fri. 1–6 P.M., Sat.–Sun. 11 A.M.–6 P.M. Totally Tots is open 11 A.M.–6 P.M. every day the museum is open. **Subway:** 3 or C to Kingston Ave., A to Nostrand Ave. (7-block walk from subway stops). Free weekend trolley shuttle from Grand Army Plaza.

Staten Island Children's Museum   STATEN ISLAND

1000 Richmond Terrace (between Tysen St. and Snug Harbor Rd.) (718) 273-2060. Nestled in the Snug Harbor Cultural Center and boasting one

of the most bucolic settings a New York institution could hope for, the museum
has a huge front lawn that is turned into a festival site every spring when the
museum hosts Meadowfair, an indoor-outdoor carnival. (The lawn also has a
large praying mantis—or "playing mantis"—sculpture for children to climb.)
Indoors, there's Block Harbor, an area for preschoolers that includes a pirate
ship for small swashbucklers; Portia's Playhouse, which provides budding star-
lets with costumes, props and a stage; and permanent exhibitions on irresistible
subjects like water and bugs (there's an Arthropod Zoo), as well as traveling
displays. In 2001, the museum expanded into a two-story turn-of-the-century
barn. The highlight of the new space is Great Explorations (open for a few
hours each afternoon), an exhibition that invites children to discover what it
was like to pioneer a tropical rain forest, the ocean depths and a snowy polar
landscape.
Admission: $5; children under 1 free. **Hours:** Tue.–Sun. noon–5 P.M.
(opens at 10 A.M. Jul.–Aug., with extended Thu. evening hours till 8 P.M.)
Directions: Staten Island Ferry to S-40 bus.

New York Hall of Science   QUEENS
47–01 111th St. (at 47th Ave.), Flushing (718) 699-0005 *www.nyhallsci.org*.
Any playground is potentially a lesson in physics. But only one playground in
New York is especially designed to teach children the scientific concepts behind
every sway of the seesaw and zoom down the slide. That's the award-winning
Science Playground at the New York Hall of Science in Queens, the largest
playground of its kind in the Western Hemisphere. Its companion area, the
Sound Playground, is understandably—and educationally—noisy.

Although these special playgrounds are open only to children over age 6, the
Hall of Science offers attractions for younger adventurers, too. The Preschool
Discovery Place allows them to explore sound, color, light and simple principles
of construction, while permanent displays in the Exhibition Hall offer their
older siblings forays into the physical world, from the atomic level on up. Marvelous Molecules offers an in-depth look at the building blocks of all life, and
the Pfizer Foundation Biochemistry Discovery Lab invites visitors to explore the
chemistry of living things by conducting experiments on subjects ranging from
why roses are red and violets are blue to how bees communicate. Recommended
for ages 7 and up, the lab is open to the public on Saturdays and Sundays from
noon to 4:45 P.M., and Thursdays and Fridays from 2 to 4:45 P.M.
Admission: $9 adults; $6 children ages 5–17 and seniors over age 62; $2.50
children ages 2–4. Science Playground entry $3 per person. Free admission Fri.
2–5 P.M. except July–Aug. **Hours:** Tue.–Thu. 9:30 A.M.–2 P.M. (till 5 P.M. in
July–Aug.); Fri. 9:30 A.M.–5 P.M.; Sat.–Sun. noon–5 P.M. (10:30 A.M.–6 P.M.
in July–Aug. Also open Mon. 9:30 A.M.–2 P.M. July–Aug. **Subway:** 7 to 111th
St. in Queens, then walk 3 blocks south.

—*Laurel Graeber*

Circuses

Big Apple Circus (800) 922-3772 *www.bigapplecircus.org*. With its local roots, intimate one-ring big top and kid-friendly mission, the Big Apple Circus has staked out its own ground between the glitz of Ringling Brothers and the artistry of Cirque du Soleil. Shows are held in the circus's quaint big top in Damrosch Park at Lincoln Center, from late October to early January. Tickets go on sale in September.

Ringling Brothers and Barnum and Bailey Circus Madison Square Garden, Seventh Ave. (at 33rd St.) (800) 755-4000 *www.ringling.com*. The classic American three-ring circus—trapeze artists, lion tamers, elephants and all—descends on Madison Square Garden every spring, running shows in March and April. Check *www.thegarden.com* for a complete schedule and ticket purchase.

Museum Programs for Children

(See "Six Great Places for Kids" *above for* **Brooklyn Children's Museum, Children's Museum of Manhattan** *and* **Staten Island Children's Museum.** *See also* **Lefferts Homestead Children's Historic House Museum** *in Prospect Park, described in the* "Brooklyn" *section of chapter* **Exploring New York.** *For admission prices, hours and directions, see the full museum listings in chapters* **Exploring New York** *and* **The Arts.***)*

American Museum of Natural History Central Park West (at 79th St.) (212) 769-5100 *www.amnh.org*. From the Dinosaur Halls to the enormous IMAX theater to the Hall of Ocean Life, with its giant blue whale suspended from the ceiling, this is a blockbuster for kids. The museum's Discovery Room, dominated by a model of an African baobab tree (with plenty of artificial creatures in its branches), offers kids the chance to play zoologist, paleontologist, geologist and anthropologist. (Ask about visiting the Discovery Room when you first arrive, since space is limited and visits are staggered to prevent overcrowding.) Check the Web site for a rundown of science and nature programs geared to kids of all ages.

Brooklyn Museum 200 Eastern Parkway, Prospect Park (718) 638-5000 *www.brooklynmuseum.org*. Kids will enjoy the largest collection of mummies outside Egypt, as well as excellent children's workshops and teen programs.

Children's Museum of the Arts 182 Lafayette St. (between Broome and Grand Sts.) (212) 941-9198 *www.cmany.org*. This museum includes interactive installations like the ever-popular Ball Pond, which invites kids to crawl through a room filled with oversized rubber balls, and two floors of art studios offering hands-on projects. **Admission:** $6; free for seniors and children under age 1. **Hours:** Wed.–Sun. noon–5 P.M. (till 6 P.M. Thu.). **Subway:** N, R to Prince St.; 6 to Spring St.

The Jewish Museum 1109 Fifth Ave. (at 92nd St.) (212) 423-3200. *www.thejewishmuseum.org.* Every Sunday, the museum offers a special Family Fun day, including everything from sing-a-longs and storytimes to art activities and theater performances. A special children's audio guide is available every day to help kids understand the museum's exhibits. Summer art and film programs are specially geared to teens.

Lower East Side Tenement Museum 90 Orchard St. (at Broome St.) (212) 431-0233 *www.tenement.org.* The museum can only be seen on a guided tour, and most of its offerings are not recommended for kids. But all that changes on weekends, when the museum offers the Confino Apartment Tour, a living history tour that allows kids to try on period clothes and talk with an actor who portrays a recent immigrant. This hour-long tour ($11 adults, $9 students and seniors) is offered four times a day on Saturdays and Sundays; advance reservations are a must.

Metropolitan Museum of Art 1000 Fifth Ave. (at 82nd St.) (212) 535-7710. *www.metmuseum.org.* The "Museum Hunt" guides, available at the information desk near the 81st Street entrance, present the special and permanent collections to kids through fun activities. Most children are entertained by the Egyptian collection (spooky mummies!). There are frequent family tours, hands-on workshops, storytelling sessions, films and more (check the Web site for the latest schedule).

MoMA 11 West 53rd St. (212) 708-9400 *www.moma.org.* Newly returned to its spectacularly renovated and expanded home in Manhattan, MoMA offers family-oriented gallery talks, "tours for tots," and special workshops and films.

P.S. 1 22-25 Jackson Ave. (at 46th Ave.), Long Island City, Queens. (718) 784-2084 *www.ps1.org.* P.S. 1, MoMA's cutting-edge affiliate, offers summer "art camps" and other programs geared to families.

Rose Center for Earth and Space 79th St. and Central Park West (212) 769-5100 *www.amnh.org/rose.* The exhibits and high-tech star shows here are always a hit with budding young astronomers. They're usually packed, so consider buying tickets in advance by calling (212) 769-5200 or ordering online.

South Street Seaport Museum 207 Front St. (between South and Water Sts.) (212) 748-8600 *www.southstseaport.org.* There's a children's center in the museum here, and almost every week brings a special children's workshop or festival. But all of the attractions in this landmark district are meant to be family-friendly. This 11-square-block development on the East River encompasses historic buildings, several piers, shops and restaurants. Kids will especially like checking out the historic ships berthed at the piers. **Admission:** $8 adults; $6 seniors and students; $4 children ages 5–12; free for children 4 and under. **Hours:** Daily 10 A.M.–5 P.M. **Subway:** J, M, Z, 2, 3, 4, 5 to Fulton St.; A, C to Broadway–Nassau.

The Whitney Museum of American Art 945 Madison Ave. (at 75th St.)
(212) 570-7710. *www.whitney.org.* The Whitney offers frequent and affordable
family workshops on weekends, encouraging adults and children to learn about
art and culture together. In addition, families can attend a free guided tour featuring sketching and discussion every Saturday at 2 P.M. (best for kids ages
7–11; reserve by calling 212-570-7745). Special print and audio guides for kids
are available at the information desks.

Music for Children
(For more information, see chapter **The Arts.***)*

Amato Opera-in-Brief 319 Bowery (at 2nd St.) (212) 228-8200.
www.amato.org. In addition to its standard performances, this company has
been staging opera for children for over 50 years. "Opera-in-Brief" performances are fully costumed, abbreviated versions of classic operas, featuring
interwoven narration so everyone can follow the story. Performances are 90
minutes long (including intermission) and should be appropriate for children 5
and up. **Prices:** $15 all seats; buy tickets in advance. **Schedule:** Usually 10 per-
formances per year, all start at 11:30 A.M. Sat, dates vary.

Carnegie Hall Family Concerts 152 W. 57th St. (at Seventh Ave.)
(212) 903-9670 *www.carnegiehall.org.* At these hour-long concerts, kids ages 5
to 12 get an introduction to music through a variety of demonstrations led by
well-known performers and groups. Parents with younger children should seek
out the "CarnegieKids" interactive morning concerts, in which preschoolers
get to play along with musicians and a storyteller. **Prices:** Family Concerts $8,
CarnegieKids $3. Buy tickets in advance, as these sell out quickly.

Lincoln Center Children's Programs
Unfortunately, there are only a few special kids' concerts at Lincoln Center
each year. Schedules can vary from season to season; parents should buy tickets
well in advance.

Growing Up With Opera (212) 769-7008 *www.operaed.org.* The Metropolitan
Opera sponsors a few shows each year for kids ages 4–6 and 6–12, often featuring question-and-answer sessions and "cast parties" with the artists afterward.

Jazz for Young People In the Time Warner Center at Columbus Circle
(212) 258-9800 *www.jazzatlincolncenter.org.* Wynton Marsalis, director of the
Lincoln Center Jazz Orchestra, is passionate about educating young fans. He
hosts and performs at educational Jazz for Young People concerts, with themes
like "Who Is Miles Davis?" or "What Is a Big Band?" In 2004, Jazz at Lincoln
Center added a new music education program called WeBop, in which children ages 2 to 5 can sing, move and play to jazz rhythms (call 212-258-9806 or
e-mail education@jalc.org to enroll).

Little Orchestra Society (212) 971-9500 *www.littleorchestra.org*. Each season, the Society sponsors three classical-music concerts geared toward children ages 6–12 at Avery Fisher Hall (plus an additional series of Lolli-Pops concerts for kids ages 3–5 at the Kaye Playhouse at Hunter College).

New York Philharmonic Young People's Concerts (212) 721-6500 *www.nyphilharmonic.org*. The Philharmonic offers four Saturday-afternoon concerts each winter, providing a fun introduction to symphonic music for 6- to 12-year-olds. Kids get the chance to make their own music at the one-hour "Kidzone Live!" sessions before each concert.

Play Spaces

Chelsea Piers West Side Hwy. at 23rd St. (212) 336-6666 *www.chelseapiers.com*. You name it—they've got it. Families can enjoy skating, bowling, batting cages and much, much more. Facilities include a toddler gym; supervised childcare for ages 18 months to 8 years (reservations required); and separate rock-climbing walls for children and teens. City kids can enroll in all kinds of classes and activities, from gymnastics to soccer to dance. Prices vary according to the activity, but none of it is cheap. (*See the box in chapter* **Sports & Recreation.**) **Subway:** C, E to 23rd St.

Lazer Park 163 W. 46th St. (between Broadway and Sixth Ave.) (212) 398-3060 *www.lazerpark.com*. In addition to the 5,000-square-foot laser tag arena, meant solely for older kids and grown-ups looking to get in touch with their inner child, there's a huge array of video and virtual-reality games. **Subway:** B, D, F, N, Q, R, V, W, 1, 2, 3, 7, 9 to 42nd St.

Puppets

The Lenny Suib Puppet Playhouse at Asphalt Green 555 E. 90th St. (between York and East End Aves.) (212) 369-8890, ext. 159. In a season that runs September to April, this theater offers puppets, magicians, clowns, ventriloquists and storytellers. **Prices:** $7. **Subway:** 4, 5, 6 to 86th St.

Puppetworks 338 Sixth Ave. (at 4th St.), Park Slope, Brooklyn (718) 965-3391 *www.puppetworks.org*. This group has been performing with hand-crafted marionettes since 1938. They generally offer three or four shows per year (like *Rumpelstiltskin*), with two performances each Saturday and Sunday. Reservations are required. **Prices:** $7 adults; $6 children. **Subway:** F to Seventh Ave..

Swedish Cottage Marionette Theater Central Park West Drive (at 79th St.) (212) 988-9093 *www.centralparknyc.org*. Puppet shows, often based on classic fairytales, are staged at 10:30 A.M. and noon Tuesday through Friday, and 1 P.M. on Saturdays. The season runs from early November through June; advance reservations are required. **Prices:** $6 adults; $5 children. **Subway:** B, C to 81st St.

Science for Children

(See "Six Great Places for Kids" *at the beginning of this chapter for the* **New York Hall of Science**. *See* "Museum Programs for Children" *earlier in this chapter for the* **American Museum of Natural History** *and the* **Rose Center for Earth and Space.***)*

Liberty Science Center 251 Phillip St. (at Communipaw Ave.), Jersey City, New Jersey (201) 200-1000 *www.lsc.org*. Each of the center's three floors is devoted to a specific theme: environment, health and invention. Visitors of all ages can touch starfish or giant insects, crawl through a 100-foot "touch tunnel" or play virtual basketball. There's also an IMAX theater screening films on topics like volcanoes of the deep sea or lions of the Kalahari. **Admission:** $10 adults; $8 children and seniors; free for children under age 2. Additional fees for IMAX and 3-D Laser Shows. **Hours:** Tue.–Sun. 9:30 A.M.–5:30 P.M. (also open Mon. in July–Aug.). **Directions:** Take the NY Waterways Ferry from North End Avenue and Vesey Street in Lower Manhattan, near the World Financial Center; or take the PATH train to Pavonia/Newport and transfer to the Hudson-Bergen Light Rail.

Sony Wonder Technology Lab 550 E. 56th St. (between Madison and Fifth Aves.) (212) 833-8100 *www.sonywondertechlab.com*. No doubt about it: This is one of the city's coolest destinations for kids, and it's absolutely free. Kids can produce their own TV shows, remix a song, analyze weather data to avert disasters, or watch HDTV. But keep in mind, this free public space dedicated to technology education just happens to be operated by Sony's retail division, and, not surprisingly, showcases only Sony products. **Admission:** Free, but advance reservations required. **Hours:** Tue.–Wed. and Fri.–Sat. 10 A.M.–6 P.M.; Sun. noon–6 P.M.; Thu. 10 A.M.–8 P.M. **Subway:** E, V to Fifth Ave.; 4, 5, 6 to 59th St.; N, R to Fifth Ave.

Theater for Children

(For the **New Victory Theater** *and* **Theatreworks/USA,** *see* "Six Great Places for Kids" *earlier in this chapter.)*

Arts Connection 520 Eighth Ave. (212) 302-7433 *www.artsconnection.org*. The affordable "Saturdays Alive" series of performances and workshops is held at the Museum of the City of New York, located at Central Park East and 104th Street. Geared to ages 5 and older, they feature craft workshops, dance performances, concerts and more. Reservations are strongly recommended; book online or call (212) 534-1672, ext. 207. **Prices:** $6, including museum admission. **Subway:** 6 to 103rd St.; 2, 3 to 100th St.

Beauty and the Beast Lunt-Fontanne Theater, 205 W. 46th St. (between Eighth Ave. and Broadway) (212) 575-9200. Disney's stage adaptation of its animated classic is more pedestrian than the breathtaking film version, but little ones will love it anyway. Even adults will go home humming the catchy show-stopper "Be Our Guest." In addition to evening performances, there are matinees on Wednesdays, Saturdays and Sundays. **Prices:** $35–$95. **Subway:** A, C, E, N, Q, R, S, W, 1, 2, 3, 7, 9 to 42nd St.

Henry Street Settlement—Abrons Arts Theater 466 Grand St. (at Pitt St.) (212) 598-0400 *www.henrystreet.org*. This historic settlement house features an arts center with an array of dance, theater and music performances for the whole family, sometimes featuring mime, puppetry and magic. One recent show was *The Ash Girl*, an Urban Youth Theater retelling of the Cinderella story. Reserve for weekend shows at least a week in advance. The settlement also offers classes for all ages in dance, music, the visual arts and theater. **Subway:** F to Delancey St.; J, M, Z to Essex St.

Kids 'N Comedy 34 W. 22nd St. (between Fifth and Sixth Aves.) (212) 877-6115 *www.kidsncomedy.com*. Monthly children's shows and comedy workshops are offered at the Gotham Comedy Club for kids ages 9 to 15. **Prices:** $15. **Subway:** F, N, R, V, 1, 9 to 23rd St.

The Lion King New Amsterdam Theater 214 W. 42nd St. (between Seventh and Eighth Aves.) (212) 282-2900. Tickets are hard to come by, but it's worth the effort. When Julie Taymor's life-size animal puppets lumber down the aisles during the opening number, it's pure enchantment. This Tony Award-winning show is a smash with kids and sophisticated adults alike. **Prices:** $25–$100. **Subway:** A, C, E, N, Q, R, S, W, 1, 2, 3, 7, 9 to 42nd St.

TADA! Youth Ensemble 120 W. 28th St. (between Sixth and Seventh Aves.) (212) 627-1733. *www.tadatheater.com*. Tada! presents one-hour original shows performed by 6- to 17-year-old actors. The schedule runs throughout the year, and frequently includes weekday and Friday-night performances. Tickets sell out quickly. Tada! also offers classes and workshops for aspiring young thespians. **Prices:** $18 adults, $8 kids ages 15 and under. **Subway:** 1, 9, to 28th St.

13th Street Repertory Theater 50 W. 13th St. (between Fifth and Sixth Aves.) (212) 675-6677 *www.13thstreetrep.org*. Located in a Greenwich Village brownstone, this 72-seat theater offers weekend-afternoon children's shows, such as *Rumple Who?*. **Prices:** $7. **Subway:** L, N, Q, R, W, 4, 5, 6 to14th St.

Vital Children's Theatre 432 W. 42nd St. (212) 268-2040 *www.vitaltheatre.org*. This program of the Vital Theatre Company offers a five-show season of high-quality children's productions on weekend afternoons from October through April. **Prices:** $14. **Subway:** A, C, E to 42nd St.

Zoos & Wildlife Centers

Bronx Zoo Wildlife Conservation Park 2300 Southern Blvd. at Bronx Park South (718) 367-1010 *www.bronxzoo.com*. *(See section "The Bronx" in chapter* **Exploring New York** *for full details.)* Every kid loves to visit the zoo, and this one is New York's best. Parents of serious young zoologists might want to sign them up for a special educational outing, such as "Breakfast with the Butterflies" or "Summer Sundaes," which highlights ways in which animals beat the heat (and features a make-your-own-ice-cream sundae finale). The most popular offering is the "Family Overnight Safari," in which families camp out overnight in the zoo and meet nocturnal animals; offered three times a year, the program runs $125 per person.

Central Park Zoo Fifth Ave. and 64th St. (212) 861-6030 *www.wcs.org. (See section* "Central Park" *in chapter* **Exploring New York** *for full listing.)* The Tisch Children's Zoo allows kids to get up close and personal with a menagerie of gentle creatures. There's also a series of special children's educational programs.

New York Aquarium for Wildlife Conservation Surf Ave. and W. 8th St., Brooklyn (718) 265-FISH *www.wcs.org. (See* "Coney Island" *in section* "Brooklyn" *in chapter* **Exploring New York** *for full listing.)* Located on a strip of coastline between Coney Island and Brighton Beach, the aquarium is worth the long schlep from Manhattan. Kids will love the narrated feedings, the sea lion and dolphin performances in the Aquatheater and the hands-on Discovery Center. The aquarium offers educational programs, including four-day summer workshops ($140 and $165) that feature art activities, strolls on the beach and the chance to observe marine animals. There are also shorter $22 programs like "Breakfast with the Animals," in which youngsters help the staff prepare food and feed the aquarium's residents. Call (718) 265-3448 to register for special programs.

Prospect Park Zoo 450 Flatbush Ave., Brooklyn (718) 399-7339 *www.prospectparkzoo.com. (See* "Prospect Park" *in section* "Brooklyn" *in chapter* **Exploring New York** *for full listing.)* This petite zoo is extremely kid-friendly, featuring giant lily pads and kid-size goose eggs to play with, plus a "barnyard" with assorted touchable animals. There are educational programs throughout the year, including overnight stays and four-day summer workshops for kids.

Queens Zoo 111th St. (at 54th Ave.), Flushing, Queens (718) 271-1500 *www.queenszoo.org.* This 11-acre park is child-oriented and interactive. Kids will enjoy the aviary, the herd of bison, and a variety of domesticated animals in the petting zoo. **Admission:** $5 adults; $1.25 seniors; $1 children ages 3–12; children under 3 free. **Hours:** Mon.–Fri. 10 A.M.–5 P.M., Sat.–Sun. 10 A.M.–5:30 P.M. **Subway:** 7 to 111th St.

Staten Island Zoo 614 Broadway (at Glenwood Pl.), Staten Island (718) 442-3100 *www.statenislandzoo.org.* The small Staten Island Zoo holds its own with a menagerie of more than 400 animals on its eight acres. There's also an aquarium, a children's zoo where kids can feed the animals, a noteworthy display of reptiles, a tropical forest exhibit and a new simulation of the African savannah at twilight featuring baboons, leopards and antelope. **Admission:** $5 adults; $4 seniors; $3 children ages 3–11; children under 3 free. **Hours:** Daily 10 A.M.–4:45 P.M.

Outdoor Attractions and Activities for Children

(See also chapter **Sports & Recreation,** *and the section* **Prospect Park** *in chapter* **Exploring New York.***)*

Central Park *(See section* "Central Park" *in chapter* **Exploring New York** *for full listing. See chapter* **Sports & Recreation** *for details on renting bikes and in-line skates.)* Central Park's Children's District (mid-park, 64th–65th St.) offers a wealth of activities, from the Carousel and Wollman Skating Rink to the Heckscher Playground. A good place to start is **The Dairy** (mid-park at 64th St.)—originally a real dairy, now an information center with a variety of activities for children. It also offers an excellent map of the park.

Perhaps the most popular children's attraction in the park lies to the east, along Fifth Avenue: the **Children's Zoo,** part of the Central Park Wildlife Conservation Center, offers pint-sized displays and a petting zoo *(see listing earlier in this chapter)*.

Around 74th Street, also on the east side of the park, lies **Conservatory Water**, a popular pond where kids and adults can rent remote-controlled boats in the afternoon. Nearby are the well-known statues of Alice in Wonderland and Hans Christian Andersen. (Check out the free **storytelling sessions** here in summer; check the online schedule for times or call 212-348-4867.) Toward the center of the park, around 79th Street, is **Belvedere Castle**; kids will love this miniature storybook castle and the Nature Observatory inside. You can also see a show at the **Swedish Cottage Marionette Theater**, located just to the west of the Castle *(see* "Puppets" *earlier in this chapter, for details)*.

If you find yourself above the 97th Street Transverse, stop at the **North Meadow Recreation Center** (mid-park, around 98th St.) to borrow one of their "field kits" for kids, packed with toys and activities to try in the park. And if you're at the very top of the park, plan to spend some time around the body of water known as **Harlem Meer**. (The **Charles A. Dana Discovery Center** can set you up for catch-and-release fishing here.) From **Conservatory Garden**, with its charming Secret Garden statue, to **Lasker Rink and Pool**, families will easily find a fun way to while away the afternoon.

New York Botanical Garden 200th St. (at Southern Blvd.), the Bronx (718) 817-8705 *www.nybg.org*. *(See the section* "The Bronx" *in chapter* **Exploring New York** *for full listing.)* The Everett Children's Adventure Garden provides eight acres and hours of entertainment, including a three-foot-high hedge maze that will delight small children. The Garden offers numerous workshops and activities, including a summer storytelling series.

KID-FRIENDLY RESTAURANTS

Little Italy

Lombardi's 32 Spring St. (near Mott St.) (212) 941-7994. The chefs at historic Lombardi's love to show off their pizza oven. If it's not too busy, they shepherd children to the rear, explain how the oven works and even allow them to toss in a chunk of coal. **Subway:** 6 to Spring St.; N, R to Prince St.

TriBeCa

Bubby's 120 Hudson St. (at N. Moore St.) (212) 219-0666. Here's a homey, loft-like neighborhood spot, serving up terrific versions of the comfort foods kids love: burgers, ribs, macaroni-and-cheese. But the real stars of the show here are the fresh-baked pies (the chocolate–peanut butter version is a legend in its own time). **Subway:** 1, 9 to Franklin St.

Greenwich Village

Peanut Butter & Co. 240 Sullivan St. (between Bleecker and 3rd Sts.) (212) 677-3995. What kid wouldn't love a restaurant that serves 21 different varieties of peanut butter sandwiches? Traditionalists stick to the Fluffernutter on white bread, but the most popular offering is the Elvis (grilled peanut butter, banana, honey and bacon). Finish your meal with make-your-own s'mores for the ultimate sugar buzz. **Subway:** A, C, E, F, V to W. 4th St.; 1, 9 to Houston St.

Midtown West

Carmine's 200 W. 44th St. (between Broadway and Eighth Ave.) (212) 221-3800. The giant helpings of pasta served at this rollicking restaurant are meant to be enjoyed family-style. It's a great value, so bring the whole clan and dig in. **Subway:** A, C, E, N, R, Q, S, W, 1, 2, 3, 7, 9 to 42nd St.

John's Pizzeria 260 W. 44th St. (between Seventh and Eighth Aves.) (212) 391-7560. Housed in what used to be the Christian Alliance Gospel Tabernacle Church, this is New York's largest pizzeria and its most beautiful. Service is friendly; you're likely to get a table without waiting; and the pies are some of the city's best. **Subway:** A, C, E, N, R, Q, S, W, 1, 2, 3, 7, 9 to 42nd St.

Virgil's 152 W. 44th St. (between Broadway and Sixth Ave.) (212) 921-9494. How could parents not appreciate being offered towels instead of napkins? Big and boisterous, Virgil's serves up respectable reproductions of barbecue styles from North Carolina to Texas. **Subway:** B, D, F, N, R, Q, S, V, W, 1, 2, 3, 7, 9 to 42nd St.

Upper East Side

The Barking Dog NYC 1678 Third Avenue (at 94th St.) (212) 831-1800. The kids will be charmed by the canine theme and dog tchotchkes. The menu features familiar all-American favorites, breakfast fare, a few British staples like shepherd's pie, and bountiful desserts. Hugely popular for weekend brunch, and very dog-friendly, of course. **Subway:** 6 to 96th St. Another branch in Midtown East at 150 E. 34th St. (near Third Ave.); (212) 871-3500.

Serendipity 3 225 E. 60th St. (between Second and Third Aves.) (212) 838-3531. This whimsical soda fountain brings back fond memories for generations of city kids. You'll find sandwiches, hot dogs, and other diner fare on the menu, but the real point is dessert. Dig into old-fashioned favorites like lemon ice box pie, a drug-store sundae, or an outrageous banana split. Expect a long, long wait. **Subway:** N, R to Lexington Ave.; 4, 5, 6 to 59th St.

Upper West Side

EJ's Luncheonette 447 Amsterdam Ave. (at 82nd St.) (212) 873-3444. It's a retro diner, with great burgers, fries and shakes. A kids' menu offers pint-size servings, plus classics like peanut-butter-and-jelly sandwiches. **Subway:** 1, 9 to 79th St.

Gabriela's 315 Amsterdam Ave. (at 75th St.) (212) 875-8532. With a bright, colorful décor and a casual vibe, Gabriela's serves up some of Manhattan's best and most affordable Mexican fare. Mom and dad can sip margaritas while perusing the children's menu. **Subway:** 1, 2, 3, 9 to 72nd St.

Popover's 551 Amsterdam Ave. (between 86th and 87th Sts.) (212) 595-8555. The real point at this warm and welcoming café is the basket of warm, fluffy popovers delivered to each table. Slather them with downhome preserves or strawberry butter. Little ones are sure to be charmed by the dozens of resident teddy bears who nestle amid the country-cute décor. **Subway:** 1, 9 to 86th St.

Sambuca 20 W. 72nd St. (between Central Park West and Columbus Ave.) (212) 787-5656. For years, locals have come here for reasonably priced family-style Italian standards. Now moms and dads have the added incentive of a "PlayDine" program: After the little ones enjoy dinner from the kids menu, they can toddle off to a supervised play area, freeing their parents to linger over grown-up conversation and a glass of wine. See www.playdine.com or www.sambucanyc.com for details on this program, which entails an extra fee and is only available during certain hours. **Subway:** 1, 2, 3, 9 to 72nd St.

Popular Theme Restaurants for Families

Hard Rock Café 221 W. 57th St. (at Broadway) (212) 459-9320. Once you pry your kids out of the souvenir store next door, service is quick and friendly, and there's an affordable kids' menu. The walls are covered with memorabilia—rock stars' guitars, platinum platters, more guitars, photos, posters. **Subway:** N, R, Q, W to 57th St.

Jekyll & Hyde Club 1409 Sixth Ave. (at 57th St.) (212) 541-9505. Jekyll & Hyde features hair-raising hourly entertainment, animated skeletons, roving actors and a conversational sphinx. The best tables for catching the action are on the first two floors of this dark old four-story mansion. Waits can be long, but children are usually enchanted. **Subway:** N, R, Q, W to 57th St.

Mars 2112 1633 Broadway (at 51st St.) (212) 582-2112. Your visit here starts with a stomach-churning mock flight to Mars, where steaming lava pools greet your arrival. At the Mars Bar, you'll find everything from planetary news and weather reports, not to mention a large menu of "Marstinis" (which parents may need). Dig into the surprisingly decent menu items, such as Big Bang bruschetta and Ziggy Stardust spaghetti. Kids are entertained by a video arcade. **Subway:** N, R, W to 49th St.; 1, 9 to 50th St.

Nightlife

By now, most visitors (as well as the majority of residents) have grown tired of tall tales and song lyrics about "the city that never sleeps." Well, like most myths and clichés, the ones about New York at night are almost always based on truth. With the possible exception of New Orleans during Mardi Gras, New York reigns as—get ready for another cliché—the nightlife capital of the world.

All platitudes aside, bar closing time *is* 4 A.M. Dance clubs often stay open until well into the morning, but stop serving at the bar. Music venues may close after the last set or keep jumping with a DJ or jukebox until the last customer has gone home. Whichever nighttime activities are on the agenda, chances are you will be exhausted before your options are.

The distinctions among bars, lounges, clubs and music venues are blurry at best. Expect live music at bars and clubs, dancing at lounges and music venues, and DJs everywhere. Because so many establishments feature a variety of activities, it is always important to check listings. *The New York Times* (Friday edition and the *Times*' city guide on the Web), *Time Out New York*, *The Village Voice*, *New York* magazine, *The New Yorker* and *The New York Press* run weekly listings.

And, by the way, the rumors are true. Smoking has been banned in all but a few establishments. If you spot a huddle on the sidewalk surrounded by a cloud of smoke, it's a sure sign that you're approaching a bar.

BARS & LOUNGES BY NEIGHBORHOOD

Many tourists concentrate on dance clubs and other places with music (*discussed later in this section*) when planning their evenings in the city. But while New York's clubs are essential to the city's nightlife, it's often in the pubs and lounges, the neighborhood watering holes and swank hot spots, that New York after dark can really be appreciated. From the most elegant hotel bars to the deepest of dives, New York has something for everyone—often all on one block.

The difference between bars and lounges is subtle and usually lies in the attitude—and maybe a few couches. Lounges also often have DJs, but not the cabaret license required to host legal dancing. Throughout the Giuliani administration raids were frequently conducted, but these days the requisite signs reading, "No dancing by order of law," are often disregarded by patrons and displayed with a wink from the management.

The following listings cover only a small fraction of the more than 1,000 bars in Manhattan. A handful were chosen from each neighborhood for their historical significance, popularity or other points of interest. Also, remember that many restaurants and hotels have great bar scenes. If you can't find a bar to your liking listed here, check the **Restaurants** and **Hotels** sections. (*For Brooklyn bars see separate listings in chapter* **Exploring New York**.)

TriBeCa/SoHo

Anotheroom 249 West Broadway (between White and Beach Sts.)
(212) 226-1418. The owner of Anotheroom (who also owns **The Room** in
SoHo, 205 Thompson St; and **The Otheroom** in the West Village, 143 Perry
St.), has perfected a simple formula: Find a small pleasant space and serve only
beer and wine. It works. Anotheroom is a tiny, oblong room, decorated in the
kind of warm, minimal style that manages to be both cozy and classy at the
same time. **Subway:** 1, 9 to Franklin St.

Canal Room 285 W Broadway (between Canal and Lispenard Sts.) (212)
941-8100. Blacked out windows and a velvet rope can't hide the thumping bass
that makes this celebrity packed lounge hop. Inside the sleek minimalist décor
resembles an episode of MTV's Cribs with crisp white Barcelona chairs and
chocolate brown leather banquettes. Behind the leafy potted palms stars such as
Lil' Kim, Demi Moore and Ashton Kutcher can often be found grooving to the
DJ's latest mix of contagious hip hop and R&B. **Subway:** A, C, E to Canal St.

Ear Inn 326 Spring St. (between Greenwich and Washington Sts.)
(212) 226-9060. Built in the 1830's, this landmark Federal-style house once
stood on the river's edge and was a favorite spot for sailors. Although landfill
has pushed the shoreline a few blocks westward, the bar still sports remnants of
its nautical past. In this friendly neighborhood atmosphere, you're likely to find
men in pinstripe suits sharing the bar with tattooed bikers.
Subway: C, E to Spring St.; 1, 9 to Houston St.

El Teddy's 219 West Broadway (between Franklin and White Sts.)
(212) 941-7070. Finding decent Mexican in this city is harder than finding a
good apartment. It's no wonder, then, that El Teddy's is constantly packed to
the gills, combining a schmaltzy 1980's wonderland décor with solid cocktails
and dining. The bar attracts after-work Wall Streeters and neighborhood residents alike. In warmer months try for a seat outside. **Subway:** 1, 9 to Franklin St.

Fanelli 94 Prince St. (at Mercer St.) (212) 226-9412. Fanelli, an unfussy place
with tiled floors, tin ceilings and a lot of old New York atmosphere (it opened
in 1872), is nestled among SoHo's glitzier restaurants and stores. The bar draws
a mixed clientele and can be crowded on weekends, but during the week the
place caters to locals, and is always laid-back. Basic but tasty bar food is available. The bartenders are friendly, and the old-fashioned mugs are perfect for a
frosty beer. **Subway:** F, S, V to Broadway–Lafayette St.; N, R to Prince St.

Liquor Store 235 West Broadway (at White St.) (212) 226-7121. The laid-
back locals who frequent this small corner bar blend congenially with the more
upscale crowd that takes over on the weekend. Big windows and little attitude
tempt you to kick back and watch the goings-on across the street at the **Bubble
Lounge.** Summertime means a happy clutter of plastic chairs—many without
tables—are scattered outside, just waiting for you to plop down and have a cold
beer. Cash only. **Subway:** 1, 9 to Franklin St.

Nancy Whiskey's Pub 1 Lispenard St. (at Sixth Ave.) (212) 226-9943 This is one of the few remaining dives in TriBeCa — the sort of place where retired utility workers, down-on-their-luck drunks and a few adventurous locals gather to play shuffleboard and chow down on a bowl a chili. And if the guy slumped over the jukebox looks like he's been here since breakfast, he probably has: Nancy Whiskey Pub starts pouring at 8 A.M. **Subway:** A, C, E to Canal

Puffy's Tavern 81 Hudson St. (between Harrison and Jay Sts.) (212) 766-9159. On a sleepy TriBeCa corner, Puffy's offers a low-key, scene-free, classic neighborhood bar. And it may actually stay that way because it's the kind of exceptionally unexceptional place that most people won't go out of their way to get to. If they did, they'd find a beautiful, welcoming, old-fashioned place with dark wood and a darts alcove, frequented by locals, old-timers and folks from the nearby financial district. **Subway:** 1, 9 to Franklin St.

SoHo: 323 323 W. Broadway (between Grand and Canal) 212-334-2232 For those jet set partiers who missed their flight to Miami for the weekend luck-ily there's SoHo:323 a bi level lounge in a land marked loft building that pays heavy homage to that painfully chic stretch of sand known as South Beach. On the first floor there's palm frond murals and feng shui furniture placement. Upstairs makeshift cabanas sit atop a wooden deck. And if you're at a loss for words you can always discuss the South Beach Diet with the model-esque clien-tele. **Subway:** A, C, E to Canal St.

Sway Lounge 305 Spring St. (between Greenwich and Hudson Sts.) (212) 620-5220. The neon sign outside may read McGoverns Bar, but this is no Hibernian homestead. Sway has the look and feel of a gigantic VIP room. Hand-picked by an oh-so-hip gatekeeper, those lucky enough to be let into this Moroccan-style lounge drink expensive cocktails and move to the beat of a dif-ferent drum 'n' bass DJ. **Subway:** C, E to Spring St.

Walkers Restaurant 16 North Moore St. (at Varick St.) (212) 941-0142. Walkers' enormous mahogany bar, high tin ceilings and good, uncomplicated cuisine recall old New York—right down to the red-and-white-checked table-cloths. This is a down-to-earth holdout in a neighborhood where prices—and attitude—snake steadily heavenward. Cash only. **Subway:** 1, 9 to Franklin St.

Lower East Side/Chinatown/Little Italy

BLVD/Crash Mansion 199 Bowery,(between Spring and Delancey) (212) 982-7767. Twenty-something women in skimpy halter-tops and the throngs of men who hope to meet make up the crowd at this massive 18,000 square foot lounge, particularly on weekends. Be prepared to shell out serious cash for private VIP rooms or bottle service. Crash Mansion is the performance space downstairs that's as slick as an airbrushed Maxim magazine cover-girl. **Subway:** F, V to Second Ave.

The Delancey 168 Delancey Street (between Clinton and Suffolk Sts.
(212) 254-9920. At the base of the Williamsburg Bridge, this 6,000-square-
foot, three-level club caters to the ranks of offbeat artists and musicians who in
advertising speak would be known as tastemakers. There's $4 Budweisers and a
sprawling tropical roof deck, sort of an alternative Garden of Eden with potted
palms, a koi fish pond, a frozen margarita machine and a view of the honking
traffic inching past. On the main floor, which has two lounges, DJ's spin from
record collections eclectic enough to appease the snobbiest of music snobs, and
in the basement, popular local bands, including the Hong Kong and the Twenty
Twos, perform. **Subway:** J, M, Z to Essex St.; F to Delancey St.

Happy Ending 302 Broome St. (between Forsyth and Eldridge Sts.)
(212) 334-9676. From the people who opened the trendy bar **Double Happi-
ness** (173 Mott St.) comes Happy Ending. The coy name alone is enough to
entice a visit to this spot in a former Chinese massage parlor. There is a bar area
with wood paneled walls, concrete floors and high-backed, red velvet banquettes, surrounded by tables that look as if they've been dunked in red glitter.
Another funky feature is the ceiling that emulates a sunset, changing colors
over the course of several hours. Expect a crowd of uptown patrons mixed in
with some locals. **Subway:** F, V to Second Ave.

Loreley 7 Rivington St. (between Bowery and Chrystie) 212-253-7077.
The melting pot result of mixing hipster Lower East Side and a German "biergarten," Loreley is a kitsch temple of unpretentious fun. Local musicians in
ironic t-shirts and German expats nibble on the mostly organic ethnic offerings
such as reasonably priced bratwurst and wiener schnitzel. Outback there's a garden with long wooden tables and benches that are perfect for enjoying a tall,
cloudy weissbier on a warm summer night. **Subway:** F, V to Delancey St.

Mare Chiaro 176 1/2 Mulberry St. (between Broome and Grand Sts.)
(212) 226-9345. At first glance, Mare Chiaro seems like the ultimate in Little
Italy authenticity: old Italian men, a jukebox that's about 85 percent Sinatra
and photos of the owner alongside Ol' Blue Eyes himself. Look more closely and
you'll notice that the crowd is largely hipsters and slumming Ivy Leaguers. It's
this crazy mix that makes Mare Chiaro such a good time. Cash only.
Subway: N, R to Prince St.; 6 to Spring St.

Max Fish 178 Ludlow St. (between Houston and Stanton Sts.)
(212) 529-3959. One of the first venues to attract bar-goers to the burgeoning
Lower East Side scene, Max Fish still draws its fair share of hipsters. Brightly lit
and without downtown attitude, Max Fish is both hip and casual at the same
time. Never lacking in interesting artwork, this spot also offers plenty of other
attractions, including pinball, video games, a pool table and cheap beer. Cash
only. **Subway:** F, V to Second Ave.

Club Mission 217 Bowery (between Prince and Rivington Sts.) 212 473 3113.
Although it's tucked amongst the homeless shelters on the Bowery, this con-

verted rescue mission is pure hip-hop "bling." On popular nights SUV's and Hummers with tinted windows clog the street outside. Inside the two level club, with decor meant to evoke a modern industrial saloon, celebrities such as P. Diddy and Wesley Snipes can be found in the VIP room perched on the faux cowhide ottomans. **Subway:** 6 to Spring St.; J, M, Z, to Bowery.

Pioneer 218 Bowery (between Prince and Spring Sts.) (212) 334-0484. Stretching the length of the ground floor of the old Prince Hotel, this Irish-run bar is a nice addition to the beautified Bowery. The large space manages to blend the spirit of the Bowery of old with the new; it is neither too chic nor too shabby. It can also accommodate large groups —you can easily seat 20 if you arrive early. A back room offers more of the traditional lounge. The music is well chosen and strictly hip, and the staff are friendly and fun. **Subway:** 6 to Spring St.; J, M, Z to Bowery.

6'S and 8'S 205 Chrystie St. (between Stanton and Rivington Sts.) No phone. A downtown take on Las Vegas this glam but divey lounge is great for eye candy. (A good thing considering the DJ spins rock n roll so loud that's it's almost to hear anything else.) Local musicians and fashion stylists sport tomorrow's asymmetrical hairstyles and deconstructed clothes while playing on the slot machines and checking their smudged makeup against the high gloss surfaces. **Subway:** F, V to Second Ave.

Welcome to the Johnsons 123 Rivington St. (between Norfolk and Essex Sts.) (212) 420-9911. Welcome to the Johnsons is a nostalgic visit to some cool kid's 70's-style basement. The orange-and-brown furniture is covered in plastic and the place is snazzed-up with macramé curtains, trophies and houseplants. The pool table, table-top video game and dirt-cheap cans of Pabst are icing. Cash only. **Subway:** F, V to Delancey St.; J, M, Z to Essex St.

East Village
(See also "The East Village's Deepest Dives" later in this section.)

Beauty Bar 231 E. 14th St. (between Second and Third Aves.) (212) 539-1389. A beauty salon for decades, it's now a bar. You can sit beneath antique hair dryers and swill Rolling Rocks, or go whole hog and get your nails done at the bar. Is it mere coincidence that many of Beauty Bar's female clientele resemble 50's pinup icon Bettie Page? **Subway:** N, Q, R, W, 4, 5, 6 to 14th St.; L to Third Ave.

The Hole 29 Second Avenue (between 2nd and 3rd Sts.) 212 473 9406. The mother of all dives with beer and plastic cups stuck to the floor, this bar attracts a who's who of waifish young models and up-and-coming fashion designers. The main attraction seems to be that the grimy anti-décor and ambiance are so foreboding that gossip columnists and outsiders don't dare set foot inside. Just be careful to check for chewing gum or vomit before you sit down in a dark corner on one of the ratty old couches. **Subway:** F, V to Second Ave.

The East Village's Deepest Dives

Neighborhood bars and local holes-in-the-wall are some of the best places to see the real New York. This is particularly true in the East Village, where dives are equivalent to town hall. Hipsters, artists and colorful residents retreat to shoot pool, chat over cheap drinks or melt into a bar stool. If you find a surly bartender and the smell of stale beer appealing, an East Village dive crawl is highly recommended.

Ace Bar 531 E. 5th St. (between Aves. A and B) (212) 979-8476. Ace is perfect for people with limited attention spans—pool, darts, pinball and video games are all provided for your enjoyment, as well as a virtual museum of over 100 children's lunch boxes.

Blue and Gold Tavern 79 E. 7th St. (between First and Second Aves.) (212) 473-8918. This is a no-nonsense beer and whisky kind of a place. On weekends the pool table can see some heated action. Also check out **Bar 81** next door. They're nearly twins.

Cherry Tavern 441 E. 6th St. (between First Ave. and Ave. A) (212) 777-1448. One of the hipper of the East Village dives, Cherry Tavern has seen a model or two in the crowd. Though there's a pool table and a good jukebox, the drink special—a shot of tequila and a can of Tecate beer for $4—may be Cherry's biggest attraction.

Holiday Cocktail Lounge 75 St. Marks Pl. (between First and Second Aves.) (212) 777-9637. This classic East Village hangout is famous for its never-changing aesthetic; quilted faux-leather booths, a jukebox and video games are worn and sprinkled with a palpable seediness. Be prepared for the bar to close at the bartender's whim.

International Bar 120 First Ave. (between 7th St. and St. Marks Pl.) (212) 777-9244. Much like **Johnny's S&P** (90 Greenwich Ave.) in the West Village, International is very local, very casual and very cheap. This tiny bar can get crowded on the weekends, but it remains unaffected.

Joe's 520 E. 6th St. (between Aves. A and B) (212) 473-9093. The jury's still out on whether this hole-in-the-wall is a dive or a honky-tonk. On the dive side it's unpretentious and homey, and on the honky-tonk side, it's known for its mostly country jukebox. It attracts a neighborhood mix of old-timers and young locals.

Marz Bar 25 E. 1st St. (at Second Ave.). This punk-art bar has been around for well over a decade, and continues to revel in its downhill slide. We're talking hardcore—yet harmless. This unpretentious little dive is a breath of fresh air for those who don't associate spending money with being cool.

Vazac's 108 Avenue B (at E. 7th St.) (212) 473-8840. Alphabet City's population of musicians, writers and actors congregates at Vazac's (a.k.a. 7B or the Horseshoe bar) to enjoy the red light–tinged, grunge-punk ambience and the loud, high-energy music.

Joey's 186 Avenue B (between 11th and 12th Sts.) (212) 353-9090. What can you say about a bar that offers not one but two Connect Four board games? A night at Joey's could be mistaken for a bustling party at home—with a hundred friends. Joey's is small and can be jam-packed, but manages a homey feel with a selection of 69 DVDs and 25 video games to play on a TV at the bar. There is also a huge deck in the backyard, enclosed in tent canvas and strewn like a yard sale with tacky coffee tables, couches and chairs. **Subway:** L to First Ave.

Lit 93 Second Ave.(between 5th and 6th Sts.) 212-777-7987. This bar/ art gallery has no sign and a grungy black façade. But inside, after midnight, there's a thriving underground art scene with celebrities such as Chloe Sevigny sporting her latest vintage getup. Here minimal does not mean slick, it simply means raw. And the only neck ties one is likely to see is not that of a banker letting lose after work but a skinny black one worn over a soiled white T-shirt. To this under 30 set, the concept of VIP rooms and expensive bottles of champagne is terribly passé. **Subway:** F, V to Second Ave.

McSorley's Old Ale House 15 E. 7th St. (between Second and Third Aves.) (212) 473-9148. Anybody who has ever read a book by Joseph Mitchell owes himself a visit to this historic bar, though it's not as old as it pretends. Have a beer and forget the food. Cash only. **Subway:** 6 to Astor Pl.; F, V to Second Ave.

Niagara 112 Avenue A (between 7th and 6th Sts.) 212-420-9517. The bartenders sporting pompadour hairdos are the star attraction on the unassuming main floor. But downstairs in the Lei Lounge it's a Gilligan's Island fantasy culled from a yard sale. Here young actresses and alternative rock stars sip tropical flavored daiquiris amongst tattered bamboo and palm fronds while go-go girls in skimpy grass skirts hula dance. **Subway:** F, V to Second Ave.

Opaline 85 Ave. A (between 5th and 6th Sts.) (212) 475-5050. Opaline is a poetic synonym for absinthe, a now-illegal liquor popular among 19th-century bohemians. The paintings inside, make you feel as though you're under the influence of that mystical, dream-inducing liquid. The bistro has an extensive wine list and an uptown menu of French cuisine, but at more down-to-earth prices. Opaline is a great place to gratify the senses of sight, sound, smell and taste. Look for live Jazz Sundays. **Subway:** F, V to Second Ave.; L to First Ave.

Otto's Shrunken Head Tiki Bar and Lounge 538 E. 14th St. (between Aves. A and B) (212) 228-2240. Sitting beneath the blowfish lamps at Otto's Shrunken Head, knees bumping split bamboo, you should probably order a Singapore sling. The parasol and grass-skirt sipping straw are a nice touch. The small room is friendly with a jukebox, not a television set, and decorated as if it were in the middle of the ocean. Otto's also doubles as a music venue hosting a variety of bands and events. **Subway:** L to First Ave.

288 Bar (a.k.a. Tom and Jerry's) 288 Elizabeth St. (at Houston St.) (212) 260-5045. This friendly neighborhood bar offers a relaxed atmosphere and more space than can normally be found in an East Village venue. There are several large tables that allow groups to sit together, and a cavernous area

in the back of the bar where you can actually talk to a group of people without feeling like you're blocking traffic. Cash only. **Subway:** F, S, V to Broadway–Lafayette St.; 6 to Bleecker St.

Von 3 Bleecker St. (between Elizabeth St. and Bowery) (212) 473-3039. Von is a compromise between old (Bowery grunge) and new (SoHo chic). A yuppyish crowd saunters in after work before giving way to a neighborhood clientele later on. With a scuffed wooden bar and tattered leather couches, Von has the air of an upper-class saloon. Its lack of pretension will make you want to stay for a while. The wine-and-beer-only drink menu is limited but well chosen. **Subway:** F, S, V to Broadway–Lafayette St.; 6 to Bleecker St.

Greenwich Village/West Village

Chumley's 86 Bedford St. (between Bleecker St. and Seventh Ave. South) (212) 675-4449. The story of Chumley's heyday as a speakeasy is as worn as its old wood tables, but it seems to keep people coming to the place in droves. The pub's three rooms are rustic, with a fireplace, sawdust on the floors and walls hung with book jackets by famous authors who used to be regulars. F. Scott Fitzgerald allegedly wrote part of *The Great Gatsby* in a corner booth. All lore aside though, today Chumley's tends to resemble an upscale frat house for young professionals swilling pints of the impressively varied beers on tap. Cash only. **Subway:** 1, 9 to Christopher St.

Hue 91 Charles St (between Hudson and Bleecker Streets) (212) 691-4170. The real action here is hidden behind the trendy nouvel Vietnamese restaurant. In a subterranean chamber, heavily guarded by bouncers and a velvet rope, models and wannabe's sprawl on daybeds and oversized cushions. The attitude is absurdly pretentious but the exotic cocktails-Dragon's Kiss (lemons, honey, plum sake and green tea) and Red River (white rum, fresh mint and raspberries)-are sure to break the ice. **Subway:** 1, 9 to Christopher St.

Luke and Leroy 21 7th Ave South (between Luke and Leroy Sts) (212) 634-0004. The modern airy décor gives this two level club and air of a suburban restaurant. But what makes it special is the progressive booking of some of the best DJ's spinning the latest hybrids and parties hosted by trendsetting junior fashionistas. For smokers there's a roped in sidewalk annex complete with an electric fireplace and a bowl of marshmallows on the mantle. **Subway:** 1, 9 to Houston St.

Play 49 Grove St (Between Bleecker St. and Seventh Ave.) (212) 243-8885. Play is meant to feel like a friend's living room, albeit a friend whose friends are famous. First you must convince the bouncers that you are fabulous enough to get into the small basement space padded with cashmere and woolen fabrics where rock bands such as Limp Bizkit and Korn have been known to hang out.

Sing, Sing a Song: Karaoke in New York

Karaoke, once considered corny by the uninitiated, has had something of a surge in popularity of late. And for good reason. There's nothing quite like belting out your favorite tune in front of a crowd, cheering you on as if you were a superstar—no matter how offensive the performance.

New York has a few karaoke options. There are karaoke lounges (often run by Japanese, Chinese or Korean Americans, but usually welcoming to all) that have karaoke every night. There are also places that rent out private rooms by the hour—a blast with a group. And then there are regular bars that have weekly or monthly karaoke nights. For more venues, check *www.murphguide.com/karaoke.htm*. If you've never done karaoke, it's about time you tried. If you have, you're probably already convinced.

Arlene Grocery 95 Stanton St. (between Ludlow and Orchard Sts.) (212) 358-1633. Come for Punk Rock/Heavy Metal Karaoke Monday nights, 10 P.M. With a live band and an enthusiastic crowd, you'll feel like a rock star, or—if you'd rather just watch—a groupie. One Monday a month it's Corporate Rock (Journey, Foreigner and the like).

Asia Roma 40 Mulberry St. (between Worth and Bayard Sts.) (212) 385-1133. This basement karaoke lounge is good for intimate groups.

Japas 55 253 W. 55th St. (between Broadway and Eighth Ave.) (212) 765-1210. At this long, skinny bar with an after-work crowd of both dilettantes and hardcore crooners, the bartenders bring you a mike where you're seated for $1 per song. Private rooms are available.

Toto Music Studio 38 W. 32nd St. (between Fifth and Sixth Aves.) (212) 594-6644. Private rooms only. A good spot for groups, the bigger rooms can literally hold dozens. Bring your own alcohol.

Village Karaoke 27 Cooper Sq. (212) 254-0066. Private rooms, a good song list and a bring-your-own-alcohol policy make this a great place to get rowdy.

Winnie's 104 Bayard St. (bet. Mulberry and Baxter Sts.) (212) 732-2384. A regular cast of folks from Chinatown shares the space with Lower East Side hipsters, rowdily handing off the microphone for both classics and Chinese pop tunes (most nights, a bartender will step out to belt a tune herself).

Then you are free to play PlayStation2, get food delivered from McDonald's or Domino's, and nurture your inner child. **Subway:** 1, 9 to Christopher St.

The Spotted Pig 314 W11th St. (between Greenwich and Washington Sts) (212) 620-0393. Modeled after British "gastropubs," (good food and good beer to compliment it) The Pig has a well curated selection of wines and brews on tap. Co-owned by chef Mario Batali (U2's Bono is rumored to be an investor) the neighborhood pub housed in the tiny ground floor of a townhouse draws rock stars and celebrities who can often be found smoking cigarettes on the bench outside amongst bushels of rosemary and sage. 1, 9 to Christopher St.

White Horse Tavern 567 Hudson St. (at 11th St.) (212) 989-3956. Located in one of the few remaining wood-framed buildings in Manhattan, the White Horse opened in 1880. It was a speakeasy during Prohibition, and legend has it that, in 1953, poet Dylan Thomas drank 18 shots of whisky, stepped outside onto the sidewalk and dropped dead. (The truth is it was about seven whiskeys, and what really killed him was a misdiagnosis of his diabetes.) Though once considered a "writer's bar," the three darkly paneled sections are now populated with more former frat boys than literary types. Cash only.
Subway: A, C, E, 1, 2, 3, 9 to 14th St.; L to Eighth Ave.

Flatiron/Union Square

40/40 6 West 25th Street; (212) 989-0040. It's not every day that a fan can rub shoulders with a multiplatinum-selling rap star, but at 40/40, Jay-Z's upscale sports lounge, the odds are better than most. The two-level $4 million interior, has 27 big-screen TV's, a Cohiba-sponsored cigar room, and two $1,500-a-night V.I.P. rooms. Here Jay-Z's rap star friends and athletes including Alex Rodriguez of the Texas Rangers and Tiki Barber of the New York Giants often hang out after local games. **Subway:** N, R, W, 6 to 23rd St.

Old Town Bar and Restaurant 45 E. 18th St. (between Broadway and Park Ave. South) (212) 529-6732. There are no gas-lit lamps or horse-drawn carriages on the streets outside this tavern. But inside, you feel as though you have entered a bygone era from New York's history. Built in 1892, Old Town is one of the city's oldest taverns. From the 14-foot pressed-tin ceiling to the mahogany bar and huge beveled mirrors, it's filled with details from another time. Even the booths tell a story: They were specially built during Prohibition with a hidden compartment for stowing liquor. **Subway:** L, N, Q, R, W, 4, 5, 6 to 14th St.

Pete's Tavern 129 E. 18th St. (at Irving Pl.) (212) 473-7676. "Oldest Original Bar in New York City Opened 1864," reads the sign behind the worn, ornate bar—a claim that's debatable. With its cracked tile floor, tin ceilings and hanging brass lamps, it has certainly retained that old New York flavor. O. Henry reportedly wrote "The Gift of the Magi" at one of the tavern's dark wooden booths. A casual crowd and friendly bartenders make this a nice place for a drink and snack. In warmer weather, the sidewalk tables are particularly pleasant. **Subway:** L, N, Q, R, W, 4, 5, 6 to 14th St.

17 37 W 17th St. (between Fifth and Sixth Aves) (212) 924-8676. At this jewel-box-sized exclusive club co-owned by soap opera star John Enos, expect to see bottle blond and blow dried personalities such as Victoria Gotti. Downstairs is an upscale rock club with bottle service and Japanese snacks; upstairs is the VIP playroom with a pool table, large screen TV's and other Soprano's style accoutrement. **Subway:** F, V to 14th St.; N, R, W, 4, 5, 6, L to 14th St.–Union Sq.

Meatpacking District/Chelsea

(For more Chelsea venues, see "Gay & Lesbian" *and* "Dance Clubs.")

Apt. 419 W 13th St. (near Tenth Ave.) (212) 414-4245. This clandestine
watering hole is worth finding. Pass through the anonymous door and discover
the apex of lounges: a sleek, modern living room in shades of electric orange
and chocolate brown. The tone is relaxed, the staff personable and the music at
a decent volume. The crowd is diverse but upscale. **Subway:** A, C, E to 14th
St.; L to Eighth Ave.

Bungalow 8 515 W. 27th St (between Tenth and Eleventh Aves.) 212-629-
3333. This ultra exclusive lounge is as hard to get into as Fort Knox. A late
night favorite amongst celebrities and the jet set it's modeled after a Hollywood
hideaway. Walls are covered with photographic murals of the Beverly Hills
Hotel's pool and manicured gardens. There are mini bars and cordless phones
beside the banquettes. And just in case you get an after-hours invitation to the
Hamptons, an in-house boutique sells bikinis and monogrammed bathrobes.
Subway: C, E to 23rd St.

Hiro 369 West 16th Street (between Eighth and Ninth Aves.)
(212) 242-4300. This vast Japanese-themed lounge at the Maritime Hotel
attracts an eclectic but fabulous crowd of art dealers, scruffy rock stars and tipsy
model. (Kirsten Dunst, Maggie Gyllenhaal, and Kate Moss attended the opening.) There's a sunken ballroom with undulating wooden ceilings were live
performances are held. Up the stairs is a dimly lit room with Japanese lanterns
and rope curtains that feels like a secret catacomb of the Asian underworld.
Subway: A, C, E to 14th St.; L to Eighth Ave.

Hogs 'n' Heifers 859 Washington St. (at 13th St.) (212) 929-0655.
Tucked away in the meatpacking district, Hogs 'n' Heifers offers a taste of Hazard County for anyone with a hankering for Budweiser and debauchery. Here
brawny bikers and yuppies ogle female bartenders dancing on the bar. If nothing
else, this place is a testament to the effectiveness of hard liquor and peer pressure in convincing women to abandon their inhibitions as well as their bras.
Cash only. **Subway:** A, C, E, 1, 2, 3, 9 to 14th St.; L to Eighth Ave.

Level V 675 Hudson Street; (between 13th and 14th Sts) (212) 699-2400.
The basement lounge of the restaurant Vento, Level V's historical architecture
is in contrast with the trendy clientele. Built as a Civil War hospital it was later
used as a stable. Now when you wander around the dark, cavernous space, it
feels like the insides of a catacomb. A tunnel of eroding stone leads past old
stalls with vaulted brick entryways that have been recast as V.I.P. nooks and red
back-painted Venetian plaster where the barn doors once were. The crowd, on
the other hand, comes blow dried hair and in the latest distressed designer
jeans. **Subway:** A, C, E to 14th St.; L to Eighth Ave.

Lot 61 550 W. 21st St. (between Tenth and Eleventh Aves.) (212) 243-6555. Housed in a vast, converted warehouse, Lot 61 is cleverly divided by sliding panels and bursting with furniture straight out of Elle Décor (don't miss the rubber sofas salvaged from insane asylums). The walls are adorned by all the right painters' works (Hirst, Landers and Salle, to name a few). And if that weren't enough eye candy, there's the drop-dead-gorgeous staff. **Subway:** C, E to 23rd St.

Lotus 409 W. 14th St. (between Ninth and Tenth Aves.) (212) 243-4420. With the no-dancing lounge scene feeling more and more tired, nightlife entrepreneurs are diversifying, creating ambitious hybrids. Lotus is a fine example, fusing a restaurant, lounge and nightclub into a single, three-level space—divided, of course, by a velvet rope or three. **Subway:** A, C, E to 14th St.; L to Eighth Ave.

Open 559 W. 22nd St. (at Eleventh Ave.) (212) 243-1851. Open was inspired by the parties that go on in converted Brooklyn warehouses colonized by artists. It has a sleek retro look. The floor is poured concrete, the bar is blond wood, and the "living room" has metal cocktail tables on which Bjork, a neighbor, has been known to tap out tunes. Drink prices are low for Manhattan, and the tunes are ambient lounge. **Subway:** C, E to 23rd St.

Passerby 436 W. 15th St. (between Ninth and Tenth Aves.) (212) 206-6847. British gallery owner Gavin Brown has converted the space next to his gallery into a bar. No sign marks the space as a bar, and tinted windows obscure any activity. Though not exactly diverse, anyone wishing to rub elbows with working artists could hardly ask for a better crowd. **Subway:** A, C, E to 14th St.

PM 50 Gansevoort Street (between Ninth Ave. and Washington St.) (212) 255-6676. A trendy, celebrity-packed nightclub that isn't tacky, PM is modeled after 1940's-era gentlemen's clubs in Haiti (but much, much harder to get into!) The converted warehouse feels tropical and raw, tricked out for a New York City runway. Two large photographic murals hang on the distressed brick walls, and lush palm trees and Caribbean-style concrete blocks line the room. Stars such as Venus Williams and Naomi Campbell can be seen cramming into the plush leather booths—designed so guests can slide out easily for maximum table-hopping. **Subway:** A, C, E to 14th St.; L to 14th St.–Union Sq.

Midtown/Murray Hill

(See also "A Grand Oasis: New York's Hotel Bars" in this chapter.)

Bliss 256 E. 49th St. (at Second Ave.) (212) 644-8750. You can't miss Bliss—just look for the garish, blue-lit sign, just the first of several features that make this two-story bar a distinctive alternative to nearby bars. The first floor features a clean, sleek, metallic bar. Wade through the thick traffic to find a stairway to the candle-lit second floor, which has a separate lounge in the back and large windows overlooking Second Avenue. **Subway:** 4, 5, 6, 7 to 42nd St.

Campbell Apartment Grand Central Terminal, 15 Vanderbilt Ave. (at 42nd St.) (212) 953-0409. Between cocktails at the Campbell Apartment, patrons crane their necks to take in the 30-foot wood-beam ceilings. They admire the deep blue Moroccan-inspired rug, the overstuffed couches set against stone walls and the huge steel safe installed by John Campbell, the original inhabitant of the space. Tucked away in Grand Central, it's sure to become a classic. **Subway: 4, 5, 6, 7 to 42nd St.**

Jimmy's Corner 140 W. 44th St. (between Sixth Ave. and Broadway) (212) 944-7819. Tucked away among big Midtown hotels is this New York gem. Covering almost every inch of wall space are posters, photos and clippings about boxing. The space at front is so small that you can barely squeeze past the regulars holding court at the bar. Everyone is friendly and the crowd is happily diverse: There are scruffy slacker types and people in suits, construction workers and, of course, boxing enthusiasts, all glad to have found this slice of authenticity in touristy Midtown. **Subway: B, D, F, N, Q, R, V, W, 1, 2, 3, 7, 9 to 42nd St.**

Landmark Tavern 626 Eleventh Ave. (at 46th St.) (212) 757-8595. When it first opened in 1868, the view from the Landmark's three-story brick building was of bustling piers and a neighborhood full of longshoremen. Since then, the river's edge has moved westward, pushed back by landfill and 12th Avenue, and the docks have gone quiet. But unlike the streets around it, the Landmark Tavern has hardly changed. Not that it still serves nickel beers, but the enormous bar—turned from a single mahogany tree—and the potbellied stove in the rear dining room remain. **Subway: A, C, E to 42nd St.**

P.J. Carney's 906 Seventh Ave. (between 57th and 58th Sts.) (212) 664-0056. A few steps from Carnegie Hall in the heart of the 57th Street tourist mecca, P.J. Carney's is an old standby for locals. The crowd fills up on shepherd's pie and 20-ounce pints of Guinness and hard cider at the bar's handful of tightly packed tables, while a grinning bartender dressed in overalls, who knows every other customer by name, glides back and forth behind a wee horseshoe-shaped bar. **Subway: N, R, Q, W to 57th St.; B, D, E to Seventh Ave.**

Rink Bar 20 W. 50th St. (between Fifth and Sixth Aves.) (212) 332-7620. Come spring, a cluster of beige and orange umbrellas sprout up like mushrooms over Rockefeller Center's legendary skating rink. The Rink Bar has a summer happy-hour scene that rivals places like Central Park's **Boathouse** and Union Square's **Luna Park**. Competitively priced nightly drink specials, like $2 Rolling Rocks on Mondays and $5 margaritas to close out the work week, offset the annoyance of often crowded quarters. **Subway: B, D, F, S, V to 47–50th St.—Rockefeller Center.**

Siberia 356 W. 40th St. (between Eighth and Ninth Aves.) (212) 333-4141. Gritty and down-to-earth, Siberia is a bar-lover's bar: no pretenses, no trendsetters—just cheap drinks and good music. A group of second-hand couches are clustered together on the large, high-ceilinged first floor surrounded by an old Pacman console and a pinball machine. Be sure to venture down the narrow stairs to the basement where bands play. **Subway: A, C, E to 42nd St.**

Upper East Side

Auction House 300 E. 89th St. (between First and Second Aves.)
(212) 427-4458. The main room in this opulent bar has a decorative fireplace,
cut-glass chandeliers, couches, Oriental rugs and window seats on either side of
the front door. Gilt-framed mirrors and a few oil paintings hang on the exposed
brick walls. The Auction House's patrons are drawn from the neighborhood, but
they tend to be older and better dressed (no baseball hats or sneakers are permitted) than at other bars in the area. **Subway:** 4, 5, 6 to 86th St.

Dorrian's Red Hand Restaurant 1616 Second Ave. (at 84th St.)
(212) 772-6660. This bar may never live down its association with Robert
Chambers, who met Jennifer Levin here in 1986 and murdered her that night
in Central Park. Despite the bad publicity, Dorrian's has recovered from the
heady days of the 80's and remains a respectable neighborhood place with an
eclectic menu and window seating at red-checkered tables. Ask the bartender
about the gory legend of the "red hand." **Subway:** 4, 5, 6 to 86th St.

Elaine's 1703 Second Ave. (between 88th and 89th Sts.) (212) 534-8103.
A meeting place for the older guard of New York's celebrity elite (think Joan
Collins and Ivana Trump). A collage of literati memorabilia covers the walls,
and *Entertainment Weekly* has been throwing its Oscar party here for years. In
addition to the famous frequenters, watch for Elaine herself, who opened these
doors almost 40 years ago and routinely table-hops to schmooze with her guests.
But you won't get the royal treatment if they don't know you.
Subway: 4, 5, 6 to 86th St.

Fitzpatrick's 1641 Second Ave. (at 85th St.) (212) 988-7141. This old Irish
pub has a friendly neighborhood feel, absent in many bars nowadays. From
10:30 A.M. until early evening, the older gents sitting at the mahogany bar
make up a family of sorts. In the evening, and especially on weekends, Fitzpatrick's comes alive, even turning people away. **Subway:** 4, 5, 6 to 86th St.

Subway Inn 143 E. 60th St. (at Lexington Ave.) (212) 223-8929. With a
worn bar, cracked red-and-white tile floor and a row of dingy, high-backed
booths, the surprise in this seediest of seedy bars is a strong showing of stylishly
outfitted young people found mixing with workers from the nearby hotels and
stores. Yet it's still a place where they serve dollar draft beers during the day.
Cash only. **Subway:** N, R to Lexington Ave; 4, 5, 6 to 59th St.

Upper West Side

If none of the following establishments appeal to you, take a walk down **Amsterdam Avenue** north of 72nd Street. There are literally dozens of bars and
restaurants to choose from.

All State Cafe 250 W. 72nd St. (between Broadway and West End Ave.)
(212) 874-1883. Inside this narrow, cozy, basement-level pub, there's a small bar

up front, with a fabulous selection of tunes on the jukebox and a fire crackling in the hearth in winter. In the back, you'll find simple wooden tables where you can pull up a chair and enjoy the neighborhood's best burger. Cash only. **Subway:** 1, 2, 3, 9 to 72nd St.

Dive 75 101 W. 75th St. (at Columbus Ave.) (212) 362-7518. Tucked away on a side street, Dive 75 merges the friendliness of a neighborhood bar with the atmosphere of a living room. A large blue aquarium separates the bar area from a small collection of tables; wooden bookshelves house a selection of board games. It's a nice alternative to the West Side's concentration of raucous frat bars. **Subway:** 1, 2, 3, 9 to 72nd St.

79th Street Boat Basin Cafe In Riverside Park at the Hudson River (212) 496-5542. The food and drinks are merely passable, but that's beside the point. When it's a breezy summer evening and there's a colorful sunset behind the houseboats bobbing in the river, there's no finer place on the West Side to down a beer. Bring the kids or even Fido—everyone's welcome. **Subway:** 1, 9 to 79th St.

West Side Brewing Company 340 Amsterdam Ave. (at 76th St.) (212) 721-2161. A nice selection of beers, surprisingly good food (make sure to order sweet-potato fries along with your sandwich), and an array of TVs tuned to the big game—what more do you need for a relaxing jeans-and-sneakers night out? **Subway:** 1, 9 to 79th St.

GAY & LESBIAN

The following listings are a selection of bars that cater to the gay and lesbian communities of New York. Also, many of the city's premier dance and cabaret venues are predominately gay or gay-friendly; several have gay or lesbian parties at least one night per week. *(See* "Dance Clubs" *and* "Cabarets and Supper Clubs" *later in this chapter.)* Check *Homo Xtra (HX)*, *Next magazine*, *HX for Her*, or *Time Out New York* for weekly events at a variety of bars, lounges and clubs.

Men

Barracuda CHELSEA 275 W. 22nd St. (between Seventh and Eighth Aves.) (212) 645-8613. This popular gay bar is often described as an oasis of East Village-style nightlife in the heart of tan-and-taut Chelsea. Barracuda's décor is decidedly low-key, producing an Alphabet City aesthetic of kitschy squalor. But don't be fooled. Despite the assumed atmosphere, aging disco-bunny muscle-queens in tank tops and skin-tight Diesel gear still abound. Cash only. **Subway:** C, E, 1, 9 to 23rd St.

Cleo's Ninth Ave. Saloon MIDTOWN WEST 656 Ninth Ave. (between 45th and 46th Sts.) (212) 307-1503. About the only dead giveaway to the gay and lesbian nature of this friendly, laid-back bar is the large rainbow flag that hangs on the back wall. Otherwise, distinguishing Cleo's from any other local dive would take a discerning eye. The beer is cheap (Budweiser is served in a can), the

Go East, Young Man

The West Village and Chelsea have always reigned as the major centers of gay nightlife in Manhattan. While these neighborhoods still boast some of the most well-known and popular spots, the East Village is giving the West Side a run for its money. The area has become home to a slew of smaller, more casual bars for men with a downtown style and attitude. If you prefer a younger, hipper crowd, this neighborhood is probably just the scene for you. (Note: Many of these bars take cash only, so hit the ATM before you go.)
Subway: L to First Ave; F, V to Second Ave.

Boiler Room 86 E. 4th St. (at Second Ave.) (212) 254-7536

The Cock 188 Ave. A (at 12th St.) (212) 777-6254

Wonderbar 505 E. 6th St. (between Aves. A and B) (212) 777-9105

Dick's Bar 192 Second Ave. (at 12th St.) (212) 475-2071

Phoenix 447 E. 13th St. (at Ave. A) 212-477-9979

jukebox has a good selection and they serve popcorn in a basket. Cash and checks only. **Subway**: A, C, E to 42nd St.

Excelsior BROOKLYN 390 Fifth Ave. (between 6th and 7th Sts.) (718) 832-1599. This warm, inviting bar with a great garden area attracts a mellow local crowd. There's plenty of action, but it's done Brooklyn-style, without all the show. Though Excelsior is definitely for the boys, the crowd can be mixed. **Subway**: F to Fourth Ave.; N, R to 9th St.

G Lounge CHELSEA 225 W. 19th St. (between Seventh and Eighth Aves.) (212) 929-1085. Smart-dressed Chelsea guys line up to get into this den of chic, with a juice bar in the back and a bar in the middle of the main room to encourage smooth cruising. G also features some of the best DJs in the city. A hot spot from the day it opened. Cash only. **Subway**: C, E, 1, 9 to 23rd St.

Hell WEST VILLAGE 59 Gansevoort St. (between Washington and Greenwich Sts.) (212) 727-1666. A nice, dimly lit lounge up the street from the popular late-night diner Florent, Hell attracts a mostly gay clientele (and a classy, not overtly cruisey one at that). It's a swell place to have a cosmopolitan as long as there's a DJ spinning. Otherwise it's those same old Erasure and Everything But the Girl songs on the jukebox—always something there to remind you of an ex-boyfriend or two. **Subway**: A, C, E to 14th St.; L to Eighth Ave.

The Monster WEST VILLAGE 80 Grove St. (between W. 4th St. and Waverly Pl.) (212) 924-3557. Located on Sheridan Square (with a view of Stonewall), the Monster is one of New York's oldest gay establishments. On the main floor, there's a huge, attractive wooden bar with plenty of seating for everyone. Moving farther in, you'll hear various patrons by the piano belting out a favorite show tune (or 10). Venture downstairs and there's another large bar and a fairly spacious dance floor. Cash only. **Subway**: 1, 9 to Christopher St.

SBNY FLATIRON/UNION SQUARE 50 W. 17th St. (between Fifth and Sixth Aves.) (212) 691-0073. SBNY is a friendly, wholesome bar—except for the go-go boys, the cruisey atmosphere and the almost exclusively male crowd. SBNY, formerly Splash, keeps its customers coming back with cozy seating around the downstairs bar and a dance floor with music that ranges from disco classics to 90's dance favorites. **Subway:** F, L, N, Q, R, V, W, 4, 5, 6 to 14th St.

The Slide EAST VILLAGE 354 Bowery (between Great Jones and E. 4th Sts.) (212) 475-7621. The Slide was conceived as a no-frills gay dive, not a trendy lounge. A laid-back East Village mélange mingles at the bar: drag queens, punk rockers, muscle men. The plank floors and wagon-wheel chandeliers in this basement space summon the vaudeville era. **Subway:** 6 to Bleecker St.

Starlight Bar and Lounge EAST VILLAGE 167 Ave. A (between 10th and 11th Sts.) (212) 475-2172. A comfortable, dimly-lit lounge with two rooms that are always packed on the weekend with a young, diverse, and mostly male crowd. You will have to squeeze through throngs of men and a wall of onlookers to reach the cozy back room, which features a DJ and plenty of couches. The Starlight hosts a party for women on Sunday night. Subway: 6 to Astor Place; L to First Avenue.

Stonewall WEST VILLAGE 53 Christopher St. (between Sixth and Seventh Aves.) (212) 463-0950. Get out your gay history books: Stonewall is the little hole in the wall where the famous riots started. (The brief version: The police raided the bar, a drag queen threw a bottle, purses flew and, over the course of a couple of days in the summer of 1969, the gay rights movement was born.) These days, the bar is a quieter, more open, less tumultuous neighborhood hangout. Cash only. **Subway:** 1, 9 to Christopher St.

Therapy MIDTOWN WEST 343 W. 52nd St. (between Eighth and Ninth Aves.) (212) 397-1700. Think XL for the uptown crowd. Apparently, Chelsea is moving to Hell's kitchen (a.k.a. Clinton if you're a real-estate developer). This upscale, beautifully designed spot is perfect for those freshly scrubbed men—you know, the kind who love their products. **Subway:** C, E to 50th St.

Townhouse MIDTOWN EAST 206 E. 58th St. (between Second and Third Aves.) (212) 826-6241. A "gentleman's club" in the truest sense of the term, this classy gay bar has the old boys' atmosphere down pat. A dress code ensures that the clientele maintains the proper image at all times. Dark wood, tapestry carpeting and paintings of hunting scenes provide the perfect backdrop for the civilized meeting and greeting that goes on here. The crowd consists of older, well-polished men in suits lounging on couches or leaning suavely against walls. Subway: 4, 5, 6 to 59th St.; N, R, W to Lexington Ave.

The Works UPPER WEST SIDE 428 Columbus Ave. (between 80th and 81st Sts.) (212) 799-7365. An ad for The Works proclaims: "89% have jobs, 73% own their own apartments, the odds are in your favor. Find your new husband here." A hint, ladies: This ad isn't aimed at you. This bar is a neighborhood fixture, and—as the ad might indicate—attracts guppies of all ages. The crowd is friendly, and the bartender swears that the chocolate martinis are delicious. Cash only. **Subway:** B, C to 81st St.

XL CHELSEA 375 W. 16th St. (between Eighth and Ninth Aves.) (212) 995-1400. This theatrical "son et lumiere" of a bar-club manages to incorporate the theatricality of Las Vegas, the finesse of modern design and the sound system of a killer club, without a slouch-inducing couch in sight. Small, flat screens punctuate the walls, showing scenes of swaying trees and vast stretching landscapes during the after-work cocktail hour, complimented by a sunset sky on the ceiling. XL will appeal to anyone who moved to New York City to live a dream. Sharp, sophisticated and 100 percent man-made, XL is a pure palace of pleasure. **Subway:** A, C, E to 14th St.; L to Eighth Ave.

Women

Cubby Hole WEST VILLAGE. 281 W. 12th St. (at W. 4th St.) (212) 243-9041. A lack of pretension characterizes this narrow room, which lives up to its matchbook's claim of being "the friendly neighborhood bar." Although it caters predominantly to casually dressed, local lesbians in their 30's and 40's, this West Village bar welcomes all. A miscellaneous collection of genders, races, ages and styles makes up the usual crowd. Cash only. **Subway:** 1, 2, 3, 9 to 14th St.

Ginger's BROOKLYN 363 Fifth Ave. (between 5th and 6th Sts.). The owners of the **Rising Café** (currently closed) have expanded their domain on Park Slope's Fifth Avenue with this casual neighborhood bar. A dimly lit space with a vaguely nautical theme, Ginger's provides just the right publike elements: tables for two, a long wooden bar that runs the length of the front room, a pool table, darts in the back and a greenly glowing jukebox replete with an eclectic selection. The clientele is representative of the neighborhood: racially mixed, straight and gay. **Subway:** F to Fourth Ave.; N, R to 9th St.

Henrietta Hudson WEST VILLAGE 438 Hudson St. (between Morton and Barrow Sts.) (212) 924-3347. A younger, less high-powered crowd than at Rubyfruit. Some nights are packed, others are dead, but the service is always pleasant and friendly. The crowd ranges from locals to bridge-and-tunnel girls. **Subway:** 1, 9 to Christopher St.

Meow Mix LOWER EAST SIDE 269 E. Houston St. (between Aves. A and B) (212) 254-0688. The epicenter of the lesbian queercore scene, Meow Mix has been featured in several films including *All Over Me* and *Chasing Amy*. It's a tiny place with a rec-room-type basement where young lesbians can go and shoot pool, flirt and drop quarters in the Ms. Pac Man machine. There's a small stage upstairs where local bands perform and the bar's restrooms feature the most exciting graffiti in town. Although primarily lesbian, there's almost always a handful of men in attendance, with no hostility toward them. Cash only. **Subway:** F, V to Second Ave.

Rubyfruit Bar and Grill WEST VILLAGE 531 Hudson St. (between W. 10th and Charles Sts.) (212) 929-3343. A mature, friendly lesbian crowd gathers here to relax at the bar or on one of the richly upholstered settees. The tables are made of such artifacts as old-fashioned sewing machines, with pedals that still work. For added privacy, there is a step-up seating area at the back of the bar area, partially enclosed by lush draperies. **Subway:** 1, 9 to Christopher St.

DANCE CLUBS

This year New York City saw an explosion of new mega dance clubs in the Meat Packing District and in the warehouses of west Chelsea, thanks in part to the favorable commercial zoning laws there. Most clubs offer an array of programming (hip hop, alternative rock, techno etc.) that changes dramatically from night to night, so phone ahead or check the club's web site for the latest updates. (See **Nightlife** introduction for resources.) Unless you're on the guest list, expect cover charges to run between $10- $30. Dress codes vary, but to be safe, the more "funky-festive" the better. (Many clubs do not allow sneakers.)

New York City still harbors the strict velvet-rope door policies that were honed during the Studio 54 era, so for best luck getting in it generally helps to have a higher ratio of women to men in the group. At very least, do not show up with a large group of hooting and hollering guys (unless it's a gay club). In the warmer months, outdoor events at venues like P.S.1 in Queens are not to be missed. And some of the best parties occur in out-of-the-way spots like Frank's Lounge and Volume in Brooklyn. Events can be found by picking up a *Time Out New York* or a *Flyer* magazine.

Avalon FLATIRON/UNION SQUARE 47 W. 20th St. (between Fifth and Sixth Aves.) (212) 807-7780. In the old chruch formerly known as the Limelight, Avalon is a muliplex-styled mega-club. Down the Habitrail-like hallways there are several chambers, each with a different style of music and atmosphere. The hip hop room has elevated banquettes and stripper poles, the chill-out room is a soothing green with comfy sofas, and VIP skyboxes with private bars are available for high rollers. But the main dance floor with marquee DJ's such as Josh Wink and the Basement Jaxx is for fans of techno and deep house. **Subway:** F, V, N, R, W to 23rd St.

Cheetah FLATIRON/UNION SQUARE 12 W. 21st St. (between Fifth and Sixth Aves.) (212) 206-7770. The former Sound Factory space has changed clientele entirely; the gay crowd stays away, while the champagne-swilling European set flocks here on weekends. The venue's tacky décor leaves a lot to be desired, but Cheetah's a good space as far as midsized clubs go. There is also a mellower downstairs lounge. **Subway:** F, N, R, V, 1, 9 to 23rd St.

Cielo WEST VILLAGE 18 Little W. 12th St. (between Ninth Ave. and Washington St.) (212) 645-5700. Unlike many big clubs, Cielo seems more tailored to the times, like a private party hidden from the uninvited. The walls and ceilings are covered with biomorphic foam tubes upholstered with retro brown ultra-suede, interspersed with Plexiglas tubes of amber light. The DJs don't spin any Top 40 hip-hop or rock; only house music with a Latin twist. Cielo frequently brings in big-name DJs like Tony Humphries and Brian Tappert but doesn't advertise. **Subway:** A, C, E to 14th St.; L to Eighth Ave.

Club Shelter MIDTOWN WEST 20 W. 39th St. (between Fifth and Sixth Aves.) (212) 719-9867. Stepping into Club Shelter, a four-level nightclub, is a little like stumbling across a secret utopia. Utopia, that is, if you like chilling out to bongo drums and dancing to really loud house music all night. On the dance floor there is an unwritten code. No groping or grabbing. Gatorade, not alcohol, is the beverage of choice, and those who hold out until 6 A.M. get free hot chocolate. When you leave, the bouncers actually smile and say good morning. No glow sticks here. This is not a rave. **Subway:** B, D, F, V to 42nd St.

Copacabana MIDTOWN WEST 560 W. 34th St. (at Eleventh Ave.) (212) 239-2672. The legendary Latin dance club that Barry Manilow once called "the hottest spot north of Havana" has reopened in a new location and is as squeaky clean as the revitalized 42nd Street. The huge bilevel club pays homage to the original where Joan Collins and Raquel Welch got their start as Copa Girls. It retains the signature white ceramic palm trees, Art Deco carpet and classic white rails around the dance floor and V.I.P. areas. Of course, the dancing is still the star attraction, with internationally acclaimed salsa and merengue bands providing the Caribbean beats. **Subway:** A, C, E to 34th St.

Coral Room CHELSEA 512 W. 29th St. (between Tenth and Eleventh Aves.) (212) 244-1965. With 1950's fashions so back in style, a nightclub with décor to match is only fitting. Coral Room looks like a punk rock version of a kitschy seaside resort in Florida. The former warehouse, painted pink and sea-foam colors, has gaudy driftwood lamps, coral-textured walls and a giant aquarium, where tropical fish swim among women dressed in bikini tops, beads and mermaid tails. Unlike some of the trendy clubs nearby, Coral Room does not cater only to those with deep pockets. **Subway:** C, E to 28th St.

Crobar CHELSEA 530 West 28th St. (between Tenth and Eleventh Aves.) (212) 629-9000. The night-life equivalent of a blockbuster film. It's a big-budget production with special effects, lots of skin and loud noises, an atmosphere that's fun if you're in the mood. Paris Hilton-Tara Reid clones clog the street in front of the entrance, marked by a wall of television monitors. Inside the multilevel club, which also has branches in Chicago and Miami, there's a coliseum-like space with a giant projection wall, flashing lights and seminude performers hanging by cords from the 60-foot ceiling. One room resembles a techno "Lord of the Rings" forest with giant bamboo-like cylinders. **Subway:** C, E to 23rd St.

Don Hill's SOHO 511 Greenwich St. (at Spring St.) (212) 219-2850. This small bar on the fringes of SoHo plays host to several popular nights featuring drag queens and dominatrixes, though Squeezebox, the club's most well known party, has left the building. As popular as ever, though somewhat straighter than it once was, Don Hill's is a safe bet if you like 70's and 80's kitsch and the crowd that goes along with it. **Subway:** 1, 9 to Canal St.; C, E to Spring St.

Exit MIDTOWN WEST 610 W. 56th St. (between Eleventh and Twelfth Aves.) (212) 582-8282. Formerly Carbon (and, before that, Mirage), Exit is one of New York's largest, least subtle clubs. With four floors and room for 5,000 partiers, Exit tries to offer everything for everyone—often at the same time. **Subway:** A, B, C, D, 1, 9 to 59th St.

La Nueva Escuelita MIDTOWN WEST 301 W. 39th St. (at Eighth Ave.) (212) 631-0588. Transsexuals, drag queens, gay men and the women who love them, and a progressive straight crowd mix it up on the dance floor. It's one of the cheaper dance venues in town—patrons pay $5–$15 on most nights and when you add the free condoms you can score in the back, it's clearly worth the price. Cash only. **Subway:** A, C, E, N, Q, R, W, 1, 2, 3, 7, 9 to 42nd St.

Marquee CHELSEA 289 Tenth Ave. (between 25th and 26th Sts.) (646) 473-0202. One of the new mega-nightspots, Marquee has its dose of pretension. But the clubby attitude keeps the atmosphere down to earth. It's a ritzy ski lodge the downtown set can endorse. The architectural firm of Philip Johnson was brought in to work on the 35-foot wishbone-shaped staircase. It leads to a lounge enclosed by a wall of glass, useful for spying on the action. And voyeurism, is essential when in a drink's toss proximity to stars such as Ben Stiller and Uma Thurman. **Subway:** C, E to 23rd St.

Mehanata CHINATOWN 416 Broadway (at Canal St.) (212) 925-2368. Mehanata (the name means little tavern) is a Bulgarian restaurant-bar-disco with Thursday night "Gogol Bordello" dance frenzies, where young and old Russians, Ukrainians and Bulgarians mix with models, artists, dot-com kids and an occasional celeb. The DJ usually plays Russian, Ukrainian and Gypsy songs, as well as Arabic and Spanish music and Euro hits from the 70's and 80's. On the dance floor, people do kicks and jump like Cossacks, swirl Ukrainian style, whistle and break plates. **Subway:** J, M, N, R, Q, W, Z, 6 to Canal St.

NV TRIBECA/SOHO 289 Spring St. (at Hudson St.) (212) 929-6868. This spot on the western bounds of SoHo is a lounge palace. Heavy scarlet curtains cloak the main parlor and a brown-marble and copper bar curves along the length of the mezzanine. NV puts on its club face every night at 10 P.M., when the $20 cover charge kicks in and DJs meld dance tracks with hip-hop and R&B. A favorite among New York's professional athletes, NV has also seen Mariah Carey do some impromptu time in the DJ booth. **Subway:** 1, 9 to Houston St.; C, E to Spring St.

Roxy CHELSEA 515 W. 18th St. (between Tenth and Eleventh Aves.) (212) 645-5156. A cavernous Chelsea club that takes its weekend parties deep into the night (and early morning). The club draws a mixed crowd and music ranging from house to trance, depending on the night. Saturdays are mostly gay and on Wednesdays the place turns into a roller disco as it was originally. Cash only. **Subway:** A, C, E to 14th St.

Ruby Falls CHELSEA 609 W. 29th St. (between Eleventh and Twelfth Aves.)
(212) 643 6464. For those on a mission to dance all night to blaring techno
and hip hop, this no-frills club is the motherlode. Star DJs from Detroit to Amsterdam keep the crowd moving with inventive mixes. And when you can't
shake your hips another second, collapse into the comfy couches strategically
located on an elevated platform so you won't miss any action on the dance
floor. **Subway:** A, C, E to 34th St.

Sound Factory MIDTOWN WEST 618 W. 46th St. (between Eleventh and
Twelfth Aves.) (212) 489-0001. Closed for a short time by federal prosecutors,
the Sound Factory re-emerged, bloodied but unbowed. It's still a hopping late-
night weekend destination that keeps the deep house pumpin' until well beyond
dawn. Not quite as enthralling as the original Sound Factory, its latest incarnation
nevertheless boasts an impressive sound system in addition to one of the more
workable dance floors in town. Cash only. **Subway:** A, C, E to 42nd St.

Spirit CHELSEA 530 W. 27th St. (between Tenth and Eleventh Aves.)
(212) 268-9477. For the post-rave set, Spirit aims to provide entertainment
through enlightenment. It's divided into three areas: Body (a dance floor and
mezzanine), Mind (a spiritual wellness center) and Soul (a restaurant). Mood-
enhancing fragrances are pumped in through vents. Best of all, there's an
"everyone's invited" policy. Expect to see groovy older folks in loose-fitting
clothing, break-dance crews with do-rags, and Euros in tinted shades. For added
momentum there are performance troupes such as Rapture that interpret Native
American mythology through dance. **Subway:** C, E to 23rd St.

Table 50 WEST VILLAGE 643 Broadway (between Bleecker and Mercer Sts)
(212) 253-2560. This speakeasy-styled dance club is tucked in a basement with
exposed foundation stones and small cavernous nooks lined with banquettes.
The intimate vibe is perfect for the sweaty dirty-dancing throngs who flock to
hear the celebrity DJs, including Mark Ronson, members of the Roots, and the
rapper Q-Tip. **Subway:** A, C, E, F, V, S to West 4th St.

13 EAST VILLAGE 35 E. 13th St. (between University Pl. and Broadway)
(212) 979-6677. This cozy second-story boîte below Union Square hosts a number of weekly parties, most notably Sunday night's long-running Shout!, a glamorous but young gathering of immaculately turned-out mods, skins, soulies and
ska babies, all frugging away to an eclectic 60's soundtrack. It's an Anglophile's
dream. Cheap drinks, comfy seating and a small dance floor help to make 13 an
off-the-beaten-path downtown gem. **Subway:** L, N, Q, R, W, 4, 5, 6 to 14th St.

Webster Hall EAST VILLAGE 125 E. 11th St. (between Third and Fourth Aves.)
(212) 353-1600. A cavernous, multilevel East Village club. On weekends you
can't get near the place, which may be just as well; 11th Street is closed to all
through traffic. Thursday is Girls Night Out, with free admission for the ladies.
Various DJs spin various sounds in various rooms.
Subway: L, N, R, 4, 5, 6 to 14th St.

POPULAR MUSIC VENUES

The following listings are a selection of the city's smaller music venues. For bigger acts, check local listings for venues like the **Bowery Ballroom**, **Irving Plaza**, the **Beacon Theater** and the **Roseland Ballroom**.

Rock, Folk & Country

Acme Underground EAST VILLAGE 9 Great Jones St. (between Lafayette St. and Broadway) (212) 677-6963. Located beneath Acme Bar and Grill, Acme Underground presents live rock and eclectic music most nights. (Weekend shows tend to be strictly 21 and over, while weekday age limits fluctuate.) There's room for a standing crowd of 225, and performers often mingle with the crowd as they walk to the stage, giving the place an intimate atmosphere. **Subway:** F, S, V to Broadway–Lafayette St.; 6 to Bleecker St.

Arlene Grocery LOWER EAST SIDE 95 Stanton St. (between Ludlow and Orchard Sts.) (212) 358-1633. With its stellar sound system, relaxed atmosphere, willingness to book unknown acts and free admission, Arlene Grocery (housed in an old bodega) has quickly become an integral part of Lower East Side bar circuit. Emerging stars such as Beth Orton and Ron Sexsmith, as well as older performers like Marianne Faithful, have used the 150-person-capacity club for intimate engagements. The club has the feel of a musicians' hangout, much like CBGB in its 1970's heyday. Cash only. **Subway:** F, V to Second Ave.

Baggot Inn GREENWICH VILLAGE 82 W. 3rd St. (between Thompson and Sullivan Sts.) (212) 477-0622. Formerly the Sun Mountain Cafe, the Baggot Inn continues the folk music tradition of long-gone 1960's coffeehouses on Bleecker Street. Occasionally, performers go electric among the flock of aspiring singer-songwriters. For the most part, however, the stage at the back of the club offers acoustic sounds, or poetry, comedy, open-mike nights and DJ events. **Subway:** A, C, E, F, V to W. 4th St.

B.B. King Blues Club and Grill MIDTOWN WEST 237 W. 42nd St. (between Seventh and Eighth Aves.) 212 997 4144. An intimate venue to experience the very best in R&B, soul, and hip hop. Aretha Franklin, Etta James, Macy Gray, DAS EFX, and the Roots are some of the pedigreed acts that regularly perform at this Times Square club. The main room is a two-tiered horseshoe space with tables surrounding the stage and a 40 foot bar for those who prefer to stand. Sundays is the gospel brunch made all the sweeter by the sounds of the World Famous Harlem Gospel Choir. **Subway:** A, C, E, N, Q, R, S, W, 1, 2, 3, 7, 9 to 42nd St.

Bitter End GREENWICH VILLAGE 147 Bleecker St. (between Thompson St. and La Guardia Place) (212) 673-7030. Bob Dylan, Joan Baez, Harry Chapin, Paul Simon and Patti Smith have graced this rickety wooden stage on their way to larger fame, and the promotional posters that line the walls give a sense of the

---

Rock Alternatives: A Music Scene Migrates to Brooklyn

It's not quite the end of the city's rock world as we know it, but Manhattan's downtown music scene is shrinking, as Brooklyn's expands. Many downtown clubs have closed in recent years, including Brownie's, Wetlands, Tramps, the Cooler, Coney Island High, Nightingales and No Moore, for reasons including skyrocketing rents and low profit margins. For musicians, the closings mean fewer places to showcase their sound, just as the city is experiencing a rock renaissance not heard since the late 1970's.

But a musical beachhead has established itself in Williamsburg and other Brooklyn neighborhoods. Clubs like Northsix (which opened in 2001 in a former steel mill), Club Luxx, Warsaw and South Paw are starting to supplant those in Manhattan as rock hothouses.

Few musicians are complaining. What Manhattan offered in sweat-soaked stages and indiscriminate crowds, Brooklyn has replied with loft-size spaces, devoted fans and, notably, dressing-room showers. Moreover, musicians say, the young club owners are less jaded, more respectful of their craft and more generous with backstage beers.

With venerable clubs like CBGB, Bowery Ballroom, Mercury Lounge and the Knitting Factory still kicking, and newer ones like Sin-é springing up, downtown remains a center for indie music. But rather than mimic that scene, Brooklyn clubs are creating their own.

Trash Bar 256 Grand St., Williamsburg (718) 599-1000

Northsix 66 N. 6th St.,Williamsburg (718) 599-5103

Pete's Candy Store 709 Lorimer St., Williamsburg (718) 302-3770

South Paw 125 Fifth Ave., Park Slope (718) 230-0236

Warsaw 261 Driggs Ave., Williamsburg (718) 387-0505

---

venue's history. Opened in 1961 as an ice cream shop, the Bitter End has maintained its informal feel and continues to present aspiring folk and rock acts for a mix of curious tourists, N.Y.U. students and each band's contingent of fans. Cash only. **Subway:** A, C, E, F, V to W. 4th St.

Bowery Ballroom LOWER EAST SIDE 6 Delancey St.(between Bowery and Chrystie Sts.) (212) 533-2111. The alternative rock and punk bands (such as the White Stripes, The Strokes, and the Yeah Yeah Yeah's) that play in this majestic old Beaux Arts building are usually one stop away from MTV and mainstream radio fame. It's oppurtune for checking out tomorrow's acts up close and personal before they're on the arena circuit. Views of the stage are best caught from the mezzanine level or else on the main floor head-bobbing with the crowds. After-parties are often held downstairs, so stick around after the show. **Subway:** F to Delancey St.; J, M, Z to Essex St.

CBGB EAST VILLAGE 315 Bowery (at Bleecker St.) (212) 982-4052. The famed CBGB's is still an ideal place to try out unknown rock bands and catch the

occasional bigger name playing an intimate show. Since its heyday (the Ramones, the Talking Heads and Blondie are some of the bands that got their start here), CB's has lost some of its hold on the rock scene, but only because other similar venues have arisen. Patrons are allowed to enter and leave the club at will, giving CB's a neighborhood-hangout feel. Cash only.
Subway: 6 to Bleecker St.; F, S, V to Broadway–Lafayette St.

CB's 313 Gallery EAST VILLAGE 313 Bowery (at Bleecker St.) (212) 677-0455. By presenting mellow, acoustic-based sounds and monthly art exhibits in a cafe setting, CB's Gallery offers an entirely different experience from its legendary progenitor, CBGB. Here you'll find tables and candles instead of a mosh pit, spoken word and poetry instead of guitar distortion and sonic shriek. Like the original CBGB, however, the gallery makes an effort to present new and unknown talent. **Subway:** 6 to Bleecker St.; F, S, V to Broadway–Lafayette St.

Continental EAST VILLAGE 25 Third Ave. (between St. Marks Pl. and 9th St.) (212) 529-6924. With a dive-bar feel, four to five aspiring rock bands nightly and a blaring sound system, the sublimely sleazy Continental is the tongue-pierced stud at the mouth of St. Marks Place. Formerly known as the Continental Divide, the bar has launched many a career—from jam-band success Blues Traveler to garage-rock renovators the Pristeens. Punk legends such as Iggy Pop, Patti Smith and the late, great Joey Ramone have been known to perform unannounced sets. Cash only. **Subway:** 6 to Astor Pl.

Fez Under Time Cafe EAST VILLAGE 380 Lafayette St. (at Great Jones St.) (212) 533-2680. Two floors below the trendy Time Cafe, Fez, which seats 150, presents indie-rockers, weekly jazz band "workshops," comedy acts and cabaret shows—all in a swank clubhouse atmosphere. It's equal parts Moroccan hashish den (hence the name), jazz club and gangster hideaway. Patrons, generally a bit older than your average rock club crowd, sit at tables or in the plush leather booths at the back. **Subway:** 6 to Bleecker St.; F, S, V to Broadway–Lafayette St.

Lakeside Lounge EAST VILLAGE 162 Ave. B (between 10th and 11th Sts.) (212) 529-8463. Enter the Lakeside Lounge and you could be in a shack on the edge of a pond deep in the country—it's trout fishing in Alphabet City. At first glance, East Village hipsters appear to dominate the front-room bar, but all are welcome. Excellent rockabilly, country and "cowpunk" bands appear most nights. Cash only. **Subway:** L to First Ave.

The Living Room LOWER EAST SIDE 84 Stanton St. (at Allen St.) (212) 533-7235. With its affordable but scrumptious vegetarian-leaning menu and its intimate folk music, the Living Room lives up to its name. The décor is makeshift, and there are games for playing with friends or for breaking the ice. Rows of tables take up most of the floor space leading up to the stage. Fans of singer-songwriter folk music will enjoy the relaxed atmosphere, the sincere performances, and the casual, parlor-room feel. **Subway:** F, V to Second Ave.

Mercury Lounge LOWER EAST SIDE 217 E. Houston St. (between Essex and Ludlow Sts.) (212) 260-4700 *www.mercuryloungenyc.com*. The Mercury Lounge attracts a varied crowd that comes to listen to everything from singer-songwriters and alterna-rockers to the latest experimental electronic music practitioners. Since the back room holds only 200 people, buying tickets at the bar ahead of time is recommended when bigger names are on the bill. Inside the performance space, there are a few highly coveted tables, but most patrons stand. Bring ID; most shows are strictly 21 and over. **Subway:** F, V to Second Ave.

Pianos LOWER EAST SIDE 158 Ludlow St. (between Stanton and Rivington Sts.) (212) 505-3733. This former piano store has fast become a mecca for the rocker bed-head boys. Hipsters talk punk, garage and indie over beers and burgers in the airy front bar, before heading into the dark bat cave of a venue at the back of the room. As the swinging dividing door opens, patrons can get a taste of the music before deciding whether or not to pay the cover. To avoid the bleeding eardrum scene, head for the upstairs lounge. Given the location, stylish décor and well-equipped venue, even when the fickle Ludlow Street lads grow tired, Pianos will certainly play on. **Subway:** F, V to Second Ave.

Rodeo Bar MURRAY HILL 375 Third Ave. (at 27th St.) (212) 683-6500 *www.rodeobar.com.* When it opened in 1987, the Rodeo Bar was one of the first places in New York to feature roots-rock made for and by local performers. Since then, it has expanded its booking policy to include touring roots-rockers as well. Long wooden railings and peanut shells on the floor add to the honky-tonk atmosphere. There is no music cover, making the Rodeo Bar a prime spot for savoring the flavor of longtime New York bar bands. **Subway:** 6 to 28th St.

Rothko LOWER EAST SIDE 116 Suffolk St (between Rivington and Delancey Sts.) No phone. To experience the thriving downtown music scene that produced bands such as the Strokes and Interpol, cram into this bare-boned live music venue. The red, minimal space has a few Rothko paintings on the wall that set the tone for the legions of young artist types and musicians in skinny ties and ripped jeans who come to hear the latest sounds. A lounge in the basement with a few padded church pews is a great spot to enjoy the cheap beer and mixed drinks. **Subway:** F to Delancey; J, M, Z to Essex St.

Sin-é LOWER EAST SIDE 148-150 Attorney St. (between Houston and Stanton Sts.) (212) 388-0077 *www.sin-e.org.* Sin-é, the former East Village club that featured burgeoning artists like Jeff Buckley and David Gray in the early 1990's, has made an apt return in style, attitude and line-up at its new Lower East Side location. After a long break while the owner opened the venerable Arlene Grocery, the new incarnation of Sin-é opened in March 2003 and almost immediately regained its reputation in the downtown indie rock scene. Acts like the Yeah, Yeah, Yeahs and the Walkmen are among the hundreds of bands that have already played here. With good acoustics, room for 225, a reasonably priced selection of wines and beers, relatively cheap cover charges, few frills and at least three or four bands a night, Sin-é's return is more than welcome. **Subway:** F, V to Second Ave.

Jazz, Blues, Experimental & World

From a distance, it seems amazing that New York should still be the place where most serious jazz players want to move to. Since the 50's, when the bohemian vogue for jazz reached its peak in this city, rents have become prohibitively overpriced for both musicians and clubowners, and the business of keeping a working band often means playing all over the world, particularly in Europe and Japan. By that logic, the best jazz musicians should probably live in the cheapest, balmiest airport hub city—Atlanta, maybe, or Salt Lake City.

But they don't, because most of them are inherently social creatures. Even when it feels as if jazz isn't producing any popular successes, there is always ferment. The tradition of younger players trailing around behind elders hasn't died out, and won't; the tradition of sitting in at late-night jam sessions has distinctly lessened, but survives; the tradition of competing on the bandstand, the friendly jostle of egos, is the glue that holds the whole thing together. There is a large, honorable family of jazz musicians in New York. It often seems fragmented, but when you see it up close, particularly at a club that jazz musicians like to hang out in (that's the Village Vanguard, the Jazz Gallery, and the Fat Cat) you realize that the aesthetic, historical and personal connections among the family members run extremely deep.

When this edition of the Guide to New York City appears, a new colossus for jazz will be up and running: the revitalized Jazz at Lincoln Center, in the Time Warner building at Columbus Circle. With its three theaters—one of them a nightly jazz club—and year-round bookings, there is a possibility that Lincoln Center's cultural capital and marketing budgets will overshadow the rest of jazz-perfomance activity in New York. But only for a little while, I'm guessing. The multitudes who follow the arts in New York will either react for or against the Lincoln Center onslaught; because there are plenty of jazz experiences that are more down-home than what's to be had in that gleaming new skyscraper, the larger entity of jazz will win either way.

In the past few years, the larger jazz clubs with kitchens have rolled back their sets to earlier starting times; the Jazz Standard, in particular, encourages you to have dinner there with its 7:30 sets, a time when jazz musicians used to be getting out of bed. And the food there, a barbecue menu created by the restauranteur Danny Meyer, is well worth it. Otherwise, it's a good idea to go see jazz later in the evening. I can' think of a late jazz set I've seen in my life that didn't improve on the early set—the musicians are looser and more intuitive, the crowd more intimate and serious about its pleasures.   — Ben Ratliff

Birdland MIDTOWN WEST 315 W. 44th St. (between Eighth and Ninth Aves.) (212) 581-3080 *www.birdlandjazz.com*. Birdland features some of the most thoughtfully booked jazz in the city. The club pays direct homage to its namesake, the legendary original Birdland at Broadway and 52nd Street. Although it's a fully functional restaurant with a Southern-tinged menu, Birdland's main attraction is music. Reservations are recommended for the music sets ($20–$35 and a $10 food or drink minimum). **Subway:** A, C, E to 42nd St.

Blue Note GREENWICH VILLAGE 131 W. 3rd St. (between Sixth Ave. and Macdougal St.) (212) 475-8592 *www.bluenote.net*. Performances by jazz heavyweights such as Tony Bennett, Oscar Peterson and Chick Corea, and exhilarating double bills are the main attractions at the Blue Note. A night at the Blue Note can easily cost you $100. Because the club's seating can make a rush-hour subway seem cozy, reservations and early arrival are essential. Record labels use Monday nights, when it's much less expensive, to break in new acts—a bargain when established musicians join in. **Subway:** A, C, E, F, S, V to W. 4th St.

CB's Lounge EAST VILLAGE 313 Bowery (at Bleecker St.) (212) 677-0455 *www.cbgb.com*. A lair for Sunday-night jazz programming, downstairs at CB's 313 Gallery, next door to the more famous rock club CBGB. Programmed by Dee Pop, once the drummer for the 80s New York band the Bush Tetras, the Sunday night "Freestyle" events here smash together all kinds of jazz. Mismatched easy chairs and a general atmosphere of a bohemian keg party are either your loss or your gain, but know that this really is a basement. As in the old days of New York jazz clubs, the bills here have three or four bands on them; the night starts at 7 and ends after 11. Get there when you want—it's never overcrowded—but save some room for the pizza, cooked on the premises. **Subway:** 6 to Bleecker St.; F/V to Second Ave.

El Flamingo CHELSEA 547 W. 21st St. (between Tenth and Eleventh Aves.) (212) 243-2121. A snazzy venue that plays up the Art Deco supper-club theme to the hilt. The main room has a good-sized dance floor that splits in half when the club hosts live music performances; the non-rhythmically inclined can watch from above. Various promoters use El Flamingo for shows, so keep an eye out for upcoming gigs. **Subway:** C, E to 23rd St.

Fat Cat WEST VILLAGE 75 Christopher Street (at Seventh Ave. S.) (212) 675-6056 *www.fatcatjazz.com*. After the closing in 2003 of Smalls, the beloved West Village club, jazz heads felt a hole in the atmosphere. Smalls was a cheap joint where young musicians could work late into the night and establish regular weekly stands to make their music grow. The club's manager, Mitchell Borden, revived the idea with the Fat Cat, a long-and-narrow room bedecked with middle Eastern rugs and African masks that takes up a third of a basement pool hall. Still relatively cheap ($15 with a drink) by New York Standards, the Fat Cat stays open all week, with jazz sets running from 10 o'clock until, on weekends, 2 or 3 in the morning. The regular bookings still constitute an index of the up-and-coming in the new jazz mainstream, with musicians like Kurt Rosenwinkel, Ethan Iverson and Robert Glasper; on Sundays there's a "Jazz Legends" night, often booked by the drummer Jimmy Cobb, who played on Miles Davis's "Kind of Blue" album. **Subway:** 1,9 to Christopher St.

55 Bar WEST VILLAGE 55 Christopher Street (at Seventh Ave. S.) (212) 929-9883 *www.55bar.com*. A bar since 1919, this small room feels thick with old-New York feeling, but it has developed a specific subgenre connotation over the past twenty years. Mike Stern, the electric guitarist of Miles Davis's 80s period, started a small principality of guitar-based jazz fusion here, and that still applies: you can hear the new guitarists here like Ben Monder, Adam Rogers, and Marvin Sewell. But you can also hear new singers, saxophonists, and other figures from the straight-ahead jazz underground; best of all it's a genuine jazz hang in the old style, boozy and low-key. Subway: 1,9 to Christopher St.

Iridium Jazz Club MIDTOWN WEST 1650 Broadway (at 51st St.) (212) 582-2121 *www.iridiumjazzclub.com*. Since it opened in 1993, this tony club has become one of the top jazz venues in the city. Success has led to a recent move and a series of "Live at the Iridium" recordings on various labels. In addition to presenting legendary guitarist Les Paul every Monday night, Iridium features both established and up-and-coming jazz stars. **Subway: 1, 9 to 66th St.**

Jazz Gallery SOHO 290 Hudson Street (at Spring) (212) 242-1063 *www.jazzgallery.org*. An upstairs space over a changing series of restaurants in one of Manhattan's quieter downtown districts, with thoughtful and judicious bookings, leaning toward new tendencies in current jazz; the club has committed itself to new and established artists including Steve Coleman, Dafnis Prieto, Jason Moran, Diego Urcola and Avishai Cohen, commissioning new works from some of them by pairing up with various public and private arts funding agencies. Except for the fact that you can't malinger there late into the night (sets tend to be at 9 and 10:30), it's a new model for what jazz clubs can do. As at an art gallery, wine is available in plastic cups; otherwise, it's not particularly a place to drink. **Subway: 1 to Houston St.; C,E to Spring St.**

The Jazz Standard FLATIRON/UNION SQUARE 116 E. 27th St. (between Park and Lexington Aves.) (212) 576-2232. Blue notes meet Blue Smoke at the new Jazz Standard. The rebirth of the club has been orchestrated by restaurateur Danny Meyer, who also owns Blue Smoke, the restaurant situated in the space above. Together, the restaurant and club offer quality jazz acts and promising barbecue fare. The softly lit basement setting, with red suede seating and smoky mirrors, is in keeping with many of the city's other jazz venues. Although patrons are spared a drink minimum, there is a $20 cover charge during the week, $25 on Fridays and Saturdays. **Subway: 6 to 28th St.**

Knitting Factory TRIBECA 74 Leonard St. (between Broadway and Church St.) (212) 219-3055 *www.knittingfactory.com*. With four spaces for live music, the Knitting Factory is host to not only the avant-garde jazz that first earned this place its reputation, but also rock, spoken word, theater, film and even children's shows. So much is going on in the Knitting Factory on any given night that there's often a bottleneck at the front door. The Main Space holds 350 patrons and can get quite crowded. The Alterknit Theater presents lesser-known acts as well as spoken word, theater and films in a space that holds 90. Free performances occur in the downstairs Tap Room, which has over 15 microbrews on tap. And the newest space, the Old Office, presents up-and-coming jazz artists in a more traditional jazz-club setting. **Subway: 1, 9 to Franklin St.**

Lenox Lounge HARLEM 288 Lenox Ave. (between 124th and 125th Sts.) (212) 427-0253 *www.lenoxlounge.com*. This Harlem Art-Deco bar is rich with musical history, including a corner banquette where Billie Holiday liked to claim a regular table. Bandleaders are mostly drawn from New York jazz's middle-aged netherworld: Musicians like Chico Freeman and James Spaulding—too old to be lions, too young to be legends. And the management doesn't rustle you out between sets; you can settle in for the evening. That's the type of peace of mind you can't buy downtown. **Subway: 2, 3 to 125th St.**

The Living Room LOWER EAST SIDE 154 Ludlow St, (212) 533-7235 *www.livingroomny.com*. As punk was to CBGBs, the new folk-pop singer-songwriter wave is to the Living Room. This is where Norah Jones played countless sets on bills with three or four other acts before her record "Come Away With Me" broke through in 2002, and various parts of her circle—including the singer/ songwriters Jesse Harris and Amos Poe—perform there still. It's moved, but it's still an informal, eclectic place with a $5 cover. **Subway: F to Delancey St.**

Nublu LOWER EAST SIDE 62 Ave. C (212) 979-9925 *www.nublu.net*. A single blue lightbulb out on Avenue C indicates a club where you might want to stay later than you intended. Run by the saxophonist Ilhan Ersahin, Nublu presents night after night of live bands alternating with DJs; the vibe is international ultra-cool, specializing in Brazilian funk, reggae, and jazz. Eddie Henderson, the trumpeter, and Seamus Blake, the saxophonist, have played there regularly, as has a charming band called Forro in the Dark, playing Northeastern Brazilian music with accordion, electric guitar, triangle, and bass drum. The room's so narrow that the band plays in the middle of it, and you have to nearly pass through them to get to the bathroom; but somehow, here, you don't mind. Subway: F/V to Second Ave.

Roulette TRIBECA 228 W. Broadway (between Franklin and N. Moore Sts.) (212) 219-8242 *www.roulette.org*. Above boisterous young professionals drinking champagne in the Bubble Lounge, serious avant-garde music takes place in Roulette. This nonprofit performance space has a mix of elegant informality and concentrated audacity, with musicians trying all sorts of new, experimental ideas. Avant-garde saxophonist John Zorn performed some of his first "game piece" compositions at Roulette, and everyone from Oliver Lake, the esteemed jazz composer, to Thurston Moore, guitarist for Sonic Youth, has appeared as part of Roulette's concert programs. Cash only. **Subway: 1, 9 to Franklin St.**

Sista's Place BROOKLYN 456 Nostrand Ave. (at Jefferson Ave.) (718) 398-1766 *www.sistasplace.org*. A cafe, performance space and meeting hall concerning itself with culture and politics, Sista's Place has a villagelike, community feeling. The jazz here—nearly every weekend—is booked by the trumpeter Ahmed Abdullah, who used to play with Sun Ra and Ed Blackwell, among others; he's brought in young musicians like Marcus Strickland and members of the 60s and 70s generation like Sonny Fortune and Odean Pope. It's a small storefront with tea, dessert, and no airs: the audience talks back to the performer, and customers are treated well from the moment they walk in. **Subway: A to Nostrand Ave.**

Smoke UPPER WEST SIDE 2751 Broadway (between 105th and 106th Sts.) (212) 864-6662 *www.smokejazz.com*. Smoke (formerly known as Augie's Pub) captures the spirit of legendary jazz jam joints like Minton's—where bebop was born in the 1940's. Up-and-coming jazz musicians blow and wail in the small, cozy storefront room. It can get quite packed, but the atmosphere is friendly and the music is almost always exciting. Jazz aficionados such as the authors Stanley Crouch and Albert Murray regularly show up, crowding in alongside Columbia University students. Cash only. **Subway:** 1, 9 to 103rd St.

S.O.B.'s TRIBECA/SOHO 204 Varick St. (at Houston St.) (212) 243-4940 *www.sobs.com.* The audience sways more than the palm fronds on the faux-tree, making S.O.B.'s one of the city's best clubs for Latin, Caribbean and Afropop music. Decorated in a Copacabana-hut style, but with disco lights, S.O.B.'s is a dancer's heaven. The club even offers salsa and tango lessons before most weekend shows. In the best New York manner, ethnic groups mix at S.O.B.'s to produce a culture greater than that of any individual subgroup. Purchase advance tickets for popular shows. **Subway:** 1, 9 to Houston St.; C, E to Spring St.

St. Nick's Pub HARLEM 773 St. Nicholas Blvd. (at 149th St.) (212) 283-9728. A legendary Harlem jazz bar, St. Nick's still serves up live jazz six nights a week, Wednesday to Monday. Saxophonist Patience Higgins and the Sugar Hill Jazz Quartet lead a popular jam session every Monday, with musicians playing well past 1 A.M. When the band takes a booze break, the jukebox cranks up, blaring both classic jazz and R&B, as well as contemporary hip-hop. Even on a Monday, seats are difficult to come by in this tiny shoebox of a bar. Cash only. **Subway:** A, B, C, D to 145th St.

Sweet Rhythm WEST VILLAGE 88 Seventh Avenue S. (at Bleecker) (212) 255-3626 *www.sweetrhythmny.com.* Rebuilt in the space of the old club Sweet Basil (1975-2001), Sweet Rhythm has updated the jazz-club paradigm for a new, more syncretic time in jazz. The club books different acts through the week, with a few regulars?including the Frank and Joe Show on Sundays, playing music influenced by Django Reinhardt and 1930s swing. As before, the club serves dinner. **Subway:** 1, 9 to Christopher St.

Terra Blues GREENWICH VILLAGE 149 Bleecker St. (between Thompson St. and La Guardia Pl.) (212) 777-7776 *www.terrablues.com.* A flight above Bleecker Street, Terra Blues is home to both local and national blues acts. Though it's named after an obscure, rural Mississippi blues genre, Terra Blues is a modern-day urban saloon with surreal sculpture and blowzy curtains framing the small stage. Musicians like playing the club and the same performers are likely to return throughout the month. **Subway:** A, C, E, F, V to W. 4th St.

Tonic LOWER EAST SIDE 107 Norfolk St. (between Delancey and Rivington Sts.) (212) 358-7503 *www.tonicnyc.com.* Downtown nightlife goes synergistic in the former kosher wine market. Tonic, which opened in early 1998, used to be a hair salon, but is now a night spot with experimental jazz, comedy nights, spoken word and occasional movie screenings. Since a more recent renovation, Tonic's roster has expanded to include avant-garde headliners like John Zorn and other Knitting Factory veterans. Cash only. **Subway:** F to Delancey St.; J, M, Z to Essex St.

Up Over Jazz Café BROOKLYN 351 Flatbush Ave. (near Seventh Ave.) (718-398-5413) *www.upoverjazz.com*. A nice alternative to Manhattan's Village Vanguards and Blue Notes: here you're really in a neighborhood club (the food, should you order it, gets delivered from the Wing Wagon downstairs) and the blood pressure of musician and audience feels lower. Nevertheless, a number of New York's better musicians have played great sets here on a regular basis, including the pianist Robert Glasper, saxophonist Marcus Strickland, and trombonist Wycliffe Gordon. **Subway:** D,Q to Seventh Ave./2,3 to Grand Army Plaza.

Village Vanguard WEST VILLAGE 178 Seventh Ave. South (between W. 11th St. and Waverly Pl.) (212) 255-4037 *www.villagevanguard.com*. Known for its intimacy, pristine acoustics and lack of pretense, the Village Vanguard is the one of the world's finest jazz venues. Since 1935, this basement hideaway has hosted a staggering lineup—from Barbra Streisand and Woody Allen to John Coltrane and Thelonious Monk. Over 100 albums bear the imprimatur "Recorded Live at the Village Vanguard." In 1965, the Mel Lewis-Thad Jones Orchestra began a Monday night big band tradition that endures under the moniker Vanguard Jazz Orchestra. Reservations are recommended. Cash only. **Subway:** 1, 2, 3, 9 to 14th St.

Zinc Bar GREENWICH VILLAGE 90 W. Houston St. (between Thompson St. and La Guardia Pl.) (212) 477-8337 *www.zincbar.com*. The Zinc Bar is a downtown venue that manages to be sophisticated yet retain an informal atmosphere. The Zinc presents some of the best up-and-coming jazz and world sounds—especially Brazilian music—in the city. The Zinc Bar can get quite crowded, so arrive early if you want to sit. Be on the lookout for two kinds of cats at the Zinc Bar: famous jazz musicians kicking back after a gig and the two felines who fearlessly roam through the crowd. **Subway:** F, S, V to Broadway–Lafayette St.

CABARET

One of the singular attractions of New York City is its busy cabaret scene. The term "cabaret" broadly applies to high-end supper clubs featuring singers who perform popular standards from the pre-rock era on. Cabaret flourishes here because of its proximity to Broadway. Theater stars often moonlight as cabaret performers, and a nightclub act can also be a stepping-stone to Broadway and sometimes even to recording careers. Cabaret intersects with the world of jazz, as more and more mainstream singers incorporate jazz flourishes into their singing. But the two worlds are still very distinct.

An evening of top-flight cabaret with a cover charge and a food and drink minimum can cost considerably more than a Broadway show. But the kind personal intimacy that the best cabaret can conjure between a performer and an audience is something that can only be experienced in a nightclub where the lights are low and the champagne is flowing.

The city's leading cabarets are the chic **Café Carlyle**, the **Oak Room** at the

Algonquin Hotel, and **Feinstein's at the Regency** (named after the popular singer and pianist Michael Feinstein, who helps book the club and sometimes performs there). Make reservations well in advance, and note that the top clubs close for all or part of the summer.

Café Carlyle In the Carlyle Hotel, 35 E. 76th St. (at Madison Ave.) (212) 570-7189 *www.thecarlyle.com*. The Café Carlyle, the Rolls-Royce of the city's cabarets (with cover charges to match), tends to book the same performers every year for extended engagements. Ruling the roost in the late spring and late fall is the singer and pianist Bobby Short, who has appeared there every year for more than three decades. In 2004, Mr. Short announced his retirement from his regular engagements there, then recanted and booked himself for another season. Now around 80, Mr. Short is an effervescent musical bon vivant with exquisite taste in songs, who, accompanied by a small swing band, brings the urbane music of Cole Porter, Cy Coleman, Duke Ellington, and many others ebulliently to life in performances that have the feel of nightly parties. **Subway:** 6 to 77th St.

Feinstein's at the Regency In the Regency Hotel, 540 Park Ave. (at 61st St.) (212) 339-4095 *www.feinsteinsattheregency.com*. Pricey and elegant, situated in the hotel's "power breakfast" room, Feinstein's at the Regency books big-name talent that has run the gamut from comedy (the Smothers Brothers) to Las Vegas legends (Keely Smith). Performers who appear there regularly and have solid followings include jazz pianist John Pizzarelli, the blue-eyed soul singer Steve Tyrell, and Michael Feinstein himself. The atmosphere might be described as "romantic library." **Subway:** N, R, W to Lexington Ave.; 4, 5, 6 to 59th St.

Oak Room In the Algonquin hotel, 59 W. 44th St. (between Fifth and Sixth Aves.) (212) 840-6800 *www.algonquinhotel.com/oakroom*. The Oak Room of the Algonquin (the site of the famous literary Round Table in the 1920's and 30's) is the regular home of singer and actress Andrea Marcovicci, a diehard romantic, who appears in the late fall resurrecting the Golden Age of American popular song, as well as excellent pop and pop-jazz singers like Karen Akers, Stacey Kent, and Paula West. **Subway:** B, D, F, S, V to 42nd St.

— Stephen Holden

Other Cabarets and Supper Clubs

(See also "A Grand Oasis: New York's Hotel Bars," earlier in this chapter.)

Bemelmans Bar In the Carlyle Hotel, 35 E. 76th St. (at Madison Ave.) (212) 744-1600. Named after illustrator Ludwig Bemelmans, who created the beloved Madeline children's books after painting the charming murals here, Bemelmans is a sumptuous, romantic spot for a classic cocktail. For a $15 cover, you can hear jazz and cabaret, sometimes barely discernible about the din of conversation. **Subway:** 6 to 77th St.

Danny's Skylight Room 346 W. 46th St. (between Eighth and Ninth Aves.) (212) 265-8133. This unadorned, crowded room in the back of Danny's Grand

Sea Palace (a good Thai place on Restaurant Row) hosts some of the city's finest cabaret performers, from fresh upstarts to great old-timers such as Blossom Dearie. As you enter Danny's, there's also a narrow piano bar, a cramped but festive spot decked out with strings of Christmas lights, where you can sing along with the theater types who've made the stools around the piano their second home. **Subway:** A, C, E to 42nd St.

Don't Tell Mama 343 W. 46th St. (between Eighth and Ninth Aves.) (212) 757-0788 *www.donttellmama.com*. This enterprising Theater District perennial is really three venues in one: two cabaret rooms and a piano bar under the same management. On weekdays, there are up to four shows a night, and on weekends, up to eight—and that's in addition to the virtually nonstop show in the bar, which features singing waiters after 9 P.M. Cover charges and minimums vary, but the piano bar has no cover. **Subway:** A, C, E to 42nd St.

The Duplex Cabaret Theater 61 Christopher St. (at Seventh Ave. South) (212) 255-5438 *www.theduplex.com*. This casual Village bar and cabaret is the oldest continuously running cabaret in the city. With three levels—a festive piano bar on the first, a lounge/game room on the second and, tucked away off to the side between the two, a small cabaret/theater—the Duplex is always hopping. The newly revitalized cabaret, which has a tiny proscenium stage with rows of crowded cocktail tables providing the seating, features many of the better rising nightclub talents. **Subway:** 1, 9 to Christopher St.

Joe's Pub 425 Lafayette St. (between Astor Pl. and 4th St.) (212) 539-8777 *www.joespub.com*. A portrait of the legendary producer Joseph Papp watches over the plush banquettes, red votives and zinc balustrades at this lovely supper club and cabaret. Joe's is a friendly watering hole, serving an Italian-American menu and offering an eclectic lineup of entertainment, from top-quality jazz performers to solo shows from pop, jazz, folk, world music, and theatrical performers of every stripe. It is a favorite hangout for record-company talent scouts on the lookout for the next big thing. DJs take over after 11 P.M. on many nights. **Subway:** 6 to Astor Pl.; N, R to 8th St.

Le Jazz Au Bar 41 E. 58th St. (between Madison and Park Aves.) (212) 308-9455. *www.aubarnewyork.com*. Entering this sleek midtown Manhattan nightclub is like descending into a movie set of a jazz club. The lighting is low, the tables packed together, the sound system excellent, the menu sparse. The club began as a jazz emporium but now leans toward cabaret-style entertainment. On the funkier side, it has seen the return of the rhythm-and-blues legend Ruth Brown, as well as appearances by the rising young jazz-gospel singer, Lizz Wright. **Subway:** N, R, W, 4, 5, 6 to 59th St./Lexington Ave.

Opia 130 East 57th St. (between Lexington and Park Aves.) (212) 688-3939. *www.opiarestaurant.com*. The new, intimate upstairs cabaret is adjacent to a popular singles bar. The menu is small but sumptuous and the talent well-chosen. The witty old-time singer, pianist and songwriter John Wallowitch holds forth on many Sundays. **Subway:** N, R, W, 4, 5, 6 to 59th St./Lexington Ave.

Rose's Turn WEST VILLAGE 55 Grove St. (between Bleecker St. and Seventh Ave. S.) (212) 366-5438. One of the friendliest cabaret and piano bars in the West Village, Rose's Turn attracts a mixed crowd—gay, straight, locals and tourists who hear the music and laughter and wander in off the street. Upstairs there are singers, comedy acts and musical revues (usually for a cover charge and a two-drink minimum). Downstairs you can just hang out at the bar or sit by the piano. Saturday nights a piano player takes requests (anything but Barry Manilow's "Mandy") and three warbling bartenders sing and tell jokes. **Subway:** 1, 9 to Christopher St.

Triad Theater 158 W. 72nd St. (between Columbus Ave. and Broadway) (212) 362-2590. The tiny Triad Theater is usually home to a show with an open-ended run, and after 10 P.M. becomes a cabaret space. What it lacks in atmosphere it makes up in sightlines and proximity to the performers. Downstairs, in the Dark Star Lounge, an average of four performers a night keep customers satisfied. Food is served in both rooms, and downstairs, in addition to the comfortable tables near the stage, there's a friendly bar that attracts neighborhood regulars. **Subway:** 1, 2, 3, 9 to 72nd St.

COMEDY CLUBS

(Many music venues and cabarets have comedy nights, such as **Luna Lounge**, **Fez Under Time Cafe** *and* **Rose's Turn**. *Check local listings for schedules.)*

Boston Comedy Club GREENWICH VILLAGE 82 W. 3rd St. (between Sullivan and Thompson Sts.) (212) 477-1000 *www.bostoncomedyclub.com*. This lesser-known basement club features comedy nightly, often with several acts on the bill. Monday is open-mike. **Price:** $8–$12 cover, two-drink minimum. **Subway:** A, C, E, F, V to W. 4th St.

Caroline's MIDTOWN WEST 1626 Broadway (at 49th St.) (212) 757-4100 *www.carolines.com*. Just when you were afraid fun had been banished from Times Square, Caroline's comes to the rescue. In 15 years, Caroline Hirsch's club has gone from a comedy fledgling to a block-long complex where many TV stars perform, often testing new material. Ask about the dinner-and-show packages. **Price:** $15–$35 cover, two-drink minimum. **Subway:** N, R, W to 49th St.; C, E, 1, 9 to 50th St.

Comedy Cellar WEST VILLAGE 117 Macdougal St. (between 3rd and Bleecker Sts.) (212) 254-3480 *www.comedycellar.com*. In the more than 20 years that it has been open, Robin Williams, Stephen Wright and Jerry Seinfeld have made surprise appearances at this intimate Greenwich Village club. **Price:** $10–$15 cover, two-drink minimum. **Subway:** A, C, E, F, V to W. 4th St.

Comic Strip Live UPPER EAST SIDE 1568 Second Ave. (between 81st and 82nd Sts.) (212) 861-9386 *www.comicstriplive.com*. You'll find 24 years' worth of autographed photos of alums such as Eddie Murphy (one of the club's discoveries), Paul Reiser and Chris Rock on the wall. New comics are so eager to perform in the no-cover Monday Talent Spotlite that twice a year they line the streets to get a lottery number. Drinks are top-dollar, but usually so are the headliners. **Price:** $12–$15 cover, two-drink minimum. **Subway:** 4, 5, 6 to 86th St.

Dangerfield's Comedy Club MIDTOWN EAST 1118 First Ave. (between 61st and 62nd Sts.) (212) 593-1650 *www.dangerfields.com*. Rodney Dangerfield's 30-year-old club feels like it's in a 1960's time warp with its swingin' red velvet and wood paneling. There's no drink minimum (a rarity in New York), affordable parking and a large menu. The featured acts are pros from the circuit, and Rodney himself performs when in town. **Price:** $12.50–$20 cover. **Subway:** N, R, W to Lexington Ave.; 4, 5, 6 to 59th St.

Gotham Comedy Club FLATIRON/UNION SQUARE 34 W. 22nd St. (between Fifth and Sixth Aves.) (212) 367-9000 *www.gothamcomedyclub.com*. With its comfortably upscale atmosphere, this Flatiron oasis beckons audiences tired of divey or over-crowded clubs. Top-notch comics who regularly emcee jokingly complain that the bathrooms here are nicer than their apartments. The room is only a few years old, but stars and TV comics perform, and there are frequent new talent nights. **Price:** $10–$15 cover, two-drink minimum. **Subway:** F, N, R, V, 1, 9 to 23rd St.

New York Comedy Club FLATIRON/UNION SQUARE 241 E. 24th St. (between Second and Third Aves.) (212) 696-5233 *www.newyorkcomedyclub.com*. It's a small, divey joint that many comedians have played at least once. Despite its size, the club does pull in pros, and on a regular night, expect truly funny performances from younger comedians. **Price:** $7–$10 cover, two-drink minimum. **Subway:** 6 to 23rd St.

Stand-Up New York UPPER WEST SIDE 236 W. 78th St. (between Broadway and Amsterdam Ave.) (212) 595-0850 *www.standupny.com*. What do Denis Leary, Jon Stewart and Comedy Central's Dr. Katz have in common? They all started at this 10-year-old club. While short on atmosphere, it's full of comedy history. There have been surprise visits from stars like Drew Carey, Robin Williams, Dennis Miller and Al Franken. **Price:** $7–$12 cover, two-drink minimum. **Subway:** 1, 9 to 79th St.

Upright Citizens Brigade Theater CHELSEA 307 W. 26th St. (at Eighth Ave.) (212) 366-9176 *www.ucbtheater.com*. The Upright Citizens Brigade, which had a series on Comedy Central, has its own 74-seat theater in Chelsea, where you can find some of the most talented performers around. They supplement their comedic arsenal with equally talented guests, like David Cross of Mr. *Show* and Janeane Garofalo. The Sunday 9:30 show is free. **Price:** $5–$7 cover. **Subway:** F, V, 1, 9 to 23rd St.

Sports & Recreation

Whether you're looking to burn some extra calories or park yourself in the bleachers, hot dog in hand, you'll find that New York is a great sports town.

For those who want to be part of the action, there are plenty of places to play throughout the city. The Parks Department alone manages hundreds of playgrounds, playing fields and tennis courts; dozens of swimming pools and recreation centers; plus golf courses, ice rinks, stadiums and zoos. (The department's Web site, *www.nycparks.com*, is extremely useful, with information on facilities and activities throughout the year.)

SPORTS & ACTIVITIES
Basketball

Pick-up, playground basketball is one of New York's great traditions. NBA stars like Stephon Marbury have honed their games on the city's blacktop courts, as have legends of more local renown, such as Earl "The Goat" Manigault and Joe "The Destroyer" Hammond.

If it's sunny, you'll find pick-up games at many city parks and playgrounds. Some of the best full-court game sites include **Riverside Park** (courts can be found at 76th, 96th and 110th Sts.), **Riverbank State Park** (Riverside Drive and 145th St.), **Central Park** (just north of the Great Lawn), **Asphalt Green** (York Ave. between 91st and 92nd Sts.), the **96th Street Playground** (96th St. between First Ave. and the FDR Dr.), and the courts at **37th Street and Second Avenue.** Just show up and ask, "Who's got winners?"

The **West 4th Street courts** (at Sixth Ave.) have been seen in more basketball-related commercials than Michael Jordan. It's always a mob scene, making it all but impossible to just walk on. Nevertheless, these courts host frequent tournaments that feature some of the city's best street talent. You may get lucky and spot a former NBA star posting up hapless opponents.

In the winter or at night, it's tougher to find a pick-up game. Your best bet is **Basketball City,** which offers six hardwood courts at 24th Street and West Street (West Side Highway) and allows walk-ins (212-924-4040, *www.basketballcity.com*). It's open Monday to Friday, 9 A.M. to 3 P.M., with a changing schedule on weekends; call to check availability and rates before going. There's also the **Field House at Chelsea Piers** (*see* "Chelsea Piers" *later in this chapter*).

Three of the city's **YMCAs** (*www.ymcanyc.org*) offer basketball, but call ahead for the schedule at each facility before showing up, as games are only scheduled on occasional nights, varying from location to location. Day passes range from $10 to $20. There's the **West Side YMCA** (5 W. 63rd St. off Central Park West; 212-787-1301), which has a decent full-length floor as well as a second, smaller

325

court; the **Vanderbilt YMCA,** which has a smaller court (47th St. between Second and Third Aves., 212-756-9600); and the **Harlem YMCA** (180 W. 135th St., 212-281-4100).

Biking

Intrepid New Yorkers bike in city traffic all the time, but you have to be alert and daring to try. If you're visiting, and you're not used to maniacal local drivers, play it safe and stick to biking in the parks.

The **Central Park Drive loop** is 6.1 miles long; this road is closed to cars 10 A.M. to 4 P.M., and, in summer, from 7 P.M. to dusk. Even when cars are permitted, there is a multi-use lane for runners, bikers and in-line skaters.

There's also a beautiful **paved multi-use recreational path** that extends along the west side of Manhattan. It parallels the Hudson River from Battery Park City up to 125th Street, then detours along St. Nicholas Avenue before returning to the river at the George Washington Bridge. More adventurous bikers can follow the bike lane over the bridge for a challenging ride along New Jersey's Palisades.

Organizations and Tours

Bike New York 891 Amsterdam Ave. (at 103rd St.) (212) 932-2300 *www.bikenewyork.org.* This 42-mile, five-borough tour of New York City takes place each year in early May. The ride begins at Battery Park and then winds its way through the Bronx, Queens and Brooklyn before it ends at Fort Wadsworth in Staten Island. There are plenty of rest stops, and the route is entirely traffic-free. Register well in advance.

The Fast and Fabulous Cycling Club *www.fastnfab.org.* Fast and Fab is a lesbian and gay bike club that sponsors regular rides. Check the calendar on the amusing Web site, and call the ride leader if you'd like to join in.

Five Borough Bicycle Club (212) 932-2300 *www.5bbc.org.* For more than a decade, this friendly bike club has been organizing free day rides in the city, and excursions farther afield—cruising to nearby beaches, the Hudson River Valley, and the Berkshires. Yearly membership fees are $15; there's a surcharge for longer trips.

Time's Up! (212) 802-8222 *www.times-up.org.* Activist in spirit, Time's Up! sponsors a number of free bicycle and in-line skate tours that challenge the traffic-centered nature of New York City. The monthly "Critical Mass" ride is an attempt to defy the dominance of motor vehicles and assert equal rights to the road. On the other hand, many of the club-sponsored rides have no political aim at all: they're simply fun and even educational. Check the Web site for a calendar of rides.

Bicycle Rentals

There are a number of rental shops around the city, most charging around $7.50 per hour, or $25–$30 per day for a decent set of wheels. You'll usually need to leave a credit-card deposit to rent.

Among the reputable choices are **Eddie's Bicycle Shop,** 490 Amsterdam Ave. (between 83rd and 84th Sts.; 212-580-2011), conveniently located near Central Park; **Larry and Jeff's Bicycles Plus,** 1690 Second Ave. (between 87th and 88th Sts., 212-722-2201); and and **Toga Bike Shop,** 110 West End Ave. (at 64th St., 212-799-9625; daily rentals only—no hourly rates). **Metro Bicycle Stores** has six locations around the city: 332 E. 14th St. (between First and Second Aves., 212-228-4344); 546 Sixth Ave. (at 15th St., 212-255-5100); 417 Canal St. (212-334-8000); 231 W. 96th St. (between Broadway and Amsterdam Ave., 212-663-7531); 360 W. 47th St. (at Ninth Ave., 212-581-4500); and 1311 Lexington Ave. (at 88th St., 212-427-4450).

In the heart of Central Park, **Loeb Boathouse,** near 74th St. and Park Drive North (212-517-2233), offers three-speed, 10-speed and tandem bikes for rent, for $10 to $20 per hour.

Billiards/Pool

At most of the pool halls listed below, you can expect to pay about $7 to $12 per player, per hour.

Amsterdam Billiard Club 344 Amsterdam Ave. (at 77th St.) (212) 496-8180. Other location: 210 E. 86th St. (between Second and Third Aves. (212) 570-4545. Upscale but not obnoxiously so. You'll find plentiful, well-kept tables, a full bar and amiable waitress service. **Subway:** West Side: 1, 9 to 79th St. East Side: 4, 5, 6 to 86th St.

Billiard Club 220 W. 19th St. (between Seventh and Eighth Aves.) (212) 206-7665. Head here for an intimate game of pool in a somewhat clubby environment, with its polished pine floor, low-key atmosphere and dark wood paneling. The 42 tables are spread out over two levels. **Subway:** 1, 9 to 18th St.

Corner Billiards 85 Fourth Ave. (at 11th St.) (212) 995-1314. Corner Billiards is your best bet in the Village. The 28 Brunswick Gold Crown Tables, a café, a microbrewery and waitress service all conspire to make this a civilized experience. **Subway:** L, N, Q, R, W, 4, 5, 6 to 14th St.

Fat Cat Billiards 75 Christopher St. (between Seventh Ave. South and Bleecker St.) (212) 675-6056. A unique, black-light-illuminated, underground pool hall in the heart of the West Village, Fat Cat is also a bargain at $3.75 per hour. **Subway:** 1, 9 to Christopher St.

Slate 54 W. 21st St. (between Fifth and Sixth Aves.) (212) 989-0096. Slate is an upscale billiards hall and restaurant with an impeccable trendy pedigree—it was featured in *Sex and the City*. Visitors can play on one of the 34 top-quality pool tables (billiards and snooker tables also available). Expect a DJ, upscale drinks, and a crowd of beautiful people. **Subway:** F, N, R, V, 1, 9 to 23rd St.

SoHo Billiard Sport Center 56 E. Houston St. (between Mulberry and Mott Sts.) (212) 925-3753. Brightly lit and pleasantly spacious, this street-level pool hall has 28 tables and a young downtown crowd. **Subway:** F, S, V to Broadway-Lafayette St.; 6 to Bleecker St.; N, R to Prince St.

128 Billiards 128 Elizabeth St. (between Grand and Broome Sts.) (212) 925-8219. If you tire of bar-hopping in the trendy Lower East Side, pop into 128 Billiards for a game on one of their 15 tables. Before 5 P.M.: $6 per hour for the first player, $3 for each additional player. After 5 P.M.: $8 per hour for the first player, $4 for each additional player. **Subway:** F to Delancey St., D to Grand St.

Boating

Downtown Boathouse West St. at Pier 26 (between Chambers and Canal Sts.) and Pier 64 (at the end of W. 24th St.) (646) 613-0375 for general info, (646) 613-0740 for daily status, *www.downtownboathouse.org*. Mid-May through mid-October, the Downtown Boathouse offers free kayaking between two piers on the Hudson River. A staff of volunteers will outfit you with a life jacket and a boat and give you some basic instruction. Once you've got a little experience under your belt, you can join them for longer kayaking trips. All trips are free, and offered on a first-come, first-served basis. **Subway:** 1, 9 to Canal St.; A, C, E to 23rd St.

Floating the Apple Hudson River (at 44th St.) (212) 564–5412 *www.floatingtheapple.org*. The aim of this club is to make the waters of New York City more accessible to boating enthusiasts. They offer a series of weekly events in Manhattan, Brooklyn and the Bronx that encourage use of the area's waterways and harbor by water-sports aficionados. The Manhattan activities originate at Pier 40 (Hudson River at Houston St.) and include youth and adult rowing programs. The club also sponsors various sailing and swimming events, including the Great Hudson River Swim from the Marina at 79th Street to Chelsea Piers at 23rd Street.

Loeb Boathouse Central Park Lake (near 74th St. and East Drive) (212) 517-2233. For a relaxing and romantic afternoon, rent a rowboat and ply the waters of one of Central Park's most scenic areas. Boats are available year-round, weather permitting. Rowboats rent for $10 for the first hour, $2.50 every 15 minutes thereafter. A $30 deposit is required, and reservations are accepted. You can also book gondola rides here. **Subway:** 6 to 77th St.; A, B, C, D to 72nd St.

Prospect Park Brooklyn (718) 282-7789. Get some exercise and a different view of the park by touring the Lullwater and the Lake on a pedal boat. A great way to spend a lazy summer afternoon. **Subway:** Q to Prospect Park or Parkside Ave.

Bowling

Bowlmor Lanes 110 University Pl. (between 12th and 13th Sts.) (212) 255-8188 *www.bowlmor.com*. It's disco bowling! Bowlmor is an authentically retro bowling alley that's been around since 1938. But it now draws a hipster crowd, with Day-Glo pins, a DJ and the occasional celebrity sighting on the lanes. Two floors of lanes and a large bar area keep the party going till 4 A.M. on weekends and Mondays. Expect to wait for a lane. Prices are $7.25 per person per game on weeknights, $7.95 on weekends. On the building's rooftop is **Pres-**

sure, a chic lounge with a martini menu, movie screens, dozens of pool tables and a fabulous Austin Powers décor. **Subway:** L, N, Q, R, W, 4, 5, 6 to 14th St.

Chelsea Piers *(See box "Chelsea Piers" in this chapter.)*

Leisure Time Bowling 625 Eighth Ave., 2nd Fl. (at Port Authority Bus Terminal) (212) 268-6909. When Leisure Time opened its modern 30 lanes a few years ago on the second floor of the Port Authority Bus Terminal, it seemed just a wee bit out of place. Now the alley is more popular than ever, with people of all ages trying to knock down a few on the lanes. Waits can be over two hours on weekends and when the weather is bad. **Subway:** A, C, E, N, R, Q, W, 1, 2, 3, 7, 9 to 42nd St.

Golf

Surprisingly, New York City offers a number of excellent golf courses, in addition to other golf resources such as driving ranges and instruction. Listed below are some of the most noteworthy and accessible of the area links. But beware: play on weekends is notoriously slow, so try to schedule your outing between Monday and Friday, preferably early in the week.

Greens fees vary from course to course, but here's a general guideline for weekends: $10 for nine holes of early-morning play (where offered); $35 for a full round before 5 P.M.; $16 for twilight rounds. Weekdays: $29 for a full round before 5 P.M.; $15 for twilight rounds; on weekdays only, there are also special discounts for senior citizens and juniors under age 18. Prices for non-residents are $8 more per round. Pull-carts rent for $4.50 with a $10 deposit, refundable at the end of play; motorized carts are $14.50 per player.

To reserve **tee times** for most of the New York City-area courses below, call **New York Golf** at (718) 225-4653. There's a $2 reservation fee per player.

Bronx

Mosholu Golf Course 3700 Jerome Ave., Bronx (718) 655-9164. Narrowly avoiding demolition last year, Mosholu is a classic inner-city course, with tenements rising above the many trees to provide a uniquely urban backdrop. Built in 1904, it is one of the oldest in the city. Nine holes were lost some years ago to the addition of parkways to the area, but it is a difficult course nonetheless: the tree-lined fairways are narrow, the medium-sized greens are fast, and there are several blind fairways in the design. Easy to reach via public transportation. **Reservations:** Two days in advance. **Subway:** 4 to Woodlawn (last stop). **Directions by car:** Major Deegan Expy. to exit 13.

Pelham Bay/Split Rock 870 Shore Rd., Bronx (718) 885-1258. Pelham Bay Park offers two excellent 18-hole courses in a bucolic setting, where pheasant, wild turkey and deer might cross your path (a red-tailed hawk nests near the 10th green on Split Rock). The Pelham Bay Course offers a links-style design, and it the easier of the two. Its signature hole is no. 9, a 433-yard par 4, requiring a shot to an extremely undulating green that is well bunkered. The Split Rock Course is more difficult because it is very wooded and has tight fairways. Water comes into play on four holes, and the terrain is rolling. The signature hole on the Split Rock Course is no. 9, a 392-yard par 4, requiring an approach shot to a green protected by what may be America's oldest living white oak tree. (Note that Split Rock will be closed in 2005 for a much-needed $14 million facelift.) **Reservations:** 10 days in advance. **Subway:** 6 to Pelham Bay Park; W-45 or M-45 bus or cab to course (as this is quite a long trip, driving is preferable). **Directions by car:** FDR Dr. to Triborough Bridge, exit toward Bronx; take 95 going North (New England Thruway); get off at Exit 8B; the course is one mile away—look for the course entrance off Shore Rd. Or take Hutchinson River Pway. to Orchard Beach/City Island.

Van Cortlandt Golf Course Van Cortlandt Park S. and Bailey Ave., Bronx (718) 543-4595. The nation's oldest public course, designed by Tom Bendelow and built in 1885. The course is well maintained, and there is a nice mix of long par 5s and short par 4s, with a few difficult par 3s. While you might drive the green on no. 6, a 292-yard par 4, watch out for no. 2, the signature 620-yard par 5 and the par 3 no. 13 that requires a shot over water to a large, undulating green. The final four holes are extremely hilly and offer a challenging end to this scenic course. In 2001 a new irrigation system was installed, vastly improving conditions on a course that sees over 63,000 rounds played per year. In addition, water hazards and sand bunkers were added to make the course more challenging. Van Cortlandt also has the distinction of being the easiest course to reach by subway from Midtown Manhattan: the 1 and 9 trains from 34th St. should get you to the course in less than an hour. **Reservations:** 10 days in advance. **Subway:** 1, 9 to 242 St.–Van Cortlandt Park (last stop); walk east 5 minutes to clubhouse. **Directions by car:** Major Deegan Expy. to W. 230th St.

Brooklyn

Dyker Beach Seventh Ave. and 86th St., Brooklyn (718) 836-9722. This is perhaps the ultimate inner-city golfing experience; the sounds of the city usually follow you along the fairway. The course has undergone a dramatic renaissance, and is now one of the best maintained in the city, despite the over 80,000 rounds played here each year. **Reservations:** Seven days in advance. **Subway:** R to 86th St.; walk along 86th Street to course or take B-64 bus or cab. **Directions by car:** Brooklyn-Queens Expy. (BQE) or Belt Pkwy. to Verrazano Bridge approach to 86th St. exit; left on 86th St.

Marine Park Golf Course 2880 Flatbush Ave., Brooklyn (718) 338-7149. Built in 1964, Marine Park was designed by the legendary Robert Trent Jones Sr., and its large and undulating greens are, according to regulars, the finest in the city. The signature hole is no. 15, a 467-yard par 4, featuring a well-bunkered fairway and requiring a downhill approach shot to a sloping green. **Reservations:** Seven days in advance. **Subway:** 2, 5 to Flatbush Ave.; then Q-35 Green bus to course. **Directions by car:** Belt Pkwy. to exit 11N (Flatbush Ave.), drive to the second traffic signal; course entrance is on the left.

Queens

Douglaston Golf Course 6320 Marathon Pkwy. (at Commonwealth Blvd.),

Queens (718) 428-1617. This short course will challenge you with narrow fairways, and its hilly nature will often result in uneven lies. While there is only one water hazard on the course, the many blind shots required make Douglaston relatively difficult. The course's signature hole is no. 18, a 550-yard par 5, requiring an approach shot to a large, well-bunkered green. **Reservations:** 10 days in advance. **Directions by car:** Long Island Expy. east to Douglaston Pkwy.; turn left, continue to 61st Ave. and make a left; turn right on Marathon; drive two blocks and course will be on the right. Or take the Grand Central Pkwy. to the Little Neck Pkwy., then take exit 32 to the course.

Kissena Park Golf Course 164–15 Booth Memorial Ave., Flushing, Queens (718) 939-4594. This is a short course (the back tees play only 4,727 yards), but the hilly terrain makes it a rather difficult one. According to the course pro, it will require every club in your bag. **Reservations:** Seven days in advance. **Subway:** 7 to Main St.– Flushing or E to Parsons Blvd.; cab from station. **Directions by car:** Long Island Expy. east to Exit 24 (Kissena Blvd.); take the service road to 164th St., turn left, go to the traffic light (Booth Memorial Ave.); turn right. You'll see the course from there.

Staten Island

La Tourette Golf Course 1001 Richmond Hill Rd., Staten Island (718) 351-1889. Once a private course, this verdant oasis from the city offers open, rolling fairways, plenty of bunkers and countless trees. The 1836 Greek-revival clubhouse is a landmark itself, and this venerable course is home to the annual New York City Amateur tournament. It is the only city course that offers a driving range on the property. **Reservations:** 10 days in advance. **Directions by car:** Brooklyn-Queens Expy. (BQE) to Belt Pkwy. to Verrazano Bridge to the Bradley Ave. exit; at second traffic signal (Wooley Ave.), turn left and proceed past the next five traffic signals; left on Richmond Hill Rd.

Silver Lake Park 915 Victory Blvd. (near Forest Ave.), Staten Island (718) 447-5686. This course is well manicured and located within a tight wooded area. The design includes several sloping, tight fairways, two water hazards and many trees lining the fairways. **Reservations:** 11 days in advance. **Directions by car:** Brooklyn-Queens Expy. (BQE) to Belt Pkwy. to Verrazano Bridge; stay on the Staten Island Expy., get off at the Clove Rd.-Victory Blvd. exit, and turn right on Clove Rd.; proceed on to Victory Blvd., travel one mile, and the course is on the left.

South Shore Golf Course 200 Huguenot Ave., Staten Island (718) 984-0101. This very picturesque course was built on hilly terrain and seems to have been cut out of the forest itself. Designed by Alfred H. Tull in 1927, the course challenges golfers with narrow fairways and large, fast greens. **Reservations:** 11 days in advance. **Directions by car:** Brooklyn-Queens Expy. (BQE) to Belt Pkwy. to Verrazano Bridge; stay on the Staten Island Expy., get off at exit 5-Rte. 440 South/West Shore Expy. exit; take Rte. 440 south to exit 4; make a left onto Arthur Kill Rd.; stay straight to Huguenot Ave.

Chelsea Piers

New York boasts the mother of all sports complexes, Chelsea Piers (extending from 17th to 23rd Streets on the Hudson River). This gargantuan facility offers everything from basketball and batting cages to golf and gymnastics. Once the city's premier passenger terminal, it is a site steeped in history; this was the intended destination of the *Titanic* (instead, the *Carpathia* arrived with the "unsinkable" ship's 675 survivors on April 20, 1912). There may be more scenic playing fields in New York, but nowhere else will you find so many activities in one location. Call (212) 336-6666 for general information, or check out *www.chelseapiers.com*.

Baseball/Softball Field House (212) 336-6500. There are four batting cages (two for righties, one for lefties, and another that serves both). Try hitting major-league heat in the fast-pitch cage, where the speed is set to about 90 mph. 10 pitches for $1.

Basketball Field House (212) 336-6500. There are two hardwood courts in the Field House. Walk-ons are welcome, but call ahead for available hours, since there is frequent league play. The cost is $7 per hour. There are also three courts in the main Sports Center, where day passes are available and pick-up sessions are available.

Bowling Chelsea Piers Bowl (212) 835-BOWL. This facility has 40 high-tech lanes. Bowl a few frames anytime, or come late on a weekend night for "Extreme Bowling," complete with Day-Glo pins and a DJ. Prices are $7 per person per game ($8 for Extreme Bowling), $4.50 for shoe rental.

Dance Field House (212) 336-6500. The 1,400-square-foot air-conditioned dance studio hosts classes in jazz, tap and modern dance.

Golf Golf Club at Chelsea Piers (212) 336-6400. This multitiered, year-round facility has to be seen to be believed. Offering 52 heated stalls and an automatic tee-up system, the driving range is a net-enclosed, artificial turf fairway stretching 200 yards out into the Hudson River. There is also a 1,000-square-foot putting area, and you can call ahead to rent a sand bunker for practice. Lessons are available at the Golf Academy, where PGA pros offer video analysis of your swing. Rates are $15 minimum for 60 balls (89 in off-peak hours); club rentals are available.

Gymnastics Field House (212) 336-6500. With 23,000 square feet of floor space, Chelsea Piers Gymnastics is the city's largest and best-equipped gymnastics training center and the only one sanctioned by USA Gymnastics for competitions. Call for class schedule and walk-on hours.

Health Club Sports Center (212) 336-6000. The 150,000-square-foot Sports Center offers two fitness studios with over 150 sports and fitness classes a week; a huge indoor running track; a 200-meter banked competition track; three basketball/volleyball courts; Manhattan's only indoor sand volleyball court; one of the largest and most challenging rock climbing walls in the world; a six-lane, 25-yard swimming pool; a separate Spinning Room; two outdoor sun decks overlooking the Hudson; extensive cardio- and strength-training areas; a boxing ring and equipment circuit; personal training; and baby-sitting. Once you're spent from all that activity, relax in the café or indulge in a spa treatment (see below). You deserve it. Day passes for non-members are a hefty $50 per day ($25 if you're with a member).

Ice Hockey/Ice Skating Sky Rink (212) 336-6100. Sky Rink, a twin-rink facility on Pier 61, operates 24/7, welcoming skaters of all ages and ability levels for recreational skating, figure skating lessons, and pick-up and league hockey. There's a complicated daily schedule ruling ice times for each activity, so call ahead or check the Web site for details. It's $22 for 80 minutes of freestyle ice skating or pick-up ice hockey (goalies play for free).

In-line Skating/Roller Hockey/Skateboarding Roller Rink (212) 336-6200. Open skating time is available on both the outdoor (weather permitting) and indoor roller rinks. Admission for a free-skate session is $7 for adults, $6 for kids; skates and protective gear can be rented. In addition to hosting numerous leagues and clinics, Chelsea Piers also offers open roller hockey on the weekends. Cost is $15 for 1 1/2 hours of pick-up play. There's also a newly expanded outdoor **Extreme Park,** offering challenging ramps, rails and launch boxes for BMX bikers, skateboarders and daring in-line skaters. A session in Extreme Park is $12.50; protective-gear rental, but no skate rental, is available.

Rock Climbing Field House (212) 336-6500. The 30-foot-high artificial rock surface offers a variety of routes that challenge climbers of all skill levels. Cost is $20 per person. Check ahead for available times. There's also a climbing wall at the Sports Center.

Soccer/Lacrosse Field House (212) 336-6500. This facility has two state-of-the-art indoor playing fields built specifically for indoor soccer and lacrosse. Measuring 55-by-110 feet, the climate-controlled, artificial turf fields are surrounded by Plexiglas boards, and equipped with goals, nets and electronic scoreboards.

Spa Origins Feel-Good Spa (212) 336-6780. Treat yourself to a massage, a facial, a manicure or a body wrap. For a menu of treatments and prices, check *www.origins.com/spa/spa-newyork.tmpl.*

General Information: Dining: There are several casual dining choices, from snack bars to the Chelsea Brewing Company (212) 336-6440. **Parking:** Available at Pier 62. **Subway:** C, E, F, V, 1, 9 to 23rd St.

Gyms & Health Clubs

There are hundreds of health clubs around the city, and most offer one-day passes to visitors. You'll save time and money if your bring your own lock, though most will rent you one and nearly all (even the Y's) will provide a towel. Make sure to bring a picture ID, too, as most require one for their records.

Health Clubs

Asphalt Green between 90th and 92nd Sts. at York Ave. (212) 369-8890 *www.asphaltgreen.org*. This nonprofit organization stands out from other gyms with its full-size Astroturf soccer field, outdoor track and Olympic-size pool. There's a full fitness center with cardio equipment and weights, plus a busy schedule of fitness classes. Day passes are $20 for the pool only, $25 for the pool and fitness center. **Subway:** 4, 5, 6 to 86th St.

Crunch Fitness *www.crunch.com*. This chain of gyms has a hip urban sensibility. There are 10 locations in Manhattan, well-equipped with cardio and weight-training equipment and featuring an array of classes (everything from serious yoga instruction to cardio strip-tease and karaoke spinning). A day pass at any of Crunch's gyms is $24.

Equinox Fitness (212) 724-6342 *www.equinoxfitness.com*. There are 13 high-end Equinox locations in Manhattan, most offering a juice bar and an athletic clothing store in addition to state-of-the-art fitness equipment. Off-peak day passes (2 P.M.–5 P.M. and after 9 P.M.) are $25, peak $35.

New York Sports Club (800) 796-NYSC for nearest location. *www.nysc.com*. This upscale chain has 16 Manhattan locations, with high-quality equipment and a wide variety of classes. Two of the Midtown locations feature pools. Day passes are $25.

Synergy Fitness *www.synergyfitclubs.com*. Synergy, a smaller chain known for their lower membership prices and neighborhood-gym feel, offers 16 clubs in the NY metropolitan area, six of which are in Manhattan. Day passes are the cheapest in town at $20.

YMCAs

New York City's YMCAs offer an affordable alternative to the health club scene, though day passes tend to be comparably priced. The gyms can often be quite crowded, but equipment is usually top-of-the-line. Check *www.ymcanyc.org* for details on programs, facilities and membership.

Harlem YMCA 180 W. 135th St. (between Lenox Ave. and Adam Clayton Powell Jr. Blvd.) (212) 281-4100. **Day pass:** $12. **Subway:** 2, 3 to 135th St.

Vanderbilt YMCA 224 E. 47th St. (between Second and Third Aves.) (212) 756-9600. **Day pass:** $25. **Subway:** 6 to 51st St.

West Side YMCA 5 W. 63rd St. (between Broadway and Central Park West) (212) 875-4100. **Day pass:** $25. **Subway:** A, B, C, D, 1, 9 to 59th St..

Horseback Riding

Claremont Riding Academy 175 W. 89th St. (between Amsterdam and Columbus Aves.) (212) 724-5100. Built in 1892, Claremont is the oldest continuously operating stable in the country. Experienced equestrians (who can walk, trot and canter comfortably) can hire horses by the hour to ride on the six miles of bridle paths in nearby Central Park. Lessons are available and there is an indoor arena for beginners. **Price:** $45 per hour. **Subway:** 1, 9 to 86th St.

Kensington Stables 51 Caton Pl., Brooklyn (718) 972-4588 *www.kensington-stables.com*. Horses can be hired here for leisurely guided rides on Prospect Park's trails. Lessons are also available. **Price:** $25 per hour. **Subway:** F to Ft. Hamilton Pkwy.

Ice Skating

Central Park—Lasker Rink Central Park at 106th St. (212) 534-7639. Located just below the scenic Harlem Meer, Lasker Rink is open for ice skating during the winter season. (It serves as Central Park's only swimming pool in the summer months.) **Subway:** 6 to E. 103rd St.; B, C to W. 103rd St.

Central Park—Wollman Memorial Rink Enter park at Sixth Ave. and Central Park South (212) 439-6900 *www.wollmanskatingrink.com*. The 33,000-square-foot Wollman Rink offers a spacious skating area and an unparalleled view of the Duck Pond framed by landmark buildings like the Plaza Hotel. **Admission:** $7.50 adults ($8 on weekends); $3.75 children under 12 and seniors. Skate rental is $3.75. **Subway:** N, R, W to Fifth Ave.

Chelsea Piers *(See box "Chelsea Piers" in this chapter.)*

Prospect Park—Wollman Rink Near the Lincoln Rd. entrance of Prospect Park (718) 287-6431. Kate Wollman Center and Rink is open for ice skating from December until March. (You can rent pedal boats here in spring and summer.) An especially nice feature of this rink is the early-bird session from 8:30–10:30 A.M. on weekdays. If you're an avid skater who hates the crowds at most public rinks, this is the place for you. **Admission:** $4. Skate rental is $3.50. **Subway:** Q to Parkside Ave.

Rink at Rockefeller Plaza 601 Fifth Ave. (between 49th and 50th Sts.) (212) 332-7654 *www.rockefellercenter.com*. Throughout the holiday season, music plays as skaters waltz around the rink under the glow of the awe-inspiring Rockefeller Center Christmas tree. Sure, the rink is cramped and crowded, but the thrill of skating at the epicenter of the city's holiday spirit is unrivaled. Visit earlier or later in the season for a less crowded experience. Call ahead for available dates and times. **Admission:** $14; $10 children under 12 (admission varies, so call ahead). Skate rental is $6. **Subway:** B, D, F, S, V to 47th-50th St.–Rockefeller Center.

In-Line Skating

Popular street-skating spots include "the cube" at Astor Place in the East Village, "the banks" under the Brooklyn Bridge (Manhattan side) and Union Square. Central Park is full of great places to skate in addition to Wollman Rink (listed below); try the main drives throughout the park, the open plaza at the north end of the Mall and the closed driveway west of the Mall. Skating in the Riverside Park grounds near 108th Street, which is permitted in the warmer months, requires a helmet, signing of a waiver and a $3 fee. Wrist and kneepads are essential, and elbow pads are recommended (212-408-0239 for info).

To rent skates, try **Blades Board & Skate** (*www.blades.com*), with locations at 160 E. 86th St. (between Third and Lexington Aves., 212- 996-1644); 120 W. 72nd St. (between Amsterdam and Columbus Aves., 212- 787-3911); and three other outlets around town. (*See also* "Chelsea Piers" *in this chapter.*)

Central Park—Wollman Memorial Rink Enter park at Sixth Ave. and Central Park South (212) 439-6100. In summer, Rollerblades replace ice skates at Wollman Rink. The rink also offers classes and guided skating tours around the park. Compared to the skating lanes in the park, the rink is fairly uncrowded, leaving room for New Yorkers to strut their stuff. Rollerblades and safety equipment (state law requires children 14 and under to wear helmets and pads) can be rented for rink use ($6) or for park use ($15 with a $100 deposit). **Admission:** $7.50 adults; $3.75 children and seniors. **Subway:** N, R, W to Fifth Ave.

Empire Skate Club of New York (212) 774-1774 *www.empireskate.org*. The Empire Skate Club is a nonprofit organization of in-line skaters dedicated to having fun and improving the skating environment in New York. The club organizes regular social skates and get-togethers in the city, trips around the eastern seaboard and farther afield, clinics, seminars, parties and skate advocacy. A year's membership is $25.

Running

While out-of-towners may think of New York City as a concrete jungle with few safe places to run, there are actually many excellent—even tree-lined and relatively bucolic—routes right in Manhattan. **East River Park** is a favorite of those living downtown, offering a scenic course that stretches along the river just across from downtown Brooklyn. The **Battery Park Promenade** offers a shady, paved path for joggers, bikers and in-line skaters, who enjoy water views while they work out. This promenade is now paved through **Hudson River Park,** all the way up the West Side of Manhattan, through Midtown, Riverside Park and all the way up to the George Washington Bridge. For runners who prefer the knee-saving qualities of a dirt path, the lower promenade at Riverside Park offers a run from 98th to 120th Street that is a little over a mile in length.

But the crown jewel of the NYC runner's kingdom is **Central Park,** unofficial home of the **New York Road Runners Club** (212-860-4455, *www.nyrrc.org*). The club sponsors many races throughout the year, usually along the Park's main Loop, the most famous race being the New York City Marathon, finishing at Tavern on the Green on the West Side. You don't have to be a member to run in club-spon-sored events (though there's usually a small fee); check *www.nyrrc.org* to find out about upcoming races.

The length of the entire **Central Park Loop**—the road that follows a circular route through the interior of the park—is 6.1 miles. This road is closed to cars 10 A.M.–4 P.M., and then again 7 P.M.–dusk. During the hours when vehicular traffic is permitted, you can run in the multi-use lane for runners, bikers and in-line skaters, though it is unprotected. Good short courses include the 3.5-mile route used by Chase's Corporate Challenge race, which begins at the Puppet Theater (roughly W. 70th St.), follows the Loop to the 102nd Street transverse, rejoins the Loop on the east side, and ends at the Rumsey Playground (where SummerStage events are held) at about East 70th Street. A popular 5K course (3.1 miles) begins at the East Drive (Loop) and 86th Street, proceeds north and across the 102nd Street transverse, back onto the Drive and finishes at the Engineer's Gate (90th St. and Fifth Ave.). The **Reservoir** run is one of the most popular courses in the city. The cinder track offers a level run of 1.6 miles and offers great views of the Man-hattan skyline at virtually every step. In spring it is especially pleasant as flowering trees line the eastern side of the course. Enter the park at 86th Street on the east or west side. Don't run in the park at night.

The best spot for a run in Brooklyn is definitely **Prospect Park.** There is a dirt path, roughly three miles, on the inside of the roadway (3.5 miles) circling the park grounds, along with other isolated trails. The **Prospect Park Track Club** has regu-lar workouts (check *www.pptc.org* for schedules); nonmembers are welcome.

Swimming

(See section "Gyms & Health Clubs" for YMCAs and private gyms with pools.)

Public Pools

Asphalt Green between 90th and 92nd Sts. at York Ave. (212) 369-8890 *www.asphaltgreen.org*. Asphalt Green has one of the biggest and newest public pools in the city, complete with a hydraulic floor that adjusts the water depth for children and those learning to swim. The 50-by-20-meter indoor pool is heated to an even 80 degrees. While nonmembers can purchase a day pass to swim, some lap-swimming lanes are always reserved for members only. Day passes are $20 to use the pool only, $25 to use the pool and other facilities. **Sub-way:** 4, 5, 6 to 86th St.

Lasker Pool Central Park, East Drive and 106th St. During the summer months, Lasker is open for community swimming, racing and lessons. At less than four feet deep, the pool is ideal for kids. You can't beat the cost, either—it's totally free. Swimmers must wear a swimsuit (no denim shorts or T-shirts). Lockers are available, but bring your own lock. **Subway:** 6 to E. 103rd St.; B, C to W. 103rd St.

Riverbank State Park Pool 679 Riverside Dr. (at 145th St.) (212) 694-3666. How's this for a funky location? Here's a pool built atop a sewage treat-ment center on the Hudson. It's not as grim as it sounds: the park is very attractive, perched 69 feet above the river, and offers many other sports in addition to swimming. The view along the river on a clear day is quite spectacular. There's an indoor Olympic-size pool, plus an outdoor lap pool and wading pool.

Municipal Pools

New York City's municipal pools require a year's membership, but it's only $25 and can be paid on the spot by personal check or money order. If you're planning on returning to the Big Apple in the next 12 months, this might be your best option.

East 54th St. Recreation Center 348 E. 54th St. (212) 397-3154 Midtown

59th Street Recreation Center 533 W. 59th St. (212) 397-3166 West Side

Asser Levy Park 23rd St. and Asser Levy Pl. (212) 447-2020 Gramercy Park

Carmine Street Recreation Center 1 Clarkson St. (212) 242-5228 Greenwich Village

Dry Dock Swimming Pool 408 E. 10th St. (212) 677-4481 Alphabet City

Hamilton Fish Recreation Center Pool 128 Pitt St. at Houston St. (212) 387-7687 Downtown

John Jay Swimming Pool 77th St. and Cherokee Pl., east of York Ave. (212) 794-6566 Upper East Side

Lenox Hill Neighborhood House 331 E. 70th St. (212) 744-5022 Upper East Side

Tennis

Public Courts

The 24 Har-tru public courts at **Central Park's** venerable Tennis Center (mid-park, 94th-96th Sts.) are among the nicest in the city, but half are booked in advance, and the rest are usually reserved on a first-come, first-served basis early each morning. Plus, you have to put up with a lot of attitude on the part of regulars who treat the Center as their own private club. But if you can handle these obstacles, playing amidst the trees of the park is a real treat. The Center, open April through November, also offers a pro shop, a locker room with showers, and a snack bar. Call (212) 360-8131 for information.

Other less crowded courts include those at **Riverside Park,** which boasts beautiful red-clay courts at the western end of 96th Street (no reservations) and recently restored hard-surface courts at 118th Street. A best-kept secret among West Siders: there are also courts just south of the George Washington Bridge in Riverside Park that do not require a permit and are usually free. Enter at 168th or 181st Street. **Riverbank State Park** also offers tennis courts in addition to its spectacular views of the Hudson River. Enter at Riverside Drive and 145th Street. East River Park (East River at Broome St.) also offers 12 hard-surface courts, perhaps the least crowded in Manhattan.

In Brooklyn, **Prospect Park Tennis Center** provides 10 Har-tru courts, located in the Parade Grounds adjacent to the southwest corner of the park, near the Park Circle. From mid-October through the end of April, a bubble structure covers these courts, and a private company rents them by the hour. (Call one day ahead to make reservations.) Also in Brooklyn are the six excellent hard-surface courts at Fort Greene Park. These are among the least used in the city, and, while there is a core group of regulars, it's relatively easy to walk on and play.

Use of all city tennis courts requires either a **season pass** ($100) or a **day pass** ($5), which can be purchased either at the Tennis Center or Paragon Sporting Goods (867 Broadway at 18th St.). Permits are less likely to be checked at the courts at Riverside and 118th and Fort Greene Park. The season is April to November, daily from 7 A.M. till 8 P.M. (light permitting).

Private Courts

Crosstown Tennis Club 14 W. 31st St. (212) 947-5780
www.crosstowntennis.com. The Crosstown facility, just steps from the Empire State Building, offers four Championship DecoTurf tennis courts, each with an 18-foot back-court area and 40-foot ceilings. **Price:** $50–$75 per hour. **Subway:** B, D, F, N, Q, R, S, V to 34th St.

Midtown Tennis Club 341 Eighth Ave. (at 27th St.) (212) 989-8572
www.midtowntennis.com. When it opened in 1965, the Midtown Tennis Club was the first indoor club in Manhattan, and it's still one of the largest and most accessible tennis sites in the city. Air-conditioned, with eight tournament Har-tru courts, and full locker-room facilities, the club offers tennis in a comfortable and relaxed atmosphere. **Price:** $45–$75 per hour indoors; $30–$40 outdoors. **Subway:** 1, 9 to 28th St.; C, E to 23rd St.

USTA National Tennis Center Flushing Meadows–Corona Park, Queens (718) 760-6200 ext. 6213 (ask for the program office) *www.usopen.org*. The USTA National Tennis Center, site of the **U.S. Open,** is the largest public tennis facility in the world, offering nine indoor courts, 18 practice courts and 18 tournament courts. All are open to the public year round except for August and September, during the U.S. Open itself. They reopen for public play one week after the last day of the Open. **Price:** $32–$48 per hour indoors (with off-peak weekday junior and senior rates); $16–$24 outdoors ($8 fee for lights for night play). **Subway:** 7 to Willets Point–Shea Stadium.

BEACHES

When you're in the depths of Manhattan's concrete canyons, it's easy to forget that miles and miles of Atlantic beaches lie beyond the city's wall of skyscrapers. There are city beaches in Brooklyn, Queens and the Bronx, as well as some very accessible spots on Long Island. If the temperature hits 90 degrees on a summer weekend, expect crowds (and that's an understatement). For millions of New Yorkers, the Atlantic provides the only way to beat the heat.

Brooklyn

Coney Island at Surf and Stillwell Aves. (718) 946-1350. *(See section* "Brooklyn" *in chapter* **Exploring New York** *for full entry.)* Have a hot dog at Nathan's, ride the Cyclone, stroll the boardwalk and spread out your towel. Though this is by far the most famous of the Brooklyn beaches, you may also want to try **Brighton Beach** right next door or **Manhattan Beach** just beyond. **Subway:** F, N, Q to Stillwell Ave.–Coney Island.

Bronx

Orchard Beach Long Island Sound (between Park Dr. and Bartow Circle) (718) 885-2275. At the turn of the century, this was a popular bathing spot for the affluent residents of Pelham Manor. A large, luxurious stand of trees skirts the beach, creating a lovely backdrop. Standing on the patio between the two halves of the old bathhouse, you can gaze over the entire expanse of sand, as idyllic as a postcard. **Subway:** 6 to Pelham Bay Park; BX 12 bus to Orchard Beach. **By car:** Hutchinson River Pkwy.; exit at City Island–Orchard Beach.

Queens

Rockaway Beach Beach 1st to Beach 149th Sts. (718) 318-4000. "Rockapulco" has a plain plank boardwalk, a pale arc of fine sand and high-rise condos. That's not to say it's without character. The beautiful old buildings, nearby hotels and ornate subway station have a kind of windswept, sunburned grandeur, and the fact that it's accessible only by bridge gives it the aura of adventure and isolation. **Riis Park,** a beach that is often overcrowded in the summer, is just west; despite the crowds, the sands are gorgeous and it's surprisingly well maintained by the National Park Service. **Subway:** A to Rockaway Park. **Directions by car:** Take Rte. 278 (BQE–Gowanus Expy.) south to Shore Pkwy. (aka Belt Pkwy.) east to Marine Pkwy.–Gil Hodges Bridge; then follow signs for Riis Park.

Long Island

Fire Island (516) 852-5200. Fire Island is a barefoot society, car-free and care-free. A barrier island, it stretches across 32 miles between the end of **Robert Moses State Park** (best bet for day-trippers, since that's the only part of Fire Island that's accessible by car) and Moriches Inlet, where the Hamptons begin. Despite an influx of tourist attention, the island has changed little in the last century. Cedar-shingled cottages are hemmed in by pines and bayberry; everyone gets around by biking and walking. The beach itself, a National Seashore, is gorgeous. **Directions:** From Penn Station, take the Long Island Railroad to Bay Shore, Patchogue or Sayville. Then take a taxi to the ferry docks in any of these towns (total price, $15–$20 round trip).

Jones Beach (516) 785-1600. Jones Beach is the single most popular site in the entire state park system, averaging nearly seven million visitors a year. This is a rollicking beach party, with radios blaring. Elsewhere in the 2,413-acre park, determined joggers, bikers and skaters swoosh along their designated paths. Surf-casters think bluefish, while anglers on the four bay piers are after fluke.

Directions: From Penn Station, take the Long Island Railroad to Freeport. Buses run every half hour from the train station to the beach ($11, includes shuttle bus). By car, take the Long Island Expy. to Meadowbrook Pkwy. south; follow signs for Jones Beach. If you drive, go early; parking lots fill quickly.

Long Beach In recent years, this seaside city has made a remarkable comeback. Smart, new high-rise oceanfront buildings have emerged, and young families, attracted by the soft sands of the Atlantic and the 53-minute commute by train to Manhattan, are moving here in droves. For the weekend visitor, the best reasons to trek to Long Beach are its wonderful sands and its boardwalk. At a little more than two miles in length, the boardwalk is Long Island's longest, featuring a block of stores and eateries. **Directions:** From Penn Station, take the Long Island Railroad to Long Beach ($11 round-trip package).

SPECTATOR SPORTS
Baseball

New York Yankees—Yankee Stadium 161st St. (at River Ave.), Bronx (718) 293-6000 *www.yankees.com*. One of the most storied venues in sports history, Yankee Stadium may be a little worn around the edges, but there's no denying its aura. The original stadium opened in 1923, as 74,200 fans packed the massive three-tiered facility and watched Babe Ruth christen his new home with a towering shot as the Yankees beat their hated rivals, the Boston Red Sox. Because Ruth was such a tremendous draw, Yankee Stadium almost immediately acquired its moniker, "The House that Ruth Built." The park was remodeled and scaled down slightly in the mid-70's, but historic touches remain, including Monument Park and the decorative white colonnade above the outfield. Some of baseball's most legendary names have played at the Stadium, including Ruth, Lou Gehrig, Joe DiMaggio, Yogi Berra and Mickey Mantle, to name but a few. It was here that Gehrig delivered his famous farewell address ("Today I consider myself the luckiest man on the face of the earth"), and here that three perfect games have been hurled (by Don Larsen, David Wells and David Cone). The current team, World Champions in 1996, 1998, 1999 and 2000, is a perennial contender to do it again—just like the "Murderer's Row" squads of the 1920's and 1930's, and the Yankees juggernaut of the 1950's and 1960's. Buy tickets in advance, and take public transportation to the stadium (traffic is a nightmare). Hardcore fans can take **stadium tours;** call (718) 579-4531 or check the Web site for details. **Tickets:** $8–$80; available through Ticketmaster, at *www.yankees.com*, at the stadium or at Yankees Clubhouse stores. **Subway:** 4, B, D to 161st St.—Yankee Stadium.

New York Mets—Shea Stadium 123–01 Roosevelt Ave. (between Grand Central Pkwy. and Van Wyck Expy.), Flushing, Queens (718) 507-6387 *www.mets.com*. While the Yankees have a certain air of invincibility and corporate efficiency, the Mets are your little brother's team. They are more colorful, more melodramatic and more unpredictable than their Bronx counterparts. The Amazin's began in 1962 as lovable losers, when the likes of Marvelous Marv

Throneberry made them the most inept team in the history of the game: 40 wins and a whopping 120 losses. But things soon turned around, as the Mets completed an improbable championship run in 1969, defeating the Orioles four games to one. In 1973 another unlikely late-season run landed them in the World Series, coining the phrase "You gotta believe!" They won their second championship in 1986, breaking hearts all over New England as the Red Sox went down in flames yet again. Though the Mets have recently fallen on hard times, it's always exciting to watch their ups and downs—you gotta believe they've always got one more come-from-behind victory up their sleeves. **Tickets:** $8-$58; available at the stadium, at *www.mets.com*, over the phone from the Mets ticket office or from Mets Clubhouse stores. **Subway:** 7 to Willets Point—Shea Stadium. **Long Island Railroad:** Stops at stadium on game days (from Penn Station, peak $5.50, off-peak $3.75, one way).

Brooklyn Cyclones—Keyspan Park 1904 Surf Ave. (between W. 17th and W. 19th Sts.), Coney Island, Brooklyn (718) 449-8497 *www.brooklyncyclones.net*. "Baseball returns to Brooklyn!" So read the tabloid headlines when the first pitch was thrown at Keyspan Park in 2001. The Cyclones, a Mets minor league affiliate, are the first professional team to play in Brooklyn since the departure of the Dodgers for Los Angeles in 1958, and baseball couldn't ask for a better venue. This gorgeous 7,500-seat ballpark is located on Surf Avenue in legendary Coney Island, offering fans an ocean view and the chance to ride the famed Cyclone roller coaster after the game. **Tickets:** $10. **Subway:** F, N, Q to Stillwell Ave.–Coney Island.

Staten Island Yankees—Richmond County Bank Ballpark 75 Richmond Terrace (718) 720-9265 *www.siyanks.com*. While the Cyclones may get all the press, a Yankees minor league squad has landed in New York City, too, and a new Big Apple rivalry has been born. Also new in 2001, their appealing 6,500-seat stadium offers views of New York Harbor and the Statue of Liberty. **Tickets:** Under $10. **Directions:** 1, 9 subway to South Ferry (or 4, 5 to Bowling Green; N, R to Whitehall); take the Staten Island Ferry across the harbor and exit from the lower deck; the ballpark is on the right.

Basketball

New York Knicks—Madison Square Garden 2 Penn Plaza (at 33rd St. and Seventh Ave.) (212) 465-6727 *www.nba.com/knicks*. Madison Square Garden is home to the Knicks, who were largely defined as Patrick Ewing's team throughout the 1990's. Though they were contenders through much of the last decade, the Knicks have recently become a high-payroll disappointment. The addition of Brooklyn's own Stephon Marbury to the starting lineup created a buzz in early 2004, but more retooling is needed before the franchise can make another serious run. Tickets are obscenely expensive, but with the team's declining fortunes, they've become easier to obtain. **Tickets:** $26.50–$1,500; available through Ticketmaster at (212) 307-7171 or at the Garden box office; for ticket info call (212) 465-JUMP. **Subway:** A, C, E, 1, 2, 3, 9 to 34th St.

New Jersey Nets—Continental Airlines Arena (Meadowlands) 50 Rte. 120 (at Rte. 3), East Rutherford, NJ (201) 935-3900 *www.nba.com/nets*. After grinding away in mediocrity for more than two decades, the Nets came out of nowhere and made it all the way to the NBA finals in 2002 and 2003. Tickets are generally easily available, though this may change if new owner Bruce Ratner is able to realize his dream of bringing the Nets to downtown Brooklyn in 2007. It would be a homecoming of sorts since the Nets called Long Island home when they were part of the old ABA from 1968 to 1976. **Tickets:** $10-$600; available through Ticketmaster online or at (201) 507-8900; for info, call (800) 7NJ-NETS or check the Web site. **Directions:** Bus service for all events at the Meadowlands Sports Complex from Manhattan's Port Authority ($6.50 round trip). By car, take the New Jersey Turnpike to exit 16W to Complex. Or take the Garden State Pkwy. south to exit 153 (153N if you're northbound), Rte. 3 east.

New York Liberty—Madison Square Garden 2 Penn Plaza (at 33rd St. and Seventh Ave.) (212) 564-WNBA *www.wnba/liberty*. The Liberty squad is a bona fide power in the WNBA. And they've built quite a fan base, one that Liberty die-hards proudly describe as noncorporate, unlike the clientele of their male counterparts. Also unlike Knicks games, it's easy to get good seats that won't cost you a second mortgage. **Tickets:** $10–$229.50; available through Ticketmaster at (212) 307-7171, or at the Garden box office. **Subway:** A, C, E, 1, 2, 3, 9 to 34th St.

Boxing

Madison Square Garden 2 Penn Plaza (at 33rd St. and Seventh Ave.) (212) 465-6727 *www.thegarden.com*. Madison Square Garden has a long and storied history of boxing, a tradition that began inside its original 19th-century building in Madison Square at 23rd Street (built in 1879, this roofless arena was also the site of chariot races) and continuing through to its present and fourth location. On March 8, 1971, one of the most anticipated sporting events of the 20th-century took place when Joe Frazier defeated Muhammad Ali in a 15-round decision for the heavyweight title. In a pale imitation of that bout in March 1999, Evander Holyfield battled Lennox Lewis to a draw in a 15-round fight. Your best hope for exciting (and affordable) boxing is the annual **Golden Gloves** tournament (April), in which kids from around the city battle for top honors in all weight divisions. **Tickets:** Available through Ticketmaster at (212) 307-7171, or at the Garden box office. **Subway:** A, C, E, 1, 2, 3, 9 to 34th St.

Church Street Boxing Gym 25 Park Pl. (between Church St. and Broadway) (212) 571-1333 *www.nyboxinggym.com*. This is New York City's premier boxing training facility, with over 10,000 square feet of gym space located in the heart of downtown Manhattan. The well-known gym has showcased many up-and-coming professional boxers, kickboxers and Thai-boxers and has worked on-site with such marquee names as Evander Holyfield, Larry Holmes and Mike Tyson. Call for a fight schedule. **Subway:** 4, 5, 6 to Brooklyn Bridge; 2, 3 to Park Pl.

Cricket

Because of the concentration of recent immigrants from cricket-playing countries (mainly from India, Pakistan and the West Indies), it's not surprising that the New York metropolitan area is considered the mecca of cricket in North America. There are 12 leagues comprising over 200 clubs, and play can be watched in a number of area parks. **Bronx:** Van Cortlandt Park, Ferry Point Park, Randall's Island, Soundview. **Queens:** Flushing Meadow Park, Baisley Park, Kissena Park, Edgemere. **Brooklyn:** Marine Park, Seaview.

Football

New York Giants—Giants Stadium (Meadowlands) 59 Rte. 120 (at Rte. 3), East Rutherford, NJ (201) 935-3900 *www.giants.com*. "Big Blue" moved to its 77,716-seat New Jersey home in 1976. The signing of rookie quarterback Eli Manning in 2004 has given fans new hope for a return to the glory days of the LT/Phil Simms era of the 80's. Tickets are available by subscription only. If you get yourself on the waiting list soon, perhaps your grandchildren will get a seat one day. **Directions:** See New Jersey Nets entry.

New York Jets—Giants Stadium 59 Rte 120 (at Rte. 3), East Rutherford, NJ (201) 935-3900 *www.newyorkjets.com*. "Gang Green" was lured to the Meadowlands after the 1983 season, so both metropolitan-area NFL franchises are actually New Jersey teams—for now. If plans for a stadium onManhattan's west side come to fruition, it will be the Jets' home by the end of the decade, as well as the venue for the main events of the 2012 Olympics, should New York win its bid to host the games. It's almost as hard to get a ticket for a Jets game as it is for those of their co-tenants: the waiting list for season tickets is currently 12 years. **Directions:** See New Jersey Nets entry.

Hockey

New York Rangers—Madison Square Garden 2 Penn Plaza (at 33rd St. and Seventh Ave.) (212) 465-6471 *www.newyorkrangers.com*. One of the "Original Six" NHL teams, the Rangers have a long tradition, although their fortunes have dimmed since winning the Stanley Cup in 1994. But win or lose, the Rangers have some of the most loyal—and vociferous—fans in the league, and games at the Garden are rowdy fun. **Tickets:** $22–$675; available through Ticketmaster at (212) 307-7171, or at the Garden box office. **Subway:** A, C, E, 1, 2, 3, 9 to 34th St.

New York Islanders—Nassau Veterans Memorial Coliseum 1255 Hempstead Tpke., Uniondale, Long Island (516) 794-9300 *www.newyorkislanders.com*. The Islanders won four successive Stanley Cups in the early 80's. Fans think back fondly on those years: the team has toiled in mediocrity since, although it is steadily improving. **Tickets:** $14–$85; available at the box office or through Ticketmaster. **Directions:** Long Island Railroad to Hempstead; walk one block to the Hempstead Bus Terminal and take N 70, N 71 or N 72 bus to Coliseum.

By car, take the Midtown Tunnel to Long Island Expy. (495) east to exit 38; Northern State Pkwy. to exit 31A; Meadowbrook Pkwy. south to exit M4, Nassau Coliseum. Parking is $6.

New Jersey Devils—Continental Airlines Arena 50 Rte. 120 (at Rte. 3), East Rutherford, NJ (201) 935-3900 *www.newjerseydevils.com*. The 2003 Stanley Cup Champions are perennially one of the best teams in the NHL, having hoisted the Cup in three of the last nine seasons. **Tickets:** $20–$90; available at the box office, or through Ticketmaster online or at (201) 507-8900. **Directions:** See New Jersey Nets entry.

Horse Racing

Aqueduct Racetrack 110th St. (at Rockaway Blvd.), Ozone Park, Queens (718) 641-4700 *www.nyra.com/Acqueduct*. The old Aqueduct, which opened in 1894, was replaced by the new "Big A" in 1959. In 1975 the inner track was constructed, allowing for winter racing. On July 4, 1972, Aqueduct was the scene of Secretariat's first event, a 5.5 furlong maiden race. **Hours:** Gates open at 11 A.M. **Admission:** Grandstand $1; Clubhouse $3; Skyline Club $4; children under 12 free. **Subway:** A to Aqueduct Racetrack; courtesy bus service to admission gate. **By car:** Midtown Tunnel to Long Island Expy. east, to Van Wyck Expy. south to exit 3, Linden Blvd.; right on Linden to track. Parking $1–$5.

Belmont Park 2150 Hempstead Tpke. (at Plainfield Ave), Elmont, Long Island (718) 488-6000 *www.nyra.com/Belmont*. In addition to hosting the Belmont Stakes each year, the final leg of the Triple Crown, Belmont Park has been the scene of many other historic events. One of America's oldest and most beautiful tracks, Belmont opened on May 4, 1905; it was here that the Wright brothers supervised an international aerial tournament before 150,000 spectators in 1910. But most important, of course, is its glorious racing past. It was here in 1973 that Secretariat won the Triple Crown, winning the race by an astonishing 31 lengths and becoming a racing legend. **Hours:** Gates open at 11 A.M. Closed Mon.–Tue. except holiday weekends (closed Wed.). Season is generally May–Jul. and Sept. to mid-Oct. **Admission:** Grandstand $2; Clubhouse $4; children under 12 free. **Directions:** Long Island Railroad; round-trip package from Penn Station includes $1 off admission. By car, take the Cross Island Pkwy. to exit 26D. Parking $2–$6.

Meadowlands Racetrack Rte. 3, East Rutherford, NJ (201) THE-BIGM *www.thebigm.com*. Harness and thoroughbred horse racing are the staples at this one-mile oval track next to Giants Stadium. The 40,000-person-capacity racetrack was built in 1976 and christened in high style when horseman Anthony Abbatiello rode across the George Washington Bridge to the Meadowlands. **Admission:** Grandstand $1–$1.50; Clubhouse, $3; Pegasus (Dining Floor) $5. **Directions:** See New Jersey Nets entry. General parking free; Clubhouse and valet parking $5.

Yonkers Raceway Central Ave., Yonkers (914) 968-4200 *www.yonkersrace-way.com*. Although the history of the modern Yonkers Raceway dates from only 1950, the Westchester oval's impressive past actually dates back to the 19th century, when it was founded as a replacement for Fleetwood Park, a Grand Circuit stop in the Bronx. The facility reopened as Yonkers Raceway and had its inaugural meet on April 27, 1950. **Hours:** Post time 7:40 P.M. Mon.–Tues. and Fri.–Sat. **Admission:** Grandstand $2.25; Empire Terrace $4.25. **Subway:** 4 to Woodlawn; B, D to Bedford Park Blvd.; 5 to 238th St.; 1, 9 to 242nd St. Take express buses from stations to track. **By car:** New York Thruway I-87 to exit 2 North, exit 4 South; Bronx River Pkwy. to Oak St., Mt. Vernon exit; Saw Mill River Pkwy. to Cross County Pkwy. to Yonkers or Central Ave. exit). Parking $2.

Soccer

New York/New Jersey MetroStars—Continental Airlines Arena 50 Rte. 120 (at Rte. 3), East Rutherford, NJ (201) 935-3900 *www.metrostars.com*. Major League Soccer began in 1996 amidst the enthusiasm generated by the World Cup. Certainly the best soccer in America is being played in MLS venues, and with the recent ban of the game-deciding shootout in favor of overtime, league officials are trying to make this a more exciting game for purists. The season runs April through September. **Tickets:** $18– $36; available through Ticketmaster online or by calling (888) 4METROTIX. **Directions:** See New Jersey Nets entry.

Tennis

Chase Championships—Madison Square Garden *www.thegarden.com* Taking place in Madison Square Garden every November, the Chase Championships is one of the WTA's top tournaments, featuring a singles field limited to the top 16 point-earners on the tour, and a similar field of eight doubles teams. The tennis is top-notch, and the Garden ambience is electric. **Tickets:** $20–$150; available through Ticketmaster at (212) 307-7171, or at the Garden box office. **Subway:** A, C, E, 1, 2, 3, 9 to 34th St.

U.S. Open—USTA National Tennis Center Flushing Meadows—Corona Park, Queens (718) 760–6200 *www.usopen.org*. The most prestigious American tournament, a Grand Slam event, is held in late August and early September at the National Tennis Center. The world's best tennis players converge on the city, hoping to vie for the championship in the spacious Arthur Ashe Stadium. Fans can pay top dollar for a seat at the showcased matches, or purchase grounds admission, which entitles them to wander from one early-round match to another; prices go up as the tournament progresses. Buy tickets well in advance; they go on sale in June. **Tickets:** Grounds admission $40; showcase match at Arthur Ashe Stadium, $46–$335. Available at the box office or through Ticketmaster online or at (866) OPEN-TIX. **Subway:** 7 to Willets Point–Shea Stadium. **Long Island Railroad:** Trains from Penn Station stop at the stadium during the Open.

Hotels, Inns, and B & B's

No doubt about it, New York is one of the most expensive hotel cities in the country. But it's not quite as bad as you may have heard. A glut of new hotel development during the past decade pushed the average hotel rate down from $237 in 2000 to a more reasonable $198 at the end of 2003. That price is for an average room, mind you—and "average" in New York usually means "tiny." For a spacious suite at a top-tier hotel, the sky's the limit. You're definitely not in Kansas anymore.

The good news is that visitors have more bargaining power these days. Rack rates remain awfully high, but hoteliers do exhibit flexibility. Resurrect your negotiating skills, especially if you'll be visiting between January and August, when hotels compete fiercely for visitors. During autumn and holiday time, you may still have to reconcile yourself to paying closer to full price, but there are some insider tips worth noting even in these seasons. For instance, hotels in Midtown West charge higher-than-usual rates for Thanksgiving, especially along the Macy's parade route; however, deals can often be had on the east side of town and downtown. And bargains abound in Financial District hotels during the holiday season, and over just about any weekend.

One more important thing you need to know: Rooms are almost invariably smaller here than in most other cities. More money will usually buy you more space, but not always. Bathrooms and closets tend to be small even at the luxury level. Space limitations (as well as hotels that are generous with space) are noted in the reviews, but if you require extra elbow room, be sure to make specific inquiries when you book.

Getting the Best Rate

It's easy to spend a fortune for the privilege of sleeping in Manhattan, but it's not necessary to do so. The city boasts many great hotels that are (relatively) reasonably priced. The best way to find them is to forsake a prime Midtown location for another part of the city. Consider staying in one of Manhattan's hip downtown neighborhoods, or in quiet Murray Hill, or in the family-friendly Upper West Side, where you'll almost always get more for your money. And doing so doesn't mean that you'll have to sacrifice convenience. Each of these neighborhoods is well connected to Midtown by mass transit. A subway or taxi can whisk you to the Theater District inside 15 minutes—with more money left in your wallet.

All hotels have official "rack rates"—sometimes published, sometimes unpublished. But you can very often do better than these official rates. Hotels frequently offer discounts and packages to get you in the door, especially if business isn't booming.

Each listing in this section includes dollar signs that reflect the average daily rate that's typically charged for a double room at each given hotel:

$ under $150
$$ $150–$249
$$$ $250–$375
$$$$ $375 and over

However, keep in mind that rates can vary dramatically depending on dates and demand. Also remember that every hotel room is subject to a hotel tax of 13.625 percent plus $2 per night.

Don't accept the first rate you're quoted; always ask politely whether the hotel can do better. Ask about special packages, discounts for seniors or AAA members, or whatever else might score you savings. Many hotels feature Internet specials and various package deals on their own Web sites, so it pays to log on before calling.

Members of the American Automobile Association should also try the **AAA Travel Agency**, which often can reward members with seriously discounted rates (*www.aaa.com,* or dial the number listed on the back of your AAA card).

You might also surf the Web to see what rates are available through agencies such as *www.quikbook.com, www.hotels.com, www.expedia.com, www.travelocity.com* or *www.orbitz.com.* But never just book a room through a reservation agency without shopping around; otherwise, you may end up paying more, not less. Compare the best rate you find online to what your travel agent can do, or what you can get by booking directly through the hotel; often, you can score a better rate by calling or surfing the hotel's own Web site.

It's best to use these online discount booking sites simply as research tools. Hotels will routinely match the rates you find online if you call them directly. And since agency bookings cost them a hefty chunk in commissions (as much as 25 percent of the room rate), they're thrilled to cut out the middleman. When you book directly, most hotels will even give you a better room than you'd get by reserving through the online agencies, since they're getting 100 percent of your hotel dollar, not 75 or 80 percent. Hotels often give their worst rooms (near the elevator, near the ice maker, on low floors, etc.) to guests who book through online discounters.

Always check the individual cancellation and change policies that accompany any reservation you make, as they can vary from booking to booking—and you'll want to avoid any unwanted surprises.

DOWNTOWN

Abingdon Guest House   VERY GOOD $$

13 Eighth Ave. (between W. 12th and Jane Sts.), West Village
www.abingdonguesthouse.com   Phone: (212) 243-5384   Fax: (212) 807-7473

Two historic town homes and one professional owner with creative vision and
impeccable taste: it all adds up to one of New York's most charming guest
houses. Located in the brownstone-lined, boutique-dotted West Village, the
Abingdon boasts an inviting residential ambiance that combines an authentic
neighborhood vibe with modern comforts. Since there's no resident innkeeper,
the house is best for independent-minded guests who prefer artistically outfitted,
one-of-a-kind accommodations and genuine New York ambiance over a generic
Midtown hotel.

Each of the nine attractive rooms has a private bath (less expensive ones
have adjacent private baths off the hall rather than en suite), cable TV, a private phone with answering machine and bold, beautiful décor. Walls are
painted in deep, vibrant hues and furnishings are well chosen for both beauty
and comfort. The best is the Ambassador Room, which boasts a grand four-
poster king, a sitting area that can sleep a third person, a wet-bar-style kitchenette and a VCR. Maid service is a daily feature on all but major holidays. On
the downside, there's no elevator, so overpackers and travelers with mobility
issues should stay elsewhere. Eighth Avenue can be a bit noisy; choose a back
room if you want maximum quiet (located at patio level, the Garden Room is a
good choice).

Rooms: Nine; four floors; all nonsmoking rooms. **Hotel amenities:** None. **Food
services:** Coffee bar at street level. **Cancellation:** Four days prior to arrival (10
days or more during holiday season; ask about Christmas/New Year's specifics).
Wheelchair access: None. **Note:** Not for children. **Subway:** A, C, E, 1, 2, 3, 9
to 14th St.

Best Western Seaport Inn   GOOD $$

33 Peck Slip (at Front St., two blocks north of Fulton St.), South Street Seaport
www.bestwestern.com/seaportinn
Phone: (212) 766-6600, (800) 468-3569 (HOTEL-NY)   Fax: (212) 766-6615

Behind a beautifully restored red-brick 1852 facade lies a perfectly unremarkable but comfortable hotel. The traditional rooms are generic but do the trick.
All have VCRs and work desks with free high-speed Internet access; some have
sleeper sofas and/or dining tables, others steam or jetted baths. Corner rooms
are largest; ask for one with a terrace and a harbor view. Experienced with visiting Wall Streeters who consider this their home away from home, the staff is
quite attentive, and rooms are kept fresh and appealing. The historic Seaport is
steps away.

Rooms: 72; seven floors; designated nonsmoking rooms. **Hotel amenities:** Dry cleaning and laundry service, exercise room, video library. **Food services:** Rates include continental breakfast. **Cancellation:** 4 P.M. day of arrival. **Wheelchair access:** ADA compliant. **Subway:** J, M, Z, 2, 3, 4, 5 to Fulton St.; A, C to Broadway–Nassau St.

Cosmopolitan Hotel—TriBeCa

GOOD **$**

95 West Broadway (at Chambers St.), TriBeCa
Phone: (212) 566-1900, (888) 895-9400

www.cosmohotel.com
Fax: (212) 566-6909

In the heart of hip TriBeCa is one of Manhattan's best cheap hotels. Make no mistake—rooms are tiny and appointments are strictly budget, but everything is very nice. A pleasant lobby area and elevator leads to well-maintained rooms furnished in a pleasant, modern IKEA-ish style, each with its own small but neat black-and-white-tiled bathroom. Linens and towels are of good quality, and mattresses are firm. All rooms have a work desk and TV, and most have an armoire (a few have wall racks instead). Rooms have one double bed or two; a few slightly larger units have two queen beds. For a few extra dollars, you can have a sitting area with a love seat, or a two-level mini-loft.

The neighborhood is one of the city's hippest, offering a wealth of first-rate restaurants at every price (including a Starbucks in the building). With the Chambers Street subway stop out the front door ready to whisk you to Times Square in five minutes, the location is practical. Services are nonexistent—but at these prices, who cares?

Rooms: 113; seven floors; no designated nonsmoking rooms. **Hotel amenities:** None. **Food services:** None. **Cancellation:** 24 hours prior to day of arrival. **Wheelchair access:** Not accessible. **Subway:** A, C, 1, 2, 3, 9 to Chambers St.

Embassy Suites New York

EXCELLENT **$$$**

102 North End Ave. (between Vesey and Murray Sts.), Battery Park City
www.embassysuites.com
Phone: (212) 945-0100, (800) 362-2779 (EMBASSY)   Fax: (212) 945-3012

This new-in-2000 all-suite hotel has emerged from the World Trade Center disaster in top form—and as a veritable hero. Located next to the World Financial Center, the hotel was relatively unscathed, and served as a 24-hour triage and rest area for rescue and recovery workers for months. It's now back to serving its original purpose, and it's looking terrific.

The hotel is ideally suited to business travelers, of course—but it has a relaxed air and a magnificent modern art collection that elevates it well above the business standard. Hudson River views and proximity to waterside parks and Statue of Liberty ferries are big pluses. While the warm, contemporary décor isn't exactly cutting edge, the hotel has substantially more panache than most of its peers—without sacrificing comfort.

Best of all is the wealth of space. Open hallways overlook a soaring, light-filled atrium and lead to extra-large two-room suites, which range from a whopping 450 to a cavernous 850 square feet. Each has a living room with dining area and pullout sofa; a wet-bar kitchenette with microwave and coffee maker; two TVs with video games; high-speed Internet access; and nice bathrooms with generous counter space. (Executive suites also have fax, CD player and an extra-large dining/meeting table.) Rates are targeted to expense accounts on weekdays, but substantial weekend discounts, slow-season packages and AAA discounts are a steal for families and other vacationers.

Rooms: 463; 14 floors; designated nonsmoking floors. **Hotel amenities:** Concierge, dry-cleaning and laundry service, coin-operated laundry, health club, business center, full conference center, executive suites for small meetings, adjacent 16-screen movie theater. **Food services:** Three restaurants, plus a bagel shop; room service; rates include full cooked-to-order breakfast. **Cancellation:** By 4 P.M. day prior to arrival. **Wheelchair access:** Fully accessible. **Subway:** E to World Trade Center; A, C, 1, 2, 3, 9 to Chambers St.

Holiday Inn Downtown/SoHo   GOOD $$

138 Lafayette St. (between Canal and Howard Sts.), Chinatown
www.holidayinn-nyc.com or *www.holiday-inn.com*
Phone: (212) 966-8898, (800) 465-4329 (HOLIDAY)   Fax: (212) 941-5832

This recently renovated chain-standard hotel overlooking Chinatown is nothing to write home about. But it's a find for shoppers in search of a SoHo location for half of what the luxury hotels charge; the boutique-lined streets of SoHo and Nolita are just a stroll away. The freshly remade rooms are unremarkable, and many are quite small, but they're clean and comfortable in a completely reliable Holiday Inn way. Nice extras include CD alarm clock radios, two-line cordless phones, coffee makers and bright bathrooms with marble countertops; suites have fax machines. Many government contractors are among the guests, so the place feels like a business hotel, but Asian decorative accents and a good Cantonese restaurant add neighborhood flair. Chinatown is fun for those who enjoy the exotica and bustle (not to mention the food), but ask for a room at the back of the hotel if you're a light sleeper. Specials can bring the rooms below the $150 price point.

Rooms: 227; 14 floors; designated nonsmoking floors. **Hotel amenities:** Concierge, dry cleaning and laundry service, meeting room. **Food services:** Chinese restaurant, bar, room service. **Cancellation:** 24 hours before arrival. **Wheelchair access:** Accessible. **Subway:** J, M, N, Q, R, W, Z, 6 to Canal St.

Holiday Inn Wall Street   EXCELLENT $$$

15 Gold St. (at Platt St.), Lower Manhattan
www.holidayinnwsd.com or *www.holiday-inn.com*
Phone: (212) 232-7800, (800) 465-4329 (HOLIDAY)   Fax: (212) 425-0330

Forget your motel preconceptions—this Holiday Inn is a first-rate choice. In fact, it's one of Manhattan's most technologically advanced hotels. The high-tech toys greet you in the small but pleasant lobby, where you can bypass the professionally staffed front desk in favor of an ATM-style machine that lets you check in with one touch. You can also download city information to your PDA at the mobile concierge or print out city info from a PC.

Rooms are very comfortable and boast conveniences galore for the traveling executive, or anybody who just likes toys. The eight-foot L-shaped workstation boasts desk-level "Plug and Play" high-speed ethernet input for laptop toters; an ergonomic chair; dual-line cordless phone with direct-dial number; and the kind of supplies you never bring but always need, like paper clips, Liquid Paper, and a thesaurus. Cellular connection services let you forward calls to your cell when you're away from your room. About half of the rooms feature their own T1-connected PC with a 14-inch flat-screen monitor, MS Word and Office applications, and full Internet access. For after-work time, there's a CD player and a TV with on-screen Internet access and Nintendo. SMART rooms feature laptop computers with carrying cases and wireless ethernet cards for mobile Internet access, Canon fax/copier/printers and other upgraded amenities.

Furnishings are surprisingly nice, if not particularly stylish; even the marble bathrooms are thoughtfully outfitted with oversized bath sheets and terry robes. The staff prides itself on service; each floor even boasts an amenity station stocked with everything from toothpaste to extra blankets.

Rooms: 138; 18 floors; designated nonsmoking floors. **Hotel amenities:** Concierge, dry cleaning and laundry service, coin-operated laundry, modern exercise room, 24-hour self-service business center, state-of-the-art executive boardroom with seating for 50, CD library. Pets accepted. **Food services:** Italian restaurant, bar, 24-hour room service, plated delivery from a range of restaurants. **Cancellation:** Before 6 P.M. day prior to arrival. **Wheelchair access:** Fully accessible. **Subway:** 2, 3 to Wall St.

Hotel Gansevoort   EXCELLENT $$$$

18 Ninth Ave. (at W. 13th St.), Meatpacking District   *www.hotelgansevoort.com*
Phone: (212) 206-6700, (877) 462-7386   Fax: (212) 255-5858

The latest fashion statement to hit the uber-trendy Meatpacking District, this brand-new silvery gray box rises up like a shiny beacon amid the neighborhood's sea of red brick and brownstone. The lobby is as ultra-cool as you'd expect, with low lighting, chocolate eel-skin-covered columns and floors that glow with illuminated red squares. The attractive rooms have a minimalist urban look, with white marble-topped dark-wood tables, tinted opaque glass closets and bathroom doors, and a dash of color in the vibrant framed neighborhood photographs that dress the walls. All rooms have CD players, multi-line phones with voicemail, high-speed Internet access, feather beds and 400-thread-count Egyptian linens. Some rooms have Hudson River views and many feature step-out Juliet balconies. Surround-sound stereo systems, balconies, DVD players and steam showers are offered in the suites.

The pièce de résistance is the 45-foot heated rooftop pool, surrounded by retractable glass walls and humming with piped-in underwater music. Adjacent to the pool is Plunge, a fabulously chic rooftop lounge with panoramic views. At presstime, an indoor/outdoor Japanese restaurant and bar called Ono (from

Jeffrey Chodorow of New York's China Grill, Asia de Cuba, Tuscan and Mix) was nearing completion.

Rooms: 187; 14 floors; designated nonsmoking floors. **Hotel amenities:** Concierge, 5,100-square foot spa; health club; rooftop pool; full business center; laundry and dry cleaning services; meeting and function rooms. **Food services:** Ono restaurant/bar; rooftop lounge, 24-hour room service. **Cancellation:** 24 hours prior to arrival. **Wheelchair access:** Fully accessible. **Subway:** A, C, E to 14th St.; L to Eighth Ave.

Larchmont Hotel
GOOD **$**

27 W. 11th St.(between Fifth and Sixth Aves.), West Village
www.larchmonthotel.com   Phone: (212) 989-9333   Fax: (212) 989-9496

New York could use a dozen more Larchmonts. This cheerful European-style hotel is an excellent value for those who don't mind sharing hall bathrooms with fellow guests in exchange for a very low rate. You'll feel the warm and welcoming vibe the instant you enter the butter-yellow lobby, where you'll be greeted by the professional staff. Each bright room is prettily furnished in rattan, with a writing desk and a wash basin, plus a TV and telephone (not a given in this price range), a ceiling fan, a library of books and a nice cotton robe and slippers for padding down the hall to the older but spotless shared bathrooms. The hotel's leafy brownstone-lined street brims with old New York charm, and several subway lines are a short walk away. Loyal guests keep this jewel booked, so reserve as far in advance as possible.

Rooms: 58 (all with shared bathrooms); six floors; smoking allowed. **Hotel amenities:** Fax service, common kitchens. **Food services:** Rates include continental breakfast. **Cancellation:** Two days prior to arrival. **Wheelchair access:** Not accessible. **Subway:** A, C, E, F, V to W. 4th St. (use 8th St. exit).

The Mercer
EXCELLENT **$$$$**

147 Mercer St. (at Prince St.), SoHo   *www.mercerhotel.com*
Phone: (212) 966-6060, (888) 918-6060   Fax: (212) 965-3838

The Mercer is so cool that it's downright frosty. Modern design buffs will love the stunning Christian Liagre–designed interiors, which are brazenly angular but comfortable; textured fabrics and African woods soften the look and add character. The high-ceilinged guest rooms are spacious and practical, with extra-large work desks that double as generous dining tables. Many rooms have exposed brick or French doors. Steel carts add storage in the big and beautiful, architecturally impressive white marble bathrooms, which boast either an oversized shower or a tub for two, plus hip Face Stockholm amenities. Flat-screen TVs with Nintendo and Sony CD players are on hand to keep you entertained (if the beautiful clientele isn't amusing enough), as well as free wireless Internet access anywhere in the building; PCs, fax machines, and DVD players can be installed upon request. Even kids get the royal treatment, with Frette-lined cribs.

No other chic SoHo hotel is so well located, and no other hotelier knows how to run a luxury boutique hotel like Andre Balazs (the power behind L.A.'s legendary Chateau Marmont). Despite the requisite chic lobby lounge, the air is more regal and exclusive than that at party scenes like the W hotels. The stylish restaurant is the domain of superstar chef Jean-Georges Vongerichten (of four-star Jean Georges).

Rooms: 75; six floors; smoking allowed. **Hotel amenities:** 24-hour concierge, laundry and dry-cleaning service, business services, CD/DVD/video library. Free access to nearby World and Crunch gyms. Pets accepted. **Food services:** Chic restaurant and bar (The Mercer Kitchen), lobby cafe and bar, 24-hour room service. **Cancellation:** Before noon the day prior to arrival. **Wheelchair access:** Fully accessible. **Subway:** N, R to Prince St.

New York City Howard Johnson Express Inn

GOOD **$**

135 E. Houston St. (at Forsyth St.), Lower East Side

www.hojo.com

Phone: (212) 358-8844, (800) 406-1411

Fax: (212) 473-3500

This new-in-2002 budget hotel is a welcome addition to the rapidly gentrifying Lower East Side. It sits on a pleasing Houston Street block, shoulder-to-shoulder with the best of the old Jewish-immigrant enclave and the newly hip 'hood; next door are Yonah Shimmel's Knish Shop (same as it ever was) and Sunshine Cinemas, a state-of-the-art indie movie complex that occupies a beautifully renovated Yiddish vaudeville house. The hotel itself offers similarly cross-pollinated appeal: It's ideal for any traveler in search of high-quality comforts or a trendy location at a low price—or both.

Management deserves kudos for outfitting a budget hotel so well. Rooms are petite (hint: You'll get the most square footage for your money if you request a room number ending in 01, 02 or 03), but furnishings and textiles are well made and attractive, beds are pleasingly firm, and work desks boast desk-level inputs and ergonomic chairs. The granite bathrooms are nicer than many you'll find in $300-a-night hotels; some even have whirlpool tubs. Coffee makers are also on hand. The staff is professional and friendly, and free continental breakfast heightens the great value. Dense with bars, live-music clubs, and affordable restaurants, the neighborhood can hop well into the wee hours, so request a room in the back of the building if you're a light sleeper.

Rooms: 46; six floors; designated non-smoking rooms. **Hotel amenities:** Laundry and dry-cleaning service. **Food services:** Rates include continental breakfast. **Cancellation:** 24 hours prior to arrival. **Wheelchair access:** ADA compliant. **Subway:** F, V to Second Ave.

New York Marriott Financial Center

GOOD **$$–$$$**

85 West St. (at Carlisle St.), Financial District

www.marriott.com

Phone: (212) 385-4900, (888) 236-2427

Fax: (212) 227-8136

Rooms are utterly unremarkable but just fine at this nondescript but well-maintained and perfectly comfortable business hotel, which deserves kudos for serving as a home base for rescue workers in the months following 9/11. It's fully open once again, and just steps from Wall Street. Some rooms have appealing views of New York Harbor and the southern tip of the island. On site is the solid, tropical-accented Roy's New York, from venerable Hawaiian chef Roy Yamaguchi. Weekend rates drop substantially, and all of Lower Manhattan's attractions are just a walk away.

Rooms: 507; 38 floors; designated nonsmoking rooms. **Hotel amenities:** Concierge, laundry and dry-cleaning service, health club with sauna and swimming pool, good business center, meeting rooms, valet parking. **Food services:** Roy's New York restaurant and bar, contemporary-style bar, room service, complimentary in-room coffee. **Cancellation:** Generally before 6 P.M. day of arrival, but up to 14–21 days in advance during big events. **Wheelchair access:** Fully accessible. **Subway:** N, R, 1, 9 to Rector St.

Ritz-Carlton New York, Battery Park

EXCELLENT $$$$

2 West St., Battery Park City
Phone: (212) 344-0800, (800) 241-3333

www.ritzcarlton.com
Fax: (212) 344-3801

The reliably refined Ritz-Carlton chain unveiled Manhattan's first-ever waterside luxury hotel in early 2002, and it's a winner. The shiny new glass-and-brick Battery Park City tower stands like a modern sentry over the Hudson River, overlooking waterfront Robert Wagner Park. Since it's just a shout from the World Financial Center and Wall Street, the hotel is geared toward high-level business travelers.

But you don't have to be a CEO to appreciate the amenity-laden rooms, which combine Ritz-Carlton's classic European style with a contemporary Art Deco look, with rich marquetry wood finishes and luxurious fabrics. Appointments emphasize luxury (think Frette linens, feather beds, the works), cutting-edge technology (including CD players, cordless phones, high-speed Internet access and technology butler service), and sweeping vistas; harbor-view rooms even feature telescopes so you can enjoy close-ups of Lady Liberty. The ultimate in luxury is reserved for the club-level floors, where additional perks include DVD/CD players with surround sound, a dedicated concierge and a private lounge with complimentary food service all day and evening. Expect impeccable service throughout. Weekend and package rates can be a relative bargain.

Rooms: 298; 38 floors (hotel occupies first 14 floors); designated nonsmoking floors. **Hotel amenities:** Concierge, fitness center, full-service spa, state-of-the-art business center with secretarial services, laundry and dry-cleaning service, conference and meeting/function rooms. **Food services:** 2 West, an elegant French-influenced steakhouse; lobby lounge with afternoon tea service; Rise, a lovely 14th-floor lounge with an alfresco deck, Statue of Liberty views, and light meals; 24-hour room service. **Cancellation:** 24 hours prior to arrival. **Wheelchair access:** Fully accessible. **Subway:** 4, 5 to Bowling Green.

60 Thompson

VERY GOOD $$$$

60 Thompson St. (between Spring and Broome Sts.), SoHo *www.60thompson.com*
Phone: (877) 431-0400 Fax: (212) 431-0200

Despite its chic modernist lines and sky-high hip factor, this super-cool SoHo hotel gets the restful residential mood just right. The entrance sets the tone: The facade is set back from the street, behind a courtyard of birch trees and blending easily with the surrounding cast-iron buildings and brownstones. Public spaces are designed for easy lounging, and guest rooms are plush, comfortable and sexy without feeling faddish. While not large, they are well equipped, with DVD and CD players, high-speed Internet access, comfortable seating areas and beautiful marble baths. The signature low-slung, wing-backed Thompson chair makes the perfect reading cradle, while the photography of Laura Resen adds artistic accents. Suites add VCRs, fax machines and Bose stereos to the mix. If money's no object, inquire about the spectacular duplex penthouse loft, with double-high windows, a stone fireplace and a private roof deck.

The restaurant, Thom (from the folks behind Indochine, Republic and Bond Street), has made a splash among the beautiful-people crowd thanks to its stylish indoor-outdoor setting and edgy Asian fusion fare. One of the best things about 60 Thompson is its wealth of alfresco spaces, which also include a patio off the clubby, intimate Thom's Bar and a beautifully landscaped rooftop garden that's home to a members-only lounge, A60, from late spring to early autumn.

Rooms: 100; 10 floors; designated nonsmoking floors. **Hotel amenities:** 24-hour concierge, dry-cleaning and laundry service, CD and DVD libraries. **Food services:** Thom restaurant, Thom Bar/breakfast room with terrace, room service. **Cancellation:** 24 hours prior to arrival. **Wheelchair access:** Fully accessible. **Subway:** C, E to Spring St.

SoHo Grand Hotel

EXCELLENT $$$$

310 West Broadway (between Grand and Canal Sts.), SoHo *www.sohogrand.com*
Phone: (212) 965-3000, (800) 965-3000   Fax: (212) 965-3244

Although built less than a decade ago, this designer hotel harkens back to SoHo's 19th-century cast-iron past with Industrial Age details (including Edison light bulbs), retro-minded furnishings with a strong Arts-and-Crafts influence, and gorgeous William Morris fabrics. Still, the overall effect is wholly modern, and comforts are 21st-century luxurious. The grand staircase that ascends from the ground floor to the lobby sets the tone from the start, as urban-industrial hardware gives way to 24-foot ceilings and two-story windows.

The understated but lovely guest rooms boast an Arts-and-Crafts ambiance with an Asian accent. Custom furnishings include saddle-stitched leather headboards; large, functional desks that resemble artists' drafting tables; and side tables fashioned after potters' stands. The natural tones are warm and soothing, textiles are plush and soft lighting abounds. Two-line cordless phones, CD players and VCRs add to the luxury, while gourmet minibars, Frette bathrobes, Egyptian cotton towels and Kiehl's toiletries in the bathrooms accent the Big

Apple vibe. The building's T shape gives many rooms entrancing views (including one north to Midtown that is worth the price of admission), but bathrooms are generally small. The chic clientele includes more than a few celebs, who prefer the slightly more relaxed vibe of this hotel over the party scene at its sister hotel, the TriBeCa Grand (below). The comfortable Grand Bar and Lounge remains a stylish hangout, while chef Gabriel Sorgi creates a classic American menu in the highly regarded Gallery restaurant. Owned by Hartz Mountain, the hotel welcomes pets, who even have their own room-service menu. (If you arrive sans pet, you can request your own goldfish for the duration of your stay.)

Rooms: 369; 17 floors; designated nonsmoking floors. **Hotel amenities:** Concierge, all-new fitness center, laundry and dry cleaning, three newly renovated meeting and function rooms, business center. Pets accepted. **Food services:** Restaurant, lounge, 24-hour room service. **Cancellation:** Before 3 P.M. the day prior to arrival. **Wheelchair access:** Fully accessible. **Subway:** A, C, E, 1, 9 to Canal St.

SoHotel

BASIC $

341 Broome St. (east of Elizabeth St.), Nolita

www.pioneerhotel.com

Phone: (212) 226-1482, (800) 737-0202

Fax: (212) 226-3525

This older, European-style hotel, the former Pioneer, is as simple and spare as they come. But if you're a budget traveler in search of a clean, quiet, friendly accommodation with a private bathroom for less than $100 per night, the SoHotel is an excellent option. Both the hotel itself and the surrounding neighborhood have seen steady improvements over the last few years, and things just keep getting better.

The SoHotel is housed in a four-story walkup just off the Bowery's light fixture/restaurant supply district, which has grown into a safe and convenient hub near SoHo, Chinatown and the Lower East Side. You'll climb one level from the street to the lobby, which is older but bright and agreeable, with a pleasantly professional staff and morning coffee. Decorative painting—stippling, colorful murals, and the like—lends an attractive accent to guest rooms that would otherwise be institutional, and hanging plants add color in the halls. Rooms have black linoleum floors, mix-and-match lamps and chairs, ceiling fans (in addition to air-conditioning), and fresh and firm platform beds (which may be a bit too firm for some). Some have simple armoires, others a rack on the wall instead of a closet. Most rooms have a minuscule but spotless bathroom with a shower stall. A few rooms have no windows, but they're blissfully silent and will even save you a few dollars. Ask for a renovated room (most are). Bring your own alarm, hair dryer, and cell phone, as amenities don't go beyond the basics.

Rooms: 125 (only 8 are singles with shared bathroom), 4 floors, smoking allowed. **Hotel amenities:** None. Food service: Morning coffee in lobby. **Cancellation:** 24 to 48 hours prior to arrival. **Wheelchair access:** Not accessible. **Subway:** F, V to Second Ave.; 6 to Spring St.

TriBeCa Grand Hotel

EXCELLENT $$$$

2 Sixth Ave. (at White and Church Sts.), TriBeCa   *www.tribecagrand.com*
Phone: (212) 519-6600, (877) 519-6600   Fax: (212) 519-6700

This chic sister to the highly successful SoHo Grand (reviewed above) is another winner in the downtown luxury category. The brick-and-cast-iron exterior is right at home in the historic neighborhood—but inside, an unabashedly modern world awaits. Designer Larry Bogdanow has styled a dramatic eight-story atrium lobby, one of the best public areas that any city hotel has to offer. The Church Lounge, with luxurious leather-and-velvet seating clusters, is a hugely popular hangout with a designer-clad downtown crowd; attached is a private 40-seat contemporary American restaurant called Trinity.

Set along open, atrium-facing corridors, the guest rooms feature similar modern design, although they've been deservedly criticized for emphasizing utilitarianism over leisure. An extra-long, built-in, L-shaped work desk with an ergonomically correct Herman Miller chair dominates each room, as does cutting-edge technology that includes a TV with wireless Internet access and VCR, Bose Wave radio with CD player, high-speed Internet access, fax/printer/copier and a two-line cordless phone, plus a second TV and upscale toiletries in the gorgeous bath. A warm gold-and-red palette, sumptuous velvet, and soft, glowing light soften the look and add luxury-level comfort. The most beautiful staff in town adds to the downtown appeal, and their professionalism is welcome relief from the chic-boutique standard. Pets are warmly welcomed by owner Hartz Mountain.

Rooms: 203; eight floors; designated nonsmoking floors. **Hotel amenities:** 24-hour concierge, fitness center, business center, laundry and dry-cleaning service, video and CD libraries, screening room, function rooms, coffee/tea/cocoa bar on each floor. Pets accepted. **Food services:** Restaurant, lounge, 24-hour room service. **Cancellation:** Before 3 P.M. the day prior to arrival. **Wheelchair access:** Fully accessible. **Subway:** 1, 9 to Franklin St.

Union Square Inn

GOOD $

209 E. 14th St. (between Second and Third Aves.), East Village
www.unionsquareinn.com   Phone: (212) 614-0500   Fax: (212) 614-0512

This budget hotel is well located a few blocks east of Union Square. It's a first-rate find for discerning travelers who want standard comforts at an affordable rate. There's no elevator, no facilities, no services to speak of, and rooms are small and lack anything resembling a view. But pillow-top mattresses, good-quality linens, contemporary redwood furniture and brand-new bathrooms tiled in pretty Italian ceramic add up to comforts that are far superior to most hotels in this price category There is dial-up Internet access from phone points in each room, and guests can use a nearby gym for $10.

Rooms: 45; five floors; designated nonsmoking floor. **Hotel amenities:** None. **Food services:** Rates include a basic continental breakfast; cafe serving light casual fare. **Cancellation:** 48 hours prior to arrival. **Wheelchair access:** Not accessible. **Subway:** L, N, Q, R, W, 4, 5, 6 to 14th St.

Wall Street Inn   VERY GOOD **$$–$$$**

9 South William St. (at Broad St.), Financial District *www.thewallstreetinn.com*

Phone: (212) 747-1500   Fax: (212) 747-1900

This serene and welcoming small hotel offers an excellent alternative for business travelers (and leisure visitors looking for a downtown perch) who prefer intimate inns over anonymous corporate hotels. This is a boutique hotel in the true rather than trendy sense. Management has done everything right here, paying close attention to the fundamentals and staying away from showy gimmicks. The plush Americana-style interiors are the perfect match for the historic building. Rooms are not overly large, but the décor is extremely attractive, the bedding is very high quality, and marble bathrooms are spacious and pretty. Nice extras include two-line phones, high-speed Internet dataports, mini-refrigerators and VCRs. Seventh-floor rooms are best, as the bathrooms have extra counter space and jetted tubs. The staff excels at offering individualized service and a personal touch. Heavily discounted weekend rates make it a veritable steal for weekenders.

Rooms: 46; seven floors; designated nonsmoking floors. **Hotel amenities:** Concierge, fitness room with sauna, business center, meeting room, laundry/dry-cleaning service, video library. **Food services:** Rates include continental breakfast. **Cancellation:** 24 hours prior to arrival. **Wheelchair access:** Accessible. **Subway:** 2, 3 to Wall St.; J, M, Z to Broad St.; N, R to Whitehall St.

CHELSEA/FLATIRON/
GRAMERCY PARK

Chelsea Lodge/Chelsea Lodge Suites   VERY GOOD **$**

318 W. 20th St. (between Eighth and Ninth Aves.)

www.chelsealodge.com, www.chelsealodgesuites.com

Phone: (212) 243-4499, (800) 373-1116   Fax: (212) 243-7852

This absolute gem of a hotel offers two kinds of lodging for discriminating budget travelers who want spotless accommodations, a dash of style and a location surrounded by excellent restaurants and nightspots. All rooms in the original walk-up brownstone are petite yet delightful doubles with a unique semi-private bath situation: Each room has a sink and a stall shower, so guests only have to share toilets. The entire building has been gorgeously renovated, and both public spaces and guest rooms overflow with country-in-the-city charm. Rooms are small, but superior comforts include high-quality bedding, smartly refinished vintage furniture, TVs, and lovely little touches like Hershey's Kisses on the fluffy pillows. Everything is like new and impeccably kept, and the staff is friendly. High ceilings make the first-floor rooms feel a bit larger.

The lodge has been such a success that the innkeepers now rent four additional studio-style suites in a nearby brownstone. Each features a queen bed, a brand-new marble bathroom, a fully outfitted kitchenette and a sitting area with TV/VCR and pullout sleeper sofa that allows the suites to accommodate up to four. Two suites share a private garden.

Rooms: 22 doubles with semiprivate bathrooms, four studios; three floors; all non-smoking. **Hotel amenities:** None. **Food services:** None. **Cancellation:** 72 hours prior to arrival. **Wheelchair access:** Not accessible. **Subway:** C, E, 1, 9 to 23rd St.

Chelsea Pines Inn

VERY GOOD **$**

317 W. 14th St. (between Eighth and Ninth Aves.)   *www.chelseapinesinn.com*
Phone: (212) 929-1023, (888) 546-2700   Fax: (212) 620-5646

This delightful walk-up on a very busy street in the heart of gay New York is targeted at gay and lesbian travelers, but all are welcome. The spotlessly kept rooms are attractively and wittily appointed. Each is named for a classic film star and features vintage poster art from the star's classic filmography. Otherwise, décor is very comfortable, everything is like new, and floral-print textiles create a pleasant, homey feeling. All rooms have minifridges and a phone with voice mail; most have queen beds and some have daybeds for extra seating/sleeping. A half-dozen deluxe rooms have breakfast areas with cafe tables and microwaves, plus a mini sound system with CD player, for just a few extra dollars. Private bathrooms are bright and freshly renovated; rooms that share baths have private showers and sinks, so budget-minded guests only have to share a hall toilet. Service is professional and friendly. Ask about special multinight packages and discounted weekly rates.

Rooms: 25 (9 with shared bathroom); 5 floors; smoking allowed in designated rooms only. **Hotel amenities:** Fax service, greenhouse-style breakfast/sitting room, back garden. **Food services:** Rates include continental breakfast; coffee, tea and cookies available throughout the day. **Cancellation:** 7 days prior to arrival; $50 cancellation fee. **Wheelchair access:** Not accessible. **Note:** Not for children. **Subway:** A, C, E to 14th St.

Colonial House Inn

GOOD **$**

318 W. 22nd St. (between Eighth and Ninth Aves.)   *www.colonialhouseinn.com*
Phone: (212) 243-9669, (800) 689-3779   Fax: (212) 633-1612

This lovely 1850's brownstone on a leafy Chelsea block was the first permanent home of the Gay Men's Health Crisis (GMHC). It's now an attractive and comfortable bed-and-breakfast that caters largely to a gay crowd but welcomes everybody. Rooms are small and simple but very nice. Almost half have private baths, and a few in the deluxe category have refrigerators and working fireplaces (Duraflame logs are supplied). All have TV, phone, radio and a comfortable bed, and everything is well tended. A surprisingly terrific collection of original abstract art (the work of owner and activist Mel Cheren) fills the public spaces, breakfast room and guest rooms, adding a thoughtful, creative air. The staff is professional and friendly, and the expanded continental breakfast features fresh baked goods. There's also a clothing-optional rooftop sun deck. All in all, an excellent choice. Book well in advance, especially for weekend stays. Inquire about discounted weekly rates.

Rooms: 20 (12 with shared bathrooms); 4 floors; smoking allowed. **Hotel amenities:** None. **Food services:** Rates include continental breakfast. **Cancellation:** Two weeks prior to arrival. **Wheelchair access:** None. **Subway:** C, E to 23rd St.

Four Points by Sheraton Manhattan Chelsea   very GOOD $$

160 W. 25th St. (between Sixth and Seventh Aves.) *www.starwood.com/fourpoints*
Phone: (212) 627-1888, (800) 325-3535   Fax: (212) 627-1611

Located in a sort of industrial no-man's-land halfway between Macy's and the Village, this new Sheraton lies a good walk away from Chelsea's liveliest concentration of restaurants and bars (it's close to the subway, however, which can whisk you to Times Square in five minutes). In fact, it would be surprisingly easy to miss this hotel amid the sewing machine stores and industrial buildings. Its Art Deco/industrial theme begins in the miniscule lobby, where leather throw pillows top Bauhaus-style chairs. The twin elevators lead to compact hallways and petite rooms, which contain dark-varnished wood furniture edged in black painted metal. The black bedspreads are offset by suede headboards and dark carpeting, resembling nothing so much as a cigar bar. Each room has a work desk, dual phone lines and Internet access. Rooms have one king or two double beds, and the mattresses are almost too firm. Each of the two junior suites has a sitting area with a leather couch, plus a north-facing balcony with great views of the Empire State and Chrysler buildings. Services are practically nonexistent, but that's the tradeoff for low prices.

Rooms: 158; 22 floors; designated nonsmoking rooms. **Hotel amenities:** Fitness center, meeting rooms, laundry and dry-cleaning service. **Food services:** Asian fusion restaurant, bar, room service. **Cancellation:** 24 hours prior to arrival. **Wheelchair access:** Fully accessible. **Subway:** 1, 9, F, V to 23rd St.

Gramercy Park Hotel   GOOD $$

2 Lexington Ave. (at 21st St.)   *www.gramercyparkhotel.com*
Phone: (212) 475-4320, (800) 221-4083   Fax: (212) 505-0535

For decades, this old-world hotel overlooking lovely Gramercy Park has hosted famous-name guests that have run the gamut from Babe Ruth and Humphrey Bogart to the Rolling Stones, Blondie and Jewel. This historic grande dame has been known for its mammoth rooms, its access to the idyllic gated park across the street and its thrillingly noirish New York vibe. Though few details were available at press time, the hotel has just been purchased by the Morgans Hotel Group, which is known for trendy, upscale properties. A major facelift seems likely; let's see.

Rooms: 509; 18 floors. **Subway:** 6 to 23rd St.

Hotel Chelsea
GOOD **$$**

222 W. 23rd St. (between Seventh and Eighth Aves.) *www.hotelchelsea.com*
Phone: (212) 243-3700

Fax: (212) 675-5531

Dozens of legendary writers, artists, actors and other creative types, ranging from William Burroughs to Sid Vicious, have stayed at or lived in this hotel since it opened in 1884. Artwork from tenants (often offered in lieu of rent in decades past) fills the lobby, enlivening every available space. The hotel is still largely occupied by residents with an artistic bent, but about 100 rooms are available to short-term visitors with a bohemian spirit. Rooms are large and eccentrically outfitted with generally older fixtures and furnishings, but usually comfortably so. The hotel is generally well kept, but the ghosts hovering in every corner of this landmark see to it that nothing is obsessively clean. Travelers in search of predictable comforts should stay elsewhere. Still, you get more space than in most New York hotels; most rooms have good light, many have kitchenettes, some have hand-carved marble fireplaces, and walls are famously thick. There's wifi access in the lobby and high-speed Internet connections available in some rooms. The staff is offbeat but friendly, attentive and used to meeting requests that range from the mundane to the extraordinary.

Rooms: 400 (usually about 100 available to travelers, some with shared bathroom); 12 floors; smoking allowed. **Hotel amenities:** Bell service (will send out dry-cleaning, pick up take-out food and so on). **Food services:** seafood-heavy El Quijote restaurant, hip bar Serena. **Cancellation:** 72 hours prior to arrival. **Wheelchair access:** ADA compliant. **Subway:** C, E, 1, 9 to 23rd St.

Hotel Giraffe
VERY GOOD **$$–$$$**

365 Park Ave. South (at 26th St.) *www.hotelgiraffe.com*
Phone: (212) 685-7700, (877) 296-0009

Fax: 212-685-7771

Designed from the ground up by supremely talented husband-and-wife team Stephen B. Jacobs (the architect) and Andi Pepper (the designer), this Flatiron District boutique beauty brims with Art Moderne–inspired elegance. Rooms aren't huge, but 10-foot ceilings create an open feeling, and honey-hued built-ins (including generous granite-topped work desks) use the available space beautifully, giving you room to spread out and reside in real comfort. All rooms have VCRs, CD players, cordless phones, wireless Internet access and windows that shut out virtually all street noise, plus gorgeous granite bathrooms. Deluxe rooms have French doors opening onto a juliet balcony, while suites add a separate living room with a long-legged coffee table that doubles for dining.

Rooms: 73; 12 floors; dedicated nonsmoking rooms. **Hotel amenities:** Concierge, business services, laundry and dry-cleaning service, video and CD libraries, rooftop garden, 1,000-square-foot penthouse suite with terrace for events. **Food services:** Sciuscia, Mediterranean restaurant and bar. Rates include continental breakfast; all-day cappuccino and snacks; cocktail hour with wine, cheese and live piano music; room service. **Cancellation:** 24 hours prior to arrival. **Wheelchair access:** Fully accessible. **Subway:** 6 to 28th St.

The Inn at Irving Place

56 Irving Pl. (between 17th and 18th Sts.)
Phone: (212) 533-4600, (800) 685-1447

EXCELLENT $$$$
www.innatirving.com
Fax: (212) 533-4611

Romance is the rule at this impeccably run, supremely elegant bed-and-breakfast inn, housed in adjoining 1834 Greek Revival brownstones on a lovely cafe-dotted Gramercy Park block. Each stunning guest room has its own layout, design and theme, usually a literary allusion (the Madame Olenska room, the Else deWolf suite and so on). No matter which one you choose, you can expect lavish high Victorian appointments that include well-chosen antiques and art, a grand non-working fireplace, Oriental rugs, luxurious fabrics and a supremely comfortable Frette-made queen bed. The bathrooms are beautiful. Modern-day luxuries include a TV with VCR (hidden in an armoire so as not to disturb the mood), a CD player, wireless Internet access and two-line phones. Deluxe rooms feature a small seating area, and the ultra-luxurious suites are larger than most Manhattan apartments, but standard rooms are sufficiently conducive to romance. The elegant staff is trained not to say no, and they usually don't. Lady Mendl's Tea Salon is a dream come true for those who like high tea—it doesn't get any better than this. Avoid rooms that overlook the basement-level restaurant's back-garden patio. And beware—there's no elevator. Otherwise, B & B fans looking for a special-occasion splurge should be thrilled; only Inn New York City (*see section* **Uptown** *later in this chapter*) comes close.

Rooms: 12; three floors; no smoking. **Hotel amenities:** Business services, laundry and dry-cleaning service, light shopping service. **Food services:** Elegant tearoom (Lady Mendl's), cocktail lounge (Cibar), 24-hour limited room service; rates include continental breakfast. **Cancellation:** 48 hours prior to arrival. **Wheelchair access:** Not accessible. **Note:** Not appropriate for children under 12. **Subway:** L, N, Q, R, W, 4, 5, 6 to 14th St.

The Inn on 23rd St.

131 W. 23rd St. (between Sixth and Seventh Aves.)
Phone: (212) 463-0330, (877) 387-2323

EXCELLENT $$
www.innon23rd.com
Fax: (212) 463-0302

This marvelous full-service bed-and-breakfast in the heart of Chelsea offers a perfect blend of genuine B & B charm and real-hotel amenities. Friendly innkeepers Annette and Barry Fisherman renovated this spacious 19th-century town house, and got everything exactly right in the process. The beautifully outfitted rooms and one suite have been decorated by Annette with an eye to both style and function. Every room is themed, but in a classy, not kitschy, way: The 40's room features Heywood-Wakefield and vintage bark cloth, while the Bamboo Room is elegantly Zen. The fifth-floor rooms all have skylights, and Ken's Cabin is a large, lodgey brick-walled room outfitted in wonderfully worn leather and delightful Americana accents, from Navajo rugs to vintage license plates. Appointments are first-class all the way. All rooms have two-line phones with voice mail and dataport, and high-speed Internet connections. Windows are double-glazed, and there are blackout shades and white-noise machines to lull you to sleep. The Inn on 23rd is child-friendly, and a

number of rooms feature pullout sofas or Murphy beds for extra travelers. A
real charmer and an excellent value.

Rooms: 14; five floors with elevator; no smoking allowed. **Hotel amenities:**
Business services, living room–style library. **Food services:** Rates include
expanded continental breakfast, plus wine and cheese on weekends. **Cancellation:** One week prior to arrival; one-night deposit is forfeited for cancellations
within the week. **Wheelchair access:** Fully accessible. **Subway:** 1, 9 to 23rd St.

The Maritime Hotel   VERY GOOD $$$
363 W. 16th St. (at Ninth Ave.)   *www.themaritimehotel.com*
Phone: (212) 242-4300   Fax: (212) 242-1188

Built in 1966, this white-on-white modern slab with porthole windows—the
former National Maritime Union—opened in 2003 as one of Manhattan's
newest trend-setting boutique hotels. It's the brainchild of two cool scenemakers: bi-coastal nightlife impresarios Eric Goode (New York's Time Café and
Bowery Bar) and Sean MacPherson (LA's Good Luck Bar and Bar Marmont).
Despite a total makeover, many original architectural elements have been preserved, including a colorful maritime-themed frieze circling the lobby at ceiling
height. Rooms are snug but well designed for maximum space and impact. Each
features gorgeous teak built-ins, including generous workspace and a platform
bed; boldly contemporary textiles in nautical hues; and its own five-foot-diameter porthole window dressed in velvet. Other fashion-forward features include
wireless Internet access, flat-screen TVs and two-line telephones, plus oversized
bath towels and upscale toiletries in the modern baths.

Rooms: 124; 12 floors; dedicated nonsmoking rooms. **Hotel amenities:** Concierge, fitness center (in the works at press time), business center, banquet room
accommodating up to 500. **Food services:** Hero lounge (the happening place to
be), lobby bar; outstanding Italian and Japanese restaurants, outdoor garden bar
and 24-hour room service. **Cancellation:** 24 hours prior to arrival. **Wheelchair
access:** ADA compliant. **Subway:** 1, 9 to 18th St.; A, C, E, L to 14th St.

W Union Square   EXCELLENT $$$–$$$$
201 Park Ave. South (at 17th St. and Union Sq. East)   *www.whotels.com*
Phone: (212) 253-9119, (877) 946-8357 (W-HOTELS)   Fax: 212-253-9229

The magnificent 1911 Beaux-Arts Guardian Life building houses the best of
New York's five W hotels. It boasts a terrific location, overlooking leafy, lively
Union Square. Architect David Rockwell has done an excellent job of transforming an office building into a luxury boutique-chic hotel, successfully fusing
original architectural details with clean-lined modernism.

Guest rooms are done in dark woods and gorgeous muted tones, with plush
fabrics, divinely comfortable beds, large worktables, high-speed Internet access
on 27-inch TVs, CD players, coffee makers, full-length mirrors and excellent
bathrooms featuring luminous mother-of-pearl countertops. Suites also have fax
machines and corner views overlooking Union Square Park. Service is personal

and reliable. Weekend and Internet-only rates are a great way to score high W style at a reasonable price.

Because it's smaller, the bright, comfortable, high-ceilinged lounge-like lobby isn't quite the frenzied scene you find at the original W New York—which many will consider a benefit. It's also cozier and warmer, with the W chain's signature wheat grass in planters used to great effect. Off the lobby is celebrity chef Todd English's Olives, which serves up very good Mediterranean-inspired nouveau fare, while sultry subterranean lounge Underbar is the domain of nightlife impresario Rande Gerber (Mr. Cindy Crawford).

Rooms: 270; 21 floors; designated nonsmoking floors. **Hotel amenities:** Concierge with W's signature "Whatever/Whenever" service, laundry and dry-cleaning service, exercise room, stunning ballroom, state-of-the-art meeting space. Pets accepted. **Food services:** Noted restaurant (Todd English's Olives), living room–style lounge, stylish subterranean Underbar, 24-hour room service. **Cancellation:** 4 P.M. day before arrival. **Wheelchair access:** Fully accessible. **Subway:** L, N, Q, R, W, 4, 5, 6 to 14th St.

MIDTOWN EAST & MURRAY HILL

The Benjamin   EXTRAORDINARY **$$$**
125 E. 50th St. (at Lexington Ave.)   *www.thebenjamin.com*
Phone: (212) 715-2500, (800) 637-8483   Fax: (212) 715-2525

The gorgeous, low-key Benjamin is a real winner. Housed within a stunning 1927 Emery Roth–designed building, the Benjamin boasts all the hallmarks of a boutique hotel, including a gracious staff. The magnificent lobby sets the tone with beautifully preserved architectural details, Venetian mirrors and a sweeping staircase leading to the mezzanine-level lounge.

The guest rooms are some of the best in town, especially for the money. They're decorated in a sophisticated neoclassical-meets-modern style, wearing rich textiles (chenille, mohair, linen) and champagne hues. But the real story is the appointments: The custom-designed Serta mattresses are dressed in Frette linens and down-filled duvets, with cushioned headboards and a choice of 11 pillow types. The kitchenettes feature microwaves, coffee makers, china and gourmet goodies. Oversized work desks are wired for high-tech travelers, with fax/printer/copiers, high-speed Internet access and outlets at desk level, ergonomic executive chairs, task lighting, two-line cordless phones and pullout undertables that are ideal for in-room dining. The 27-inch TVs feature Web TV and video games. Service is excellent, and rooms are blissfully free of street noise. The white marble bathrooms are on the small side, but use space efficiently. Suites add a divine sitting room with a full sofa, a super-cozy wingback mohair chair and a CD player; some have their own terraces.

Rooms: 209; 26 floors; dedicated nonsmoking floors. **Hotel amenities:** Concierge; full-service Affinia Wellness Spa with gym; laundry and dry-cleaning service; business services, executive boardroom and function rooms. Pets accepted. **Food services:** Restaurant, lounge; 24-hour room service. **Cancellation:** Before 6 P.M. day of arrival. **Wheelchair access:** Fully accessible. **Subway:** 6 to 51st St.

Crowne Plaza at the United Nations

VERY GOOD $$

304 E. 42nd St. (east of Second Ave.)   *www.unitednations.crowneplaza.com*

Phone: (212) 986-8800, (800) 879-8836   Fax: (212) 986-1758

A striking 1931 neo-Tudor building houses one of Manhattan's best chain hotels, located and designed to appeal to discerning diplomats. It also makes sense for visitors who want to be near Midtown, but not in the thick of it. Rooms are outfitted in a very comfortable and surprisingly high-quality traditional style. Italian marble baths and bedside controls for climate and lighting, a coffee maker, and well-chosen belle époque poster art and vintage black-and-white New York scenes add to the feeling of luxury. Select rooms and suites also have whirlpool tubs and pullout sofas or love seats. Triple-paned windows shut out street noise entirely. High-speed Internet access and dual-line speaker phones with voice mail and dataports are other pluses. Weekend, holiday and promotional rates can often score bargain hunters an excellent value.

Rooms: 300; 20 floors; designated nonsmoking floors. **Hotel amenities:** Concierge, fitness center with sauna, business center, laundry and dry-cleaning service, meeting and function rooms. **Food services:** Restaurant and bar, lounge for light dining, room service. **Cancellation:** 24 hours prior to arrival. **Wheelchair access:** Fully accessible. **Subway:** S, 4, 5, 6, 7 to 42nd St.

Fitzpatrick Grand Central Hotel

VERY GOOD $$$

141 E. 44th St. (at Lexington Ave.)   *www.fitzpatrickhotels.com*

Phone: (212) 351-6800, (800) 367-7701   Fax: (212) 818-1747

This lovely hotel from the Dublin-based Fitzpatrick hotel group is notable for its distinctive Emerald Isle personality, its warm hospitality and its excellent location, just steps from Grand Central Terminal. The small but welcoming lobby leads to elegant guest rooms that far surpass the business-hotel standard with elegant half-canopied beds, luxury fabrics, very pleasing and spacious baths, minifridges, coffee makers, two-line phones, fax machines, wireless Internet access and plush terry robes. The Liam Neeson penthouse offers Waterford- and marble-adorned ultra-luxury, including many amenities imported from Ireland. The Garden Suites are not quite as luxurious, but outdoor patios and big, beautiful baths make them a worthwhile splurge. Check for special packages and heavily discounted Internet rates, especially for weekend stays.

Rooms: 151; 10 floors; designated nonsmoking floors. **Hotel amenities:** Concierge, exercise room, laundry and dry-cleaning service, small meeting room, car service. **Food services:** Authentic Wheeltapper Irish pub, 24-hour room service. **Cancellation:** 24 hours. **Wheelchair access:** Fully accessible. **Subway:** S, 4, 5, 6, 7 to 42nd St.

Four Seasons Hotel New York

EXCELLENT $$$$

57 E. 57th St. (between Park and Madison Aves.)
Phone: (212) 758-5700, (800) 487-3769

www.fourseasons.com
Fax: (212) 758-5711 (guest) or
(212) 350-6302 (reservation)

This ultra-modern, I.M. Pei–designed hotel is a haven of supreme luxury for international CEOs and superstars. Pei's sleek 52-story limestone tower is filled with 1930's-meets–21st-century glamour and a soothingly sophisticated ambiance. The combination of stunning spaces, first-class amenities and impeccable Four Seasons service makes this one of the city's most outstanding (though shockingly expensive) places to stay.

The money-is-no-object ostentation begins the moment you step into the soaring, streamlined lobby with its reflective marble floors and backlit onyx ceiling. All but the cheapest rooms are large—500 to 600 square feet, 800 in suites—and sumptuously designed in a lovely cream-on-white style that harkens back to the Golden Age of Hollywood. Standout features include lustrous silks, warm English sycamore furnishings that include an oversized dining/work table, spacious dressing areas, massive Florentine marble baths with lush oversized towels and soaking tubs that fill in 60 seconds, fax/printer/copier combos, Bose CD/alarm clocks, DVD players, plasma TVs, multi-line phones with voice mail, and high-speed Internet access. Floor-to-ceiling windows frame breathtaking views (and bedside-controlled window treatments allow you to shut them out); a lucky handful of rooms have balconies, too. The custom Sealy PostureLux mattresses offer such a good night's sleep that many guests purchase them as a big-ticket souvenirs to take back home.

Rooms: 364 (21 with balconies); 52 floors; designated nonsmoking floors. **Hotel amenities:** 24-hour concierge; full-service spa and fitness center with steam, whirlpool and sauna; full-service business center; laundry and dry-cleaning service; health club; extensive meeting and conference space. **Food services:** New York Times three-star Fifty Seven Fifty Seven restaurant and martini bar, Lobby Lounge for afternoon high tea, light fare and cocktails; 24-hour room service. **Cancellation:** 24 hours prior to arrival. **Wheelchair access:** Fully accessible. **Subway:** 4, 5, 6 to 59th St.; E, V to Fifth Ave.

The Helmsley Middletowne

GOOD $$

148 E. 48th St. (between Lexington and Third Aves.) www.helmsleyhotels.com
Phone: (212) 755-3000, (212) 888-1624, (800) 221-4982 Fax: (212) 832-0261

A converted apartment building that still feels like one, the Middletowne doesn't have room service, an exercise room or even much of a lobby. What it does have are large, relatively affordable rooms and suites (both junior suites and full one- and two-bedrooms). Every room has a refrigerator (most have wet bars, too), two-line phones, older but nice bathrooms and generous closet space. Furnishings are older and lack any style, but mattresses are fresh and firm, and carpets, textiles and linens are like new. The one- and two-bedroom suites are big enough to call home, and full galley kitchenettes make it so (some cabinets are without dishware, though). The location is pleasant and convenient, and the long-employed staff is friendly and strives to meet your needs.

Rooms: 192 (includes 42 suites); 18 floors; designated nonsmoking floors. **Hotel amenities:** Laundry and dry-cleaning service, meeting room. **Food services:** Rates include a basic continental breakfast. **Cancellation:** 24 hours prior to arrival. **Wheelchair access:** Fully accessible. **Subway:** 6 to 51st St.

Hotel Elysée

VERY GOOD   **$$$**

60 E. 54th St. (between Park and Madison Aves.)   *www.elyseehotel.com*
Phone: (212) 753-1066, (800) 535-9733   Fax: (212) 980-9278

Built in 1926, this charming and intimate hotel makes a lovely choice for travelers who want a boutique hotel without pretensions. Styled like a small European hotel, it offers rooms and suites that are generously sized and traditionally decorated in dark woods and soft, pretty pastels. Entry halls and vestibules make the rooms feel residential and buffer guests from hallway noise (as do the thick walls). All accommodations have firm beds, well-maintained marble baths, good closet space, VCRs, two-line phones and high-speed Internet access. A handful of junior suites have nonworking fireplaces, while two deluxe rooms and a suite have terraces. Rooms with two doubles are especially large and suitable for families and shares; suites also have sleeper sofas and some offer kitchenettes and small dining areas. Complimentary breakfast and weekday evening wine and cheese are served in the supremely comfortable, elegant sitting room, which recalls the French Empire with its rich velvets and reds and golds. The service is intimate and attentive, and the location is the very best part of Midtown—in the heart of it all but not too bustling. The legendary Monkey Bar is as stylish as ever.

Rooms: 101; 15 floors; designated nonsmoking floors. **Hotel amenities:** Laundry and dry-cleaning service, sitting room, clubby library (where a PC offers free Internet access), free access to nearby health club, video library. **Food services:** Monkey Bar restaurant and bar, room service; rates include continental breakfast and evening wine and hors d'oeuvres. **Cancellation:** 24 hours prior to arrival. **Wheelchair access:** 2 rooms. **Subway:** E, V to Lexington Ave.

Kimberly Hotel

VERY GOOD   **$$$**

145 E. 50th St. (between Lexington and Third Aves.)   *www.kimberlyhotel.com*
Phone: (212) 755-0400, (800) 683-0400   Fax: (212) 486-6915

This low-profile hotel was conceived as an apartment building but was recast as a hotel during construction. The practical effect of this quick change is plenty of space for guests. The very pleasing hotel boasts mostly apartment-style one-bedroom and two-bedroom/two-bath suites featuring all the comforts of home, including a well-equipped kitchen with full-size appliances; a living room with a dining area and Oriental rugs; marble bathrooms; and large, nicely appointed rooms. One-bedroom suites run about 600 square feet, two-bedroom suites a whopping 1,200 square feet, making them perfect for families and business travelers looking to stay awhile. All rooms have mini-fridges. Video games are on hand to please the kids; fax machines, high-speed Internet access and two-line phones are on hand for business travelers. A number of attractive and comfortable standard doubles with especially nice bathrooms and deep soaking tubs are also available, but the best values are clearly the suites. The traditional décor isn't stylish, but the comfort level is high. Service is refined and attentive. On site is George O'Neill's, a classic steakhouse, and the chic nightclub VUE, built in the 1920's as an opera house. The Kimberly's ongoing promotions and package rates are excellent; almost no one pays full rack rate here, so be sure to mine for discounts.

Rooms: 185 (mostly suites); 30 floors; designated nonsmoking floors. **Hotel amenities:** Concierge, laundry and dry-cleaning service, business center, penthouse meeting suite, free access for adults to nearby health club with swimming pool. **Food services:** Two restaurants, two bars, room service. **Cancellation:** 24 hours prior to arrival, 48 hours on weekends. **Wheelchair access:** Fully accessible. **Subway:** 6 to 51st St.

The Kitano New York   EXCELLENT $$$–$$$$

66 Park Ave. (at 38th St.)   *www.kitano.com, www.summithotels.com*
Phone: (212) 885-7000, (800) KITANO-NY (548-2666)   Fax: (212) 885-7100

This elegant Japanese-owned hotel is a sea of tranquility in the bustle and chaos of New York City. Botero's voluptuous bronze sculpture "Dog" greets you at the entrance—and the art collection only gets better from there. The clean-lined lobby exudes luxury with deep-grained mahogany, rich suede-upholstered sofas and fabulous art. The overall feeling is one of warmth, sophistication and Zen-like repose.

The modern guest rooms and suites are clean-lined, natural-hued havens of Japanese luxury and practicality. The building's corner location grants impressive cityscape views to most rooms. Though the windows do open, they seem to hermetically seal each room from street noise. Other luxury extras include large work desks with fax machines and high-speed Internet access, Web TV, heated towel racks in the marble baths, bathrobes, umbrellas for borrowing and green tea (a hot pot is provided). If you're the adventurous sort, book New York's only authentic Tatami Suite; its bedroom can be transformed into a Japanese tea ceremony room. Nadaman Hakubai, the hotel's elegant kaiseki restaurant, is exceptional, and the largely Japanese staff offers flawless service. Weekend packages and special Internet rates are the way to go for vacationers in search of a special getaway.

Rooms: 149; 19 floors; designated nonsmoking floors. **Hotel amenities:** Concierge, business services, laundry and dry-cleaning service, boardroom, meeting space, free access to nearby health club. **Food services:** Nadaman Hakubai restaurant, continental cafe, lounge with live jazz (Wed.–Fri.), room service. **Cancellation:** 24 hours prior to arrival. **Wheelchair access:** Fully accessible. **Subway:** S, 4, 5, 6, 7 to 42nd St.

Le Marquis

GOOD $$$–$$$$

12 E. 31st St. (between Fifth and Madison Aves.)   www.lemarquisny.com
Phone: (212) 889-6363, (866) MARQUIS (627-7847)   Fax: (212) 889-6699

This lovely boutique hotel, new in 2002, unites style and comfort. The tone is set in the classic-goes-contemporary lobby, dressed in the warm cherry woods and deep blues that pervade the hotel. In the back is a delightful living room–style lounge where you're invited to pull a book off the shelf, check your e-mail on a PC with free high-speed Internet access, or sink into a sofa, put your feet up and watch a classic flick on the 40-inch flat-screen TV.

The smallish guest rooms are beautifully outfitted with custom furnishings that include armoires, efficient work desks and platform beds wearing goose-down and fine linens. Further in-room luxuries include Nintendo, two-line cordless phones, free high-speed Internet access and DVD/CD players. The sparkling white, cobalt-accented bathrooms boast double-wide glassed-in shower stalls with rainshower heads (a few have standard tub/shower combos).

Rooms: 120; 14 floors; designated nonsmoking floors. **Hotel amenities:** 24-hour concierge, laundry and dry-cleaning service, exercise room with Finnish sauna, high-tech conference room. **Food services:** Chic Bar 12:31, serving light Thai fare; room service. **Cancellation:** 24 hours prior to arrival. **Wheelchair access:** ADA compliant. **Subway:** N, R to 28th St., 6 to 33rd St.

Library Hotel

VERY GOOD $$$

299 Madison Ave. (at 41st St.)   www.libraryhotel.com
Phone: (212) 983-4500, (877) 793-7323   Fax: (212) 499-9099

One of the best boutique hotels in town is this biblio-themed charmer, located just a stone's throw from the New York Public Library, the hotel's inspiration. The Library Hotel is intimate and beautifully outfitted in a classic-goes-contemporary style; the unifying theme establishes a tone of both luxury and joyful discovery. The floors are categorized by the Dewey Decimal system, with each room's "subject" reflected in the framed photography and books within: Romance Languages, Ethics, Botany, Fairy Tales, Erotic Literature, African Religion and so on. Would-be astronauts might like the Astronomy room (Neil Armstrong did), while those with a penchant for the past might prefer the Twentieth Century room (on the History floor) or the Dinosaurs room (Math and Science). The Love room (on the Philosophy floor) is a must for romancing couples, who can read Shakespeare's sonnets to each other. Fiction and nonfiction books covering a range of subjects also fill the cozy penthouse-level library; overall, the hotel's collection numbers more than 6,000 titles.

The guest rooms themselves are understated but beautiful, done in a rich and restful natural palette. Mahogany built-ins provide a wealth of work and storage space; bathrooms aren't very big, but they're smartly designed. Amenities include VCRs (the full library of the American Film Institute's top 100 films is on hand for you to borrow), free bottled water, two-line cordless phones and free high-speed Internet access.

Rooms: 60; 14 floors; designated nonsmoking rooms. **Hotel amenities:** Laundry and dry-cleaning service, business center, penthouse-level conference room, library lounge with fireplace, penthouse-level terrace, free access to New York Sports Club. **Food services:** Rates include continental breakfast, all-day cappuccino and cookies, weekday wine and cheese. **Cancellation:** 24 hours prior to arrival. **Wheelchair access:** ADA compliant. **Subway:** S, 4, 5, 6, 7 to 42nd St.

The Lombardy   EXCELLENT $$–$$$

111 E. 56th St. (between Park and Lexington Aves.)   *www.lombardyhotel.com*
Phone: (212) 753-8600, (800) 223-5254   Fax: (212) 754-5683

Built in 1926 by William Randolph Hearst for his mistress, silent film star Marion Davies, the Lombardy is a marvelous vestige of old New York, one of its last genuine apartment hotels. The Lombardy is a co-op residence made up of individually owned apartments—75 one-bedrooms and 40 studios—that are rented as hotel rooms, along with a full spectrum of hotel services. The superior products here are the huge one-bedroom suites, which average 850 square feet. Décor varies dramatically since they're individually owned, but almost all have been beautifully renovated, some remarkably so. Studios, which average about 450 square feet, are a bit of a crapshoot décor-wise, but owners are held to a high standard, and you still get a lot for your money. All units have fully equipped kitchenettes in separate rooms; all have fridges, microwaves and coffee makers, and many have stovetops and/or dishwashers. Bathrooms are usually marble and always pleasant, but not large; on the other hand, most New Yorkers would kill to have this much closet space. Other common features include dining areas and work desks; maid service is also a part of the package. A standout is no. 402, a glorious one-bedroom outfitted with marble floors, two glorious marble baths, a new kitchen and a museum-worthy collection of mid-century and modern furnishings and art.

The hotel runs like a well-oiled machine: The entire place is immaculately kept, the fiercely loyal staff is solicitous to residents and hotel guests alike, and management always strives to improve an already-stellar property. Smoking is allowed in all rooms (unless the owner prohibits it), but the hotel is so well maintained that it's hard to smell a whiff anywhere. The excellent on-site restaurant, L'Etoile, is a mid-priced neighborhood favorite.

Rooms: 115 (mostly suites); 14 floors; smoking allowed. **Hotel amenities:** Concierge, day spa and salon, laundry and dry-cleaning service, exercise room, business center, meeting and function space. **Food services:** Restaurant and lounge, room service. **Cancellation:** 24–48 hours prior to arrival, depending on season. **Wheelchair access:** Fully accessible. **Note:** Children under 12 not accepted. **Subway:** 4, 5, 6 to 59th St.

Morgans   VERY GOOD $$–$$$

237 Madison Ave. (between 37th and 38th Sts.)   *www.morganshotelgroup.com*
Phone: (212) 686-0300, (800) 606-6090   Fax: (212) 779-8352

Ian Schrager's first boutique hotel opened in 1984 as a low-profile "anti-hotel" without a sign or a staff member experienced in hotel management. There's still little to give away its quiet Murray Hill location except for the limos occasionally dropping off some high-profile type, but today the staff is experienced and competent. Andrée Putman's interiors eschew the over-the-top, theatrical elements of Schrager's other Philippe Starck–designed hotels in favor of a low-key, grown-up sensibility. Hotel restaurants don't get more popular than the perennially hot—and surprisingly good—Asia de Cuba, but since it's tucked away with a separate entrance, the scene doesn't intrude on the hotel's tranquil domestic tone.

Rooms are not huge, but low-to-the-ground furnishings and beautiful maple-eye built-ins—including cushioned window seats for both lounging and out-of-sight luggage storage—make them feel spacious, and the colors are serene and restful. The beds are luxurious, with 300-thread-count Egyptian cotton sheets, down comforters, Scottish wool blankets and suede headboards. Other extras include spacious work desks, high-speed Internet access, two-line phones with direct-dial numbers, and CD players (on request). The small bathrooms feature black-and-white checkered tile and stainless-steel sinks; most have double-wide stall showers, so request a tub when booking if you want one. Though you might not expect it from such a cool place, there are lots of family-friendly amenities on hand, including jogging strollers, playpens, cribs, toys and other baby gear; babysitting can be arranged.

Rooms: 113; 19 floors; designated nonsmoking floors. **Hotel amenities:** 24-hour concierge, business services, dry-cleaning and laundry service, state-of-the-art meeting space. **Food services:** Asia de Cuba restaurant, Morgans Bar, 24-hour room service; rates include continental breakfast served in the cozy Living Room. **Cancellation:** 24 hours prior to arrival. **Wheelchair access:** ADA compliant. **Subway:** S, 4, 5, 6, 7 to 42nd St.

Murray Hill Inn

BASIC $

143 E. 30th St. (between Lexington and Third Aves.)   *www.nyinns.com*
Phone: (212) 545-0879, (212) 693-6900   Fax: (212) 545-0103

The rooms here are small, spare and about as stylish as your great-aunt Erma's house. But this well-managed walk-up hotel, sister to the Union Square Inn (see "Downtown") and the Amsterdam Inn (see "Upper West Side"), makes an excellent choice for travelers on a strict budget. In late 2003, all rooms were refurbished with new furniture, fabrics, hardwood floors and satellite TVs, plus new bathrooms with Italian tile (most units used to share, but almost all have private baths now). The mostly tiny rooms are outfitted with a single bed, bunks or a double; a phone; a wall rack for hanging clothes; and a dresser. Facilities and services are virtually nonexistent, as is standard for New York's cheapest hotels. Management is planning to offer wireless Internet access in early 2005.

Rooms: 50 (4 with shared bathrooms); five floors; designated nonsmoking floors. **Hotel amenities:** None. **Food services:** None, but complimentary continental breakfast offered at nearby coffee shops. **Cancellation:** 72 hours prior to arrival. **Wheelchair access:** Not accessible. **Subway:** 6 to 33rd St.

The New York Palace   EXCELLENT $$$$
455 Madison Ave. (between 50th and 51st Sts.)   *www.newyorkpalace.com*
Phone: (212) 888-7000, (800) NY-PALACE (697-2522)   Fax: (212) 303-6000

Founded by the notorious Helmsley hoteliers, the Palace is now owned by the
Sultan of Brunei, and it's a superior choice. The Palace mostly occupies a high-
rise modern tower presiding over the stunning Villard Houses (1882), a land-
mark that holds the hotel's boldly decorated public spaces as well as the Villard
Bar & Lounge, one of the city's most stylish watering holes (the famed Le
Cirque 2000 restaurant moved out in late 2004).

   The hotel boasts what are essentially three levels of service and amenities.
There are the "deluxe" standard rooms, nine executive floors geared to business
travelers, and the Towers, which is virtually a boutique hotel in its own right.
The main hotel and executive rooms are a spacious 300 square feet, and feel
even larger. They're not stylish, but they are extremely comfortable. They boast
generous work desks and bedside side tables, both with pullout undertables that
make the useable space even larger, and a bedside control panel that adjusts
lighting, temperature, a "Do Not Disturb" sign and the like. The rooms in the
Towers average a larger 400 square feet and are done in either classic or modern
Deco design. Towers guests also benefit from more personalized services. You
don't have to be in the Towers, though, to enjoy spectacular views; ask for a
room overlooking St. Patrick's or book one of the four glorious triplex suites,
each with its own elevator, gorgeous designer décor and breathtaking panoramic
vistas via 18-foot windows. High-speed Internet access is offered in all rooms
(it's free in the Towers) as well as three phone lines.

Rooms: 897; 55 floors; designated nonsmoking floors. **Hotel amenities:**
Concierge, business center, meeting and function rooms, fitness center with a
view, laundry and dry cleaning. **Food services:** Restaurant (Istana; at press time,
a replacement for Le Cirque 2000 had not been announced), two bars, 24-hour
room service. **Cancellation:** 24 hours prior to arrival. **Wheelchair access:** Fully
accessible.

Omni Berkshire Place   EXCELLENT $$$–$$$$
21 E. 52nd St. (at Madison Ave.)   *www.omnihotels.com*
Phone: (212) 753-5800, (800) THE-OMNI (843-6664)   Fax: (212) 754-5018

The Omni may not have a high profile, but this tranquil and refined luxury
hotel is first-rate on all fronts, from the comfortably traditional décor to the
impeccable service. Built by internationally renowned architectural firm Warren & Wetmore in 1926, the hotel underwent a complete $70 million renova-
tion in 1995. In mid-2003, the guest rooms were upgraded again, with rich color
schemes, luxurious fabrics and plush touches like down duvets and pillows, 300-
thread-count sheets and pillow-topper mattresses. The marble-and-granite bathrooms are substantially larger than those in most other historic luxury hotels,
and they now feature wall-to-wall mirrors. Even standard rooms are large, and
appointments include TVs with Internet access and Nintendo, CD players, fax
machines, robes and umbrellas, free high-speed Internet connectivity, plus a

bedside superphone that controls the lights, TV, music and more. Get Fit rooms feature their own portable treadmills. A serene air pervades all of the public spaces and guest floors, and double-glazed windows mean that even the second-floor meeting rooms on the Madison Avenue side are ultra-quiet.

Management is first-class and Omni corporate (which manages just 40 hotels) keeps a tight rein, so service is first-rate. Extensive business services are available for corporate travelers, and the neighborhood is prime shopping territory. Discounts and special packages abound for savvy travelers.

Rooms: 396; 21 floors; one designated smoking floor. **Hotel amenities:** Clef d'Or concierge, full-service business center, good fitness center with sun deck, laundry and dry-cleaning service, extensive meeting and function space (including executive boardroom), Omni Kids program. Pets are accepted. **Food services:** Restaurant, bar, lounge for afternoon tea and light fare, 24-hour room service. **Cancellation:** 24 hours prior to arrival. **Wheelchair access:** Fully accessible. **Subway:** 6 to 51st St.; E, V to Fifth Ave.

The Roger Williams   GOOD $$–$$$
131 Madison Ave. (at 31st St.)   *www.rogerwilliamshotel.com*
Phone: (212) 448-7000, (888) 448-7788   Fax: (212) 448-7007

This pleasing hotel presides over lower Madison Avenue like a temple of sleek modern design. The two-story lobby sets a tranquil tone that's carried into the compact but smartly designed guest rooms. Architect Rafael Viñoly has used space well, with blond built-ins that include platform beds, entertainment centers and user-friendly worktables. Task lighting, shoji-like window coverings and white-on-white Belgian linens are other nice touches. Many guests prefer the baths with the double shower stalls over the tub/shower combos. In 2004, the hotel underwent a renovation; a new fitness center and a new restaurant were added, and guest rooms were revamped. Each one is now outfitted with a new flat-screen TV, plus new furniture and fabrics. Amenities include wireless high-speed Internet access, VCRs, CD players and down comforters and pillows. Penthouse rooms also have semi-private terraces with memorable views of Midtown.

Rates are slashed during slow periods, and some type of discount or value-added package is almost always available, so be sure to ask. Free breakfast adds to the good value at any time of year. The concierge is more connected than most in this price range.

Rooms: 183; 16 floors; designated nonsmoking floors. **Hotel amenities:** Concierge, laundry and dry-cleaning service, exercise room, business center, mezzanine-level guest lounge, CD and video libraries. **Food services:** Restaurant (under construction at press time); cookies and 24-hour self-serve cappuccino bar; room service at lunch and dinner Mon.–Fri. (dinner only on Sat.); rates include continental breakfast. **Cancellation:** 24 hours prior to arrival. **Wheelchair access:** Fully accessible; ADA compliant. **Subway:** 6 to 33rd St.

The St. Regis, New York

EXTRAORDINARY $$$$

2 E. 55th St. (at Fifth Ave.)
Phone: (212) 753-4500, (800) 325-3535

www.stregis.com
Fax: (212) 787-3447

Commissioned by industrialist John Jacob Astor and opened in 1904 when 55th Street was still considered the suburbs, the St. Regis still reigns supreme as the pinnacle of Gilded Age wealth, grace and civility. This Beaux-Arts landmark is a monument to conspicuous consumption with 22K gold leaf, Italian marble, rich mahogany paneling, Louis XVI antiques and Waterford crystal covering every square inch (apparently, even the walls of the boiler room are marble). A complete restoration in 1991 ensured thoroughly modern conveniences, but the style remains unabashedly Old World. The St. Regis isn't for you if you prefer understatement, but there's no arguing with it as one of New York's most glorious and well-run hotels.

After checking in, you are escorted to your floor, where you will be greeted by an elegant butler who will see to your every need during the course of your stay. Prefer soy milk with your morning coffee? No problem. Want your room prepared for an afternoon nap every day at 3 PM? It's a snap. Even the smallest guest room is at least 430 square feet, and brims with luxury features: high ceilings, silk wall coverings, king beds dressed in 300-thread-count Egyptian cotton sheets, bedside controls, VCRs, high-speed Internet access, executive work desks with fax machines, and glamorous bathrooms with double sinks and ultra-plush bathrobes with a sexy retro flair.

With its Maxfield Parrish mural and legendary bar nuts, the King Cole Bar is the most well-heeled of Midtown watering holes, and Astor Court is a winner for formal high tea. And event spaces don't come more glorious than those at the St. Regis. Among the multiple breathtaking venues is the St. Regis Rooftop, one of New York's most sought-after spaces for society weddings and other once-in-a-lifetime events.

Rooms: 315; 18 floors; designated nonsmoking floors. **Hotel amenities:** Concierge, 24-hour Maitre d'Etage butler service, business center, fitness center with saunas, laundry and dry-cleaning service, extensive meeting and function space. **Food services:** King Cole Bar, Astor Court tea lounge, 24-hour room service. **Cancellation:** 24 hours (72 hours in Dec.). **Wheelchair access:** Fully accessible. **Subway:** E, V to Fifth Ave.

70 Park Avenue Hotel

EXCELLENT $$$

70 Park Ave. (at E. 38th St.)
Phone: (212) 973-2400, (877) 707-2752

www.70parkavenuehotel.com
Fax: (212) 973-2401

Convenient to Midtown (it's only four blocks from Grand Central, a short walk to Times Square and close to Fifth Avenue shopping), this is one of Manhattan's newest boutique hotels. It's all about very stylish serenity. The lobby, complete with fireplace, is a cozy space meant to feel like a living room. The rooms are compact, but mirrors on opposing walls create an infinity effect. Flameless, rechargable Candellas glow softly when removed from their base, allowing you to set the mood when you're nestled in your suede-backed armchair or working at the leather-topped desk. The hotel makes a special effort to cater to female guests: the minibar stocks everything from panty hose to nail files and polish; the bathroom lighting is soft and indirect; the maid leaves under-eye cream on your pillow at turndown; and there's even an in-house yoga channel (call the desk to request your yoga mat). This almost makes up for the lack of on-site gym facilities (there's a fitness center a block and a half away with all the standard classes). Linens and towels are of exceptional quality, mattresses are firm, and ergonomic headboards support your neck when you're sitting up in bed to read. Each room has a work desk, a high-definition 42-inch flat-screen TV, a DVD/CD player, wireless Internet access, and a high-tech KioPhone with Internet, e-mail, electronic room service and more. The armoire has metal mesh doors to allow your clothes to "breathe"; here you'll also find designer robes, an iron and ironing board, and an umbrella. Rooms have either one or two queen-size or double beds; 18 rooms have extra-large spa bathrooms. The penthouse suite has a wraparound balcony.

Rooms: 205; 17 floors; with designated nonsmoking rooms. **Hotel amenities:** Concierge, laundry and dry-cleaning service, meeting and function rooms. **Food services:** New American restaurant and bar; complimentary wine hour in lobby; 24-hour room service. **Cancellation:** 24 hours prior to arrival. **Wheelchair access:** Fully accessible. **Subway:** 4, 5, 6, 7, S to 42nd St.–Grand Central.

Sheraton Russell Hotel

45 Park Ave. (at 37th St.)
Phone: (212) 685-7676, (800) 325-3535

GOOD $$$–$$$$
www.sheraton.com
Fax: (212) 889-3193

This serene and intimate hotel is richly residential in feeling and exceptionally well run. Don't let the chain-hotel name fool you: offering accommodations under the Sheraton brand since the 1940s, the Russell is intertwined with New York history (in fact, the property originally belonged to the family for which the surrounding Murray Hill neighborhood is named) and has its own independent spirit—not to mention a comforting sense of permanence in a city where hotels change owners and names like hats.

The civilized tone is set in the mahogany-paneled lobby, plus a gorgeous living room with cozy sofas, shelves of books for borrowing and a gas fireplace. The spacious, high-ceilinged rooms are comfortably and traditionally decorated, with swagged drapes and dark furnishings, but the tone is light and the atmosphere inviting. Features include high-speed Internet access, coffee makers, decent closet space and soundproofing that successfully banishes street noise. Each room also has Sheraton's "Sweet Sleeper Bed," with an extra-soft top mattress, a duvet and feather down pillows. Nearly half of the rooms are designated as club-level "Smart" rooms, equipped as virtual offices; they boast some of the best work desks in the city with a leaf that pulls out for more workspace or in-room dining, a swiveling ergonomic chair, fax/printer/copier, desk-level inputs and Bose Wave radios. Suites also have queen sleeper sofas, cordless phones and second TVs. The only downsides? Service can be uneven, and regular rates are a bit too high given the strong competition at the over-$300 mark.

Rooms: 146; 10 floors; designated nonsmoking floors. **Hotel amenities:** Clefs d'Or concierge, living room-style lounge, fitness room, business center, laundry and dry-cleaning service, boardroom. **Food services:** Breakfast room, bar and cocktail lounge, 24-hour room service. **Cancellation:** 24 hours prior to arrival. **Wheelchair access:** Fully accessible. **Subway:** 6 to 33rd St.

Swissôtel New York—The Drake   EXTRAORDINARY $$$$
440 Park Ave. (at. 56th St.)   www.swissotel.com
Phone: (212) 421-0900, (888) 737-9477 (73-SWISS)   Fax: (212) 371-4190

A new-in-2001 lobby wearing a gorgeous contemporary European look completed a total facelift that transformed the 1929-vintage Drake from Depression-era dowager into the most stylish roost on Park Avenue. The high-ceilinged guest rooms wear a similarly warm and elegant Regency-goes-modern style, with bold furnishings and art, plus textiles in rich coffee tones, ethnic-inspired patterns and splashes of vibrant color. Amenities include triple-paned windows, two-line phones, high-speed Internet access, an oversized work desk with fax machine and desk-level inputs, a club chair or other seating area, coffee maker, bathrobes and an umbrella for rainy days. More than 100 rooms are one- or two-bedroom suites with wet bars, and some Park Avenue suites feature terraces. VCRs, CD players and fridges are available on request.

Terrific accommodations aside, the Drake is worth a stay for its superior facilities alone. Q56 restaurant attracts a stylish foodie crowd with a smart contemporary interior and a first-rate global seafood menu. Ditto for Parisian chocolatier Fauchon, which operates a gorgeous retail boutique featuring sweets flown in daily, plus a dainty salon serving lunch and afternoon tea. The spa and fitness center is also a standout, featuring an extensive workout facility and one of New York's few hydrotherapy rooms. All and all, an extraordinary hotel—and destined to get even better now that stellar Singapore hotelier Raffles is in charge. Check online, because Internet specials can be a steal.

Rooms: 495; 21 floors; designated nonsmoking floors. **Hotel amenities:** Clefs d'Or concierge; full-service Park Avenue Spa & Fitness center; laundry and dry-cleaning service; full-service, state-of-the-art business and conference center with full secretarial support; extensive meeting and function space. Pets accepted. **Food services:** Q56 restaurant and bar, Fauchon Salon de The for afternoon tea, 24-hour room service. **Cancellation:** 24 hours prior to arrival. **Wheelchair access:** Fully accessible. **Subway:** 4, 5, 6 to 59th St.

Thirty Thirty   GOOD $-$$
30 E. 30th St. (between Park and Madison Aves.)   www.thirtythirty-nyc.com
Phone: (212) 689-1900, (800) 497-6028   Fax: (212) 689-0023

The former home of the Martha Washington women's hotel (model for the Tom Hanks and Peter Scolari roost in the vintage sitcom *Bosom Buddies*) and legendary nightclub Danceteria (where Madonna launched her career) has been transformed into a sleek modern hotel that's ideal for budget travelers who want a great value and a dash of panache. An industrial-chic lobby leads to smallish but comfortable rooms that boast a hip khaki look and brand-new everything; even the hallways have a smart modern style. Nice features include cushioned headboards, firm mattresses, good bedside lighting, roman shades on the windows, built-in wardrobes and nicely tiled baths that are pretty spacious considering the low price tag. There are dataports in each room and high-speed Internet access from a kiosk in the lobby. Most rooms are either queens or twin-bedded rooms, and a few larger rooms have kitchenettes. A brand-new executive level features extra-spacious rooms with either one king or two queen beds, CD player, coffee maker and a gorgeous granite bath; some have sleeper sofas.

Rooms: 243; 12 floors; one designated smoking floor. **Hotel amenities:** Concierge, dry-cleaning and laundry service, free access to nearby gym. Pets are accepted. **Food services:** Restaurant and bar. **Cancellation:** 24 hours prior to arrival. **Wheelchair access:** Fully accessible. **Subway:** 6 to 33rd St.

W New York—The Court

130 E. 39th St. (at Lexington Ave.)
Phone: (212) 685-1100, (877) W-HOTELS (946-8357)

VERY GOOD **$$$**
www.whotels.com
Fax: (212) 889-0287

W New York—The Tuscany

120 E. 39th St. (between Lexington and Park Aves.)
Phone: (212) 686-1600, (877) W-HOTELS (946-8357)

VERY GOOD **$$$**
www.whotels.com
Fax: (212) 779-7822

These side-by-side sister hotels are superior to their uptown counterpart, the original W New York on Lexington Avenue, and a little less of a scene than the W Union Square and the W Times Square (both also reviewed in this chapter). The beautifully designed rooms are both substantially larger and significantly improved in both form and function. The cosmopolitan-chic look features sumptuous textiles in a restful palette with just a few sexy red accents; pillowtop mattresses dressed in gorgeous linens with a cozy thermal throw; a plush chaise for lounging; and big, bold, angular furnishings that include an oversized worktable. Rooms look the same at both properties, but the Tuscany gives you a bit more space in both bedroom and bath. In-room luxuries include DVD/CD players, cordless phones and high-speed Internet access.

It used to be that the Court was the trendy crowd's activity hub, with the highly praised restaurant Icon and the hot Wetbar in residence. But the arrival of the W Cafe in the Tuscany's living room-style lobby as well as Cherry, a bar from nightlife impresario Rande Gerber, has upped the volume of the scene at the Tuscany, too. However, the Tuscany does remain the more laid back of the two.

Rooms: 198 rooms, 16 floors at the Court; 120 rooms, 17 floors at the Tuscany; designated nonsmoking rooms. **Hotel amenities:** 24-hour concierge with W's signature "Whatever/Whenever" service, stylish fitness center SWEAT,

laundry and dry-cleaning service, meeting and function rooms. **Food services:**
Icon restaurant, Wetbar at the Court; W Cafe, Cherry bar at the Tuscany;
24-hour room service. **Cancellation:** 24–72 hours prior to arrival, depending
on reservation. **Wheelchair access:** Fully accessible. **Subway:** S, 4, 5, 6, 7 to
42nd St.

Waldorf=Astoria, A Hilton Hotel   EXCELLENT $$$–$$$$
301 Park Ave. (between 49th and 50th Sts.)   *www.waldorfastoria.com*
Phone: (212) 355-3000, (800) WALDORF (925-3673)   Fax: (212) 872-7272

Waldorf Towers, A Conrad Hotel   EXCELLENT $$$$
100 E. 50th St. (at Park Ave.)   *www.waldorf-towers.com*, *www.conradhotels.com*
Phone: (212) 355-3100, (888) WA-TOWER (928-6937)   Fax: (212) 872-7272

Sure, everybody knows the legendary Plaza—but many would prefer this grande
dame over that tourist magnet any day of the week. For good reason: This mammoth block-square hotel is now in the capable hands of the Hilton Hotels group,
and it's as gorgeous and glamorous as ever. Rates are actually rather reasonable in
the main hotel, considering the old New York pedigree, beautifully appointed
rooms and first-class dining and amenities. No two rooms are alike; they range
from 200-square-foot deluxe units to 900-square-feet suites. Overall, you can
expect a high-ceilinged room or suite that's generally large by city standards, outfitted in a fresh hybrid Deco-traditional style and very comfortable. Marble bathrooms are the norm, and 21st-century touches include two-line phones and
fax/printer/copiers for laptop toters; most have high-speed Internet access (some
have only dataports). Business-class rooms add nightly turndown service and on-
screen Web access, while Astoria-level rooms feature dedicated concierge service
and complimentary continental breakfast and evening hors d'oeuvres. Don't
expect anything resembling personal attention in a hotel of this size, but the
place runs remarkably smoothly considering that it's practically big enough to
need its own ZIP code.

Operated under the Conrad Hotels flag (Hilton's ultra-luxury brand), the
exclusive Waldorf Towers occupies floors 28 through 42. This is where globe-
trotting celebrities and world leaders stay (including every president from Herbert Hoover to Bill Clinton); they're ushered in through a separate entrance
and attended to around the clock. With themes ranging from French Provincial
to opulent Asian, these elegant rooms and suites boast original art and antiques,
crystal chandeliers and the like, plus full dining rooms, kitchens and maid's
quarters in many. In addition to the lavish decor, there are practical features like
coffee makers, high-speed Internet access, fax/printer/copier combos and two-
line phones. It's the ultimate in residential hotel living—which is why legends
ranging from the Duke of Windsor and wife, Wallis Simpson, to Frank Sinatra
called the Towers home for so many years.

Rooms: 1,245 in the Astoria, 180 in the Towers; 42 floors; designated nonsmoking floors. **Hotel amenities:** Concierge, theater desk, fitness center with
massage services, laundry and dry-cleaning service, legendary Starlight Ballroom

and extensive meeting space; butler service and Clefs d'Or concierge in Towers. **Food services:** Bull & Bear, an excellent choice for steaks, chops and classic cocktails; Oscar's for American brasserie food, including Sunday brunch; Inagiku for nouveau Japanese; Peacock Alley for Sunday Brunch; Cocktail Terrace for afternoon tea and cocktails; Sir Harry's Bar; 24-hour room service. **Cancellation:** 24 hours prior to arrival. **Wheelchair access:** Fully accessible. **Subway:** 6 to 51st St.

MIDTOWN WEST & TIMES SQUARE

The Algonquin   VERY GOOD **$$–$$$**
59 W. 44th St. (between Fifth and Sixth Aves.)   *www.algonquinhotel.com*
Phone: (212) 840-6800, (888) 304-2047   Fax: (212) 944-1419

Birthplace of *The New Yorker* magazine and "*My Fair Lady*," home to Dorothy Parker's literary Round Table of the 1920s, this legendary hotel closed its doors briefly during the summer of 2004 for renovations. They swung open again to reveal updated rooms and thoroughly refreshed public areas (but don't worry; the ambience of that great mahogany-paneled lobby was left largely intact). Michael the bellman and Matilda the cat are still in residence, and the beloved New Yorker cartoon wallpaper remains in the hallways.

Since no two rooms are exactly alike, each unit got a custom redesign treatment in the renovation process. Some received all-new furnishings; other retain an original armoire or chair. Plush carpeting, new window treatments, black-and-white photo prints of the hotel and bedding in vibrant color schemes give the high-ceilinged rooms a fresh new look. You'll find luxurious 350-thread-count sheets and duvets on the new all-white beds. Most bathrooms still have their original short but deep soaking tubs, but now have more space, new vanities and great shower curtains imprinted with Al Hirschfeld drawings. Rooms now sport conveniences such as high-speed Internet access and two-line speakerphones with dataports and voice mail. Many have flat-screen plasma TVs. Terry robes, fresh fruit and umbrellas are other nice touches. Rooms with window seats set into bay windows are especially charming. For the ultimate in historic appeal, book one of the delightfully outfitted literary-themed suites, which also boast VCRs and CD players.

Off the glorious mahogany-paneled lobby is the Oak Room, still one of the city's premier cabaret rooms. Be sure to check out the rotating collection of Al Hirschfeld drawings in the equally atmospheric Blue Bar, which offers good service, excellent pub fare and clubby appeal. The Round Table Room restaurant serves a new menu of American/continental fare, but still offers classics like Lobstor thermidor and the Dorothy Parker sirloin steak.

Rooms: 174; 12 floors; designated nonsmoking floors. **Hotel amenities:** Concierge, fitness center, business services, laundry and dry-cleaning service, five meeting and function rooms. **Food services:** American/Continental restaurant, lobby lounge for light meals and cocktails, Blue Bar pub, room service. **Cancellation:** 24 hours prior to arrival. **Wheelchair access:** ADA compliant. **Subway:** B, D, F, S, V to 42nd St.

Americana Inn   BASIC $

69 W. 38th St. (at Sixth Ave.)   *www.newyorkhotel.com*
Phone: (212) 840-6700, (888) HOTEL-58 (468-3558)   Fax: (212) 840-1830

Shoestring accommodations convenient to the Theater District don't get better than the Americana, run by the same reliable hotel group behind Midtown's Travel Inn and the Belvedere as well as the Upper West Side's Lucerne (all recommended in this chapter). Linoleum floors and fluorescent lighting create an institutional feel, but rooms and shared bathrooms are bright and spotless, service is professional and an elevator (uncommon in many budget-basic hotels) makes luggage-toting easy. Every room has generic but like-new furniture, a comfortable bed with a nice bedspread, a TV, a telephone and a sink. The Garment District location is central, but ask for a room in the back to avoid street noise.

Rooms: 50 (all with shared bathroom); 5 floors; designated nonsmoking rooms. **Hotel amenities:** None. **Food services:** Common kitchen with fridge and microwave on each floor. **Cancellation:** 24 hours prior to arrival. **Wheelchair access:** None. **Subway:** B, D, F, N, Q, R V, W to 34th St.

Belvedere Hotel   GOOD $$

319 W. 48th St. (between Eighth and Ninth Aves.)   *www.newyorkhotel.com*
Phone: (212) 245-7000, (888) HOTEL-58 (468-3558)   Fax: (212) 245-4455

Here's a nice mid-priced hotel in the heart of the Theater District, just steps away from the Broadway theaters and hip Ninth Avenue, Manhattan's newest Restaurant Row.

A Deco-inspired lobby that's more beautiful than most in this price range leads to rooms that are good-sized, cheerfully decorated and very comfortable. Beds (either a queen or two doubles) are nice and firm, the cherrywood furnishings are better than average, linens are of good quality and towels are fluffy. The smallish bathrooms are well maintained and boast massaging shower heads. Each room has a small kitchenette with a minifridge, a microwave, and a coffeemaker, plus video games and Web TV; about a quarter of the rooms have high-speed Internet access. Executive-level rooms and suites also feature luxurious king beds with fluffy down comforters, a work desk with an ergonomic chair and CD player. The staff is efficient and friendly. Many guests are European leisure travelers.

Rooms: 400; 17 floors; designated nonsmoking floors. **Hotel amenities:** Concierge, self-serve business center, laundry and dry-cleaning service, self-serve laundromat, fitness center, conference room. **Food services:** Brazilian restaurant Churrascaria Plataforma; cafe and lounge. **Cancellation:** 24 hours prior to arrival. **Wheelchair access:** Fully accessible. **Subway:** C, E to 50th St.

Big Apple Hostel   BASIC $

119 W. 45th St. (between Sixth and Seventh Aves.)   *www.bigapplehostel.com*
Phone: (212) 302-2603   Fax: (212) 302-2605.

Manhattan's best hostel is budget-basic all the way, but it's spotlessly clean, well managed and cheap as can be (usually around $30 per person in a dorm room, less than $85 for a private single or double). The location is fabulous, just steps from Times Square in the heart of the Theater District. Dorm rooms feature four metal bunks and little else; linens are provided, but plan to bring your own towels. The tiny private doubles are not quite so spartan; you can expect a full-size bed, a phone, an alarm-clock radio and a small TV with cable. Shared bathrooms are better than average, as are the common spaces, which include a well-equipped kitchen and a small furnished patio with a barbecue grill. Book well in advance, since the hostel is increasingly popular with families, who like the dorm-style accommodations and central-to-everything location (Mom and Dad can usually score a dorm for four, thus turning it into a "private" room), as well as international tourists who can afford better but prefer spending their money in more lasting ways. In the dog days of summer, you'll be grateful that air-conditioning was recently added throughout the entire property. There's no elevator for guest use, so be prepared to haul your luggage.

Rooms/beds: 112 dorm beds, 11 private rooms (all with shared bathrooms); 7 floors; no smoking allowed. **Hotel amenities:** Luggage storage. **Food services:** Common kitchen. **Cancellation:** One day prior to arrival. **Wheelchair access:** Not accessible. **Subway:** 1, 2, 3, 9, N, R, S to 42nd St.

The Blakey New York   VERY GOOD $$–$$$

136 W. 55th St. (between Sixth and Seventh Aves.)   *www.blakeynewyork.com*
Phone: (212) 245-1800, (800) 735-0710   Fax: (212) 582-8332

This newly overhauled Midtown hotel was transformed from the bright and brassy Gorham (known for its great family amenities, not its looks) into a much more adult-friendly property that caters first and foremost to business travelers and groups. Ira Drukier and Richard Born (the names behind the trend-setting Maritime, Chambers and Mercer hotels, as well as the more down-to-earth Wellington and Holiday Inn Midtown) have created a completely new animal. From the forest green ultra-suede walls and tartan-patterned carpeting in the hallways, it would seem that the Blakey has been reborn as a warm and cozy English hunting lodge. Well, close enough. This fresh, new incarnation is a winner with its top-notch location and traditional look. Even though the Blakey is geared to business travelers, the room amenities are perfect for families. Every unit room has a king bed or two doubles, a work desk, a two-line phone, Frette bathrobes, a 27-inch flatscreen TV, free high-speed Internet access, a DVD/CD player and a large marble bath, plus a fully outfitted kitchenette with microwave, coffee maker and dishes. Spacious one-bedroom suites have a twin daybed in the living room and two TVs. Cribs are available and kids under 18 stay free.

Rooms: 117; 17 floors; designated nonsmoking floors. **Hotel amenities:** Concierge, business services, fitness room, laundry and dry-cleaning service, meeting room with garden terrace. **Food services:** Abboccato, a new Italian restaurant and bar (from the owners of Molyvos and Oceana), breakfast room with buffet spread (not included in rates), room service. **Cancellation:** 24 hours prior to arrival. **Wheelchair access:** ADA compliant. **Subway:** B, D, E to Seventh Ave.; F, N, R, Q, W to 57th St.

Broadway Inn   VERY GOOD $$
264 W. 46th St. (at Eighth Ave.)   www.broadwayinn.com
Phone: (212) 997-9200, (800) 826-6300   Fax: (212) 768-2807

Here's a find for folks who want bed-and-breakfast comforts and charm without sacrificing a Theater District location. Part full-service hotel, the Broadway Inn is a haven of tranquility and good taste just off garish, neon-lit Times Square. The big draw is the phenomenal service—some of the best the city has to offer in this price range—and the charming ambiance. The simple rooms are impeccably maintained and tastefully decorated with an Art Deco flair. Beds are firm, linens are of good quality, and bathrooms are pleasant and spotless. With a sleeper sofa, microwave, minifridge and lots of closet space, the suites are a good bet for longer stays or shares. Continental breakfast is served in the charming sitting room/lobby, where brick walls, book-lined shelves, an overstuffed sofa and classical music set a restful, homey tone. Wireless Internet access is also offered in the lobby. Children are welcome (a nice change from the B & B norm). Rates are a bit high in the fall, but reasonable the rest of the year, especially considering the quality and location. An A+ for cleanliness, reliability and service. This is a walk-up, however, so stay elsewhere if you require an elevator. And while the rooms are relatively quiet, this is a noisy corner of the city; ask for a back-facing room if you want to ensure quiet.

Rooms: 41; four floors; no smoking allowed. **Hotel amenities:** Concierge, fax and copy services. **Food services:** Rates include continental breakfast; guest discounts at two nearby restaurants. **Cancellation:** 48 hours to 3 weeks prior to arrival, depending on reservation. **Wheelchair access:** Not accessible. **Subway:** A, C, E to 42nd St.

Bryant Park Hotel   VERY GOOD $$$–$$$$
40 W. 40th St. (between Fifth and Sixth Aves.)   www.bryantparkhotel.com
Phone: (212) 869-0100, (877) 640-9300   Fax: (212) 869-4446

Directly across from Bryant Park, one of the city's most civilized squares, this boutique hotel made its debut in 2001. It's housed in the majestic 1924 American Radiator Building (immortalized by Georgia O'Keeffe during her New York years), whose breathtaking gilt-edged facade has been impeccably restored. The unapologetically modern-minimalist lobby comes as something of a shock, but a pleasant one.

The hotel was conceived as a high-ticket ultra-luxury palace; after the economy's downturn, the hotel couldn't score those $400-plus reservations, so value-minded luxury travelers will get a lot for their money here. But don't be surprised if service doesn't equal that at the St. Regis. Extra-high ceilings, super-white walls and blond-wood floors give the large, airy rooms and suites the look of finished luxury lofts. Furnishings are bold and angular, softened by ultra-luxury textiles—cashmere-covered goose-down, Tibetan rugs, phenomenal 400-thread-count Egyptian linen—and bold, autumn accent colors. Bathrooms are luxurious in a clean-lined, high-quality way, with a beautiful blend of travertine, stainless steel and teak furnishings, plus the most beautiful sinks to occupy any hotel bathroom. Amenities include high-speed Internet access, VCRs, Bose CD players, digitally downloadable movies, cordless phones and fax machines. Expect your fellow guests to be a well-heeled mix of uber-trendy fashion and media folks.

Rooms: 129; 22 floors; designated nonsmoking floors. **Hotel amenities:** 24-hour concierge, state-of-the-art fitness center, laundry and dry-cleaning service, boardroom, 70-seat screening room. **Food services:** Ilo restaurant, Lobby Lounge, Cellar Bar, 24-hour room service. **Cancellation:** 48 hours prior to arrival. **Wheelchair access:** Fully accessible. **Subway:** B, D, F, S, V to 42nd St.

Buckingham Hotel

VERY GOOD **$$**

101 W. 57th St. (at Sixth Ave.)
www.buckinghamhotel.com
Phone: (212) 246-1500, (888) 511-1900
Fax: (212) 246-1311

Staying in this all-suite hotel (a residence since 1929) is like having your own New York City pied à terre. Suites are not as sharply decorated as the hip, music-themed lobby and public spaces suggest, but they do boast hardwood floors, colonial-style furnishings and comfortable beds, and housekeeping is spotless. Studios are generously sized (360 to 405 square feet) and feature a sleeping area with a plump queen bed, a fully furnished dining or sitting area, a nice kitchenette, and a small but bright bathroom. The 450- to 650-square-feet one-bedrooms boast a large living room with dining area, a separate bedroom with a nicely dressed queen or king, and a fully outfitted kitchen complete with dishwasher. All units, no matter what the size, feature a cordless phone and a fully equipped entertainment center with 27-inch TV with cable and VCR, plus a Sony CD stereo and high-speed Internet access. One-bedrooms also have a work desk.

A gorgeous contemporary stained-glass window overlooking 57th Street adds a touch of the majestic to the Buckingham. In the lobby you'll be greeted by a staff that's friendly, if small; no matter, because they've managed to earn a guest book full of accolades. The week's cultural happenings are posted in the stylish elevator, evidence of the hotel's thoughtful management and artistic flair. The Buckingham is real deal considering its generous spaces, newness, extensive amenities and A-1 location (Carnegie Hall is just down the block). Short-term stays enjoy daily maid service, while long-term stays benefit from cheaper rates and weekly maid service.

Rooms: 85; 17 floors; designated nonsmoking rooms. **Hotel amenities:** Concierge, fitness center with sauna, self-service business center. **Food services:** None. **Cancellation:** 24 hours prior to arrival. **Wheelchair access:** ADA compliant. **Subway:** B, D, F, S, V to 42nd St.

Chambers

VERY GOOD $$$$

15 W. 56th St. (between Fifth and Sixth Aves.)   *www.chambers-ahotel.com*
Phone: (212) 974-5656, (866) 204-5656   Fax: (212) 974-5657

Celebrity architect David Rockwell envisioned this boutique hotel as an uptown version of a downtown loft—and he largely succeeded. Unfinished concrete and a phenomenal (and somewhat controversial) modern art collection set a SoHo tone, while rich fabrics and furniture add Fifth Avenue polish. The hotel has made such an impression that comedian Chris Rock quipped, "The Four Seasons is a nice place to stay if Chambers is booked."

The lobby is streamlined and fairly straightforward; the magnificent art collection starts on the mezzanine-level lounge. Each guest-floor hallway wears a specially commissioned artwork or installation by a noted contemporary artist, including Katerina Grosse, Sheila Pepe and filmmaker John Waters; some simply installed a piece, while others actually used the entire hallway as their tableau. Modeled after an artist's loft, each guest room has carefully chosen furniture and objects that emphasize the cutting edge, plus at least four original artworks. The result is a stimulating combination of rough-hewn and luxurious. Turkish rugs, mohair, faux furs and hand-painted velvet soften the look, but some may consider the concrete slabs, hand-troweled walls and unfinished base moldings a bit much. Iridescent tiles, rainwater showerheads and deep tubs add luxury to the monolithic concrete bathrooms. Technology includes high-speed Internet access, cordless phones and CD/DVD players. You can even request in-room personal yoga instruction and personal shopping services from Henri Bendel.

Another notable feature is Geoffrey Zakarian's exciting restaurant Town, a *New York Times* three-star winner, which also provides room service.

Rooms: 77; 15 floors; two designated smoking floors. **Hotel amenities:** Concierge, fitness room (plus free access to New York Sports Club), laundry and dry-cleaning service, CD and DVD libraries. **Food services:** Town restaurant with bar, room service. **Cancellation:** Before 3 P.M. day prior to arrival. **Wheelchair access:** Fully accessible. **Subway:** B, D, E to Seventh Ave. St.; F, N, R, Q, W to 57th St.

City Club Hotel

VERY GOOD $$$

55 W. 44th St. (between Fifth and Sixth Aves.)   *www.cityclubhotel.com*
Phone: (212) 921-5500, (888) 256-4100   Fax: (212) 944-5544

Hotelier Jeff Klein has created a boutique hotel for the new millennium. It's housed behind a modest 1904 facade on Hotel/Club Row, directly across the street from the Royalton. In some ways, this delightfully discreet hotel is the anti-Royalton: The City Club is all about restful solitude rather than a party scene. Guests are greeted with a small, simple lobby where the adornments are limited to a floor-to-ceiling painting by modern master Richard Giglio. A skylight peeks through to a mezzanine-level lounge, which is sometimes used as a tea salon.

The spacious guest rooms are all about cocooning. Interior designer-to-the-stars Jeffrey Bilhuber has created a restful look that beautifully blends traditional furnishings and textiles with midcentury-modern lines and finishes. A gorgeous soft palette adds to the serene ambiance. Custom furnishings include a marvelous window seat, cushioned from floor to ceiling and overflowing with fluffy pillows, plus a movable table for working or dining. Plump feather beds are dressed in lovely Frette linens. High-tech luxuries include DVD and CD players, two-line cordless phones, free high-speed Internet access and TVs hidden behind floor-length mirrors (an interesting and space-saving element, but unfortunately it means you won't get an ultra-crisp picture). Done in chocolate marble and chrome, bathrooms are outfitted with a double-wide shower or a tub, plus Hermès toiletries and robes. The art is an appealingly eclectic mix of original modern art, old New York photos, Broadway playbills from the 50's, and framed LPs from the 80's. Unfortunately, a few signs of wear are showing here and there. The impressive new duplex suites boast his-and-hers bathrooms and terraces with glorious Manhattan views. Also on site is *New York Times* two-star winner DB Bistro Moderne from chef Daniel Boulud.

Rooms: 65; seven floors; designated nonsmoking floors. **Hotel amenities:** 24-hour concierge, complimentary access to nearby health club, laundry and dry-cleaning service, CD and DVD libraries. **Food services:** DB Bistro Moderne restaurant, room service. **Cancellation:** 24 hours prior to arrival. **Wheelchair access:** ADA compliant. **Subway:** B, D, F, V, 7 to 42nd St.

Comfort Inn Midtown   GOOD $–$$

129 W. 46th St. (between Sixth Ave. and Broadway)
www.comfortinn.com, www.applecorehotels.com
Phone: (212) 221-2600, (800) 567-7720   Fax: (212) 764-7481

This modest but comfortable hotel prides itself on being Manhattan's only wholly smoke-free chain hotel. It's plain but pleasant, and offers good value and a great location for theater goers. A marble-and-mahogany lobby leads to petite but pleasant guest rooms that wear cheerful Shaker-style décor and boast coffee makers, video games and TV Internet access, nice marble-and-tile bathrooms (some of which only have showers). Facilities are better than most in this price category. Rates can soar on occasion, but rooms are usually value priced in the low $100s. Complimentary continental breakfast adds to the bargain, as does free wi-fi access. A nice choice for non-smoking budget-minded travelers.

Rooms: 79; nine floors; no smoking allowed. **Hotel amenities:** Fitness room, self-service business center, laundry and dry-cleaning service, meeting room. **Food services:** Rates include continental breakfast. **Cancellation:** 24 hours prior to arrival. **Wheelchair access:** Not accessible. **Subway:** B, D, F, N, Q, R, S, V, W, 1, 2, 3, 7, 9 to 42nd St.

Crowne Plaza Manhattan

GOOD $$$

1605 Broadway (between 48th and 49th Sts.)   www.crowneplaza.com
Phone: (212) 977-4000, (800) 243-6969   Fax: (212) 333-7393

Towering over Times Square is the international flagship of Holiday Inn's upscale brand. Style-setting designer Adam Tihany infused the public spaces with new zest in 1999, but they're still more chain-generic than chic. Expect anonymous but comfortable accommodations outfitted with standard comforts like coffee makers and work desks. Sightlines are one of the towering glass monolith's best assets; no guest rooms are located below the 16th floor, so most offer views and quiet. There's no better perch for watching the Thanksgiving Day parade float by or the New Year's Eve ball drop. Another excellent attraction is the massive 34,000-square-foot New York Sports Club fitness center, which features a 50-foot skylit lap pool. On the downside, the hotel always bustles with convention and group business, and its huge size can make the service slow and chaotic at times; don't expect anything resembling personalized attention. Rack rates are too high, so hold out for discounts and special offers.

Rooms: 770; 46 floors; designated nonsmoking floors. **Hotel amenities:** Concierge, tour desk, business center, secretarial services, New York Sports Club, laundry and dry cleaning, 29,000 square feet of meeting and function space. **Food services:** One restaurant, two bars, room service. **Cancellation:** Before 6 P.M. day prior to arrival. **Wheelchair access:** Fully accessible. **Subway:** 1, 9 to 50th St.; N, R, W to 49th St.

Doubletree Guest Suites Times Square

VERY GOOD $$$

1568 Broadway (at 47th St. and Seventh Ave.)   www.nyc.doubletreehotels.com
Phone: (212) 719-1600, (800) 222-TREE (222-8733)   Fax: (212) 921-5212

This all-suite hotel's central location at the neon heart of Times Square and its extensive amenities make it a good choice for families, business travelers and theater lovers alike. Don't expect much in the way of personality, but suites are spacious, attractive and contemporary. They're remarkably quiet, given the location; the ceilings are low but you don't feel cramped. Each suite has a separate bedroom, a living room with a sleeper sofa (great for the kids), a table that does double duty for dining and working, a wet bar with microwave and coffee maker, high-speed Internet connectivity and two TVs with video games. For business travelers, a dozen conference suites with good workstations are set up for small meetings (for up to eight). A floor of childproof suites caters to families, as do a range of special amenities, including a well-outfitted playroom, a children's room-service menu and a kid-friendly staff. Theatergoers will appreciate the connected concierge; those who want half-price tickets need only step out the front door to reach the TKTS discount ticket booth. All in all, a terrific choice, especially for those who want their space and a heart-of-it-all location. Inquire about theater packages. And help yourself to Doubletree's fresh-baked chocolate-chip cookies, which are always available at the front desk.

Rooms: 460 (all suites); 43 floors; designated nonsmoking floors. **Hotel amenities:** Concierge, tour desk, business center, fitness center, laundry and dry-cleaning service, meeting and function rooms. **Food services:** Broadway-themed restaurant and lounge, room service. **Cancellation:** 24 hours prior to arrival. **Wheelchair access:** Fully accessible. **Subway:** 1, 9 to 50th St.; N, R, W to 49th St.

Hilton New York   GOOD $$–$$$
1335 Sixth Ave. (between 53rd and 54th Sts.)   *www.newyorktowers.hilton.com*
Phone: (212) 586-7000, (800) HILTONS (445-8667)   Fax: (212) 315-1374

The largest hotel in New York is a virtual city unto itself, with traffic congestion in the lobby, guests from all over the globe, a staff that speaks 30 languages, even a 24-hour foreign currency exchange office. Rooms are small, as are bathrooms, but wall-to-wall windows frame pleasing city views, especially on the upper floors, and you'll find all the reliable mid-level comforts that the Hilton name guarantees. A recent $90 million renovation has left things feeling fresh and sophisticated, and the Rockefeller Center location suits business and leisure travelers alike. The newer Times Square sister hotel (see below) is preferable, but this is by no means a bad choice—as long as you don't mind crowds and conventioneers. The hotel plays host to countless business and society functions in its whopping four floors of ballroom and meeting space.

Hallways are incredibly long, so expect a hike from your room to the nearest elevator. Standard rooms come with either a queen, a king or two double beds; all rooms have marble baths, 27-inch TVs, coffee makers, high-speed Internet access and two phones with voice mail and dataport. You may find it worthwhile to spend a few extra dollars on an Executive-Floor room, which allows you to bypass the throngs with private check-in and awards you with a dedicated concierge, complimentary breakfast, and all-day snacks and evening hors d'oeuvres in the Executive Lounge.

Rooms: 2,041; 46 floors; designated nonsmoking rooms. **Hotel amenities:** Concierge, theater and tour desks, full-service business center, fitness center and full-service day spa, laundry and dry-cleaning service, kid's "Vacation Station" in summer, meeting and function rooms. **Food Services:** Two restaurants (one Italian, one American), two bars, room service. **Cancellation:** 24 hours prior to arrival. **Wheelchair access:** Fully accessible. **Subway:** B, D, E to Seventh Ave.

Hilton Times Square   EXCELLENT $$$
234 W. 42nd St. (between Broadway and Eighth Ave.)
www.timessquare.hilton.com
Phone: (212) 840-8222, (800) HILTONS (445-8667)   Fax: (212) 840-5516

New in 2000, this Hilton gracefully rises above the clamor of Times Square, thanks to clever design that puts all guest rooms above the 22nd floor. As a result, even the cheapest room is peacefully quiet and comes with a great view. As soon as you enter the 21st-story Sky Lobby, you'll realize that this isn't just another Hilton. Co-opted from the pervasive boutique-hotel movement is a living room–style lobby with extra-high ceilings, cozy seating nooks, original contemporary art, a chic open bar, a stylish restaurant and an air of sophistication. Guest accommodations surpass the chain-hotel norm with larger-than-standard rooms (330 to 360 square feet) that hold a king or two double beds, smart décor featuring blond wood furnishings, an attractive natural palette and original art. Each room has an easy chair with ottoman, a generous work desk, a coffee maker, expansive marble counters in the spacious bathrooms, and technology that includes complimentary high-speed Internet access, desk-level inputs and CD players. Suites, which average a large 660 square feet, are especially comfortable and stylish, and make a worthy splurge.

Rooms: 444; 24 floors (hotel on floors 21-44); designated nonsmoking floors. **Hotel amenities:** Concierge, business center, secretarial services, fitness room, laundry and dry-cleaning service, kid's "Vacation Station," meeting and function space. **Food services:** Restaurant (called Above), Pinnacle lobby bar, 24-hour room service. **Cancellation:** 24 hours prior to arrival. **Wheelchair access:** Fully accessible. **Subway:** A, C, E, N, Q, R, S, W, 1, 2, 3, 7, 9 to 42nd St.

Hotel Casablanca

VERY GOOD $$–$$$

147 W. 43rd St. (east of Broadway)

www.casablancahotel.com

Phone: (212) 869-1212, (888) 922-7225

Fax: (212) 391-7585

Thanks to a designer with a deft touch, this Moroccan-spiced hotel avoids kitsch in favor of an exotic look that's downright enchanting. The Casablanca is so welcoming and tranquil that it's hard to believe you're in the eye of the Times Square storm. Rooms are not large, but high-quality details—including polished rattan furnishings, Murano glass light fixtures, gorgeous Andalusian tile in the bathrooms (which have either a tub or an oversized shower), North African art, two-line phones, VCRs, CD players and ceiling fans—speak to the care that has gone into this place. While spaces are small, they're just fine for two—and the Casablanca suits a romantic mood.

The second floor is home to Rick's Cafe, an extremely inviting lounge with a serve-yourself cappuccino machine, a roaring fireplace in winter and a small alfresco patio in warmer months. Complimentary breakfast, all-day coffee and cookies, and weekday wine and cheese add to the excellent value. Furthermore, the staff is exceptionally warm, and there's no better perch from which to watch the ball drop on New Year's Eve. Check for weekend, seasonal and Internet specials (as low as $179).

Rooms: 48; six floors; designated nonsmoking floors. **Hotel amenities:** Business center, free use of nearby New York Sports Club, laundry and dry-cleaning service, state-of-the-art conference room, video library. **Food services:** Rates include continental breakfast, all-day cappuccino at Rick's Cafe, and weekday wine and cheese. **Cancellation:** Before 5 P.M. day prior to arrival. **Wheelchair access:** ADA compliant. **Subway:** B, D, F, N, Q, R, S, V, W, 1, 2, 3, 7, 9 to 42nd St.

Hotel Edison   BASIC $–$$

228 W. 47th St. (between Broadway and Eighth Ave.) *www.edisonhotelnyc.com*
Phone: (212) 840-5000, (800) 637-7070   Fax: (212) 596-6850

Located in the heart of the Theater District since it opened in 1931, the Edison has long been a beacon for budget-minded travelers looking for a central location. Unfortunately, popularity seems to have gone to its head—this mammoth hotel has raised its rates substantially in the last few years, though it's often still possible to snag a room for less than $200. Still, it continues to be a good choice for travelers who want to be in the middle of the action. Rooms don't even register on the personality meter—think run-of-the-mill motor lodge—but they're reasonably comfortable and very well kept. Amenities are pretty barebones, though the hotel is adding wifi access in late 2004. Most double rooms feature two twins or a full bed, but there are some queens; request one at booking and show up early in the day for your best shot at one. Quad rooms suit families well. Off the grand, block-long, Art Deco–muraled lobby is the perennially popular and cheap Cafe Edison, a Polish deli and de facto canteen for up-and-coming theater types. Service is virtually nonexistent, so don't expect much.

Rooms: 850; 22 floors; designated nonsmoking floors. **Hotel amenities:** Theater/transportation desk, laundry and dry-cleaning service, exercise room. **Food services:** Two restaurants (one Polish deli, one continental), the Rum House bar. **Cancellation:** 24 hours prior to arrival. **Wheelchair access:** Fully accessible. **Subway:** A, C, E, N, Q, R, S, W, 1, 2, 3, 7, 9 to 42nd St.

Hotel Metro   VERY GOOD $–$$

45 W. 35th St. (between Fifth and Sixth Aves.)   *www.hotelmetronyc.com*
Phone: (212) 947-2500, (800) 356-3870   Fax: (212) 279-1310

The Metro is one of Midtown's best affordable options. The entire hotel brims with bright and jaunty Art Deco style, and rooms are larger and better-outfitted than others at this price. First-quality comforts include attractive neo-Deco furniture, fluffy pillows and towels, and small but beautifully appointed marble bathrooms, most with an oversized shower stall (junior suites have whirlpool tubs). There's Wi-Fi Internet access, plus dataports in the rooms for dial-up connections. Everything is spotless, and beautifully framed black-and-white photos add a touch of glamour. The Metro comes to the rescue of moderate-income families with the clever family room, a two-room suite that has a second bedroom in lieu of a sitting area. Rooms with two doubles do the trick for families on a budget.

The lobby lounge is especially comfortable and inviting, as is the library-style back lounge. Be sure to head up to the rooftop terrace on pleasant days, where you can enjoy a breathtaking vista of the Empire State Building. The Metro Grill restaurant is surprisingly stylish and good. Despite the low rates, the hotel is very popular with the fashion and media crowds, who know a good value when they see one.

Rooms: 179; 13 floors; designated nonsmoking floors. **Hotel amenities:** Fitness room, laundry and dry-cleaning service, meeting room. **Food services:** Restaurant and bar, alfresco rooftop bar weekdays in summer, room service; rates include continental breakfast. **Cancellation:** 24 hours prior to arrival. **Wheelchair access:** Accessible. **Subway:** B, D, F, N, Q, R, S, V, W to 34th St.

The Hudson GOOD $$$

356 W. 58th St. (between Eighth and Ninth Aves.)
www.hudsonhotel.com, www.morganshotelgroup.com
Phone: (212) 554-6000 (800) 444-4786 Fax: (212) 554-6054

Many trendy types love the Hudson, but it's not for everybody. From the team of Ian Schrager (the man who powered the boutique hotel movement) and designer Philippe Starck, the Hudson emphasizes scene over service, just like most of its cooler-than-thou peers. Schrager attracts star-studded events and premier parties to its wealth of riotously designed public spaces, including the ivy-draped lobby, the second-level Private Park deck and the 15th-floor Sky Terrace (two of the best alfresco spaces in the city), and the white-hot Hudson Bar with its glowing floor and frescoed ceiling. These spaces often overflow with revelers, so you must love a party to enjoy the Hudson.

Beware, though—guest rooms are small. The tiniest doubles are a real squeeze at just 144 square feet. Even some of the "deluxe" doubles occupy just 200 or so square feet. If you're a heavy packer or need space to spread out, stay elsewhere. But style hounds will prize the beauty and efficiency of Starck's design. Rooms were modeled on the retro-romantic idea of the early 20th-century ocean liner, with rich detailing that includes African makore paneling, hardwood floors, white-leather steamer trunk upholstery, and white-on-white beds dressed in down and 300-count Egyptian cotton, plus tiny but gorgeous white-marble baths. Technology includes a CD player, satellite radio, two-line phones and high-speed Internet access. Expect zero in the way of personal attention.

Rooms: 1,000; 24 floors; designated nonsmoking rooms. **Hotel amenities:** 24-hour concierge, fitness center, business center, laundry and dry-cleaning service, indoor and outdoor lounging and event space, state-of-the-art conference center, welcome gift for kids, in-room spa services. **Food services:** Hudson Cafeteria restaurant, Hudson Bar, library lounge with cognac/brandy bar, 24-hour room service, refreshment lounge on every floor. **Cancellation:** 24 hours prior to arrival. **Wheelchair access:** Not accessible. **Subway:** A, B, C, D, 1, 9 to 59th St.

The Iroquois New York GOOD $$$–$$$$

49 W. 44th St. (between Fifth and Sixth Aves.) *www.iroquoisny.com*
Phone: (212) 840-3080, (800) 332-7220 Fax: (212) 398-1754

For those of you who like the intimacy of a boutique hotel but prefer to pass on the highbrow modernism that seems to go hand-in-hand with the concept these days, there's the Iroquois. This understated hotel is a favorite among business and leisure travelers thanks to its domestic, clubby ambiance.

The rooms and suites are outfitted in a traditional French town-house style, with a soft color scheme. Nice touches include jacquard textiles, 300-count Frette linens and robes, CD players, TVs with VCRs and video games, two-line phones, complimentary high-speed Internet access and Italian marble baths. Rooms are too small for the money, though, even in the deluxe category. About half of the rooms have an executive-size work desk with desk-level jacks, so request one when booking. Rack rates are ridiculously high, but Internet and seasonal specials can lower prices appreciably (as low as $209). Film buffs will enjoy the themed James Dean Suite; the tragic star of *Rebel Without a Cause* lived in suite 803 from 1951 to 1953. Dinner at intimate, elegant Triomphe, chef Steven Zobel's *New York Times* two-star winner, is a must.

Rooms: 114; 12 floors; designated nonsmoking floors. **Hotel amenities:** Concierge, fitness room with Finnish sauna, library-style business center and lounge with PC with free Internet access, laundry and dry-cleaning service, meeting and function rooms, video library. **Food services:** Triomphe restaurant and bar, 24-hour room service. **Cancellation:** 24 hours prior to arrival. **Wheelchair access:** ADA compliant. **Subway:** B, D, F, S, V to 42nd St.

La Quinta Manhattan   GOOD $–$$
17 W. 32nd St. (between Fifth and Sixth Aves.)
www.lq.com, www.applecorehotels.com
Phone: (212) 736-1600, (800) 551-2303   Fax: (212) 563-4007

Meet the first East Coast outpost of the best limited-service chain of the West, La Quinta. It opened in 2003 following a $2.5 million renovation of the 1904 Beaux-Arts building. Rooms are newly renovated and well equipped, with such nice perks as video games on the TV, coffee maker and free high-speed Internet access. Public spaces also feel fresh and attractive; in fact, the lobby even feels somewhat stylish. The staff is friendly, and management company Apple Core Hotels has been reliably providing cut-rate rooms to budget-conscious visitors for a good half-decade now. The hotel is located in the heart of Manhattan's bright Korean restaurant row, so good eats abound; the Theater District is an easy 10-minute walk away. The indoor/outdoor rooftop SkyBar for cocktails and light refreshments adds additional appeal.

Rooms: 182; 12 floors; designated nonsmoking floors. **Hotel amenities:** Concierge, fitness room, self-service business center, laundry and dry-cleaning service, meeting room. **Food services:** Korean restaurant, Dae Dong; indoor/outdoor rooftop bar; rates include continental breakfast. **Cancellation:** 24 hours prior to arrival. **Wheelchair access:** Not accessible. **Subway:** B, D, F, N, Q, R, S, V, W, 1, 2, 3, 7, 9 to 42nd St.

Le Parker Meridien   EXTRAORDINARY $$$$
118 W. 57th St. (between Sixth and Seventh Aves.)   *www.parkermeridien.com*
Phone: (212) 245-5000, (800) 543-4300   Fax: (212) 307-1776

The Parker may be the most successful hotel in New York at fusing chic modern style with classic, full-service functionality. The attitude embodied in their tagline—"Uptown. Not Uptight"—is immediately apparent in the soaring neo-classical lobby, a stage set for classic modern furnishings, pinwheel art from Brit bad-boy Damien Hirst and a hip staff. The hotel overflows with top-notch facil-ities, including a massive 15,000-square-foot health club and spa, a glass-enclosed penthouse-level swimming pool, two terrific restaurants (Norma's for all-day gourmet breakfast and charming Seppi's for excellent and moderately priced Alsatian French) and a *Jetsons*-inspired cocktail lounge. Two concierges on staff have Clef d'Or designation, so service is first-rate, and the Parker is leg-endary for being the most pet-friendly hotel in town.

Rooms are spacious and outfitted in chic Scandinavian-modern style. Features include comfy platform feather beds, extra-large worktables with ergonomically correct (and beautiful) Aeron chairs and desk-level inputs, plus a wealth of tech-nology that includes a 32-inch TV with video games, DVD/CD player and VCR, cordless phones and free high-speed Internet access. Bathrooms sport warm slate-gray tile and good mirrors. Junior suites are beautifully configured for work and play, with a cozy seating area with pullout sofa, extra work space and a swivel entertainment center that caters to both living area and bedroom.

Rooms: 730; 41 floors; designated nonsmoking floors. **Hotel amenities:** Clefs d'Or concierge, full-service business center, 15,000-square-foot Gravity fitness center and spa, penthouse-level pool, laundry and dry-cleaning service, meeting and function rooms. Pets accepted. **Food services:** Two restaurants, lounge, 24-hour room service. **Cancellation:** Before 3 P.M. day prior to arrival. **Wheelchair access:** Fully accessible. **Subway:** F, N, R, Q, W to 57th St.

The Mansfield   GOOD $$–$$$
12 W. 44th St. (between Fifth and Sixth Aves.)   *www.mansfieldhotel.com*
Phone: (212) 277-8700, (800) 255-5167   Fax: (212) 764-4477

The Mansfield shows just how distinctive a small hotel can be. This 1905 hotel beautifully fuses romance and modernism in rooms that are very inviting despite their small size. The public spaces are dressed mainly in period style, with their original terrazzo floors and mahogany balustrades beautifully maintained. A more heavily modern fusion look takes over in the rooms, where natural-fiber rugs cover ebony-stained floors, contemporary metal-mesh sleigh beds wear gor-geous Belgian linens and bathrooms are stylishly updated with limestone and stainless steel. Framed prints and wood Venetian blinds keep a nostalgic cast. Nice plusses include VCRs, CD players, robes and down comforters and pillows. Free wireless Internet access is available in all public spaces and guest rooms.

A lovely fireplace-lit library doubles as a breakfast room and all-day lounge for serve-yourself cappuccino and tea. The stylish M Bar makes a romantic cocktail spot. Management is thoughtful and keeps the place in excellent shape. Rack rates are too high, but specials dipped as low as $189 at press time, so always ask.

Rooms: 124; 12 floors; designated nonsmoking floors. **Hotel amenities:** Fax ser-vice, laundry and dry cleaning, small meeting room, video and CD libraries. **Food services:** M Bar with light menu, lounge with complimentary continental breakfast, plus cappuccino, tea and cookies during the day; room service in evenings. **Cancellation:** 24 hours prior to arrival. **Wheelchair access:** Not accessible. **Subway:** B, D, F, S, V to 42nd St.

Millennium Broadway   VERY GOOD $$$–$$$$

145 W. 44th St. (between Broadway and Sixth Ave.) *www.millennium-hotels.com*
Phone: (212) 768-4400, (800) 892-7444   Fax: (212) 768-0847

The Millennium is built for business, but it's ideal for any visitor who wants an attractive, well-mannered hotel in the heart of the Theater District. A vast, mahogany-and-marble lobby leads to the original Millennium rooms, in the main building. They are large and attractively outfitted in a smart Art Deco style, with rich red mahogany and black lacquer furnishings; good-quality mattresses, comforters and goose-down pillows; comfy streamlined club chairs; two-line phones and spacious marble baths. But the real perks come in the Premier tower. These designer rooms combine sleek design, coziness and 21st-century technology in one beautiful package. White sycamore predominates, giving the rooms a feeling of openness and light, accented by green glass and natural-fiber textiles (such as a sumptuous merino wool throw). The Premier tower is not as tall as the Millennium, so the views are not as good, and some of the closets are small—but bathrooms are big and beautiful, CD players and fax machines are the norm, and the custom bedding is heaven-sent. Premier guests also have access to their own lounge with a 24-hour dedicated concierge, complimentary continental breakfast and evening cocktails and canapes, and a flat-screen TV.

Rack rates are high at the Millennium, but one of its greatest appeals are terrific package rates—especially on weekends—so be sure to inquire.

Rooms: 752; 52 floors (21 floors in Premier tower); designated nonsmoking floors. **Hotel amenities:** Concierge, fitness center with sauna, full-service business center with secretarial services, laundry and dry-cleaning service, 110,000-square-foot Millennium Conference Center with meeting and function rooms, restored 1903 Hudson Theatre for presentations and events. **Food services:** Charlotte restaurant (celebrated for its weekend brunch), cocktail lounge, room service. **Cancellation:** 24 hours prior to arrival. **Wheelchair access:** ADA compliant. **Subway:** B, D, F, N, Q, R, S, V, W, 1, 2, 3, 7, 9 to 42nd St.

The Muse   EXCELLENT $$$

130 W. 46th St. (between Fifth and Sixth Aves.)   *www.themusehotel.com*
Phone: (212) 485-2400, (877) NYC-MUSE (692-6873)   Fax: (212) 485-2900

With its emphasis on both comfort and functionality, the Muse is ideal for travelers who want the scale and personalized service of a boutique hotel but find no appeal in their often steely and unwelcoming modern design (and the typical dose of attitude). A modern exterior gives way to a warm, wood-paneled lobby where management has done away with the traditional front desk in favor of full concierge service that makes everyone feel like a VIP. After a welcoming hassle-free check-in, you'll be led to your inviting room, which features modern furnishings in warm woods with classic lines. Bathrooms are handsome and well outfitted. Perks include plump feather beds and duvets (hand-screened by a contemporary artist), CD players, high-speed Internet access (plus wireless access throughout the hotel), cordless phones, coffee makers, plush bathrobes and business cards personalized with your in-house direct-dial number. Select rooms also have balconies, DVD players, wide-screen TVs, exercise equipment and desktop computers. Service is excellent.

Don't miss the gorgeous David Rockwell–designed District, a stellar New American brasserie. All in all, the Muse is a hidden gem that's well worth seeking out; value-added packages are usually available. Pets are more than welcome—they receive their own amenity-filled treat basket upon arrival, and the concierge will be happy to point out all of the city's pooch-friendly hotspots, from parks to restaurants.

Rooms: 200; 19 floors; three designated smoking floors. **Hotel amenities:** Concierge, business services, fitness room, laundry and dry-cleaning service, meeting rooms. Pets accepted. **Food services:** District restaurant and bar, room service. **Cancellation:** 24 hours prior to arrival. **Wheelchair access:** ADA compliant. **Subway:** B, D, F, V to 47th-50th Sts.

New York Marriott Marquis

GOOD $$$

1535 Broadway (between 45th and 46th Sts.)   www.marriott.com
Phone: (212) 398-1900, (800) 843-4898   Fax: (212) 704-8930

This hulking monolith looks like a cross between a convention hall and a parking garage. It takes a good 10 minutes to ascend a variety of escalators and always-packed elevators from street level to your room. But once you get there, your room will be surprisingly spacious (by New York standards, anyway). Rooms are sparkling fresh after a total renovation in 2004; they sport plush new carpeting, fabrics and furniture for a bright, clean, contemporary Deco look. Business travelers will appreciate the well-designed work space, coffee maker, two-line phones and high-speed Internet access; an executive floor is available for those who need extra attention. You can't expect personalized service at a hotel of this size, of course—but the location couldn't be better for theatergoers. Skyline views are stellar from the revolving rooftop lounge, even if service isn't. Rack rates are way too high, so be sure to mine for discounts.

Rooms: 2,000; 49 floors; designated nonsmoking floors. **Hotel amenities:** Concierge, tour desk, full-service business center, health club with sauna, laundry and dry-cleaning service, guest laundry, 100,000 square feet of function space with 54 meeting rooms. **Food services:** Four restaurants (one American buffet, one steakhouse, one sushi bar, one rooftop revolving restaurant and lounge), three lounges, Starbucks coffee bar, room service. **Cancellation:** 6 P.M. day of arrival. **Wheelchair access:** Fully accessible. **Subway:** N, Q, R, S, W, 1, 2, 3, 7, 9 to 42nd St.

The Paramount   GOOD $$–$$$

235 W. 46th St. (between Broadway and Eighth Ave.) *www.morganshotelgroup.com*
Phone: (212) 764-5500, (800) 225-7474   Fax: (212) 354-5237

Style over square footage is the mantra here. The Paramount is the bargain choice for travelers who want to sample boutique-hotel style at a reasonable rate. The minuscule rooms are all whites and grays, with compact stainless-steel bath, a cartoonish cafe table and chairs, a swiveling armoire hiding a small TV and VCR, two-line phones, and a low-slung platform bed dressed in 300-count Egyptian cotton. Be prepared, because it's a tight fit—you'll need a suite if you can't manage to pack light. These rooms are only for visitors who really value style over space; otherwise, you're much better off elsewhere.

The Paramount will only exist in its current incarnation until early 2005. Ian Schrager's Morgans Hotel Group just sold this property to Becker Ventures, which owns the Hard Rock Hotel in Chicago. It will soon close and undergo a complete transformation. Look for New York's first Hard Rock Hotel to debut here in the near future.

Rooms: 610; 19 floors; designated nonsmoking floors. **Hotel amenities:** 24-hour concierge, business center, fitness room, laundry and dry-cleaning service, meeting room, welcome gift for kids, video library. **Food services:** Mezzanine restaurant, two bars, Dean & Deluca coffee bar, room service. **Cancellation:** Before 6 P.M. day prior to arrival. **Wheelchair access:** Not accessible. **Subway:** A, C, E, N, Q, R, S, W, 1, 2, 3, 7, 9 to 42nd St.

Park Central New York   VERY GOOD $$–$$$

870 Seventh Ave. (at 56th St.)   *www.parkcentralny.com*
Phone: (212) 247-8000, (800) 346-1359   Fax: (212) 707-5557

A massive $65 million renovation completed in late 2001 turned a formerly dowdy hotel into a very nice place to stay. Of 935 guest accommodations, the hotel has just 20 suites; the rest are generous double/doubles and kings that are quite large, especially by city standards. Expect contemporary décor, full-sized closets with an oversized floor-to-ceiling mirror, nice bathrobes, windows that open, TV with Nintendo, a writing desk and good black granite counter space in the bathroom, plus extra-thick walls and floors that encourage sleepability. Big Apple–themed art sets an appealing tone. Management is making an earnest effort to keep the hotel feeling fresh and new. The five business concierge floors add free continental breakfast and evening hors d'oeuvres (served in a private lounge), plus a spacious workstation, a coffee maker and a fax machine. High-speed wireless Internet access is also available on the business concierge floors for an additional fee. The hotel is generic, but the comforts are all there—and the A-1 location, just three blocks from Central Park and halfway between the Theater District and Fifth Avenue shopping, couldn't be better. A nice alternative to such chaotic behemoths as the Marriott Marquis.

Rooms: 935; 25 floors; designated nonsmoking floors. **Hotel amenities:** Concierge, fitness center, laundry and dry-cleaning service, extensive and newly renovated meeting and conference facilities. **Food services:** Casual bistro-style restaurant and bar, lobby lounge, room service. **Cancellation:** 24 hours prior to arrival. **Wheelchair access:** Fully accessible. **Subway:** N, R, Q, W to 57th St.

The Peninsula New York   EXTRAORDINARY $$$$
700 Fifth Ave. (at 55th St.)   www.peninsula.com
Phone: (212) 956-2888, (800) 262-9467   Fax: (212) 903-3949

Set in a stunning neoclassical building with a grand Beaux Arts lobby, this is one of New York's best ultra-luxury hotels. Guest rooms have extra-large room configurations, monster-size marble bathrooms and state-of-the-art wiring. No other hotel so successfully fuses old New York style with 21st-century luxury.

The décor is exquisite, a dramatic but sublimely comfortable fusion of Art Nouveau lines, elegant Asian accents and contemporary art. Mahogany is polished to a high sheen and silks are lustrous. A wealth of beautifully designed storage space and a CEO-sized work desk with desk-level outlets and free high-speed Internet access, a leather executive chair and fax/printer/copier adds a practical edge to the elegance. But the technology isn't limited to business travelers: in the bathroom, a tub-level panel lets you control the room-wide sound system, answer the phone and even watch TV (in all but the cheapest rooms). A bedside console controls the mood lighting, climate, TV, "Do Not Disturb" sign—in short, does everything but tuck you in. There's even an outside climate display next to the door so you know if you need to take an umbrella, and a complimentary "water bar" offering five bottled choices.

The spectacular tri-level spa is a big asset, offering a full range of services, a complete health club and a swimming pool with panoramic skyline views. Service is flawless. Very expensive, but worth it if you can afford it.

Rooms: 239; 23 floors; designated nonsmoking rooms. **Hotel amenities:** 24-hour concierge; complete fitness center, full-service spa and sun deck; business center; laundry and dry-cleaning service; meeting and function rooms. Small pets are accepted. **Food services:** The well-regarded FIVES restaurant and bar, featuring "Atlantic Rim" (continental/Pacific Rim) cuisine; library-style Gotham Bar & Lounge for afternoon tea, cocktails, and light fare; indoor/outdoor rooftop Pen-Top Bar & Terrace with Fifth Avenue views; 24-hour room service. **Cancellation:** 24 hours prior to arrival. **Wheelchair access:** Fully accessible. **Subway:** E, V to Fifth Ave.

The Plaza   GOOD $$$–$$$$
768 Fifth Ave. (at Central Park South)   www.fairmont.com
Phone: (212) 759-3000, (800) 441-1414   Fax: (212) 759-3167

If ever a hotel has earned the right to be officially declared a landmark, it is the Plaza. Designed and built by Henry J. Hardenbergh, the stately French Renaissance hotel—which sits at one of the world's most glamorous intersections—has hosted countless famous names and events since 1907, from the visits of Mark Twain and "Diamond" Jim Brady to the nuptials of Michael Douglas and

Catherine Zeta-Jones. No doubt you already know what the Plaza looks like, thanks to films such as *North by Northwest, Funny Girl* and *Home Alone 2*. Unfortunately, hordes of tourists in the public spaces often undermine the historic elegance.

The Plaza is in need of renovation, and hopefully it will soon get the facelift it deserves, as the hotel was just sold to Elad Properties in 2004 (prompting speculation that Elad might turn some guest rooms into condominiums). It'll be interesting to see what Elad has in store, for the rooms and public spaces are looking rather worn around the edges, and the quality of accommodations can vary dramatically. The beautifully renovated Waldorf is a better choice—but still, this is the Plaza. Modern touches include high-speed Internet access, fax machines, two-line speaker phones, Frette bathrobes and TVs with video games. Even the smallest room is a reasonable size, and the building's U-shape means that every one gets a measure of fresh air and sunlight.

After a stylish culinary and design reinvention, the dated Edwardian Room has been reinvented as OneCPS, but other dining-and-cocktail options remain pleasingly Old World, including the gilded Palm Court for tea, the surprisingly good Oyster Bar for seafood and the legendary Oak Bar. A day spa boasts a full-service menu, a state-of-the-art gym and his-and-hers tiled Jacuzzis.

Rooms: 805; 19 floors; designated nonsmoking rooms. **Hotel amenities:** Concierge, theater desk, 8,000- square-foot full-service spa and fitness center, full-service business center, laundry and dry-cleaning service, extensive meeting and function space, including the Grand Ballroom. Small pets accepted. **Food services:** OneCPS restaurant, Oyster Bar English-style pub, Palm Court restaurant, Oak Room, Oak Bar, 24-hour room service. **Cancellation:** 24 hours prior to arrival. **Wheelchair access:** Fully accessible. **Subway:** N, R, W to Fifth Ave.; 4, 5, 6 to 59th St.

Red Roof Inn   VERY GOOD $–$$
6 W. 32nd St. (between Fifth and Sixth Aves.)
www.redroof.com, www.applecorehotels.com
Phone: (212) 643-7100, (800) 567-7720, (800) 733-7663   Fax: (212) 643-7101

The first Big Apple outpost of one of Middle America's favorite motel chains has been a red-hot success thanks to comfortable, freshly outfitted rooms, a better-than-budget lobby and amenities, and professional service. Don't expect anything in the way of style or luxury; Red Roof earns its "Very Good" rating with reliable comforts, including relatively spacious bedroom and bathroom configurations, and in-room features (including coffee makers and Web TV) that emphasize comfort and convenience. The pleasant public spaces include a mezzanine-level lounge, a business center and an exercise room. There's also Wi-Fi Internet access throughout the building. Lined with affordable Korean restaurants and other mid-priced hotels, the bright, safe and bustling block is just a stone's throw from Macy's, the Empire State Building and a clutch of subway lines. You can usually score a rate in the low $100s in all but the business seasons (and sometimes even then); your best bet is to price-compare by calling both toll-free numbers and checking online rates.

Rooms: 172; 17 floors; designated nonsmoking floors. **Hotel amenities:** Concierge, mezzanine-level lounge, exercise room, business center, laundry and dry-cleaning service, meeting room. **Food services:** Rates include continental breakfast. **Cancellation:** Before 3 P.M. day prior to arrival. **Wheelchair access:** Accessible. **Subway:** B, D, F, N, Q, R, S, V, W to 34th St.

Ritz-Carlton New York, Central Park

EXCELLENT $$$$

50 Central Park South (at Sixth Ave.) *www.ritzcarlton.com*
Phone: (212) 308-9100, (800) 241-3333 Fax: (212) 207-8331

The former St. Moritz was reborn in 2002 as Ritz-Carlton's glamorous uptown outpost, and it's a star. This is not the place to parade through the lobby in your faded jeans and flip-flops. Unlike its sister hotel in Battery Park (reviewed earlier in this chapter), which wears a contemporary sheen, this hotel bespeaks opulent, old-money formality from the gilded front doors through the glittering lobby (which is often filled with the sweet sounds of a harpist).

Even standard guest rooms are a sizeable 425 square feet and boast just about every imaginable luxury: Feather beds wear custom-designed 300-count Frette linens; minibars come stocked with Dean & Deluca munchies and Opus One wine. State-of-the-art technology includes a 27-inch flat screen TV, a DVD player, high-speed Internet access and multi-line cordless phones. The marble baths feature a deep tub, separate shower and Frederic Fekkai bath products. If you can afford a park-facing room, you'll be rewarded with majestic views. The Ritz-Carlton's faultless service is in full swing; you can even call on the Bath Butler to draw you a custom soak. The Ritz's Club Level is always worth the price of admission, since you'll enjoy dedicated concierge service and an elegant park-view lounge with five complimentary food presentations a day, including an expanded continental breakfast. Famous for its age-defying treatments, the La Prairie Spa has quickly earned a regular spot on the city's "best" lists.

Rooms: 277; 33 floors; designated nonsmoking floors. **Hotel amenities:** Concierge, 24-hour technology butler, full-service business center, fitness center, full-service La Prairie at the Ritz-Carlton spa, laundry and dry-cleaning service, conference and meeting/function rooms, car service, meeting space, DVD library of Academy Award–winning films. **Food services:** Atelier restaurant (jacket required in evening); Star Lounge for the legendary afternoon tea service, cocktails and light meals; 24-hour room service. **Cancellation:** 24 hours prior to arrival. **Wheelchair access:** Fully accessible. **Subway:** F to 57th St.

Sofitel New York

EXCELLENT $$$–$$$$

45 W. 44th St. (between Fifth and Sixth Aves.) *www.sofitel.com*
Phone: (212) 354-8844, (800) SOFITEL (763-4835) Fax: (212) 354-2480

This sophisticated French import is the best among a large crop of new luxury hotels. The good impression begins as soon as you enter the curvilinear tower and step into the stunning lobby, with its soaring ceilings, fluted columns and streamlined Art Moderne club chairs. This is one handsome hotel.

The Sofitel is beautifully run, too. The front desk is at the far end of the ballroom-sized lobby, tucked away to the side, which gives the entrance a serene quality. The bilingual staff (they are required to speak both English and French, at minimum) is thoughtful, efficient and attentive. Filled with well-chosen and gorgeously displayed Parisian- or New York–themed gifts, even the boutique is something special.

Sofitel's thoroughly French perspective also adds a fashionable flair to the guest rooms, where the dramatic design seamlessly blends Art Deco and contemporary elements. Amenities include first-rate soundproofing, desk-level inputs with high-speed Internet access, CD players, Web TV and plush robes. The spacious bathrooms are done in honey-hued marble with separate tub and shower, plus a well-lit beveled mirror. All standard rooms have queen-sized beds; king beds are available only in suites.

Rooms: 398; 29 floors; designated nonsmoking floors. **Hotel amenities:** Concierge, business center, laundry and dry-cleaning service, ballroom, state-of-the-art meeting and function space, including a grand ballroom. **Food services:** Stylish French brasserie and bar, Gaby, with outdoor terrace; 24-hour room service. **Cancellation:** 24 hours prior to arrival. **Wheelchair access:** Fully accessible. **Subway:** B, D, F, S, V, 4, 5, 6, 7 to 42nd St.

Super 8 Hotel Times Square   VERY GOOD $–$$
59 W. 46th St. (between Fifth and Sixth Aves.)
www.super8.com, www.applecorehotels.com
Phone: (212) 719-2300, (800) 567-7720   Fax: (212) 790-2760

This smart new addition to the Theater District hotel scene is a joint venture between Apple Core hotels (the company behind a few value-priced Midtowners, including the Comfort Inn Midtown, La Quinta Manhattan and the Red Roof Inn, all recommended in this chapter) and the Super 8 chain, best known for its reliable highway motor lodges and making its first foray into the Big Apple. The partnership really pays off for budget-conscious travelers, who can enjoy reliable comforts and a central location for a terrific price (usually in the low to mid $100s, sometimes even less). The spacious rooms boast a king bed or two doubles, all-new furnishings, brand-new bathrooms, coffee makers, and TV with on-screen Web access and video games. The décor won't win any awards, but it's fresh and pleasant. Value-minded families will love the family suite, which features one double bed in each of two adjoining rooms (no fussing with a pullout sofa). Service is professional, and free continental breakfasts adds to an already excellent value. The location, within shouting distance of the bright lights of Broadway, is excellent.

Rooms: 206; 12 floors; designated nonsmoking rooms. **Hotel amenities:** Concierge, exercise room, business center, laundry and dry-cleaning service, meeting room. **Food services:** Rates include continental breakfast. **Cancellation:** Before 3 P.M. of the day prior to arrival. **Wheelchair access:** Accessible. **Subway:** B, D, F, S, V, 4, 5, 6, 7 to 42nd St.

Travel Inn   GOOD $–$$
515 W. 42nd St. (between 10th and 11th Aves.)   *www.newyorkhotel.com*
Phone: (212) 695-7171, (800) 869-4630   Fax: (212) 967-5025

Now that far-west Midtown is rife with chic restaurants and resident yuppies, this agreeable motor inn isn't so far removed anymore. The rooms here are large, clean, bright and comfortable, if nondescript. Even the smallest room is spacious and has a good-sized bathroom; those with two double beds make well-priced shares for families. In-room perks include TV with video games and on-screen Internet access. But the best reason to stay here is the absolutely free parking—with in and out privileges—since virtually every other hotel in town charges anywhere from $25 to $50 a day. The rooftop outdoor pool and well-furnished sun deck—another otherwise-nonexistent perk in the Big Apple—is a refreshing summertime treat that makes the Travel Inn a worthwhile choice even for those who don't have their own wheels. The Javits Convention Center is just three blocks away. What's more, Internet and other specials often drop prices (as low as $99 at press time).

Rooms: 160; seven floors; designated nonsmoking rooms. **Hotel amenities:** Exercise room, rooftop swimming pool and sun deck, meeting room, Gray Line tour desk. **Food services:** Coffee shop, room service. **Cancellation:** 48 hours prior to arrival. **Wheelchair access:** Not accessible. **Subway:** A, C, E to 42nd St.

W Times Square   VERY GOOD $$$–$$$$
1567 Broadway (at 47th St.)   *www.whotels.com*
Phone: (212) 930-7400, (877) 946-8357 (W-HOTELS)   Fax: (212) 930-7500

The flagship hotel for Starwood's designer-label chain, the newest W hotel is also the hippest of a very sleek bunch. A sleek, mod-inspired lobby—with Zen-like water features for an air of groovy tranquility—leads to guest rooms that unite modern linearity with luxury-level comfort. Unfortunately, they're smaller and somewhat less elegant than those at the W Union Square, and low-ceilinged hallways add to the penned-in feeling. Perks include cloud-fluffy pillowtop beds; luminous resin cubes serving as nightstands; TV with on-screen Internet access, VCR and DVD; CD stereo; a coffee maker and joyfully stocked minibar (with such goodies as Gummi bears and Slinkys); high-speed Internet access, two-line cordless phones and a large worktable; sexy bathrooms with circular sinks, suspended as if in midair, and lightweight cotton pique bathrobes; and lighting that makes everybody look great.

Supermod seafood restaurant Blue Fin won two precious *New York Times* stars out of the gate, and the Whiskey Bar is an even better realization than nightlife impresario Rande Gerber's original hotspot. You can bring the W lifestyle home by flexing your credit card at W The Store, on the lobby level. The hotel is a favorite gathering spot for the style-conscious entertainment crowd whose offices fill the surrounding heart-of-Broadway blocks.

Rooms: 509; 57 floors; designated non-smoking floors. **Hotel amenities:** Concierge with W's signature "Whatever/Whenever" service, business center, exercise room, spa, laundry and dry-cleaning service, meeting rooms. **Food services:** Blue Fin restaurant, Whiskey Bar, 24-hour room service. **Cancellation:** 24 hours prior to arrival, depending on reservation. **Wheelchair access:** Fully accessible. **Subway:** N, R, W to 49th St.

Westin New York Times Square   VERY GOOD $$$

270 W. 43rd St. (at Eighth Ave.)   *www.westinny.com, www.westin.com*
Phone: (212) 201-2700, (866) 837-4183, (800) WESTIN1 (937-8461)
Fax: (212) 201-2701

Built in 2002, this tower contains nearly 900 rooms, all of which boast the single best reason to stay at this well-outfitted chain hotel: Westin's truly celestial Heavenly Bed, a custom Simmons Beautyrest® pillowtop mattress dressed in layer upon layer of fluffy down and crisp white linen. The hotel's 45-story-high "prism" façade—featuring 8,000 sheets of glass in 10 colors—scored a lot of ink when the hotel first opened; cutting-edge architecture or no, it sure does evoke an 80's-era disco. A big, bright lobby and oversized elevators lead to spacious and attractive (if rather generic) contemporary guest rooms, each featuring an executive-style work desk with high-speed Internet connectivity, a 27-inch TV with on-screen Web access, a cordless phone and the signature Heavenly Bath, with plush velour robes and oversized bathsheets. Heavenly Cribs are even on hand for the kids. The Executive Club offers oversized rooms with upgraded furnishings and amenities, plus a soaring atrium-style executive lounge serving complimentary continental breakfast and evening hors d'oeuvres.

Shula's Steak House—the city's first upscale outlet from the Miami Dolphins' legendary head coach Don Shula's well-regarded chain—is another plus. The hotel, developed as part of the neon-bright renovation of the "new" Times Square, is perfectly located for sightseeing, dining and theater-going.

Rooms: 863; 45 floors; designated non-smoking floors. **Hotel amenities:** Concierge, theater ticket desk, business center, full-service spa and fitness center, laundry and dry-cleaning service, extensive meeting and function space. **Food services:** Shula's Steak House, Bar 10 lounge and sushi bar, 24-hour room service. **Cancellation:** Before 4 P.M. day of arrival. **Wheelchair access:** Fully accessible. **Subway:** A, C, E, N, Q, R, S, W, 1, 2, 3, 7, 9 to 42nd St.

UPPER EAST SIDE

The Carlyle   EXTRAORDINARY $$$$
35 E. 76th St. (at Madison Ave.)   www.thecarlyle.com
Phone: (212) 744-1600, (888) 767-3966   Fax: (212) 717-4682

The discreet and elegant Carlyle epitomizes Upper East Side glamour. About half
of the hotel is occupied by permanent residents, while the other half is made up of
rooms and suites available to short-term guests with deep pockets. The softly lit
lobby is distinctly discreet, which heightens the exclusive residential feel. Generations of famous faces and power brokers have been attracted by this low-profile
ambiance, as well as the impeccable attention to detail and the unmatched service.

Individually decorated rooms and suites are luxuriously appointed, but not in
the gilded, big-money way of luxury palaces like the St. Regis. Think understated, traditional, rare, and you'll get the picture: chintz, satin, antiques, original Audubon prints and oils depicting English country scenes on the walls, Oriental rugs over gleaming wood floors. There is a full roster of amenities you
have every right to expect at this price level, including jetted tubs, Kiehls bath
products and high-speed Internet access, plus many less common luxuries, such
as terraces, grand pianos and/or full kitchens. Many regulars prefer the high-
floor tower rooms; they're not large, but the light and the views—particularly
those overlooking Central Park—are enthralling.

Cafe Carlyle is New York's premier cabaret room, although the legendary
Bobby Short is ending his regular run here at the end of 2004. But you can
always expect a first-rate lineup of song stylists (and a whopping cover charge);
Woody Allen is usually in the house on Monday, swinging on clarinet with the
Eddy Davis New Orleans Jazz Band. Jazz vocalists also entertain a well-heeled
crowd at the glamorous Bemelmans Bar. The French restaurant Dumonet, from
celebrated chef Jean-Louis Dumonet, is well-regarded. Pets are welcome; in fact,
the staff will even walk Bowser for you.

Rooms: 180; 33 floors; designated nonsmoking floors. **Hotel amenities:**
Concierge; attractive fitness center with whirlpool, sauna and spa services; business services; laundry and dry-cleaning service; high-end retail shops, meeting
and function rooms. Pets accepted. **Food services:** Elegant French restaurant
(Dumonet); Bemelmans Bar; Café Carlyle supper club; The Gallery for afternoon tea and light fare; 24-hour room service. **Cancellation:** 24 hours prior to
arrival. **Wheelchair access:** Fully accessible. **Subway:** 6 to 77th St.

Hotel Wales   GOOD $$-$$$
1295 Madison Ave. (between E. 92nd and 93rd Sts.)   www.waleshotel.com
Phone: (212) 876-6000, (866) 925-3746   Fax: (212) 860-7000

Built in 1901, this recently renovated but still quirky hotel offers relatively
affordable accommodations in a corner of the Upper East Side called Carnegie
Hill. Most guest rooms are not large; luckily, almost half are suites. Ample
amenities—including VCRs, CD players and pillowy beds with Belgian

linens—up the appeal substantially. Contemporary touches combine with Victorian details for a pleasing look. Original woodwork is beautifully refinished, the walls wear warm and pretty hues, and the furnishing accents the heritage without adding frills. All-day snacks laid out in a sunny lounge and the presence of the wonderful Sarabeth's restaurant make the Wales a pleasing place to stay. Free bottled water is another nice touch, as are the $15 discounted day passes at the nearby 92nd Street YMCA. Be aware, however, that the nearest subway stop is a 10-minute hike from the hotel.

Rooms: 87; 10 floors; one designated smoking floor. **Hotel amenities:** Lounge, rooftop terrace, exercise room, in-room spa treatments, laundry and dry-cleaning service, fax service, complimentary video and CD libraries. Small pets accepted. **Food services:** Sarabeth's restaurant, room service, continental breakfast served in lounge for a $9-per-person charge; rates include help-yourself cappuccino, tea and cookies. **Cancellation:** 24 hours prior to arrival. **Wheelchair access:** Not accessible. **Subway:** 6 to 96th St.

The Lowell   EXCELLENT $$$$
28 E. 63rd St. (between Madison and Park Aves.)   *www.lhw.com*
Phone: (212) 838-1400, (800) 221-4444   Fax: (212) 319-4230

The low-profile Lowell is the hidden jewel of the Upper East Side—small, quiet, private, residential, elegant and service-oriented. Even though it's at the Midtown end of the Upper East Side, it feels like a secret hideaway from the moment you enter the intimate, Deco-influenced French Empire lobby. Two-thirds of the accommodations are suites; each has a well-equipped kitchenette or a full kitchen. Each guest room is unique, with individual appointments ranging from wood-burning fireplaces to Jacuzzis. Chintzed to the max, the Lowell suites are just right for honeymoons and other special occasions. The Hollywood Suite has a 41-inch TV, a full selection of Hollywood classics on video and a delightful collection of movie paraphernalia, while the Garden Suite boasts not one but two ultra-romantic terraces. The new Manhattan Suite (formerly known as the Madonna Suite, after the star had it outfitted with a gym during a lengthy stay) has two terraces, a huge marble bathroom with Jacuzzi and steam shower and four TVs. Expect a full slate of luxuries in any accommodation. Warmth is the order of the day from the first-rate staff, who leave complimentary Fiji water at turndown.

Rooms: 70; 17 floors; designated nonsmoking rooms. **Hotel amenities:** 24-hour concierge, good fitness center, secretarial services, laundry and dry-cleaning service, limousine service, meeting and function rooms, video library. **Food services:** Post House steakhouse, Pembroke Room for continental cuisine and tea, 24-hour room service. **Cancellation:** 48 hours prior. **Wheelchair access:** Accessible. **Subway:** N, R, W to Lexington Ave.; 4, 5, 6 to 59th St.

The Mark   EXCELLENT $$$$
25 E. 77th St. (at Madison Ave.)   *www.mandarinoriental.com*
Phone: (212) 744-4300, (800) THE-MARK (843-6275)   Fax: (212) 744-2749

Boasting an intricate Art Deco facade and outfitted in an elegant English-Italian neoclassical style, the Mark is nevertheless lighter and more contemporary in feeling than its chief neighborhood rival, the Carlyle, and most other hotels in the super-luxury category. Rooms are a comfortable mix of classic and contemporary design, with luxurious textiles; pillowy king-sized beds dressed in Belgian and Frette linens; a stylish, oversized and well-lit bathroom, most with separate tub and shower; plus modern features like high-speed Internet access, VCRs, fax machines and two-line phones with cordless handsets. About three-quarters of the rooms and suites have full kitchens or kitchenettes. Service is beyond reproach, and Mark's is one of the city's best hotel restaurants. An excellent choice on all counts. And get ready, shoppers, because the location is in prime platinum-card spending territory.

Rooms: 180; 15 floors; designated nonsmoking floors. **Hotel amenities:** Clefs d'Or concierge, fitness center with sauna and steam, full-service business center, laundry and dry-cleaning service, meeting and function rooms, complimentary weekday-morning shuttle to Wall Street. **Food services:** Mark's Restaurant, which serves a memorable Asian afternoon tea; intimate and romantic Mark's Bar; 24-hour room service. **Cancellation:** 24 hours prior to arrival. **Wheelchair access:** Fully accessible. **Subway:** 6 to 77th St.

The Melrose Hotel, New York   GOOD $$$
140 E. 63rd St. (at Lexington Ave.)   *www.melrosehotel.com*
Phone: (212) 838-5700, (800) MELROSE (635-7673)   Fax: (212) 888-4271

A literary landmark—thanks to poet Sylvia Plath's novel of tormented youth, *The Bell Jar*—the former Barbizon is now under the guiding hand of the Dallas-based Melrose Hotel group. At the southern end of the residential Upper East Side, just three blocks from Bloomingdale's, its location is a prime asset. The hotel is in very good shape. Rooms are not distinctive, but they're comfortably outfitted with firm beds, soft pastels, and attractive wrought-iron furnishings, nice bathrooms, high-speed Internet access, two-line phones and CD/cassette stereos. On the downside, many are small. Still, rooms are light and bright, and housekeeping is immaculate. Deluxe rooms buy you more space and a foldout love seat.

In the top-of-the-line Tower Suites, located on the 18th and 19th floors, the hotel's Moorish architecture is in evidence, particularly the intricate detailing and Romanesque arches of the nicely furnished terraces attached to about half of these rooms. Views are stunning, décor is slightly more luxurious, and Jacuzzi tubs and Dolby surround-sound stereos are among the extras.

Rooms: 306; 22 floors; designated nonsmoking floors. **Hotel amenities:** Concierge, 34,000-square-foot Equinox Fitness Club and Spa with pool on site (use fee charged), laundry and dry-cleaning service, CD library, board room seating ten. **Food services:** Restaurant, lobby lounge serving lunch and dinner, "Sign & Dine Around" program with nearby restaurants, room service. **Cancellation:** 24 hours prior to arrival. **Wheelchair access:** Fully accessible. **Subway:** F, N, R, W to Lexington Ave.; 4, 5, 6 to 59th St.

The Pierre

EXCELLENT $$$$

2 E. 61st St. (at Fifth Ave.)   *www.fourseasons.com/pierre*

Phone: (212) 838-8000, (800) 819-5053, (800) PIERRE-4 (743-7731)
Fax: (212) 940-8109

This well-mannered, very European-style residential hotel is enormously
appealing. A stay in the beautifully restored 1930s Georgian-style building will
make you feel regal. The Old World ambiance is extremely formal—with doormen worthy of the Queen's Guard and white-gloved elevator operators—but
not uninvitingly so. Opulent, almost museum-like public spaces give way to
guest rooms that are individually appointed in a supremely elegant classical
style featuring English chintzes, Oriental toiles and dark woods polished to a
high sheen. Ceilings are high, so even the smaller rooms feel light, airy and
spacious. The rooms are less about business and technology (rooms are wired
for high-speed Internet access, but amenities like VCRs and fax machines are
mostly on request) and more about supreme comfort. The staff will graciously
fulfill any request. Services include elevators staffed around the clock; anytime
laundry, dry cleaning and pressing; packing and unpacking service; even special
menus and amenities for well-heeled kids. Grand suites are apartment-like and
uniquely appointed; many include full dining rooms, park views and/or terraces. The most thrilling rooms are those with views over Central Park, which
is just across the street. For a memorable experience, take traditional high tea
in the distinctive Rotunda Room, with its trompe l'oeil murals by Edward Mel-
carth. Keep in mind, though, that this is the kind of hotel where you must be
willing to dress smartly, or you will feel out of place.

Rooms: 253; 41 floors; designated nonsmoking floors. **Hotel amenities:** 24-hour
concierge, theater desk, 24-hour elevator operator, full-service business center,
fitness center, Dominique Salon (with spa services), laundry and dry-cleaning
service, two grand ballrooms and extensive meeting and function space. **Food
services:** Cafe Pierre for elegant continental dining and cocktails; Rotunda for
breakfast, light fare and afternoon tea; 24-hour room service. **Cancellation:**
Before 3 P.M. day prior to arrival. **Wheelchair access:** ADA compliant. **Subway:** N, R, W to Fifth Ave.

The Regency Hotel

EXCELLENT $$$$

540 Park Ave. (at E. 61st St.)   *www.loewshotels.com*
Phone: (212) 759-4100, (800) 23-LOEWS (235-6397)
Fax: (212) 688-2898, (212) 826-5674

For decades, the Regency has been a favorite among visiting Hollywood elite—
including Audrey Hepburn, Elizabeth Taylor and Princess Grace. And now the
hotel has new polish, grace and energy following a recent $35 million remake.
The ornate spaces, both public and private, radiate warmth and contemporary
luxury; this is a Park Avenue address where you can feel comfortable putting
your feet up. Plush materials—rich mahogany, deep-hued leather, silks and velvets—do much of the work. A strong lineup of amenities helps, too. The rooms

have large granite-top work desks with ergonomic chairs and fax/printer/copiers, digital two-line phones, high-speed Internet access, CD players, extra TVs in the bathrooms and beds that beckon with Frette linens and goose-down duvets. About half of the rooms have microwaves, and fridges can be supplied. Though well equipped, the bathrooms are quite small.

Under the guiding hand of the Loews hotel chain, the Regency just may be the best choice in the luxury category for visiting families. Children's services and amenities include a dedicated "kid concierge," who will help with finding a favorite video, Play Stations, a baby-sitter or other requests. Dog-walking and other pet-friendly services also make the Regency ideal for travelers with Rover in tow. The 540 Park restaurant is considered to be the original New York home of the power breakfast, while Feinstein's at the Regency is one of the city's top cabaret rooms.

Rooms: 351; 21 floors; designated nonsmoking floors. **Hotel amenities:** Concierge, full-service fitness center (personal training and massage available), salon, full-service business center, laundry and dry-cleaning service (including overnight service), meeting and function rooms, limousine service; in-room fitness gear (such as weights) available. Pets accepted. **Food services:** 540 Park restaurant, Feinstein's at the Regency supper club, Library lounge, 24-hour room service. **Cancellation:** Before 6 P.M. day of arrival. **Wheelchair access:** Fully accessible. **Subway:** N, R, W to Lexington Ave.; 4, 5, 6 to 59th St.

The Stanhope, Park Hyatt New York

995 Fifth Ave. (at E. 81st St.)
Phone: (212) 774-1234, (888) 591-1234

VERY GOOD $$$$
www.parkhyatt.com
Fax: (212) 517-0888

This bright and elegant member of the posh Park Hyatt chain is ideal for museum lovers, since the Metropolitan Museum of Art is just across tony Fifth Avenue, and the Frick, the Guggenheim, the Whitney and other Museum Mile institutions are within easy walking distance. That's enough reason to stay, but the Stanhope offers many additional incentives, too—most notably, a feeling of privacy and accessible Old World luxury. The Versailles-inspired lobby displays Louis XIV antiques and museum-quality tapestries, while the newly refurbished rooms are done in a very pleasing French Empire style with touches like gold-leaf candelabra wall sconces. Amenities include CD players and high-speed Internet connectivity; bathrooms are small but well-outfitted. The location keeps the clientele pleasantly mixed between business travelers and vacationers. Sidewalk cafe seating in warm weather adds to the appeal.

Rooms: 185; 17 floors; designated nonsmoking floors. **Hotel amenities:** Concierge, fitness room, business center, laundry and dry-cleaning service, meeting and function rooms, personal shopping service, complimentary car service to Midtown Tue.–Fri. **Food services:** Contemporary American restaurant with alfresco café in summer, Tahitian-style bar serving light meals, 24-hour room service. **Cancellation:** 48 hours prior to arrival. **Wheelchair access:** Fully accessible. **Subway:** 6 to 77th St.

UPPER WEST SIDE

Amsterdam Inn   BASIC $
340 Amsterdam Ave. (at W. 76th St.)   *www.amsterdaminn.com*
Phone: (212) 579-7500   Fax: (212) 579-6127

This sister property to the Murray Hill Inn (reviewed earlier in this chapter) is a
similarly wallet-friendly choice. The narrow rooms are outfitted with little more
than a bed, a wall rack for hanging clothes and a set of drawers; only a small TV
and a telephone make them more luxurious than monk's quarters. About half the
rooms have private baths (the rest share); the four deluxe rooms also have kitchenettes. Visitors opting for a double with private bathroom will find slightly nicer
rooms at the Murray Hill Inn, but the Amsterdam is a fine option, too, and the
upscale residential neighborhood is absolutely terrific. Note, however, that some
"doubles" have single beds with a pull-out trundle rather than a real bed for two,
so find out exactly what you're reserving. Facilities and service are virtually
nonexistent, as in most of New York's cheapest hotels, but Wi-Fi Internet access is
planned for 2005.

Rooms: 25 (12 with shared bathrooms); four floors; smoking allowed. **Hotel
amenities:** 24-hour reception desk. **Food services:** None. **Cancellation:** 48 hours
prior to arrival. **Wheelchair access:** Not accessible. **Subway:** 1, 9 to 79th St.

Country Inn the City   VERY GOOD $$
270 W. 77th St. (between Broadway and West End Ave.)
www.countryinnthecity.com   Phone: (212) 580-4183   Fax: (212) 874-3981

This beautifully outfitted guest house is a true delight, offering both amenity-
laden accommodations and a true taste of New York living to discerning visitors
who want more personality than your average hotel offers. Tucked away on a
leafy block just off Broadway, this 1891 limestone town house features four spa-
cious and impeccable studio suites, each outfitted by innkeepers with an eye for
design and a nose for practicality. Apartments are bright and elegant, and
homey features include wood floors covered with Oriental rugs, a beautifully
dressed queen bed (two are four-posters, one a romantic canopy bed) with a
high-quality mattress, a cozy sitting area facing a nonworking fireplace, and
bright colors, original art and well-chosen collectibles. Modern appointments
include a fully equipped galley kitchen, a cafe-style dining table for two and a
private phone with answering machine.

    There are a few downsides, though: There is no resident innkeeper, so this
option is best for independent types who don't need anything in the way of per-
sonal service. As in most New York brownstones, there's no elevator, either.
And while each kitchen comes stocked with coffee and basic breakfast fixings,
you're likely to have to purchase a few things on your own if you're staying
beyond the three-night minimum. Lastly, maid service is offered only every
three or four days for long-term stays, so be prepared to pick up after yourself

and make your own bed. Last-minute travelers should be sure to check online or inquire about late-booking specials.

Rooms: Four; five floors; smoking not allowed. **Hotel amenities:** None. **Food services:** Stocked breakfast pantry. **Cancellation:** 30 days prior to arrival; $30 cancellation fee if apartment is not rebooked. **Wheelchair access:** Not accessible. Note: Limit two occupants per apartment; no children under 12; credit cards not accepted; three-night minimum stay. **Subway:** 1, 9 to 79th St.

Excelsior Hotel   GOOD $–$$

45 W. 81st St. (between Columbus Ave. and Central Park West)
www.excelsiorhotelny.com
Phone: (212) 362-9200   Fax: (212) 580-3972

This attractive hotel has a lot going for it, most notably an amazing location: It sits across the street from the Rose Center for Earth & Space, on a block of regal apartment buildings, with a prime entrance to Central Park in one direction, the boutiques and restaurants of Columbus Avenue in the other. This is the Upper West Side's very best residential territory.

But the appeal doesn't end with the address. A richly wood-paneled lobby that looks like it belongs in a far more expensive hotel leads to freshly outfitted, traditionally styled guest rooms and suites that are good-sized, comfortable and well outfitted with good-quality bedding and textiles, and a fax/copier/printer on the work desk. There's high-speed Wi-Fi Internet access throughout the hotel. The plush library-style lounge—with gorgeous leather seating nooks, fireplace, books and games, and a large flat-screen TV with VCR and DVD player—is another plus. Service isn't faultless, but it's perfectly acceptable considering the fine amenities, first-class location and reasonable rates.

Rooms: 196; 16 floors; designated nonsmoking rooms. **Hotel amenities:** Concierge, exercise room, entertainment room/library, laundry and dry-cleaning service, conference room. **Food services:** Breakfast buffet served in library (for a charge). **Cancellation:** Before 4 P.M. day prior to arrival. **Wheelchair access:** Not accessible. **Subway:** 1, 9 to 79th St.

Hotel Beacon   VERY GOOD $$

2130 Broadway (at W. 75th St.)   *www.beaconhotel.com*
Phone: (212) 787-1100, (800) 572-4969   Fax: (212) 724-0839

The focus at the Beacon isn't on amenities or service but on room size and value for dollar—and on those counts, it scores extremely well. Built in 1929 for permanent residents, the Beacon has grown into an Upper West Side staple since becoming a full-fledged hotel more than a dozen years ago. Almost half of the rooms are apartment-sized suites, but even the standard configurations can easily accommodate four in two double beds. Every room and suite features a modern kitchenette with cooktop, coffee maker, minifridge (a full-size fridge in suites), microwave (plus a stove in suites) and a full complement of cookware and dishes; and a new marble bathroom; plus a pullout sleeper sofa in suites.

The gargantuan two-bedroom/two-bath suites are value-priced for larger families. The décor is generic, but there's no arguing with the comfort level. The location, at the heart of one of Manhattan's most desirable and family-friendly neighborhoods, and just a stone's throw from some of New York's finest gourmet markets, is first-rate. Rooms in the front, facing Broadway, can't avoid street noise, so ask for a back unit or a high floor.

Rooms: 236; 25 floors; designated nonsmoking rooms. **Hotel amenities:** Concierge, laundry and dry-cleaning service, coin-operated laundry, meeting room seats up to 75. **Food services:** 24-hour coffee shop. **Cancellation:** 24 hours prior to arrival. **Wheelchair access:** Fully accessible. **Subway:** 1, 2, 3, 9 to 72nd St.

Inn New York City   EXCELLENT $$$$
266 W. 71st St. (between Broadway and West End Ave.)
www.innnewyorkcity.com   Phone: (212) 580-1900   Fax: (212) 580-4437

This one-of-a-kind, four-suite luxury inn just may be the most romantic place to stay in the city. Its only peer is the Inn on Irving Place, but this place has an air of private luxury and personalized hospitality that's unparalleled. There are no public spaces whatsoever—no front desk, no concierge, no lobby—so upon entering the beautifully restored brownstone, you'll feel like you're the treasured guest of a doting, and very rich, friend with impeccable taste. Each of the four suites takes up an entire floor, and you may not ever see your fellow guests.

Each suite has a unique theme and tailored amenities, plus 12-foot ceilings, a fully equipped gourmet kitchenette, sumptuously outfitted sleeping quarters, a terrific bathroom, beautifully chosen antiques and only the plushest textiles, CD players and VCRs. The Opera Suite has a baby grand piano, a working fireplace in the bedroom, a Jacuzzi tub in the bath and French doors leading to a private terrace. One entire room of the ultra-romantic, Victorian-style spa suite is dedicated to the art of bathing, with a monster Jacuzzi tub (big enough for a party), a fireplace, a glass-block shower and a cedar-lined sauna, plus a vintage barber chair for character. The skylit, somewhat masculine and extremely handsome Library Suite is ideal for small families or shares, since pocket doors can convert the mammoth living room into a second bedroom. The duplex Vermont Suite is also available for month-long stays.

The discreet service is impeccable; the innkeepers will leave you entirely alone if you prefer, or will be at your service with the push of a button (they live in the building). The Inn is very expensive, but simply stunning—you will get your money's worth.

Rooms: Four suites; four floors; smoking not allowed. **Hotel amenities:** Copy and fax services, dry-cleaning service, washer/dryers in three suites (maid will do laundry for Opera Suite guests). **Food services:** Stocked breakfast cupboard in each suite. **Cancellation:** 14 days prior to arrival, $50 cancellation fee. **Wheelchair access:** Not accessible. Note: Best for children over 12. Two-night minimum; one-night stays command an additional $100 fee. **Subway:** 1, 2, 3, 9 to 72nd St.

The Lucerne

EXCELLENT $$–$$$

201 W. 79th St. (at Amsterdam Ave.)   *www.newyorkhotel.com*

Phone: (212) 875-1000, (800) 492-8122   Fax: (212) 579-2408

A landmark 1903 terra-cotta building houses one of the city's best mid-priced hotels. The bright and comfortably furnished marble lobby leads to extremely well-maintained rooms that are generally spacious; even the standards are large enough to accommodate a king or queen bed, or two doubles for shares or small families. Outfitted in an attractive and comfortable Americana style, all rooms have TVs with Nintendo and Web TV, dial-up Internet access (high-speed in some rooms), coffee makers and a bathroom with spacious travertine counters. One-bedroom suites have granite-counter wet-bar kitchenettes with microwaves, plus sleeper sofas, extra sitting room and TVs; the deluxe king suite also has a Jacuzzi tub. Corner units are especially light and bright. Management is fanatical about excellent service; in fact, the service is otherwise unrivaled in this price range. The upscale residential neighborhood is excellent, and the subway is less than a block away, ready to whisk you to Midtown in minutes. Check for special rates, as low as $155 at press time.

Rooms: 250; 14 floors; designated nonsmoking floors. **Hotel amenities:** Laundry and dry-cleaning service, fitness room, penthouse meeting space. **Food services:** French-Mediterranean restaurant, room service. **Cancellation:** 24 hours prior to arrival. **Wheelchair access:** Fully accessible. **Subway:** 1, 9 to 79th St.

Mandarin Oriental New York

EXTRAORDINARY $$$$

80 Columbus Circle (at W. 60th St.)   *www.mandarinoriental.com*

Phone: (212) 805-8800, (800) 526-6566   Fax: (212) 805-8882

The most talked-about hotel in New York resides in the most talked-about brand-new building, the Time Warner Center at Columbus Circle. Who can even remember that scruffy white misfit, the New York Coliseum, which sat decaying in this spot for years? This patch of New York real estate couldn't have undergone a more dramatic change. The building houses the headquarters of media giant Time Warner, a host of multi-million-dollar condos, several levels of shops and a pair of stunning Lincoln Center jazz theaters. The hotel occupies floors 35 through 54 in the northwestern tower of this massive modern structure.

The hotel made its debut in late 2003 and immediately won raves. Enter via a subdued ground-level elevator in the building's lobby; when you step out on the 35th floor, the hotel's actual lobby, you'll be overwhelmed by panoramic views. The lobby is elegantly spare, with sleek marble, a hand-blown glass centerpiece from Dale Chihuly, and giant walls of glass that capture amazing views over Central Park.

All guest rooms have sweeping views of Central Park, the Hudson River or the Manhattan skyline. Each unit boasts some $27,000 worth of high-tech perks, including three multi-line phones with voice mail and dataports; high-speed Internet access; and flat-screen LCD TVs with surround-sound stereo, CD/DVD players and a laptop connection. The oversized marble bathrooms also have flat-screen TVs. All suites and most rooms feature bathtubs with picture windows overlooking the Hudson or the park. Other posh touches include Italian linens, bathrobes and an in-room CD library. The decor features cherrywood and black-leather furnishings, plus red, bamboo, black and silvery gray drapes, bedding and sidetables. Stunning Asian accents, like Chinese lanterns and Japanese prints, work beautifully with the classic New York glamour. The 48 suites dwell on the corners of the building on floors 43 to 54, boasting the most dramatic views of all.

The reception area leads right to the Asiate restaurant and the Lobby Lounge, which seem to be suspended in midair above the park and cityscape below. With these breathtaking views, it'll take effort to focus on your meal, but the Japanese/French fare at Asiate is divine (desserts are simply perfect).

Rooms: 251; 19 floors; designated nonsmoking floors. **Hotel amenities:** Concierge; 14,500-square-foot spa; fitness center with river-view 75-foot lap pool; full business facilities; 7,000 square feet of meeting and function rooms, including a pillar-less ballroom with park views; laundry and dry-cleaning service. **Food services:** Asiate restaurant; Lobby Lounge, for casual fare and cocktails; MObar, an intimate lounge; 24-hour room service. **Cancellation:** 24 hours prior to arrival. **Wheelchair access:** Fully accessible. **Subway:** A, B, C, D, 1, 9 to 59th St.

Trump International Hotel & Tower   EXTRAORDINARY $$$$
1 Central Park West (at Columbus Circle)   *www.trumpintl.com*
Phone: (212) 299-1000, (888) 44-TRUMP (448-7867)   Fax: (212) 299-1150

Think what you want about brash real-estate developer, reality TV star and Page Six favorite Donald Trump. But it's hard to find fault with the jewel of a hotel that bears his name. It is simply spectacular.

The hotel is housed in a mirrored tower at Columbus Circle, overlooking Central Park; park views are most prized, of course, but the tower's freestanding situation awards all rooms with light, and three sides offer at least a glimpse of the green. Rooms with city views over Broadway lose a bit of the magic but retain their status as an unreserved cocoon of contemporary luxury.

About three-quarters of the accommodations are suites. High ceilings, floor-to-ceiling windows, and smart design maximize space. The look is definitely sumptuous, but in a restrained, meditative way with warm beiges and honey hues predominating. A recent freshening has lightened the look up even more. Appointments include TV with VCR and video games, CD stereo, two-line phones, complimentary high-speed Internet access and fax, a clothes steamer, a Jacuzzi tub in the marble bath and a telescope for taking in the thrilling views. Most rooms and all suites also have top-of-the-line Euro-style kitchens stocked with Limoges china and crystal. If you don't feel like relying on run-of-the-mill room service or hiking all the way down to the lobby level to dine at glorious *New York Times* four-star winner Jean Georges, one of Jean-Georges's sous-chefs will prepare your meal en suite. What's more, guests are assigned a personal concierge for the course of their stay, so expect to have your every need met and your every preference noted. A superior hotel experience, just like its brand-new neighbor across the street, the Mandarin Oriental.

Rooms: 167; 52 floors (hotel rooms housed on floors 3 through 17); designated nonsmoking floors. **Hotel amenities:** Concierge; Trump Attaché butler service; 6,000-square-foot health club with spa services, swimming pool, steam and sauna; full-service business center; laundry and dry cleaning; meeting and function rooms; CD library. **Food services:** Jean Georges restaurant, 24-hour room service. **Cancellation:** 24 hours prior to arrival. **Wheelchair access:** Fully accessible. **Subway:** A, B, C, D, 1, 9 to 59th St.

B & B BOOKING AGENTS AND SHORT-TERM APARTMENT RENTALS

Independent-minded travelers who are looking for home-style accommodations and a high value-to-dollar ratio can often do well by booking a bed-and-breakfast room (either hosted or unhosted) or a private apartment through a rental agency. Accommodations can run the gamut from spartan to splendid, from studios to multibedroom homes (which makes this a great option for families). And while they're great for long-term stays, they're also a fine option for shorter trips, as many agencies require just a two-, three- or four-night minimum, and rates on full studio apartments can start as cheaply as $90 or $100 a night.

Another advantage to reserving through a booking agency rather than a formal hotel is that taxes are often lower (usually just 8.25 percent instead of the standard 13.625 percent plus $2 per night hotel tax). Sometimes tax is eliminated altogether on longer stays, thanks to a loophole in the tax laws; ask for the details on sales tax when you book.

If you opt for this style of accommodation, be prepared to be largely on your own. You won't have the services that a hotel offers, like maid service. In fact, many accommodations that call themselves bed-and-breakfasts don't even offer breakfast as part of the package ("guest house" would be a better term), so ask. In fact, get all promises in writing and an exact total up front to avoid any misunderstandings. And try to pay by credit card if you can, so you can dispute payment if the agency fails to live up to its promises.

You'll probably have the best luck with Judith Glynn's **Manhattan Getaways** (212-956-2010; *www.manhattangetaways.com*), which offers consistently reliable apartments and service in excellent locations throughout the city. The following agencies are also usually reliable bets:

Abode Apartment Rentals (212) 472-2000, (800) 835-8880, *www.abodenyc.com*

A Hospitality Company (212) 813-2244, (800) 987-1235,
www.hospitalityco.com

City Sonnet (212) 614-3034, *www.citysonnet.com*

Homestay New York (718) 434-2071, *www.homestayny.com*

Manhattan Lodgings (212) 677-7616, *www.manhattanlodgings.com*

New York Habitat (212) 255-8018, *www.nyhabitat.com*

If you're a self-sufficient traveler interested in arranging an apartment swap with a New Yorker, your best source is **Craig's List** at *www.newyork.craigslist.org*.

BEYOND MANHATTAN
THE BRONX

Le Refuge Inn   GOOD $
586 City Island Ave. (between Sutherland and Cross Sts.), City Island
www.lerefugeinn.com   Phone: (718) 885-2478   Fax: (718) 885-3363

This pleasant old 19th-century house on the main strip of enjoyably funky City Island in the far reaches of the Bronx makes for a pleasant country-in-the-city-style getaway. The warmth of the welcome, the delightful French meals prepared by Normandy-born innkeeper and chef Pierre Saint-Denis (who also presides over Le Refuge Restaurant on the Upper East Side), and the chamber concerts on Sunday afternoons are the best reasons to visit. M. Saint-Denis imbues the inn with the genuine ambiance of his homeland.

Rooms: Six (some with shared bathrooms); three floors; no smoking allowed. **Hotel amenities:** None. **Food services:** Rates include continental breakfast; prix-fixe dinner $45, Sunday brunch $19.50. **Cancellation:** 10 days prior to arrival. **Wheelchair access:** Not accessible. **Directions:** 6 to Pelham Bay Park; then transfer to City Island Bus No. 29 toward City Island (third stop).

BROOKLYN

Bed & Breakfast on the Park   VERY GOOD $$–$$$
113 Prospect Park West (between 6th and 7th Sts.), Park Slope *www.bbnyc.com*
Phone: (718) 499-6115   Fax: (718) 499-1385

A beautifully restored town house, built in 1895 and situated right across the street from Prospect Park, is the setting for Brooklyn's best bed-and-breakfast inn, one of the finest in the entire city. The house is enchantingly and lavishly outfitted with antiques, oriental rugs, fine oil paintings and stained glass. The rooms are individually appointed, but each is ultra-romantic in its own way; the most sumptuously outfitted suites stumble into the $$$ price category. Breakfast is vast and satisfying. Be prepared when you pay your bill: A 10 percent staff gratuity is requested.

Rooms: Seven (all with private bathrooms); four floors; no smoking allowed.

Hotel amenities: None. **Food services:** Rates include full breakfast. **Cancellation:** 11 days prior to arrival, subject to cancellation fee. **Note:** Two-night minimum (three nights on select weekends). **Wheelchair access:** Not accessible. **Subway:** F to Seventh Ave.

New York Marriott at the Brooklyn Bridge   VERY GOOD $$$
333 Adams St. (between Tillary and Willoughby Sts.), Downtown Brooklyn
www.marriott.com
Phone: (718) 246-7000, (888) 436-3759   Fax: (718) 246-0563

This Marriott, which occupies seven floors of a big office tower adjacent to the Metro Tech Center (and just minutes from the Lower Manhattan Financial District), is a prime symbol of downtown Brooklyn's booming gentrification. It's attractive and well-outfitted, with nods to its home borough that pull it out of the chain-generic doldrums. Behind the front desk is a mural of the Brooklyn Bridge, and artwork and photos of Brooklyn or by Brooklyn artists adorn the walls throughout the hotel.

Once you reach your room, it's strictly Marriott, but all the bases are well covered. Perks include high-speed and wireless Internet access. Even though the hotel is built over busy Adams Street, the rooms are tranquil. Nearly a dozen major subway lines converge in this area, so citywide access is easy, and you can be in Manhattan inside ten minutes. Weekend rates often fall into the $$ range.

Rooms: 376; seven floors; designated nonsmoking floors. **Hotel amenities:** Concierge, business center, health club with lap pool, dry-cleaning service, meeting and function rooms, valet parking. **Food services:** Restaurant, cocktail lounge, room service. **Cancellation:** Before 6 P.M. day of arrival. **Wheelchair access:** Fully accessible. **Subway:** M, R to Court St.; 2, 3, 4, 5 to Borough Hall; A, C, F to Jay St.–Borough Hall.

STATEN ISLAND

Harbor House   GOOD $
1 Hylan Blvd.(at Edgewater St.)   *www.nyharborhouse.com*
Phone: (718) 876-0056   Fax: (718) 420-9940

Built in 1890, the Harbor House is not luxurious in any way, but it does have wonderful views over the harbor to Manhattan, taking in the Verrazano Bridge and Lady Liberty as well. (One smart man rented the whole place for the Fourth of July and had his family there to watch the fireworks.) The house feels more like a beach house than anything else, and you can lie in bed and look out to the water. Rooms tend to be large, with a TV, dresser, armoire and ceiling fan, but no phone. (There's a phone in the main hall; local calls are free for guests.)

Rooms: 11 (six with shared bathroom); three floors; no smoking allowed. **Hotel amenities:** None. **Food services:** Rates include continental breakfast. **Cancellation:** One night non-refundable deposit. **Wheelchair access:** Not accessible. **Directions:** Staten Island Ferry to S-51 bus to Hylan and Bay Street; walk across Bay Street and down one block.

AIRPORTS

(For directions to airports, see chapter **Visiting New York***.)*

La Guardia Airport

Crowne Plaza Hotel La Guardia   GOOD   **$$–$$$**
104-04 Ditmars Blvd. (at 23rd Ave.), East Elmhurst   *www.crowneplaza.com*
Phone: (718) 457-6300, (800) 227-6963   Fax: (718) 899-9768

This recently renovated airport hotel features classic-contemporary rooms that
have ample amenities. Closets aren't large and ceilings are low but the soundproofing is very good; rooms feature coffee makers (ideal for that early-morning
flight), Nintendo on the TV and wireless Internet access. A extra few dollars
will garner you an Executive Level room, which comes with access to a complimentary breakfast, evening hors d'oeuvres and slightly upgraded accommodations. An airline screen shows up-to-date flight information.

Rooms: 358; seven floors; designated nonsmoking rooms. **Hotel amenities:**
Concierge; full-service business center; fitness center with swimming pool,
sauna and whirlpool; laundry and dry-cleaning service, guest laundry; meeting
space, including conference theater with high-speed Internet access, complimentary airport shuttle. **Food services:** Restaurant, bar, room service. **Cancellation:** Before 6 P.M. day of arrival. **Wheelchair access:** Fully accessible.

New York La Guardia Airport Marriott   GOOD   **$$**
102-05 Ditmars Blvd. (at 23rd Ave.), East Elmhurst   *www.marriott.com*
Phone: (718) 565-8900, (800) 882-1043   Fax: (718) 898-4955

Here's a competent and comfortable, if not particularly colorful, hotel near La
Guardia's terminal, which keeps the noise level down (hotels near the runways
are much noisier). All of the familiar Marriott and airport-hotel trappings are
here, including an executive concierge level and an airline monitor.

Rooms: 437; nine floors; designated nonsmoking floors. **Hotel amenities:**
Concierge; business center; fitness center with swimming pool, sauna and
whirlpool; dry-cleaning service; extensive meeting and function space. **Food
services:** Restaurant, sports bar, room service; complimentary airport shuttle.
Cancellation: Before 6 P.M. day of arrival. **Wheelchair access:** Fully accessible.

J.F.K. Airport

Holiday Inn New York—J.F.K. Airport   GOOD   **$–$$**
144-02 135th Ave. (Van Wyck Expressway, exit 2), Jamaica
www.holidayinnjfk.com, *www.sixcontinentshotels.com*
Phone: (718) 659-0200, (800) 692-5350   Fax: (718) 322-2533

Situated on the airport's periphery, this Holiday Inn offers some serenity. It has
quiet rooms, a pleasant pool area and even a Japanese garden. In fact, if you
have a room facing away from the airport, you'd hardly know you were there.

Rooms aren't exactly charming, but they are clean, comfortable and decently sized; bedding is quite comfortable, and bathrooms are plain but adequate.All units have wireless Internet access through the TV.

Rooms: 360; 12 floors; designated nonsmoking rooms. **Hotel amenities:** Concierge, business center, fitness center; indoor/outdoor pool with sauna and whirlpool; laundry and dry-cleaning service, guest laundry, meeting and function rooms, 24-hour courtesy airport transportation. **Food services:** Restaurant, sports bar, room service. **Cancellation:** Before 6 P.M. day of arrival. **Wheelchair access:** Fully accessible.

Radisson Hotel J.F.K. Airport   GOOD $–$$
135-30 140th St., Jamaica   *www.radissonjfk.com*
Phone: (718) 322-2300, (800) 333-3333   Fax: (718) 322-5569

Rooms here are traditionally decorated and moderately attractive; mattresses are good, but your sleep may be undermined by noise from the Belt Parkway just outside. Other in-room perks include high-speed Internet access, on-demand video games and a coffee maker; junior suites add a pullout sofa, fridge and a spacious work desk. A bar in the lobby serves sandwiches and beer.

Rooms: 386; 12 floors; designated nonsmoking floors. **Hotel amenities:** Concierge, business center, fitness room, laundry and dry-cleaning service, meeting and function rooms. **Food services:** restaurant, bar with large-screen TV, room service, complimentary airport transportation. **Cancellation:** Before 6 P.M. on day of arrival.**Wheelchair access:** Fully accessible.

Newark Liberty International Airport, Newark NJ
Newark Airport Marriott   GOOD $$$
Newark International Airport   *www.marriott.com*
Phone: (973) 623-0006, (800) 228-9290   Fax: (973) 623-7618

The only hotel on Newark Airport property, this Marriott has the company's familiar combination of comforts and corporate-traveler-friendly amenities. Most important, the windows offer virtually complete soundproofing against airplane noise. Rooms aren't particularly spacious, but they're perfectly adequate and feature in-room coffee makers and high-speed Internet connectivity.

Concierge-level rooms have additional amenities and a separate lounge serving complimentary continental breakfast and evening hors d'oeuvres. A telescope helps you keep track of the air traffic, and an airline monitor in the lobby helps you keep track of flight schedules.

Rooms: 597; 10 floors; designated nonsmoking floors. **Hotel amenities:** Concierge; business center; health club with swimming pool, sauna and whirlpool; laundry and dry-cleaning service, guest laundry facilities; extensive meeting and function space, complimentary airport shuttle. **Food services:** Three restaurants (steakhouse, pub and an American grill), room service. **Cancellation:** Before 6 P.M. day of arrival. **Wheelchair access:** Fully accessible.

HOTELS BY PRICE

$$$$ Very Expensive

The Carlyle	Upper East Side	EXTRAORDINARY
Chambers	Midtown West	VERY GOOD
Four Seasons Hotel New York	Midtown East	EXCELLENT
Hotel Gansevoort	Meatpacking District	EXCELLENT
The Inn at Irving Place	Gramercy Park	EXCELLENT
Inn New York City	Upper West Side	EXCELLENT
Le Parker Meridien	Midtown West	EXTRAORDINARY
The Lowell	Upper East Side	EXCELLENT
Mandarin Oriental New York	Upper West Side	EXTRAORDINARY
The Mercer	SoHo	EXCELLENT
The Mark	Upper East Side	EXCELLENT
The New York Palace	Midtown East	EXCELLENT
The Peninsula New York	Midtown West	EXTRAORDINARY
The Pierre	Upper East Side	EXCELLENT
The Regency Hotel	Upper East Side	EXCELLENT
Ritz-Carlton New York, Battery Park	Battery Park	EXCELLENT
Ritz-Carlton New York, Central Park	Midtown West	EXCELLENT
60 Thompson	SoHo	VERY GOOD
The St. Regis New York	Midtown East	EXTRAORDINARY
The Stanhope, Park Hyatt New York	Upper East Side	VERY GOOD
Swissôtel New York-The Drake	Midtown East	EXTRAORDINARY
Trump International Hotel & Tower	Upper West Side	EXTRAORDINARY
Waldorf Towers, A Conrad Hotel	Midtown East	EXCELLENT

$$$–$$$$

Bryant Park Hotel	Midtown West	VERY GOOD
The Iroquois New York	Midtown West	GOOD
The Kitano New York	Murray Hill	EXCELLENT
Millennium Broadway	Times Square	VERY GOOD
Omni Berkshire Place	Midtown East	EXCELLENT
The Plaza	Midtown West	GOOD
Sheraton Russell Hotel	Murray Hill	GOOD
Sofitel New York	Midtown West	EXCELLENT
SoHo Grand Hotel	SoHo	EXCELLENT
Tribeca Grand Hotel	TriBeCa	EXCELLENT
Waldorf=Astoria, A Hilton Hotel	Midtown East	EXCELLENT
W Times Square	Times Square	VERY GOOD
W Union Square	Union Square	EXCELLENT

$$$ Expensive

The Benjamin	Midtown East	EXTRAORDINARY
City Club Hotel	Midtown West	VERY GOOD

Crowne Plaza Manhattan	Midtown West	GOOD
Doubletree Guest Suites Times Square	Times Square	VERY GOOD
Embassy Suites New York	Battery Park City	EXCELLENT
Fitzpatrick Grand Central Hotel	Midtown East	VERY GOOD
Hilton Times Square	Times Square	EXCELLENT
Holiday Inn Wall Street	Financial District	EXCELLENT
Hotel Elysée	Midtown East	VERY GOOD
Hudson	Midtown West	GOOD
Kimberly Hotel	Midtown East	VERY GOOD
Library Hotel	Midtown East	VERY GOOD
The Lombardy	Midtown East	EXCELLENT
The Maritime Hotel	Chelsea	VERY GOOD
Melrose Hotel	Upper East Side	GOOD
Morgans	Murray Hill	VERY GOOD
The Muse	Midtown West	EXCELLENT
New York Marriott at the Brooklyn Bridge	Brooklyn	GOOD
New York Marriott Marquis	Times Square	GOOD
Newark Airport Marriott	Newark	GOOD
70 Park Avenue Hotel	Murray Hill	EXCELLENT
W New York-The Court	Midtown East	VERY GOOD
W New York-The Tuscany	Midtown East	VERY GOOD
Westin New York Times Square	Midtown West	VERY GOOD

$$–$$$

The Algonquin	Times Square	VERY GOOD
Bed & Breakfast on the Park	Brooklyn	VERY GOOD
The Blakey New York	Midtown West	VERY GOOD
Crowne Plaza Hotel La Guardia	Queens	GOOD
Hilton New York	Midtown West	GOOD
Hotel Casablanca	Times Square	VERY GOOD
Hotel Giraffe	Flatiron District	VERY GOOD
Hotel Wales	Upper East Side	GOOD
Le Marquis New York	Murray Hill	GOOD
The Lucerne	Upper West Side	EXCELLENT
The Mansfield	Midtown West	GOOD
New York Marriott Financial Center	Financial District	GOOD
Paramount	Times Square	GOOD
Park Central New York	Midtown West	VERY GOOD
The Roger Williams	Midtown East	GOOD
Wall Street Inn	Financial District	VERY GOOD

$$ Moderate

Abingdon Guest House	West Village	VERY GOOD
The Belvedere	Midtown West	GOOD
Best Western Seaport Inn	Lower Manhattan	GOOD

Broadway Inn	Midtown West	VERY GOOD
Buckingham Hotel	Midtown West	VERY GOOD
Chelsea Lodge Suites	Chelsea	VERY GOOD
Country Inn the City	Upper West Side	VERY GOOD
Crowne Plaza at the United Nations	Midtown East	VERY GOOD
Four Points by Sheraton Manhattan	Chelsea	VERY GOOD
Gramercy Park Hotel	Gramercy Park	GOOD
The Helmsley Middletowne	Midtown East	GOOD
Holiday Inn Downtown/Soho	Chinatown	GOOD
Hotel Beacon	Upper West Side	VERY GOOD
Hotel Chelsea	Chelsea	GOOD
The Inn on 23rd St.	Chelsea	EXCELLENT
New York La Guardia Airport Marriott	Queens	GOOD

$–$$

Chelsea Pines Inn	Chelsea	GOOD
Chelsea Lodge/Chelsea Lodge Suites	Chelsea	VERY GOOD
Comfort Inn Midtown	Midtown West	GOOD
Excelsior Hotel	Upper West Side	GOOD
Holiday Inn New York-J.F.K. Airport	Queens	GOOD
Hotel Edison	Times Square	BASIC
Hotel Metro	Midtown West	VERY GOOD
La Quinta Manhattan	Midtown West	GOOD
Radisson Hotel J.F.K. Airport	Queens	GOOD
Red Roof Inn	Midtown West	VERY GOOD
Super 8 Hotel Times Square	Times Square	VERY GOOD
Thirty Thirty	Murray Hill	VERY GOOD
Travel Inn	Midtown West	GOOD

$ Inexpensive

Americana Inn	Midtown West	BASIC
Amsterdam Inn	Upper West Side	BASIC
Big Apple Hostel	Times Square	BASIC
Colonial House Inn	Chelsea	GOOD
Cosmopolitan Hotel-Tribeca	Tribeca	GOOD
Harbor House	Staten Island	GOOD
Larchmont Hotel	West Village	GOOD
Le Refuge Inn	The Bronx	GOOD
NYC Howard Johnson Express Inn	Lower East Side	GOOD
SoHotel	Nolita	BASIC
Murray Hill Inn	Murray Hill	BASIC
Union Square Inn	East Village	GOOD

According to former *New York Times* food critic, William Grimes, "The quality, range and sheer number of the city's restaurants has made New York the world's most exciting place to eat. Paris may have more French restaurants, and Rome more trattorias, but no city on earth offers the adventurous eater more variety and depth than New York at the present moment."

For more than 30 years, New Yorkers have been relying on restaurant reviews in the *Times* for the most trustworthy advice about where to eat in their hometown. The 300 or so restaurants included here have all been reviewed by the major food critics of the *Times*: William Grimes, Eric Asimov and Frank Bruni. Since 1992 Eric Asimov has been responsible for finding those quintessential New York restaurants that serve high quality food at reasonable prices (his reviews are clearly identified by the term **"$25 & Under"** which appears at the top of the review). Restaurants with stars have been reviewed by Mr. Bruni since 2004 and by Mr. Grimes before then. Some original reviews have been updated in the "Eating Out" and "Good Eating" columns that appear weekly in the newspaper and those changes are reflected here. In addition, Mr. Grimes and Mr. Asimov have done recent updates for this *Guide*.

(Note: The best restaurants in Brooklyn, Queens and the other boroughs can be found in the chapter **Exploring New York**.)

Using This Guide

What the Stars Mean:

☆ ☆ ☆ ☆   Extraordinary
☆ ☆ ☆   Excellent
☆ ☆   Very Good
☆   Good

Price Range: The dollar signs that appear at the top of each review are based on the cost of a three-course dinner and a 15 percent tip (but not drinks).

$	$25 and under
$$	$25 to $40
$$$	$40 to $55
$$$$	$55 and over

$25 & Under: At these restaurants you can get a complete meal, exclusive of drinks and tip, for $25 or less; recently, as a concession to inflation, some restaurants have been included where only an appetizer and main course total $25.

Abbreviations: Meals: B = Breakfast, Br = Brunch, L = Lunch, D = Dinner. LN = Late Night (restaurants open till midnight or later). Credit cards: AE = American Express; DC = Diner's Club; D = Discover; MC = Master Card; V = Visa; if there is no credit card information it means that at least three of these cards are accepted.

The Best Restaurants in New York City

☆ ☆ ☆ ☆—EXTRAORDINARY

Alain Ducasse

Daniel

Jean Georges

Le Bernardin

☆ ☆ ☆—EXCELLENT

Aquavit

Atelier

Babbo

Biltmore Room

Bolo

Bouley

Café Boulud

Chanterelle

Craft

Danube

Felidia

Fiamma Osteria

Fifty Seven Fifty Seven

The Four Seasons

Gotham Bar and Grill

Gramercy Tavern

Honmura An

JoJo

Kuruma Zushi

La Grenouille

Le Cirque 2000

L'Impero

March

Masa

Next Door Nobu

Nobu

Oceana

Patria

Patroon

Picholine

Pico

RM

Spice Market

Sushi Yasuda

Tabla

Town

Veritas

☆ ☆—VERY GOOD

Ada

Aix

Amma

Amuse

Aquagrill

Artisanal

Balthazar

Bambou

Bayard's

Beacon

Beppe

Bice

BLT Steak

Blue Fin

Blue Hill

Blue Ribbon Sushi

Brasserie

Brasserie 360

Bread Tribeca

Café des Artistes

Café Sabarsky

Capitale

Casa Mono

Centolire

'Cesca

Chelsea Bistro & Bar

Chez Josephine

Cho Dang Gol

Chola

Churrascaria Plataforma

Circus

City Hall

Compass

David Burke

  & Donatella

DB Bistro Moderne

Django

Diwan

Eight Mile Creek

Eleven Madison Park

Esca

Estiatorio Milos

Firebird

Fleur de Sel

Fresh

Gabriel's

Guastavino's

Hangawi

The Harrison

Hatsuhana

Heartbeat

Hearth

Icon

Il Gattopardo

Il Valentino

I Trulli

Jack's Luxury Oyster

  Bar

Jefferson

Joe's Shanghai

Kai
Kang Suh
Kittichai
Le Colonial
Le Madri
Le Perigord
Lever House Restaurant
Lutèce
Manhattan Ocean Club
Marseille
Matsuri
Maya
Megu
Mercer Kitchen
Mesa Grill
Michael Jordan's
Michael's
Mi Cocina
Mix in New York
Moda
Molyvos
Nadaman Hakubai
New York Noodle Town

Nice Matin
Nick & Toni's Café
Nicole's
Odeon
Orsay
Otabe
Otto
Ouest
Paola's
Parioli Romanissimo
Park Avenue Café
Park View at the
   Boathouse
Payard Patisserie
Petrossian
Ping's Seafood
Remi
Riingo
Ruby Foo's
Salaam Bombay
Savoy
Sea Grill
71 Clinton Fresh Food

Shun Lee Palace
66
Smith & Wollensky
Solera
Sumile
Surya
Sushi Seki
Tamarind
Thalia
Tocqueville
Tribeca Grill
Triomphe
Tuscan
"21" Club
Union Pacific
Union Square Café
Upstairs at "21"
Wallsé
WD-50
Wolfgang's Steakhouse
Zarela

☆—GOOD

Acqua Pazza
Agave
Alfama
Asia de Cuba
Asiate
Avra
Azafron
Baldoria
Barbalùc
Barrio
Blue Smoke
Blue Water Grill
Branzini
Brasserie 8 1/2
Butter
Calle Ocho
Chubo
Coup
Dawat
Delmonico's
Dim Sum Go Go
District
Dock's Oyster Bar
Frank's
Geisha
Goody's
Hacienda de Argentina

Hue
industry (food)
Ixta
Jane
Jarnac
Jean-Luc
Jubilee 51
Kloe
Lamu
Landmarc
La Nonna
Lentini
Les Halles Downtown
Le Zinc
Lotus
Lozoo
Mas
Meet
Morrells
92
NL
Noche
Ola
Olives
Parish & Company
Pastis
Patroon

Peasant
Provence
Public
The Red Cat
Redeye Grill
Rocco's on 22nd
Salón Mexico
Scalini Fedeli
Sciuscià
Sparks Steak House
Strip House
Suba
Suenos
The Tasting Room
Tavern on the Green
36 Bar and Barbecue
325 Spring Street
Thom
V Steakhouse
Verbena
Viceversa
Voyage
Zitoune
Zocalo
Zona Rosa

MANHATTAN RESTAURANTS, A-Z

Acqua Pazza   ☆   **$$$**   ITALIAN SEAFOOD
36 W. 52nd St. (between Fifth and Sixth Aves.)   (212) 582-6900
A solid Italian seafood restaurant where the welcome is warm, and the waiters
fuss in a friendly way. The kitchen is dedicated to seafood—there's no meat on
the menu, period. For excitement, go straight to the homemade pampanelle,
thin ribbons of pasta tinted black on one side with cuttlefish ink. The main
courses, too, can be show-stoppers, when the kitchen does not slip into the bad
habit of cooking fish medium-well rather than medium-rare. **Price range:**
Entrees $17–$29. **Meals:** L (Mon.–Fri.), D (Mon.–Sat.). Closed Sun. **Subway:**
1, 9 to 50th St.; N, R, W to 49th St.

Acquario   **$25 & Under**   MEDITERRANEAN
5 Bleecker St. (near Bowery)   (212) 260-4666
Acquario is a small, warm place straight out of the Village's bohemian past. A
couple of Acquario's large appetizers can easily make a light meal. Try the fresh
sardines, which have a strong, briny aroma but a mild, wonderfully nutty flavor.
The most alluring dish is the Portuguese fish stew. **Price range:** Entrees,
$12–$18. Cash only. **Meals:** D. Closed Sun. **Subway:** 6 to Bleecker St.

Ada   ☆ ☆   **$$$$**   INDIAN
208 E. 58th St. (between Second and Third Aves.)   (212) 371-6060
Ada aims to elevate the status of Indian cuisine in New York. The décor steers
clear of Indian fabrics and beaded curtains; the owner is intent on giving the
food an upgrade as well. Spices are used with great delicacy in most dishes, and
they penetrate every fiber of tandoori-cooked meats, which arrive in a state of
melting tenderness. The dessert menu uses a few Indian ingredients strategi-
cally, with some success. **Price range:** Prix fixe, $55 or $65. **Meals:** L, D. **Sub-
way:** 4, 5, 6 to 59th St.

Agave   ☆   **$$$**   SOUTHWESTERN
140 Seventh Ave. S. (near Charles St.)   (212) 989-2100
The cuisine at Agave is billed as New Southwestern, and it comes in handsome
surroundings. Eating here is an impetuous, slightly mad adventure, a blur of
spices, colors and textures. The cuisine, by design, has a large trash element to
it: one of the best things on the menu is a sloppy bowl of three melted cheeses
poured over pieces of spicy chorizo. **Price range:** Entrees, $14–$23. **Meals:** D.
Subway: 1, 9 to Christopher St.

Aix   ☆ ☆   **$$$**   FRENCH
2398 Broadway (near 88th St.)   (212) 874-7400
The chef at Aix — a bustling, cheery place with three dining levels — treats
Provence as a repository of images and taste sensations, which he freely reinter-
prets, sometimes ingeniously, sometimes not. Main courses, like broiled squab
and venison, are robust. Aix has the kind of wine list you hope for in a restau-

rant celebrating the South of France, and the dessert menu reflects the avant-garde school, whose adherents believe that diners should be challenged, not coddled. **Price range:** Entrees, $22–$29. **Meals:** D. **Subway:** 1, 9 to 86th St.

Ajisai $25 & Under   JAPANESE/SUSHI
1466 First Ave. (near 76th St.)   (212) 717-5464
Ajisai's pleasant dining room, with cross-hatched burgundy walls and comfortable red banquettes, conveys a feeling of warmth and ease. The sushi and sashimi selection is not extensive, but the quality is superb. Non-sushi dishes are also good, including stewed pork belly, soft and tender enough to cut with chop sticks. **Price range:** Entrees, $14–$20; sushi and sashimi dinners, $12–$27. **Meals:** L, D. Closed Mon. **Subway:** 6 to 77th St.

aKa Café $25 & Under   FUSION
49 Clinton St. (near Rivington St.)   (212) 979-6096
This storefront offshoot of 71 Clinton Fresh Food takes the familiar downtown sandwich-and-wine bar into a stratosphere of unexpected flavor combinations. The signature lamb tongue sandwich is one of the most successful offerings, a balance of savory, sweet and rich. The back-lighted bar is the central feature of an otherwise minimally decorated room; yet the menu grabs the attention right away, even though it offers no more than soups, salads and sandwiches. **Price range:** Everything is $5–$7. **Meals:** D. Closed Sun. **Subway:** F, J, M to Delancey St.

Alain Ducasse at the Essex House   ☆☆☆☆ $$$$ FRENCH
155 W. 58th St. (between Sixth and Seventh Aves.)   (212) 265-7300
The service here has a polish and grace befitting the jewel box of a dining room. The easier, happier atmosphere emanates, ultimately, from the kitchen. Chef Alain Ducasse has always sworn allegiance to the philosophy that ingredients should rule the kitchen and his menu abounds in simple classic preparations. The payoff is evident every night at the Essex House, where Mr. Ducasse offers the kind of food that brings diners to their knees. **Price range:** Prix-fixe and tasting menus, $145-160 (lunch "menu salad," $65; truffle menu, $300). **Meals:** L (Thu. & Fri.), D. Closed Sun. **Subway:** F, N, Q, R, W to 57th St.

Alfama   ☆ $$$ PORTUGUESE
551 Hudson St. (near Perry St.)   (212) 645-2500
The food at this warm and inviting place can be robust and blunt, but it can also reach a level of elegance that manages to retain the forceful flavors so characteristic of Portuguese cuisine. The sautéed fresh cod with broa, the Portuguese corn-and-wheat bread, is lively and delicious. Prawns with a lemon-shellfish bread pudding is another superb dish. The selection of more than 100 Portuguese wines may be the best in the city. Desserts are a high point, particularly the disco voador, a wonderful sweet tart of ground walnuts and almonds. **Price range:** Entrees, $16–$25. **Meals:** L, D. **Subway:** 1, 9 to Christopher St.

Alias $25 & Under   BISTRO
76 Clinton St. (at Rivington St.)   (212) 505-5011
This offbeat bistro finds and exalts the big, warm flavors of classic combinations. Simple roast chicken is renewed, full of flavor, and served with mashed
potatoes enlivened with a purée of porcini mushrooms. Homey, hearty dishes
shine. Alias hews closely to the traditional bistro role of offering predictably satisfying food, but it does so creatively. **Price range:** Entrees, $17–$20. **Meals:** D.
Subway: F to Delancey St.

Alta $25 & Under   MEDITERRANEAN
64 West 10th St. (at Sixth Ave.)   (212) 505-7777
Each meal at Alta is a natural, unforced pleasure; the elements of food, wine
and ambience all come together with a menu of small plates, using flavors and
ingredients from around the Mediterranean. Some of the dishes are traditional:
a pile of tiny deep-fried smelts would be right at home in any seaside Greek taverna. Each plate brings with it unexpected flavor combinations. Beautifully
roasted piquillo peppers are stuffed with goat cheese and served over a pestolike
sauce, an excellent marriage of pungencies. **Price range:** Entrees, $10–$14.
Meals: L, D. **Subway:** A, C, E, F, V to West 4th St.

Amma   ☆☆ $$–$$$ INDIAN
246 E. 51st St. (between Second and Third Aves.)   (212) 644-8330
Amma's menu is a whirlwind tour of India that extends geographically from the
northwestern frontier to Goa, and stylistically from refined Mogul cooking to
lunchbox fare and street snacks. Amma does away with redundant curries, vin-
daloos and pilafs, replacing them with a wide variety of homey dishes and
seductive entrees from the tandoor. There's a great emphasis on condiments and
breads, which include the standard parathas and nans, but also a sweetly chewy
kulcha stuffed with crab meat. Save room for the satiny mango cheesecake.
Price range: Entrees $12–$28; tasting menu $50. **Meals:** L, D. **Subway:** E, V to
Lexington Ave./53rd St.; 6 to 51st St.

Amuse   ☆☆ $$ NEW AMERICAN
108 W. 18th St. (near Sixth Ave.)   (212) 929-9755
Amuse is short for amuse-bouche, the French term for the bite-size pre-appetiz-
ers intended to titillate the palate. Here the entire menu is designed around
small tastes. There are a half dozen choices in four price categories, $5, $10,
$15, and $20. With each increase in price, the preparations become more com-
plex. **Price range:** Dishes in four categories: $5, $10, $15 and $20. **Meals:** L, D,
LN. Closed Sun. **Subway:** F to 14th St.; 1, 9 to 18th St.

Anh $25 & Under   VIETNAMESE
363 Third Ave. (near 27th St.)   (212) 532-2858
The dining room is dim and stylish: one wall of fieldstones and polished
wooden louvers looks as if it came from a Frank Lloyd Wright catalog. Many of
the dishes on the menu may seem familiar. Yet the kitchen renders them
expertly, capturing Vietnamese cuisine's low-key delicacy with just the right

light touch. Main courses are often a letdown at Vietnamese restaurants, but Anh's exhibit a winning subtlety. **Price range:** Entrees, $7–$14. **Meals:** L, D. **Subway:** 6 to 28th St.

Aquagrill ☆☆ $$$ SEAFOOD
210 Spring St. (at Sixth Ave.) (212) 274-0505

Aquagrill has the comfortable air of a neighborhood place, the sort of restaurant that ought to be serving burgers and beer. Instead there's an oyster bar in front and the menu is refreshingly original. Devoted almost entirely to fish, it offers unusual dishes like "snail-snaps" (bite-size popovers with a single snail) and salmon in falafel crust. Soups are also satisfying. **Price range:** Entrees, $18.50–$26. **Meals:** Br, L, D. Closed Mon. **Subway:** C, E to Spring St.

Aquavit ☆☆☆ $$$$ SWEDISH
13 W. 54th St. (between Fifth and Sixth Aves.) (212) 307-7311

Marcus Samuelsson, Aquavit's restlessly inventive executive chef, has a distinctive style in which precisely defined flavors talk back and forth to each other rather than blending into a single smooth harmonic effect. The menu sparkles with bright thoughts. Herring, of course, is on the menu, a reminder that, to the Swedes, this fish is a form of cultural expression that is part of the genetic code. But Mr. Samuelsson's pièce de résistance is his pellucid arctic char, pinkish orange and delicately smoked. **Price range:** Pre-theater menu, $39; prix fixe and tasting menus, $67–$110. **Meals:** L, D. **Subway:** B, D, E to Seventh Ave.

Arezzo ☆ $$$ ITALIAN
46 W. 22nd St. (between Fifth and Sixth Aves.) (212) 206-0555

A modest low-ceiling dining room with a coal-burning oven is the setting for Tuscan and Piedmontese cuisine, with some modernizing. The oven, source of the more traditional dishes, produces what may be the best appetizer on the menu, a focaccina, a flatter relative of the famed focaccia, split in half and spread with a mixture of robiola cheese, potato and spinach, then drizzled with truffle oil. Pea-flavored cavatelli with a sauce of hot and sweet sausages is among the best pastas. Arezzo has a lot of desserts, but the pastry chef outdoes himself with a very dense, intensely flavored bitter-chocolate panna cotta. **Price range:** Lunch: apps., $7–$12; entrees, $14–$22. Dinner: apps., $9–$18; entrees, $17–$35; desserts, $8.50. **Meals:** L, D. Closed Sun. **Subway:** N, R to 23rd St.

Artisanal ☆☆ $$$$ BISTRO
2 Park Ave. (at 32nd St.) (212) 725-8585

Artisanal is a big, very good-looking brasserie with more varieties of cheese (nearly 200) than most human beings will encounter in a lifetime. About half the menu at Artisanal is honest bistro cooking. The other half shows some genuinely inspired flashes, like rabbit in riesling sauce. After the entrees comes the moment of truth. You will have plenty of help putting together a good cheese plate, and Artisanal makes all of its 140 or so wines available by the glass, so no cheese need be eaten without the mathematically precise wine pairing. **Price range:** Entrees, $16–$36. **Meals:** L, D, LN. **Subway:** 6 to 33rd St.

Asia de Cuba   ☆   **$$$**   ASIAN/LATIN AMERICAN
237 Madison Ave. (near 37th St.)   (212) 726-7755
You won't eat very well at Asia de Cuba. But the manic energy of the place
makes every night feel like a party. There aren't many main dishes to recom-
mend. But who can think about all that when desserts are exploding all over the
room? Guava Dynamite is just guava mousse wrapped in a chocolate tuile, but
the sparkler on top is seductive. **Price range:** Entrees, $22–$34.
Meals: L, D, LN. **Subway:** 6 to 33rd St.

Asiate   ☆   **$$$$**   FRENCH/ASIAN FUSION
Mandarin Oriental Hotel, Time Warner Center, 35th floor,
Columbus Circle (entrance on 60th St., west of Broadway)   (212) 805-8881
Dining at Asiate begins with a whoosh! as the elevator shoots up 35 floors to
the restaurant's glassed-in perch, where tables are arranged so that most diners
overlook Central Park. No extravagance was spared in the luxurious design, and
the waiters are deft. Alas, the fusion cuisine seems to have gotten muddled in
the rarefied air. The chef feels the need to load every dish with his entire culi-
nary arsenal. But when the kitchen does pull off the acrobatics, it can be mar-
velous. **Price range:** $65 prix-fixe. **Meals:** L (Mon.–Fri.), D (Mon.–Sat.).
Closed Sun. **Subway:** 1, 9, A, B, C, D to 59th St./Columbus Circle.

Atelier   ☆☆☆   **$$$$**   FRENCH
Ritz-Carlton Hotel, 50 Central Park S. (at Sixth Ave.)   (212) 521-6125
Atelier has firmly established itself as one of the city's finest French restaurants.
The menu embraces both minimalist spa dishes like steamed black sea bass in a
lemon verbena jus and a punchy, explosively flavorful oxtail crèpinette stuffed
with wild mushrooms and coated, almost like a candy apple, in a sticky, syrupy
reduction. The dessert offerings deliver fireworks and fun. The dining room is
quiet and civilized, with relaxed but efficient service. Atelier is committed to
luxury and indulgence, but the experience, like the sauces, never weighs heav-
ily. **Price range:** $72 three-course prix-fixe; $95 six-course tasting menu; $128
chef's tasting menu. **Meals:** D. **Subway:** N, R, Q, W to 57th St.; F to 57th St.

August   **$25 & Under**   BISTRO/FRENCH
359 Bleecker St. (at Charles St.)   (212) 929-4774
The soft yet insistent fragrance of wood smoke makes a tantalizing first impres-
sion upon entering this slender, rustic dining room. The dishes are classics and
are generally prepared with precision and care, but appetizers can misfire. The
odds of success are better with main courses, like a superb skate grenobloise.
Bass à la grecque is a small triumph. Service is friendly and an enclosed garden
doubles the seating. **Price range:** Entrees, $14–$24. **Meals:** L, D. **Subway:** 1, 9
to Christopher St.

Avra   ☆   **$$$**   GREEK/SEAFOOD
141 E. 48th St. (between Third and Lexington Aves.)   (212) 759-8550
Greek cuisine is a modest thing, a fairly limited catalog of simple pleasures, and

Avra gives it honest, honorable representation. Fresh fish, barely touched, is the selling point here. In the open kitchen, a ball of fire blasts each side of a sea bass or red snapper imprisoned in a grilling basket; the fish gets a squirt of lemon, a drizzling of olive oil and a sprinkling of herbs, then heads to the table. The seafood counter offers about a dozen fish. Lamb loin chops are tender and flavorful, and spanakopita is a flawless layering of good feta, firm spinach and leeks, with crackling-fresh leaves of phyllo dough. **Price range:** Entrees, $18.50–$26. **Meals:** L, D. **Subway:** S, 4, 5, 6, 7 to 42nd St.

Azafrán   ☆ $$ SPANISH/TAPAS
77 Warren St. (near W. Broadway)   (212) 284-0577
Azafrán, an unassuming neighborhood spot, aims to do the right thing by tapas. Despite its austere setting and punishing acoustics, Azafrón succeeds where many have failed. Almost anything involving shrimp steps immediately to the head of the class. Close rivals are the croquettes, stuffed with a rich béchamel sauce and nuggets of Spanish ham, Manchego cheese or mushrooms. **Price range:** Entrees, $11–$22. **Meals:** D. Closed Mon. **Subway:** 1, 2, 3, 9 to Chambers St.

Babbo   ☆☆☆ $$$$ ITALIAN
110 Waverly Pl. (at Washington Square Park)   (212) 777-0303
Celebrity chef Mario Batali is an indulgent ruler. Babbo remains his throne, from which he bestows his most lavish favors and intense flavors upon an appropriately grateful dining public. But while it's an absolutely terrific restaurant, it is not a wholly transcendent dining experience. That's partly because of the thundering rock music, and partly because the tables are wedged so tightly together. Although Babbo could be easier on the ears and elbows, it cannot be much better to the belly. Mr. Batali is here almost nightly, promising adventure to those who want it, safety to those who don't. The pasta, made in house, is always perfect. And the desserts (especially the pine nut crostata and the famous saffron panna cotta) are wonderful. Call exactly one month ahead for reservations. **Price range:** Pastas $17–$24; entrees $23–$32.50; tasting menus $59 and $65. **Meals:** D. **Subway:** A, C, E, F, V to W. 4th St.

Baldoria   ☆ $$$ ITALIAN
249 W. 49th St. (between Seventh and Eighth Aves.)   (212) 582-0460
Baldoria (meaning "rollicking good time") is a big slice of neighborhood Italian, New York style. It serves feel-good food in a feel-good atmosphere that inclines diners to overlook shortcomings. When it's good, Baldoria is quite good. The greens and the tomatoes are always fresh and flavorful. Pastas, too, perform strongly, especially trenette with prosciutto, peas and onions in a light cream sauce. Standard appetizers are respectable, as are main courses like sweet sausages with pepper and onions. Get the costata di manzo, an incredibly flavorful rib chop, juicy, tender and perfectly cooked. **Price range:** Entrees, $18–$32. **Meals:** D. Closed Sun. **Subway:** C, E, 1, 9 to 50th St.

Bali Nusa Indah   **$25 & Under**   INDONESIAN
651 Ninth Ave. (near 45th St.)   (212) 765-6500
Bali Nusa Indah offers fresh and lively Indonesian dishes in a tranquil and
pretty setting. Most of the food is forcefully spiced, yet respectful of the flavors
of each dish. Among the dishes worth trying are Javanese fisherman's soup; nasi
goreng, the wonderful Indonesian version of fried rice; and sea bass broiled in a
banana leaf. There are exceptional desserts as well. **Price range:** Entrees,
$6–$13.50. **Meals:** L, D. **Subway:** A, C, E to 42nd St.

Balthazar   ☆☆   **$$$**   FRENCH BISTRO
80 Spring St. (at Crosby St.)   (212) 965-1414
Everybody who's been to Balthazar seems to have a story about being hung up
on by the reservationist or snubbed by a waiter tending to a more important
guest. Yet everyone returns. Balthazar is no longer hip, but it's still bustling and
it's now acquired the feel of an authentically worn brasserie. The space is loud,
yet within your cocoon, you can hear your companions. The Balthazar salad of
romaine, frisée, asparagus, ricotta salata and truffle oil is as good as ever. And
the crisp, salty French fries are still the best in the city. **Price range:** Entrees
$16–$36. **Meals:** B, L, D. **Subway:** 6 to Spring St.; N, R, W to Prince St.

Bambou   ☆☆   **$$$**   CARIBBEAN
243 E. 14th St. (between Second and Third Aves.)   (212) 505-1180
The best Caribbean food in the city is served in a room with such cozy elegance,
it feels as if a warm breeze is blowing through it. There is no better way to begin
a meal here than with the eggplant soup, a thick dark liquid with the scent of
curry and the deep, intoxicating taste of coconut. Bambou shrimp, each
encrusted in coconut, are sweet and tasty, the tropical fruit plate glows with color
and the coconut crème brûlée is fabulous. **Price range:** Entrees, $18–$26. **Meals:**
D. **Subway:** L to Third Ave.; N, Q, R, W, 4, 5, 6 to 14th St.

Bandol   **$25 & Under**   FRENCH
181 E. 78th St. (between Third and Lexington Aves.)   (212) 744-1800
Bandol, named for a fine Provençal wine, offers dreamy Mediterranean flavors.
The food is very good, the atmosphere warm and neighborly. Even the overly
familiar dishes like lamb shank, salmon and scallops have clear, direct flavors
that convey their appeal rather than their popularity. Among the appetizers,
the pissaladiére, a tart of onions, olives and anchovies, is so good that you
could eat two and call it a meal. Coq au vin is lighter than usual, grilled steak
is juicy and flavorful, and the tender lamb shank offers primal enjoyment.
Price range: Entrees, $16–$22. AE only. **Meals:** Br, L, D. **Subway:** 6 to 77th St.

Bao Noodles   **$25 & Under**   VIETNAMESE
391 Second Ave. (at 22nd St.)   (212) 725-7770
The narrow dining room floor is patched here and there to connote age, each
place at the bar is set with chopsticks, and the wood banquets and benches
almost seem like Asian church pews. The menu goes beyond the standard

dishes, offering some unusual variations that are a welcome change. The Hue clam salad is spicy enough to make the mouth glow. The hoisin sauce has real character. Other menu highlights include a carefully spiced grilled pork chop, which tastes subtly of anise. But strangely, the noodle soups are lackluster. **Price range:** Entrees, $5–$9. **Meals:** L, D. **Subway:** 6 to 23rd St.

Barbuto   **$25 & Under**   ITALIAN/NEW AMERICAN
775 Washington St. (at West 12th St.)   (212) 924-9700
At this spare Italian restaurant, the menu, which changes daily, emphasizes ties between a brand of California cuisine and the rustic, intensely seasonal cooking of the Italian countryside. The main courses are under $20 and almost all appetizers are under $10. The risotto is perfectly textured and carries the concentrated flavors of shiitake mushrooms, asparagus and chicken stock. Grilled rabbit is moist and absolutely delicious. **Price range:** Entrees, $14–$19. **Meals:** L, D. **Subway:** A, C, E, to 14th St., L to 8th Ave.

Bar Jamón   **$25 & Under**   SPANISH
125 East 17th St. (at Irving Pl.)   (212) 253-2773
The name means "ham bar" in Spanish; it holds barely 25 people, and the crowd spills onto the sidewalk. It is a tapas bar-with no tables, just wooden counters running perpendicular to a small counter in the front of a boxy room. There are no reservations, no orderly lines and not enough stools. Two barmen take orders for food and pour *cuartos de vino*, small carafes of wine. One ham, aged 14 months, is slightly oily yet wonderfully mellow; the older, aged 18 months, had a stiffer, more leathery texture, but the flavor was more reticent. Thick salami-size rounds of chorizo have the texture of firm kielbasa and go well with pickled peppers. **Price range:** Entrees, $3–$12. **Meals:** D. **Subway:** 4, 5, 6, N, R, Q, L to Union Square.

Barking Dog Luncheonette   **$25 & Under**   DINER
1678 Third Ave. (at 94th St.)   (212) 831-1800
1453 York Ave. (between 77th and 78th Sts.)   (212) 861-3600
With its dark wood paneling, comfortable booths, bookshelves and low-key lighting, the Barking Dog looks more like a library than a luncheonette. That, in part, explains its appeal to adults, along with its up-to-date American menu, which ranges from hamburgers, fried chicken and meatloaf to leg of lamb and roasted trout. If the children begin to fidget while waiting for the rich, bountiful desserts, distract them with the restaurant's dog tchotchkes, which can be a parent's best friend. **Price range:** Entrees, approx. $11. Cash only. **Meals:** B, Br, L, D, LN. **Subway:** Third Ave.: 6 to 96th St. York Ave.: 6 to 77th St.

Bar Pitti   **$25 & Under**   ITALIAN
268 Sixth Ave. (near Houston St.)   (212) 982-3300
This casual café offers superbly simple Tuscan fare and draws a fashion-conscious crowd. Bar Pitti's ease with people and with food is what makes it seem so Italian; its atmosphere of jangly controlled frenzy makes it a wonderful New York experience. Outdoor seating on Sixth Avenue is remarkably pleasant. The

menu is small and familiar, and almost all the main courses are superb.
Price range: Entrees, $10.50–$19. Cash only. **Meals:** L, D, LN. **Subway:** A, C,
E, F, S to W. 4th St.

Barrio   ☆ $$$ BISTRO
99 Stanton St. (at Ludlow St.)   (212) 533-9212
Barrio's round-the-clock, seven-day schedule makes it a cross between a diner
and a bistro. The lunch menu is mostly given over to soup, sandwiches and salads. But the soup could be a thick, silken blend of rutabaga and parsley root,
sneakily spiced with cayenne and ginger, and the sandwiches outperform their
bargain price. The prix-fixe makes it possible to enjoy lunch with substantial
main courses like braised veal cheeks. **Price range:** Entrees, $13–$27. **Meals:**
Open 24 hours. **Subway:** F to Second Ave.

Bayard's   ☆ ☆ $$$$ FRENCH
1 Hanover Sq. (between Pearl and Stone Sts.)   (212) 514-9454
Bayard's may be the most distinctive, romantic dining room in Manhattan, and
the food suits the surroundings. Chef Eberhard Müller grows his own produce,
and it features prominently on the menu. When this approach works, it works
spectacularly. The knockout wine list is a lengthy document, peppered with bargains, that many restaurants would kill for. The solid dessert list offers classics as
well as highly inventive ones. **Price range:** Entrees, $29–$38. **Meals:** D. Closed
Sun. **Subway:** 2, 3 to Wall St.

Bayou $25 & Under   CAJUN/SOUTHERN
308 Lenox Ave. (between 125th and 126th Sts.)   (212) 426-3800
This handsome Creole restaurant would do any New Orleans native proud.
With its brick walls, retro brass lamps and woody touches, Bayou looks like
countless other neighborhood bars and grills, but its big picture windows offer
an unusual New York panorama, unimpeded by tall buildings. The short menu
includes standout appetizers like chicken livers in a rich port wine sauce. The
sautéed snapper Alexandria, sprinkled with roasted pecans and drenched with
lemon butter, is moist and altogether delicious. For dessert, bread pudding with
a vanilla-whiskey sauce is excellent. **Price range:** Entrees, $12.95–$21.95.
Meals: L, D. **Subway:** 2, 3 to 125th St.

Beacon   ☆ ☆ $$$ NEW AMERICAN
25 W. 56th St. (between Fifth and Sixth Aves.)   (212) 332-0500
This classy-looking Midtown restaurant offers civilized dining in a beautiful setting. Organized around an open kitchen and a huge wood-burning oven, it delivers uncomplicated big-flavored food emphasizing fresh, seasonal ingredients.
Meat and fish pick up a smoky tang from the oven, roasted vegetables are served
with entrees and even desserts feature roasted fruits. Two of the best entrees are
triple lamb chops, rubbed with cumin and pureed picholine olives, and a plain
trout roasted with a bright vinaigrette of chervil, parsley, cilantro and shallots.
For dessert, a carmelized apple pancake grabs the brass ring. **Price range:**
Entrees, $19–$32. **Meals:** L, D. Closed Sun. **Subway:** N, R, W to Fifth Ave.

Beppe ☆☆ **$$$** ITALIAN
45 E. 22nd St. (between Broadway and Park Ave. S.) (212) 982-8422
The comfortable rustic Tuscan room at Beppe has exposed brick walls, wood
beams and a wood-burning fireplace. The chef is at his very best with the Tus-
can dishes: Order anything made with farro, the nutty whole grain, which is
served in soup and a risotto-style dish. The fried chicken would make a cook of
the Deep South proud, and the 11-herb pasta is filled with flavor. For dessert,
try a Tuscan riff on ice cream sandwiches, made with toasted buccellati, the
Tuscan version of panettone. (*Marian Burros*) **Price range:** Pasta, $16–$20;
Entrees, $23–$29. **Meals:** L, D. Closed Sun. **Subway:** 6 to 23rd St.

Bice ☆☆ **$$$** ITALIAN
7 E. 54th St. (between Fifth and Madison Aves.) (212) 688-1999
With a main dining room done in beige and wood with brass sconces and indi-
rect lighting, Bice is the handsomest Italian restaurant in town. If you have lots
of money, good ears and a desire to see the fast and the fashionable, this offshoot of a Milanese restaurant is for you. Fresh pastas, risotto, and uncomplicated main courses—veal chop, chicken paillard and duck breast with mango—
are all recommended. The mostly Italian wine list is well chosen. **Price range:**
Avg. entree, $24–$31. **Meals:** L, D, LN. **Subway:** E, F to Fifth Ave.

The Biltmore Room ☆☆☆ **$$$$** GLOBAL FUSION
290 Eighth Ave. (near W. 25th St.) (212) 807-0111
With its glossy interior, all marble and mirrors, the Biltmore Room may be the
best restaurant ever to come out of far left field. The general drift here is Asian,
with dishes that jet-hop from Japan to India to Thailand, but the kitchen can
easily slip into a Moroccan or Italian idiom, or slyly rework a Maryland crab
cake. Here and there, a single, ingenious touch energizes and transforms an otherwise straightforward dish, like the red-pepper crostini that accompanies a simple salad of heirloom tomatoes, served with a little fennel and arugula, and drizzled with olive oil. **Price range:** Entrees $24–$32. **Meals:** D. Closed Sun.
Subway: 1, 9, C, E to 23rd St.

Bistro le Steak **$25 & Under** BISTRO/STEAK
1309 Third Ave. (at 75th St.) (212) 517-3800
Bistro le Steak hardly strikes a false note. It does look Parisian. The friendly
staff conveys warmth and informality, and the food is both good and an excellent value. Steak is the specialty, but other simple bistro specialties are consistently satisfying and desserts are terrific. **Price range:** Entrees, $15–$30. **Meals:**
L, D. **Subway:** 6 to 77th St.

BLT Steak ☆☆ **$$$** STEAK/AMERICAN
106 E. 57th St. (at Park Ave.) (212) 752-7470
BLT's decor resembles Peter Luger after a session with "Queer Eye for the
Straight Guy." In addition to well-seared meats and a serious wine list, there's a
surprisingly soft touch in the cooking, a sensitivity to acute flavors and seasonal
ingredients. The focus is on dry-aged meats, but oddly, the beef is the most

underwhelming part of the menu. Veal chop, rack of lamb and Dover sole may seem like tame choices, but here they are stunning. And the kitchen really excels with soups, salads and side dishes. It's difficult to save room for dessert, but it would be a shame to miss the best chocolate tart in New York City. **Price range:** Entrees $22–$72. **Meals:** D. Closed Sun. **Subway:** 4, 5, 6 to 59th St.

Blue Fin ☆☆ $$$ SEAFOOD
W Times Square Hotel , 1567 Broadway (at 47th St.) (212) 918-1400
At Blue Fin, from the operation that runs Blue Water Grill, Isabella's and Ruby Foo's, the theme is fish. And because it's part of an empire that buys a lot of fish, it gets first dibs. The quality is unmistakable. There are 20 varieties of sushi and sashimi, but the main menu is where Blue Fin impresses the most. The most impressive entree is a crisply sautéed fillet of Atlantic black bass served on a creamy shrimp and asparagus risotto. Desserts are first-class. **Price range:** Entrees, $11–$38. **Meals:** L, D, LN. **Subway:** N, Q, R, W to 49th St.; B, D, F, V to 47th St.

Blue Hill ☆☆ $$ NEW AMERICAN
75 Washington Pl. (at Sixth Ave.) (212) 539-1776
A few steps below sidewalk level, Blue Hill almost shrinks from notice. But the quiet, adult setting admirably suits a style of cooking that is both inventive and highly assured. There are dull spots on the menu, but the overall standard is high enough to make up for the excruciating banquette seating. Poached duck deserves to be the restaurant's signature: a skinned duck breast, poached in beurre blanc and duck stock, is paired with leg meat done as a confit, then crisped at the last minute and placed over pureéd artichokes. For dessert, chocolate bread pudding is a conversation-stopper. **Price range:** Entrees, $18–$23. **Meals:** D. Closed Sun. **Subway:** A, C, E, F, S to W. 4th St.

Blue Ribbon Sushi ☆☆ $$$ JAPANESE/SUSHI
119 Sullivan St. (between Prince and Spring Sts.) (212) 343-0404
Blue Ribbon Sushi has good fish and an awesome list of sakes, but beyond that it has very little in common with a classic Japanese sushi bar. If you have ever felt like a clumsy foreigner and worried about doing the wrong thing, this is the sushi bar for you. The menu is enormous, and almost everything is good, from a pretty seaweed salad to broiled yellowtail collar. But the high point of the meal is always sushi and sashimi. The sushi chefs are at their best when inventing interesting specials. Just name the price you are willing to pay and let them amaze you. **Price range:** Entrees, $11.75–$27.50. **Meals:** D, LN. Closed Mon. **Subway:** C, E to Spring St.; N, R to Prince St.

Blue Smoke ☆ $$ BARBECUE
116 E. 27th St. (between Park and Lexington Aves.) (212) 447-7733
In this rustic dining room, Danny Meyer has taken on the quixotic quest of building a fine barbecue emporium in Manhattan. The beef ribs are among the best you'll find anywhere, but the brisket, the staple dish of Texas barbecue, is

texturally more reminiscent of corned beef than fine Texas brisket. Desserts are direct, uncomplicated, huge. **Price range:** Entrees, $12–$23. **Meals:** D, LN. **Subway:** 6 to 28th St.

Blue Water Grill   ☆   **$$**   SEAFOOD
31 Union Sq. W. (at 16th St.)   (212) 675-9500
Built as a bank in 1904, this is a big, breezy room with a sidewalk café and a casual air. Along with pleasant service, large portions and reasonable prices can come large crowds and long waits. Shrimp and oysters are good choices; so is the grilled fish. Desserts are not among the happy surprises, but the brownie sundae would make most people very happy. **Price range:** Entrees, $18–28. **Meals:** Br, L, D, LN. **Subway:** L, N, Q, R, W, 4, 5, 6 to 14th St.

Bolo   ☆☆☆   **$$$$**   SPANISH
23 E. 22nd St. (between Broadway and Park Ave. S.)   (212) 228-2200
After showing some slippage over the decade since it opened, Bolo is newly energized. The Spanish-influenced menu has been updated. The wine list has been improved and more tightly focused. And the new tapas menu shows star chef Bobby Flay at his best. The humble fig in Mr. Flay's hands becomes an opulent sauce that doubles the richness of the walnut romesco stuffing in an entree of pork tenderloin. Mr. Flay also delivers what may be the finest cheesecake known to humankind. **Price range:** Entrees, $27.50–$31. **Meals:** L, D. **Subway:** N, R, 6 to 23rd St.

Bouley   ☆☆☆   **$$$$**   FRENCH
120 West Broadway (at Duane St.)   (212) 964-2525
Many diners arrive expecting transcendence, for this is the province of David Bouley, one of America's most celebrated chefs. But the electricity has dimmed, and the service includes dispiriting bits of sloppiness. You'll eat well, no question about that, for there is serious talent in the kitchen and a commitment to the best ingredients. The staff excels at preparing fish, including a black sea bass slow-roasted to moist perfection and served in a bouillabaisse seasoned with vanilla. And the desserts still weave a decadent spell. Bouley is elegant, warm and inviting, but without a crucial flame. **Price range:** Entrees, $34–$42; five-course tasting menu, $75. **Meals:** L, D. **Subway:** A, C, 1, 2, 3, 9 to Chambers St.

Bouterin   ☆   **$$$$**   FRENCH
420 E. 59th St. (between First Ave. and Sutton Pl.)   (212) 758-0323
Serving Provençal food in a Provençal atmosphere, this restaurant can be charming. The best dishes are the chef's old family recipes, like the hearty vegetable soupe au pistou, which tastes the way it might if had been made on a wood-burning oven on a Provençal farm, the tarte a la Provençale, and sea bass in a bold bouillabaisse sauce. The daube of beef, too, is delicious, the beef slowly stewed in red wine and garlic. **Price range:** Entrees, $20–$32. **Meals:** D. **Subway:** 4, 5, 6 to 59th St.; N, R to Lexington Ave.

Brasserie   ☆☆   **$$$**   BISTRO/FRENCH
100 E. 53rd St. (at Lexington Ave.)   (212) 751-4840
The old Brasserie (which closed in 1995 after a kitchen fire) was a part of the city's
fabric. When patrons enter the new restaurant, their jaws drop. The staircase down
to the dining room has been transformed into a gentle slope of translucent steps. In
futuristic booths along the side of the room, the tables are slabs of translucent lime-
green acrylic. The Brasserie is ready for a new life, and the chef delivers sensible,
well-executed food with up-to-date touches but not too many neurotic kinks. For
dessert try the chocolate beignets. **Price range:** Entrees, $14–$28. **Meals:** B, Br, L,
D, LN. **Subway:** 6 to 51st St.

Brasserie 8 1/2   ☆   **$$$**   BRASSERIE/FRENCH
9 W. 57th St. (between Fifth and Sixth Aves.)   (212) 829-0812
Visually, Brasserie 8 1/2 is a knockout. The dining room could be a galactic mess
hall, with a white terrazzo tile floor and black leather booths. The traditional
brasserie menu can be seen in a mostly standard raw bar selection, an iced
seafood platter and a weekly rotation of specials like bouillabaisse on Fridays
and confit of suckling pig on Thursdays. For dessert try the arresting
milk–chocolate crème brûlée. **Price range:** Entrees, $18–$30. **Meals:** B, Br, L,
D, LN. **Subway:** N, R to Fifth Ave.

Brasserie 360   ☆☆   **$$$**   FRENCH/SUSHI
200 E. 60th St. (near Third Ave.)   (212) 688-8688
A three-building complex across from Bloomingdale's has been transformed
into a bright, bustling brasserie. Downstairs, diners enter a brasserie so French it
could be installed in a museum. Upstairs, in a quiet, intimate room, is a smart-
looking sushi bar. Diners, both upstairs and down, get both menus. The
brasserie offers small surprises. Upstairs, the sushi bar offers dependably fresh
fish of about 20 species, including one or two less common fry, like spotted sar-
dine. **Price range:** Entrees, $19–$29; sushi, $3–$6 a piece; sushi rolls, $4–$8.
Meals: L, D. **Subway:** 4, 5, 6 to 59th St.

Bread Bar at Tabla   **$25 & Under**   NEW AMERICAN/FUSION
11 Madison Ave. (at 25th St.)   (212) 889-0667
Bread Bar, Tabla's less formal, less expensive cousin, radiates a beauty of its own
that shines right through its dim and noisy dining room. Bread Bar serves home-
style dishes and street snacks full of authentic flavors in a family style, with
dishes arriving as they are ready. Chicken tikka is a dream, moist and full of gin-
gery, peppery flavor. For dessert, the coffee kulfi pop is a triumph. **Price range:**
Small dishes, $6–$9; large dishes, $10–$18. **Meals:** L, D. **Subway:** 6, N, Q, R,
W to 23rd St.

Bread Tribeca   ☆☆   **$$**   ITALIAN
301 Church St. (at Walker St.)   (212) 334-8282
Most of the food is a pleasure. Taking its cue from Liguria, the restaurant offers
food that is simply prepared and delicious. The chef shows a very sure hand
with fish, and his fritto misto may be one of the best in the city. If you think the

only kind of pizza crust worthy of the name is rolled as thin as possible and baked in a brick oven, stick with the pizza margherita and pizza with prosciutto and arugula. **Price range:** Entrees $13–$25. **Meals:** L, D. **Subway:** 1, 9 to Franklin St.

Bukhara Grill $25 & Under   INDIAN
230 E. 58th St. (between Second and Third Aves.)   (212) 339-0090
217 E. 49th St. (between Second and Third Aves.)   (212) 888-2839
The northern Indian cooking here is mostly superb, with the sort of precise, res-onant, yet subtle spicing that is all too rare in Indian restaurants. Bukhara's extensive, fairly priced wine list also stands out. Try the slender, lively kebabs made entirely of minced vegetables, and excellent curries like pepper chicken, a rich dish with distinct layers of black pepper, ginger and chili flavors. **Price range:** Entrees, $12–$28. **Meals:** L, D. **Subway:** 49th St.: E, F, 6 to 51st St. 58th St.: 4, 5, 6, N, Q, R, W to Lexington Ave.–59th St.

Butter   ☆ $$$ NEW AMERICAN
415 Lafayette St. (near Astor Pl.)   (212) 253-2828
Upstairs at Butter is a professionally run vaulted dining room that looks like a cross between a chalet and a sauna. Downstairs is a dim and smoky lounge. The chef has put together a serious contemporary American menu with all the req-uisite high-end ingredients and global touches. Appetizers struggle to hold up the food end. Main courses, especially fish dishes, are more sure-footed. A lamb chop and loin are juicy enough, and a beef fillet will do the job of placating beef lovers. The amiable list of desserts does not break new ground, though some offer appealing architecture. **Price range:** Entrees, $27–$30. **Meals:** D, LN. **Subway:** 6 to Astor Pl.; N, R, to 8th St.

Cabo Rojo $25 & Under   PUERTO RICAN
254 10th Ave. (near 25th St.)   (212) 242-1202
Cabo Rojo offers stellar variations on Puerto Rico's favorite themes: sweet, salt, sour, fire. Baked pork chops are tender and fragrant with sofrito, the island's national seasoning. There's a touch of it beneath in picadillo con maduros (ground meat with plantains) and in the gravy that adorns the beef stew. Gen-erous servings of rice and beans (some days pigeon peas) come with every order. **Price range:** $3–$9.25. **Meals:** B, L, D. Closed Sun. Cash only. **Subway:** C, E to 23rd St.

Café Boulud   ☆ ☆ ☆ $$$$ FRENCH
20 E. 76th St. (near Madison Ave.)   (212) 772-2600
Café Boulud is sleek and easy; this is your opportunity to find out what hap-pens when a chef at the top of his form stretches out and takes chances. The menu, which changes frequently, is divided into four sections: La Tradition (classic country cooking), La Saison (seasonal dishes), Le Potager (vegetar-ian choices), and Le Voyage (world cuisine). What that really means is, any-thing goes. Most days there are 30 or more dishes, and none are ordinary.

Soup is a sure thing, and the wine list explores little-known vineyards. **Price range:** Entrees, $24–$32. **Meals:** L, D. **Subway:** 6 to 77th St.

Cafécito $25 & Under   CUBAN
185 Avenue C (at 12th St.)   (212) 253-9966
Cafécito offers authentic Cuban dishes, tempered by contemporary American dietary customs. The restaurant is always pleasant. The menu is slender and the choices among appetizers are few: the best selection is masitas de puerco, chunks of pork marinated in mojo, the Cuban garlic-and-citrus condiment. Ropa vieja, the classic Cuban dish, starts with a routine piece of beef and adds flavor in the form of a light tomato-and-wine sauce, mixed with onions and peppers cooked until soft, and plenty of cumin. **Price range:** Entrees, $5–$14. **Meals:** L, D. **Subway:** L to First Ave.

Café des Artistes   ☆ ☆ $$$$ CONTINENTAL
1 W. 67th St. (between Central Park West and Columbus Ave.) (212) 877-3500
On a bad day, or in a bad decade, Café des Artistes, in business since 1917, can seem lackluster. Then it can snap back to life, and even disillusioned diners rediscover what makes it one of the city's best-loved restaurants. At the moment, Café des Artistes seems to be experiencing a mild resurgence. The menu retains old standbys like pot-au-feu, Dover sole and a classic Wiener schnitzel. The setting still enchants, with lush floral displays and Howard Chandler Christy's pastel murals of naked beauties prancing through romantic landscapes. Service is warm and friendly, but the focus can zoom in and out. **Price range:** Entrees $29–$37. **Meals:** L (Mon.–Fri.), D. **Subway:** 1, 9 to 66th St.

Café Sabarsky   ☆ ☆ $$ AUSTRO-HUNGARIAN
Neue Gallerie, 1048 Fifth Ave. (near 86th St.)   (212) 288-0665
At this authentic Viennese café, the end of the meal is the beginning, really. The rest of the menu presents some tried and true Austro-Hungarian staples, but the goulash, herring sandwiches and boiled beef are merely a warm-up to the desserts. The house specialty is a Klimt torte, neatly stacked layers of hazelnut cake alternating with firm, bittersweet chocolate. It deserves classic status, along with the linzer torte and the Sacher torte, both flawless. The coffee comes from Meinl's in Vienna, and it may be the best in the city: rich, robust and deep. **Price range:** Entrees, $10–$25. **Meals:** L, D. **Subway:** 4, 5, 6 to 86th St.

Calle Ocho   ☆ $ $ SPANISH/DINER
446 Columbus Ave. (between 81st and 82nd Sts.)   (212) 873-5025
At this homage to South American cooking, the kitchen makes food like complicated ceviches and seductive shrimp chowders. It is hard to resist the beauty of camarones, big shrimp brushed with rum and beautifully arranged around a heap of fried seaweed, or crisp chicken cooked in lime. The dining room is handsomely decorated, and there is a big, separate bar in front. **Price range:** Entrees, $16–$24. **Meals:** Br, D. **Subway:** B, C to 81st St.; 1, 9 to 79th St.

Capitale ☆☆ **$$$$** NEW AMERICAN
130 Bowery (near Grand St.) (212) 334-5500
In a city with no shortage of grand dining rooms, Capitale takes the cake. Formerly the Bowery Savings Bank, it is almost preposterously opulent, a gilt-encrusted temple with 45-foot-high coffered ceilings. The menu wanders hither and yon in a sometimes disorienting way, but sometimes the gambles pay off. **Price range:** Entrees, $24–$45. **Meals:** D. Closed Sun. **Subway:** J, M, Z to Bowery; N, Q, R, W, 6 to Canal St.

Carnegie Deli **$$** DELI
854 Seventh Ave. (at 55th St.) (212) 757-2245
A quintessential New York City experience, from pickles to pastrami. Carnegie's sandwiches are legendarily enormous, big enough to feed you and a friend and still provide lunch for tomorrow. That doesn't stop people from trying to eat the whole thing, a sight that must gratify the notoriously crabby waiters. The pastrami is wonderful, of course, but so are the cheese blintzes with sour cream, which are only slightly more modest. **Price range:** Entrees, $10–$20. Cash only. **Meals:** B, L, D, LN. **Subway:** N, R, Q, W to 57th St.

Casa Mono ☆☆ **$$$** TAPAS
52 Irving Pl. (at 17th St.) (212) 253-2773
In Casa Mono, a tapas bar-restaurant with a New York sensibility, Joe Bastianich and Mario Batali have another hit on their hands. It has an agreeable buzz, with a smoothly functioning dining room and a sommelier knowledgeable about the well-priced list of Spanish wines. The place is small, and there is a serious crush. The stars of the tapas menu are fried squid and the far more unusual fried pumpkin croquetas stuffed with goat cheese. Watch out, though: enough of these little plates and you have a considerable bill. **Price range:** Tapas $3–$17. **Meals:** L, D. **Subway:** L, N, Q, R, W, 4, 5, 6 to 14th St.

Celeste **$25 & Under** PIZZA/ITALIAN
502 Amsterdam Ave. (near 85th St.) (212) 874-4559
Celeste is that rare bird: a true neighborhood restaurant. The atmosphere is convivial. The staff is pleasant and efficient. And the food is sublime. Start with a pizza from the wood oven at the back, though it is worth it to ask for a well-done crust. Entrees are a weak spot. Far better are salads. Pastas are good as well. The best of these is the raviolini — pillowy little ravioli stuffed with ricotta and spinach in a butter-sage sauce. **Price range:** Entrees, $8–$15. **Meals:** Br, D. Cash only. **Subway:** 1, 9 to 86th St.

Centolire ☆☆ **$$$** ITALIAN
1167 Madison Ave. (near 86th St.) (212) 734-7711
Centolire is a large, good-looking trattoria with a warm, beating heart. The food, doled out in substantial portions, is honest, well executed and deeply satisfying. One of Centolire's gimmicks is the coccio, or crock, that appears as a little symbol next to several dishes. It's shorthand for rustic, and most of the dishes

cooked in the coccio are also covered in a thick bread dough, crosta di pane, that transforms them into an Italian potpie. The menu divides appetizers, pastas and entrees into two categories, Old World and New World. The pastas, old or new, have a rough-hewn integrity that makes them impossible not to order. **Price range:** Entrees, $12–$34. **Meals:** Br, L, D. **Subway:** 4, 5, 6 to 86th St.

'Cesca   ☆☆ $$$ ITALIAN
164 W. 75th St. (between Amsterdam and Columbus Aves.)   (212) 787-6300
'Cesca strikes a pitch-perfect tone: a little more stylish than a common neighborhood restaurant, but not formal enough to require a jacket. Patrons feel a pleasant sense of bustle, but the well-spaced tables and wraparound booths are islands of repose. Tom Valenti, a very assured chef, emphasizes honest, uncomplicated food with strong, clearly defined flavors. A scattering of celery leaves and first-rate capers from Salina make Mr. Valenti's vitello tonnato a revelation. There is a solid list of pastas and risottos with a decidedly rustic bent. The big-hearted entrees can bring down a weak-kneed diner at 50 yards. **Price range:** Pastas and risottos $18–$25; entrees $19–$32. **Meals:** L (Tue.–Fri.), D (Tue. - Sun.). Closed Mon. **Subway:** B, C, 1, 2, 3, 9 to 72nd St.

Chanoodle $25 & Under   CHINESE
79 Mulberry St. (at Canal St.)   (212) 349-1495
This is a bright and inviting restaurant on the western edge of Chinatown that pays its respects to the international tastes of recent Hong Kong immigrants with some unusual fusion dishes, like an exceptional blend of roast pork, soothing, sweet coconut milk, sliced mushrooms, delicate circles of tofu and clear-colored ginkgo nuts. More conventional choices from the enormous menu include thin, glossy noodles with shreds of roast duck, and a lively beef lo mein. **Price range:** Entrees, $4–$15. **Meals:** L, D. **Subway:** 6, N, R, Q to Canal St.

Chanterelle   ☆☆☆ $$$$ FRENCH
2 Harrison St. (at Hudson St.)   (212) 966-6960
Few restaurants are as welcoming or comfortable to enter as Chanterelle, and there's a soft, casual edge to the atmosphere and the service. Chef David Waltuck favors an opulent style. His strong suits are depth and intensity of flavor, and he doesn't shy away from thick, rich sauces in his quest to ravish the palate. The menu changes every four weeks and includes splendid dishes like a simple, pristine beef fillet, drenched in a red wine and shallot sauce with more layers of flavor than a complex Burgundy. There are always some thrilling desserts like a courageously bitter chocolate tart, served with a pastry ice-cream cone filled with banana malt ice cream. **Price range:** Three-course prix-fixe, $75; five-course tasting menu, $89 or $139 with matching wines. **Meals:** L, D. Closed Sun. **Subway:** 1, 9 to Franklin St.

Chelsea Bistro & Bar   ☆☆ $$$ BISTRO/FRENCH
358 W. 23rd St. (between Eighth and Ninth Aves.)   (212) 727-2026
With a cozy fireplace, a great wine list and really good French bistro food, this is a find in the neighborhood. If the first thing you eat here is the fabulous mussel

and clam soup, you will be hooked forever. The fricassee of lobster and sea scallops is almost as good. The hanger steak is fine and rare, with a dense red-wine sauce. The restaurant serves predictable and good classic New York bistro desserts. The bread pudding is slightly less conventional, if only because it is enlivened with a shot of rum. **Price range:** entrees, $17.95–$27; pre-theater prix-fixe, $28.50. **Meals:** D, LN. **Subway:** C, E to 23rd St.

Chennai Garden $25 & Under   INDIAN
129 East 27th St. (at Lexington Ave.)   (212) 689-1999
This bright, boxy restaurant offers kosher vegetarian food with an inexpensive all-you-can-eat lunch buffet. By night, the menu emphasizes South Indian specialties, like dosas, huge crepes rolled into cylinders around fillings like potatoes mashed with onions, and utthappam, smaller pancakes studded with onions and topped with vegetable mixtures. It also offers vegetarian specialties from Gujarat, on the western end of India's midsection, and the Punjab, to the north. **Price range:** Entrees, $6–$9. **Meals:** L, D. **Subway:** 6 to 28th St.

Chez Josephine   ☆☆ $$$ BISTRO/FRENCH
414 W. 42nd St. (between Ninth and 10th Aves.)   (212) 594-1925
This Theater Row pioneer has been entertaining us with its colorful parade of musicians, singers and dancers for more than a decade and is still going strong. Its reliably pleasing bistro fare and attentive service add to the charm. Favorite entrees include lobster cassoulet; sautéed calf's liver with honey mustard sauce and grilled onions; and grilled salmon with a coulis of fine herbs. **Price range:** Avg. entree, $19. **Meals:** D, LN. Closed Sun. **Subway:** A, C, E to 42nd St.

Chibitini $25 & Under   JAPANESE/SAKE BAR
63 Clinton St. (at Rivington St.)   (212) 674-7300
This sake bar, seating only about 20 people in a small, slender room, has more than two dozen selections, almost all available by the glass. It's worth examining the wide range of flavors and textures. The best deals on the menu are the bento box dinners; by far the best centerpiece for them is ground veal flavored with ginger and pine nuts, and wrapped in cabbage leaves like German rouladen. Among the other choices, the best is rectangular slices of lush yellowfin tuna, seared like tataki. **Price range:** Entrees, $4–$14. **Meals:** D. **Subway:** F to Delancey St.

Cho Dang Gol   ☆☆ $$ KOREAN
55 W. 35th St. (between Fifth and Sixth Aves.)   (212) 695-8222
Cho Dang Gol serves uniquely rustic food that is very different from what is available at other Korean restaurants in the surrounding blocks. The specialty here is fresh soybean curd, made daily at the restaurant. The kitchen makes each dish with extreme care, but for the uninitiated, searching out the best dishes is not easy. Try cho-dang-gol jung-sik. It arrives in three bowls: one with rice dotted with beans, another with "bean-curd dregs" (which hardly conveys its utter deliciousness) and the third with a pungent soup-stew containing pork, seafood, onions and chilies. Also excellent is chung-kook-jang, soybean-paste

stew with an elemental flavor, and doo-boo doo-roo-chi-gi, a combination of
pork, pan-fried kimchi, clear vermicelli and big triangles of bean curd.
Price range: Entrees, $6.95–$17.95. **Meals:** L, D, LN. **Subway:** B, D, F, N, Q,
R, W to 34th St.

Chola ☆☆ $$ INDIAN
232 E. 58th St. (between Second and Third Aves.)   (212) 688-4619
The menu at this modest, crowded restaurant roams across the Subcontinent,
offering special dishes from the Jews of Calcutta, fiery dishes beloved by the English and wonderful vegetarian dishes like dosa from South India. Uthappam is a
scallion-laced vegetable pancake that is among the great pancakes of the world.
Continue with a fine dish from Kerala, konju pappas, shrimp in a chili-laden
sauce. Among the excellent desserts are kulfi, a grainy frozen dessert flavored with
nuts and saffron, and rasmalai, an addictive, sweet sort of homemade cheese. Best
of all is the extraordinary Indian coffee: strong, milky and sweet. **Price range:**
Entrees, $10.95–$24.95. **Meals:** L, D. **Subway:** 4, 5, 6 to 59th St.; N, R, W to
Lexington Ave.

Chubo ☆ $$ ASIAN FUSION
6 Clinton St. (near Houston St.)   (212) 674-6300
Chubo is so tiny that diners can watch chef Claude Chassagne toiling in the
kitchen on their behalf. The restaurant's low profile is good news for diners who
like to drop in and eat without fuss. Mr. Chassagne has come up with a clever
format for his often inspired French-Asian fusion cooking, with five appetizers,
five entrees and five desserts. For $24 you can order one dish from any two cate-
gories. For $28 you get three. Half the pleasure lies in seeing how much Mr.
Chassagne can do with humble ingredients and a price ceiling for a three-course
dinner that would barely buy an entree in Midtown. The answer is, a lot more
than you might think. **Price range:** Two courses $24; three courses $28. **Meals:**
D, Sun. brunch. Closed Mon. **Subway:** F to Delancy St.; J, M, Z to Essex St.

Churrascaria Plataforma ☆☆ $$$ LATIN AMERICAN/STEAKHOUSE
316 W. 49th St. (between Eighth and Ninth Aves.)   (212) 245-0505
Two things are required to truly appreciate this all-you-can-eat Brazilian restaurant: a large appetite to keep you eating and a large group to cheer you on. The
salad bar is extraordinary, a long two-sided affair anchored at the corners by four
hot casseroles. Go easy; this is only the appetizer. The waiters will entice you
with ham, sausage, lamb, wonderfully crisp and juicy chicken legs, pork ribs,
even the occasional side of salmon, which is delicious in its caper sauce. But it is
beef that has pride of place: sirloin, baby beef, top round, skirt steak, brisket,
short ribs, special top round. **Price range:** All-you-can-eat rodizio meal, $38.95;
children under 10, $19.50. **Meals:** L, D, LN. **Subway:** C, E to 50th St.

Circus Restaurant ☆☆ $$$ BRAZILIAN
808 Lexington Ave. (near 62nd St.)   (212) 223-2965
An upscale Brazilian restaurant that turns into a party every night. Circus serves
the food your mother might cook if you were raised in São Paulo or Bahia. It is a

warm and cozy place, usually packed with Brazilians eager for a taste of home. The camarao na moranga is excellent, a heap of tiny, tender rock shrimp sautéed with fresh corn, hearts of palm, shallots, peas and coconut milk, mixed with cheese and baked in an acorn squash. Among the sweet, tropical desserts, the best is caramelized bananas with ice cream. **Price range:** Entrees, $15–$23. **Meals:** L, D, LN. **Subway:** N, R, W to Lexington Ave.; 4, 5, 6 to 59th St.

City Hall ☆☆ $$$ AMERICAN

131 Duane St. (near Church St.)   (212) 227-7777

The cavernous dining room has the spare quality of an old steakhouse; the clean details, loud music and hip clientele give it an up-to-date air. The menu includes all the old classics, from iceberg lettuce to baked Alaska, but there is more to City Hall than old-fashioned fare. The plateau de fruits de mer, which feeds six to eight, is a behemoth so impressive that people invariably gasp as it is carried across the room. You also can't go wrong with oysters at City Hall, raw or cooked. Among the meat dishes there is a huge double steak, still on the bone and served for two. **Price range:** Entrees, $18–$32. **Meals:** L, D. Closed Sun. **Subway:** A, C, 1, 2, 3, 9 to Chambers St.

Col Legno $25 & Under ITALIAN

231 East Ninth St. (between Second and Third Aves.)   (212) 777-4650

The visual focus here is the wood-burning oven in the rear, which also perfumes the air with the warm, appetizing scent of smoke. The individual pizzas are excellent, the crust smooth and elastic, burnished brown around the circumference. The best dish is the pappardelle in a robust sauce made with ground wild boar. Meat courses are simply prepared and satisfying. Try the meaty, slightly gamy grilled quail, subtly flavored with sage and a judicious touch of truffle oil, served with firm grilled polenta. **Price range:** Entrees, $9–$17. **Meals:** D. **Subway:** L to Third Ave.

Congee $25 & Under CHINESE

98 Bowery (between Grand and Hester Sts.)   (212) 965-5028

Congee is little more than thin rice porridge, bland as milquetoast, yet it arouses strong feelings. Perhaps it is a reaction to the ingredients typically added to the dish, which can range from humble organ meats to bits of exquisite lobster. Congee, the restaurant, is not much to look at. But the food is fresh and vivid, with clear spicing and pure flavors. Congee's congee is outstanding. If your soul does not cry out for congee, the extensive menu includes more than 200 dishes. **Price range:** Entrees, $7–$19. **Meals:** L, D. **Subway:** J, M, Z to Bowery; N, Q, R, W, 6 to Canal St.

Congee Village $25 & Under CHINESE

100 Orchard St. (between Delancey and Broome Sts.)   (212) 941-1818
1848 Second Ave. (near 95th St.)

The best congee in New York is in these friendly restaurants. Congee, also known as jook, is nothing more than Chinese porridge. More than two dozen versions of congee are served here, some with additions as exotic as fish maws or frog. At the uptown location, most of the rest of the menu is devoted to generic sweet and crispy Chinese-American dishes and a selection of surf-and-turf meals. The downtown restaurant offers excellent Cantonese and Hong Kong dishes. **Price range:** Congee, $2.50–$4.75; entrees, $5.50–$16.95. **Meals:** L, D, LN. **Subway:** Downtown: F to Second Ave. Uptown: 6 to 96th St.

Cooke's Corner $25 & Under   EUROPEAN/AMERICAN
618 Amsterdam Ave. (at 90th St.)   (212) 712-2872
This charmingly subdued little restaurant, with its small, well-designed menu and intelligent wine list, caters to grown-ups and makes no apologies for it. The menu is quietly satisfying with attention to details. Main courses include a juicy, flavorful roast chicken served over polenta with a mushroom stew, and beef, braised for four hours until remarkably tender. **Note:** Some daily specials are priced at $25, far more than the regular menu items. **Price range:** Entrees, $12–$25. AE only. **Meals:** D. Closed Mon. **Subway:** 1, 9 to 86th St.

Craft   ☆ ☆ ☆ $$$$ NEW AMERICAN
43 E. 19th St. (between Broadway and Park Ave. South)   (212) 780-0880
This is a handsome restaurant, with a clean, vaguely Mission-influenced look . Craft offers a vision of food heaven, a land of strong, pure flavors and back-to-basics cooking techniques. But Craft is also one of the most baroque dining experiences in New York: diners build their own meals , with side dishes and even sauces presented as options. The saving grace is the high quality of the ingredients and their masterly handling by the kitchen. The oysters sparkle. The veal, a humble cut of meat wrapped around some simple roast vegetables, has an honesty and a depth of flavor that will stop you cold. And in a city famous for steak worship, the frighteningly large porterhouse ranks as one of the finest large-scale hunks of beef you'll encounter. For dessert, try a light, chiffonlike steamed lemon pudding or the custardy pain perdu, which can easily handle anything thrown at it. **Price range:** Entrees, $22–$36. **Meals:** L, D. **Subway:** L, N, Q, R, W, 4, 5, 6 to 14th St.

Craftbar $25 & Under   NEW AMERICAN
47 E. 19th St. (between Park Ave. S. and Broadway)   (212) 780-0880
In looks and service alone, Craftbar sets itself leagues beyond the typical sandwich shop. Its snacks, soups, salads and sandwiches, supplemented each day by a meat, a fish and a pasta dish, exude the simplicity of a wine bar, where needs are joyfully met. Sandwiches are uniformly excellent; warm pressed sandwiches rely on blends of flavors as with earthy duck ham, hen of the woods mushrooms and mild taleggio cheese. For dessert, coconut panna cotta is light and flavorful. **Price range:** Entrees, $14–$18. **Meals:** L, D, LN. **Subway:** 4, 5, 6, L, N, Q, R, W to Union Sq.

Crispo $25 & Under   ITALIAN
240 W. 14th St. (between Seventh and Eighth Aves.)   (212) 229-1818
Crispo's dining room—dark and cozy, with the electric-lamp glow of modern-

ized rusticity — fills early. The fresh and unassuming menu comes as a welcome antidote to the greenhorn staff. The pastas, also available as half orders, vary in quality. Crispo's spaghetti carbonara is an absolute model of the form, and in many ways, the restaurant's best dish. **Price range:** Entrees, $12.50–$17. **Meals:** D. Closed Sun. **Subway:** A, C, E, 1, 2, 3, 9 to 14th St.

Crudo $25 & Under   SPANISH
54 Clinton St. (near Rivington St.)   (646) 654-0116
Crudo, where each dish revolves around raw fish, is hardly bigger than a slender piece of sashimi. With flattering lighting, raw walls of brick and textured plaster and vintage Eames chairs, Crudo has all the makings of a great first-date restaurant. The menu lists only 10 dishes, in either small or large portions. The best dishes playfully mix sweet and salty flavors and gracefully blend textures. **Price range:** Small dishes, $6–$10; large, $9–$17. **Meals:** D. Closed Sun., Mon. **Subway:** F to Delancey St.; J, M, Z to Essex St.

Cubana Café $25 & Under   CUBAN
110 Thompson St. (at Prince St.)   (212) 966-5366
For a quick inexpensive bite and a glass of wine, or better yet, an excellent mojito, Cubana Café is a good bet. Cuban-style food is the central theme and the heart of the menu. The best dish is a whole roasted red snapper served with a chunky mango salsa, a decidedly Nuevo touch. Ropa vieja, a traditional dish of tender, shredded beef, gets much of its flavor from olives, as well as sautéed onions and peppers. **Price range:** Entrees, $8–$14. **Meals:** L, D. **Subway:** 6 to Spring St.

Da Andrea $25 & Under   ITALIAN
557 Hudson St. (near Perry St.)   (212) 367-1979
Da Andrea is a dependably good local favorite, one with ambition. Before anything, order a plate of tigelle. It's a plate of thin, warm biscuits fresh from the oven. You slice a biscuit open, sprinkle grated Parmesan cheese on the steaming bread, fold some thin-sliced prosciutto onto one side, close the covers and eat the melting flavors. The pastas are made daily and are worth exploring. The entrees are less assured. The lamb shank, however, is terrific. **Price range:** Entrees, $12–$16.50. **Meals:** D. **Subway:** 1, 9 to Christopher St.

Da Ciro $25 & Under   ITALIAN
229 Lexington Ave. (near 33rd St.)   (212) 532-1636
An excellent, often overlooked little Italian restaurant. Specialties, cooked in a wood-burning oven, include terrific pizzas. Also excellent is a casserole of wild mushrooms baked in a crock with arugula, goat cheese, olives, tomatoes and mozzarella. The pastas are simple but lively, and full-flavored desserts like bitter chocolate mousse cake and hazelnut semifreddo more than hold their own. **Price range:** Entrees, $15.50–$28. **Meals:** L, D. **Subway:** 6 to 33rd St.

Dakshin $25 & Under   INDIAN
1713 First Ave. (near 89th St.)   (212) 987-9839
Much Indian food in Manhattan is bland, so it is a great pleasure to find lively
spicing in more than a few dishes at Dakshin, like jhinga jal toori, small but flavorful shrimp in a sauce of tomatoes and onions made tangy by mustard greens
and enhanced by the nutty, slightly bitter aroma of curry leaves. Dakshin's
breads are excellent, especially mint paratha and garlic nan, made smoky in the
clay oven. Among the meat main courses, try the chicken Chettinad, with the
chicken in a thick sauce made lively by black pepper and curry leaves. Dakshin's
vegetable dishes also excel. **Price range:** Entrees, $7–$17. **Meals:** L, D.
Subway: 4, 5, 6 to 86th St.

Daniel   ☆ ☆ ☆ ☆ $$$$ FRENCH
Mayfair Hotel, 60 E. 65th St. (between Madison and Park Aves.) (212) 288-0033
This is a top-flight French restaurant, sumptuous and rather grand, but still very
much the personal expression of its chef and owner, Daniel Boulud. His menu is
overwhelming, with a dozen appetizers and ten main courses supplemented by a
daily list of specials and assorted tasting menus. The influences come from all
over the Mediterranean, and as far afield as Japan and India, pulled in and made
French with total assurance. The dessert menu is remarkable for its elegance
and restraint; it is also highly advisable to study the cheese trolley when it rolls
around. It is possible to spend lavishly on wine, but there is also a strong selection of half bottles, wines by the glass and modestly priced bottles. Service, con-
fident and expert, goes a long way to explain the neighborhood's love affair with
Daniel. Diners feel well cared for. The tone is pitch-perfect, and as a result,
patrons feel at ease. **Price range:** Prix-fixe and tasting menus, $78–$140.
Meals: L, D. Closed Sun. **Subway:** 6 to 68th St.

Danube   ☆ ☆ ☆ $$$$ AUSTRIAN
30 Hudson St. (at Duane St.)   (212) 791-3771
David Bouley does not do things in a small way. Using fin-de-siècle Vienna as a
culinary source, and a repository of romantic images, he has created Danube,
the most enchanting restaurant New York has seen in decades. This is an opiate
dream of lush fabrics, deeply saturated decadent colors and lustrous glazed surfaces. If ever a restaurant was made for a four-hour meal, Danube is it. After
anchoring the menu with a handful of classics, Mr. Bouley has conjured up his
own private Austria or, in some cases, taken leave of the country altogether
with impressive appetizers like a delicate, complexly orchestrated dish of raw
tuna and shrimp. More typically, he has lightened, modernized and personalized
traditional dishes, or invented new ones using traditional ingredients, often
with stunning results. Two traditional desserts are both impeccable: a Czech
palacsintak, or crêpe, and a Salzburger nockerl, a mound-shaped soufflé dusted
in confectioners' sugar and served with raspberries. **Price range:** Entrees,
$29–$35. **Meals:** L, D. **Subway:** A, C, 1, 2, 3, 9 to Chambers St.

David Burke & Donatella ☆☆ $$$$ FUSION

133 E. 61st St. (between Park and Lexington Aves.) (212) 813-2121

Crisp and angry lobster. "Bronx style" filet mignon of veal. A cheesecake lollipop tree with bubble-gum whipped cream. These off-the-wall menu items can only be the work of one man, David Burke, who whizzes around the kitchen preparing complex dishes of immense fussiness that really shouldn't work, but do. Mr. Burke seems to know what he's doing and when his complex combinations work, the depth of flavor in the dish is a joy. The restaurant itself is grand enough to be quite at home in Palm Beach. **Price range:** Entrees $20–$36; tasting menu $65. **Meals:** L (Mon.–Fri.), D. **Subway:** N, R, W, 4, 5, 6 to 59th St.

Dawat ☆ $$$ INDIAN

210 E. 58th St. (between Second and Third Aves.) (212) 355-7555

Most of the vegetable dishes here—the small baked eggplant with tamarind sauce, the potatoes mixed with ginger and tomatoes, the homemade cheese in spinach sauce—are excellent. The set lunches are a bargain. **Price range:** Entrees, $15.95–$23.95. **Meals:** L, D. **Subway:** 4, 5, 6 to 59th St.; N, R to Lexington Ave.

DB Bistro Moderne ☆☆ $$$$ BISTRO

55 W. 44th St. (between Fifth and Sixth Aves.) (212) 391-2400

Daniel Boulud's newest venture is a lively, even raucous restaurant that tries to pass for a bistro but can't quite disguise its high-class leanings. The cooking, although simplified to suit the bistro concept and even countrified on occasion, plays to Mr. Boulud's strength, his refined rusticity. He simply shows that rock-solid technique, good ingredients and a sound idea translate into gustatory bliss. Gazpacho is clean, crisp and clear, and roasted duck breast has great depth of flavor. Years of catering to an Upper East Side clientele have also given Mr. Boulud a supernatural hand with salads and spa fare. There are excellent light desserts, as well as richer ones like clafoutis tout chocolat, a small round chocolate cake, runny in the center, that could win over the most hardened chocolate skeptic. **Price range:** Entrees, $28–$32. **Meals:** L, D. Closed Sun. **Subway:** B, D, F, S to 42nd St.

Delmonico's ☆ $$$ ITALIAN/NEW AMERICAN

56 Beaver St. (at Williams St.) (212) 509-1144

Opulent, old-fashioned and dignified, the huge rooms at this American icon are rich with stained wood and soft upholstery, and the tables are swathed in oceans of white linen. The best dishes are in the section headed "Pasta, Risotti." Linguine with clams is a classic that is very well done. Ricotta and spinach ravioli may lack delicacy, but they are generous little pockets topped with clarified butter and fresh sage, and they make a satisfying meal. The rib-eye may not have the pedigree of a porterhouse or Delmonico, but it is big, tasty and perfectly cooked. **Price range:** Entrees, $21–$34. **Meals:** L, D. **Subway:** 2, 3 to Wall St.; 4, 5 to Bowling Green; J, M, Z to Broad St.

Dim Sum Go Go   ☆   **$$**   CHINESE
5 E. Broadway (at Chatham Sq.)   (212) 732-0797
Dim Sum Go Go is a bright, happy extrovert clinging to the edge of Chinatown
like a goofy sidekick. There's a sameness to the dim sum lineup that's hard to
ignore; the better, more inventive food can be found on a larger menu abound-
ing in pleasant surprises. Bean curd skin is one of them, stuffed with bits of
black mushroom and chopped spinach, then folded like a crepe and fried. The
restaurant's interior design has a clean, streamlined look, with perforated steel
chairs, bright red screens and a clever wall pattern taken from medieval scrolls
with dining scenes. **Price range:** Entrees $8.95–$16.95. **Meals:** L, D. **Subway:** J,
M, N, R, Q, W, 6 to Canal St.

District   ☆   **$$$$**   NEW AMERICAN
130 W. 46th St. (between Sixth and Seventh Aves.)   (212) 485-2999
There's a theatrical aspect to dining at District. The walls look like flats, and
ropes behind the banquettes create the illusion that the scenery might be raised
at any moment. It is witty, sophisticated and surprisingly cozy, especially if you
land one of the wraparound booths. When the kitchen hits the marks, it's worth
the ticket. The main courses sing at top volume, especially the fearsome chicken
cannelloni. For dessert, a tall, fluffy cheesecake with huckleberry compote scores
a direct hit. **Price range:** Entrees, $21–$37.50. **Meals:** B, L, D. **Subway:** B, D, F,
N, Q, R, S, W, 1, 2, 3, 7, 9 to 42nd St.

Divane   **$25 & Under**   TURKISH
888 Eighth Ave. (at 52nd St.)   (212) 333-5888
To the frequent question of where to eat before the theater, Divane is the new
answer. Rarely has satisfying simplicity been offered with such focus. The menu
consists of a selection of grilled meats and fishes, with only four appetizers. Each
appetizer is superb, starting with lahmacun, thin crisp pide bread topped with
spicy lamb, onion and parsley, which adds fresh herbal grace notes. Swordfish
kebabs are juicy and perfectly seasoned, while sea bass is moist and delicious.
Kadaif, a syrupy confection topped with crisp strands of pastry, is right on track.
Price range: Entrees, $14–$18. **Meals:** L, D. **Subway:** C, E to 50th St.

Diwan   ☆☆   **$$**   INDIAN
148 E. 48th St. (near Lexington Ave.)   (212) 593-5425
Diwan has the somewhat impersonal appearance of a hotel restaurant, but it is
unmistakably Indian. The chef has shaken up the menu, adding unusual fare
like venison and wild boar chops. The tandoori dishes are superb, putting to
shame the usual dry, orange-tinged chickens that have come to symbolize
Indian cooking in New York. Diwan's tandoori halibut is a revelation. **Price
range:** Entrees, $11–$25. **Meals:** L, D. **Subway:** 6 to 51st St.

Django   ☆☆   **$$$**   GLOBAL
480 Lexington Ave. (at E. 46th St.)   (212) 871-6600
Django got off to a bad start when it first opened, serving uninspired cuisine in a

blandly agreeable setting. But a new chef, a new look and a new sense of daring have turned things around. The menu is now slanted toward the Mediterranean, with special emphasis on Morocco. The excellent "toro" tagine includes chunks of rib-eye slowly stewed until they achieve melt-in-the-mouth consistency. Served in a traditional peaked clay vessel, it's a spice pot of exotic flavors and aromas. **Price range:** Entrees $21–$29. **Meals:** L (Mon.–Fri.), D (Mon.–Sat.). Closed Sun. **Subway:** S, 4, 5, 6, 7 to 42nd St.

Djerdan Burek $25 & Under   BALKAN
221 W. 38th St. (between Seventh and Eighth Aves.)   (212) 921-1183
Djerdan Burek, one of the newest in an ever-changing population of hole-in-the-wall eating establishments in the garment district, offers what a sandwich board in front sweetly calls "Balkanian food." The menu includes pastas, American-style sandwiches and salads, along with the small but most interesting section of Balkan specialties. If the bureks come straight from the oven, they are superb, the phyllo crust light and delicately flaky. Good as the bureks are, the stuffed cabbage is even better. **Price range:** $2–$10.50. **Meals:** B, L. Closed Sat., Sun. Cash only. **Subway:** A, C, E, 1, 2, 3, 9 to 34th St.

Dock's Oyster Bar   ☆ $$$ SEAFOOD
633 Third Ave. (at 40th St.)   (212) 986-8080
2427 Broadway (at 89th St.)   (212) 724-5588
These bustling fish houses give you your money's worth, with sparkling shellfish bars from which to choose shrimp or lobster cocktails or oysters and clams on the half shell. Favorites among starters are the Docks clam chowder, Maryland crab cakes and steamers in beer broth. Engaging entrees include grilled red snapper with coleslaw and rice, grilled salmon steak with coleslaw and steamed potatoes and Caesar salad with grilled tuna. Steamed lobsters come in one- to two-pound sizes, and there is a New England clambake on Sunday and Monday nights. **Price range:** Entrees, $15–$29. **Meals:** Br, L, D, LN. **Subway:** Midtown: 4, 5, 6, 7, S to 42nd St. Uptown: 1, 9 to 86th St.

Eight Mile Creek   ☆☆ $$$ AUSTRALIAN
240 Mulberry St. (at Prince St.)   (212) 431-4635
When a restaurant announces that it will be serving Australian cuisine, you expect good comic material, not good food. The joke stops when the kangaroo salad arrives: large cubes of the tender, richly flavored loin languish in a marinade flavored with coriander seed, smoked paprika and poached garlic, and then are seared and served on lettuce-leaf wrappers. The menu is short, but the chef makes every dish count. Oyster pie is a pastry-wrapped stew of precisely cooked oysters, still plump and juicy, suspended in a cream sauce chunky with salsify and leeks. Australia without lamb is an impossibility, and the chef merely braises a whopping big shank and surrounding it with parsnips, chanterelles and roasted apple. **Price range:** Entrees, $17–$23. **Meals:** D. **Subway:** N, R to Prince St.

El Cid $25 & Under   SPANISH
322 W. 15th St. (between Eighth and Ninth Aves.)   (212) 929-9332
El Cid is delightful, with delicious food and a professional staff that handles any
problem with élan. Tapas are a highlight, and you can make a meal of dishes
like grilled shrimp that are still freshly briny; tender white asparagus served cool
in a delicate vinaigrette; and chunks of savory marinated pork with french fries.
The paella is exceptional. The simple décor features hard surfaces that amplify
noise, producing a rollicking party atmosphere as the room gets crowded. And it
does get crowded. **Price range:** Entrees, $14.95–$27.95. AE/D only. **Meals:** L,
D. Closed Mon. **Subway:** A, C, E to 14th St.; L to Eighth Ave.

Eleven Madison Park   ☆☆ $$$$ CONTINENTAL
11 Madison Ave. (at 24th St.)   (212) 889-0905
Eleven Madison Park occupies the stately ground floor of a grand Art Deco building near the Flatiron building. The restaurant is an homage to the area's past, and
the menu is a thoughtful return to Continental cuisine. The best main courses are
skate grenobloise and the choucroute of salmon and trout. Sweetbreads are spectacular, too. Desserts are irresistible. **Price range:** Entrees, $19–$32. **Meals:** L, D.
Subway: 6 to 23rd St.

El Fogon $25 & Under   SPANISH/PUERTO RICAN
183 E. 111th St. (between Lexington and Third Aves.)   (212) 426-4844
The Puerto Rican specialties are fabulous at this friendly neighborhood hangout, which generally offers two interesting main courses each day. Corned beef
is ground fine and served in a rich sauce with olives, squash, peppers and
onions, enhancing its briny, smoky flavor. Roasted pork is moist and garlicky
and chicken fricassee is a beautifully flavored stew. Each dish comes with white
rice and plump red beans; for an extra $1, try a remarkably flaky and crisp
pastelillo, the Puerto Rican version of empanadas. **Price range:** Avg. entree, $6.
Cash only. **Meals:** L, D. Closed Sun. **Subway:** 6 to 110th St.

Emily's $25 & Under   SOUTHERN
1325 Fifth Ave. (at 111th St.)   (212) 996-1212
This pleasant but institutional restaurant offers a diverse Southern menu and
draws an integrated crowd. If you go, go for the meaty, tender baby back pork ribs,
subtly smoky and bathed in tangy barbecue sauce, or the big plate of chopped
pork barbecue. The best sides include savory rice and peas (actually red beans)
and peppery stuffing, and all dishes come with a basket of fine corn bread. Sweet
potato pie is the traditional dessert, and Emily's version is nice and nutmeggy.
Price range: Entrees, $10–$25. **Meals:** Br, L, D, LN. **Subway:** 6 to 110th St.

Emo's $25 & Under   KOREAN
1564 Second Ave. (near 81st St.)   (212) 628-8699
Emo's pulls few punches, offering robust, spicy, authentic fare that is full of flavor. The highlights here are the superb main courses, like oh jing uh gui, wonderfully tender cylinders of barbecued squid scored to resemble pale pine cones

and touched with hot sauce. A variation of this is jae yook gui, barbecued pork in a delectable smoky, spicy sauce. An American-style bar lines the entryway to the spare, narrow but airy dining room. **Price range:** Entrees, $11–$18. **Meals:** L, D. **Subway:** 6 to 77th St.

Empire Diner $$ DINER
210 10th Ave. (at 22nd St.)   (212) 243-2736
One of the early entries in the modern revival of America's love affair with diners was this campy Art Deco gem that attracted a hip late-night crowd in the 1980's. Nowadays, the Empire is a tourist destination. The up-to-date diner basics with some Mediterranean touches are not bad at all—better than at most diners, in fact—which is reflected in the prices. **Price range:** Entrees, $10–$17. **Meals:** B, Br, L, D, LN. **Subway:** C, E to 23rd St.

Esca   ☆☆ $$$ ITALIAN/SEAFOOD
402 W. 43rd St. (at Ninth Ave.)   (212) 564-7272
At Esca—the name means "bait"—the most important word in the Italian language is *crudo*. It means raw, and that's the way the fish comes to the table in a dazzling array of appetizers that could be thought of as Italian sushi. By changing olive oils, adding a bitter green, or throwing in minced chilies, the chef works thrilling variations on a very simple theme. The menu changes daily depending on what comes out of the sea. Look hard enough, and you can find a dish like guinea hen or roast chicken, but it seems perverse to order anything but seafood. The lemon-yellow walls and sea-green tiles give it a bright, cool look, and the solid wooden table in the center of the dining room, loaded down with vegetable side dishes, strikes a rustic note while communicating the food philosophy: fresh from the market, and prepared without fuss. **Price range:** Entrees, $17—$26. **Meals:** L, D. Closed Sun. **Subway:** A, C, E to 42nd St.

Esperanto $25 & Under   PAN-LATIN
145 Ave. C (at 9th St.)   (212) 505-6559
This is a warm and welcoming place with Latin food that can be surprisingly subtle and delicate. Bolinho de peixe, deep-fried balls of codfish, are exceptionally light, crisp and flavorful, with a terrific dipping sauce galvanized by spicy mustard. Esperanto's main courses are sturdy and hard to mess up, like a good and beefy steak bathed in chimichurri, the Argentine condiment of garlic and parsley. Esperanto serves potent caipirinhas and mojitos, a sort of Cuban mint julep—and don't miss the stellar coconut flan. **Price range:** Entrees, $9 to $14. AE only. **Meals:** D, LN. **Subway:** L to First Ave.

Estiatorio Milos   ☆☆ $$$$ GREEK/SEAFOOD
125 W. 55th St. (between Sixth and Seventh Aves.)   (212) 245-7400
The restaurant is clean, spare, blindingly white, and the entire focus is on the display of gorgeous fish by the open kitchen. Choose one and it is grilled simply and brought to the table. All the fish are cooked whole, and the lamb

chops are excellent. Appetizers are wonderful, too. The octopus, charred and sliced, mixed with onions, capers and peppers, is truly delicious. Thick homemade yogurt is the ideal way to end these meals. **Price range:** fish for main courses is sold whole and by weight, from $25–$34 a pound. **Meals:** L, D, LN. **Subway:** B, D, E to Seventh Ave.; N, Q, R, W to 57th St.

Felidia   ☆☆☆ $$$$ NORTHERN ITALIAN
243 E. 58th St. (between Second and Third Aves.)   (212) 758-1479

Felidia offers itself in the guise of an old-fashioned restaurant, but there's a professional polish in the dining room and high ambition in the kitchen. The seasonal menu concentrates on the foods of Italy's northeast: Friuli, the Veneto as well as Istria, now part of Croatia, and the home of owners Felice and Lidia Bastinich. This is robust food served in generous portions, revolving around game, organ meats, and slow-cooked sauces. This is not to say you can't eat lightly. Felidia serves lots of seafood, including lobster and crabmeat salad, and an impressive spiced monkfish in clam broth. Despite her expanding career as a television chef and cookbook writer, Ms. Bastianich has managed to keep standards admirably high at Felidia. **Price range:** Entrees, $27–$35. **Meals:** L, D. Closed Sun. **Subway:** 4, 5, 6 to 59th St.; N, R to Lexington Ave.

Fiamma Osteria   ☆☆☆ $$$ ITALIAN
206 Spring St. (near Sullivan St.)   (212) 653-0100

Fiamma Osteria is a beautifully realized restaurant, highly satisfying in every way. The upstairs dining room has a subdued atmosphere with rich, saturated reds and browns; the downstairs room is lighter, brighter and louder, more brasserie than restaurant. The food lives up to the setting. The chef stays firmly rooted in the core principles of Italian cooking, putting prime ingredients on a sparely designed stage and letting them speak with minimum interference. The pastas at Fiamma are exceptional, especially the raviolini stuffed with braised veal shank in a potent, highly reduced veal sauce enriched with formaggio de fossa. The dessert showstopper is a layered hazelnut chocolate torte on a crackling pastry base, served with gianduja gelato and chocolate sauce. **Price range:** Entrees, $21–$32. **Meals:** L, D. **Subway:** C, E to Spring St.

50 Carmine $25 & Under   ITALIAN
50 Carmine Street (at Bedford Street)   (212) 206-9134

The dining room here is without a hint of character, but the chef, schooled in rustic Italian cooking, gives 50 Carmine all the color and intrigue not conveyed by its décor. Emphasis is on seasonal ingredients, and the menu of dishes soar when they succeed. The deceptively simple pasta with many cheeses is astoundingly good. Rabbit with Umbrian chickpeas comes in an almost perfect tomato sauce. The fricassee of lamb with braised artichokes is a study in complementary flavors. The wine list is surprisingly expensive, but service is friendly and responsive. **Price range:** Entrees, $12–$14. **Meals:** D. **Subway:** A, C, E, F, V to West 4th St.

Fifty Seven Fifty Seven ☆☆☆ **$$$$** AMERICAN

Four Seasons Hotel, 57 E. 57th St. (between Park and Madison Aves.)

(212) 758-5757

With its solicitous service in a memorable public space, Fifty Seven Fifty Seven sets a new standard for an old tradition. The menu changes frequently, but it still offers something for absolutely every taste. The food is decidedly American with a modern bent. Vegetarians will find many choices; dieters will find starred offerings low in fat and salt. And those with an appetite for meat and potatoes have many options, from rack of veal in a red wine sauce to grilled beef tenderloin with rosemary cream potato pie. The visually restrained desserts are rich in flavor and texture, but the chocolate desserts are the greatest triumph. **Price range:** Entrees, $25–$32. **Meals:** B, L, D. **Subway:** 4, 5, 6 to 59th St.; N, R to Lexington Ave.

Firebird ☆☆ **$$$** RUSSIAN

365 W. 46th St. (between Eighth and Ninth Aves.) (212) 586-0244

This jewel box of a restaurant boasts a dining room as ornate and luxurious as a Fabergé egg, and a staff so polished, it really does seem that you have entered some more serene and lavish era. The caviar arrives with its own private waiter who turns the service into a performance, pouring hot butter onto the plate, spooning on the caviar and then delicately twirling the blini around the roe. Firebird continues to offer imaginatively updated Russian classics. Desserts, once a weak point, have improved greatly. **Price range:** Entrees, $26–$38. **Meals:** L, D. **Subway:** A, C, E to 42nd St.

First **$25 & Under** NEW AMERICAN

87 First Ave. (between 5th and 6th Sts.) (212) 674-3823

Ambitious, creative contemporary American fare at relatively modest prices, served late into the night. First also offers an intelligently chosen list of wines and beers and worthwhile weekly specials, like its Sunday night pig roast. **Price range:** Avg. entree, $17. **Meals:** D, LN. **Subway:** F to Second Ave.

Fish **$25 & Under** SEAFOOD

280 Bleecker St. (at Jones St.) (212) 727-2879

The simple menu at Fish focuses on chowders, an expanded raw bar, lobster rolls and grilled fish. The bar is dim, the beer is flowing, and the illusion of waterfront dissolution, which gives oyster bars such character, is intact. There are few places to find fresher or better oysters on the half shell. Simple dishes are the best. You'll love the casual, rakish feel of Fish, waiters in white aprons, rickety tables, the scent of horseradish in the air. **Price range:** Entrees, $9–$28 (for steak). **Meals:** L, D, LN. **Subway:** 6 to Bleecker St.

Fleur de Sel ☆☆ **$$$$** FRENCH

5 E. 20th St. (between Fifth Ave. and Broadway) (212) 460-9100

Who doesn't pine for that little neighborhood restaurant, tucked away on a side street, where the lighting is subdued, the chef is French and the food is terrific? Well, here it is. The fixed-price menu is perfectly calibrated to the small room, and the chef knows in a quiet sort of way how to create excitement on the plate. Large ravioli stuffed with bits of sweetbread and cepes do the trick, each package containing a rich, meaty ooze. The raspberry feuillete is a disarmingly simple-looking thing, but the pastry melts on the tongue, and the ganache is almost criminally delicious. **Price range:** Three courses, $52. **Meals:** L, D. **Subway:** N, R to 23rd St.

Flor's Kitchen $25 & Under   VENEZUELAN
149 First Ave. (near 9th St.)   (212) 387-8949

Tiny, bright and colorful, this new Venezuelan restaurant offers many snacking foods like empanadas criollas, smooth, crisp pastries with fillings like savory shredded beef or pureed chicken. The arepas—corncakes with varied fillings—include a wonderful chicken and avocado salada. Two sauces—one made with avocado, lemon juice and oil; the second, a hot sauce—make dishes like chachapas (corn pancakes with ham and cheese) taste even better. Soups are superb, and desserts are rich and homespun. **Price range:** Entrees, $4–$9. **Meals:** L, D, LN. **Subway:** F to Second Ave.; L to First Ave.

The Four Seasons   ☆☆☆ $$$$ NEW AMERICAN
99 E. 52nd St. (between Park and Lexington Aves.)   (212) 754-9494

Few restaurants occupy as honored a position in New York as the Four Seasons, now in its fifth decade as a destination for the high, the haute, and almost any-body feeling celebratory. The two rooms, designed by Philip Johnson, are as cool and elegant as ever, understated examples of the best of mid-century style. By day, the Grill Room is power central for the worlds of finance, fashion and publishing. Food is almost beside the point. By night, the shimmering Pool Room takes over. While the kitchen nods in the direction of recent trends, offering many dishes with an Asian accent, for example, it is at its best with ele-gant classics, like broiled Dover sole or fabulously tender rack of lamb with ethereal mashed potatoes. **Price range:** Entrees, $34–$55. **Meals:** L, D. Closed Sun. **Subway:** E, F to Lexington Ave.; 6 to 51st St.

Frank $25 &   Under   ITALIAN
88 Second Ave. (near 5th St.)   (212) 420-0202

This sweet, unpretentious restaurant, with its crowded, ragtag dining room, has been packed from the moment it opened. Start with an order of insalata Caprese, ripe tomatoes and mozzarella di bufala; among the entrees, try the polpettone, a savory meatloaf, with a classic, slow-cooked gravy, and orecchi-ette with fennel and pecorino Toscano. If you go early, you can expect special touches, like a free plate of tiny potato croquettes, or a dish of olive oil fla-vored with orange rind with your bread. **Price range:** Entrees, $6.95–$14.95.Cash only. **Meals:** Br, L, D, LN. **Subway:** F to Second Ave.

Frank's   ☆ $$$ STEAKHOUSE
85 10th Ave. (at 15th St.)   (212) 243-1349

A paradise for carnivores. The bare brick walls and long bar announce this as a restaurant whose only desire is to serve big portions to hungry people. Three or four shrimp in a cocktail would probably provide enough protein for an average person: they are giant creatures of the sea, and absolutely delicious. The T-bone steak has the fine, funky flavor of meat that has been dry-aged for a long time and the steak fries are long and thick. The same family has been running Frank's since 1912; they will make you feel at home. **Price range:** Entrees, $18–$30. **Meals:** L, D. **Subway:** A, C, E to 14th St.; L to Eighth Ave.

Fresh ☆☆ $$$$ SEAFOOD
105 Reade St. (near W. Broadway) (212) 406-1900
It's a bold and playful shuffling of ingredients that makes Fresh, an airy seafood restaurant, so intriguing. There are straightforward cooking moments, but Fresh rises and falls on its more expressive dishes. The chef treats pieces of fish like meat. Kobe toro, tuna that is thick and buttery rich, tastes as babied as the legendary Kobe beef. Conventional cuts of seafood earn a more delicate treatment. Occasional inconsistencies in the food are a problem, and service can be surprisingly amateurish in an otherwise professional operation. **Price range:** Entrees, $19–$34. **Meals:** D. **Subway:** 1, 2, 3, 9 to Chambers St.

Funky Broome $25 & Under CHINESE
176 Mott St. (between Broome and Kenmare Sts.) (212) 941-8628
From its odd name to its brightly colored interior, Funky Broome suggests youth and energy rather than conformity. Though the menu is largely Cantonese and Hong Kong, Funky Broome has stirred it up a bit with some Thai touches and by making mini-woks centerpieces. Some of the dishes are unusual and good, like plump and flavorful oysters stuffed with green onions and steamed in a red wine sauce. Seafood dishes are excellent, and Funky Broome can breathe new life into hoary old dishes like crisp and tender beef with broccoli. **Price range:** Entrees, $6.95–$15.95. **Meals:** L, D, LN. **Subway:** 6 to Spring St.

Gabriela's $25 & Under MEXICAN
685 Amsterdam Ave. (at 93rd St.) (212) 961-0574
311 Amsterdam Ave. (at 75th St.)
There really is a Gabriela, and she makes terrific, authentic Mexican dishes. Taquitos al pastor, tiny corn tortillas topped with vinegary roast pork, pineapple salsa and cilantro, are a wonderful Mexican street dish. Gabriela's pozole, the traditional Mexican soup made with hominy, is an entire meal in itself, served in a huge bowl with chunks of tender pork or chicken. Entrees all come with tortillas so fragrant that the aroma of corn rises with the steam. Gabriela's also offers superb desserts, including capirotada, a buttery bread pudding with lots of honey. **Price range:** Entrees, $5.95–$14.95. **Meals:** B, L, D. **Subway:** 93rd St.: 1, 2, 3, 9 to 96th St.; 75th St.: 1, 2, 3, 9 to 72nd St.

Gabriel's ☆☆ $$$ ITALIAN
11 W. 60th St. (between Broadway and Columbus Ave.) (212) 956-4600
This clubby and comfortable restaurant offers great big portions and fabulous friendly service. Although the food is called Tuscan, it is far too American for that, too original. None of the pastas are ordinary, but the real winner here is

homemade gnocchi, little dumplings so light they float into your mouth and
down your throat. Among the entrees, the best dish is the sea bass cooked in a
terra-cotta casserole. Desserts, with the exception of the wonderful sorbets and
gelatos, are not very exciting. **Price range:** Entrees, $18–$32. **Meals:** L, D.
Closed Sun. **Subway:** A, B, C, D, E, 1, 9 to 59th St.

Geisha   ☆ $$$ JAPANESE FUSION
33 E. 61st St. (between Fifth and Madison Aves.)   (212) 813-1113
Geisha features low lounge sofas, lots of gauzy Asian fabrics and a projector
showing Japanese cartoons. Music thumps, and on your way through the bar
you hear things like, "Did you see that babe?" Once you reach the table, your
oasis, matters improve, for some very good cooks toil in Geisha's kitchen. The
sushi is prepared competently, but the fun lies elsewhere. Dumplings are stuffed
with black tiger shrimp and bathed in a green curry broth rich with kaffir lime.
Skate is poached, then laid in a pool of browned butter infused with ponzu and
sake. Go at lunch for a serene experience. **Price range:** Entrees $19–$33.
Meals: L, D. Closed Sun. **Subway:** N, R, W to Fifth Ave./59th St.; 4, 5, 6 to
59th St.

Gonzo $25 & Under   PIZZA/ITALIAN
140 W. 13th St. (between Sixth and Seventh Aves.)   (212) 645-4606
Gonzo specializes in antipasti and pizzas, but offers a conventional Italian menu,
too. The dining room is loud, but dim, and almost Gothic with a high, paneled
ceiling and tapestries. Gonzo clearly has an audience. They come for the pizzas,
which arrive irregularly shaped. The crust is thin and curled, with doughy flavor
and elasticity, crisp and surprisingly light. **Price range:** Pizzas, $13–$15. **Meals:**
D, LN. Closed Mon. **Subway:** F, V, 1, 2, 3, 9 to 14th St.

Good $25 & Under   LATIN AMERICAN
89 Greenwich Ave. (at Bank St.)   (212) 691-8080
It's possible to eat unusually, eclectically and very well here. Crisp peanut
chicken is a welcome old dish, while grilled calamari, a newcomer, takes its
cue from Asia, arriving in a lime-and-mint dressing. Also good are the grilled
flank steak and sauteed rock shrimp, flavored with garlic. The service is warm
and professional. **Price range:** Entrees, $10–$17. **Meals:** L, D. Closed Mon.
Subway: 1, 2, 3, 9 to 14th St.

Goody's   ☆ $ CHINESE
1 East Broadway (at Chatham Sq.)   (212) 577-2922
Goody's pride is the crab meat version of soup dumplings, xiao long bao,
tinted pink by the seafood that glows through the sheer, silky skin. But there
are other unusual dishes, like fabulous turnip pastries, yellowfish fingers in
seaweed batter, and braised pork shoulder, a kind of candied meat. This dish is
so rich that it must be eaten in small bites. Goody's kitchen also works magic
with bean curd, mixed with crab meat so it becomes rich and delicious. **Price
range:** $15–$20. **Meals:** L, D. **Subway:** J, M, N, Q, R, W, Z, 6 to Canal St.

Gotham Bar and Grill ☆☆☆ $$$$ NEW AMERICAN
12 E. 12th St. (between Fifth Ave. and University Pl.)   (212) 620-4020
A cheerful, welcoming restaurant in an open, high-ceilinged room with a
lively bar along one side. Waiters anticipate your every wish and make you
feel remarkably well cared for. The food seems modern but is almost classic in
its balance. The signature dish is seafood salad, a spiral of scallops, squid,
octopus, lobster and avocado that swirls onto the plate like a mini-tornado.
Main courses are more straightforward, like rosy slices of duck breast set off by
a single caramelized endive and a sweet potato purée. Desserts, like the wonderful chocolate cake, are intense and very American. **Price range:** Entrees,
$28–$38. **Meals:** L, D. **Subway:** F, L, N, Q, R, W, 4, 5, 6 to 14th St.

Gradisca $25 & Under ITALIAN
126 W. 13th St. (between Sixth and Seventh Aves.)   (212) 691-4886
Gradisca epitomizes the local trattoria, downtown style. The dining room is rustic, but the waiters conform to a more modern stereotype: young, hip and lanky
in tight black T-shirts. The menu offers simple, delicious flavors, like piadinas,
round, unleavened flatbreads, cooked on a griddle and then stuffed with things
like prosciutto and fresh mozzarella (a marvelously nutty combination), or
spinach and pecorino. There are two superb main courses: sliced leg of lamb in a
red wine sauce, and a big pork chop under a cloud of crisp leeks. Dessert standouts include a deliciously dense, bittersweet chocolate torte and a satisfying
amaretto semifreddo. **Price range:** Entrees, $12–$20. Cash only. **Meals:** D.
Subway: F, 1, 2, 3, 9 to 14th St.

Gramercy Tavern ☆☆☆ $$$$ NEW AMERICAN
42 E. 20th St. (between Broadway and Park Ave. South)   (212) 477-0777
The large and lively tavern has redefined grand dining in New York. Chef Tom
Colicchio cooks with extraordinary confidence, creating dishes characterized by
bold flavors and unusual harmonies. To experience Mr. Colicchio's cooking at
its best, consider the chef's extraordinary market menu. It is expensive, but perfect for special occasions. For a less expensive alternative, the handsome bar in
front offers a casual but excellent menu. On a recent visit, the restaurant lived
up to its three stars, with consistently fresh, inventive new American dishes;
desserts also remain a highlight. **Price range:** Prix-fixe and tasting menus,
$65–$90. **Meals:** L, D. **Subway:** N, R, 6 to 23rd St.

Grand Sichuan $25 & Under CHINESE
229 Ninth Ave. (at 24th St.)   (212) 620-5200
The owner of this terrific restaurant hands out a 27-page pamphlet that explains
five Chinese regional cuisines and describes dozens of dishes the restaurant
serves. The eating is as interesting as the reading, with wonderful dishes like
sour stringbeans with minced pork and tea-smoked duck. While Sichuan food is
indeed spicy, that is only part of the story, as you see when you taste a fabulous
cold dish like sliced conch with wild pepper sauce, coated with ground Sichuan
peppercorns, which are not hot but bright, effervescent and almost refreshing.
Price range: Entrees, $5.95–$16.95. **Meals:** L, D. **Subway:** C, E to 23rd St.

Grand Sichuan Eastern $25 & Under   CHINESE
1049 Second Ave. (near 56th St.)   (212) 355-5855
The newest of the Grand Sichuan restaurants, a bright, boxy storefront that
conforms largely to the Chinatown school of interior design, has added 96
dishes to the menu under the heading "New Sichuan Food." Some are scorch-
ing. While the new dishes are intriguing, do not let a trip to Grand Sichuan
pass without checking in on old favorites. There's nothing better than paper-
thin slices of cured pork with tender garlic shoots, except possibly the tea-
smoked duck — likely the best barbecue in New York. **Price range:** Entrees,
$7–$17. **Meals:** L, D. **Subway:** 4, 5, 6 to 59th St.; N, R, W to Lexington Ave.;
E, V to Lexington Ave.

Guastavino's   ☆ ☆ $$$$ NEW AMERICAN
409 E. 59th St. (between First and York Aves.)   (212) 980-2455
This dazzling transformation of the Queensboro Bridge vaults gives New Yorkers
a glimpse of a swaggering international restaurant style where the scenes are
loud, lively and up to the minute, and the food often runs second to the design.
A long, low-slung bar draws an Upper East Side crowd; the main restaurant is a
300-seat brasserie, clamorous and casual, with a glorious shellfish display in front
of the kitchen. Guastavino's kitchen feeds a lot of people out there, and they do
a more than respectable job. At its best, these are well-conceived, well-executed
dishes that really can compete with the surroundings. **Price range:** Entrees,
$14–$30. **Meals:** L, D. **Subway:** 4, 5, 6 to 59th St.; N, R to Lexington Ave.

Gumbo Café $25 & Under   NEW ORLEANS/AMERICAN
950 Columbus Ave. (near 107th St.)   (212) 222-2378
Even though Gumbo Café serves only a few basic New Orleans dishes, the flavors are so soulfully deep that you want to savor each bite to its depths. Jambal-
aya is smoky but complex; as in a paella, the rice forms a crucial basis for
sausage, chicken and vegetables, and is amplified by a blend of garlic, peppers,
tomato, basil and other spices. The gumbo is also excellent. Don't skip the
house-made desserts: the eggy pecan tart, the light, not-too-sweet lemon
merengue pie and the spicy sweet potato pie are each wonderful in their own
way. **Price range:** Entrees, $6–$10. **Meals:** L, D. **Subway:** 1, 9 to 110th St.

Gus's Figs Bistro and Bar $25 & Under   MEDITERRANEAN
250 W. 27th St. (between Seventh and Eighth Aves.)   (212) 352-8822
This restaurant captures the dreamy, generous, sun-soaked aura that makes the
Mediterranean so endlessly appealing. The chef excels at blending flavors and
textures in main courses like moist, flavorful chicken, braised in a clay pot and
served over creamy polenta. Top dishes include tender pieces of lamb served
over a soft bread pudding made savory with goat cheese and pine nuts and
sweetened with figs; and pan-roasted cod with grilled leeks, orange sections
and pomegranate vinaigrette. **Price range:** Entrees, $13–$19.50. **Meals:** L, D,
LN. **Subway:** C, E, 1, 9 to 28th St.

Habib's Place $25 & Under   NORTH AFRICAN
130 St. Marks Pl. (near Ave. A)   (212) 979-2243
Habib's Place is colorful and commodious with a menu that runs the gamut of familiar Middle Eastern and North African specialties. But couscous is the thing, served in handsome ceramic tagines. Alternatives include superb kebabs. The lamb shawarma is especially noteworthy. Falafel is so fresh you can taste the cumin, coriander, garlic and onion in the chickpea blend. **Price range:** $3–$12. **Meals:** L, D, LN. Cash only. **Subway:** 6 to Astor Pl.

Hacienda de Argentina   ☆ $$$ ARGENTINE
339 E. 75th St. (between First and Second Aves.)   (212) 472-5300
The dining room is crowded with heavy Old World oak furniture, burnished candelabra, gilt mirrors and, inexplicably, a full suit of armor. The restaurant aims for a faithful rendition of Argentina's distinctive beef-crazy cuisine, an odd mixture of grilled steaks, sausages and offal influenced by the cooking of Italian, Spanish and German immigrants. (There's a notable lack of enthusiasm for vegetables.) Sink your teeth into the juicy, tender, beautifully marbled shell steak, then proceed directly to the flourless torte made with intense Belgian chocolate. **Price range:** Entrees $13.50–$35.75. **Meals:** D. **Subway:** 6 to 77th St.

The Half King $25 & Under   PUB/AMERICAN
505 W. 23rd St. (between 10th and 11th Aves.)   (212) 462-4300
Owned by Sebastian Junger, author of *The Perfect Storm*, this unconventional writers' bar serves Irish pub grub, elevated from its proletarian moorings while retaining its heartiness and simplicity. Main courses include a superbly flavorful pork roast and a surprisingly delicate fillet of sole. Desserts are good and rustic, like a rough-hewn berry, peach and apple crumble. A small garden in the rear is pleasant at lunch or at breakfast. **Price range:** Entrees, $9–$16. **Meals:** B, L, D. **Subway:** C, E to 23rd St.

Hangawi   ☆☆ $$ KOREAN/VEGETARIAN
12 E. 32nd St. (between Fifth and Madison Aves.)   (212) 213-0077
Hangawi leaves you feeling cleansed and refreshed, as if you had come from a spa instead of a vegetarian Korean restaurant. Diners remove their shoes on entering and sit at low tables with their feet dangling comfortably into the sunken space beneath them. They are surrounded by unearthly Korean music, wonderful objects and people who move with deliberate grace. Many of the exotic greens, porridges and mountain roots on the menu can be sampled by ordering the emperor's meal, which includes a tray of nine kinds of mountain greens surrounded by 10 side dishes. **Price range:** Entrees, $14.95–$24.95. **Meals:** L, D. **Subway:** 6 to 33rd St.

The Harrison   ☆☆ $$$ NEW AMERICAN
355 Greenwich St. (at Harrison St.)   (212) 274-9319
With a clean, all-American look for the interior, the Harrison offers a modestly priced menu poised carefully between new American and fusion cooking. The

food may speak with an accent, but it's American food. Shell steak gets some inspired Italian tailoring, a rich, crunchy topping of crisped pancetta with bitter radicchio and balsamic vinegar. Likewise, chicken crisped in the pan with lemon-mustard sauce has the immediacy of a slap in the face. For desserts, the quince and apple crisp is a rip-roaring mainstream pleaser. **Price range:** Entrees, $9–$28. **Meals:** L, D. Closed Sun. **Subway:** 1, 2 to Franklin St.

Hatsuhana ☆☆ $$$ JAPANESE/SUSHI
17 E. 48th St. (between Fifth and Madison Aves.)   (212) 355-3345
237 Park Ave. (at 46th St.)   (212) 661-3400
Of all the city's sushi bars, Hatsuhana is the one that best bridges the gap between East and West. It is a comfortable and welcoming restaurant where you can depend on being served high-quality sushi whether you speak Japanese or not. Real connoisseurs sit at the downstairs sushi bar and enjoy extraordinary chu toro, tuna that is richer than maguro but less rich than toro, and ika uni, pure white squid cut into long strips as thin as spaghetti. The quality of the cooked food is excellent, too. The Park Avenue location is not nearly as good as the 48th Street location. **Price range:** Avg. entree, $30. **Meals:** L, D. Closed Sun. **Subway:** S, 4, 5, 6, 7 to 42nd St.

Havana Central $25 & Under   CUBAN/PAN-LATIN
22 E. 17th St. (between Fifth Ave. and Union Square W.)   (212) 414-4999
Somewhere in the imagination resides a fantasy of pre-Castro Havana. Enter Havana Central. The long, narrow room is exciting and loud, with sounds echoing off the high ceiling. The lighting is as warm as a tropical sunset. The menu takes liberties. The best dishes, though, are those that stay close to the Cuban ideal. Service is friendly but can be slow. **Price range:** Apps., $4–$8.75; entrees, $9–$22. **Meals:** L, D, LN. **Subway:** L, N, R, Q, W, 4,5, 6 to 14th St.

Havana NY $25 & Under   LATIN AMERICAN
27 W. 38th St. (between Fifth and Sixth Aves.)   (212) 944-0990
This bustling Cuban restaurant serves tasty, inexpensive food in pleasant sur-roundings. The food is typically robust, flavored with lusty doses of garlic and lime, yet it can be delicate, too, as in an octopus salad, which is marinated in citrus until tender like a ceviche. Chilean sea bass, is moist and subtly flavored, and grilled skirt steak is excellent. All the main courses are enormous, served with rice, beans and sweet plantains. Service is swift and likable. **Price range:** Entrees, $8.95–$12.95. **Meals:** L, D. Closed Sat., Sun. **Subway:** B, D, F, N, Q, R, S, W to 34th St.

Heartbeat ☆☆ $$$ NEW AMERICAN
149 E. 49th St. (at Lexington Ave.)   (212) 407-2900
New York's hippest spa food brings models to mingle with moguls in a slick set-ting. You could describe Heartbeat that way, but it would be doing the restaurant a disservice; this is a very comfortable, crowded and surprisingly quiet room with

good service and good food. This approach works best when the food is simply left alone. Try the simple grills, the good meats and the Japanese-accented dishes. **Price range:** Entrees, $18–$30. **Meals:** B, Br, L, D. **Subway:** 6 to 51st St.; E, F to Lexington Ave.

Hearth ☆☆ $$$ ITALIAN
403 E. 12th St. (at First Ave.)   (646) 602-1300
Its name suggests an expansive coziness—Tuscany and your grandmother's house wrapped in one, with a little smoked bacon on the side. Banished are the garnish, the layered sauce, the architectural tuna. This disciplined, almost stoical, cooking is mostly pleasing in its simplicity, with dishes like ribollita, duck pappardelle and game bird terrine. No wild-card ingredients, no fussy presentations: just good, familiar food given a little luster. The wine and beer lists are beguiling. **Price range:** Entrees $18–$26. **Meals:** D. Closed Mon. **Subway:** L to First Ave.

Heidelberg $25 & Under GERMAN
1648 Second Ave. (near 85th St.)   (212) 628-2332
Heidelberg is swathed in history, presenting its worn and faded face without touch-ups or apologies. With waiters in lederhosen, chandeliers made of deer antlers and sturdy oil paintings dulled by decades of smoke, Heidelberg is almost a stereotype of a German beer hall. Yet it is a friendly, laid-back place, and just right for the sort of hearty rib-sticking fare that Yorkville-ites once took for granted. Go directly to the entrees. The sauerbraten, a tender beef roast redolent of vinegar and cloves is superb. **Price range:** Entrees, $9–$25. **Meals:** L, D. **Subway:** 4, 5, 6 to 86th St.

Hell's Kitchen $25 & Under MEXICAN
679 Ninth Ave. (near 47th St.)   (212) 977-1588
This restaurant makes creative use of Mexican flavorings and cooking techniques, adding ingredients and dishes from the global palette of contemporary American cooking. The appetizer of tuna tostadas is brilliant. Quesadillas are like small main courses. They retain their Mexican identity even with creative enhancements. The best main course is a pork loin flavored with chili. For dessert try the intense fruit sorbets, served over fruit with a surprising touch of chili. With the loud music and hopping bar, acoustics are surprisingly good. **Price range:** Entrees, $13–$18. **Meals:** D, LN. **Subway:** C, E to 50th St.

Holy Basil $25 & Under THAI
149 Second Ave. (between 9th and 10th Sts.)   (212) 460-5557
This is one of the best Thai restaurants in the city, turning out highly spiced, beautifully balanced dishes like green papaya salad, elegant curries and delicious noodles. The dining room looks more like a beautiful church than a restaurant, jazz usually plays in the background and the wine list offers terrific choices. **Price range:** Entrees, $8–$16. **Meals:** D, LN. **Subway:** F to Second Ave.; L to First or Third Ave.

Honmura An   ☆☆☆ $$$ JAPANESE/NOODLES

170 Mercer St. (between Houston and Prince Sts.)   (212) 334-5253

Making the buckwheat noodles known as soba is not easy, but the soba chefs at
Honmura An have clearly put in their time—the soba in this spare, soothing
space is wonderful and worth the high price. Many appetizers, as well as good
tempura, are worth trying here, but nothing is remotely on a par with the noodles. To appreciate how fine they are, you must eat them cold. The noodles are
earthy and elastic, and when you dip them into the briny bowl of dashi (dipping
sauce), land and sea come, briefly, together. Honmura An also makes excellent
udon, fat wheat noodles. Served hot, in the dish called nabeyaki, they virtually
redefine the dish. **Price range:** entrees, $13–$22. **Meals:** L, D. Closed Mon.
Subway: N, R to Prince St.; F, S to Broadway–Lafayette St.

Hue   ☆ $$ VIETNAMESE

91 Charles St. (at Bleecker St.)   (212) 691-4170

Everyone at Hue seems to know that the appetizers and entrees are theatrical
props, that the lemon-basil martinis are at least as important as the pho bo and
that no one over 30 belongs there. But quite a few of the props are edible,
because Hue, unlike many feverishly social restaurants, does care about the
food. Skip the adequate but distracting sushi menu; it's far more rewarding to
zero in on Vietnamese dishes like cari ga xao lin, large pieces of chicken sim-
mered in a clay pot with sweet coconut milk, long beans and eggplant. For
dessert, go with the magnificent fried coconut ice cream, a cross between baked
Alaska and a jelly doughnut. **Price range:** Entrees $13.95–$23.95. **Meals:** L, D.
Subway: 1, 9 to Christopher St.

Icon   ☆☆ $$ NEW AMERICAN

130 E. 39th St. (between Lexington and Park Aves.)   (212) 592-8888

Icon has a mildly lurid décor and a lighting philosophy perfectly designed for
illegal trysts and furtive meetings. It is attached to the W Court Hotel, ensuring
a steady flow of youngish, stylish diners. Visually, it is soothing to the nerves.
Aurally, it's touch and go. As the evening progresses, a thumping rock soundtrack forces diners to shout across the table, and the noise from Wet Bar across
the lobby becomes intrusive. The food at Icon is better than the setting might
suggest. Desserts are not flashy; quiet good taste is more the style. **Price range:**
Entrees, $19–$25. **Meals:** B, Br, L, D. **Subway:** S, 4, 5, 6, 7 to 42nd St.

Il Gattopardo   ☆☆ $$$ ITALIAN

33 W. 54th St. (between Fifth and Sixth Aves.)   (212) 246-0412

There is nothing the least bit fussy about Il Gattopardo (The Leopard), a tiny,
almost spartan Neapolitan restaurant where an emphasis on simplicity often
translates into high satisfaction. The uncomplicated elegance of its meatballs
stirs the soul. The appetizer selection includes many of the menu's highlights,
baby artichokes with Parmesan and smoked mozzarella. Pastas succeed as well.
The Genovese sauce is superb. **Price range:** Entrees, $18–$32. **Meals:** L, D.
Closed Sun. **Subway:** E, V to Fifth Ave.

Il Mulino $ $ $ $ ITALIAN
86 W. 3rd St. (between Sullivan and Thompson Sts.)   (212) 673-3783
Big portions (and prices), long waits, a halcyon atmosphere. Dinner might
begin with a dish of shrimp fricassee with garlic; bresaola of beef served over
mixed greens tossed in a well-seasoned vinaigrette, or aromatic baked clams ore-
ganato. The pasta roster includes fettuccine Alfredo; spaghettini in a robust
Bolognese sauce; trenette tossed in pesto sauce; and capellini all'arrabbiata, or
in a spicy tomato sauce. The menu carries a dozen veal preparations, along with
beef tenderloin in a shallot, white wine and sage sauce; and broiled sirloin.
Price range: Entrees, $24 and up. **Meals:** L, D, LN. Closed Sun. **Subway:** A, C,
E, F, S to W. 4th St.

Il Valentino   ☆☆ $ $ ITALIAN
Sutton Hotel, 330 E. 56th St. (between First and Second Aves.) (212) 355-0001
In a city where purely pleasant restaurants have become increasingly rare, Il
Valentino feels like an oasis. The food is reliable, you don't have to wait for
your table and you can hear your friends when they talk. The timbered ceiling
and terra-cotta floor give the room a cool rustic feeling, and the food is simple,
tasty Tuscan fare. The artichoke salad is delicious, and the Caesar salad impressive. But it is the pastas that really shine. Marinated grilled lamb chops in a
mustard seed sauce and osso buco are also excellent. **Price range:** entrees,
$16–$25. **Meals:** L, D. **Subway:** 4, 5, 6 to 59th St.; N, R to Lexington Ave.

industry(food)   ☆ $ $ $ BISTRO
509 E. 6th St. (near Ave. A)   (212) 777-5920
Despite the grave pretensions of its name, despite the lapses of discipline in the
kitchen, industry(food) is at base an unpretentious, likable neighborhood
restaurant. The menu features some gutsy pairings, like roast chicken with tasso
ham and black-eyed peas, and braised veal cheeks with celery root purée.
Desserts require you to tread carefully. **Price range:** Entrees, $17–$24. **Meals:**
D, LN. **Subway:** F to Second Ave.; 6 to Astor Pl.

Inside $25 & Under   NEW AMERICAN
9 Jones St. (between 4th and Bleecker Sts.)   (212) 229-9999
The handsome wood bar in front and the professional greeting bespeak the
comfort of a more expensive restaurant, yet the almost bare white walls make
the dining room feel airy and streamlined. With dishes based on no more than
three seasonal and simple ingredients, Inside can keep prices gentle. Main
courses are streamlined. Newport steak is thick and beefy, and tender braised
lamb with cinnamon and olives achieves an almost Moroccan balance of savory
and sweet. For dessert, try the panna cotta or a steamed chocolate pudding with
rhubarb. **Price range:** Entrees, $13–$18. **Meals:** Br, D. **Subway:** 6 to Bleecker St.

Isola $25 & Under   ITALIAN
485 Columbus Ave. (between 83rd and 84th Sts.)   (212) 362-7400
When Isola is crowded, its dining room can be unbearably loud, but the restaurant offers some of the best Italian food on the Upper West Side, with lively

pastas like spaghetti in a purée of black olives and oregano, and fettuccine with crumbled sausages and porcini mushrooms. The wine list is nicely chosen. **Price range:** Entrees, $9.95–$18. **Meals:** Br, L, D. **Subway:** B, C to 81st St.

I Trulli ☆☆ $$$ ITALIAN

122 E. 27th St. (between Lexington Ave. and Park Ave. South) (212) 481-7372
This is New York City's best and most attractive restaurant dedicated to the cooking of Apulia. It serves interesting, unusual food in an understated room that is both elegant and warm; there is also a beautiful garden for outdoor dining. The rustic food from Italy's heel does not have the subtle charm of northern Italian food or the tomato-and-garlic heartiness of Neapolitan cuisine. Pastas have a basic earthy quality; orechiette are a house staple made by the owner. **Price range:** Entrees, $18–$32. **Meals:** L, D. Closed Sun. **Subway:** 6 to 28th St.

Itzocan Bistro $25 & Under MEXICAN

1575 Lexington Ave. (at 101st St.) (212) 423-0255
This is a boxy little corner with hospitable service and quiet, engaging cooking that takes the bistro repertory and adds Mexican touches that tweak the dishes in unexpected directions but do not overwhelm them. The tile floor is old and scarred, and the tables and chairs are nothing fancy, but Mexican candelabras and a portrait of Frida Kahlo add warm touches. Main courses are almost all winners, and modestly priced, too. It's hard to imagine a better roast chicken than Itzocan's. Seafood pozole, a pot of spicy broth thick with hominy, mussels, shrimp and fish, is perhaps the dish truest to the Mexican flavorings of corn and chilies. **Price range:** Entrees, $12–$16. **Meals:** D. **Subway:** 6 to 103rd St.

Jack's Luxury Oyster Bar ☆☆ $$$ SEAFOOD

246 E. Fifth St. (at Second Ave.) (212) 673-0338
Jack's is a New Orleans oyster bar that has been given a downtown twist or two. Diners can order oysters on the half shell, littleneck clams and a shrimp cocktail, and make a light meal at the bar with a glass of riesling or a cold beer. Those in search of a full meal find themselves staring at a menu with one entree and one dessert, for Jack's has only six upstairs tables and what must be the smallest restaurant kitchen in Manhattan. The chef gives a refined French touch to homey Southern dishes, or reverses the equation by throwing Louisiana heat into a French recipe. **Price range:** Entrees $25. **Meals:** D. Closed Sun. **Subway:** F to Second Ave.; 6 to Astor Pl.

Jane ☆ $$ NEW AMERICAN/BISTRO

100 W. Houston St. (at Thompson St.) (212) 254-7000
Jane is a restaurant with the soul of a café. It sets itself modest goals, and for the most part it delivers, at a fair price. Grease-free fried clams come with a hot-cold accompaniment of sweet-corn "dip," a cool, creamy slush that nicely offsets a pungent rice-wine vinegar dipping sauce steeped in habañero peppers. Entrees do not, on balance, live up to the appetizers. An exception is the dark, richly gamy hanger steak, swimming in a red wine sauce and onion marmalade. At dessert time the bias is toward American flavors, but with a little twist here and

there, like the lemon-thyme sauce that brightens a dense cylinder-shaped cheesecake. **Price range:** Entrees, $17–$21. **Meals:** D. **Subway:** C, E to Spring St.; N, R to Prince St.; F, S to Broadway–Lafayette St.

Jarnac ☆ $$$ FRENCH

328 W. 12th St. (near Greenwich St.)   (212) 924-3413

Jarnac is in many ways a dream bistro. A small and attractive restaurant, it sits on a tranquil corner of the far West Village, with windows that open out and offer prime viewing of the neighborhood. The menu is short, sweet and French. The wine list has personality. At its best, Jarnac offers nicely executed food with an original twist. One of the best dishes is roasted poussin with butter walnut sauce that looks grim. Don't look, eat. **Price range:** Entrees, $20–$24. **Meals:** Br, D. Closed Mon., Sun. brunch only. **Subway:** A, C, E to 14th St.

Jean Claude $25 & Under   BISTRO/FRENCH

137 Sullivan St. (between Prince and Houston Sts.)   (212) 475-9232

The dining room is authentically Parisian, with the scent of Gitanes and the sound of French in the air. For these low prices you don't expect to find appetizers like seared sea scallops with roasted beets or main courses like roasted monkfish with savoy cabbage, olives and onions. **Price range:** Entrees, $12–$16. Cash only. **Meals:** D. **Subway:** C, E to Spring St.; N, R to Prince St.; F, to Broadway–Lafayette St.

Jean Georges ☆☆☆☆ $$$$ NEW AMERICAN

Trump Hotel, 1 Central Park West (at 60th St.)   (212) 299-3900

Chef and co-owner Jean-Georges Vongerichten has created an entirely new kind of four-star restaurant. He has examined all the details that make dining luxurious, and refined them for an American audience. Even if the restaurant has become as much a meeting place for the rich and powerful as a culinary showcase, Jean Georges remains deeply impressive. And while some restaurants are more concerned with who is in the room than what is on the plate, the people at Jean Georges neither fawn nor intimidate; all over the dining room, waiters bend over the food, carving or pouring, intent only on their guests' pleasure. **Price range:** Prix-fixe and tasting menus, $45–$115. **Meals:** L, D. Closed Sun. **Subway:** A, B, C, D, 1, 9 to 59th St.

Jean-Luc ☆ $$ BISTRO/FRENCH

507 Columbus Ave. (near 84th St.)   (212) 712-1700

New York has lots of technically correct bistros, but they often lack a certain something: personality. Night after night, Edmond Kleefield, better known as Jean-Luc, meets and greets, circulates from table to table, and holds forth on any topic that comes into his head. The noise level can be deafening. The "mouthwatering" tournedos of beef really does deserve special billing. Pan-seared magret of duck carries a recommendation, as does the poussin with candied root vegetables. **Price range:** Entrees, $17–$25. **Meals:** D. Closed Mon. **Subway:** 1, 2, B, C to 86th St.

Jefferson ☆☆ $$$ NEW AMERICAN/ASIAN

121 W. 10th St. (near Greenwich Ave.)   (212) 255-3333

Nowhere has fusion cuisine put down stronger roots than at Jefferson. The cuisine, served in a spacious dining room, is billed as New American. This America thrives on immigrant energies. In culinary terms, that means ravioli made from edamame, with ginkgo nuts and mascarpone cheese, or scallops crusted in rice shavings and dressed with a white miso tangerine sauce. The menu includes a gentle spin on fairly traditional dishes. At a time when restaurants all over town are simplifying and, in many cases, dumbing down, Jefferson has smartened up. **Price range:** Entrees, $20–$28. **Meals:** D. Closed Sun. **Subway:** 1, 9 to Christopher St.

Jewel Bako $25 & Under   SUSHI

239 E. 5th St. (between Second and Third Aves.)   (212) 979-1012

The first taste at Jewel Bako will leave no doubt that here is great sushi. Add the welcoming charm of the owners and the warmth of the chef, and you come close to the ideal for a neighborhood sushi bar. The chef focuses on the freshest and best ingredients; order à la carte, allowing him to guide you. Each piece of sushi seems an almost perfect unit of rice and fish, often with a dot of complementary flavoring, like an almost smoky vinegar jelly, a touch of hot chili or a breezy hint of shiso. There is a refreshing dessert of stewed mission figs, served cool in a sweetened white wine and shiso broth. **Price range:** Sushi and sashimi selections, $12–$29; à la carte, $3–$4.50 a piece; some specials higher. **Meals:** D. Closed Sun. **Subway:** F to Second Ave.

Joe Allen $$ NEW AMERICAN

326 W. 46th St. (between Eighth and Ninth Aves.)   (212) 581-6464

Chili and celebrities in the heart of Broadway. The food's not great, but it's not expensive either. This is the place for safe, unpretentious American food in Restaurant Row. You need to reserve both before and after the theater. **Price range:** Entrees, $9–$24. **Meals:** Br, L, D. **Subway:** A, C, E to 42nd St.

Joe's Ginger $25 & Under   CHINESE

113 Mott Street (at Hester Street)   (212) 966-6613

Chinatown at its best. At Joe's Ginger four hungry souls can eat like ravenous hogs for around $100. There are two varieties of soup dumplings: pork and pork and crab. Both are delicious, but the crab version, its filling enriched by roe and as delicate beneath its topknot of pastry as a tiny cloud, is the winner by a nose. The brilliant lion's head, three pork meatballs served in a braise of dark soy sauce and surrounded by steamed baby bok choy, is reliably excellent. **Price range:** Entrees, $4–$21. **Meals:** L, D. **Subway:** 6, N, R, Q to Canal St.

Joe's Shanghai ☆☆ $ CHINESE

24 W. 56th St. (between Fifth and Sixth Aves.)   (212) 333-3868
9 Pell St. (between Mott St. and Bowery)   (212) 233-8888

These spartan restaurants serve awesome xiao lung bao—Shanghai soup dumplings, modestly listed on the menu as "steamed buns". The chef has perfected the art of wrapping hot liquid in pastry: the filling is rich, light and swimming in hot soup. Everybody orders them, but there are many other wonderful dishes, including smoked fish, strongly flavored with star anise, vegetarian duck, thin sheets of braised tofu folded like skin over mushrooms, and drunken crabs, raw marinated blue crabs with a musty, fruity flavor that is powerful and unforgettable. **Price range:** A la carte $9.50 and up. **Meals:** L, D. **Subway:** Downtown: J, M, N, Q, R, Z, 6 to Canal St. Midtown: N, R, W to Fifth Ave.

Jo Jo ☆☆☆ $$$$ NEW AMERICAN
160 E. 64th St. (between Lexington and Third Aves.)   (212) 223-5656
Jo Jo has shown, with extraordinary grace, how a restaurant can age without looking old. The place looks sumptuous; at the same time, it still has the heart of a bistro. The style of service is not overformal. The menu is a fairly short read, and the wine list makes a serious effort to please the $50 customer. Chef Jean-Georges Vongerichten's food never clamors for attention. A few signature dishes remain, including the renowned roast chicken with chickpea fries. **Price range:** Entrees, $18–$35; prix fixe and tasting menus, $20–$65. **Meals:** L,D. **Subway:** 6 to 68th St.; N, R to Lexington Ave.

Josie's $25 & Under NEW AMERICAN
300 Amsterdam Ave. (at 74th St.)   (212) 769-1212
565 Third Ave. (at 37th St.)   (212) 490-1558
Much of the food at Josie's is billed as organically raised; the surprise is that so much of the food is so good, with highlights like light potato dumplings served in a lively tomato coulis spiked with chipotle pepper, ravioli stuffed with sweet potato purée, superb grilled tuna with a wasabi glaze and wonderful gazpacho. Josie's offers many reasonably priced wines, some organic beers and freshly squeezed juices, including tart blueberry lemonade. Even the organic hot dogs are good. **Price range:** Entrees, $9.50–$16. **Meals:** L, D, LN. **Subway:** 1, 2, 3, 9 to 72nd St.; 6 to 33rd St.; 4, 5, 6, 7 to 42nd St.

Jubilee $25 & Under FRENCH
347 E. 54th St. (between First and Second Aves.)   (212) 888-3569
Small, crowded and exuberant, this is a great East Side find. It offers simple and good bistro food, like steak frites and roast chicken. The restaurant makes something of a specialty of mussels, offering them in five guises with terrific french fries or a green salad, all for reasonable prices. **Price range:** Entrees, $13.50–$24. **Meals:** L, D. **Subway:** E, F to Lexington Ave.; 6 to 51st St.

Jubilee 51 ☆ $$$ FRENCH BISTRO
329 W. 51st St. (between Eighth and Ninth Aves.)   (212) 265-7575
Jubilee 51 has the hallmarks of a classic bistro: a pressed-tin ceiling; soft lighting; and a dark and moody bar. The only thing missing is clouds of smoke. A cursory glance at the menu reveals escargots, moules, omelettes, steak frites and tarte Tatin, although there are contemporary notes like tuna tartare with miso seaweed salad. Generally the cooking is most successful when it sticks to traditional fare (like a sweet and creamy chicken liver paté). But the kitchen does

tend to overcook things, and desserts are uneven (luckily, the silken crème brûlée is everything you could hope for). **Price range:** Entrees $19–$27. **Meals:** L (Tue.–Fri.), D, Sat. -Sun. brunch. **Subway:** 1, 9 to 50th St.

Kai   ☆ ☆ $$$$ JAPANESE
822 Madison Ave. (at 69th St.)   (212) 988-7277

Kai is short for kaiseki, the traditional meal of refined little bites that grew up around the tea ceremony. The simplest of the three prix fixe formulas here includes a cup of fragrant, floral jasmine tea, a small plate of tiny bites (deai) that might include rich slices of duck or sliced bamboo shoots, soup, and a small plate of sashimi with freshly grated wasabi. The executive chef has grafted French ideas onto kaiseki cuisine, and he has done so with an elegant hand. Yogan yaki, small, dice-size cubes of aged prime beef, bears a family resemblance to filet mignon with béarnaise sauce. Chilled soba noodles, made at the restaurant, always round out the meal, followed by desserts and green tea. **Price range:** Prix fixe $55–$85. **Meals:** L, D. Closed Sun. **Subway:** 6 to 68th St.

Kang Suh   ☆ ☆ $$ KOREAN
1250 Broadway (at 32nd St.)   (212) 564-6845

This is the most accessible of the Korean restaurants in the small Koreatown locally known as Sam Ship Iga (32nd St.). Downstairs is a sushi bar, upstairs a huge menu of Korean dishes. Two things make this special: it's open 24 hours and you can grill your own food over live charcoal at the table. **Price range:** Entrees, $6.99–$30. **Meals:** Open 24 hours. **Subway:** B, D, F, N, Q, S, R to 34th St.

Katsu-Hama $25 & Under   JAPANESE
11 E. 47th St. (between Madison and Fifth Aves.)   (212) 758-5909

Katsu-Hama doesn't offer much in the way of atmosphere or creature comforts, but it is an authentic Japanese experience. To enter it, you need to walk through a takeout sushi restaurant (Sushi-Tei) and pass through a curtain divider; there, you encounter an almost entirely Japanese crowd who've come for the restaurant's specialty: tonkatsu, or deep-fried pork cutlets. The best variation is unadorned, dipped into a special condiment that resembles freshly made Worcestershire sauce blended with sesame seeds. **Price range:** $8.95–$13.95, including soup and rice. **Meals:** L, D. **Subway:** S, 4, 5, 6, 7 to 42nd St.

Katz's Deli $ DELI
205 E. Houston St. (at Ludlow St.)   (212) 254-2246

A wonderful Lower East Side artifact, originator of the World War II slogan, "Send a salami to your boy in the Army," and one of the few delis that still carves pastrami and corned beef by hand, which makes for delicious sandwiches. **Price range:** Entrees, $5–$10.95. **Meals:** B, Br, L, D, LN. **Subway:** F to Second Ave.

Kittichai   ☆ ☆ $$ THAI
60 Thompson St. (at Broome St.)   (212) 219-2000

Orchids twist in an ersatz spider web overhead, buoyant votive candles skitter across the surface of a dark reflecting pool and dim lighting makes everyone look good. Delicious, colorful cocktails are carried by servers wearing fetching pajamalike black outfits. Luckily, the gustatory pleasures at Kittichai rise almost to the level of the visual ones. The restaurant's Thai soul asserts itself with kaffir lime and lemon grass, Thai basil and Thai chili peppers, coriander and coconut. Among the best entrees is a divinely moist Chilean sea bass under a caramelized sheen of palm sugar and red curry paste. **Price range:** Entrees $14–$27. **Meals:** L, D. **Subway:** A, C, E, 1, 9 to Canal St.; N, R, W to Prince St.

Kori $25 & Under   KOREAN
253 Church St. (near Leonard St.)   (212) 334-0908

Kori succeeds in merging East and West, old and new. It seems a wholly personal expression of its owner and chef, Kori Kim: up-to-date and appealing to Americans but tied to Korean traditions. She learned to cook in a big, traditional Korean family in Seoul, but it is hard to imagine Ms. Kim serving food at home as polished as her dubu sobegi, a tofu croquette stuffed with savory ground Asian mushrooms and beautifully presented like a rectangular gift box. Galbi jim is a wonderful stew of short ribs with sweet dates, chestnuts and turnips. **Price range:** Entrees, $12.95–$21. **Meals:** L, D, LN. **Subway:** 1, 9 to Franklin St.

Kuruma Zushi   ☆ ☆ ☆ $$$$ SUSHI
7 E. 47th St. (between Fifth and Madison Aves.)   (212) 317-2802

Few restaurants are more welcoming to diners who do not speak Japanese, and few chefs are better at introducing people to sushi than Toshiro Uezu, proprietor of Kuruma Zushi. One of New York City's most venerable sushi bars, it serves only sushi and sashimi and is, admittedly, expensive. But after eating at Kuruma Zushi it is very hard to go back to ordinary fish. **Price range:** Entrees, $25–$100. **Meals:** L, D. Closed Sun. **Subway:** S, 4, 5, 6, 7 to 42nd St.

La Grenouille   ☆ ☆ ☆ $$$$ FRENCH
3 E. 52nd St. (near Fifth Ave.)   (212) 752-1495

La Grenouille is the most frustrating restaurant in New York. This is not because the food is bad or the service unpleasant. Just the opposite, in fact, the restaurant displays such flashes of brilliance that each failure is a deep disappointment. It is also one of the few New York restaurants that still serves many of the French classics, including quenelles de brochette, perfectly grilled Dover sole and the best souffles in New York. Each meal offers moments of joyful excellence, but many dishes are entirely forgettable. You can count on a good meal at La Grenouille. If you're lucky, however, you may get a great one. **Price range:** Three course prix-fixe dinner $80; lunch $45, Tasting menu $100. **Meals:** L, D. Closed Sun., Mon. **Subway:** E, F to Fifth Ave.

La Locanda dei Vini $25 & Under   ITALIAN
737 Ninth Ave. (near 50th St.)   (212) 258-2900

La Locanda serves pastas and meat dishes that stand out for their simplicity and flavor, and offers an enticing and unusually arranged wine list. Try one of the large and alluring salads, like insalata rifredda, essentially an Italian version of the frisée salad. Pastas can be excellent. Sliced leg of lamb, served like all the main courses with roasted potatoes and sauted broccoli rape, is past the point of pink, but the sauce imbues the meat with flavor. The same is true of veal shoulder. La Locanda also makes its own desserts. **Price range:** Pastas and entrees, $11–$21.50. **Meals:** L, D. **Subway:** C, E to 50th St.

La Nacional $25 & Under   SPANISH
239 West 14th St. (between Seventh and Eighth Aves.)   (212) 243-9308
La Nacional has no signs. The doorway to the street is unmarked, and you enter a cluttered hallway and stand before an equally unmarked interior door. The small rustic dining room serves tapas and a few main courses, including paella. Main courses are simple enough: a chewy but flavorful steak that is about as good as a $15 steak gets, a clutch of tiny lamb chops bathed in garlic, an equally garlicky codfish in vinegar and oil and a soothing seafood casserole, served with a saffron-scented broth, which is an excellent approximation of bouillabaisse. La Nacional's paella is as beautiful to look at as it is to eat. **Price range:** Entrees, $13–$15. **Meals:** L, D. **Subway:** L to 6th Ave.

Landmarc   ☆ $$ AMERICAN BISTRO
179 W. Broadway (at Leonard St.)   (212) 343-3883
Landmarc is a comfortable neighborhood haunt where nothing is high concept. The space is comfortably dim, which softens its industrial edges. If you are in a bistro mood, there is foie gras terrine, and if you're hankering for American fare, there is a grilled pork chop with spinach and apples. Simple, competent cooking goes a long way. There's a lengthy menu and a wine list with a strong selection of half bottles. **Price range:** Entrees $12–$30. **Meals:** L (Mon.–Fri.), D (Mon.–Sat.). Closed Sun. **Subway:** 1, 9 to Franklin St.

La Nonna   ☆ $$$ ITALIAN
133 W. 13th St. (between Sixth and Seventh Aves.)   (212) 741-3663
La Nonna is a warm, inviting place with a no-nonsense menu of thoroughly traditional Tuscan dishes, with an emphasis on meat and fish roasted or grilled in a wood-burning oven. A moist and tender marinated Cornish hen makes the best advertisement for the oven, but pasta turns out to be the most dependable category on the menu. A standout is strozzapreti, slightly sticky dumplings of Swiss chard and spinach firmed up with ricotta and Parmesan cheese, then doused with butter and sage. **Price range:** Entrees, $16.50–$24.50. **Meals:** L, D. **Subway:** F, 1, 2, 3, 9 to 14th St.

La Palapa $25 & Under   MEXICAN
77 St. Marks Pl. (at First Ave.)   (212) 777-2537
This bright and cheerful restaurant shows off the regional glories of Mexico rather than the familiar one-dimensional margarita-fueled Tex-Mex dishes. Tacos are authentically Mexican, made with soft corn tortillas, and are also artful, with fillings like chili-rubbed chicken, shrimp in adobo sauce or mild poblano chili with epazote and onions. The real excitement comes with the main courses, like thin slices of duck breast, fanned out in a wonderful sesame

mole, or chicken enchiladas in a soupy tomatillo sauce that is very spicy. For dessert, try rich Mexican chocolate ice cream and a spicy chili-laced peach sorbet. **Price range:** Entrees, $12–$19. **Meals:** L, D, LN. **Subway:** 6 to Astor Pl.

La Palapa Rockola $25 & Under   MEXICAN
359 Avenue of the Americas (at West 4th St.)   (212) 243-6870
With brick walls and wood beams, dim lighting and photos devoted to actresses of the golden age of Mexican cinema, La Palapa Rockola has a different mood and feel. The food is excellent. You won't go wrong starting with a taco, and chicken enchiladas with tomatillo sauce are bright and lively, topped with white onion that adds a sweet harmony. The barbacoa de cordero (lamb shank) is cooked slowly until the meat is soft as jam and flavored with anise-scented avocado leaves and mild ancho chilies. Given the wide variety of tequilas on the drinks menu, most patrons seem able to rise to the festive atmosphere. **Price range:** Entrees, $14–$20. **Meals:** L, D. **Subway:** A, C, E, F, V to West 4th St.

Lavagna $25 & Under   MEDITERRANEAN
545 E. 5th St. (at Ave. B)   (212) 979-1005
Lavagna's food is fresh and generous, with honest, straightforward flavors. The simple rectangular dining room is casual and inviting, but can get loud when it's crowded. Pastas are best, both simple dishes like rigatoni with crumbled fennel sausage, peas, tomatoes and cream, and more complicated ones like fresh pappardelle with rabbit stew. Cacciucco, the Tuscan fish soup scented with saffron and anise, and served with mussels, cockles and chunks of fish, is a great value. **Price range:** Entrees, $11–$16.50. Cash only. **Meals:** D, LN. Closed Sun. **Subway:** F to Second Ave.

Layla $$$ MEDITERRANEAN/MIDDLE EASTERN
211 West Broadway (at Franklin St.)   (212) 431-0700
For months after Sept. 11, Layla remained closed, but finally reopened in the spring with a new chef and a new menu. Now the attitude of the Middle East is conveyed more through spices and flavorings than the usual repertory of regional dishes. Alongside the chunky hummus and earthy merguez, served with slivers of dates, are appetizers like pistou, the Provencal vegetable soup, and fried sardines. Among the main courses, dishes that you would have expected to find at the old Layla, like a Moroccan tagine of duck with couscous and toasted pistachios, are supplemented by scallop-size cylinders of monkfish, wrapped in prosciutto, with pesto-flavored risotto. **Price range:** Entrees, $20–$29. **Meals:** L, D. **Subway:** 1, 9 to Franklin St.

Le Bernardin   ☆☆☆☆ $$$$ FRENCH/SEAFOOD
155 W. 51st St. (between Sixth and Seventh Aves.)   (212) 489-1515
Most restaurants grow into their stars. Not Le Bernardin: at the ripe old age of three months, it had all four stars bestowed upon it. The restaurant has been in the spotlight ever since. Its hallmark is impeccably fresh fish cooked with respect and simplicity. Most of the problems that plague other great establish-

ments are solved here: there are no rude reservations takers, no endless waits for tables, no overcrowding in the dining room. The waiters know their jobs and keep their distance. Dinners are appropriately paced. When you reserve a table at Le Bernardin, you can count on being seated promptly, served beautifully and fed fabulously. Le Bernardin once showed New York how to eat fish; now it is showing the city how a four-star restaurant should behave. **Price range:** Dinner prix-fixe, $77; tasting menu, $95–$125. **Meals:** L, D. Closed Sun. **Subway:** N, R to 49th St.; 1, 9 to 50th St.

Le Cirque 2000   ☆☆☆ $$$$ FRENCH/ITALIAN
New York Palace Hotel, 455 Madison Ave. (between 50th and 51st Sts.)
(212) 303-7788

As pure spectacle, there is nothing in New York like Le Cirque. First and foremost, it is a social institution and an emblem of status. Diners check in, have their self-esteem validated by Sirio Maccioni and settle in for a sumptuous evening surrounded by their own kind. More than any restaurant, Le Cirque is a one-man show. Diners put themselves in Mr. Maccioni's practiced hands, not the kitchen's. The menu moves back and forth between two poles: an almost rustic simplicity and sometimes heavy, lavishly presented fancy food. One of Le Cirque's signature dishes, black sea bass wrapped in sheets of crisp, paper-thin potato and lavished with Barolo sauce, is still excellent, and simpler dishes deliver, like beef short ribs, a mighty cube of savory meat in a rich reduction sauce. At dessert time, ridiculous sugar sculptures and chocolate trees make their way to tables where diners grin like kids at a birthday party. **Price range:** Entrees, $28–$39. **Meals:** L, D. **Subway:** 6 to 51st St.; E, F to Lexington Ave.

Le Colonial   ☆☆ $$ VIETNAMESE
149 E. 57th St. (between Lexington and Third Aves.)   (212) 752-0808.
Vietnamese cuisine, as interpreted here, is sedate Asian fare that is more delicate than Chinese food, less spicy than Thai and notable mostly for its abundance of vegetables and its absence of grease. Spring rolls at Le Colonial are so delicate you tend to forget that they are fried. The beef salad, the only really spicy dish here, is excellent. **Price range:** Entrees, $14–$23. **Meals:** L, D. **Subway:** 4, 5, 6 to 59th St.; N, R, W to Lexington Ave.

Le Gigot $25 & Under   FRENCH
18 Cornelia St. (between 4th and Bleecker Sts.)   (212) 627-3737
This little restaurant pulses with the welcoming spirit of a Parisian hangout. The Provence-inflected food adds to the illusion, with excellent bistro fare like leg of lamb in a red wine reduction; lamb stew; endive salad with apples, walnuts and Roquefort, and rounds of baguette smeared with goat cheese and smoky tapenade. The best desserts are the sweet, moist, caramelized tarte Tatin, the excellent bananas flambé, and the great little cheese course, not usually available in a restaurant like this. **Price range:** Entrees, $12–$17. AE only. **Meals:** Br, L, D. Closed Mon. **Subway:** A, C, E, F, S to W. 4th St.

Le Madri ☆☆ **$$$** ITALIAN

168 W. 18th St. (between Sixth and Seventh Aves.) (212) 727-8022

Le Madri opened in 1989 to a great deal of heat and fanfare. Those stylish days are long gone. And yet, Le Madri has evolved rather than ossified. The food is better than ever. The dining room is cozier and quieter. The menu combines a respect for Italian traditions with an international sensibility. Most of the pastas are distinct and lively. The best entrees are an impressive prime rib of beef and an outstanding grilled rack of lamb. **Price range:** Entrees, $14–$38. **Meals:** L, D. **Subway:** 1, 9 to 18th St.

Lentini ☆ **$$$** ITALIAN

1562 Second Avenue (at 81st St.) (212) 628-3131

Location and atmosphere make this a neighborhood restaurant. Some of the dishes do, too. But look more closely at the menu, scan the ambitious wine list and its equally ambitious prices, and it becomes clear that Lentini wants to be more than a nice little local standby. Pastas are a very good bet. Tomato sauces can be light or so concentrated that you can almost slice them like terrine. The swordfish, miraculously, comes out perfectly moist. **Price range:** Entrees, $18–$30. **Meals:** D. **Subway:** 4, 5, 6 to 86th St.

Le Périgord ☆☆ **$$$$** FRENCH

405 E. 52nd St. (at First Ave.) (212) 755-6244

Le Perigord is a French restaurant the way French restaurants used to be. The waiters, well on in years, wear white jackets. The even more senior captains wear tuxedos. On the dessert trolley you know that you will find floating island, chocolate mousse and tarte Tatin. Some nights, the restaurant can seem like a cross between Fawlty Towers and Katz's Delicatessen. The diners do not seem to mind. Inside Le Perigord, they can swaddle themselves in a quietly civilized atmosphere, a million miles removed from the tumult of the city outside. **Price range:** Three-course prix-fixe, $57. **Meals:** L, D. **Subway:** 6 to 51st St.; E, F to Lexington Ave.

Les Halles Downtown ☆ **$$$** FRENCH

15 John St. (near Broadway) (212) 285-8585

The small white floor tiles and the stamped-tin ceiling feel as New York as the Bowery, and a long mahogany bar along one wall, with drinkers hunched over their beers and aperitifs, seems in keeping with the true brasserie spirit. The benchmark dishes, the ones that would be criminal to botch, come through with flying colors. The côte de boeuf is the king of meats at Les Halles. It is intended for two, and it may be the most impressively succulent slab of beef on the menu. Mussels are also a feature, and fish and chips, somewhat surprisingly, score high. **Price range:** Entrees, $10–$26. **Meals:** L, D. **Subway:** A, C, J, M, Z, 2, 3, 4, 5 to Fulton St.—Broadway-Nassau.

Le Tableau $25 & Under   MEDITERRANEAN
511 E. 5th St. (between Aves. A and B)   (212) 260-1333

This simple storefront restaurant turns out superb Mediterranean fare. Unconventional dishes stimulate the mouth with new flavors and textures, like a spicy calamari tagine that incorporates anchovies, hummus and olive purée. Main courses are familiar, yet they are presented in inventive ways. Desserts can be excellent, like a mellow pumpkin bread pudding, a honey-nut tart and an apple tajine. The dining room is dimly lighted with candles and can become noisy, especially when a jazz trio begins playing in the late evening. **Price range:** Entrees, $9.50–$14.75. Cash only. **Meals:** Br, D. Closed Mon. **Subway:** F to Second Ave.

Lever House Restaurant   ☆☆ $$$$ NEW AMERICAN
390 Park Ave. (entrance on E. 53rd St.)   (212) 888-2700

It took nerve to put a restaurant in Lever House, for great architecture can be tough on a restaurant. But amazingly, the restaurant holds its own. In a reckless gamble, Marc Newson, the designer, more or less thumbed his nose at the severely elegant architecture around him, creating a retro-futuristic dining room that is calculated to keep patrons slightly on edge. The kitchen, by contrast, sticks to a clean, New American style. Tuna carpaccio with wasabi creme fraiche may not be the most original dish in town, but this rendition is perfection. Wild salmon is prepared with a simple herb butter, earthy mushrooms and sweet carrots, and the result is a dish that cannot be improved upon. **Price range:** Entrees $26–$42. **Meals:** L (Mon.–Fri.), D. **Subway:** 6 to 51st St.; E, V to Lexington Ave./53rd St.

Le Zie 2000 $25 & Under   ITALIAN
172 Seventh Ave. (at 20th St.)   (212) 206-8686

This modest, often crowded little trattoria offers some terrific Venetian dishes, like an inspired salad that features pliant octopus and soft potatoes acting in precise textural counterpoint. The chef has a sure hand with pastas like rigatoni with rosemary, served al dente in a perfectly proportioned sauce. Risotto with squid is also superbly cooked. Striped bass fillet with fennel and white beans is moist and wonderfully flavorful. Desserts are a weak point. **Price range:** Entrees, $8.50–$16.95. Cash only. **Meals:** L, D. **Subway:** 1, 9 to 23rd St.

Le Zinc   ☆ $$ BISTRO
139 Duane St. (between Church St. and West Broadway)   (212) 513-0001

The low-key bistro menu, with an Asian accent here and a down-home touch there, qualifies as upmarket Manhattan comfort food. It's solid, reliable and reassuring, served in portions so abundant that appetizers often seem like entrees in training. And the price is right. Le Zinc offers a menu-within-a-menu of charcuterie, and there's no doubt about it, the terrines here are superior. Main courses make the usual bistro stops, with competently executed dishes like skirt steak in a red wine reduction and skate with brown butter and capers. **Note well:** Le Zinc takes no reservations. **Price range:** Entrees, $12–$19. **Meals:** Br, L, D, LN. **Subway:** 1, 9 to Franklin St.

Le Zoo $25 & Under
BISTRO/FRENCH

314 W. 11th St. (at Greenwich St.)   (212) 620-0393

This little restaurant can get crowded, loud and zoolike, but the food is good and often creative. You might reasonably expect to find steak frites and pâté de campagne, but there are instead such combinations as monkfish with honey and lime sauce. The dessert selection is small and classically French, offering satisfying choices. The restaurant does not take reservations. **Price range:** Entrees, $12.50–$16. **Meals:** D, LN. **Subway:** 1, 9 to Christopher St.

L'Impero   ☆ ☆ ☆ $$$
ITALIAN

45 Tudor City Pl. (near 42nd St.)   (212) 599-5045

L'Impero digs deeply into the robust, generous spirit of the Italian countryside, turning out dishes full of flavors that are joyous and highly refined, served in a dining room that emanates a gracious warmth. Though you can opt for a conventional appetizer-main course approach, L'Impero's $48 tasting menu is great. Flavors are loud and assertive in the pastas. Spaghetti with sea urchin is well worth trying. Main courses quietly satisfy rather than excite. **Price range:** Entrees, $16–$27. **Meals:** L, D. Closed Sun. **Subway:** 4, 5, 6, 7 to 42nd St.

Lombardi's $25 & Under
PIZZA

32 Spring St. (between Mulberry and Mott Sts.)   (212) 941-7994

The dining room reeks of history at this reincarnation of the original Lombardi's, which is often credited with introducing pizza to New York City. The old-fashioned coal-oven pizza is terrific, with a light, thin, crisp and gloriously smoky crust topped with fine mozzarella and tomatoes. The garlicky clam pizza is exceptional. **Price range:** Pizzas, $10.50–$20. Cash only. **Meals:** L, D, LN. **Subway:** 6 to Spring St.

Loreley $25 & Under
GERMAN

7 Rivington St. (at Bowery)   (212) 253-7077

Loreley calls itself a biergarten, but the "garten" part is a bit of a fraud: the only green is on the umbrellas advertising German beers. Loreley is a hymn to carbohydrates and fat: well-made mashed potatoes; excellent sour bread; thick, springy spaetzle noodles; and juicy sausages with just the right snap. Many menu items are variations on the sausage theme: plump bratwurst, slim hot-dog-like würstchen, even "currywurst," a Berlin street-food specialty of sliced bratwurst covered with a ketchup-based, curry-spiced sauce. Seasonal or not, two rich stews are the best things on the menu at Loreley: a creamy veal goulash and classic chicken paprika. **Price range:** Entrees, $9–$17. **Meals:** L, D. **Subway:** 6 to Spring St.

Lozoo   ☆ $$
CHINESE

140 W. Houston (near Sullivan St.)   (646) 602-8888

Lozoo, a coolly contemporary restaurant and lounge that specializes in refined Shanghai cooking, is idiosyncratic, ambitious and nervy. Lozoo, whose name means green tea in Mandarin, presents the kind of dishes that might be served at a banquet in Shanghai. The play of textures is complex and deceptive. One of the best appetizers is baby escargots in crispy tofu. Also try the poached pork belly with marinated bamboo strips and fat tsai, a fuzzy black tree fungus. **Price range:** Entrees, $15–$20. **Meals:** D. **Subway:** 1, 9 to Houston St.

Luca $25 & Under   ITALIAN
1712 First Ave. (near 89th St.)   (212) 987-9260
This superb neighborhood Italian restaurant is spare but good-looking, with beige walls and rustic floor tiles. The menu offers dishes skillfully cooked to order that emphasize lusty flavors. The antipasto for two is very generous and very good. Pastas, like bigoli with a buttery shrimp-and-radicchio sauce, are terrific, as are main courses like grilled calamari and crisp grilled Cornish hen. **Price range:** Entrees, $8.50–$19.95. **Meals:** D. **Subway:** 4, 5, 6 to 86th St.

Lunchbox Food Company $25 & Under   DINER/AMERICAN
357 West St. (near Clarkson St.)   (646) 230-9466
The Lunchbox Food Company is one fine-looking diner, yet this is no humble coffee shop. Lunchbox takes a connoisseur's attitude toward ingredients and preparations, but offers simple, tasty food for reasonable prices. Partisans of the classic tuna sandwich might sneer at the fancy-pants tuna blended with sherry vinaigrette and layered with roasted tomatoes and almond-arugula pesto on grilled olive bread. But what sounds overly complex is pure pleasure in the mouth. Lunchbox doesn't mess around with its burger. **Price range:** Breakfast, $1.75–$5.75. Lunch, $8–$9. Dinner entress, $15–$19. **Meals:** B, Br, L, D, LN. **Subway:** 1, 9 to Houston St.

Lupa $25 & Under   ITALIAN
170 Thompson St. (near Houston St.)   (212) 982-5089.
Crowded and clamorous, Lupa serves intensely delicious Roman trattoria food. Appetizers range from the classic to the bizarre: Prosciutto di Parma arrives in thin, nutty slices, a reminder of why this combination became popular in the first place. Pastas are simple and tasty, and saltimbocca, thin slices of veal layered with prosciutto, is good and juicy. The resident wine expert takes great delight in directing you to the perfect choice on Lupa's 130-bottle wine list, and the best dessert choice is something from the cheese tray. **Price range:** Entrees, $9–$15. **Meals:** L, D. Closed Mon. **Subway:** F, S to Broadway–Lafayette St.

Luzia's $25 & Under   PORTUGUESE
429 Amsterdam Ave. (between 80th and 81st Sts.)   (212) 595-2000
Luzia's began life as a takeout place. Then the neighborhood fell in love with the cozy restaurant and started staying for dinner. Luzia's serves wonderful Portuguese comfort food, like caldo verde, shrimp pie and cataplana, the soupy stew of pork and clams. It also produces remarkably delicious non-Portuguese dishes, like beef brisket that is tender and peppery. Luzia's has a great flan, and a nice list of Portuguese wines. **Price range:** Entrees, $20–$25. **Meals:** Br, L, D. Closed Mon. **Subway:** 1, 9 to 79th St.

Maia   **$25 & Under**   TURKISH
98 Avenue B (at Sixth Street)   (212) 358-1166
This Turkish meyhane (literally, "wine house") recreates the larger cultural
chemistry of a successful watering-hole back home—the refreshment, but also
the music, the dance and the social intercourse. The meze are dainty and piquant
enough to tease you into lingering under the ceiling fans, waiting for the band or
the belly dancer to show. They also serve dishes like the Circassian cerkez
tavugu—poached chicken breast smothered in a sauce of coarsely ground walnuts, garlic and bread—a rustic dish whose subtlety is a soothing counterpoint to
the spicier meze. Another standout is kuzu "karsky," a thick cut of roasted lamb
loin. **Price range:** Entrees, $12–$21. **Meals:** D. **Subway:** F to Second Ave.

Mama's Food Shop   **$25 & Under**   AMERICAN
200 E. 3rd St. (between Aves. A and B)   (212) 777-4425
A simple takeout shop and restaurant where you point at what you want and
they dish it up. But the food is outstanding: grilled salmon, fried chicken and
meatloaf. Vegetable side dishes are especially good, like brussels sprouts, carrots,
beets and mashed potatoes. **Price range:** Entrees, $7–$8.50. Cash only.
Meals: L, D. Closed Sun. **Subway:** F to Second Ave.

Mandler's   **$25 & Under**   SANDWICHES
26 East 17th St. (between Fifth Ave. and Broadway)   (212) 255-8999
Mandler's serves European-style sausage sandwiches—and serves them fast. It is
simply a boxy room with a very high ceiling and a counter in the rear, but it
combines functionality with a certain industrial style. Each order requires multiple choices. Aside from a dozen sausages, you must select from five kinds of
bread, 11 toppings and seven sauces. Most of the sausages are almost delicate,
gently but insistently flavored. Peppadew is the trademarked brand name for a
sauce made of South African peppers that are simultaneously sweet and spicy
and seem to improve most of the sausages. **Price range:** Entrees, $8–$11. **Meals:**
L, D. **Subway:** 4, 5, 6, N, R, Q, L to Union Square.

Manhattan Ocean Club   ☆☆   **$$$$**   SEAFOOD
57 W. 58th St. (between Fifth and Sixth Aves.)   (212) 371-7777
Tony, comfortable and trim as a luxury yacht, this is the steakhouse of fish restaurants. Eating here is an indulgence, and the prices are high. Soups like the
creamy clam chowder are less expensive but no less delicious. Simple preparations are the most appealing but one of the best dishes is the oysters buried in
tiny morels covered with cream and baked in the shell. The dish is an edible def-
inition of luxury. Desserts are almost all big and sweet. **Price range:** Entrees,
$22.50–$31. **Meals:** L, D. **Subway:** N, R, W to Fifth Ave.

March   ☆☆☆   **$$$$**   NEW AMERICAN
405 E. 58th St. (near First Ave.)   (212) 754-6272
When everything is clicking, there are few places better than this cozy,
antique-filled town house. The usual three-course restaurant menu is replaced

with one that allows you to choose either four or seven smaller courses. At March, no dish is more than a few bites, but those are so pretty and powerful that you are almost always satisfied. The most popular items are Beggars' purses, diminutive dumplings filled with caviar, truffles or foie gras. **Price range:** Lunch prix fixe, $39. Dinner prix fixe, $72–126. **Meals:** L, D. **Subway:** 4, 5, 6 to 59th St.; N, R to Lexington Ave.

Marseille   ☆ ☆   **$$$**   FRENCH/MEDITERRANEAN
630 Ninth Ave. (near 44th St.)   (212) 333-3410
Marseille, named for France's most Arab-influenced city, is a spacious, confi-dent-feeling brasserie on the western edge of the theater district, with blue Moroccan floor tiles and apricot-colored walls. The chef has a fondness for couscous, preserved lemon, dates and lamb, ingredients that he uses for local color rather than in any systematic way. He goes flat out in a very rich seafood lasagna layered with crab meat, cockles and mussels in a buttery mussel sauce; also excellent is roasted chicken, marinated in olive oil, garlic and smoked paprika. For dessert, try the renowned crunchy peanut butter tart. **Price range:** Entrees, $16–$24; tasting menu, $65. **Meals:** D. **Subway:** A, C, E to 42nd St.

Marumi   **$25 & Under**   JAPANESE/SUSHI
546 La Guardia Pl. (between 3rd and Bleecker Sts.)   (212) 979-7055
This versatile, reliable Japanese restaurant near N.Y.U. offers a cross-section of casual Japanese dining. The service is swift, efficient and charming and will even go the extra mile in preventing bad choices. It's rare that you get such an interesting assortment of sushi at an inexpensive restaurant, like mirugai, or geoduck clam. Other worthwhile dishes are broiled eel, noodle soups and the economic bento box meals. **Price range:** Entrees, $9–$15. **Meals:** L, D. **Subway:** A, C, E, F, S to W. 4th St.

Mas   ☆   **$$$**   FRENCH
39 Downing St. (at Bedford St.)   (212) 255-1790
Mas, which serves seasonal, French-influenced food, has the tantalizing aura of a clandestine discovery. The menu emphasizes organic meat and produce from local or regional providers. The vegetables are reliably and wonderfully fresh, but the dishes into which they are woven are less certain propositions. While some work beautifully, others are poorly executed, like the rubbery vegetarian terrine. But there are real flashes of excellence, like the astonishingly moist squab baked in a clay shell. The wine list is serious, and the selection of arti-sanal cheeses is impressive. **Price range:** Entrees $26–$34. **Meals:** D. Closed Sun. **Subway:** 1, 9 to Houston St.

Masa   ☆ ☆ ☆   **$$$$**   JAPANESE
In the Time Warner Center, Columbus Circle, 4th floor   (212) 823-9800
Masa is New York's most expensive restaurant, and dining here is like visiting a secret clubhouse. The room is quiet and self-contained, with just 26 seats. Behind the sushi bar is Masayoshi Takayama, who welcomes you warmly. There

is no menu, so courses just begin appearing. After a parade of salads and cooked foods, the sushi begins to arrive. Sometimes it is a wisp of halibut brushed with nikiri sauce. Or calamari, sprinkled with sea salt, and yuzu. All of it is pristine, vibrant and utterly delicious. A large part of the experience is watching Mr. Takayama work; he never loses pace with your meal, even though he is serving everyone in the room. You must request a seat at the sushi bar. Service can be more slipshod at the tables, and they offer none of Mr. Takayama's splendid theater and lasting charm. Our verdict is four stars when dining at the sushi bar and three stars at the tables. **Price range:** $300 prix-fixe. **Meals:** L, D. **Subway:** 1, 9, A, B, C, D to 59th St./Columbus Circle.

Matsuri ☆☆ $$$ JAPANESE

In the Maritime Hotel, 369 W. 16th St. (212) 243-6400

By tradition, Japanese cuisine calls for a contemplative setting. But Matsuri pretty much throws all that out the window. Youthful and exuberant, and stylish as all get-out, it occupies a warehouse-size basement that feels as much like a club as it does a restaurant. The visuals are impressive. Huge paper lanterns, crazily squashed and lopsided, hang from a vaulted ceiling; the walls are faced with lustrous jade-green ceramic tiles. Most of the menu is dedicated to traditional sushi and sashimi, with nearly 30 species of fish, including shad and pink snapper. The star appetizer is a small bowl of crunchy lotus-root slices braised in a thick sake-soy sauce. The sake selection is magnificent. **Price range:** Sushi and sashimi $5–$7 per piece; entrees $12–$23. **Meals:** D. **Subway:** A, C, E, L, 1, 2, 3, 9 to 14th St.

Max $25 & Under ITALIAN

51 Ave. B (near 4th St.) (212) 539-0111

Max's draw is exactly what has always attracted people to neighborhood Italian restaurants: well-prepared food, served with warmth. Best of all, Max is cheap. Fettuccine al sugo Toscano has a wonderfully mellow meat sauce with layers of flavor that unfold in the mouth, while rigatoni Napoletano is served southern Italian style, with meatballs and sausages left intact in the sauce. Order the sauce on the side of the Neopolitan-style meatloaf, because the meatloaf is fascinating, stuffed with mozzarella, hard-boiled egg and prosciutto, making for a savory, moist and delicious combination. **Price range:** Entrees, $8.95–$14.95. Cash only. **Meals:** L, D, LN. **Subway:** F to Second Ave.

Maya ☆☆ $$$ MEXICAN/TEX-MEX

1191 First Ave. (between 64th and 65th Sts.) (212) 585-1818

Some of New York's most interesting Mexican food is served in this bright, festive but often noisy room. Try some of the more unusual dishes, like rock shrimp ceviche, seafood salad, and roasted corn soup with huitlacoche dumpling. The most impressive main courses are chicken mole (the dark sauce is truly complex) and pipian de puerco, grilled pork marinated in tamarind and served on a bed of puréed roasted corn. Desserts are not impressive. **Price range:** Entrees, $18.50–$24.50. **Meals:** D. **Subway:** 6 to 68th St.

Meet   ☆ $$$ NEW AMERICAN/MEDITERRANEAN
71-73 Gansevoort St. (at Washington St.)   (212) 242-0990

As its name suggests, Meet wants to be a place where people meet. Ideally, these would be young, good-looking people. In an effort to attract this crowd, the owners have fashioned a visually arresting dining room. Diners who keep their attention riveted on the plate will find honest bistro fare with a contemporary spin. The kitchen is the conscience of Meet. If you like to eat, come before 8, when the waiters still control the operation. If you like to meet, come later. **Price range:** Entrees, $16–$24. **Meals:** D, LN. **Subway:** A, C, E to 14th St.

Megu   ☆ ☆ $$$$ JAPANESE
62 Thomas St. (at West Broadway)   (212) 964-7777

From its flamboyant décor to its overwhelming menu, Megu is oblivious to the lines between extravagance and excess. If it reined itself in, it might be one of the most thrilling dining experiences in the city. The chef puts top-tier ingredients to often sumptuous use, creating a nonstop carnival of sensations. The Crown Gems, for example, feature blackfin tuna with ruby-colored flesh so meltingly tender that it evaporates on your tongue. The Kobe beef is so flavorful that it almost makes you swoon. Megu shows as little inhibition with prices as it does with everything else, except portions. You can easily spend $100 a person and find yourself hungry again three hours later. **Price range:** Sushi $5–$20 per piece; other dishes $15–$180. **Meals:** D. Closed Sun. **Subway:** 1, 2, 3, 9 to Chambers St.

Meltemi $25 & Under   GREEK/SEAFOOD
905 First Ave. (at 51st St.)   (212) 355-4040

This attractive neighborhood Greek restaurant offers big portions of simply prepared seafood, like grilled octopus with oil and lemon, and typical Greek offerings like grilled whole porgy and red mullet. Appetizers are generous, and two portions can easily feed four people. Grilled seafood is the centerpiece here. The enthusiastic staff adds to Meltemi's enjoyable atmosphere. **Price range:** Entrees, $14.95–$28.95. **Meals:** L, D. **Subway:** 6 to 51st St.; E, F to Lexington Ave.

Mercer Kitchen   ☆ ☆ $$$$ FRENCH
Mercer Hotel, 99 Prince St. (at Mercer St.)   (212) 966-5454

Jean-Georges Vongerichten strikes again in this chic SoHo restaurant filled with models and movie stars. The space is so mysteriously beautiful it makes each vegetable shimmer like a jewel in the dark. The food is equally innovative. The kitchen occasionally spins out of control, but desserts are simple and appealing, especially the fruit terrines and the rich and fascinating custard with a slice of carmelized pineapple. **Price range:** Entrees, $19–$35. **Meals:** Br, L, D, LN. **Subway:** N, R to Prince St.

Mermaid Inn $25 & Under   SEAFOOD
96 Second Ave. (near 5th St.)   (212) 674-5870

The Mermaid Inn offers a dead-on rendition of a casual fish shack, where the well-seasoned, simple preparations and small, intelligent wine list meet all the style and attitude requirements of the East Village. The front room has maybe two dozen seats and a bar with weathered beams and old marine charts. A larger rear room eases the crowding, but the acoustics in the room, with its high-timbered ceiling and brick walls, are dreadful. **Price range:** Entrees, $14–$21. **Meals:** D, LN. Closed Sun. **Subway:** F to Second Ave.; 6 to Astor Pl.

Mesa Grill ☆☆ **$$$$** SOUTHWESTERN
102 Fifth Ave. (between 15th and 16th Sts.) (212) 807-7400
Mesa Grill is a downtown favorite, crowded and clamorous at lunch, and even more crowded and clamorous at night. Chef-owner Bobby Flay goes after big flavors and he knows how to get them; he also uses chilies and spices for flavor, not for heat. Sixteen-spice chicken is a subtly handled, tingling orchestration of flavors, with an off-sweet sauce of caramelized mangos and garlic. New arrivals keep the menu fresh. The margarita list is an inspirational document, with a list of fine tequilas that can either be sipped on their own or used to upgrade a standard margarita. **Price range:** Entrees, $24–$39. **Meals:** Br, L, D. **Subway:** F, L, N, Q, R, W, 4, 5, 6 to 14th St.

Metsovo **$25 & Under** GREEK
65 W. 70th St. (near Columbus Ave.) (212) 873-2300
Instead of seafood, this romantic restaurant, named after a town in northwestern Greece, specializes in hearty stews, roasts and savory pies from the hills that form a spine through the region. Try the Epirus mountain pies, which are offered with different fillings each day. Tender chunks of baby lamb and a mellow stew of robust goat blended with thick yogurt and rice are also good. Once you get through the house specialties, though, you're back in familiar territory. You may never receive the same selection of desserts twice, so hope for the luscious fig compote, or the wonderfully thick and fresh yogurt. **Price range:** Entrees, $10.50–$23.95. **Meals:** D. **Subway:** 1, 2, 3, 9 to 72nd St.

Mexicana Mama **$25 & Under** MEXICAN
525 Hudson St. (at W. 10th St.) (212) 924-4119
While this colorful restaurant's small menu doesn't register high on a scale of authenticity, the food succeeds in a more important measure: it tastes good. Rather than using the traditional mutton or goat, for example, a dish like barbacoa is made with beef, braised and then cooked slowly in a corn husk until it is fall-away tender, like pot roast. Authentic? No. Tasty? Definitely. Other worthy dishes include pollo con mole, a boneless chicken breast that is surprisingly juicy, with a terrific reddish-brown mole. **Price range:** Entrees, $8–$17. Cash only. **Meals:** L, D. **Subway:** 1, 9 to Christopher St.

Michael Jordan's Steak House ☆☆ **$$$$** STEAKHOUSE
23 Vanderbilt Ave. (in Grand Central Terminal) (212) 655-2300
The real star of this place is Grand Central Terminal. You sit in comfort on the balcony gazing at the starry ceiling while harried commuters dash madly through the marble halls below. The menu is what you would expect, but the food, for the most part, is equal to the space. Shrimp cocktail is excellent, the

meat robust, prime, aged and old-fashioned. All the standard cuts are available, but the flavorful rib eye steak is best. The hamburger is absurd; it's so enormous it looks more like an inflated basketball. Desserts are not inspiring. **Price range:** Entrees, $18–$34. **Meals:** L, D. **Subway:** S, 4, 5, 6, 7 to 42nd St.

Michael's ☆☆ $$$$ NEW AMERICAN
24 W. 55th St. (between Fifth and Sixth Aves.)   (212) 767-0555
Home of the power lunch. All of publishing goes to Michael's because the room is attractive and filled with good art. The menu offers one of the city's finest selections of fancy salads (some large enough to feed a small nation). The best food on the menu is unabashedly American, including grilled chicken, grilled lobster, good steaks and chops, and California cuisine. There are several daily fish selections. For dessert, the classic collection of tarts and cakes is very enticing. **Price range:** Entrees, $22–$34. **Meals:** B, L, D. Closed Sun. **Subway:** N, R, W to Fifth Ave.

Mirchi $25 & Under   INDIAN
29 Seventh Ave. (near Morton St.)   (212) 414-0931
A vast majority of Indian restaurants in Manhattan settle for a dreary sameness; Mirchi tries to break the imprisoning mold, and it succeeds often enough for its failures to be forgiven. The clean and simple design, casual service and loud music suggest other youth-oriented restaurants with bar crowds, yet the food is strictly Indian, with not even a hint of fusion. Portions are quite large and spicing is forceful, with occasionally very high heat (the word mirchi means hot, as in chilies). **Price range:** Entrees, $9–$19. **Meals:** L, D. **Subway:** 1, 9 to Houston St.

Miss Maude's Spoonbread Too $25 & Under   SOUTHERN
547 Lenox Ave. (near 137th St.)   (212) 690-3100
This bright restaurant celebrates the virtues of family meals without childish nostalgia. Meals begin with a basket of mildly spicy corn bread and are served Southern style, with large portions of two sides. The smothered pork chops are thin but flavorful enough to stand up to the peppery brown gravy. Close behind are the excellent fried shrimp with traces of cornmeal in the delectable crust. Side dishes are all excellent. **Price range:** Dinners, $9.95–$12.95. **Meals:** Br, L, D. **Subway:** 2, 3 to 135th St.

Mix in New York   ☆☆ $$$$ FRENCH/AMERICAN
68 W. 58th St. (between Fifth and Sixth Aves.)   (212) 583-0300
Somewhere deep in the kitchen of Mix, a chef with wholesome and honest instincts is struggling for attention. But he has a lot of visual and conceptual clutter to break through, courtesy of Alain Ducasse and Jeffrey Chodorow, two overheated imaginations working to make Mix a nonstop thrill ride. The good news is that after all the effort, there is the food: upmarket, down-home dishes with powerful flavors. **Price range:** Mix prix-fixe $48 or $58. **Meals:** L (Mon.–Fri.), D. **Subway:** A, B, C, D, 1, 9 to 59th St.; N, R, Q, W to 57th St.

Moda ☆☆ $$$ ITALIAN

Flatotel, 135 W. 52nd St. (between Sixth and Seventh Aves.) (212) 887-9880

Moda's coolly stylish dining room has a subtly minimalist look with warm touches. The menu reflects a commitment to prime ingredients and a quiet determination not to let style overrule substance. The menu format is flexible, with dishes categorized as small plates and big plates, with side dishes like whipped Parmesan potatoes or polenta with truffle oil and Gorgonzola. The easy dessert choice is a modest-looking bittersweet chocolate cake that's halfway toward being a pudding. **Price range:** Entrees, $14–$28. **Meals:** L, D. **Subway:** 1, 2 to 50th St.;N, R, W to 49th St.; B, D, E to Seventh Ave.

Molyvos ☆☆ $$$ GREEK

871 Seventh Ave. (near 55th St.) (212) 582-7500

Molyvos is pleasingly informal and spacious. While familiar Greek dishes dominate the menu, it's worth trying some of the more recent additions, like one called Greek fava, yellow split peas, mashed and whipped to a froth and served as an almost lighter-than-air flan. The best main courses tend to be the most straightforward. The kitchen gives special care to fresh fish grilled simply over wood, like a light, lemony branzino and the slightly richer, more strongly flavored dorade royale. Baby lamb chops are perfect with no more than a sprinkling of salt and pepper. **Price range:** Entrees, $19–$35. **Meals:** L, D. **Subway:** N, R, Q, W to 57th St.; B, D, E to Seventh Ave.

Morrells ☆ $$ NEW AMERICAN

900 Broadway (near 20th St.) (212) 253-0900

Morrells is a greatly expanded version of the little wine bar and café next to the Morrells wine store in Rockefeller Center. Diners face a nonstop bombardment of fine wines before, during and after the meal. The rules of the game require wine to be woven into the texture of virtually every dish, sometimes discreetly, sometimes as pure gimmick. When the wine makes a natural fit, the conceit seems clever. The wine in a reduction sauce casts a spell over the superlative Kobe-style beef from Lobell's. **Price range:** Entrees, $21–$28. **Meals:** L, D. Closed Sun. **Subway:** N, R to 23rd St.

Moustache $25 & Under MIDDLE EASTERN

90 Bedford St. (between Grove and Barrow Sts.) (212) 229-2220

265 E. 10th St. (between First Ave. and Ave. A) (212) 228-2022

These small, excellent Middle Eastern restaurants specialize in "pitzas," pizzalike dishes made with pita dough, including lahmajun, the Turkish specialty with a savory layer of ground lamb on crisp crust, and zaatar, a crisp individual pizza topped with a smoky, aromatic combination of olive oil, thyme, sesame seeds and sumac. A sandwich of sliced lamb in pita bread with onion and tomato is brought to life by a minty lemon mayonnaise. **Price range:** $3–$12. Cash only. **Meals:** L, D, LN. **Subway:** Bedford St.: 1, 9 to Houston St. E. 10th St.: L to First Ave.

Mughlai $25 & Under   INDIAN

320 Columbus Ave. (at 71st St.)   (212) 724-6363

Mughlai offers tantalizing glimpses of the pleasures of Indian food. Its menu offers the litany of familiar dishes, yet it also invites diners to try uncommon regional dishes, which are almost always better. Dal papri, potatoes and chickpeas blended in a tangy tamarind-and-yogurt sauce and served cool, is a superb appetizer. Pepper chicken, a dish from the southwestern state of Kerala, is another adventure. Also excellent are baghare baigan, small eggplants in an aromatic sauce of ground peanuts, sesame, tamarind and coconut. **Price range:** Entrees, $6.95–$18.95. **Meals:** L, D. **Subway:** 1, 2, 3, 9 to 72nd St.

Nadaman Hakubai   ☆☆ $$$$ JAPANESE

Kitano Hotel, 66 Park Ave. (at 38th St.)   (212) 885-7111

A visit to this restaurant is like a quick trip to Japan. Kaiseki cuisine, associated with the tea ceremony, is food for the soul as well as the body, meant to feed the eye with its beauty and the spirit with its meaning. The courses follow a strict order and each is intended to introduce the coming season. Unless you are an extremely adventurous eater, you will probably not like every dish, but an evening in one of the private tatami rooms can be immensely rewarding. Kaiseki dinners in the main restaurant are not particularly recommended. **Price range:** $100 minimum per person, for a minimum of four people. **Meals:** B, L, D. **Subway:** S, 4, 5, 6, 7 to 42nd St.

Nam $25 & Under   VIETNAMESE

110 Reade St. (at W. Broadway)   (212) 267-1777

Nam's high ceiling, stylishly draped chairs, candles and cleverly backlighted old pictures of Vietnam make it feel almost Parisian. The menu offers some seldom-seen recipes like banh la, fragile rectangular noodles stuffed with minced shrimp, wrapped in banana leaves and steamed, giving them a deliciously cheeselike richness. More familiar dishes are also well rendered, like goi du du, or green papaya salad, which is pungent and refreshing, augmented by paper-thin slices of salty dried beef. **Price range:** Entrees, $9–$16. **Meals:** L, D. **Subway:** 1, 2, 3, 9 to Chambers St.

Natchez $25 & Under   NEW ORLEANS

31 Second Avenue (at 2nd St.)   (212) 460-9171

Natchez offers the New Orleans vernacular, with a spare menu with fewer than a dozen dishes each night. Many of the better selections on it have clear Louisiana antecedents, like the exceptional gumbo, thickened Cajun-style, with filé powder rather than okra. Filet mignon is decent enough, and the potato-crusted redfish fillet is served with sumptuous smoked mashed potatoes and a lively tomato chili marmalade. Natchez has a short wine list, and serves cocktails from the Patio bar next door, which is connected by a doorway. **Price range:** Entrees, $10–$20. **Meals:** L, D. **Subway:** F to Second Ave.

New Green Bo   **$**   CHINESE
66 Bayard St. (between Mott and Elizabeth Sts.)   (212) 625-2359
This bright, plain restaurant in Chinatown looks like many other bright, plain restaurants in the neighborhood, except that it offers delicious Shanghai specialties like soup dumplings, smoked fish and eel with chives.
Price range: Entrees, $2.75–$24. Cash only. **Meals:** L, D, LN. **Subway:** J, M, N, Q, R, W, Z, 6 to Canal St.

New York Noodle Town   ☆☆   **$**   CHINESE
28 1/2 Bowery (near Bayard St.), Chinatown   (212) 349-0923
With its bustle and clatter, its shared tables and its chefs wreathed in billows of steam rising from the cauldrons of soup in the front of the restaurant, New York Noodle Town is as close as you can get to Hong Kong without leaving Manhattan. It serves Chinatown's most delicious food. Everything is good, from the superb roast suckling pig to the superlative deep-fried soft-shell crabs. All the noodle dishes are wonderful, and the roasted meats are also amazing. No meal at Noodle Town is complete without one of the salt-baked specialties.
Price range: Entrees, $4–$20. Cash only. **Meals:** B, L, D, LN. **Subway:** J, M, N, Q, R, W, Z, 6 to Canal St.

Next Door Nobu   ☆☆☆   **$$$$**   JAPANESE
105 Hudson St. (near Franklin St.)   (212) 334-4445
Slightly more casual than Nobu, Next Door Nobu takes no reservations and does not serve lunch. But the food is as accomplished (and as expensive) as Nobu's. It strives for its own identity, with an emphasis on raw shellfish, whole fish served for an entire table, noodles, and texture. The few meat dishes on the menu are memorable. Mochi ice cream balls are the most appealing way to end a meal. Mochi, the pounded rice candy of Japan, is stretchy and sticky when warm, but hardens into a cold tackiness when frozen. **Price range:** Noodle dishes, $10–$15; hot dishes, $8–$32; sushi and sashimi, $3–$8 a piece. **Meals:** D, LN. **Subway:** 1, 9 to Franklin St.

Nha Trang   **$25 & Under**   VIETNAMESE
87 Baxter St. (between Canal and Bayard Sts.)   (212) 233-5948
148 Centre St. (at Walker St.)   (212) 941-9292
Nha Trang was one of the pioneering Vietnamese restaurants in Chinatown, and it's still one of the best. Spring rolls are perfectly fried, while steamed ravioli, glistening paper-thin rice noodle crepes wrapped around minced pork and ground mushrooms, is another excellent appetizer. Vietnamese rice noodle soups are big enough to be an entire meal. **Price range:** Entrees, $5–$11. Cash only. **Meals:** B, Br, L, D. **Subway:** J, M, N, Q, R, W, Z, 6 to Canal St. (for both locations).

Nice Matin   ☆☆   **$$**   FRENCH
201 W. 79th St. (at Amsterdam Ave.)   (212) 873-6423
Nice Matin gives the Upper West Side a splash of Provençal sunshine and a heady introduction to the cuisine of Nice, home of the pissaladière, pan bagnat

and, if we are to believe the menu, a whopping big burger topped with comté cheese, smeared with aioli. When it's crowded, the brutal acoustics preclude conversation. **Price range:** Entrees, $15.75–$24.75. **Meals:** Br, L, D. **Subway:** 1, 9 to 79th St.

Nick & Toni's ☆☆ $$$ MEDITERRANEAN
100 W. 67th St. (between Broadway and Columbus) (212) 496-4000
Nick & Toni's is a lot like the neighborhood it serves: casual, crowded and noisy. But there is one thing that sets it apart from most of the neighborhood's restaurants: the food is really delicious. Nick & Toni's starts with good ingredients and leaves them alone. The menu changes constantly, but there are a few perennials, like the mussels and the impeccable Caesar salad. Often there is a fine pasta with just the right number of baby clams. Desserts are simple and seasonal. **Price range:** Entrees, $11–$28. **Meals:** L, D. **Subway:** 1, 9 to 66th St.

Nick's Family-Style Restaurant $25 & Under PIZZA/ITALIAN
1814 Second Ave. (near 94th St.) (212) 987-5700
Nick's — a small, pleasant corner spot with brick walls, a pressed tin ceiling and hearty service — adheres to all the Italian family-style macaroni-and-gravy hokum. What separates Nick's from some of the others is a track record of taking food seriously, especially pizza. The crust is beautifully thin and crisp, blackened in spots and smoky. Tomato sauce is well seasoned, and toppings are excellent. **Price range:** Entrees, $11–$22. **Meals:** L, D. **Subway:** 6 to 96th St.

92 ☆ $$ NEW AMERICAN
45 E. 92nd St. (between Fifth and Madison Aves.) (212) 828-5300
One virtue of 92 is that it fulfills the diner role without overthinking it. The place has fat leather banquettes that look as if they might have been taken from a 1930's train station, cozy booths and dark wooden tables. There's onion soup, along with cheeseburgers, and the fried onion rings have a sweet-hot Thai dipping sauce. Macaroni and cheese deserves applause, and the fine-grained meatloaf is dense and flavorful. The daily specials shine, especially the expertly handled fish and chips and the generous slab of pork ribs. The best of the desserts is the classic chocolate sundae and a firm, unctuous chocolate-pudding cake. **Price range:** Entrees, $19–$29. **Meals:** Br, L, D. **Subway:** 6 to 96th St.

NL ☆ $$$ DUTCH/INDONESIAN
169 Sullivan St. (near Houston St.) (212) 387-8801
A Dutch restaurant seems like an inside joke. But NL, which is short for Netherlands, has the last laugh, serving a clever mix of beloved Dutch standbys, Indonesian dishes that have gained honorary Dutch citizenship and invented dishes that use homey Dutch ingredients like herring, potatoes, cheese and the yogurt cream known as hangop. Sauerkraut risotto sounds forbidding, but it turns out to be one of the best things on the menu: the sauerkraut, distributed in fine threads, adds piquancy without bullying the dish. For dessert, try poffertjes, soft, puffy mini-pancakes sprinkled with powdered anise and served with a

scoop of vanilla butter. **Price range:** Entrees, $18–$25. **Meals:** D.
Subway: 1, 9 to Houston St.

Nobu ☆☆☆ $$$$ JAPANESE
105 Hudson St. (at Franklin St.) (212) 219-0500

Chic, casual and pulsing with energy, Nobu cannot be compared with any other restaurant. The kitchen incorporates new ingredients into old dishes and retools traditional recipes; the result is something that seems like a Japanese dish but is not. The best time to eat at Nobu is lunchtime. Order an Omakase meal and let the chefs choose your meal for you. If dishes like Funazushi, a freshwater trout buried in rice for a year, do not appeal to you, just tell the waiter the foods you do not eat. No kitchen turns out a more spectacular plate of sushi. Desserts include a warm chocolate soufflé cake with siso syrup and green tea ice cream that comes in a bento box. **Price range:** Avg. $60–$75 per person. **Meals:** L, D.
Subway: 1, 9 to Franklin St.

Noche ☆ $$$ PAN-LATIN
1604 Broadway (near 49th St.) (212) 541-7070

Broadway could use more places like Noche, a multilevel pan-Latin restaurant with a striking design, a spirited atmosphere and excellent value. The background music is loud, and some nights, live mambo music starts around 9. Main courses are a carnivore's delight, especially the pork dishes. Apart from shrimp, the seafood dishes don't stand up to the meat selections. **Price range:** Entrees, $15–$22. **Meals:** L, D. Closed Sun. **Subway:** N, R, W to 49th St.

Oceana ☆☆☆ $$$$ SEAFOOD
55 E. 54th St. (between Park and Madison Aves.) (212) 759-5941

The good ship Oceana — a two-story town house decorated to resemble a yacht — has found a new surge of energy. Oysters on the half shell, each topped with a dollop of sturgeon caviar, are perfection. But the more complicated appetizers show what the kitchen can do. Perhaps the most impressive entree is loup de mer, topped with a thin golden crouton and poised on a bed of coconut-flavored basmati rice. In restaurant years Oceana, which opened over a decade ago, is entering late middle age, but it shows no sign of faltering. **Price range:** Dinner, three courses, $68; six-course tasting menu, $110. **Meals:** L, D. Closed Sun.
Subway: E, V to Fifth Ave.

Odeon ☆☆ $$ BISTRO/NEW AMERICAN
145 West Broadway (at Thomas St.) (212) 233-0507

TriBeCa's first great American bistro is still cooking after all these years. The neighborhood has certainly changed, but time has stood still in the dining room. It is still unpretentious and comfortable, and it still feels as if it is filled with artists. It's great for burgers, omelets, pasta and roast chicken in a slightly funky setting; it's even greater for a martini. And it's still a destination until 3 A.M.
Price range: Avg. entree, $18. **Meals:** Br, L, D, LN.
Subway: A, C, 1, 2, 3, 9 to Chambers St.

Ola ☆ $$

NUEVO LATINO

304 E. 48th St. (near Second Ave.)   (212) 759-0590

At Ola, a narrow set of steps decorated in Spanish tile leads to a small, crowded bar, and onward to a long, booth-lined room that feels like a superdiner. If you can manage to land one of the secluded booths at the very back, there's a slim chance you might be able to hear the conversation at the table. Ola stands for "of Latin America." This vague affiliation allows the chef to do whatever on earth he wants, as long it has a Latin flavor. The tapas menu makes plenty of room for novelty items. Like so many dishes on the menu, these are often shameless and irresistible. **Price range:** Entrees, $10–$22. **Meals:** L, D. Closed Sun. **Subway:** 6 to 51st St.

Olives ☆ $$$

MEDITERRANEAN

281 Park Ave. South, in the W Union Square Hotel (at 17th St.) (212) 353-8345

The food here is easy to like but hard to respect. Do not look for light, because you won't find it, not even hidden under a cheese shaving. But it's hard to beat chef Todd English for sheer palate-engulfing flavor. Both venison and veal feature prominently in two of the better pastas, chestnut ravioli in a venison Bolognese sauce with creamy spinach, and mezzaluna, or pasta half-moons, stuffed with artichokes and blanketed under a ragu of braised veal breast and roasted tomatoes. Desserts are the kind that make diners feel pleasantly guilty. **Price range:** Entrees, $18–$30. **Meals:** B, Br, L, D. **Subway:** L, N, Q, R, W, 4, 5, 6 to 14th St.

O Mai $25 & Under

VIETNAMESE

158 Ninth Ave. (near 20th St.)   (212) 633-0550

The restaurant has no sign out front, only potted bamboo plants. Behind them, bathed in soft, amber light, sits a crowded storefront. The din is incredible and the mood bright, everyone laughing. It is a heavily stylized place that serves traditional, delicate Vietnamese fare, little of it blunted for the Western palate. The best available entrees are a roasted duck with lime-ginger dipping sauce and that bird's less expensive cousin, a roasted chicken, served with the same sauce. They are simple meals, beautifully cooked. **Price range:** Entrees, $6–$17. **Meals:** D. **Subway:** C, E to 18th St.

One If By Land, Two If By Sea $$$$

CONTINENTAL

17 Barrow St. (between W. 4th St. and Seventh Ave. South)   (212) 255-8649

Considered by many to be the most romantic restaurant in New York, it is almost always booked. The lights are low, the gas fireplaces burn even in the summer and a pianist serenades you with music. Known mainly for the 1950's specialty Beef Wellington, the food has grown more ambitious of late. The seared tuna is fresh and rosy, and the lightly smoked and roasted rack of lamb is a fine piece of meat. **Price range:** Prix-fixe, $64–75. **Meals:** D. **Subway:** 1, 9 to Christopher St.

Orsay ☆☆ **$$$** FRENCH/BRASSERIE
1057 Lexington Ave. (at 75th St.) (212) 517-6400
Orsay looks as if it was ordered from a kit, with a lot of shiny brass, pristine leather banquettes and authentic French waiter costumes. But the cuisine has a fresh, wayward bent and an international style. Orsay's hickory-chip smoker gives a dark, woodsy bite to salmon and to a dense, deeply flavored duck sausage. Oddly enough in this traditional setting, it's the traditional brasserie and bistro dishes that disappoint, but the restrained raspberry napoleon, with just a few pastry layers defining the form, is a perfectly executed classic. **Price range:** Entrees, $15–$26. **Meals:** Br, L, D. **Subway:** 6 to 77th St.

Otabe ☆☆ **$$$** JAPANESE
68 E. 56th St. (between Park and Madison Aves.) (212) 223-7575
In the back room this is a very upscale Benihana; the elegant front dining room serves kaiseki-like cuisine. The kaiseki dinner is a lovely and accessible introduction to a ceremonial Japanese cuisine that is traditionally served in many small courses meant to reflect the season. Less ambitious eaters might want to sample fewer dishes. Desserts are the big surprise at Otabe; more French than Japanese, they are original, beautiful and very delicious. The teppan room has a separate menu, and each course is cooked before your eyes by your personal chef. **Price range:** Entrees, $14.50–$65. **Meals:** L, D. **Subway:** 4, 5, 6 to 59th St.; E, F, N, R to Lexington Ave.

Otto ☆☆ **$** PIZZA/ITALIAN
1 Fifth Ave. (at 8th St.) (212) 995-9559
Otto is advertised as an enoteca and pizzeria, which is more and less than the truth. There is a serious all-Italian list. There are also a lot of pizzas, some traditional, others unique to Otto, and all cooked on top of the griddle rather than in an oven. But Otto may be the only pizzeria in New York where it's possible to skip the pizza entirely. The menu is devised, ingeniously, to stave off boredom, with separate categories devoted to antipasti, bruschettas, pizzas, fried appetizers, cheeses and desserts. **Price range:** Starters, $4–$8; pizzas, $7–$14. **Meals:** L, D. **Subway:** N, R to 8th St.; A, C, E, F, V, S to W. 4th St.

Ouest ☆☆ **$$$** NEW AMERICAN/BISTRO
2315 Broadway (at 84th St.) (212) 580-8700
Long before the food arrives, Ouest (pronounced WEST), with disarming confidence, has most diners eating out of the palm of its hand. Pray for a booth, however, because the upstairs balcony seating is dark, cramped and loud. The cooking has a sane, rooted quality that makes it appropriate for what is, when all is said and done, a neighborhood restaurant. The food has a solid, uncomplicated appeal, especially the special section of the menu devoted to simple grilled meats. **Price range:** Entrees, $16–$27. **Meals:** D. **Subway:** 1, 9 to 86th St.

Our Place Shanghai Tea Garden   **$25 & Under**   CHINESE
141 E. 55th St. (at Third Ave.)   (212) 753-3900
With its elevated service and thick linens, Our Place has the feel of a fine yet
informal banquet. The Shanghai dishes are rich and satisfying, beautifully
rendered, yet accessible to Americans, who make up most of the clientele.
The waiters are supremely attentive, dividing portions onto plates, putting
umbrellas into drinks for young children and generally offering to do anything
short of feeding you. Silver-dollar-size steamed soup dumplings are well-seasoned and nicely textured. The kitchen excels at tofu dishes, and noodle
dishes are superb. **Price range:** Entrees, $9.95–$24.95. **Meals:** L, D.
Subway: E, F to Lexington Ave.; 6 to 51st St.

Oyster Bar and Restaurant   **$$$**   SEAFOOD
Grand Central Terminal (Lexington Ave. at 42nd St.)   (212) 490-6650
Today, there is really only one restaurant in the city where diners can experi-
ence the oyster in its full glory. For a certain kind of dining, nothing can beat
the Oyster Bar at Grand Central Terminal, in business since 1913. Everything
about the experience — the din and the tumult, the oyster shuckers working
double-time, the vaulted tile ceilings — is almost transcendentally New York.
The problems start if you leave the oyster trail. The service can be charmingly
inept or uncharmingly inept. **Price range:** Entrees, $20–$30. **Meals:** L, D.
Closed Sun. **Subway:** 4, 5, 6, 7 to 42nd St — Grand Central Terminal.

Paladar   **$25 & Under**   CARIBBEAN/MEXICAN
161 Ludlow St. (near Stanton St.)   (212) 473-3535
Paladar's menu hews closely to Mexican and Caribbean dishes. Standout appe-
tizers include sopes, thick but delicate corn tortillas covered in avocado salsa
and a fragrant sauce of fermented black beans, and a savory quesadilla with
chorizo and roasted tomatoes, flavored with a smoky chipotle salsa. Seafood is a
highlight, with excellent choices like roasted mahi-mahi in an orange-chili
vinaigrette over coconut-flavored rice. **Price range:** Entrees, $9–$14. **Meals:** D,
LN. **Subway:** F, J, M, Z to Delancey St.–Essex St.

Palm   **$$$$**   STEAKHOUSE
837 Second Ave. (between 44th and 45th Sts.)   (212) 687-2953
250 W. 50th St. (between Broadway and Eighth Ave.)   (212) 333-7256
Great steak, rude waiters, high prices and the world's best hash brown potatoes.
The walls are covered with caricatures, the floor is covered with sawdust and if
you want to experience what people think is the real New York rush, this is the
place for you. **Price range:** Entrees, $16–$35. **Meals:** L, D. **Subway:** Second
Ave.: S, 4, 5, 6, 7 to 42nd St. W. 50th St: C, E, 1, 9 to 50th St.

Pam Real Thai Food   **$25 & Under**   THAI
404 W. 49th St. (at Ninth Ave.)   (212) 333-7500
At this sweet little restaurant, your palate will revel in the kitchen's sure-
handed spicing. Shredded green papaya salad, for instance, is not only both

tangy and sweet but fiery as well, strewn with chewy dried shrimp and tiny red chilies, with a faint sense of pungent fish sauce in the background. Pam's curries are superb: try chu chee curry with pork, with its underlying flavor of coconut milk laced with chili heat. **Price range:** Entrees, $7–$14. Cash only. **Meals:** L, D. **Subway:** C, E to 50th St.

Paola's   ☆☆ $$ ITALIAN
245 E. 84th St. (between Second and Third Aves.)   (212) 794-1890
Paola's is one of the city's best and least-known Italian restaurants. It makes some of the city's finest pasta, and the wine list is wonderful. No meal is complete without an order of carciofi alla giudea, a fine version of baby artichokes fried in the style of the Roman ghetto. But pastas are the soul of the menu. Filled pastas such as cazunzei and pansotti are wonderful. Desserts, except the ricotta cake, seem like an afterthought. **Price range:** Pastas, $12.95–$14.95; entrees, $16.95–$26.95. **Meals:** L, D. **Subway:** 4, 5, 6 to 86th St.

Paradou $25 & Under   FRENCH/SANDWICHES
8 Little W. 12th St. (near Ninth Ave.)   (212) 463-8345
The full-scale arrival of Italian wine-and-panini shops in the last few years has been a great thing. Paradou is a panini shop born of a different Mediterranean coast where the specialty is "sandwichs grillés," as they would say in Provence. Named for a Provençal bistro, Paradou excels where it counts, with a delicious range of sandwiches, some distinctly French, and some Mediterranean. The sampler of five tartines for $10 is the best deal. The larger grilled sandwiches, served on pressed, toasted baguettes with a small green salad, make surprisingly substantial meals. **Price range:** Tartines, salads and sandwiches, $5–$15; larger plates, $12–$20. **Meals:** D, LN. **Subway:** A, C, E to 14th St.

Parish & Company   ☆ $$ NEW AMERICAN
202 Ninth Ave. (at 22nd St.)   (212) 414-4988
Parish & Company's very eclectic mix-and-match menu roams far and wide but never seems to lose its way. It is a model neighborhood restaurant for tough times. The tables are covered in brown paper, and the restaurant will win no beauty contests. But Parish & Company, modest and overachieving, pays attention to detail. The menu offers most dishes in appetizer and entree sizes, making it possible to create a meal consisting of many small bites. **Price range:** Entrees, $13–$19. **Meals:** L, D, LN. **Subway:** C, E to 23rd St.

Park Avenue Café   ☆☆ $$$$ NEW AMERICAN
100 E. 63rd St. (near Park Ave.)   (212) 644-1900
After a decade, the restaurant feels a little past its prime. But Upper East Siders still treat it as a beloved neighborhood fixture where they can relax and eat sanely reinterpreted, high-spirited American food. Pastas are among the best dishes on the menu, but the most sinfully indulgent experience is the formidable terrine of foie gras, served folksy style in a glass jar with fig jam smeared on the hinged lid. The signature "swordchop" still holds its place on the menu. It is juicy and big-flavored. For dessert, try the cherry tart or the beautifully realized

chocolate cube. **Price range:** Entrees, $19.50–$42. **Meals:** L, D. **Subway:** N, R, W to Lexington Ave.; 4, 5, 6 to 59th St.

Park View at the Boathouse   ☆☆ $$$ NEW AMERICAN

Loeb Boathouse, Central Park, E. 72nd St. entrance   (212) 517-2233

Is this Manhattan's most romantic spot? Very possibly. Situated in the Loeb Boathouse next to Central Park's prettiest lake, it combines country charm with views of skyscrapers peeking over the trees. There is interesting, eclectic food and a good wine list here. The setting is so swell that you feel lucky to be there. Live jazz at the adjacent café is a real bonus. **Price range:** Entrees, $18–$30. **Meals:** Br, L, D. **Subway:** B, C, 1, 2, 3, 9 to 72nd St.

Pastis   ☆ $$$ BISTRO/FRENCH

9 Ninth Ave. (at Little W. 12th St.)   (212) 929-4844

Virtually every dish here could qualify for protection by the French Ministry of Culture. And all are good. It's a deliberate invitation to simple pleasures. Pastis needs to work on its steak frites, but rabbit pappardelle is a pleasant surprise, a superior plate of firm pasta with a sweetly meaty sauce. For dessert, the crêpes suzette rise up in glory, and the floating island floats, a cloud with just enough substance to support its light custardy sauce. **Price range:** Entrees, $14–$17. **Meals:** L, D, LN. **Subway:** A, C, E to 14th St.; L to Eighth Ave.

Patria   ☆☆☆ $$$$ NUEVO LATINO

250 Park Ave. South (20th St.)   (212) 777-6211

The tone here is a little quieter than it used to be, a little less like a big, nonstop party. And the food is superb. The menu is fun, high flying and inventive, but the ideas never spin out of control. Colombian pan de bono, chewy round rolls made from cornmeal, are flavored very mildly with Colombian queso fresco, but they assume lethal power when a waiter brings over a crock filled with nata, a potent mixture of butter, sour cream and roasted garlic. Ceviche maintains a delicate balance between acid, spice and fruit. An excellent entree is roast chicken in a smoky chipotle sauce flavored with huitlacoche, or corn fungus. For dessert, the honors go to three little flans, vanilla, corn and pineapple. **Price range:** Entrees, $10–$32; prix-fixe and tasting menus, $20–$79. **Meals:** L, D. **Subway:** 6, N, Q, R, W to 23rd St.

Patroon   ☆ $$$$ NEW AMERICAN

160 E. 46th St. (between Lexington and Third Aves.)   (212) 883-7373

Today's Patroon looks more like the dining room of an airport hotel than an up-to-date "21" Club. This is not to suggest that Patroon has become inexpensive. It's a steakhouse with steakhouse prices, but the menu has been pruned of almost all excess and, for that matter, individuality. Oysters on the half shell are superb, although the selection is slim. But a jumbo crab cake is practically all meat, a thoroughly satisfying mouthful of pure flavor. As far as beef goes, little things tend to go wrong, although fish dishes are excellent. **Price range:** Entrees, $20–$42. **Meals:** L, D. **Subway:** S, 4, 5, 6, 7 to 42nd St.

Payard Pâtisserie ☆☆ $$$ BISTRO/FRENCH

1032 Lexington Ave. (at 73rd St.)   (212) 717-5252

This is the ultimate Upper East Side bistro, a whimsical café and pastry shop, complete with mirrors, mahogany and hand-blown lamps. A recent visit showed that chef Philippe Bertineau is still going strong, with inventive, impeccably executed dishes like a twice baked cheese soufflé with Parmesan cream sauce, sardines stuffed with quince chutney, and a simple sirloin steak with four-peppercorn sauce. **Price range:** Entrees, $17–$25. **Meals:** Br, L, D. Closed Sun. **Subway:** 6 to 77th St.

Pearl Oyster Bar $25 & Under SEAFOOD

18 Cornelia St. (between Bleecker and W. 4th St.)   (212) 691-8211

It's just a marble counter with a few small tables, but Pearl has won over its neighborhood with its casual charm and Maine-inspired seafood. The restaurant is modeled on the Swan Oyster Depot in San Francisco, and when packed exudes a Barbary Coast rakishness. The menu changes seasonally, but grilled pompano was sweet and delicious, while scallop chowder was unusual and satisfying. Lobster rolls are big and delicious, and blueberry pie is sensational. Don't forget the oysters. **Price range:** Entrees, $17–$25. MC/V only. **Meals:** L, D. Closed Sun. **Subway:** A, C, E, F, S to W. 4th St.

Pearson's Texas Barbecue $25 & Under BARBECUE

170 E. 81st St. (between Lexington and Third Aves.)   (212) 288-2700

Pearson's Texas Barbecue sticks close to the rustic tradition: worn wood floors, plastic chairs and Formica tables are the real thing. But the Pearson's brisket will never be mistaken for, say, a good Texas version, or even for the brisket at Pearson's Queens outpost, now housed in a sports bar in Jackson Heights. No such inconsistency mars Pearson's superb hot links, cut lengthwise into thin slices, smoky, savory and just spicy enough. Modestly smoky pork ribs, cooked until the exterior is barely crisp, are very good, as is an occasional special of beef back ribs. Food comes on compartmentalized platters, and sometimes in plastic takeout containers. Nothing is cooked to order. **Price range:** Entrees, $12–$24. **Meals:** D. **Subway:** 4, 5, 6, to 86th St.

Peasant ☆ $$$ ITALIAN

194 Elizabeth St. (between Prince and Spring Sts.)   (212) 965-9511

Peasant has built a following by sticking to some very simple premises. Keep the food simple, rustic and Italian. Cook it over a wood fire. Serve abundant portions. Be nice. That's about it. When the formula works, Peasant sends out highly satisfying food, with the rich tanginess that wood smoke imparts. It adds a sublime crunch to the excellent crust of Peasant's little pizzas. The pasta at Peasant is good, not great. The desserts include a few surprises. The best choices are vanilla-soaked bread pudding and a heroically proportioned peach pie with a rough lattice crust. **Price range:** Entrees, $19–$24. **Meals:** D. Closed Mon. **Subway:** N, R to Prince St.; 6 to Spring St.

Petrosino $25 & Under   ITALIAN
190 Norfolk St. (near E. Houston St.)   (212) 673-3773
Petrosino presents a cross section of Italian regional dishes and a modest but
excellent list of southern Italian wines. But what really stands out are the bold
flavors in lively, forthright dishes that are unmarred by fussiness or pretension.
Service is warm and responsive. Petrosino's open spirit is reflected in the dining
room, which achieves a well-calibrated dimness that makes everybody look
good. The prices don't look so good. Some careful limbo dancing is required to
qualify as $25 & Under. **Price range:** Pastas and entrees, $12–$22. **Meals:** Br,
D, LN. Cash only (A.T.M. on premises). **Subway:** F to Delancey St.

Petrossian   ☆ ☆ $$$$ NEW AMERICAN/RUSSIAN
182 W. 58th St. (at Seventh Ave.)   (212) 245-2214
Nobody in New York City serves better caviar, and nobody does it with more
style. The dark room is covered with Art Deco splendor, the waiters wear blue
blazers and an obsequious air, and the caviar arrives with warm toast, blini and
beautiful little spoons. Vodka is served in icy little flutes that make it taste
somehow better. Should you desire something else, the food is good and surprisingly affordable. **Price range:** Entrees, $24–$34. **Meals:** Br, L, D. **Subway:** N, R,
Q, W to 57th St.

Picholine   ☆ ☆ ☆ $$$$ MEDITERRANEAN/FRENCH
35 W. 64th St. (between Broadway and Central Park West)   (212) 724-8585
Picholine, named after a Mediterranean olive, focuses on the food of southern
France, Italy, Greece and Morocco. Meals begin with good house-made breads,
bowls of the tiny olives and olive oil. Salmon in horseradish crust is a signature
dish and it is excellent. But there are also robust dishes from the north, like
daube of beef short ribs with a horseradish potato purée, and a hearty cassoulet.
The kitchen also has a way with game, and a wonderfully extravagant cheese
cart. **Price range:** Entrees, $26–$36; prix-fixe, $58; four-course tasting menu,
$70 ($90 for seven courses). **Meals:** L, D. Closed Sun. **Subway:** 6 to 66th St.

Pig Heaven $25 & Under   CHINESE
1540 Second Ave. (near 80th St.)   (212) 744-4333
Pig Heaven has a sleekly modern look, with a handsome bar, almond-shaped
hanging lamps and a table of ceramic and carved decorative pigs. Its terrific
Chinese-American food is spiced and presented in ways that please Westerners,
yet it is fresh and prepared with finesse. The best place to start is the pork selection, particularly roasted Cantonese dishes like suckling pig, strips of juicy meat
under a layer of moist fat and wafer-thin, deliciously crisp skin.
Price range: Entrees, $7.95 to $18.95. **Meals:** L, D. **Subway:** 6 to 77th St.

Ping's Seafood   ☆ ☆ $$ CHINESE
22 Mott St. (between Worth and Mosco Sts.)   (212) 602-9988
Near the door, a high-rise of stacked fish tanks offers the menu headliners, a stel-
lar cast that includes but is by no means limited to lobsters, eels, scallops, sea bass

and shrimp. The preparations are minimal and the results are maximal. Shrimp in the shell, crackling crisp and salty, come to the table piping hot, exhaling a delicate, fragrant steam. One of the more appealing rituals at Ping's is winter melon soup. You must call a day ahead, since the melon, which flourishes in the summer despite its name, has to steam for six hours. It is the perfect emblem for Ping's, an exotic package with thrilling secrets inside. **Price range:** Entrees, $6.95–$30. **Meals:** Br, L, D. **Subway:** J, M, N, Q, R, W, Z, 6 to Canal St.

P.J. Clarke's $25 & Under   AMERICAN
915 Third Ave. (at 55th St.)   (212) 317-1616
When the family that had owned P.J. Clarke's since 1949 sold the place, it was hard not to believe that an era had ended. But the saloon spirit is certainly intact. The big bar in front is still a riot of noise with bartenders in white aprons sending out perfectly pulled pints of Guinness. The worn wood floor and red-and-white checked tablecloths are all still there. The old vibe that made Clarke's such a hangout lives on, and diners seem to be enjoying themselves. **Price range:** Entrees, $8–$33. **Meals:** L, D, LN. **Subway:** 6 to 51st. St.; E, V to Lexington Ave.

Po $25 & Under   ITALIAN
31 Cornelia St. (near Bleecker St.)   (212) 645-2189
At this small, vivacious, reasonably priced trattoria, the parade of lush flavors begins with the bruschetta offered at the start of each meal, a slice of toasted Italian bread piled high with tender Tuscan white beans. Appetizers are a strong point and salads, too, are exceptional. A paillard of lamb, as long as a skirt steak, is almost beefy, daubed with aioli and served over sweet grape tomatoes. Desserts include a sublimely dense terrine of dark chocolate with a core of rich marzipan.   **Price range:** Entrees, $12.50–$16. AE only. **Meals:** L, D / Closed Mon. **Subway:** A, C, E, F, S to W. 4th St.

Pongal $25 & Under   INDIAN/KOSHER/VEGETARIAN
110 Lexington Ave. (near 27th St.)   (212) 696-9458
The delectable vegetarian cuisine of South India is the specialty at Pongal, where the food is kosher as well. The centerpiece dishes are the daunting dosai, huge crepes made of various fermented batters that are stuffed and rolled into cylinders that can stretch two-and-a-half feet. But they are light and delicious, filled with spiced mixtures of potatoes and onions. Pongal also serves a wonderful shrikhand, a dessert made of yogurt custard flavored with nutmeg, cardamom and saffron. **Price range:** Entrees, $7.95–$13.95. **Meals:** L, D. **Subway:** 6 to 28th St.

Pop's Pierogi $25 & Under   POLISH
190 Bleecker Street (at Macdougal St.)   (212) 505-0850
Pop's Pierogi specializes in the innumerable variations on the dumplings that are street foods in Russia and in the surrounding countries in Eastern Europe and along the Black and Caspian Seas. The namesake pierogi, little half-moon Polish boiled dumplings, come 12 to the order with stuffings such as savory beef,

cabbage sautéed until almost sweet, and soft cheese that actually is sweet. Pel-
meni, carefully wrought little dumplings that look like a cross between tortellini
and shiu mai, are even better. Other stuffed dishes are larger, such as kutabi, a
thin pastry skin stuffed with meat and samsa, big, golden half moons filled with
ground lamb. **Price range:** Entrees, $2–$8. **Meals:** L, D. **Subway:** A, C, E, F, V,
to West 4th St.

Provence ☆ $$$ FRENCH
38 Macdougal St. (near Prince St.) (212) 475-7500
A crowded French café straight out of the French countryside, but while the
atmosphere is charming and rustic, the food feels tired. Mussels gratinées, baked
on the half shell and sprinkled with almonds and garlic, are very tasty. Bourride,
a pale fish soup, is thickened with aioli; don't miss it. Pot au feu, a sometime
special, is also a fine example of hearty country cooking, and the bouillabaisse,
served only on Fridays, is superb. **Price range:** Entrees, $15.50–$26. AE only.
Meals: L, D. **Subway:** N, R to Prince St.

Prune $25 & Under ECLECTIC
54 E. 1st St. (near First Ave.) (212) 677-6221.
The idiosyncratic name (the chef and owner's childhood nickname) is perfect
for this unconventional little place. You could describe the food as homey, or
as faintly European. Thin slices of duck breast taste deliciously of smoke, vinegar and black pepper, and are served with a small omelet flavored with rye.
Roasted capon is as conventional a dish as Prune offers, yet it is marvelously
juicy, served over a slice of toast imbued with garlic. Desserts are terrific, like
cornmeal poundcake drenched in a rosemary syrup, with a poached pear. **Price
range:** Entrees, $10–$17. **Meals:** D. Closed Mon. **Subway:** F to Second Ave.

Public ☆ $$ GLOBAL FUSION
210 Elizabeth St. (between Prince and Spring Sts.) (212) 343-7011
A triumvirate of New Zealand chefs practice a style of global fusion cuisine that
walks the line between freewheeling and reckless. Some dishes, like the grilled
foie gras placed on a "scone," are a mess, but sometimes the roll of the dice
comes up seven. Pickled chilies provide an unexpected, thrilling jolt in an
Asian-style entree of roasted duck breast with bok choy and a light sesame-soy
dressing. Public has the wines to stand up to big meats: the list is heavy on
mighty Australian shirazes and New Zealand pinot noirs. Understatement is not
in the plan. **Price range:** Entrees $18–$25. **Meals:** D, Sat.– Sun. brunch. **Subway:** N, R, W to Prince St.; C, E to Spring St.

The Red Cat ☆ $$ BISTRO/AMERICAN
227 10th Ave. (near 23rd St.) (212) 242-1122
A lot of restaurants make a big noise about being warm, welcoming and accessible.
The Red Cat, with little ado, manages to be all three. It is stylish, but not snooty,
cool but relaxed. The menu reflects the spirit of the place with a lineup of solid,
well-executed American bistro dishes, with a little trick or twist on each plate. The
obligatory steak dish comes with a ragout of roasted shallots, tomatoes and cracked

olives. The short dessert list does not disappoint. **Price range:** entrees, $15–$24. **Meals:** D, LN. **Subway:** C, E to 23rd St.

Redeye Grill   ☆ $$$ NEW AMERICAN
890 Seventh Ave. (at 56th St.)   (212) 541-9000
The boisterous room seems as big as Grand Central Terminal and is lively at almost any hour. There's something for everyone on the vast menu, from smoked fish to raw clams, Chinese chicken, pasta, even a hamburger—late into the night. The small grilled lobster, served with a little potato cake and pristine haricots verts, is lovely. The steak of choice here would be the hanger steak, tender slices piled onto a biscuit. The plain Jane cream-cheese bundt cake is usually the best of the desserts. **Price range:** Entrees, $18–$29. **Meals:** Br, L, D, LN. **Subway:** N, R, Q, W to 57th St.

Remi   ☆☆ $$$ ITALIAN
145 W. 53rd St. (between Sixth and Seventh Aves.)   (212) 581-4242
Remi's stunning Gothic interior and the kitchen's enticing and inventive Northern Italian fare make it easy to understand its continued popularity. The diverse menu includes excellent pastas and main courses like garganelli blended with Coho salmon in balsamic sauce; veal-and-spinach-filled cannelloni in rosemary sauce; and salmon in a horseradish crust, finished with red wine sauce. **Price range:** Entrees, $16–$28. **Meals:** L, D. **Subway:** B, D, E to Seventh Ave.

Riingo   ☆☆ $$$ JAPANESE FUSION
205 E. 45th St. (between Second and Third Aves.)   (212) 867-4200
Riingo's brand of fusion cuisine blends the varied pasts of three chefs. Against a backdrop of American-Japanese cooking, whiffs of France, Korea, Sweden, Ethiopia and even Mexico emerge. One half of the vast menu lists appetizers, main courses and side dishes; on the other is a selection of more than 40 types of nigiri, sashimi and maki. The conventional sushi is excellent, but it is impossible to pass up selections like tuna foie gras, smoked char and rice-puff-crusted shrimp. Beneath Riingo's clutter is a three-star restaurant trying to get out. **Price range:** Entrees $14–$42. **Meals:** L (Mon.–Fri.), D. **Subway:** S, 4, 5, 6, 7 to 42nd St.

Risa $25 & Under   PIZZA/ITALIAN
47 E. Houston St. (near Mulberry St.)   (212) 625-1712
Risa's pizzas taste as good as they look. The crust is thin and light, with a gentle, crisp snap. The cheese and tomato pie is impeccably fresh, and other toppings only enhance. Designer pies, like one made with speck (a smoked ham), arugula and mascarpone, are notable for their subtlety. Even truffle oil, a domineering ingredient that often crowds out other flavors, is used lightly. Beyond pizzas, Risa offers pastas that are fine if not especially unusual. Appetizers are a weak link, although calamari is full of flavor and texture, and an arugula and fennel salad is appropriately refreshing. **Price range:** Pizzas, $9–$12; entrees, $8.50–$19.50. **Meals:** L, D, LN. **Subway:** F, S to Broadway–Lafayette St.

RM ☆☆☆ $$$$ SEAFOOD

33 E. 60th St. (between Fifth and Madison Aves.) (212) 319-3800

In some ways, Rick Moonen, the long-time chef at Oceana, has sought to recreate his old workplace at RM, as with the yachtlike setting. He is that rare chef whose creations are both gutsy and academic. Each dish is a carefully controlled, reasoned construction. Not everything succeeds, but the few clunkers are the exceptions. Good entree choices include poached halibut with fennel cream, walleyed pike wrapped in potato slices and skate encrusted with pistachio. **Price range:** Three-course prix fixe, $55; six-course tasting menu, $100. **Meals:** L, D. Closed Sun. **Subway:** N, R, W to Fifth Ave.

Rocco's on 22nd ☆ $$$ ITALIAN/AMERICAN

12 E. 22nd St. (between Park Ave. and Broadway) (212) 353-0500

Patrons clamor for a table here because they want to step into the world of *The Restaurant*, the TV show that made a star of Rocco DiSpirito. Serious diners enter with foreboding, since the series showed how awful the homestyle food was in the early days. But as the more hopeless members of the team departed, the restaurant got down to the actual work of preparing and serving food, and at the moment most of it is more than respectable. Mama's meatballs, juicy and mildly spiced, are about as good as meatballs can get. **Price range:** Pastas $14–$19, entrees $19–$26. **Meals:** D. Closed Sun. **Subway:** N, R, W, F, V, 6 to 23rd St.

Royal Siam $25 & Under THAI

240 Eighth Ave. (between 22nd and 23rd Sts.) (212) 741-1732

Royal Siam's generic décor of mirrored walls, Thai posters and glass-topped tables belie some of the most flavorful and attractively prepared Thai cooking around. Dishes to look for include tom yum koong, or shrimp and mushroom soup in a lemony seafood broth; tod mun pla, fish cakes paired with a bright peanut sauce; and nuur yunk namtok, or grilled steak served sliced on a bed of mixed greens with cucumber and tomato. **Price range:** Entrees, $8.95–$14.95. **Subway:** C, E to 23rd St.

Ruby Foo's ☆☆ $$ PAN-ASIAN

1626 Broadway (between 49th and 50th Sts.) (212) 489-5600

2182 Broadway (at 77th St.) (212) 724-6700

The Upper West Side branch has everything it takes to make the neighborhood happy: fabulous décor, interesting pan-Asian food and the sort of atmosphere that appeals to families with children as well as singles on the prowl. The décor suggests the mysterious East as imagined by a 1940's B-movie producer. The menu offers everything from dim sum to sushi with side trips through Thailand, tailored to American tastes. But it is the Southeast Asian dishes that really sing. The green curry chicken has a fiery coconut-based sauce that is irresistible. Desserts are purely American and purely wonderful, especially the raspberry-passion fruit parfait. **Price range:** Entrees, $9.50–$19.50. **Meals:** Br, L, D, LN. **Subway:** Midtown: 1, 9 to 50th St. Uptown: 1, 9 to 79th St.

Salaam Bombay Indian Cuisine ☆☆ $$ INDIAN
317 Greenwich St. (near Duane St.) (212) 226-9400

Salaam Bombay looks much like every other upscale Indian restaurant in New York City, large and pleasant. But it departs from tradition and showcases the richness of regional Indian cooking. At lunch there's a big, affordable buffet. At dinner an interesting assortment of vegetable dishes is where this kitchen really shines. The best is ringna bataka nu shaak, a Gujarati eggplant and potato dish cooked with curry leaves and lots of spices. Also try kadhai jhinge, shrimp stir-fried with tomatoes, onions and lots of fresh and fragrant spices. For dessert, shrikhand, a dreamy, custardlike dessert, has a mysterious flavor that imparts a certain sense of wonder. **Price range:** entrees, $9.95–$19.95. **Meals:** L, D. **Subway:** A, C, 1, 2, 3, 9 to Chambers St.

Salón México ☆ $$$ MEXICAN
134-136 E. 26th St. (near Lexington Ave.) (212) 685-9400

Salón México, a dim, starkly decorated restaurant, is a highly personal, quirky homage to the foods and pleasures of Mexico. Most of the modernized dishes are handled with restraint and good taste. But the heart and soul of the menu lies in the more orthodox dishes like a poblano chili stuffed with shrimp and scallops, or duck breast in a pumpkin-seed sauce. **Price range:** Entrees, $15–$26. **Meals:** L, D. **Subway:** 6 to 28th St.

Salt $25 & Under NEW AMERICAN
58 Macdougal St. (near Houston St.) (212) 674-4968

Salt, a small American bistro in SoHo, soothes rather than challenges and is drawing in youthful crowds nightly. The menu offers two main-course options: conventional entrees or Protein Plus 2 plates where diners select a simple main course and two side dishes. Protein Plus 2 is the way to go, whether pairing a whole dorade royale with buttery Yukon Gold potatoes and roasted brussels sprouts, or smoky slices of roasted duck breast with puréed butternut squash and braised beets and carrots. The chef-composed main courses were less successful. **Price range:** Entrees, $13.50–$20.50. **Meals:** Br, D. **Subway:** F, V to Broadway–Lafayette St.

San Domenico ☆☆☆ $$$$ ITALIAN
240 Central Park South (between Broadway and Seventh Ave.) (212) 265-5959

This dignified and comfortable spot is one of a handful of American restaurants trying to showcase the cooking of the aristocratic northern Italian kitchen. Most of the appetizers are so seductive that you will eat every meal in a flush of joyful anticipation. The restaurant's signature dish is uovo in ravioli con burro nocciola tartufato: a single large puff filled with ricotta and spinach perfumed with truffle butter. Snuggled inside is an egg that spurts golden yolk as you begin to eat. But you could also come to San Domenico and treat it like a trattoria, choosing only simple dishes and enjoying the care with which they are cooked. **Meals:** L, D. **Subway:** A, B, C, D, 1, 9 to 59th St.

Savoy   ☆☆   **$$$**   NEW AMERICAN
70 Prince St. (at Crosby St.)   (212) 219-8570
Savoy looks like a funky old aluminum-sided diner. But the upstairs dining room, where cooking is done right in the fireplace, is one of the city's coziest rooms. The menu dances around the globe, borrowing where it will. The results can be wildly uneven but are usually charming. If you are unlucky you may end up with one of the occasionally gummy risottos or doughy pastas. Order a salad, however, and you will instantly be seduced. Desserts are excellent and change with the market. If you have an adventurous spirit, you will discover a sense of fun that is missing in most modern restaurants. **Price range:** Entrees, $19–$26. **Meals:** L, D. **Subway:** N, R to Prince St.; F, S to Broadway–Lafayette St.

Scalini Fedeli   ☆   **$$$$**   ITALIAN
165 Duane St. (Hudson St.)   (212) 528-0400
Scalini Fedeli (which means "steps of faith") has no edge. What it has, instead, is old-fashioned grace. The pleasing food rarely takes flight, and when it does, the dish is likely to be disarmingly simple. The main courses are satisfying, decorous and rather unassuming. For dessert, the panna cotta takes a back seat to the dense chocolate tart. **Price range:** Dinner, three courses, $60. **Meals:** L, D. **Subway:** A, C, 1, 2, 3, 9 to Chambers St.

Schiller's Liquor Bar   **$25 & Under**   NEW AMERICAN
131 Rivington St. (at Norfolk St.)   (212) 260-4555
With walls tiled like subway stations, mirrors carefully marred, and blissful golden lighting, Schiller's Liquor Bar allows you to eat deliciously as you glow at the center of the universe, and for not a lot of money. After 7, reservations are not accepted, so prospective diners clog the paths between tables, wandering and jostling tattooed servers as they try not to spill their drinks. The best dishes are main courses, all familiar yet uncommonly well-executed. Rotisserie chicken is that rare bird that actually tastes like chicken. The sturdy, straightforward desserts do their job admirably, whether fine lemon meringue pie, soft as a cloud, or rich chocolate cream pie. **Price range:** Entrees, $11–$22. **Meals:** L, D. **Subway:** F to Delancey St.

Sciuscià   ☆   **$$$**   ITALIAN/MEDITERRANEAN
Hotel Giraffe, 365 Park Ave. South (near 26th St.)   (212) 213-4008
A slightly mad cheeriness pervades Sciuscià, an eccentric subterranean restaurant that can seem like an Italian version of Alice's tea party. With its truly hideous surroundings, it manages to please the palate, if not the eye. The great strength of the chef's Italian-accented Mediterranean menu is pasta. Paccheri is served with a wonderful sweet sauce of stewed pork belly and onions. Cavatelli come with mussels in a spicy tomato sauce with a real zip. The appetizers, on the whole, put in a stronger showing than the main courses. **Price range:** Entrees, $14–$28. **Meals:** L, D. **Subway:** 6 to 28th St.

Sea Grill ☆☆ $$$ SEAFOOD

19 W. 49th St. (in Rockefeller Center) (212) 332-7610

During the winter the main draw here is a view of the Rockefeller Center skating rink. In warm weather, the skating rink becomes an outdoor extension of the restaurant, with canvas umbrellas and potted shrubs. Much of the menu has a brasserie feel to it, with a changing daily menu of day-boat fish that are simply grilled, sauteed or seared. A fresh breeze blows over the rest of the menu as well, with the accent on vibrant flavors and simple preparations. The crab cake is justly renowned: a lumpy-looking thing, more ball than patty, displaying the rough-hewn virtues that distinguish a real crab cake from a thousand prettified pretenders. **Price range:** Entrees, $21–$29. **Meals:** L, D. Closed Sun. **Subway:** B, D, F, S to 47th-50th St.–Rockefeller Center.

71 Clinton Fresh Food ☆☆ $$ BISTRO/NEW AMERICAN

71 Clinton St. (near Rivington St.) (212) 614-6960

New chef Matt Reguin has wisely chosen not to venture far from the sort of elegantly composed contemporary American dishes that won Wylie Dufresne so much applause. A fat square of Arctic char is lacquered with a glaze just sweet enough to bring out the sweetness of the fish itself, which is offset by salty, spicy rounds of chorizo and slivers of green onion. Mr. Reguin also likes to add fruit to the mix, serving a sour cherry chutney with wonderfully tender slices of venison, creamy lentils and sublimely smoky mushrooms. The restaurant remains as crowded as ever, and its appeal is undimmed. **Price range:** Entrees, $15–$22. **Meals:** D. Closed Sun. **Subway:** F to Delancey St.; J, M, Z to Essex St.

Shanghai Pavilion $25 & Under CHINESE

1378 Third Ave. (at 79th St.) (212) 585-3388

This glossy restaurant on the Upper East Side is sleek and inviting, its cool, modernistic black and red color scheme warmed by brick. The food is lively and balanced, emphasizing the lightness and delicacy for which Shanghai cooking is known. The crab and pork soup dumplings are superb, bright and rich. Call a day ahead to order two Shanghai banquet specialties: beggar's chicken, a famous dish in which the bird is boned, stuffed with pork and preserved vegetables, rubbed with spices and encased in clay; or eight treasures duck, a boneless duck stuffed with eight ingredients until it is as plump as a pillow. **Price range:** Entrees, $8–$36. **Meals:** L, D. **Subway:** 6 to 77th St.

Shore $25 & Under SEAFOOD/NEW AMERICAN

41 Murray St. (at Church St.) (212) 962-3750

Shore is as unpretentious a New England fish shack as you can imagine with a TriBeCa address. The dining room, with wicker chairs and tables covered in butcher paper, is adorned with photos of the New England seashore. Chowder is the place to start, and a platter of impeccably fresh oysters is just the right supplement. The fried clam roll is pleasing because the clams are crisp and full of flavor. Brook trout stuffed with crab meat and bread crumbs is a classic diner preparation, but far more delicate, and an occasional special of baked Chatham cod shows how good cod can be if cooked just long enough to allow its reticent flavors to emerge. **Price range:** Entrees, $14–$29. **Meals:** L, D. **Subway:** 4, 5, 6, N, R, to Brooklyn Bridge/City Hall.

Shun Lee Palace   ☆ ☆ $$$ CHINESE
155 E. 55th St. (between Lexington and Third Aves.)   (212) 371-8844
No restaurant in New York City can produce better Chinese food. And no restaurant in New York City does it so rarely. Shun Lee is a New York institution, with a cool opulence that is almost a caricature of a Chinese-American palace. The spareribs are long, meaty, almost fat-free and perfectly cooked. The chefs do impressive things with whole fish, and the owner likes to appear with live fish and suggest various ways the kitchen might prepare them. A recent visit served as a reminder that no one quite matches Shun Lee for its blend of showmanship and culinary quality. **Price range:** Entrees, $9–$30. **Meals:** L, D. **Subway:** E, F to Lexington Ave.; 6 to 51st St.

Shun Lee West $$$ CHINESE
43 W. 65th St. (at Columbus Ave.)   (212) 595-8895
A cavernous Chinese restaurant near Lincoln Center that is always packed. The kitchen can do great things, but they are rarely produced for a clientele that sticks mostly to the familiar. If you want the best food, call ahead and discuss the menu. Good Peking duck. **Price range:** Avg. entree, $19. **Meals:** Br, L, D, LN. **Subway:** 1, 9 to 66th St.

66   ☆ ☆ $$$$ CHINESE
241 Church St. (near Leonard St.)   (212) 925-0202
Jean-Georges Vongerichten's most polished production yet may be 66. It is an elegantly understated room subdivided into discrete dining areas by frosted glass panels. The design is flawless. The food is hit and miss, although it's hard to imagine, in principle, a more appealing menu. Diners can wander at will among noodles, soups, dim sum, small vegetable plates, clever appetizers, and larger entree-like dishes, ordering entirely by whim. Make the right choices, and you'll have the meal of your life. **Price range:** Entrees, $18–$40. **Meals:** L, D. **Subway:** 1, 9 to Franklin St.

Smith & Wollensky   ☆ ☆ $$$$ STEAKHOUSE
797 Third Ave. (at 49th St.)   (212) 753-1530
This is a place for two-fisted eating. It is also one of the few steakhouses that never lets you down: the service is swell, the steaks are consistently very, very good (if rarely great) and the portions are huge. The sirloins are aged for around two weeks to intensify the flavor and give the meat a dry edge. Beyond that, if you have noncarnivores to feed, the restaurant knows how to do it. The lobsters, clams, oysters and chicken are excellent too. Desserts, unfortunately, leave a great deal to be desired. **Price range:** Entrees, $18.50–$65. **Meals:** L, D, LN. **Subway:** 6 to 51st St.; E, F to Lexington Ave.

Snack $25 & Under   GREEK
105 Thompson St. (at Prince St.)   (212) 925-1040
This is one of Manhattan's smallest restaurants. But taste the stifado, a delicately spiced stew of braised lamb, and you know right away that Snack is worth squeezing into. Start with the impeccable cold appetizers: hummus, melitzanes salata, taramosalata, tzatziki and skordalia. Other gems among the small selection of main courses include keftedes, or savory veal meatballs, and juicy roast chicken. Desserts are simple and satisfying. **Price range:** Entrees, $8–$13. Cash only. **Meals:** L, D. **Subway:** N, R to Prince St.

Snack Taverna $25 & Under   GREEK
63 Bedford St. (at Morton St.)   (212) 929-3499
Snack Taverna is simple and clean, adhering so closely to the casual traditions of the taverna that the intriguing Greek wines are served in juice glasses. It has effectively deconstructed the classic flavors of Greek cooking and reintegrated them in stylish dishes that are presented with an almost French elegance. Moussaka, made with a light béchamel, is meatless, with prunes added to the eggplant and potatoes for moisture and substance. Taramosalata and tzatziki are uncommonly tangy and delicious, and braised lamb shoulder is tender as can be, with mint, roasted potatoes and dandelion greens. **Price range:** Entrees, $17–$19. **Meals:** D. **Subway:** 1, 9, to Christopher St.

Soba Nippon $25 & Under   JAPANESE/SUSHI
19 W. 52nd St. (between Fifth and Sixth Aves.)   (212) 489-2525
Few places make better noodles than Soba Nippon. The owner has his own buckwheat farm and soba noodles are made daily at the restaurant. Try the cold soba noodles served plain, on a flat basket with a dipping sauce of fish stock and soy. Eventually, a small, simmering pot of liquid is placed on the table: this is the broth in which the noodles were boiled. Pour the broth into the dipping sauce, add the scallions and wasabi, and drink. It's marvelous. **Price range:** Entrees, $8–$17. **Meals:** L, D. **Subway:** E, F to Fifth Ave.

Soba-Ya $25 & Under   JAPANESE/NOODLES
229 E. 9th St. (between Second and Third Aves.)   (212) 533-6966
Noodles are the focus at this bright, handsome little Japanese restaurant. The soba noodles — buckwheat, pale tan and smooth — are served hot in soups or cold, a better bet for appreciating their lightness and clear flavors. Appetizers are excellent, differing night to night but sometimes including cooked marinated spinach, rice with shreds of marinated sardines and fried squares of marvelously fresh tofu. **Price range:** Noodles and rice bowls, $6.50–$14. **Meals:** L, D. **Subway:** 6 to Astor Pl.; N, R to 8th St.

Soho Steak $25 & Under   BISTRO/FRENCH
90 Thompson St. (near Spring St.)   (212) 226-0602
This thoroughly French little restaurant, drawing a young, good-looking crowd, emphasizes meat but is no simple steakhouse. It is a cleverly conceived, bustling

bistro that serves creative dishes for lower prices than you might imagine. Steak frites, of course, is top-notch. Few places offer this much value for this kind of money. **Price range:** Entrees, $14–$16. Cash only. **Meals:** Br, D. **Subway:** C, E to Spring St.

Solera ☆☆ $$$ TAPAS/SPANISH

216 E. 53rd St. (between Second and Third Aves.) (212) 644-1166

Solera looks so cozy it is almost impossible not to be drawn into the long room, with its terra-cotta tiles and romantic lighting. Pull up a chair and prepare to be seduced by the food and wine of Spain. The appetizers are all fine, but octopus with paprika and olive oil is consistently amazing. There are several versions of paella, all delicious but the seafood is the most impressive. Best of all are the crisp little lamb chops served with a ragout of beans and polenta laced with cheese. **Price range:** Entrees, $25–$35; tapas, $3–$9.50. **Meals:** L, D, LN. Closed Sun. **Subway:** E, F to Lexington Ave.; 6 to 51st St.

Sparks Steak House ☆ $$$$ STEAKHOUSE

210 E. 46th St. (between Second and Third Aves.) (212) 687-4855

Even within the two-fisted genre of New York steakhouses, few places are as decidedly masculine as Sparks. Yet, even though a dinner at Sparks brings out the raucous bond trader in even the mildest-mannered diner, it all feels exactly right. The bar is crowded with people waiting for tables — and there always seems to be a wait. The kitchen has been inconsistent in the past, but when things are right, the thick, salt-crusted prime sirloins and lamb chops are superb. Stick with the steakhouse classics and take time to explore the superb wine list. Service is friendly but at times careless. **Price range:** Entrees, $20–$90. **Meals:** L, D. Closed Sun. **Subway:** 4, 5, 6, 7 to 42nd St.

Spice Market ☆☆☆ $$$ PAN-ASIAN

403 W. 13th St. (at Ninth Ave.) (212) 675-2322

Spice Market is a bustling former warehouse transformed by worn teak beams and balustrades, soaring palms and lavender silk lanterns. Its casual, exotic luxury provides the perfect setting for Chef Jean-George Vongerichten's reworked and polished take on street food. A succession of stimulating textures and vivid flavors flutter on your palate. Sweet shrimp fritters are dotted with crunchy bits of long bean and tempered by a relish of peanut and cucumber. Thai chicken wings are coated in a hot, sticky sauce, fragrant with chilies, soy, lime and fish sauce. To cap off the extraordinary pleasure, order the Thai jewels for dessert: it's a colorful, wonderful mess of flavors. **Price range:** Entrees $6–$29. **Meals:** D. Closed Sun. **Subway:** A, C, E, L to 14th St.

The Spotted Pig $25 & Under NEW AMERICAN

314 West 11th St. (at Greenwich St.) (212) 620-0393

This is one of the most crowded little restaurants in New York, but it shows a winning confluence of casual yet imaginative food served in an easygoing, almost rustic atmosphere where the menu is ever changing. It may have the best version of vitello tonnato in New York, made with thin slices of pork, served in a thick, soulful, tuna-imbued mayonnaise with capers and anchovies. Roast cod is enlivened by a sharp parsley sauce, and a mean cheeseburger is charred crisp around the exterior and sharpened with Roquefort. **Price range:** Entrees, $13–$19. **Meals:** L, D. **Subway:** 1, 9 to Christopher St.

Strip House ☆ $$$ STEAKHOUSE
13 E. 12th St. (between Fifth Ave. and University Pl.)   (212) 328-0000
Strip House is not so much a steakhouse as a catalog of hip references to the idea of a steakhouse. with a cheery, comfortable atmosphere. The filet mignon and New York strip steaks are acceptable, but the swaggering porterhouse comes through in a big way, seared aggressively to achieve a deep crunch, all rubescent tender meat within. For dessert, the caramelized apple tart with mascarpone ice cream and brown sugar hard sauce is as good as it sounds. **Price range:** Entrees, $22–$32. **Meals:** D. **Subway:** F, L, N, Q, R, W, 4, 5, 6 to 14th St.

Suba ☆ $$ SPANISH/ECLECTIC
109 Ludlow St. (near Delancey St.)   (212) 982-5714
The descent to the dining room at Suba is a series of twists and turns along a staircase made from industrial grating. The chef takes Spain as a departure point, but quickly speeds off to points unknown. Some of this is wildly misconceived. Some of it is wonderful. None of it is boring. Goat cheese is everywhere on the menu, most successfully in a kind of napoleon consisting of thin black-pepper tuiles, serrano ham, quince paste and cheese. Try the flourless chocolate cake served with a coffee-avocado shake. It's a minor triumph. **Price range:** Entrees, $18–$25. **Meals:** D. **Subway:** F to Delancey St.; J, M, Z to Essex St.

Sueños ☆ $$ MEXICAN
311 W. 17th St. (between Eighth and Ninth Aves.)   (212) 243-1333
This outpost of new-wave Mexican cuisine sports a hot tropical color scheme, folk-art dioramas and a rock garden open to the elements. Fresh tortillas (stained red ocher by mild chilies) and guacamole are prepared at what looks like a street vendor's stand. The kitchen keeps things light and subtly spicy. Unfortunately, the staff simply falls apart when the dining room fills up. **Price range:** Entrees $17–$23. **Meals:** D, Sun. brunch. **Subway:** 1, 9 to 18th St.

The Sultan $25 & Under TURKISH
1435 Second Ave. (near 74th St.)   (212) 861-2828
This friendly storefront restaurant offers mainstream Turkish dishes that are notable for their fresh, lively flavors. Meals begin with a basket of puffy house-made bread studded with tiny black sesame seeds, and a dish of tahini blended with pekmez, a thick grape syrup. Kebabs are universally good here, especially the lamb yogurt kebab, and whole trout is grilled perfectly, then filleted at the table. The dessert menu is predictable yet well prepared.
Price range: Entrees, $11.95–$16.95. **Meals:** L, D. **Subway:** 6 to 77th St.

Sumile   ☆☆   **$$$**   JAPANESE FUSION
154 W. 13th St. (at Seventh Ave.)   (212) 989-7699
At Sumile (SOO-mee-lay), the menu format is simplicity itself. There are about
20 dishes, all priced at $14, with a supplement for a few dishes that use expen-
sive ingredients. Three dishes make a substantial meal. The sashimi dish is an
inspired bit of stagecraft: Neat slices of fish, daubed in red, are arranged in an
imitation Japanese rock garden, with rice grains for sand. While some dishes
lack balance, others are beyond praise. Aged sake adds layers of yeasty opulence
to sliced duck breast, arranged over blanched cabbage in foie gras whipped into
a froth. The dining room feels light and airy, with white marble floors and pure
white walls expanding the sense of space. It's smart design for smart food. **Price
range:** Entrees $14–$28. **Meals:** D. **Subway:** A, C, E, L to 14th St.

Supper   **$25 & Under**   ITALIAN
156 E. 2nd St. (near Ave. A)   212) 477-7600
Decorated in standard-issue mismatched tables and chairs with brick walls, tile
flooring and antique chandeliers, Supper is divided into a sidewalk area, a rear
dining room, and a front dining room centered on an open kitchen. Consider
sharing a pasta as an appetizer, especially tajarin d'ortice, the Piedmontese name
for tagliatelle prepared simply with mint and butter. On weekends, Supper
serves bollito misto, the Northern Italian feast of boiled meats. For dessert, light
and sumptuous hazelnut panna cotta is the clear highlight. **Price range:**
Entrees, $7–$14. Cash only. **Meals:** D, LN. **Subway:** F, V to Delancey St.

Surya   ☆☆   **$$**   INDIAN
302 Bleecker St. (between Seventh Ave. South and Grove St.) (212) 807-7770
The restaurant named for the sun (in Tamil) has a small garden in the back
along with a sleek interior. Its menu features mostly south Indian dishes,
often filtered through the technique of France. The main courses have a bold
freshness. But what is most splendid about Surya is the entirely meatless side
of the menu. It is, in fact, difficult to come up with a more exciting place to
eat vegetables in New York City. Don't eat a meal at Surya without ordering
the okra, sautéed in a thick mixture of tomatoes, onion, garlic and kokum (a
sour Indian fruit). Try the dosai, too, and the exceptional desserts. **Price
range:** Entrees, $11–$24. **Meals:** Br, D. **Subway:** 1, 9 to Christopher St.

Sushi Seki   ☆☆   **$$$**   JAPANESE/SUSHI
1143 First Ave. (near 62nd St.)   (212) 371-0238
Sushi Seki will produce traditional sushi if you wish, but its specialty is a mod-
ern style in which each piece is topped with a little sauce. It is a respectful adap-
tation that stays true to the essentials without being bound by the approved
methods. Yellowtail, for example, comes with garlic sauce and also a sliver of
jalapeño. The rear dining room is quiet and feels slightly removed from the
action at the sushi bar, where sushi is prepared with artistry, dedication and
panache. **Price range:** Entrees, $8–$20; sushi, $18–$35. **Meals:** D, LN. Closed
Sun. **Subway:** N, R, W to Lexington Ave.; 4, 5, 6 to 59th St.

Sushi Yasu $25 & Under JAPANESE
Washington Jefferson Hotel, 324 W. 51st St. (212) 765-1818
This is a serious, no-nonsense place where visiting businessmen can get a traditional Japanese meal, drink themselves silly if they like, and follow it up with a
breakfast of grilled fish and miso soup the next morning. The sushi is straightforward and very good, and the lunch prices especially are excellent. The lunch
menu includes some home-style dishes, like a fried pork cutlet served over rice
with poached eggs and a sweet brown sauce, or una-don, with grilled eel, or the
yakinu-kudon, with grilled short ribs. **Price range:** Entrees, $12–$20; omakase
(chef's choice) meal, $50–$70. **Meals:** L, D. **Subway:** C, E, to 50th St.

Sushi Yasuda ☆☆☆ $$$ JAPANESE/SUSHI
204 E. 43rd St. (between Second and Third Aves.) (212) 972-1001
In one of the city's dreariest restaurant neighborhoods, Sushi Yasuda glows like a
strange mineral, with a cool, celery-green façade. Inside, the mood is quiet, con-
templative, austere. But Sushi Yasuda has a lot of downtown in its soul. The
exemplary service has an open, friendly quality to it. The menu is a purist's par-
adise of multiple choices among fish species—nearly 30, a startling number for a
small restaurant—and elegantly presented appetizers and side dishes. But sushi
is only half the story. The daily menu includes a small sheet of special appetiz-
ers, and they are worth jumping for. **Price range:** Sushi, $3–$6.50 a piece.
Meals: L, D. Closed Sun. **Subway:** S, 4, 5, 6, 7 to 42nd St.

Svenningsen's $25 & Under SEAFOOD
292 Fifth Ave. (near 30th St.) (212) 465-1888
Svennignsen's owner buys excellent seafood and puts it to righteous use. A half-
dozen mighty-size cherrystones taste as if they were pulled from the sea only
minutes before. Or try a dark, buttery lobster stew, or a lighter, saltier, but no
less attractive seafood chowder. Among the entree options, crab cakes are per-
haps the best. Look at the gentle interaction between those serving and those
eating. No, it's not a pretty room. But it is a kind one. **Price range:** Entrees,
$14.50–$21.50. **Meals:** L, D. **Subway:** F, N, R, Q, V, W to 34th St.

Sylvia's $ SOUTHERN
328 Lenox Ave. (between 126th and 127th Sts.) (212) 996-0660.
Tour buses pull up in front for a sanitized taste of Harlem. The food's not fabu-
lous, but it offers everything you expect: fried chicken, collard greens and sweet
potato pie. Best for the gospel brunch on Sunday. **Price range:** Entrees,
$8.95–$13; gospel brunch: $15.95. **Meals:** Br, L, D. **Subway:** 2, 3 to 125th St.

Tabla ☆☆☆ $$$$ AMERICAN-ASIAN FUSION
11 Madison Ave. (near 25th St.) (212) 889-0667
The newest of Danny Meyer's restaurants, Tabla vibrates with sound and sizzles
with color. At the bar downstairs, cooks grill roti and naan in odd and interest-
ing flavors. Upstairs, the dining room is darkly sensuous with walls stained in
shades of jade and coral. Then the food arrives—American food, viewed
through a kaleidoscope of Indian spices. The powerful, original and unexpected

flavors evoke intense emotions. Those who do not like Tabla tend to dislike it with a passion. Ignore them and abandon yourself to the joys of a fine restaurant. **Price range:** Three-course prix-fixe dinner, $52 (plus a few supplements). **Meals:** L, D. Closed Sun. **Subway:** 6 to 23rd St.

Tagine $25 & Under   MOROCCAN

537 Ninth Ave. (near 40th St.)   (212) 564-7292

Tagine is a low-budget operation. The dim, alluring dining room seems a blizzard of colors and styles and the languorous service may lead you to believe that food is not the focus here, but you'll relax when the food arrives. Zaalouk, an eggplant purée rich with the dusky aroma of cumin, is wonderful on freshly baked bread. The restaurant's signature tagines, fragrant stews served in traditional earthenware vessels with conical lids, are the least satisfying of the main courses, though the chicken tagine and lamb shank are quite good. Desserts can be excellent, like semolina cake soaked in orange blossom water. **Price range:** Entrees, $13–$19.50. **Meals:** L, D, LN. **Subway:** A, C, E to 42nd St.

Tamarind   ☆☆ $$ INDIAN

41-43 E. 22nd St. (between Broadway and Park Ave. South)   (212) 674-7400

Tamarind, named for the sweet-and-sour fruit, looks and feels fresh. It is stylishly decorated, and the menu treats Indian cuisine as a genuine culinary language, like French, able to assimilate nontraditional ingredients and techniques. Quality varies on the extensive dinner menu, but on balance, the winners outnumber the losers by about 3 to 1. For whatever reason, anything involving shrimp succeeds wildly, like shrimp balchau, an exotic shrimp cocktail with a smoothly fiery chili-masala sauce wrapped around tiny chunks of firm tomato. Vegetarian dishes also seem to bring out the best at Tamarind. The ingenious lunch menu offers five set menus, each representing a coherent Indian meal. **Price range:** Entrees, $15–$26. **Meals:** L, D. **Subway:** 6 to 23rd St.

The Tasting Room   ☆ $$$ NEW AMERICAN

72 E. 1st St. (between First and Second Aves.)   (212) 358-7831

When the Tasting Room is not caught up in its own spell, it serves good food at a moderate price in a pleasant atmosphere, with a clever format. What sets the restaurant apart is its ferociously ambitious, nicely priced wine list. The menu allows diners to combine several tasting portions into a meal or to order the usual appetizer and main course. At the Tasting Room, bolder is better. Try rabbit or a simple pan-roasted sea bass. For dessert, Renée's Mother's Cheesecake is a cheesecake to die for; in comparison, the menu is a mere footnote. **Price range:** Entrees, $13–$29. **Meals:** D. Closed Sun. **Subway:** F to Second Ave.

Tavern on the Green   ☆ $$$$ NEW AMERICAN

Central Park West (at 67th St.)   (212) 873-3200

This is America's largest-grossing restaurant, a wonderland of lights, flowers, chandeliers and balloons that can make a child out of the most cynical adult. Patrick Clark, who died in February 1998, was a terrific chef, and he's left a culinary legacy for his successors to follow. But even he was not able to overcome the tavern's unaccountably rude and lax service. Even so, the people keep coming for the glittery setting. **Price range:** Entrees, $21.75–$34. **Meals:** Br, L, D. **Subway:** 6 to 66th St.

Temple $25 & Under   KOREAN
81 St. Marks Pl. (near First Ave.)   (212) 979-9300
Temple manages to offer many authentic Korean flavors while fitting in well with the youth-oriented culture of the East Village. Temple is tiny, with one row of tables along one side of the room and a small counter along the other. The dish called ku jol pan is fun and delicious: a pile of delicate palm-size pancakes strewn with sesame seeds, surrounded by little dishes of food, to be wrapped in the pancakes and dipped into a tangy soy-and-wasabi sauce. There are many other worthy choices, including kimchi stew, a spicy soup with tofu, kimchi and bits of pork. Meals end with a refreshing cup of cinnamon-ginger iced tea. **Price range:** Entrees, $9–$14. **Meals:** L, D. **Subway:** 6 to Astor Place.

Thalia   ☆☆ $$$ NEW AMERICAN
828 Eighth Ave. (at 50th St.)   (212) 399-4444
Thalia is the Muse of comedy, and also a confusing name for a serious restaurant. Executive chef Michael Otsuka practices an intelligent form of fusion cooking, with a strong Asian influence. He has faith in the power of simple ingredients and flavors, and the wit to use them in inventive ways. A spoonful of wasabi granita, cold and crunchy, with a piercing heat, sets off Kumamoto oysters brilliantly. Foie gras fatigue disappears the moment you lay eyes on foie gras mousse, sprinkled with chopped pistachio and accompanied by figs drenched in port. It looks like dessert but it's twice as rich—damnation on a small plate. **Price range:** Entrees, $17–$29. **Meals:** L, D. **Subway:** C, E to 50th St.

36 Bar and Barbecue   ☆ $$ KOREAN
5 W. 36th St. (near Fifth Ave.)   (212) 563-3737
The aroma of wood smoke, sweet and penetrating, makes a powerful first impression at 36 Bar and Barbecue, a tiny, enormously appealing Korean barbecue restaurant. It is shooting for a younger, hipper and more mixed clientele than its neighbors, but the food, and the manners, remain traditional. The marinated beef short ribs are exceptionally tender. **Price range:** Entrees, $8–$19. **Meals:** L, D, LN. **Subway:** B, D, F, N, Q, R, V, W to 34th St.

Thom   ☆ $$$ FUSION/NEW AMERICAN
Thompson Hotel, 60 Thompson St. (near Broome St.)   (212) 219-2000
The menu here is certainly not boring, although the chef seems to have a weakness for sweets. Pan-broiled beef fillet, with short ribs braised in cabernet, meets the sweetness challenge and emerges triumphant. Fermented chilies added a subtle fire to shrimp in a thick curry sauce. The pastry chef also comes up with a few winning combinations, like toasted almond anglaise served with a warm plum cake, rich and light at the same time. **Price range:** Entrees, $19–$29. **Meals:** D. **Subway:** A, C, E to Canal St.

325 Spring Street   ☆   **$$$**   BRASSERIE
325 Spring St. (at Greenwich St.)   (212) 414-1344
The owner has decided that truffles will give his restaurant personality, so he
has signed the great French chef Clément Bruno, although his title is honorific
(the kitchen is actually run by two chefs de cuisine). Mr. Bruno lends his presti-
gious name and in return gets to showcase his cuisine and his line of truffle oils,
on sale up front. Diners get a menu with very high highs (like the pizza with
Comté cheese and shavings of summer truffles), and some pretty low lows (like
the grilled tuna). The setting is gorgeous, with a dining room done in a 1930's
moderne style reminiscent of a great ocean liner. **Price range:** Entrees $16–$36.
Meals: D. Closed Sun. **Subway:** F, V to Broadway/Lafayette; N, R, W to Prince
St.; C, E to Spring St.

Tocqueville   ☆ ☆   **$$$$**   FRENCH
15 E. 15th St. (between Fifth Ave. and Union Sq. West)   (212) 647-1515
Tocqueville is a quiet haven of good taste, good food and good service. The
spacing between tables is generous, given the floor space, and the service, which
could easily feel intrusive and hovering, achieves a laudable transparency. Billy
Bi soup, the oddly named classic from France's Atlantic coast, is beyond praise.
Desserts do honor to the menu, especially the upside-down banana tart, a small
palisade of fat banana chunks encircling a disk of almond shortbread, teamed up
with a ball of brown-sugar ice cream. **Price range:** Entrees, $22–$28. **Meals:** L,
D. Closed Sun. **Subway:** L, N, Q, R, W, 4, 5, 6 to 14th St.

Topaz Thai   **$25 & Under**   THAI
127 W. 56th St. (between Sixth and Seventh Aves.)   (212) 957-8020
This restaurant offers fine Thai cooking. Soups, like the delicious tom kha gai,
made with chicken stock, coconut milk, chili peppers and lime, are particularly
good, as are spicy dishes like the soupy jungle curry made with scallops and
green beans. The restaurant has a peculiar nautical theme courtesy of a previous
tenant—Art Deco paneling, triangular sconces and wooden captain's chairs.
Price range: Entrees, $8–$18. **Meals:** L, D. **Subway:** N, R, Q, W to 57th St.

Town   ☆ ☆ ☆   **$$$**   NEW AMERICAN
Chambers Hotel, 15 W. 56th St. (between Fifth and Sixth Aves.)
                                                              (212) 582-4445
Town has an unmistakable sense of style. It's a civilized, very adult setting that
suits the chef's elegant, clean cooking. He manages to enliven his dishes with
just the half twist that makes them distinctive, as in a simple roasted skate
served with three sorbet-shaped quenelles: pea-peppermint, apple-miso, and
eggplant with hazelnut oil and quatre-épices. A risotto of escargots doused with
black truffle broth seems unfair. How can it fail? The dessert list is strong, and
one is a showstopper: it starts with a basket of sugar-powdered beignets filled
with molten chocolate. Then comes a perfect frozen dome with a matte-brown
cocoa surface, a chilled version of café brûlot, a flaming liqueur-laced coffee.
Price range: Entrees, $21–$29. **Meals:** L, D. **Subway:** N, R, Q, W to 57th St.

Tribeca Grill ☆☆ $$$ NEW AMERICAN

375 Greenwich St. (at Franklin St.)   (212) 941-3900

Robert De Niro's first venture into the restaurant business in what the neighbors sometimes call Bob Row is a cool, casual outpost of modern American cuisine with an almost constant flow of celebrity guests. And the food's good. The big, airy space with exposed bricks, colorful banquettes and comfortable tables centers on a massive handsome mahogany bar. The beguiling fare remains a steady lure. **Price range:** Entrees, $12–$29. **Meals:** Br, L, D. **Subway:** 1, 9 to Franklin St.

Triomphe ☆☆ $$$ FRENCH/NEW AMERICAN

Iroquois Hotel, 49 W. 44th St. (between Fifth and Sixth Aves.) (212) 453-4233

In a city with flash to spare, this restaurant has a rare commodity: charm. And the food, simple and understated, matches the room. Again and again, Triomphe quietly strikes the right note, as with a subtle herb broth that nicely underlines the natural sweetness of acorn-squash wontons covered in shavings of Parmesan cheese. When the main ingredient calls for more, the chef opens up the flavors. A hefty rib-eye steak comes with fat grilled cepes and a muscular brandy demi-glace, and a thick slab of salmon gets the works: a caviar-dotted beurre blanc, a scattering of grilled shrimp and parsnip whipped potatoes. **Price range**: Entrees, $23–$32. **Meals:** B, L, D. **Subway:** B, D, F, to 42nd St.

Tsuki $25 & Under SUSHI/JAPANESE

1410 First Ave. (near 75th St.)   (212) 517-6860

Tsuki is a modest storefront that has a warm family feeling. As at many sushi bars, non-sushi items are available. Try a bowl of the house-made tofu, served warm with ginger and soy. Sushi, though, is the thing, and for a neighborhood restaurant, Tsuki has an extensive list of fish. Those include fine, delicately flavored red snapper, and the richer, slightly oily horse mackerel. You'll love Tsuki's bonito, served with a dab of mayonnaise and grated ginger. **Price range:** Sushi, $3–$6.50 a piece; chef's selection, $36 and up. **Meals:** D. AE only. **Subway:** 6 to 77th St.

Turkuaz $25 & Under TURKISH

2637 Broadway (at 100th St.)   (212) 665-9541

The dining room here is draped in billowy fabric so that it resembles an Ottoman tent, and the staff is adorned in traditional Turkish costumes. Cold appetizers are excellent, and main courses tend to be simple and elementally satisfying, like beyti kebab, spicy chopped lamb charcoal-grilled with herbs and garlic. Desserts include a neat variation on rice pudding, served with the top caramelized like crème brûlée. **Price range:** Entrees, $8.50–$18.50. **Meals:** D. **Subway:** 1, 9 to 103rd St.

Tuscan ☆☆ $$$$ ITALIAN

622 Third Ave. (at 40th St.)   (212) 404-1700

The former Tuscan Steak, now simply called Tuscan, is a much better restaurant. Tuscan retains the party atmosphere and the throbbing bar scene on the mezzanine level. But the large, stylish dining room now emphasizes variety rather than abundance. Nearly half the menu is devoted to an assortment of well-made antipasti. The restaurant's signature dish is bocconcini, miniature footballs of buttery polenta dough, reeking of truffle, that are deep-fried and completely seductive. **Price range:** Entrees, $19–$44. **Meals:** D. Closed Sun. **Subway:** 4, 5, 6, 7 to 42nd St.

"21" Club   ☆☆ $$$$ AMERICAN
21 W. 52nd St. (between Fifth and Sixth Aves.)   (212) 582-7200
Of all the restaurants in New York City, none has a richer history. American royalty has been entertaining at "21" for most of this century. The restaurant continues to be operated like a club where unknowns are led to the farthest dining room as the more favored clients are pampered and petted. Nothing much else has changed either: the tablecloths are still red and white checked, the toys are still hanging from the ceiling, and it still looks like the speakeasy it once was. The menu has been modernized but with mixed results. The basics are still superb, however. Great steak, rack of lamb, Dover sole, and the "21" burger, and several traditional desserts such as rice pudding and crème brûlée are all worthwhile. **Price range:** Entrees, $24–$39. **Meals:** L, D. Closed Sun.
Subway: E, F to Fifth Ave.

26 Seats $25 & Under   FRENCH
168 Ave. B. (11th St.)   (212) 677-4787
This sweet little French restaurant is intimate yet relatively comfortable, and the waitresses are friendly and kind to children. The menu's French country offerings are both satisfying and a good value, like the pissaladière, a flat, wafer-thin crusted tart of caramelized onions, made pungent with anchovy fillets and olives, or the savory garlic sausage paired with boiled potato and hard-boiled eggs, all dressed in a balsamic vinaigrette. The main courses are well-executed versions of familiar recipes, with the occasional pleasing twist. For dessert, a wedge of apple tart is the best choice. **Price range:** Entrees, $11–$16.50. AE only **Meals:** D. Closed Mon. **Subway:** L to First Ave.

Union Pacific   ☆☆ $$$$ SEAFOOD
111 E. 22nd St. (between Park and Lexington Aves.)   (212) 995-8500
Is chef Rocco DiSpirito spending more time at Rocco's on 22nd Street, his television-created spaghetti parlor, than at his premier restaurant, which opened in 1997? The unevenness of the cooking here brings up the question. Some dishes seem poorly thought out, like turkey schnitzel, and other seem as if no one has tasted them before putting them on the menu. But some of the food is spectacular, a sophisticated blend of unexpected ingredients, like fluke carpaccio drizzled with sweet cashew purée and a coriander vinaigrette. A pleasing remodeling job has turned a cold, uninviting space into something warm and welcoming. **Price range:** Entrees $24–$39; prix-fixe $68 and $75. **Meals:** L (Mon.–Fri.), D (Mon.–Sat.). **Subway:** N, R, W, 6 to 23rd St.

Union Square Café   ☆☆ $$$ NEW AMERICAN
21 E. 16th St. (between Fifth Ave. and Union Sq. West)   (212) 243-4020
Union Square's pioneering fusion of fine food and wine, casual atmosphere and
stellar service has made it the most influential restaurant of its time in the city,
certainly one of the most popular, and a top destination for tourists. The wine
list is still outstanding and still full of bargains. Don't miss the signature fried
calamari, nicely complemented with an incisive, creamy anchovy mayonnaise.
Although there are several foreign accents heard on the menu, Italian dominates, especially in the pasta dishes, which put many Italian restaurants to
shame. Desserts aim for an artful blend of homey and exotic, most memorably
in the banana tart with a caramel shellac, a Union Square standby. **Price range:**
Entrees, $18.50–$28. **Meals:** L, D. **Subway:** L, N, Q, R, W, 4, 5, 6 to 14th St.

United Noodles $25 & Under   PAN-ASIAN
349 E. 12th St. (near First Ave.)   (212) 614-0155
United Noodles is a simple, narrow storefront that radiates a happy warmth as it
plays host, nightly, to an incredible mix of people. They all enter its stylish interior on the strength of its inexpensive and interesting menu of deconstructed
Asian food. The cold soba sashimi — which amounts to a plate of sashimi
thrown into a blender, dressings and all, with cold soba noodles — is a brilliant
fusion dish: Honmura An meets Nobu. **Price range:** Entrees, $9–$15. **Meals:** D.
Subway: L to First Ave.

Upstairs at "21"   ☆☆ $$$$ NEW AMERICAN
21 W. 52nd St. (between Fifth and Sixth Aves.)   (212) 265-1900
The new upstairs dining room at the "21" Club is a club within a club, a small,
windowless room ruled by its own peculiar rituals, meant to suggest a vanished
world of privilege and high style. It gives the chef the opportunity to cook the
kind of food that could never fly in the conservative dining room downstairs.
The evening begins with three amuse-bouches for each diner. Meals come in
two formats, a four-course à la carte dinner and a tasting menu of six courses.
The chef makes every effort to dazzle, and he is successful about half the time.
One sparkling instance is sea scallops, sashimi style, with a creamy mussel dressing and osetra caviar. **Price range:** Four-course prix fixe, $85; six-course tasting
menu, $125. **Meals:** D. Closed Sun., Mon. **Subway:** E, V to Fifth Ave.

Uskudar $25 & Under   TURKISH
1405 Second Ave. (near 73rd St.)   (212) 988-2641
This restaurant is the model of a successful neighborhood institution, and it has
achieved that status without the burgers, pastas and steaks that form the default
menu of most local hangouts. The selection of appetizers includes excellent
Middle Eastern spreads: patlican, smoky eggplant mashed with garlic, sesame
paste and herbs; and ezme, a blend of tomatoes, onions, parsley and walnuts.
Kebabs are uncommonly juicy, but the best dishes are the stews, like hunkar
begendi, a hearty lamb stew. Uskudar makes excellent desserts, especially

kadayif, shredded wheat crowned with ground walnuts and drenched in honey.
Price range: Entrees, $12.95–$15.95. **Meals:** L, D. **Subway:** 6 to 77th St.

V Steakhouse   ☆ $$$–$$$$ STEAK/AMERICAN
In the Time Warner Center, Columbus Circle, 4th floor   (212) 823-9500
It's hard to imagine a restaurant as convoluted as this, the latest enterprise from
Jean-George Vongerichten. The disappointing appetizers and the desserts are so
needlessly complicated that they require tableside coaching from your servers.
At least the main courses are robustly satisfying. There are big, thick, high-qual-
ity hunks of meat, and the kitchen is skilled at preparing them. Unfortunately,
they're undercut by a selection of a dozen homemade condiments like tamarind
ketchup. The décor overdoses on faux opulence; it's like the nexus of the Best
Little Whorehouse in Texas and Tavern on the Green, somewhat redeemed by a
sweeping view of Central Park. **Price range:** Entrees $19–$62. **Meals:** L, D.
Subway: 1, 9, A, B, C, D to 59th St./Columbus Circle.

Vatan $25 & Under   INDIAN/VEGETARIAN
409 Third Ave. (at 29th St.)   (212) 689-5666
This astounding Indian restaurant transports you to a bright, animated Indian
village with thatched roofs and artificial banyan trees. Vatan specializes in the
rich, spicy yet subtle vegetarian cuisine of Gujarat. For one price, a parade of little dishes is served, which might include khaman, a delicious fluffy steamed
cake of lentil flour with black mustard seeds; delicate little samosas; patrel, taro
leaves layered with spicy chickpea paste and steamed, and much more.
Price range: $19.95. **Meals:** D, LN. Closed Mon. **Subway:** 6 to 28th St.

Verbena   ☆ $$$ NEW AMERICAN
54 Irving Pl. (near 17th St.)   (212) 260-5454
The newly remodeled Verbena looks attractive. The tight dining room retains
its very adult sense of calm and style, and a cool, breezy and secluded courtyard
garden has been created in the back. But dishes take a long time to arrive at the
table, and what arrives does not always thrill. The bolder dishes sometimes hit
and sometimes miss. The sirloin steak is a remarkably rich, tender cut, beautifully charred outside. Your waiter will ask if you are interested in the baked-to-
order Bing cherry upside-down cake. Say yes. **Price range:** Entrees, $14.50–
$28. **Meals:** Br, D. **Subway:** L, N, Q, R, W, 4, 5, 6 to 14th St.

Veritas   ☆ ☆ ☆ $$$$ NEW AMERICAN
43 E. 20th St. (near Park Ave. South)   (212) 353-3700
Small, spare and elegant, Veritas could be called a wine cellar with a restaurant
attached, because at Veritas, the wine is more important than the food. The
1,300 entries on its wine list include many rarities at extremely reasonable
prices. The room often seems overcrowded, but Veritas offers clean and unfussy
food that works well with its wine. Main courses, to suit the powerful wines, are
robust, powerful and simple—with surprisingly little red meat on the menu. The
intensity does not abate with desserts. Try a startlingly delicious praline parfait

with a polished reduction of clementines. **Price range:** Prix-fixe dinner, $62. **Meals:** L, D. Closed Sun. **Subway:** 6 to 23rd St.

Viceversa ☆ **$$** ITALIAN
325 W. 51st St. (Between Eighth and Ninth Aves.) (212) 399-9265
With its crisp earth-colored awnings and gleaming façade, Viceversa (pronounced VEE-chey-VAIR-suh) stands out on one of Manhattan's grungier blocks like a Versace suit. The menu is honest and unpretentious, a solid lineup of mostly northern Italian dishes presented in a perfectly straightforward manner. Casoncelli alla bergamasca deserves star billing in Viceversa's strong ensemble cast of pastas: it is a ravioli filled with chopped veal, crushed amaretti, raisins and Parmesan, then topped with butter, crisped sage leaves and crunchy bits of fried pancetta. **Price range:** Entrees, $16.50–$22.50. **Meals:** L, D. **Subway:** C, E to 50th St.

Virgil's Real BBQ **$25 & Under** BARBECUE
152 W. 44th St. (between Broadway and Sixth Ave.) (212) 921-9494
Virgil's is a wildly popular shrine to barbecue joints around the country. If the food isn't quite authentic, the formula comes close enough and it works. And the place smells great, as any barbecue place should. Highlights on the menu include hush puppies served with a maple syrup butter; smoked Texas links with mustard slaw; barbecued shrimp and Texas red chili with corn bread. For main fare, big barbecue platters carry enticing selections of Owensboro lamb, Maryland ham, Carolina pork shoulder, Texas beef brisket and more. **Price range:** Entrees, $10.95–$18.95. **Meals:** L, D, LN. **Subway:** B, D, F, N, Q, R, S, W, 1, 2, 3, 7, 9 to 42nd St.

Voyage ☆ **$$$** BISTRO
117 Perry St. (near Greenwich St.) (212) 255-9191
The menu at Voyage is a culinary tour that wanders from Africa to South America to the American South. It offers global down-home cooking, in which A-list ingredients are combined with more marginal ones. Truffled scallops, almost ludicrously classy in Voyage's simple surroundings, find themselves face - to-face with creamy grits and red-eye gravy, a high-low matchup that works brilliantly. Like many other downtown restaurants, Voyage has not quite decided whether it's a lounge or not. The service can be casual to a fault. **Price range:** Entrees, $14–$28. **Meals:** D. **Subway:** 1, 9 to Christopher St.; 6 to 28th St.

Wallsé ☆ ☆ **$$$** AUSTRIAN
344 W. 11th St. (at Washington St.) (212) 352-2300
It is a treat to find a restaurant that sails along so assured and unfettered. The menu is a stimulating blend of elegance and brawn: Delicately poached lobster and light asparagus soup coexist happily with venison and lingonberries, goulash and potato pancakes. If you are not tempted by goulash with spaetzle (a perfect dish), you can have wild striped bass, topped with a tuft of freshly grated horseradish. There is an excellent, but not overreaching cheese menu. Despite

Wallsé's liberal use of lobster and foie gras, it maintains a neighborhood demeanor. **Price range:** Entrees $23–$30. **Meals:** L (Mon.–Fri.), Sun. brunch, D. **Subway:** A, C, E, L to 14th St.

WD-50   ☆☆ $$$ NEW AMERICAN
50 Clinton St. (near Rivington St.)   (212) 477-2900
At WD-50, Wylie Dufresne seems to have decided that the simple, elegant style that seduced diners and critics at his first restaurant, 71 Clinton Fresh Food, was too easy to like. This time, he challenges his customers, provoking them with risky flavor combinations and ingredients in unfamiliar roles. Mr. Dufresne, one of the most distinctive culinary talents in New York, has a restless artistic temperament, and a total lack of fear. Mr. Dufresne's new digs, carved out of what used to be a bodega, isn't particularly comfortable or attractive. The view on the plate is much more appealing. **Price range:** Entrees, $22–$28. **Meals:** D. Closed Sun. **Subway:** F to Delancey St.; J, M, Z to Essex St.

Wolfgang's Steakhouse   ☆☆ $$$$ STEAK/AMERICAN
4 Park Ave. (at E. 33rd St.)   (212) 889-3369
For decades, Wolfgang Zwiener was the head waiter at Peter Luger, the most celebrated steakhouse in New York. He and his co-owners replicate the Luger process at Wolfgang's: steaks hang in a dry-aging box for weeks, then are cooked under a high-temperature broiler that produces a deeply charred exterior. The porterhouse is sized as Steak for Two, Three or Four, and it's many wonderful things at once: crunchy, tender, smoky, earthy. Wolfgang's doles out mammoth portions straight through dessert, including a delicious slice of cheesecake that's big enough for its own treadmill. Service is gruff but efficient, and the noise level under the gorgeous vaulted tile ceilings can be deafening. **Price range:** Entrees $29.95–$37.95. **Meals:** L, D (dinner only on Sat.). Closed Sun. **Subway:** 6 to 33rd St.

Wu Liang Ye $25 & Under   CHINESE
338 Lexington Ave. (between 39th and 40th Sts.)   (212) 370-9647
215 E. 86th St. (at Third Ave.)   (212) 534-8899
36 W. 48th St. (between Fifth and Sixth Aves.)   (212) 398-2308
Though each of these branches of a Chinese restaurant chain differs slightly in menu and atmosphere, they all specialize in lively, robust Sichuan dishes, notable for their meticulous preparation. Sliced conch is one of their more unusual dishes, firm, chewy and nutty, served with spicy red oil. Four kinds of dumplings are all delicate and flavorful. **Price range:** $7.50–$20. **Meals:** L, D, LN. **Subway:** Call for directions to each location.

Yakiniku JuJu $25 & Under   JAPANESE
157 E. 28th St. (between Third and Lexington Aves.)   (212) 684-7830
This small and friendly restaurant specializes in cook-it-yourself shabu-shabu, sukiyaki and Japanese barbecue. Try an appetizer of "salted squid guts," chewy and salty squid cut into cylinders the size of small anchovies and immersed in a

pasty liquid; or takoyaki, croquettes stuffed with pieces of octopus and flavored with dried seaweed, ginger and a fruity sauce. The large main courses include yakiniku, in which you cook pieces of meat and vegetables directly on the grill; shabu-shabu, in which you swish the meat and vegetables through boiling broth; and sukiyaki, the traditional Japanese stew. **Price range:** Dinner for two, $30–$46; for four, up to $80. **Meals:** D. **Subway:** 6 to 28th St.

Yang Pyung Seoul $25 & Under   KOREAN
43 W. 33rd St. (between Fifth Ave. and Broadway)   (212) 629-5599
With a reputation for smoothing the head and soothing the stomach hae jang gook is a specialty at Yang Pyung Seoul, a bright, friendly place. The broth is deep and flavorful, full of ultra-tender tripe and earthy house-made blood sausage. The menu offers some rarely seen North Korean dishes. One of these, kimchi with seafood, is cool, bright and refreshing. **Price range:** Entrees, $8–$15. **Meals:** 24 hrs. **Subway:** B, D, F, N, Q, R, S, V, W to 34th St.

Zarela   ☆☆ $$$ MEXICAN/TEX-MEX
953 Second Ave. (between 50th and 51st Sts.)   (212) 644-6740
Bright, bold and raucous as a party, the sort of place that looks like a typical Mexican taquería. Happily, it is not. Zarela Martinez has written several excellent Mexican cookbooks, and she serves some of the city's most exciting and authentic Mexican food. Among the best dishes are a fiery snapper hash, crisp flautas, tamales and fajitas. Good side dishes include creamy rice baked with sour cream, cheddar cheese, corn and poblano chilies. **Price range:** Avg. entree, $24. **Meals:** L, D. **Subway:** 6 to 51st St.; E, F to Lexington Ave.

Zerza $25 & Under   MOROCCAN
304 E. Sixth St. (between First and Second Aves.)   (212) 529-8250
The menu and the décor here are distinctively Moroccan. Zerza's strongest dishes are among the mezze, or small plates. Grilled merguez, perched atop a carrot purée sweetened with honey, is a typical and enticing Moroccan combination of sweet and savory. The best main courses are the tagines, stews served in earthenware pots with distinctive conical lids, although they can sometimes be painfully cloying. Tender duck with roasted pears and figs achieves a good balance. Service is friendly and well-meaning though sometimes disorganized, and the background music occasionally threatens to seize the foreground. **Price range:** Entrees, $10–$16. **Meals:** L, D. **Subway:** 6 to Astor Place.

Zitoune   ☆ $$ MOROCCAN
46 Gansevoort St. (at Greenwich St.)   (212) 675-5224
Zitoune, which is Arabic for olive, is a lively bistro serving updated Moroccan cuisine. The chef may be English, but you'd never guess from the subtle touch he brings to traditional Moroccan tagines, briks, briwats and bsteeyas. Lamb tagine, one of those dishes that simply must be done right at a restaurant like this, is excellent, complexly spiced and cooked nearly to the melting point. Zitoune's best dessert, a made-to-order bsteeya packed with dried fruit and nuts,

is worth the extra 20 minutes it requires. **Price range:** Entrees, $8–$20.50.
Meals: L, D. **Subway:** A, C, E to 14th St.

Zócalo   ☆ $$$ MEXICAN
174 E. 82nd St. (between Third and Lexington Aves.)   (212) 717-7772
Most of the action at Zócalo is at the colorful, convivial bar in the front of the
restaurant. But in a rear sky-lighted room filled with colorful folk art, it is possible to enjoy Mexican food that is often interesting, though rarely challenging or
unusual, in relative tranquillity. Familiar dishes are well rendered, like chunky
guacamole and chicken quesadillas and enchiladas. **Price range:** Entrees,
$17.50–$24. **Meals:** D. **Subway:** 4, 5, 6 to 86th St.

Zona Rosa   ☆ $$$ MEXICAN
40 W. 56th St. (between Fifth and Sixth Aves.)   (212) 247-2800
With a lackluster location and a bland room, Zona Rosa is often overlooked.
But that's a shame, for the kitchen has subtlety and sophistication. The quesadillas are thin, delicious tortillas wrapped around a scant but powerful filling
of Oaxacan cheese, almonds and spinach. The black bean soup doesn't look like
much, but it contains a spectrum of sensations, and the shrimp ceviche is piled
in a glassy red marinade that enlivens your palate. There's an extraordinary
tequila menu; many cocktails rely on salt and citrus rather than sweetness, making them excellent partners to the food. **Price range:** Entrees $18–$27. **Meals:**
L (Mon.–Fri.), D (Mon.–Sat.). Closed Sun. **Subway:** N, R, Q, W to 57th St.

Zum Schneider $25 & Under   GERMAN
107 Ave. C (at 7th St.)   (212) 598-1098
Essentially an indoor beer garden, Zum Schneider packs young people in
nightly. The simple menu hews closely to the Bavarian formula of wurst, pork
and cabbage, but it has accomplished the unlikely feat of making a German
place cool. Try the pfannkuchen soup. The best of the main courses is a plump,
rosy smoked pork chop. The bar offers a dozen excellent seasonal draft beers, all
German, and 10 more in bottles. **Price range:** Entrees, $7–$12, with $3 and $6
appetizer portions.

A Guide to Restaurants by Cuisine

AMERICAN
BLT Steak ☆☆
City Hall ☆☆
Fifty Seven
  Fifty Seven ☆☆☆
Gumbo Cafe
The Half King
Landmarc
Lunchbox Food
  Company
Natchez
P.J. Clarke's
Taste
"21" Club ☆☆
V Steakhouse ☆
Wolfgang's
  Steakhouse ☆☆

ASIAN FUSION
Asiate ☆
Chubo ☆
Spice Market ☆☆☆

AUSTRALIAN
Eight Mile Creek ☆☆

AUSTRIAN
Café Sabarsky ☆☆
Danube ☆☆☆
Wallsé ☆☆

BALKAN
Djerdan Burek

BARBECUE
Blue Smoke ☆
Pearson's Texas
  Barbecue
Virgil's Real BBQ

CAJUN
Bayou

CARIBBEAN
Bambou ☆☆
Island Spice
Paladar

CHINESE
Chanoodle
Chinese Mirch
Congee
Congee Village
Dim Sum Go Go ☆
Funky Broome
Goody's
Grand Sichuan
Grand Sichuan Eastern
Joe's Ginger
Joe's Shanghai ☆☆
Lozoo ☆
New Green Bo
New York Noodle
  Town ☆☆
Our Place
Pig Heaven
Ping's Seafood ☆☆
Shanghai Pavilion
Shun Lee Palace ☆☆
Shun Lee West
66 ☆☆
Wu Liang Ye

CONTINENTAL
Café des Artistes ☆☆
Eleven Madison
  Park ☆☆
One if By Land

DELI
Carnegie Deli
Katz's Deli

DINER
Barking Dog
Empire Diner

DUTCH
NL ☆

EAST EUROPEAN
Danube ☆☆☆
Pop's Pierogi

FRENCH
Aix ☆☆
Alain Ducasse ☆☆☆
Alias
Artisanal ☆☆
Atelier ☆☆☆
August
Balthazar ☆☆
Bandol
Barrio ☆
Bayard's ☆☆
Blue Hill ☆☆
Bouley ☆☆☆
Bouterin ☆
Brasserie ☆☆
Brasserie 360 ☆☆
Café Boulud ☆☆☆
Chanterelle ☆☆☆
Chelsea Bistro
  & Bar ☆☆
Chez Josephine
Daniel ☆☆☆☆
DB Bistro Moderne ☆☆
Django ☆☆
Fleur de Sel ☆☆
Jarnac ☆
Jean Claude
Jean Georges ☆☆☆☆
Jean-Luc ☆
JoJo ☆☆☆
Jubilee
Jubilee 51 ☆
La Grenouille ☆☆☆
Le Bernardin ☆☆☆☆
Le Cirque 2000 ☆☆☆
Le Gigot
Le Périgord ☆☆
Les Halles Downtown ☆
Le Tableau
Le Zinc ☆
Le Zoo
Marseille ☆☆
Mas ☆
Mercer Kitchen ☆☆
Nice Matin ☆☆
Orsay ☆☆

Paradou
Pastis ☆
Payard Pâtisserie ☆ ☆
Picholine ☆ ☆ ☆
Provence ☆
325 Spring Street ☆
Tocqueville ☆ ☆
Triomphe ☆ ☆
Union Pacific ☆ ☆ ☆

GERMAN
Heidelberg
Loreley
Zum Schneider

GLOBAL FUSION
The Biltmore
  Room ☆ ☆ ☆
Django ☆ ☆
Public ☆

GREEK
Avra ☆
Estiatorio Milos ☆ ☆
Meltemi
Metsovo
Molyvos ☆ ☆
Snack
Snack Taverna

INDIAN
Ada ☆ ☆
Amma ☆ ☆
Bread Bar at Tabla
Bukhara Grill
Chennai Garden
Chola ☆ ☆
Dakshin
Dawat ☆
Diwan ☆ ☆
Mirchi
Mughlai
Pongal
Salaam Bombay ☆ ☆
Surya ☆ ☆
Tabla ☆ ☆ ☆
Tamarind ☆ ☆
Vatan

INDONESIAN
Bali Nusa Indah
NL ☆

ITALIAN
Acqua Pazza ☆
Azalea ☆
Babbo ☆ ☆ ☆
Baldoria ☆
Barbalúc ☆
Bar Pitti
Beppe ☆ ☆
Bice ☆ ☆
Bread Tribeca ☆ ☆
Campagna ☆ ☆
Celeste
Centolire ☆ ☆
'Cesca ☆ ☆
Col Legno
Crispo
Dan Andrea
Delmonico's ☆
Esca ☆ ☆
Fiamma Osteria ☆ ☆ ☆
Felidia ☆ ☆ ☆
50 Carmine
Frank
Gabriel's ☆ ☆
Gonzo
Gradisca
Hearth ☆ ☆
Il Gattopardo ☆ ☆
Il Valentino ☆ ☆
Il Mulino
Isola
I Trulli ☆ ☆
La Locanda
La Nonna ☆
Lentini ☆
Le Cirque 2000 ☆ ☆ ☆
Le Madri ☆ ☆
Le Zie
L'Impero ☆ ☆ ☆
Lupa
Max
Moda ☆ ☆
Nick's Family-Style
Otto ☆ ☆
Paola's ☆ ☆

Peasant ☆
Petrosino
Po
Remi ☆ ☆
Risa
Rocco's on 22nd ☆
San Domenico ☆ ☆ ☆
Scalini Fedeli ☆
Sciuscia ☆
Tuscan ☆ ☆
Viceversa ☆

JAPANESE
Ajisai
Blue Ribbon Sushi ☆ ☆
Chibitini
Hatsuhana ☆ ☆
Honmura An ☆ ☆ ☆
Jewel Bako
Kai ☆ ☆
Katsu-Hama
Kuruma Zushi ☆ ☆ ☆
Marumi
Masa ☆ ☆ ☆
Matsuri ☆ ☆
Megu ☆ ☆
Minca
Nadaman Hakubai ☆ ☆
Next Door Nobu ☆ ☆ ☆
Nobu ☆ ☆ ☆
Otabe ☆ ☆
Soba Nippon
Sushi Hatsu ☆ ☆
Sushi Seki ☆ ☆
Sushi Yasu
Sushi Yasuda ☆ ☆ ☆
Tsuki
Yakiniku JuJu

JAPANESE FUSION
Geisha ☆
Riingo ☆ ☆
Sumile ☆ ☆

KOREAN
Cho Dang Gol ☆ ☆
Emo's
Hangawi ☆ ☆
Kang Suh ☆ ☆

Kori
Muzy
Temple
36 Bar and Barbecue ☆
Yang Pyung Seoul

LATIN AMERICAN
Asia de Cuba ☆
Bohio
Cafecito
Calle Ocho ☆
Chicama ☆☆
Churrascaria
  Plataforma ☆☆
Circus ☆☆
Cuba Libre
Cubana Cafe
El Fogon
Esperanto
Flor's Kitchen
Good
Hacienda de
  Argentina ☆
Havana Central
Havana NY
La Fonda Boricua
National Café
Noche
Patria ☆☆☆

MEDITERRANEAN
Acquario
Branzini ☆
Gus's Figs Bistro & Bar
Lavagna
Layla
Marseille ☆☆
Meet ☆
Nick & Toni's ☆☆
Olives ☆
Picholine ☆☆☆
Savoy ☆☆
Sciuscia ☆
Tappo ☆
Zona Rosa ☆

MEXICAN/TEX-MEX
Dos Caminos ☆
Gabriela's

Hell's Kitchen
Itzocan Bistro
Ixta ☆
La Palapa
La Palapa Rockola
Maya ☆☆
Mesa Grill ☆☆
Mexicana Mama
Paladar
Salon Mexico ☆
Suenos ☆
Zarela ☆☆
Zocalo ☆
Zona Rosa ☆

MIDDLE EASTERN
Habib's Place
Layla
Moustache
Tagine
Turkuaz
Zitoune ☆

NEW AMERICAN
Alias
Amuse ☆☆
Barbuto
Beacon ☆☆
Bread Bar at Tabla
Butter ☆
Capitale ☆☆
City Hall ☆☆
Cooke's Corner
Craft ☆☆☆
Craftbar
David Burke &
  Donatella ☆☆
Delmonico's ☆
District ☆
First
The Four
  Seasons ☆☆☆
Gotham Bar
  and Grill ☆☆☆
Gramercy
  Tavern ☆☆☆
Guastavino's ☆☆
Heartbeat ☆☆
Icon ☆☆

industry(food) ☆
Inside
Jane ☆
Jean Georges ☆☆☆☆
Jefferson ☆☆
Joe Allen
Josie's
Kloe ☆
Lever House
  Restaurant ☆☆
Man Ray ☆
March ☆☆☆
Meet ☆
Merge
Michael's ☆☆
Mix in New York ☆☆
Montrachet ☆☆
Morrells ☆
92 ☆
Odeon ☆☆
Ouest ☆☆
Parish & Company ☆
Park Ave. Café ☆☆
Park View ☆☆
Patroon ☆
The Red Cat ☆
Redeye Grill ☆
Salt
Savoy ☆☆
Schiller's Liquor Bar
Screening Room ☆☆
71 Clinton Fresh
  Food ☆☆
The Spotted Pig
The Tasting Room ☆
Tavern on the Green ☆
Thalia ☆☆
Thom
Town ☆☆☆
Tribeca Grill ☆☆
Triomphe ☆☆
"21" Club ☆☆
Union Square
  Café ☆☆
Upstairs at "21" ☆☆
Veritas ☆☆☆
Voyage ☆
Wyanoka
WD-50 ☆☆

PAN-ASIAN
Asia de Cuba ☆
Ruby Foo's ☆☆
Tabla ☆☆☆
United Noodles

PAN-LATIN
Bolivar ☆☆
Cabo Rojo
Calle Ocho ☆
Esperanto
Ola ☆
Patria ☆☆☆
Suba ☆

PORTUGUESE
Alfama ☆
Luzia's

RUSSIAN
Firebird ☆☆
Petrossian ☆☆

SANDWICHES
aKa Café
Mandler's
Paradou

SCANDINAVIAN
Aquavit ☆☆☆

SEAFOOD
Aquagrill ☆☆
Atlantic Grill ☆
Avra ☆
Blue Water Grill ☆
Dock's ☆
Esca ☆☆
Estiatorio Milos ☆☆
Fish
Fresh ☆☆
Jack's Luxury Oyster
    Bar ☆☆
Le Bernardin ☆☆☆☆

Manhattan Ocean
    Club ☆☆
Meltemi
Mermaid Inn
Oceana ☆☆☆
Oyster Bar
RM ☆☆☆
Sea Grill ☆☆
Shore
Svenningsen's
Union Pacific   ☆☆

SOUTHERN
Bayou
Emily's
Hog Pit
Miss Maude's
Sylvia's

SOUTHWESTERN
Agave ☆
Mesa Grill ☆☆

SPANISH
Azafron ☆
Bolo ☆☆☆
Crudo
El Cid
El Fogon
La Nacional
Solera ☆☆
Suba ☆
Xunta

STEAKHOUSE
Bistro Le Steak
BLT Steak
Churrascaria
    Plataforma ☆☆
Frank's ☆
Michael Jordan's ☆☆
Palm
Smith &
    Wollensky ☆☆
Soho Steak

Sparks ☆
Strip House ☆
Wolfgang's ☆☆

SUSHI
Blue Ribbon Sushi ☆☆
Geisha ☆
Hatsuhana ☆☆
Jewel Bako
Kuruma Zushi ☆☆☆
Marumi
Sushi Seki ☆☆
Sushi Yasuda ☆☆☆

THAI
Holy Basil
Kittichai ☆☆
Pam Real Thai Food
Royal Siam
Topaz Thai

TAPAS
Bar Jamon
Casa Mono ☆☆

TURKISH
Divane
Maia
The Sultan
Turkuaz
Uskudar

VEGETARIAN
Hangawi ☆☆
Pongal
Vatan

VIETNAMESE
Anh
Bao Noodles
Hue ☆
Le Colonial ☆☆
Nam
Nha Trang
O Mai

Index

523